T0330147

EFFICIENCY, FINANCE, AND VARIETIES OF INDUSTRIAL POLICY

―――

INITIATIVE FOR POLICY DIALOGUE AT COLUMBIA:
CHALLENGES IN DEVELOPMENT AND GLOBALIZATION

INITIATIVE FOR POLICY DIALOGUE AT COLUMBIA:
CHALLENGES IN DEVELOPMENT
AND GLOBALIZATION

JOSÉ ANTONIO OCAMPO AND JOSEPH E. STIGLITZ,
SERIES EDITORS

EFFICIENCY, FINANCE, AND VARIETIES OF INDUSTRIAL POLICY

GUIDING RESOURCES, LEARNING, AND TECHNOLOGY FOR SUSTAINED GROWTH

Akbar Noman and
Joseph E. Stiglitz, Editors

COLUMBIA UNIVERSITY PRESS

NEW YORK

Columbia University Press
Publishers Since 1893
New York   Chichester, West Sussex
cup.columbia.edu

Library of Congress Cataloging-in-Publication Data
Names: Noman, Akbar, editor. | Stiglitz, Joseph E., editor.
Title: Efficiency, finance, and varieties of industrial policy : guiding
resources, learning and technology for sustained growth / Akbar Noman
and Joseph Stiglitz, eds.
Description: New York : Columbia University Press, [2017] | Includes index.
Identifiers: LCCN 2016033888 | ISBN 9780231180504 (cloth : alk. paper) |
ISBN 9780231542777 (E-book)
Subjects: LCSH: Sustainable development. | Economic development. |
Industrial policy. | Development banks—Finance.
Classification: LCC HC79.E5 E3324 2016 | DDC 338.9/27—dc23
LC record available at https://lccn.loc.gov/2016033888

Columbia University Press books are printed on permanent
and durable acid-free paper.

Printed in the United States of America

Cover image: ©zhaojiankang/iStockPhoto

INITIATIVE FOR POLICY DIALOGUE AT COLUMBIA: CHALLENGES IN DEVELOPMENT AND GLOBALIZATION

JOSÉ ANTONIO OCAMPO AND JOSEPH E. STIGLITZ, SERIES EDITORS

The Initiative for Policy Dialogue (IPD) at Columbia University brings together academics, policymakers, and practitioners from developed and developing countries to address the most pressing issues in economic policy today. IPD is an important part of Columbia's broad program on development and globalization. The *Initiative for Policy Dialogue at Columbia: Challenges in Development and Globalization* book series presents the latest academic thinking on a wide range of development topics and lays out alternative policy options and trade-offs. Written in a language accessible to policymakers and students alike, this series is unique in that it both shapes the academic research agenda and furthers the economic policy debate, facilitating a more democratic discussion of development policies.

Many of the most fundamental and frequent controversies in economics revolve around the issues of the salience and significance of market failures and the role of the state in overcoming them. They arise in a particularly acute form in the literature on industrial policies. Broadly understood, "industrial policy" refers to public policy measures aimed at influencing the allocation and accumulation of resources, and the choice of technologies. A particularly important set of industrial policies, at the center of many of the papers in this volume, comprises those targeted at activities that promote learning and technological upgrading. They are sometimes more accurately labeled as "learning, industrial and technology" (LIT) policies.

There has been a resurgence of interest in industrial policies in recent years, and such policies have even come to be advocated by the World Bank. This revival prompted IPD and Japan International Cooperation Agency (JICA) to establish a joint task force on industrial policies motivated in part by the neglect of research into industrial policies in the long period the subject was neglected. Issues requiring further exploration included those pertaining to development finance and the links between the recent literature on industrial policies and that on growth and structural transformations. So did new empirical work on experiences with industrial policies; and new insights into the debate on static vs. dynamic efficiency and on mitigation of risks.

This volume hopes to inform the policy choices facing countries both in the advanced world and in emerging markets and less developed countries, and to help them design institutions and policies appropriate for them.

For more information about IPD and its upcoming books, visit www.policydialogue.org.

CONTENTS

EFFICIENCY, FINANCE, AND VARIETIES
OF INDUSTRIAL POLICY

CHAPTER 1

Learning, Industrial, and Technology Policies

AN OVERVIEW

Akbar Noman and Joseph E. Stiglitz

Many of the most fundamental and frequent controversies in economics revolve around two related sets of issues: the salience and significance of market failures and the role of the state in overcoming them. They arise in a particularly acute form in the literature on industrial policies. Broadly understood, industrial policy refers to public policy measures aimed at influencing the allocation and accumulation of resources, and the choice of technologies. A particularly important set of industrial policies, at the center of many of the chapters in this volume, comprises those targeted at activities that promote learning and technological upgrading. They are sometimes more accurately labeled as *learning, industrial and technology* (LIT) policies. We use the term to cover both deliberate and self-described industrial policies as well as policies that have a similar effect though they are not labeled as "industrial policies" (this is particularly well illustrated by Antonio Andreoni's contribution, chapter 9).

Industrial policies became virtually ousted from the set of policy prescriptions proffered by economists—even if they were often resorted to in practice—in the heyday of neoliberalism, with the Washington consensus policies heavily biased in favor of largely unfettered markets.[1] There has been a resurgence of interest in industrial policies in recent years, and such policies have even come to be advocated by the World Bank.[2] This revival prompted the Initiative for Policy Dialogue (IPD) and Japan International Cooperation Agency (JICA) to establish a joint task force on industrial policies. The task force's work was motivated in part by the neglect of research into industrial policies in the long period the subject was in exile from academic research and policy analysis, and especially from that of multilateral organizations. Issues requiring further exploration included those pertaining to development finance and the links between the recent literature on industrial policies and that on growth and structural transformations. There has been, moreover, new empirical work on different experiences with industrial policies and new insights into the debate on static vs. dynamic efficiency and on mitigation of risks.

The historical experience of advanced economies at or near the frontier of technology, attests to the vital role that industrial policies played in sustained economic growth and transformation.[3] This provides compelling testimony to the critical role of governments in fostering sustained economic progress. Moreover, there are good theoretical reasons for the type of public policy interventions that constitute what we have called LIT and industrial policies. These are elaborated in chapter 2 by Mario Cimoli and Giovanni Dosi, and in chapter 3 by José Antonio Ocampo. Before we turn to these and the other chapters that comprise this volume, it would be apposite to comment on one objection to industrial policies: What may be good in theory may be vitiated by the risks of poor design and implementation. The answer to this objection is, first, that while industrial policies are not *sufficient* by themselves for success in economic development, both historical experience and theory indicate that they are virtually *necessary*. Second, yes there are risks stemming from institutional imperfections and political economy "failures," but such problems are by no means confined to industrial policy as demonstrated, for example, by many failed programs of macroeconomic stabilization or of liberalization and privatization. The challenge for public policy is to get the risk–reward ratio right. That industrial policy has the potential to provide plentiful rewards and that there are ways to obtain them and mitigate risks of failure are amongst the central contentions of this collection of essays.

The rest of the volume comprises three parts. Part I elaborates on the conceptual and theoretical foundations of LIT or industrial policies. Part II focuses on an aspect that has been relatively neglected in the recent literature, even as its importance has been widely recognized: development finance, in particular development banks. The primary focus of part III is on experiences and experiments with industrial policies, their lessons, and proposals about their design and implementation. In this overview, we pay particular attention to part I. This quick sketch cannot, of course, do justice to the chapters and is aimed more at whetting the appetite and drawing some salient links between the various contributions than at providing a summary.

Chapter 2 by Cimoli and Dosi draws heavily on Cimoli, Dosi, and Stiglitz (2009). It begins by noting that LIT policies and *associated institution building* play a vital role in sustained economic progress and transformation. At the outset Cimoli and Dosi emphasize the pervasiveness of market failures, noting that the conditions required for the standard normative welfare theorems to hold are far from the conditions that prevail in the real world: "The whole world can be seen as a huge market failure!" They recognize that the question in practice is more one of whether the deficiencies are sufficiently serious to warrant active policy intervention, including in shaping institutions. They observe that this way of posing the question shifts the burden of proof away from those who believe that the presumption should be to avoid interventions in markets.

In particular, Cimoli and Dosi point to the severe shortcomings of markets in dealing with knowledge and information. Knowledge is essentially a public good (in the sense of Samuelson). But the nexus of technology, learning, and information is at the heart of sustained growth and catch-up. Cimoli and Dosi further note that most firms are operating below "best practice" even within the same economy and that this pervasive phenomenon raises the question of whether the standard production possibility curve makes sense even within a sector or a country. Most importantly, they argue that comparative advantage "needs to be re-examined: a country's comparative advantage is based in part on its comparative learning capabilities." Many of the policies that "enhance economy-wide learning are the opposite of those derived from the standard neoclassical model."[4] Cimoli and Dosi also point to the trade-offs that may arise between static efficiency and the dynamics of learning and technology along similar lines to the more detailed elaboration of that theme in the contribution by Ocampo (see below).

A particular kind of information problem that developing countries face is called the *coordination problem*. In well-functioning market economies, prices serve this role. Even there, prices often fail to provide the necessary coordination, but in the context of development, industrial policies can help overcome coordination problems of the sort recognized in the early development literature (e.g., Nurkse 1953; Gerschenkron 1962; Rosenstein-Rodan 1943; Hirschman 1958; and Prebisch 1963).

While stressing that there are no "magic policy bullets," Cimoli and Dosi identify broad types of policy prescriptions revolving around the "necessity of nurturing infants." In particular, Cimoli and Dosi provide a taxonomy identifying seven broad "domains of policy intervention" and how they map into different policy measures and institutions. They recognize that policy frameworks need to pay attention to building the "capabilities" of actors and also to curb rent seeking and inertia. They argue that in achieving development objectives, incentives via altering prices such as protection or subsidies are not likely to be sufficient. In this context, they contrast the stylized Latin American experience with that of the East Asian "tigers" (Japan, Korea, Taiwan, and Singapore).

Cimoli and Dosi then turn to how to motivate learning and accumulation of capabilities and the increase in productive capacity. They emphasize that while innovation may give rise to rents, these rents may incentivize research, and rents may be necessary for financing innovation in the absence of a well-functioning financial market. Even innovation rents today do not automatically get reinvested into producing innovation in the future. They elaborate on the three aspects of strategies designed to promote innovation and the accumulation of capabilities: carrots, sticks, and competition.

Cimoli and Dosi's last two sets of policy prescriptions pertain to avoiding the natural resource curse and the imperative of consistency between macroeconomic and industrial polices.

Cimoli and Dosi, as well as Ocampo in chapter 3, also note that the world has changed in ways that provide challenges to the effective implementation of some of the "old" policies that worked in the past. In particular, they point to the constraints imposed by globalization and changes in global rules such as those reflected in World Trade Organization (WTO) commitments and bilateral and "plurilateral" investment and trade treaties. Both Cimoli and Dosi and Ocampo examine in distinctive ways how these constraints impact industrial policies and how the adverse effects can be mitigated. After noting the several loopholes and flexibilities that developing countries can exploit, they make a case against bilateral trade and investment treaties and in favor of a reform of the international rules governing trade and intellectual property rights. Both chapters conclude with a call for a reform of the current framework of such international rules.

The contribution by José Antonio Ocampo (chapter 3) provides a grand sweep of the literature on economic growth and structural change and places the role of industrial policies in that broader context. He contrasts the neoclassical focus on static efficiency with what is needed for sustained growth: "Economic growth in developing countries is intrinsically tied to the dynamics of production structures and to the specific policies and institutions created to support them. The major focus is on the *dynamic efficiency* of economic structures, defined as their capacity to generate new waves of structural change . . . ."

Ocampo makes extensive use of the "old" and "new" literature on growth and development. He first addresses the methodological issues that arise in (1) distinguishing between what Madison (1991) refers to as "proximate" and "ultimate" causes and (2) the direction of causality given the simultaneous movement of a series of variables with growth (investment, production structures, technology, human capital, etc.).

Ocampo then sketches the regularities characterizing the growth process, providing a succinct discussion of five sets of stylized facts that are of special importance in understanding growth and their implications: (1) the persistence of large intercountry difference in several dimensions; (2) the large discontinuities that generally characterize growth (which often tends to come in spurts); (3) the importance of elastic factor supplies in the development process; (4) the path dependence of growth; and (5) the variability of successful trade policy packages, which argues against the simplistic generalizations about what constitutes "good" trade policy that have been all too common.

Ocampo then distinguishes "framework conditions" (macroeconomic stability, basic institutions, human capital, infrastructure) that are *necessary* for growth from the active determinants of the growth momentum, the ability to generate *continually* new dynamic activities. He argues that it is "the *system-wide* processes," including interactions among (1) innovations and learning and (2) complementarities, linkages, or networks among production activities that matter the most.

He concludes that "the key to rapid growth in the developing world is the combination of *strategies aimed at the dynamic transformation of productive structures* with appropriate macroeconomic conditions and stability . . ." (emphasis added).

Both of these papers on conceptual and theoretical foundations also point to the importance of development finance, especially the role of development banks in providing long-term capital for new activities of the sort they emphasize. The four chapters of part II are devoted to development finance, a topic that has been widely recognized as important in the recent literature on industrial policies but elsewhere has received rather scant attention. Together, the four chapters not only present the theoretical case for development banks—explaining why conventional financial market institutions fail to meet certain societal needs—but also demonstrate that a number of successful development banks have made a difference in the development of their countries. Of course, there have been failures of development banks in the past, sometimes associated with politically connected lending. Unfortunately, there is a paucity of research on development banks (perhaps reflecting the long period during which they were out of favor). The key question is: Why have some banks succeeded and others failed?

João Carlos Ferraz in chapter 4 notes that the 2008 financial crisis and its lingering aftermath have brought renewed attention to development banks, including notably for the countercyclical role they have played. Had they not continued to provide finance, the economic crises in these countries would have been deeper. But that is secondary to the main purpose of development banks, which is to overcome financial market imperfections, especially for longer-term investment and structural transformation. (Of course, avoiding the volatility of private finance has long been held as one of the advantages of development banks.)

Over the years, development banks have been subject to extensive criticism. Ferraz tackles head on some of these, such as the alleged crowding-out effect of development banks: that they crowd out private banks, which (under the standard neoliberal framework) are presumptively better at allocating scarce capital. On the contrary, he asserts they can also "crowd in" private finance. Other criticisms are associated with political interference and cronyism and the inability of any public institution to outsmart the private sector in "picking winners." He suggests ways— institutional designs—in which the risks of these potential problems can be mitigated (e.g., clear segregation of functions, independent board members, banking supervision).

Ferraz shows that development banks have become a major source of finance within the global economy, with a combined asset base of the 23 members of the International Development Finance Club (IDFC) of around $2.8 trillion in 2013. As a ratio of GDP, the sizes of national development banks vary greatly, with their asset base ranging from 0.5 percent of GDP in Indonesia to more than 14 percent in China, Brazil, and Germany.

Ferraz chooses four of the largest development banks for a more detailed analysis of their structure, behavior, and performance in recent years. These are the China Development Bank (CDB), Kreditanstalt fur Wiederaufbau (KfW) in Germany, BNDES in Brazil and the Japan Finance Corporation (JFC). He finds many more similarities than differences among them and judges them on the whole to be success-ful in achieving their developmental objectives while turning in a "very sound financial performance . . . based on a strong asset base" in 2013. JFC appears to be an exception, with negative profits and the highest nonperforming loans ratio. But even that is modest, at less than 3 percent of loans being nonperforming. CDB and BNDES had the best financial performance among the four banks, with returns on equity exceeding 15 percent and a nonperforming loans ratio of 0.01 and 0.48 percent, respectively. Ferraz concludes that development banks "are one of the pil-lars of a resilient financial system . . . relevant for countries at all stages of development."

While development banks have typically been thought of as insti-tutions relevant for developing countries, they have in fact played an important role even in advanced European economies. Stephany Griffith-Jones and Giovanni Cozzi (chapter 5) ask how development banks can promote investment, particularly in Europe. They begin by noting that the global private financial sector has been wanting in per-forming any of the functions that it is supposed to perform, and thus increased attention needs to be paid to "the positive role that effective public development banks can play." Griffith-Jones and Cozzi pro-vide a succinct analytical case for development banks, beginning with the endemic and serious failures in financial markets, in particular as elaborated by Stiglitz in his writings. Notwithstanding these failures—well documented in practice and well explained in theory—there was a strong belief in some quarters in the efficiency of financial markets. These beliefs, combined with political pressure from the financial sector, led to excessive financial liberalization and a push against public lending institutions. There are many ironies: the World Bank, a public devel-opment bank, encouraged countries to close down their development banks, arguing that they can't work; and during and after the financial crisis, government *had* to take on a massive *financial* role—had it not, the private financial system would have collapsed. Even today, in the United States, the government underwrites virtually all home mortgages. After elucidating the types of failures that financial markets are prone to, Griffith-Jones and Cozzi hone in on the roles that development banks do play and need to play—and how development banks can effectively play these roles—in promoting the kinds of industrial policies, enhanc-ing dynamic efficiency, that the earlier contributions of Cimoli and Dosi and of Ocampo have emphasized.

Griffith-Jones and Cozzi then simulate alternative scenarios for Europe and the global economy, employing the Cambridge Alphametrics Model (CAM) for the period until 2020 to show the "very positive impact that a greater role of development banks—together with slowing down of excessive fiscal consolidation—can have on investment, growth and employment . . . and debt to GDP ratios."

Go Shimada, in chapter 6, examines the role of development banks in Japan. Shimada begins with a nuanced discussion of the pros and cons of development banks. On the rationale for such banks he emphasizes, in particular, the financial market imperfections stemming from information asymmetries, externalities, and the risks of long-term investments, especially when there are economies of scale. Among the cons he notes are the difficulties of assessing loan applications, especially given the need to focus on economic and social benefits instead of simple profitability; and the risks of political capture or rent seeking. The main part of the chapter is a detailed case study of the "vital role" of development banks in Japan's industrial policies after World War II. The government "played an important role in both collecting deposits and allocating finance to industrial development." The former reflected the special importance of the postal banks in Japan, which held about 20 percent of the total bank deposits even as late as the 1980s.

Shimada's analysis of development banking in Japan is embedded in an insightful discussion of Japan's postwar recovery and development. The Reconstruction Finance Bank (RFB) was established in 1947, and its financing, particularly of coal and steel industries, was a "crucial contributing factor" to Japan's postwar reconstruction. But it succumbed to rent-seeking activities of the sort that reflect corruption rather than creation of value, and after a corruption scandal, it was shut down and replaced by the Japan Development Bank (JDB). Shimada says that the lessons learned from the "capture" of RFB were used in the design of the JDB— in particular, to insulate it from the influence of assorted outside agencies—and that this much greater autonomy and the high quality of its project appraisal and supervision processes were vital to its success. Also crucial was the fact that JDB lending "was embedded in the government's industrial policy." Shimada provides a detailed discussion of JDB operations. Starting with "basic industries" (electricity, iron and steel, shipbuilding and coal), it shifted to financing manufacturing industries that were deemed to have high spillovers and complementarities; hence, this "was not an unadulterated picking the winner out of thin air type of intervention." Shimada also finds that JDB played a role in overcoming asymmetries of information in the financial markets in Japan. JDB loans lowered risks for other banks by signaling government support, and the information was seen as reliable because "JDB's lending had broader aims than profit maximization."

The paper notes the context specificity of successful development banks in other countries such as Brazil, China, Malaysia, Korea, and Taiwan in the way they overcame "issues such as rent seeking and political capture, and to complement the work of markets" as a lead-up to the question of lessons from Japan's experience. Shimada stresses the importance of autonomy and loan appraisal expertise (including the development of the institutional capacity to make such appraisals), aspects of development banking that other scholars of development have noted. But he also emphasizes the importance of a "a strong network among the institution's stakeholders"; a "good division of labor with other . . . banks"; clarity in the "division of labor inside the [bank's] institutional framework"; the need to renew and reform the institution to fight the tendency to institutional ossification; and focus on supporting activities with large "vertical and horizontal externalities," observing that such externalities contribute to strengthening the networks that play a central role in the success of development banks.

The last chapter on development banks, chapter 7 by Deepak Nayyar, examines the Indian experience and its lessons. Nayyar places the Indian experience in a broad historical and cross-country context. He begins with a discussion of "catch-up" industrialization, development finance, and industrial policy in general terms, noting that the "economic logic of development banks is simple. In . . . latecomers to industrialization, capital markets are imperfect . . . . [N]ew firms . . . find it exceedingly difficult to obtain finance for their initial investment, let alone to cover the losses of the learning period . . . [T]he problem is compounded when such investments are characterized by lumpiness and . . . gestation lag[s]." He traces the historical origins of development banking to the financial institutions that emerged in Europe from around the middle of the nineteenth century that served as role models for the development banks in postwar Germany and Japan, and he provides a quick sketch of the founding of development banks starting with Mexico and Chile in the 1930s and ending with the China Development Bank in 1994.

Nayyar then turns to the Indian experience. That turns out to be both complicated and mixed. He distinguishes three phases: the late 1940s to mid-1960s; the 1980s; and the late 1990s onward. He comments that the "first phase, which kick-started industrialization, was the most significant." In this phase, three national (federal) level development financial institutions (DFIs)[5] and a number of state level development banks were established. The second, in the 1980s, saw a number of refinancing, sector-specific or specialized institutions (for agriculture, housing, small-industries, urban development, rural electrification, exports and imports, power, railways, renewable energy, and tourism). India seems to have ended up with an extraordinarily complex and multidimensional network of numerous DFIs before scaling back sharply in the third phase beginning in the late 1990s. Except for India Infrastructure Finance Company Limited (IIFCL), the development banks became also—and in some cases, only—commercial banks. By the end of the 2000s there was a sharp reduction in the role of development banking. The only remaining long-term lending financial institution exclusively lending to industry is the Small Industries Development Bank of India (SIDBI), and the only institution that still lends to the industrial sector generally rather than to specific subsectors is the Life Insurance Corporation (LIC). Both are profitable as are the refinancing institutions that continue to exist. Among the sector-specific institutions, the Export-Import (EXIM) bank, Rural Electrification (REC), Power Finance Corporation (PFC), Indian Railways Finance Corporation (IRFC), and Housing and Urban Development Corporation (HUDCO) are active and profitable.

The importance of DFIs in financing investment in manufacturing was very considerable even after the initial kick-starting phase in the 1950s and 1960s: 10 percent in 1970–71; 30 percent in 1980–81; 36 percent in 1990–91; and 49 percent in 2000–01 before collapsing to 6 percent in 2005–06 and recovering to 14 percent in 2012–13. The proportion was much higher for the private sector: 25 percent in 1970–71 and 75 percent in 2000–01 (thus public funding of investment in manufacturing either via development banks or directly—including retained earnings of public sector enterprises—was extremely important). Nayyar attributes the decline of development banks to financial sector reforms "influenced, if not driven by the World Bank." The cost of borrowing for DFIs rose significantly with a sharp reduction in concessional financing by the Reserve Bank of India and in government-guaranteed bonds. Thus "eroding profitability was a self-fulfilling prophecy . . . [c]ompounded by their past sins which led to an accumulation of nonperforming assets." Nayyar's chapter also stresses that the weaknesses of DFIs in India include notably inadequate protection from political capture and that their lending had feeble links to industrial policies. The industrial policies, in turn, had their own weaknesses, especially the absence of mechanisms to ensure that the rents to which they gave rise were used productively (the importance of which was emphasized by several other contributions to this volume including notably by Ocampo and by Cimoli and Dosi). Nayyar concludes that the weaknesses of the relationship between DFI lending and industrial policies and the deficiencies of the latter in India provide important lessons for development finance.

While there have been and continue to be many highly successful development banks, there are also many examples of failures mainly on account of political capture and rent seeking. They are high-risk, high-rewards institutions that require a state broadly committed to pursuing developmental goals (sometimes referred to as a *development state*) to realize their potential. Other notable examples of success, not covered in this volume, include the Development Bank of Ethiopia in recent years (Abebe and Schaefer 2015)[6] and development banks in Pakistan during the 1950s and 1960s (Noman 1991 and 2015, Papanek 1967).

Noman (2015) proposes some ways of mitigating the risks that arise in contexts of "messy" governance, such as in Pakistan in more recent times. These include a tightly defined, narrow mandate of lending for low-hanging fruits of incontrovertible "winners" (such as lending to help move firms to the "best practice" frontier within some sectors in the country; in the case of Pakistan, technological upgrading of its textile sector). Other ways of risk mitigation proposed in that paper include regular and frequent public disclosure in parliament of lending and loan repayments as well as appropriate civil society representation on the board.

Mitigation of risks is also an important concern of chapter 8 in part III by Justin Yifu Lin, chief economist of the World Bank from 2008 to 2012. The fact that the chief economist of the World Bank devoted so much of his tenure to the advocacy of industrial policies shows how much the Bank—and development thinking more broadly—has changed since the heyday of neoliberalism and the Washington Consensus.[7] He focuses not so much on the risks pertaining to development banking as on those associated with industrial policies more broadly. (This is a revised version of work Lin has already published, but we consider it worth reproducing here, especially since its earlier version was discussed at a meeting of the Task Force that resulted in this volume).

Justin Yifu Lin in chapter 8 argues that historical experience since around the beginning of the nineteenth century shows that industrial policies are necessary for catching up but that more often than not they have been unsuccessful in developing countries in the postwar period beginning in the 1940s. He proposes that industrial policies be embedded in what he terms *new structural economics* whose conceptual basis is rooted in historical experience. Lin pithily summarizes the gist of his arguments as follows:

> (1) Sector-targeted industrial policy is essential to achieve dynamic structural change and rapid, sustained growth in the economy; (2) most industrial policies fail because they target industries that are not compatible with the country's comparative advantage; (3) successful industrial policies should target industries that are the countries' latent comparative advantage; (4) historical experiences show that in the catching-up stage, successful countries industrial policies, in general, have targeted the industries in countries with a similar endowment structure and somewhat higher per capita income; and (5) the growth identification and facilitation framework [GIF] based on new structural economics, is a new, effective way to target latent comparative advantage industries and support their growth.

The gist of the GIF is to identify the latent comparative advantage that is to be exploited by identifying well-established industries in rapidly growing countries with a per capita income not much higher than twice the level of the country at hand.

There was a particularly lively discussion at the meeting of the task force where Lin's paper was discussed. There was a widely shared consensus that there is much to be said for Lin's approach and that it serves to guard against the risk of "picking losers." However, some participants questioned his analysis of past successes, some of which involved leapfrogging and more active promotion of *dynamic* comparative advantage— seemingly going more against the comparative advantage of the moment than Lin's framework allows. Also questions were raised about whether factor endowments as reflected in per capita incomes were adequate indicators of what constitutes "nearness" or latent comparative advantage, especially in a context of mobility of capital and highly skilled labor, rapid technological change, and evolving global value chains. Perhaps the most important "endowment" of a country was assets that were not mobile—institutions and learning capacities that were embedded in local institutions. It was these that countries needed to take into account as they struggled to shape their long-term (dynamic) comparative advantage; and in doing so, they also needed to take into account how what they chose to do would affect their learning abilities, which would, in turn, determine their future evolution.[8]

The remainder of part III contains a collection of papers on various aspects of industrial policies pursued in the past and proposed future practice.

Antonio Andreoni in chapter 9 shows that the term *industrial policy* applies to a wide variety of policy interventions and that virtually all countries can be said to have industrial policies. He comments that "understanding the 'policy context' in which industrial policies are designed, implemented . . . is critical for disentangling the varieties of industrial policy we observe today." He develops a methodology for analyzing the variety of industrial policy models and policy packages and applies this methodology to six country cases: United States, Japan, Germany, Brazil, China, and South Africa.

Whilst Andreoni provides a general historical overview and briefly sketches the particular history in each of his six cases, his main focus is on present and very recent policies, especially those adopted after the 2008 crisis. For example, in the United States, the several industrial policy actions identified by Andreoni include two programs run by the Small Business Administration (SBA); a subset of initiatives under the *American Recovery and Reinvestment Act;* measures to overcome shortages of science, technology, engineering, and mathematics (STEM) graduates; clean energy initiatives; and a "new industrial policy package" since 2010 that includes "a number of selective measures aimed at strengthening the domestic manufacturing base as well as its presence in the international market." These include a new National Network for Manufacturing Innovation (NNMI), which is a "web of . . . institutes working on the development and adoption of advanced manufacturing technologies," as well as a number of high-tech initiatives (Materials, Genome, Robotics, etc.). The post-2010 industrial policy package in the United States also includes initiatives to promote exports.

We have chosen to illustrate the broad sense in which industrial policies can be said to be pursued with examples from the United States because there is probably greater resistance to the idea of industrial policy in that country than anywhere else, or at any rate in any of the other countries in Andreoni's sample. The label *industrial policy* is not applied to any of the policies, though they are clearly just that.

In concluding, Andreoni, while noting the differences among his six countries, remarks that "Despite the variety of . . . industrial policy . . . all countries are adopting a mix of selective sectoral policies and manufacturing system policies . . . [that] go beyond sectoral boundaries and focus on linkages across sectors." He adds that all six countries "have increasingly strengthened their technological and financial support to the overall manufacturing . . . system."

In a broadly similar vein, in chapter 10, Akio Hosono follows up his overview of the literature on the critical importance of learning and innovation for growth and development by examining different approaches effective in "promoting learning to attain transformation with good quality growth." He does so by examining five case studies of highly varied approaches which he classifies into two categories: learning a specific capacity/capability and learning to learn.[9] The case studies pertain to (1) small-scale farmers in horticulture in Kenya; (2) rural infrastructure development in Bangladesh; (3) rural livelihood improvement (*seikatsu kaizen*) programs in Japan and some developing countries; (4) the One Village, One Product (OVOP) initiative in Japan and its dissemination to Thailand and Malawi; and (5) Just-in-Time, Total Quality Management, and *Kaizen* in Japan, the United States, Singapore, and some other countries. This last receives the greatest attention.

The richness of Hosono's chapter lies particularly in the details, and hence it is least amenable to summarizing. The upshot in Hosono's words is as follows: "The case studies illustrate how learning and the accumulation of knowledge capabilities play a vital role . . . . Several approaches for learning . . . were identified . . . that not only promote learning but also facilitate learning to learn." Hosono also notes several common features of these different approaches, e.g., easy entry points; focus on learning by doing and mutual learning, and the intrinsic contribution of learning to the particular objective being pursued. He also emphasizes the importance of learning for a green economy and more generally for "high-quality" growth.

In chapter 11, Carlota Perez makes a case for natural resource (NR) based industrialization. Perez provided an excellent abstract of her paper, and we can do no better than to quote it:

This chapter argues that development is a moving target, and that windows of opportunity to both "catch up" and "leap ahead" present themselves at certain times and in specific regions due to technological revolutions and paradigm shifts. Having examined the historical precedents, it observes that the exploitation and processing of natural resources (NR), once seen as a "curse" for developing nations, present such an opportunity for Latin America and other resource-rich countries at this stage in the diffusion of the ICT revolution. The factors changing the context and conditions around NR are analyzed, from the new nature of markets and the growing influence of environmental factors to the significant increase in technological dynamism and potential for innovation in developing countries brought about by ICT and market segmentation. Examining the specificity of Latin America in its ability to respond to these different conditions, and identifying the capabilities gained in the previous opportunity with import substitution, the article argues that success today would depend upon building natural resource-based networks of innovation aimed at the dynamic Asian markets. Given the low labor intensity of most NR processing industries, a dual-integrated strategy of "resource-intensive industrialization" is proposed which promotes both top-down economic growth for global positioning and bottom-up wealth creation in each corner of the territory generating employment and well-being for all. It is finally argued that such a converging process of growth and innovation is both possible and necessary to ensure that Latin America benefits from the current window of opportunity while building a platform of innovative potential, networks and social capabilities in order to be able to leap forward with the next technological revolution. The many obstacles and limitations are not ignored; they can only be faced successfully if the nature of the opportunity is fully recognized.

At the time the article was written, Latin America was experiencing a natural resource boom—a boom that has since ended. It is evident that some countries availed themselves more of the kinds of ideas Perez advocates than did others and that some diversified more than others; with the collapse of natural resource prices, those that didn't diversify have experienced particularly marked slowdowns and even recessions.

Nobuya Haraguchi in chapter 12 seeks to "better understand how comparative advantage, productivity growth, and country-specific conditions drive industrial development." To do so, in his empirical work Haraguchi undertakes regression analysis of "the evolving patterns of manufacturing industries and corresponding changes in productivity." The availability of data limits the coverage to 73 countries. His conclusion can be summarized as follows: "the development patterns of manufacturing industries . . . indicate the existence of comparative advantage, whose shift is associated with changes in GDP per capita. Even successful countries like . . . Korea have generally followed these patterns." This chapter thus complements and buttresses the earlier one by Justin Yifu Lin (chapter 8). Haraguchi adds: ". . . our research suggests how different schools of thought on industrial development, such as comparative advantage, technological development and functional approaches, all have a place in explaining the performance of industrial development and account for different aspects of development. Future research is needed to further investigate the country-specific conditions and how they are translated into long-term country-specific advantages."

In chapter 13, Ming Leong Kuan uses the new data of the European Commission's World-Input-Output Database (WIOD) to examine whether and to what extent there is a symbiotic relationship between manufacturing and services that necessitates geographical proximity. He analyzes manufacturing-services linkages across countries and over time and finds strong colocational tendencies. He concludes: "Although international trade and ICT advancements have increased the potential for cross-border flows of services, manufacturing-services linkages have not fragmented to the extent that some countries can specialize as manufacturers while others focus on exporting intermediate services to them." Kuan adds that for "developing countries seeking to bypass industrialization by undertaking a services-led path of development, an assessment will need to be made on whether the development of services can be sustainable without the presence of a healthy producer sector . . . countries neglect their manufacturing sector at their own risks."

Of course, the service sector is a catchall that includes not just intermediate services but also tourism, health, and education. There are some countries, such as Namibia, that have successfully diversified a rich natural resource economy with some manufacturing (often related to their natural resource base, as suggested by Perez), but even more importantly with a successful tourism sector.

The set of papers emerging from the work of the joint IPD-JICA Task Force that are published here aim to make a contribution to the case for the vital role of government interventions of the industrial policy variety in promoting sustained economic growth in countries at all stages of development but especially those that need to catch up with countries at the frontier of economic prosperity. The studies show that industrial policies carry with them risks—as do all other policies; but the benefits can be great, especially if industrial policies are well thought through and well implemented. Part of successful design is to have policies that can be implemented within the countries' institutional capacities and to have policies that enhance those institutional capacities. Countries and policy analysts have learned much from the failures and successes of the past, with the result that in many countries, industrial policies have played a vital role in their development. They have learned how to structure institutions, such as development banks, that bring expertise to the development process and minimize the risks that undermined some earlier attempts at industrial policy. As Stiglitz has repeatedly emphasized, all countries have industrial policies; it is just that some countries don't know it—and because they aren't aware of how each of their policies, from expenditure to tax policies to their underlying legal/economic framework, affects the structure of the economy, there is a risk of ill-conceived policies, reflecting the interests of special interests.

The degrees of risk and rewards and the particular mix of appropriate policies will, of course, vary according to the specific context of each economy. Hopefully this volume will serve to inform the policy choices facing countries both in the advanced world and in emerging markets and less developed countries, and will help them design institutions and policies appropriate for them.

NOTES

1. See, e.g., Serra and Stiglitz (2008).

2. See, e.g., Stiglitz, Lin, and Monga (2013) and Stiglitz, Lin, and Patel (2013). Also see, e.g., Chang (2002 and 2015), Lin (2012), Cimoli et al. (2009), Noman et al. (2012), Noman and Stiglitz (2015), Greenwald and Stiglitz (2006), Stiglitz and Greenwald (2014), Mazzucato (2013), O'Sullivan et al. (2013), Primi (2015), Economic Commission for Africa (2016), and several other readings listed in the References.

3. Perhaps the most comprehensive and convincing of the works making this point is by Chang (2002). More recently, Mazzucato (2013) has argued convincingly in her

book *The Entrepreurial State* that most of the important innovations have originated through government support. Much has been written about the role of industrial policy in the fastest growing economies of East Asia, notably the seminal works of Alice Amsden (1989) and Robert Wade (1990). Another notable example but one focused on Europe is that of Alexander Gerschenkron (1962).

4. Cimoli and Dosi also point to the importance of tacit knowledge and its implications for organizational and institutional innovations. See also Stiglitz and Greenwald (2014).

5. These three were the Industrial Finance Corporation of India (IFCI), Industrial Credit and Investment Corporation of India (ICICI), and Industrial Development Bank of India (IDBI).

6. Stiglitz and Noman; Abebe and Schaefer (2015).

7. In many ways, the succession of chief economists of the World Bank traces out the evolution of developmental thinking. Hollis Chenery focused on developmental planning, and toward the end of Robert McNamara's regime as World Bank president, there was considerable discussion of inequality. Chenery was followed by Anne Krueger, Stanley Fischer, and Larry Summers. Michael Bruno represented a transition period, leading to Stiglitz' active opposition to the Washington consensus policies that had been pushed by his predecessors, with a renewed emphasis on structural transformation and industrial policies. Successor chief economists (Nicholas Stern, Francois Bourguignon, Justin Lin, and Kaushik Basu) maintained similar positions. See Stiglitz (1998a, 1998b, 1998c, 2016).

8. See Greenwald and Stiglitz (2014) for a more extensive elaboration.

9. The concept of learning to learn was first introduced by Stiglitz (1987).

REFERENCES

Abebe, Girum, and Florian Schaefer. 2015. "Review of Industrial Policies in Ethiopia: A Perspective from the Leather and Cut Flower Industries." In *Industrial Policy and Economic Transformation in Africa*, ed. Akbar Noman and Joseph E. Stiglitz. New York: Columbia University Press.

Amsden, Alice. 1989. *Asia's Next Giant*. Ithaca, N.Y.: Cornell University Press.

——. 2001. *The Rise of the Rest: Challenges to the West from Late-Industrializing Economies*. London: Oxford University Press.

Chang, Ha-Joon, ed. 2001. *Joseph Stiglitz and the World Bank: The Rebel Within*. London: Wimbledon.

Chang, Ha-Joon. 2002. *Kicking Away the Ladder: Development Strategy in Historical Perspective*. London: Anthem.

——. 2015. "Is Industrial Policy Feasible and Necessary in Africa?" In *Industrial Policy and Economic Transformation in Africa*, ed. Akbar Noman and J. E. Stiglitz. New York: Columbia University Press.

Cimoli, Mario, G. Dosi, and J. E. Stiglitz. 2009. "The Political Economy of Capabilities Accumulation: The Past and Future of Policies for Industrial Development." In *Industrial Policy and Development*, ed. M. Cimoli, G. Dosi, and J. E. Stiglitz. New York: Oxford University Press.

Economic Commission for Africa. 2016. *Transformative Industrial Policy for Africa.* Addis Ababa, Ethiopia: United Nations Economic Commission for Africa.

Gerschenkron, Alexander. 1962. *Economic Development in Historical Perspective: A Book of Essays.* Cambridge, Mass.: Harvard University Press.

Greenwald, Bruce, and J. E. Stiglitz. 1986. "Externalities in Economies with Imperfect Information and Incomplete Markets." *Quarterly Journal of Economics* 101, 2 (May 1986): 229–64.

——. 2006. "Helping Infant Economies Grow: Foundations of Trade Policies for Developing Countries." *American Economic Review* 96, 2: 141–46.

——. 2014. *Creating a Learning Story: A New Approach to Growth, Development and Social Progress.* New York: Columbia University Press.

Hirschman, A. O. 1958. *The Strategy of Economic Development.* New Haven, Conn.: Yale University Press.

Khan, M., and S. Blankenburg. 2009. "The Political Economy of Industrial Policy in Asia and Latin America." In *Industrial Policy and Development: The Political Economy of Capabilities Accumulation,* ed. Mario Cimoli, G. Giovanni Dosi, and J. E. Stiglitz. London: Oxford University Press, 336–77.

Lin, Justin Yifu. 2012. *New Structural Economics: A Framework for Rethinking Development Policy.* Washington, D.C.: World Bank.

Madison, Angus. 1991. *Dynamic Forces in Capitalist Development: A Long-Run Comparative View.* London: Oxford University Press.

Mazzucato, Mariana. 2013. *The Entrepreneurial State: Debunking Public vs. Private Sector Myths.* London: Anthem.

Noman, Akbar. 1991. "Industrial Development and Efficiency in Pakistan: A Revisionist Overview." *Pakistan Development Review* 30, 4: 849–61.

——. 2015. "The Return of Industrial Policy and Revival of Pakistan's Economy: Possibilities of Learning, Industrial and Technology Policies." *The Lahore Journal of Economics* 20 (September 2015): 31–58.

Noman, Akbar, and J. E. Stiglitz, eds. 2015. *Industrial Policy and Economic Transformation in Africa.* New York: Columbia University Press.

Noman, A., K. Botchwey, H. Stein, and J. E. Stiglitz, eds. 2012. *Good Growth and Governance in Africa: Rethinking Development Strategies.* New York: Oxford University Press.

Nurkse, Ragnar. 1953. *Problems of Capital Formation in Underdeveloped Countries.* New York: Oxford University Press.

O'Sullivan, E., A. Andreoni, G. Lopez-Gomez, and M. Gregory. 2013. "What Is New in the New Industrial Policy? A Manufacturing System Perspective." *Oxford Review of Economic Policy* 29, 2: 432–62.

Papanek, Gustav F. 1967. *Pakistan's Development: Social Goals and Private Incentives.* Cambridge, Mass.: Harvard University Press.

Prebisch, Raúl. 1951. "Theoretical and Practical Problems of Economic Growth" (E/CN.12/221). Mexico City: Economic Commission for Latin America (ECLA).

——. 1963. *Towards a Dynamic Development Policy for Latin America.* United Nations E/CN.12/680/Rev.1, New York.

Primi, Annalisa. 2015. "The Return of Industrial Policy: (What) Can Africa Learn from Latin America?" In *Industrial Policy and Economic Transformation in Africa,* ed. A. Noman and J. E. Stiglitz. New York: Columbia University Press.

Rosenstein-Rodan, P. N. 1943. "Problems of Industrialization of Eastern and South-Eastern Europe." *The Economic Journal* 53, June-September.

Serra, Narcis, and J. E. Stiglitz. 2008. *The Washington Consensus Reconsidered: Towards a New Global Governance.* New York: Oxford University Press.

Stiglitz, Joseph E. 1987. "Learning to Learn, Localized Learning and Technological Progress." In *Economic Policy and Technological Performance*, ed. P. Dasgupta and P. Stoneman. London: Cambridge University Press, 125–53.

——. 1998a. "An Agenda for Development in the Twenty-First Century." In *Annual World Bank Conference on Development Economics 1997*, ed. J. E. Stiglitz and B. Pleskovic. Washington DC, World Bank, 17–31.

——. 1998b. "More Instruments and Broader Goals: Moving Toward the Post-Washington Consensus." In *Development Issues in the 21st Century*, ed. G. Kochendorfer-Lucius and B. Pleskovic. Berlin: German Foundation for International Development, 1999, 11–39. Also Chapter 1 *in Joseph Stiglitz and the World Bank: The Rebel Within*, ed. Ha-Joon Chang, London: Wimbledon, 2001, 17–56. (Originally presented as the 1998 WIDER Annual Lecture, Helsinki, January 1998; also keynote address at Villa Borsig Winter Workshop, February 1998.)

——. 1998c. "Towards a New Paradigm for Development: Strategies, Policies and Processes." 9th Raul Prebisch Lecture delivered at the Palais des Nations, Geneva, October 19, 1998, UNCTAD. Chapter 2 in *Joseph Stiglitz and the World Bank: The Rebel Within*, ed. Ha-Joon Chang, London: Wimbledon, 2001, 57–93.

——. 2016. "The State, the Market, and Development." WIDER Working Paper, February 2016, originally presented at a conference celebrating WIDER's thirtieth anniversary, December 2015.

Stiglitz, Joseph E. and Bruce Greenwald. 2014. *Creating a Learning Society: A New Approach to Growth, Development, and Social Progress.* New York: Columbia University Press. Reader's Edition published in 2015.

Stiglitz, Joseph E., Justin Yifu Lin, and Celestin Monga. 2013. "Introduction: The Rejuvenation of Industrial Policy." In *The Industrial Policy Revolution I: The Role of Government Beyond Ideology*, ed. J. Esteban, J. Y. Lin, and J. E. Stiglitz. Houndmills, UK: Palgrave Macmillan.

Stiglitz, Joseph E., J. Y. Lin, and E. Patel, eds. 2013. *The Industrial Revolution II: Africa in Twenty-first Century.* Houndmills, UK: Palgrave Macmillan.

Wade, Robert. 1990. *Governing the Market: Economic Theory and the Role Government in East Asian Industrialization.* Princeton, N.J.: Princeton University Press.

PART I

Theoretical and Conceptual Foundations

CHAPTER 2

Industrial Policies in Learning Economies

Mario Cimoli and Giovanni Dosi

Industrial policies, written large, and institution building are crucial ingredients among the conditions hindering or fostering the process of knowledge accumulation and its effective economic exploitation along the great transformation (Polanyi, 1957) which first led parts of the Western world toward an industrial economy and later fostered both the movement of the "endless frontier" of technological and organizational innovation and, together, the catch-up of some out of many laggard economies.

There are two complementary ways to introduce their analysis.

First, one may just build on the simple empirical observation that no example can be found in history of a process of development nested in an environment even vaguely resembling the institution-free tale of economic interactions that one finds in a good deal of contemporary economic theory. On the contrary, all historical experiences of sustained economic growth—starting at least from the English Industrial Revolution—find their enabling conditions in a rich set of complementary institutions, shared behavioral norms, and public policies. And, more narrowly, discretionary public policies have been major ingredients of national development strategies, especially in catch-up countries, throughout the history of modern capitalism.

Conversely, from a symmetric perspective, there are extremely sound theoretical reasons supporting the notion that *institutions and policies always matter* in all processes of technological learning and economic coordination and change.

We start from the latter issue and outline some theoretical foundations for institution building and policies (section 1). Next, we briefly discuss the nature and dynamics of technological knowledge, as such a fundamental driver of development (section 2). Technological learning, however, does not occur within isolated entities and even less so with isolated individuals. Rather, technological and organizational learning occurs within webs of firms and nonprofit institutions. Indeed, the emergence and development of national systems of production and innovation entail major coordination challenges, in that policies foster (or don't) the coevolution of technological capabilities, organizational forms, and incentive structures. Section 3 discusses a taxonomy of such policies, and analyzes the dilemmas typically facing emerging economies—in particular the potential conflict between revealed "comparative advantages" and notional opportunities for future learning. Section 5, takes a historical perspective and tries to distill the lessons from successful instances of industrialization useful for the design of current and future industrial policies. Finally, in section 6 such lessons are translated into a series of policy prescriptions concerning, among others, science and technology policies, infant-industry measures, intellectual property rights, and trade policies.

1. THE GENERAL THEORETICAL FRAMEWORK

A MISLEADING POINT OF DEPARTURE: MARKET FAILURE

Conventionally, one would start from the very general question "When are public policies required?" from the point of view of the theory, and, as known, the standard answer would be "when there are market failures" of some kind. However, albeit quite common, the market failure language tends to be quite misleading in that, in order to evaluate the necessity and efficacy of any policy, it takes as a yardstick those conditions under which standard normative ("welfare") theorems hold. The problem with such a framework is not that market failures are irrelevant. Quite the contrary: the problem is that hardly any empirical setup bears a significant resemblance with the yardstick in terms of, e.g., market completeness, perfectness of competition, knowledge possessed by economic agents, stationarity of technologies and preferences, "rationality" in decision making, etc. (The list is indeed very long!) In a profound sense, when it is judged with standard canons, *the whole world can be seen as a huge market failure!*

Indeed, this is implicitly recognized in any serious policy discussion, where the argument about policy almost never is about whether the situation at hand is actually "optimal," but rather about whether the problems with the incumbent institutional setup are sufficiently severe to warrant active policy measures. In all that, most often the demand for "proofs for failures" mainly plays as a device to put the burden of the evidence away from the believers in the dogma that in general "more market is always better than less."

It has been more than sixty years since Robert Solow showed persuasively that most of the increases in standards of living were due to technological progress and learning, and since Kenneth Arrow, Richard Nelson, and Christopher Freeman began the analysis of endogenous technological learning.

But the full disruptive implications of their work for the neoclassical model, which was central for instance to Solow's analysis, have still not been taken onboard. And the implications for policy have been even less absorbed into mainstream thinking.

Note that just taking seriously the role of information challenges all the standard results and conclusions.

Equilibrium might not exist. When it does exist, it could look markedly different from that depicted by the standard model. Supply might not equal demand. There could be credit rationing and unemployment. Equilibrium might not be characterized by a single price. There might be price dispersions. Price might systematically exceed marginal cost. And market equilibrium, even when it formally exists, is not in general Pareto efficient.

The impact on both theory and policy is profound.

Indeed, information can be thought of as a particular kind of knowledge (see, among others, Stiglitz and Greenwald (2014) and Dosi and Nelson (2010)), with the properties of the latter having even more profound effects.

On the micro side is overwhelming evidence that most firms are operating below "best practices" (see Dosi 2007; Dosi and Nelson 2010). Does a production possibilities curve based on the assumption that firms are all efficient—or that their knowledge is fixed—make sense? Is it a useful tool *at all*? Even within a single sector and a single country? The answer is emphatically negative, and more so across countries.

Together, comparative advantages need to be reexamined: a country's long-term comparative advantage is based in part on its comparative learning capabilities.

In a learning economy, there is no presumption that the market economy, on its own, is efficient—in either a static or dynamic sense.

Indeed, the presumption is to the contrary. That means that there are policies that can lead to higher sustained growth. But many of the policies that enhance economywide learning are the opposite of those derived from the standard neoclassical model. A focus on short-run allocative efficiency may lead to slower growth. Industrial policies—including interventions in trade—typically will be desirable, and there may even be a permanent part of an economy's policy framework, not just in the early catch-up stage.

Much nearer are the empirical realities of markets and nonmarket institutions which govern production, exchanges, and economic coordination in modern economies. In the following we discuss both issues of (1) the *boundaries* between market and nonmarket forms of economic organization and (2) *embeddedness* of markets themselves into *complementary* nonmarket institutions.

Let us start from the simplest domains.

A RATHER UNIVERSAL ROLE OF INSTITUTIONS: DETERMINATION OF BOUNDARIES BETWEEN NONMARKET AND MARKET INTERACTIONS

Which types of social activities are subject to (1) decentralized production and (2) money-mediated exchanges, and which ones are not? There is an impressive range from the economically banal to the morally outrageous. "Strategic" goods? Pharmaceuticals? "Natural" monopolies? Public utilities? Education? Child care? Retirement benefits? Health care? Human organs? Blood? Husbands and wives? Political votes? Children? Court rulings?

In another work one of us (Nelson 2005) discusses precisely the *governance structure* of a few goods and services wherein their provision has often relied on, in part or entirely, nonmarket mechanisms.

Clearly the question of the determination of market boundaries applies to both developed and developing countries but is particularly crucial in emerging and ex-centrally planned economies where the boundaries between market and nonmarket institutions have still to be clearly defined. Far from the fury of market fundamentalism, our basic view there is that nonmarket institutions (ranging from public agencies to professional associations, from trade unions to community structures) are at the core of the very constitution of the whole socioeconomic fabric.

Their role goes well beyond the enforcement of property rights. Rather, they offer the main governance structure in many activities where market exchanges are socially inappropriate or simply ineffective. At the same time, they shape and constrain the behavior of economic agents toward competitors, customers, suppliers, employees, government officials, etc. They are also instrumental in curbing the "self-destruction perils" flagged long ago by Polanyi (1957) and Hirschman (1982).

Moreover, notice that even when one encounters a prevailing "market form" of governance, the latter is embedded in a rich thread of nonmarket institutions.

Pharmaceutical is a very good case in point. Here in all countries with an effective, for-profit pharmaceutical industry, one finds government programs that support biomedical research, generally at universities and public laboratories. Together, the university parts of these programs are associated also with scientific training for people who go on to work in pharmaceutical companies after finishing their education. Moreover, in virtually all countries, public funds and programs play a major role in the procurement of pharmaceuticals. And, finally, in virtually all countries there are various forms of regulation of pharmaceuticals that go well beyond a textbook guarantee of property rights and integrity of exchanges.

Or consider aircraft and airline services. In all countries that have major aircraft production, government funds play a significant role in R&D. And in most countries both the airports and the traffic control system are not only funded but also run by government agencies. Even in the simple case of trucking and the use of automobiles, the public sector plays a major role: it builds and maintain roads, regulates safety, and inspects vehicles, while a large share of the police is traffic police.

Indeed, even when the conditions that allow markets to work reasonably well are fulfilled—in terms of distribution of information, norms of interaction, etc.—we propose that their role should be evaluated not only in terms of allocative efficiency (whatever that means in ever-changing economies) but also as environments that continuously allow the experimentation of new products, new techniques of production, and new organizational forms. In this perspective, markets, *when they work,* operate as (imperfect) mechanisms of selection. Also at this level, the ways in which the institutional architecture organizes the interactions among economic agents and the ways in which policies regulate behaviors and forms of competition have a paramount importance.

2. THE GENERATION, ADOPTION, AND ECONOMIC EXPLOITATION OF NEW SCIENTIFIC AND TECHNOLOGICAL KNOWLEDGE

While the importance of institutions and policies is ubiquitous in all processes of economic coordination and change, this is particularly so with respect to the generation and use of information and knowledge. As we know since the early works of Nelson (1959) and Arrow (1962), they are in many respects similar to a "public good" in that the use of information is

- *Nonrival* (the fact that one uses it does not prevent others from using it too)
- Nonexcludable (were it not for institutional provisions such as patent-based monopoly rights of exploitation)

Moreover, the generation of information is subject to sunk, up-front costs of production and basically zero cost of reproduction.

If anything, there are increasing returns to the use of information, in the sense that the more we use it, the easier it is and dynamically the higher is the likelihood of learning and producing ourselves "better," "novel," in some sense "innovative" further pieces of information.

Note that these very properties of information *intrinsically* entail phenomena of *market failures*, to use the jargon just criticized above (also in that marginal prices are of no guidance to efficient market allocation and equilibria might even fail to exist).

Further insights may be gained by distinguishing between sheer information and knowledge. Knowledge includes (1) the preexisting cognitive categories that allow information to be interpreted and put to use and (2) search and problem-solving heuristics irreducible to well-defined algorithms.

All forms of knowledge have a significant tacit aspect, highly complementary to codified information, which makes them person- or organization-embodied and rather sticky in their transmission. Indeed, this is one of the fundamental reasons why technological catch-up by developing countries remains a challenging task even in an era of globalization and free-information flows.

It happens that all processes of generation of new scientific and technological knowledge as well as of technological imitation and adaptation involve a rich variety of complementary actors, often including business firms but, together, public training and research institutions, "communities of practice," technical societies, and trade unions, among others.

In a fundamental sense, institutions and policies addressing technological learning have to do with the construction of *national systems of production and innovation.*

In fact, the process of catch-up involves innovation in an essential way. The innovating activities that drive the process or course differ from the innovation that is the focus of a good deal of research and technological learning in advanced economies. The new technologies, and new practices more generally, that are being taken onboard, while new to the country playing catch-up, generally are well established in countries at the frontier. And much of the innovation that is required is organizational and institutional. But what is going on in catch-up most certainly is innovation in the sense that there is a break from past familiar practices, considerable uncertainty about how to make the new practice work effectively, a need for sophisticated learning by doing and using, and a high risk of failure as well as a major potential payoff from success.

Together, the dynamics of industrialization rest upon major structural transformations that entail a changing importance of different branches of economic activity as generators of both technological and organizational innovations. The recent literature on innovation highlights the diversity in the sources of learning opportunities and the complementarities among them (Dosi 1988a; Cimoli and Dosi 1995; Mowery and Nelson 1999). In fact, in each epoch there appear to be technologies whose domains of application are so wide and their role so crucial that the pattern of technical change of each country depends to a good extent on the national capabilities in mastering production, imitation, and innovation in such crucial knowledge areas (e.g., in the past, mechanical engineering, electricity, and electrical devices and nowadays also information technologies); what Freeman and Perez (1988) call *new technoeconomic paradigms.* Moreover, the linkages among production activities often embody structured hierarchies whereby the most dynamic technological paradigms play a fundamental role as sources of technological skills, problem-solving opportunities, and productivity improvements. Thus, these core technologies shape the overall absolute advantages and disadvantages of each country. The patterns of change for each country in these technologies does not average out with the technological capabilities in other activities, but are complementary to them. These core technologies often also imply the construction of basic infrastructures and networks common to a wide range of activities (such as the electricity grid, road system, and telecommunication information networks). Historical evidence strongly supports the view that self-sustained technological dynamism in catch-up countries is hardly possible without a progressive construction of a widening manufacturing sector involving also indigenous skills in a set of core technologies.

3. COMPLEMENTARITIES, INCENTIVES, AND COORDINATION HURDLES

So far, we addressed some basic motivations underlying the policies and institutions affecting primarily the mechanism of knowledge accumulation. But what about *coordination* problems, stemming in a first instance from the very interrelatedness among multiple heterogeneous agents?

Of course, the distinction is not as clear as that: coordination involves also demand (Keynesian) feedbacks and requires reasonable degrees of incentive compatibility among agents as well as coordination in learning processes. However, the fundamental coordination issues here are the *matching* between decentralized behaviors, the radically different outcomes that such processes might entail depending on the institutions in which they are nested, and the importance of policies in all that.

Interestingly, the basics are quite clear to some founding figures of development economics as a discipline (including Nurske, Gerschenkron, Rosenstein-Rodan, Hirschman, and Prebisch).

Consider the following remarks by Nurske (1953, 13–14):

> In our present context it seems to me that the main point is to recognize how a frontal attack of this sort—a wave of capital investments in a number of different industries—can economically succeed while any particular industry may be blocked or discouraged by the limitation of the pre-existing market. Where any single enterprise might appear quite inauspicious and impracticable, a wide range of projects in different industries may succeed because they will all support each other, in the sense that the people engaged in each project, now working with more real capital per head and with greater efficiency in terms of output per man-hour, will provide an enlarged market for the products of the new enterprises in other industries. In this way the market difficulty, and the drag it imposes on individual incentives to invest, is removed or at any rate alleviated by means of a dynamic expansion of the market thorough investment carried out in a number of different industries.

Together consider the remarks by Gerschenkron (1962, 10–11):

> Industrialization process begins only if the industrialization movement can proceed, as it were, along a broad front, starting simultaneously along many lines of economic activities. This is partly the result of existence of complementarity and indivisibilities in economic process. Railroads cannot be built unless coal mines are opened up at the same time; building half a railroad will not do if an inland center is to be connected with a port city. Fruits of industrial progress in certain lines are received as external economies by other branches of industry whose progress in turn accords benefit to the former. In viewing the economic history of Europe in the nineteenth century, the impression is very strong that only when industrial development could commence on a large scale did the tension between the preindustrialization conditions and the benefits expected from industrialization become sufficiently strong to overcome the existing obstacles and to liberate the forces that made for industrial policies.

Similar insights are behind Rosenstein-Rodan's *big push* theory (Rosenstein-Rodan, 1943; cf. also the contemporary revisitation in Murphy, Shleifer, and Vishny, 1989): As one discusses in Hoff and Stiglitz (2001), a crucial feature on which the relevance of big push models rest is diffused externalities, where the interaction effects occur through system-wide variables such as aggregate demand, industrial demand for inputs, or search costs.

These are all domains where appropriate mixes of policies may and do help—as historical experiences have shown—to "delock" from the past and foster novel developmental trajectories ultimately yielding dynamic *national and sectoral systems* of production and innovation.[1] It has been so in the past, and as we shall argue below, there is little reason to believe that it will be radically different in the future, notwithstanding so-called globalization.

Indeed, institutions can be seen as the *social technologies* (Nelson and Sampat 2001; Stiglitz and Greenwald 2014) mastering externalities and matching and mismatching patterns between innovative activities, underlying incentives structures, investment, saving propensities, labor training, and socially distributed skills. In turn, the institutions governing such externalities and complementarities also govern interaction rules among agents, shaping their beliefs and the information they may access, their "ethos" and behavioral rules. (For a more detailed discussion, see Hoff and Stiglitz 2001.)

THE INSTITUTIONAL DEVELOPMENT OF TECHNOLOGICAL CAPABILITIES, ORGANIZATIONS, AND INCENTIVE STRUCTURES: COEVOLUTIONARY DYNAMICS

A fundamental element in countries that successfully caught up with the leaders during the nineteenth and twentieth centuries was active government support of the catch-up process, involving various forms of protection and direct and indirect subsidy. The guiding policy argument has been the need of domestic industry—in the industries of the day judged critical in the development process—for some protection from advanced firms in the leading nations. Alexander Hamilton's argument (1791) for infant-industry protection in the new United States was virtually identical to that put forth decades later by List (1841) regarding Germany's needs. Gerschenkron's (1962) famous essay documents the policies and new institutions used in continental Europe to enable catch-up with Britain. The same story also fits well with the case of Japan, and of Korea and Taiwan somewhat later. In many countries these policies engendered not successful catch-up but a protected inefficient home industry. However, they also were the hallmark during the twentieth century of all the countries that have achieved their catch-up goals.[2] We need to learn more about both the circumstances under which infant-industry protection leads to a strong indigenous industry and the conditions under which it is self-defeating; indeed several contributions to this project shed new light on the issue.

These policies obviously angered companies in the leading countries, and their governments, particularly if the supported industry not only supplied its home market but also began to invade the world market. While the case made after World War II for free trade was mostly concerned with eliminating protection and subsidy among the rich countries, (and at that time there was sympathy for the argument that some infant-industry protection was often useful in developing countries), the more recent international treaties increasingly have been used against import protection and subsidy in countries seeking to catch up from far behind.

Our belief is that Hamilton and List were and continue to be right that successful catch-up in industries where international trade is considerable requires some kind of infant-industry protection or other modes of support.

Moreover, during the nineteenth and early twentieth centuries, many developing countries operated with intellectual property rights regimes which did not restrict seriously the ability of their companies to effectively copy technologies used in the advanced countries. There are many examples where licensing agreements were involved, but we believe that for the most part these were vehicles through which technology transfer was effected for a fee or other considerations, rather than instances of aggressive protection of intellectual property by the company in the advanced country.

Like infant-industry protection and subsidy, conflicts tended to emerge largely when the catch-up company began to encroach onto world markets, or even to export to the home market of the company with the patent rights. Increasing instances of this clearly were a major factor in inducing the treaty on Trade Related Intellectual Property Rights. But this treaty makes vulnerable to prosecution not just companies in developing countries that are exporting, but also companies that stay in their home markets.

Given that, what are the different domains of policy intervention and how do they map into different policy measures and related institutions? Table 2.1 summarizes an exploratory taxonomy.

As a last resort, policies and other activities of "institutional engineering" affect together (1) the technological capabilities of individual and corporate organizations, and the rate at which they actually learn; (2) the economic signals that they face (including, of course, profitability signals and perceived opportunity costs); (3) the ways they interact with one another and with nonmarket institutions (e.g., public agencies, development banks, training and research entities).

It happens that all major developed countries present, indeed, relatively high degrees of intervention—whether consciously conceived as industrial policies or not—that affect all the above variables. And this applies, even more so, to the period when today's developed countries were catching up with the international leader. What primarily differentiates the various countries are the instruments, the institutional arrangements, and the philosophy of intervention.

In another work, one of us considers the case of Japanese policies, especially in relation to electronic technologies, after World War II, as a paradigmatic example of catch-up policies (Dosi 1984).

Interestingly, Japan appears to have acted comprehensively upon all the variables categorized in our taxonomy above. A heavy discretionary intervention on the structure of signals (also involving formal and informal protection against imports and foreign investments) recreated the

Table 2.1 Some Classification of the Variables and Processes That Institutions and Policies Act on (in General and with Particular Reference to Technological Learning)

Domains of Policy Intervention	Policy Measures	Related Institutions
(1) Opportunities of scientific and technological innovation	Science policies, graduate education, "frontier" technological projects	Research universities, public research centers, medical institutes, space and military agencies, etc.
(2) Socially distributed learning and technological capabilities	Broader education and training policies	From primary education to polytechnics, to U.S.-type "land-grant colleges," etc.
(3) Targeted industrial support measures, affecting, e.g., types of firms, etc.—first the structure, ownership, modes of governance of business firms (e.g., domestic versus foreign, family-owned versus publicly owned companies, etc.)	From the formation of state-owned firms to their privatization, from "national champions" policies to policies affecting multinational corporations' investments, all the way to the legislation affecting corporate governance	State-owned holdings, public merchant banks, public "venture capitalist," public utilities
(4) The capabilities of economic agents (in the first instance business firms) in terms of the technological knowledge they embody, the effectiveness and speed with which they search for new technological and organizational advances, etc.	Cf. especially points (2) and (3) and R&D policies; policies affecting the adoption of new equipment; etc.	
(5) The economic signals and incentives profit-motivated agents face (including actual and expected prices and profit rates, appropriability conditions for innovations, entry barriers, etc.)	Price regulations; tariffs, and quotas in international trade; intellectual property rights (IPR) regimes, etc.	Related regulatory agencies, agencies governing research and production subsidies, trade-controlling entities, agencies granting and controlling IPRs
(6) Selection mechanisms (overlapping with the above)	Policies and legislation affecting antitrust and competition; entry and bankruptcy; allocation of finance; markets for corporate ownership; etc.	Antitrust authorities, institutions governing bankruptcy procedures, etc.
(7) Patterns of distribution of information and of interaction among different types of agents (e.g. customers, suppliers, banks, shareholders, managers, workers)	Governance of labor markets, product markets, bank-industry relationships, etc., all the way to collectively shared arrangements for within-firms information-sharing mobility and control, forms of cooperation and competition among rival firms, etc. (cf., for example, the historical differences between Japanese and Anglo-Saxon firms)	

"vacuum environment" that is generally enjoyed only by the technological leader(s). However, this was matched by a pattern of fierce oligopolistic rivalry between Japanese companies and a heavy export orientation which fostered technological dynamism and prevented any exploitation of protection simply in terms of collusive monopolistic pricing.

It is tempting to measure this Japanese experience—notwithstanding, recent, mostly macroeconomic difficulties—with others, on average less successful, such as the European ones, which heavily relied upon one single instrument, financial transfers (especially R&D subsidies and transfers on capital account), leaving to the endogenous working of the international market both the determination of the patterns of signals and the response capabilities of individual firms. Certainly, there are country-specific features of the Japanese example which are hardly transferable. However, that case, in its striking outcome, points at a general possibility of reshaping the patterns of comparative advantages as they emerge from the endogenous evolution of the international markets.

The comparison between the experience of Far Eastern countries and Latin American ones is equally revealing (cf., among others, Amsden 1989 and 2001; Wade 1990; Kim and Nelson 2000; Dosi, Freeman, and Fabiani 1994).

In a nutshell, Korea—as well as other Far-Eastern economies—has been able to "twist around" absolute and relative prices and channel the resources stemming from "static" comparative advantages toward the development of activities characterized by higher learning opportunities and demand elasticities (Amsden 1989).[3] And they did that in ways that penalized rent-seeking behaviors by private firms. In fact, the major actors in technological learning have been large business groups—the *chaebols*—which were able at a very early stage of development to internalize skills for the selection of technologies acquired from abroad, their efficient use, and their adaptation and, not much later, were able to grow impressive engineering capabilities (cf. Kim 1993).

This process has been further supported by a set of institutions and networks for improving human resources (Amsden 1989). All this sharply contrasts with the Latin American experience, where the arrangement between the state and the private sector has often been more indulgent over inefficiencies and rent accumulation and less attentive to the accumulation of socially diffused technological capabilities and skills.

Ultimately, success or failure appears to depend on the combinations of different institutional arrangements and policies, insofar as they affect learning processes by individuals and organizations, on one hand, and selection processes (including of course market competition), on the other.

Certainly, the historical experience shows a great variety of country and sector-specific combinations between the types of policies illustrated above. Some subtle regularities nonetheless emerge.

First, a regularity, holding from nineteenth-century Europe and the United States all the way to contemporary times, is the centrality of public agencies, such as universities, and public policies in the generation and establishment of new technological paradigms.

Second, "incentives are often not enough." A crucial role of policies is to affect the capabilities of the actors, especially in the foregoing case of new technological paradigms, but also in all cases of catch-up whereby no reasonable incentive structure might be sufficient to motivate private actors to surmount big technological lags.

Third, market discipline is helpful insofar as it weeds out the low performers and rewards the high performers within particular populations of firms. However, nothing guarantees that too high selective shocks will not wipe out the entire populations themselves, thus also eliminating any future learning possibility.

Fourth, policies—especially those aimed at catch-up—generally face the need to balance measures aimed at capability building (and also at protecting the "infant learner") with mechanisms curbing inertia and rent seeking. For example, the latter are indeed one of the major elements missing in the old Latin American experience of import substitution while the former are what is lacking under many more recent "liberalization" policies.

Fifth, historically, a successful catch-up effort in terms of per capita income and wages has always been accompanied by catch-up in the new and most dynamic technological paradigms, irrespective of the initial patterns of comparative advantages, specialization, and market-generated signals. Our conjecture is that, ceteris paribus, the structural need for policies affecting *also* the patterns of economic signals (including relative prices and relative profitabilities) as they emerge from the international market will be greater, the higher the distance of any one country from the technological frontier. This is what Amsden (1989) has provocatively called policies of deliberately "getting the prices wrong." Conversely, endogenous market mechanisms tend to behave in a "virtuous" manner for those countries that happen to be on the frontier, especially in the newest and most promising technologies. This is broadly confirmed by historical experience: unconditional free trade often happened to be advocated and fully exploited only by the technologically and politically leading countries.

SOME FUNDAMENTAL TRADE-OFFS FACING INSTITUTIONS AND POLICIES IN LEARNING ECONOMIES

In a world characterized by technical change (both *continuous* change along defined technological trajectories and *discontinuous* change related to the emergence of new technological paradigms), technological lags and leads shape the patterns of intersectoral and interproduct profitability signals and thus also the patterns of microeconomic allocation of resources. The latter, however, may affect the long-term macroeconomic dynamism of each country, in terms of both rates of growth of income consistent with the foreign balance constraint and of technological innovativeness. In the last resort, this happens because the effects of a multiplicity of signals (related to profitability, long-term demand growth, and technological opportunities) upon microeconomic processes of adjustments are likely to be *asymmetric*. In other words, we elaborate on this point by distinguishing between the notions of (1) *allocative* efficiency, (2) *innovative* (or "Schumpeterian") efficiency, and (3) *growth* efficiency of particular patterns of production (Dosi, Pavitt, and Soete 1990; Stiglitz and Greenwald 2014). There we argue that, especially in countries far from the technological frontier, patterns of allocation of resourcesthat are "efficient" on the grounds of the incumbent distribution of technological capabilities and relative prices might well entail negative long-term effects in terms of demand elasticities of the goods one country will be able to produce (the "growth efficiency") and of the innovative potential associated with that (the criterion of "innovative efficiency"). Whenever trade-offs between different notions of efficiency arise, "suboptimal" or "perverse" macroeconomic outcomes may emerge. Since the *future* pattern of technological advantages and disadvantages is also related to the *present* allocative patterns, we can see at work here dynamic processes which Kaldor called of *circular causation*. Economic signals related to intersectoral profitabilities—which lead in a straightforward manner to comparative advantages and relative specializations—certainly control and check the allocative efficiency of the various productive employments, but may also play a more ambiguous or even perverse role in relation to long-term macroeconomic trends.

Note that these possible trade-offs have little to do with the information efficiency of market processes (even if, of course, various forms of information asymmetries are likely to make things worse). Rather it is the general condition of an economic system that technological opportunities vary across products and across sectors. Moreover, within each technology and each sector the technological capabilities of each firm and each country are associated with the actual process of production and innovation in the area. Thus, the mechanisms regarding resource allocation *today* affect also where technical skills will be accumulated, (possibly) innovation undertaken, economics of scale reaped, etc. However, the potential for these effects differs widely across technologies and sectors. This is another aspect of the irreversibility of economic processes: present allocative choices influence the direction and rate of the future evolution of technological coefficients. Whenever we abandon the idea of technology as a set of blueprints and we conceive technical progress as a joint product with manufacturing, it is possible to imagine an economic system that is dynamically better off than otherwise (in terms of productivity, innovativeness, etc.), if it evolves in disequilibrium vis-à-vis conditions of allocative efficiency.

It is rather easy to see how such trade-offs between allocative efficiency and innovative efficiency can emerge. The patterns of specialization (with their properties of allocative efficiency) are determined, for each country, by the relative size of the sector-specific technology gaps (or leads) (see in Dosi, Pavitt, and Soete 1990). Whenever the gap is highest in the most dynamic technologies (i.e., those characterized by the highest technological opportunities), allocative efficiency will conflict directly with innovative efficiency. We would suggest that the likelihood of such trade-offs between the two notions of efficiency is proportional to the distance of each country from the technological frontier in the newest, most dynamic, and most pervasive technologies.[4]

A similar argument applies to the trade-offs between allocative and growth efficiency: ultimately countries may well end up by "efficiently" specializing in the production of commodities which a relatively small or even decreasing number of world consumers want to buy, thus tightening their ability to grow consistently with some foreign balance constraint.[5]

Under conditions of nondecreasing (often increasing) returns, there is no straightforward way in which markets can relate the varying growth and innovative efficiencies of the various commodities to relative profitability signals for the microeconomic agents.[6]

This also defines a fundamental domain for policies.

A detailed understanding of, and intervention upon, patterns of signals, rules of allocative responses, and forms of institutional organization of the "economic machine" are particularly important in those phases of transition from a technological regime (based on old technological paradigms) to a new one. These historical periods define a new set of opportunities and threats for each country: the patterns of international generation and diffusion of technologies become more fluid as do, consequently, the international trade flows and the relative levels of per capita income.

The contemporary economy, we believe, is undergoing such a change. In the process, comparative advantages become the self-fulfilling prophecy of a successful set of institutional actions and private strategies: ex post, technological and economic success makes optimal from the point of view of the economist what ex ante is in a political dream.

4. POLICY LESSONS FROM THE PAST AND WISDOM FOR THE FUTURE

The lessons from the past are useful insofar as they apply also to the future. Hence, any normative conclusions have to be qualified with some words on the possible discontinuities that globalization implies vis-à-vis previous development patterns. In particular, what about the millenarian notion according to which discretionary industrial, technology, and trade policies *might have been necessary* in a world of nation states that constrained the full display of market forces, but are redundant or harmful nowadays? In fact, the evidence (cf., among many others, Castaldi et al. 2009; Stiglitz 2006) suggests that the secular divergences in technological capabilities, growth rates, and levels of per capita income (across and within countries) have continued, if not increased, under the last decades of globalization. Countries differ—possibly even more so than in the past—in their capabilities of absorption of production technologies and product design capabilities developed in "frontier" countries. If anything has changed, it is that under multiple forms of localized increasing returns, greater degrees of international integration fostered by globalization—when left to themselves—may well lead to phenomena of increasing national and international differentiation with self-reinforcement and lock-in onto particular production activities, specialization patterns, and technological capabilities (or lack of them). Globalization is by itself no recipe for some sort of natural catch-up in technological capabilities or for easy convergence in incomes. On the contrary, more interdependent economies are likely to require *more and more sophisticated* measures of policy intervention by the weaker countries. It was already so when Hamilton was trying to design an industrialization strategy for the new-born United States in a world of British-dominated globalization, and it continues to be so nowadays.

Moreover, yet other aspects of unbridled globalization, which cannot be discussed at length here, add to the demands for policy governance. So, as we comment in Stiglitz (2006), in the new millennium, and in the last part of the previous one, income distribution has dramatically changed against wages and in favor of profits, with 59 percent of the world population living in countries with increasing inequality and only 5 percent living in countries with increasing equality (ILO 2004; Cornia, Addison, and Kiiski 2005). Further, globalization has favored the transformation of employment in both developed and developing countries working against organized labor and against employment guarantees; it has made acute the conflict between the requirements of international competitiveness and social norms (e.g., on work safety, working hours, environmental protection, child labor); it has brought pressure on national government to dismantle social welfare systems in countries that have them and against their establishment in countries that do not have them yet; and globalization has made it harder to impose fiscal levies on "mobile factors," i.e., capital, as compared to "immobile" ones, i.e., labor; on all these points see in Stiglitz (2002 and 2006); and Rodrik (1997).

Of course, the urgency to govern these consequences of the contemporary regime of international economic and political relations complements the more specifically "developmental" reasons motivating industrialization policies. Concerning the latter, while the basic historical lessons, to repeat, continue to hold, the political and ideological context has indeed changed, entailing also the actual *or perceived* disempowerment of national or even supernational institutions (such as the European Union) of many of the policy instruments that historically allowed the governance of the political economy of industrial development. Needless to say, also the mechanisms and degrees of disempowerment differ across the world. In some cases, it is an item of packages imposed at gunpoint from the outside; in other (even less justifiable!) cases, it is a self-inflicted hardship paddled by "market talibans." Indeed, there is nothing new in the fact that countries that have been successful in reaching the technological and income frontier next tend to "kick away the ladder" (Chang 2002) which allowed them to get there in the first place and to rebuild a free-market virginity. What is specific to this globalization wave is the formation of an increasingly "globalized" ruling class, often with a degree in economics obtained in Anglo-Saxon countries (generally the United States), taking home also policy medicines that the country of origin itself frequently finds too unpalatable to swallow.

However, such disruptive sides of the current globalization mode luckily are short of the point of no return. Fortunately, policy making continues to have a lot of unexploited degrees of freedom, and in different ways this applies from Brasilia to Brussels to Washington, D.C. As the orgy of market fanaticism is wearing out, finally hit by the evidence of its failure, this chapter comes at a high time of renewed reflection and tries to offer a fresh look at the policies and institutions fostering technological and organizational learning and industrialization across and within countries.

Extensive empirical evidence on development is seen as a process that links microlearning dynamics, economywide accumulation of technological capabilities, and industrial development. Different learning patterns and different national "political economies" yield different patterns of industrialization. However, it happens that all the countries that are nowadays developed undertook indeed relatively high degrees of intervention to support the accumulation of technological capabilities and the transformation of their organizations of production especially in the early period of industrialization.

From the start of this chapter we emphasized the futility of the search for any "magic bullet" driving industrialization. The process of accumulation of technological and organizational capabilities does play a crucial role—as highlighted by many contributions to Cimoli et al. (2009) and theoretically analyzed in Stiglitz and Greenwald (2014)—but such a process has to be matched (1) by a congruent political economy offering an incentive structure conducive to learning-based rent seeking while curbing rent seeking *tout court* and (2) by a congruent macroeconomic management. By the same token, it is futile to search for any magic policy recipe for automatically yielding industrialization and catch-up.

However, as one is able to identify some regularities in the ingredients and processes driving industrialization, so one can trace some basic ingredients and principles that *successful* policy arrangements historically had and have in common. We spell out some of them.

EMULATION AND SOMETIMES LEAPFROGGING
AS A GENERAL PRINCIPLE INSPIRING POLICIES

Emulation—we borrow the term from Reinert (2007)—is the purposeful effort of imitation of frontier technologies and production activities irrespective of the incumbent profile of comparative advantages. It often involves explicit public policies aimed at "doing what rich countries are doing" in terms of the production profile of the economy, and it always involves microeconomic efforts—on the part of individuals and, more so, firms—to learn how to do things others in frontier countries are already able to do. It is a familiar story over the last three centuries. It dates at least to the case of England vis-à-vis the Low Countries in the period preceding the industrial revolution, and it applies all the way to the contemporary Chinese industrialization.

Emulation concerns primarily—as it ought to—products and processes based on new technological paradigms. In one epoch it meant mechanized textile production and the construction of the related machines. Later it was steel production, electricity-based products and machinery, and internal combustion engines. Nowadays it has to do with, first, information and telecommunication technologies.

In fact, it sometimes happened that catch-up countries not only emulated the leading ones, but also "leapfrogged" in some of the newest and most promising technologies. It happened in the nineteenth-century United States and Germany which forged ahead of England in electromechanical engineering, consumer durables, and synthetic chemistry.

But why should everyone emulate frontier technologies in the first place, rather than being guided by one's own comparative advantages? Or, as the skeptics often put it, isn't it absurd to suggest that everybody should specialize in information and communications technologies (ICT) production?

This very question, in our view, reveals a dangerous albeit widespread confusion over absolute versus comparative advantages. Typically, relatively backward economies display an *absolute disadvantage in everything*; i.e., they are less efficient in the production of every commodity, and in fact the disadvantage in many commodities is likely to be infinite in the sense that they are not able to produce them at all. Catch-up entails closing the gap in production knowledge and learning how to produce novel goods (which at the beginning are generally novel only for the catch-up country, even if they are considered old for the world). This is particularly important with respect to new technological paradigms because such technologies are most often *general purpose*: they influence directly or indirectly most production activities. For example, it was so in the past (and it continues to be so nowadays) in the case of mechanical engineering and electricity as it is today for the case of ICT technologies.

Moreover, goods and pieces of equipment based on the new technological paradigms generally entail higher elasticity of demand and richer opportunities for further technological advance (cf. Castaldi et al. 2009; Cimoli, Dosi, and Stiglitz 2009b). Hence emulation of frontier countries in these activities implies, other things being equal, higher growth possibilities, a greater potential for productivity growth, and eventually domestic product innovation.

The issue of *comparative advantage* is a quite distinct one. The point is made also in Reinert (2007). It is trivially true that any economy has comparative advantages in something or other. So, when one is comparing an advanced ICT economy and a Stone Age one, it is straightforward that the latter is likely to have a comparative advantage in stone-intensive products! However, the distribution of the overall (world) income between the two depends first on the magnitude of absolute advantages (i.e., seen the other way round of the *technological gaps*) between the two economies. Learning and catch-up affect precisely the profile of such advantages and gaps. In the process, changing comparative advantages are only the by-product of the different rates at which learning occurs in different activities.

THE COMPLEMENTARITY BETWEEN TECHNOLOGICAL LEARNING AND THE DEVELOPMENT OF PRODUCTION CAPACITY

As we discussed above, the difference between technological knowledge and sheer information bears important implications in terms of "stickiness" and difficulty in the transmission of the former—embodied as it generally is into specific people, organizations, and local networks. A consequence is also that learning rarely occurs "off line," especially in the initial phases of industrialization. Rather it goes together with the acquisition of production equipment, and with the efforts of learning how to use it and how to adapt it to local conditions (see Bell and Pavitt 1993). In turn, this goes hand in hand with the training of workers and engineers and the formation of managers capable of efficiently running complex organizations.

Of course, no policy maker is in the position to fine-tune the details of the production activities and the patterns of learning which the economy has to exploit. Such details of the actual dynamics depend a good deal on the details of corporate strategies and (why not?) on chance. So, to give an example, there was no way that the Korean policy makers could know, or even less plan, say, a learning push in semiconductor memories rather than microprocessors. However, policy makers ought to be acutely aware of the fact that future capabilities build upon, refine, and modify incumbent ones: hence the policy goal of building *good path dependencies*. The point resonates with similar advice given by Rodrick and Hausmann (2006) when addressing the patterns of product diversification along the development process.

5. SOME POLICY PRESCRIPTIONS

THE NECESSITY OF NURTURING INFANT INDUSTRIES

Consider again the caricature of the Stone Age economy and the ICT one, and allow them to interact. Two properties are quite straightforward. First, the patterns of economic signals will be quite biased in favor of stone-intensive products in one country and ICT-intensive products in the other (i.e., precisely their current comparative advantages). Hence if the former who wants to enter the ICT age has to purposefully *distort market signals* as they come from international exchanges (on the assumption that there are some—it could well be that the ICT economy is unwilling to absorb any stone product). Second, it is quite unlikely that the stone producers, even under the "right" kind of signal, will be able to instantly acquire the knowledge to competitively produce ICT products.

Certainly, all individuals take a long time to learn new skills. Turning violinists into football players and vice versa is rather hard, if at all possible. And, even more so, this applies to organizations and organization building. Even when the transformations are possible, they require time, nurturing, and care. If a newly born violinist, who is an ex-football player, is made to compete with professional violinists, he will make a fool of himself. If a catching-up company is suddenly made to compete with the world leaders, it will most likely disappear. Often, it is already a daunting task to learn how to make—no matter how inefficiently—a product that indeed might be rather standard in technologically more sophisticated economies. To demand also competitive efficiency is similar to asking the violinist to run the 100 meters in around 10 seconds after some quick training rounds.

Safeguarding the possibility of learning is indeed the first basic pillar of the *infant-industry logic*.

On the incentive side, to repeat, market signals left to themselves are often not enough. Indeed, they frequently *discourage* the accumulation of technological capabilities insofar as they ought to occur in activities currently displaying significant comparative *disadvantages* and thus also unfavorable current profitabilities. Also note that financial markets are meager instruments, if at all, for translating a future and uncertain potential for learning into current investment decisions (see Stiglitz 1994; Stiglitz and Greenwald 2014). Thus, there are sound learning-related reasons why historical evidence shows that, just prior to industrial catching-up, average industrial import tariffs are relatively low; they rise rapidly in the catching-up phase, and they fall after a mature industrialization. Indeed, it is during the catching-up phase that the requirement of distorting (international) market signals is more acute, precisely because there are young and still relatively fragile learning infants. Before there were no infants to speak of; after, there are adults able to swim into the wild international ocean by themselves.

Some decades ago, there was the old adage "What is good for General Motors is good for the United States." By turning it upside down, the developmental policy heuristic becomes "Let us make 'good' (that is viable and, in the future, profitable) for Toyota, Sony, etc., and later Samsung, Lenovo, etc., what is good for Japan, Korea, China, etc." Doing that, however, does not involve only signal distortion. As many of the Latin American experiences have shown, this is far from enough. Partly, it has to do with the fact that many forms of protection entail the *possibility* of learning but not, in the language of Khan and Blankenburg (2009), the *compulsion* to innovate as distinct from the sheer incentive to just exploit a monopoly rent, no matter how inefficient and lazy is the potential learner (more on this below). Partly, it has to do with the *conditions of capabilities accumulation and the characteristics of the actors involved*.

After all, even under the best intentions and incentives, the violinist will take time both to learn and to develop his football skills only in a team. In turn, most often, the team will not be the making of sheer self-organization, especially when production entails relatively complex products, as it usually does. At the same time, a violin player might not be the best candidate to play football, irrespective of the incentive structure. Out of metaphor, and contrary to the "De Soto conjecture," industrialization might have rather little to do with the sheer award of property rights and with the establishment of firms as legal entities (cf. Hobday and Perini, 2009). Of course, the legal context does matter and is likely to be a conducive condition (even if cases such as China show the possibility of a fast takeoff even under a regime of poor property right protection and a blurred rule of law). However, this is far from sufficient. In fact, it is quite misleading to think that all over the world there are plenty of sources of technological knowledge just waiting to be exploited, with the lag being due mainly to institutional and incentive-related forces. In fact, irrespective of the opportunities for entrepreneurial exploitation of technological knowledge which the international knowledge frontier *notionally* offers, the fundamental gap regards precisely the *lack of capabilities* in exploring and exploiting them. This is a crucial bottleneck for development. Such gaps apply to rather simple capabilities which even casual visitors of developing countries notice (whenever walking out of IMF paid hotels) regarding, at the early stages of development, (even rather basic activities such as accessing the Internet or processing a credit card) and apply, more so, to firm-level capabilities such as drilling an oil well (or, at early stages, even keeping an existing well working). As discussed above (as well as in Mazzoleni and Nelson 2009), "horizontal" policies of education and training, together with the activities of technical support to firms by public institutions, can go a long way in the capability-enhancing direction. But even that is not likely to be enough. In fact, policies are often bound to get their hands *explicitly* dirty with respect to the *nature, internal structure, and strategies of a few corporate agents themselves.*

Both fostering the emergence and, on a few occasions, explicitly building technologically and organizationally competent firms are indeed fundamental infant-industry nurturing tasks.

Needless to say, the absence or existence of mature technological capabilities and the dynamic capabilities for changing them (cf. Teece, Pisano, and Shuen 1997) in any one country are not a binary variable. However, the distribution is highly uneven. So one could list several dozen countries which can hardly show any. Other countries do display some technologically progressive organizations in a bigger sea of less dynamic firms. In fact, even the most developed countries present only a fraction of technologically dynamic organizations within a much greater population of firms. (Note that all this applies to both high-technology and low-technology sectors as conventionally defined.) In a sense, industrialization has to do with the properties of changing distributions between "progressive" and "backward" firms. How do policies affect such a dynamic? Dahlman (2009) reports on China and India, but the historical lesson goes well beyond these two countries' cases. Policies happened to involve

1. State ownership
2. Selective credit allocation
3. Favorable tax treatment to selective industries
4. Restrictions on foreign investment
5. Local context requirements
6. Special IPR regimes
7. Government procurement
8. Promotion of large domestic firms

In a nutshell, this is the full list of the capital sins that the market faithful are supposed to avoid!

There is here again a widespread misunderstanding to be dispelled, which goes under the heading of "picking the winner" or "national champion" fallacies. Why should governments foster national oligopolists or monopolists in the first place? And how could governments be more "competent" than the market in selecting who is technologically better or worse?

There certainly are unintentional or even counterintentional outcomes of discretionary industrial policies. Of course, untainted pro-market advocates typically quote among OECD countries the failures of the computer support programs and the Concord project in Europe as archetypes of such government failures to be put down on the table against market failures. Economists more sympathetic to the positive role of the public visible hand, including the authors, would find it easy to offer the cases of Airbus or ST Microelectronics in Europe, Petrobras and Embraer in Brazil, etc., among many others, as good counterexamples. However, our point goes well beyond this. The picking-the-winner idea basically builds on the unwarranted myth that there are many competitors out there in the market, and that the government has the arrogance of knowing better than the market in its selection. This is often far from reality in developed countries and, even more so, in catch-up ones. When the U.S. government sponsors Boeing, cutting every possible "fair trade" corner, and the European Union matches up with EADS/Airbus, there is little resembling governments messing around with the "invisible hand of markets," selecting politically appointed winners out of a multitude of candidates instead of letting competition work its way. Rather we observe the "public hand" shaking, twisting, helping a quite *visible* corporate hand, often represented by one or very few members of international oligopolies with their own capabilities and strategic orientations which might or might not match the long-term interests of the countries where they are located. This applies, *much more so,* to developing countries where often governments face the task of helping the birth and growth of *one or very few* candidates to eventually join the same quite-exclusive clubs.

And in fact it happens that the major vehicles of learning and catching up in all episodes of successful industrialization, with the possible exception of little Singapore, have been *domestic* firms—sometimes alone, sometimes in joint venture with foreign multinational corporations (MNCs)—but rarely MNCs themselves. This holds from German and American industrialization all the way to current China—possibly the case nearest to a two-pronged strategy, both fostering the development of domestic firms and trying to squeeze out of foreign MNCs as much technological knowledge as possible.

An ensemble of infant-industry nurturing measures, we have suggested, has been a major ingredient of development policies throughout the history of industrialization, and it continues to be so today. Historically, the infant learners had to be shielded or helped in the domestic and international markets, essentially in their interactions with the more efficient and more innovative firms from frontier countries. This also happens to a large extent today. However, the unique feature of the current "Sinocentric" world, as Castro (2009) puts it, is that many catch-up countries are, so to speak, caught between two fires: the developed world is still ahead of them, but at the same time China quickly reduces its absolute disadvantages across the board, in both more traditional productions and activities based on the newest technological paradigms. And it does so at rates higher than its catch-up in wages (notwithstanding the fast growth of the latter). The outcome is an absolute *cost* advantage in an expanding set of goods including those which were or are central to industrial production of many low- and middle-income countries. In that respect the magnitude and the speed of Chinese industrialization risk exerting a sort of crowding-out effect vis-à-vis the industrializing potential of many other countries. So, e.g., Brazil—a country indeed on the upper tail of

the distribution of industrializers in terms of technological capabilities—
turns out to be a very high-wage country compared to China, but so
also are other less developed Latin America countries, and even African
countries are losing cost-based international (and domestic) competitiveness vis-à-vis China. Is this a reason to give up the infant-industry nurturing philosophy? In our view, it is not. On the contrary, it adds to the
reasons urging to practice various combinations of the capital policy sins
mentioned above. And it ought to push toward a more explicit use of the
domestic or regional markets as venues of culture of an emerging national
industry even when the latter tends to be squeezed on the international
arena between advanced productions and Chinese exports.

INFANT INDUSTRIES UNDER THE NEW
INTERNATIONAL TRADE REGIME

There is another big novelty in the current organization of international
economic relations, namely, the regulatory regime stemming from the
World Trade Organization (WTO) and the Trade-Related Aspects of
Intellectual Property Rights (TRIPS) agreements (more on them below).
This historically unprecedented regime indeed implies a significant
reduction in the degrees of freedom developing countries can enjoy in
their trade policies, while notably all catch-up countries in the preceding
waves of industrialization could exploit a large menu of quotas, tariffs,
and other forms of nontariff barriers. Just as an illustration, note that in
developing countries the average industrial tariffs have fallen from nearly
35 percent in the early 1980s to 12 percent at the turn of the millennium
(conversely, in developed countries they have halved from around 8 percent
to 4 percent: *for industrial goods*, agriculture is quite a different matter).
Together, there are also stronger constraints on what is admissible in
terms of subsidies and other discretionary forms of support to firms and
industries. Countries' members of WTO who do not comply may be
hit by countervailing duties and other retaliatory measures. As a consequence, quite a few of the instruments for industrial policy—which have
been a common practice at least from the times of the U.S. Declaration
of Independence all the way to the development of domestic technological capabilities in China and India—have been outlawed in the new international trade regime. In turn this state of affairs makes it more difficult
for new players—new firms, new sectors, new emerging economies—to
enter existing industries.

What can be done? *Quite a few things can be done also within the incumbent agreements,* full as they are of loopholes and provisions for exceptions generally put there by the negotiators of developed countries with an eye on their special interests, ranging from dubiously defined antidumping measures to national safety and security considerations. Developed countries (in fact, frequently, *the very representatives of special industrial interests* in person, mostly from the United States, the European Union, and Japan) have been quick to exploit these provisions. Developing countries have rarely done so, as they are overwhelmed by the power of the money, the political clout, the lawyers' sophistication, the power of blackmail by stronger states. At least equally common has been so far the unawareness of these opportunities for pragmatic management, certainly thickened—we caricature on purpose—by Chicago-trained ministers of the economy truly believing that all problems come from the fact that trade liberalization has not gone far enough, and directors-general of the ministry of trade who had been taught that the Heckscher-Ohlin-Samuelson theorem on gains from trade is the last word on the subject. In this respect, we believe that if catching-up countries could display the same amount of pragmatism (someone would say *cynicism*) currently practiced by, e.g., U.S. representatives at the WTO, then many degrees of freedom could be regained *even under current rules.* In that BRICS countries (Brazil, Russia, India, China, and South Africa) could play a very important role. Notwithstanding the deep differences among these economies and political systems, they have the skills to negotiate, together with the sheer economic size, the technological capabilities to imitate (or even to forge ahead in new technological paradigms, as in the case of Russia). When (unfortunately too rarely) a BRICS country has put the cards on the table, it has been remarkably successful. Recall the example of the Brazilian negotiations with Big Pharma on the conditions of production and distribution of retroviral drugs. Indeed, this is a case to be studied, improved upon, and repeated more often.

There are other things that must be avoided at all costs. Among them, *shy away from bilateral agreements.*

In brief, bilateral agreements are WTO-plus, and, in terms of Intellectual Property Rights (IPR), 'TRIPS-plus' agreements, whose bottom line is to close the loopholes, exceptions, and safeguard clauses of the original WTO and TRIPS deals, freezing them in favor of the companies and industries from the developed world. So, a bilateral agreement, most often with the United States, offers "preferred country clauses," typically concerning textile exports and the like, which we know do not matter much, if at all, since Chinese exports are more competitive even if one takes away all tariff on the developing country's export. On the other subtler side, the provisions of the bilateral agreement often involve the unconditional acceptance of the IPR regime imposed by the developed partner (we shall come back to that) and curbs on imports from third countries of commodities produced under the various waivers still contemplated under the WTO. So, e.g., if the Brazilian government is able to have internationally recognized its possibility to produce and sell, say, a certain pharmaceutical drug, then the bilateral agreement is generally preventing the signee from buying it, forcing the country to accept all the conditions (and prices!) of Pfizer, Glaxo, etc. In the short term, the neglect of the issue of any minister of finance and trade of, say, Colombia, Morocco, or Jordan—the names are from the list of countries that signed bilateral trade treaties with the United States—appears to be quite reasonable. No firm in these countries would be able in the near future to produce, say, any retroviral drug, but at the same time such deals increase the obstacles to catching-up for the whole group of industrializing countries. Come as it may, bilateral agreements give very little to the country signing them, because in any case China tends to be better and cheaper in the productions concerning the upside of the agreement, and China puts in place many obstacles to the possibilities of technological learning ahead for the developing country, with added constraints to those countries already trying to catch up.

While there are significant and still largely unexploited degrees of freedom unintentionally provided by the current international trade institutions and rules, the straightjacket is likely to remain too tight. As Dahlman (2009) remarks, if China and India "had liberalized from the beginning it is unlikely that they would be the strong economic powers that they have become. To a large extent, some of the strengths of both countries are that they developed strong capabilities before they liberalized." The point applies of course also to the countries which are beginning now their process of capability accumulation. But then the conclusion is that some trade renegotiation is going to be necessary. It is reasonable, e.g., to switch to a regime whereby the objects of multilateral agreement are *average* industrial tariffs as distinct from tariffs that are line-by-line or apply to specific products and sectors.

The system is simpler than the current structure of tariff commitments and would also reconcile multilateral discipline with policy flexibility since countries would be subject to an overall average ceiling while maintaining degrees of freedom for discretionary sectoral strategies. In practice, it would have the effect of balancing tariff increases and reductions, since a country would need to lower its practiced tariffs on some products in order to be able to raise them on others. This would encourage governments to view tariffs as temporary instruments and to focus their efforts to ensure that they effectively serve the purpose they are designed for, i.e., to provide a breathing space for infant industries before they mature and catch up with their counterparts in more advanced countries.

Moreover, within such a logic, the average ceiling itself ought to depend on the levels of technological and economic development, raising as the catch-up process is put in motion and falling as industrialization becomes ripe.

MANAGEMENT OF THE DISTRIBUTION OF RENTS FAVORABLE TO LEARNING AND INDUSTRIALIZATION

The other side of infant-industry nurturing policies discussed above regards the rent distribution profile that they entail. We have already emphasized that offering an opportunity of learning via, say, a temporary trade barrier does not imply per se the incentive to do so, rather simply exploiting the rents stemming from the protection. As outlined by Khan and Blankenburg (2009), successful industrialization policies have all come with rent management strategies providing for *compulsions* for learning and accumulation of both technological capabilities and production capacity. There are three sides to such strategies.

First, on the "carrot" side, policies must be able to transfer resources to the progressive actors: fiscal policies, subsidies, preferential credits, and grants are among the possible means. In fact, fiscal policies are particularly important in the transfer of resources from those activities which benefit from (cyclical or, even more so, trend) improvements in the terms of trade of natural resources, in the form of export levies, royalties indexed on the final price of the commodities, and fines and taxes discouraging environmental damage. Moreover, the construction of industrialization-friendly financial institutions is of paramount importance. In some historical cases, it has meant steering in a pro-development fashion the financing strategies of large private conglomerates, such as the Korean chaebols. In other historical examples it involves state-owned development banks such as BNDES in Brazil. Conversely, the absence of industry-friendly intermediation of finance is a major bottleneck for both learning and investment, as witnessed by most Latin American countries over the most recent decades.

Second, on the "stick" side, governments must have the credibility to commit to developmental rents for periods that are sufficiently long but not too long (of course how long will depend on the sectors; the nature of the technologies; the distance from the international frontier; the initial capabilities of managers, technicians, workers; etc.). Of course, the critical requirement is the credible commitment to stop all rent-yielding measures after some time and, in any case, to withdraw them and impose sanctions on firms and industries failing to achieve technological investment or export targets. A good case to the point has been the carrot-and-stick allocation of scarce foreign currency to firms in Korea in the first industrialization phase as a function of export targets.

Third, the nurturing of domestic oligopolists has to be matched by measures fostering competition. There is a general lesson coming from the experiences of Korea, and some decades before Japan, whereby quasi-monopolistic or oligopolistic domestic firms were forced, quite early on, to compete fiercely on the international markets. And, together, above some threshold of industrial development, antitrust policies are an important deterrent against the lazy exploitation of infant-industry protection.

Indeed, the management of rent distribution in its relation with industrial learning is one of the most difficult and most crucial tasks of any industrialization strategy, as it concerns the overall distribution of income, wealth, and political power across economic and social groups. For example, well beyond the pitfalls of single policy measures, one of the deeper underlying weaknesses of the industrialization process in most Latin American countries has been the absence of pro-development social coalitions with the strength of channeling resources toward industry (i.e., both industrial firms and urban workers). In this respect, the recent episodes of resistance to export levies by land owners in Argentina is just another symptom of a quite diffused anti-industrial political economy, often linking together agricultural, financial, and mining interests.

TIGHT INTELLECTUAL PROPERTY RIGHTS REGIMES NEVER HELP INDUSTRIALIZATION AND SOMETIMES HARM IT

We have already mentioned that all past episodes of successful industrialization have occurred under conditions of *weak* IPR protection.

(For the overall analysis of the relationships between IPR and development, see Cimoli et al. 2013.) All catching-up countries—including, to repeat, at one time also the United States and Germany—have done so through a lot of imitation, reverse engineering, and straightforward copying. But these activities are precisely what strong property rights protection is meant to prevent. How effective IPRs are in achieving this objective depends a lot on the technologies and the sectors (see Dosi, Marengo, and Pasquali 2006), but certainly when they are effective, they are likely to represent an obstacle to domestic technological learning. Conversely, if IPR protections *may* represent an incentive to innovate in *frontier* countries—a claim indeed quite controversial, not supported by particularly robust evidence (for a discussions see Cimoli et al., 2013; Dosi, Marengo, and Pasquali 2006)—there is no evidence that they have any positive effect in spurring innovative activities in catch-up countries. Certainly, successful industrializers at some point start innovating and also patenting, but typically—a century ago as well as today—they fill their patent claim in frontier countries where their strongest competitors are likely to be based. At the same time, the domestic IPR regime has been characteristically weak. The situation, however, has recently changed with TRIPS agreements which have basically extended the tightest IPR rules of developed countries to all the signing countries, including developing ones, and has been made even worse by the already mentioned bilateral agreements. Further, TRIPS has taken away the possibility of differentiation of the regime of protection across products and technologies. For example, even countries such as Italy and Switzerland were not granting IPR protection to pharmaceuticals (indeed an area where patents are very effective appropriability devices) until the 1980s! This is not possible any longer under the new TRIPS rules. Finally, one is witnessing an unprecedented aggressiveness in IPR enforcement by developed world MNCs, even when the stakes are low and the moral outrage is rampant, as in the case of retroviral drugs to be used with third world patients.

What can catch-up countries do?

In principle, the first and easiest thing to do is to *be aware* and never buy the story that "IPRs are good for development because they are good for innovation." On the contrary, in many technological areas they are largely irrelevant for both innovation and technological catch-up. In other areas such as *drugs*, IPRs are definitely harmful for imitation and capability building in catch-up countries (while they have indeed a dubious effect on the rates of innovation in frontier countries). A consequence of such an awareness is also the need of greater efforts to build institutional capabilities and a clear technology acquisition strategy to orient negotiations and dispute settlements.

Second, and relatedly, TRIPS agreements contain a series of loopholes, safeguard clauses, and exceptional provisions, e.g., concerning compulsory licensing, which catch-up countries have still to learn how to exploit.

Third, the most advanced among catch-up countries ought to strive to offer to relatively less developed countries appealing regional agreements which could be viable alternatives to the bilateral agreements with the United States (and the European Union) generally containing IPR provisions even stricter than those of TRIPS.

Fourth, in this case, as in the trade of goods, already discussed, a new wave of multilateral negotiations is likely to be needed that is aimed at

1. Reducing the breadth and width of IPR coverage
2. Expanding the domain of *unpatentability*, from scientific knowledge to algorithms to data
3. Conditioning the degrees of IPR protection on the relative level of economic and technological development of each country

After all, the current international IPR regime is largely the response to the special appropriability interest of a small *subset* of developed countries' firms—basically Big Pharma and biotechnology, Microsoft and Hollywood. A reform in the directions just indicated would benefit catch-up countries, but also the first-world consumers, without doing any harm to the overall rate of innovation.

AVOID THE NATURAL RESOURCE CURSE

The availability of natural resources—from mineral to hydrocarbons to agricultural land and forestry—at first look appears as a blessing, an easy shortcut to development, especially in times of rising terms of trade such as the current ones. In fact, they may turn out in the long run to be a curse. Exports of natural resources may induce the "Dutch disease." It was noticed, around forty years ago in the gas-exporting Netherlands, that exchange rate appreciation was "crowding out" manufacturing by making it internationally less competitive. Insofar as industry is at the core of technological learning, it also reduces the future learning potential.

Production activities in natural resources are typically capital intensive with a reduced demand of skilled labor. They favor polarization in
income distribution. The big stakes involved in exploration and mining
rights are easily conducive to corruption among bureaucrats and politicians. And the problem has been recently compounded by privatization
generally occurring under rapacious terms in favor of foreign mining
companies and to the exclusive domestic benefit to a few corrupted officials. Of course, in modern history resource abundance has sometimes
fueled growth, the most noticeable case being in the nineteenth-century
United States. However, this occurred precisely through a resource-
intensive *industrialization* process (Wright 1997). Without that, resource
abundance can sustain growth for some time, especially when terms of
trade improve and sectoral productivity is rising. However, in the long
term, the small size in terms of the overall employment of the resource-
exploiting sector, the failure to tackle income inequality, and the scarce
overall learning efforts tends to erode the economic benefits derived from
natural resource exports. In fact, to avoid the resource curse, rents have
to be purposefully distributed against comparative advantages, fostering
diversification of production in knowledge-intensive activities.

THE NECESSARY CONSISTENCY BETWEEN MACROECONOMIC AND INDUSTRIAL POLICIES

As extensively discussed in several chapters of Cimoli, Dosi and Stiglitz
(2009a) addressing the Latin American experience over the last two
decades, there are macroeconomic policies that kill most learning efforts
together with most forms carrying the related learning capabilities.
Sudden and indiscriminate dismantling of trade barriers can easily do
that, especially if it comes together with reckless nonmanagement of
exchange rates, characterized by vicious cycles of appreciation followed
by sudden devaluations. And the cycles have been only amplified by the
stubborn refusal to utilize controls over capital movements, especially
short-term movements. Blind trust in the "magic of the marketplace" and
the associated lack of fiscal policies and demand management increase
output volatility. In turn, the latter, together with the endemic financial
fragility of many developing countries' firms, means induced waves of
corporate mortality and with that also the disappearance of the capabilities of technological accumulation. And even among surviving firms,
behavior tends to become more short-term, and the economy tends to

respond more to financial signals than to long-term learning opportunities (see more in Ocampo and Taylor 1998; Stiglitz et al. 2006). The comparative tales of Latin American countries as compared to, say, Korea or Malaysia tell the importance of the vicious feedbacks between macro policy shocks prescribed by orthodox recipes and micro dynamics (in Latin America) versus the virtuous feedbacks between more interventionist and Keynesian macro policies and the continuing industrial expansion even under severe financial crises (e.g., in Korea).

A NEW DEVELOPMENT PACT: THE COURAGE OF IMAGINING A NOVEL INTERNATIONAL "CONSENSUS"

Even before the Great Recession, the credibility of the so-called Washington Consensus was fading away and the damages incurred by the almost religious implementation of such an extremist version of economic orthodoxy became all the more apparent. The times of *antipolicy* consensus are over, buried by the weights of the economic failures in addition to the massive social disruptions. In this chapter, rather than propose amendments to the failed consensus, we build on a different diagnosis of the obstacles to and drivers of development, centered on the conditions for the accumulation of technological and organizational knowledge and on the political economy sustaining or hindering it. Far too much reliance has been put in the current analyses of development on a highly simplified and indeed misleading economic model whereby technology is just information in principle freely available to every country and every economic agent in the world. On the contrary, even a slightly more sophisticated understanding of the nature of productive knowledge has crucial economic ramifications. These ramifications put in the forefront the enormous asymmetries in the international distribution of such knowledge; the difficulties in its accumulation; and the interactions between what economic agents know how to produce and search for, the incentives they have to do so, and the role of public policies in shaping both.

The analysis, from different angles, offers a rich alternative menu of industrial policies—in their broadest definition. Many such policies may be implemented, albeit with daunting difficulties, even under the current regime of international economic relations, largely built under the political atmosphere of the Washington Consensus. Indeed, the Great Recession has brought into the forefront the need for industrial policies, written large, also for developed economies. In fact, public policies have played and continue to play a major role driving innovation in all frontier economies (see Mazzucato 2013, which draws a broad fresco; and Nelson, 1982, 1994, and 2004 for a germane perspective). Here we would like to conclude with a comprehensive and daring policy vision. This alternative view is also inspired by an alternative view of the patterns of international economic relations.

Indeed, here is a *new pact*.

First, on the "take" side for developing countries there ought to be much greater provision for *managed trade*—a term used for too long to protect rented interests of *first*-world lame ducks—in order to allow, on the contrary, *infant-industry nurturing*, with time limits and under transparent conditions. The lower the distance from the international technological frontier, the lower also the degrees of "nurturing" that should be allowed. Together, the new WTO pact should prescribe much more stringent conditions under which "antidumping" measures can be called for. (Notice that under current practices the punitive measures may be implemented first, while waiting for the definitive ruling with the likely consequence that the developing country's firm dies before having its rights recognized.)

Second, one does not need to be a development-friendly economist to acknowledge the antidevelopment bias of agricultural trade policies in all developed countries. There is a curious paradox here. Agriculture is the sector that most resembles textbook economics, made of many small, price-taking producers with little possibility of monopolistic rents. This sector is indeed the one in which all developed countries massively "distort market signals" and with no gains in terms of learning opportunities of any kind. There is just a pure rent transfer with a huge loss by a multitude of developing countries' farmers and developed countries' consumers. Any new trade deal is bound to involve the dismantling of arrangements that are massively damaging the cotton producer of West Africa, the Brazilian soya producer, and the Detroit or London consumer, without any dynamic benefit for any economy.

Third, it is urgent to reform of intellectual property rights regimes at the international level and domestically within developed countries toward a *reduction* of IPR protection in terms of domains of patentability and patent scope, together with some proportionality between degrees of development and degrees of IPR protection. Again, it is a "win-win" reform that finds an increasing number of advocates both in frontier countries and in a part of *frontier firms*, worried that the current system might simply lead to patent "arms races," stockpiling otherwise useless patent tickets, just waiting to be used for threat or retaliation. And the rates of innovation stagnate, while the costs of litigation soar: in fact, in the United States, litigation costs are estimated to be around one-third of the total RCD expenditure of the U.S. industry.

Fourth, untamed globalization of production activities has been a powerful vehicle for a huge income transfer from labor to *first-world* capital. The transfer of production, say, within NAFTA, from the United States to Mexico, or from OECD countries to China, has meant much lower wage costs. In the change, relatively little goes to the wage of the Mexican or Chinese worker, very little is the price gain for the U.S. or European shopper at Wal-Mart; most goes to the companies that dislocate the production and/or intermediate the product. And the relocation has also indirect effects since it makes it harder and harder for the first-world workers to negotiate on wages, working conditions, and pensions or even to defend the status quo. Symmetrically, in most developing countries the nearly "unlimited supply of labor" puts the bargaining power of local workers to nearly zero. One outcome has been that wages in the United States have stagnated for at least 15 years, despite steady productivity growth, and the widening gap between productivity and wages has certainly not gone to the workers of Tijuana or Shanghai. The new pact should correct for all that and allow for the possibility of developed countries to require for their imports the fulfillment of standards concerning child labor, work conditions and working hours, right to unionize, and environmental respect. Unconditional free-traders would certainly consider those measures to be protectionism in disguise.

In fact, in our view, these measures are going to be beneficial also to catch-up countries, to their workers, and to their environment. Indeed, they would contribute to re-dress a worldwide tendency toward ever-growing income inequalities, within a larger pro-development international deal fostering knowledge accumulation and industrialization in catch-up countries.

NOTES

This chapter largely draws upon M. Cimoli, G. Dosi, and J. E. Stiglitz,. 2009a. (2— in particular Cimoli, Dosi, Nelson and Stiglitz 2009a and Cimoli, Dosi and Stiglitz 2009b—and upon Stiglitz and Greenwald 2014.

The research leading to this work has enjoyed the long-term backing of the Initiative for Policy Dialogue (IPD), Columbia University.

1. More on this notion in Lundvall (1992), Nelson (1993), and Malerba (2002). See also Dosi (1999).

2. For a broad historical overview of the role of policies in some now developed countries, see Reinert (2004).

3. On the "perverse" importance of rent seeking in the development process, cf. Khan (2000a) and (2000b).

4. Somewhat similar conclusions on the crucial importance of the distance from the international technological frontier in terms of required mix of policy measures can be drawn also on the grounds of "neo-Schumpeterian" models of growth: cf. Aghion and Howitt (2005).

5. In Dosi, Pavitt, and Soete (1990) and Cimoli (1988), one argues this proposition on the ground of a model nesting a Kaldor-Thirlwall growth dynamic onto diverse technology gaps at commodity level. A similar proposition, however, can be shown to hold under more conventional assumptions: see Rodrik (2005).

6. Putting the same argument in a language more familiar to the economist, the widespread possibility of trade-offs among allocative, Schumpeterian, and growth efficiencies arises from the fact that the general case is one of nonconvexity of production and consumption possibility sets and dynamic increasing returns and path dependencies of technological advances. On the point, within a growing literature, see the complementary arguments of Atkinson and Stiglitz (1969); David (1988); Arthur (1994); Dosi, Pavitt, and Soete (1990); Krugman (1996); Antonelli (1995); Cimoli (1988); and Castaldi and Dosi (2006).

REFERENCES

Aghion, P., and P. Howitt. 2005. "Appropriate Growth Policy: A Unifying Framework." The 2005 Joseph Schumpeter Lecture. European Economic Association Congress. Amsterdam, August 25, 2005.

Amsden, A. 1989. *Asia Next Giant.* Ithaca, N.Y.: Cornell University Press.

——. 2001. *The Rise of the Rest. Challenges to the West from Late-Industrializing Economies.* London: Oxford University Press.

Antonelli, C. 1995. *The Economics of Localized Technological Change and Industrial Dynamics.* Boston: Kluwer.

Arrow, K. 1962. "Economic Welfare and the Allocation of Resources for Invention." In *The Rate and Direction of Inventive Activity*, R. Nelson, ed. Princeton, N.J.: Princeton University Press.

Arthur, W. B. 1994. *Increasing Returns and Path Dependence in the Economy.* Ann Arbor, Mich.: University of Michigan Press.

Atkinson, A., and J. Stiglitz. 1969. "A New View of Technological Change." *Economic Journal* 79: 573–78.

Bell, M., and K. Pavitt. 1993. "Technological Accumulation and Industrial Growth: Contrasts Between Developed and Developing Countries." *Industrial and Corporate Change* 2: 157–210.

Castaldi, C., and G. Dosi. 2006. "The Grip of History and the Scope for Novelty: Some Results and Open Questions on Path Dependence in Economic Processes."

In *Understanding Change*, ed. A. Wimmer and R. Kössler. London: Palgrave Macmillan, 99–128.

Castaldi C., M. Cimoli, N. Correa, and G. Dosi. 2009. "Technological Learning, Policy Regimes, and Growth: The Long-Term Patterns and Some Specificities of a 'Globalized' Economy." In Cimoli, Dosi, and Stiglitz, 2009a, 39–78.

Castro, A. 2009. "The Impact of Public Policies in Brazil along the Path from Semi-Stagnation to Growth in a Sino-Centric Market," in Cimoli, Dosi, and Stiglitz, 2009a, 257–76.

Chang, H. J. 2002. *Kicking away the Ladder: Development Strategy in Historical Perspective*. London: Anthem.

Cimoli, M. 1988. "Technological Gaps and Institutional Asymmetries in a North-South Model with a Continuum of Goods." *Metroeconomica* 39: 245–74.

Cimoli, M., and N. Correa. 2005. "Trade Openness and Technological Gaps in Latin America: A 'Low Growth' Trap." In Ocampo 2005, 45–70.

Cimoli, M., and G. Dosi. 1995. "Technological Paradigms, Patterns of Learning and Development. An Introductory Roadmap." *Journal of Evolutionary Economics* 5: 243–68.

Cimoli M., G. Dosi, and J. E. Stiglitz, eds. 2009a. *Industrial Policy and Development. The Political Economy of Capabilities Accumulation*. New York: Oxford University Press.

Cimoli M., G. Dosi, and J. E. Stiglitz. 2009b. "The Future of Industrial Policies in the New Millennium: Toward a Knowledge-Centered Development Agenda". In Cimoli, Dosi, and Stiglitz 2009a, 541–60.

Cimoli, M., G. Dosi, K. Maskus, R. L. Okediji and J. Stiglitz, eds. 2013. *Intellectual Property Rights and Development*. London: Oxford University Press.

Cimoli, M., G. Dosi, R. R. Nelson, and J. E. Stiglitz. 2009. "Institutions and Policies Shaping Industrial Development: An Introductory Note." In Cimoli, Dosi, and Stiglitz, 2009a, 19–38.

Cornia, G. A., T. Addison, and S. Kiiski. 2005. "Income Distribution Changes and Their Impact in the Post-World War II Period." In *Inequality, Growth, and Poverty in an Era of Liberalization and Globalization*, ed. G. A. Cornia. New York: Oxford University Press, 26–55.

Dahlman, C. J. 2009. "Growth and Development in China and India: The Role of Industrial Innovation Policy in Rapid Catch-up." In Cimoli, Dosi, and Stiglitz, 2009a, 303–335.

David, P. A. 1988. "Path Dependence: Putting the Past into the Future of Economics." Stanford University, Institute for Mathematical Studies in the Social Science, Technical Report 533.

Dosi, G. 1984. *Technical Change and Industrial Transformation*. London: Macmillan and New York: St. Martin Press.

——. 1988a. "Sources, Procedures and Microeconomic Effects of Innovation." *Journal of Economic Literature* 26(3): 1120–71.

——. 1988b. "Institutions and Markets in a Dynamic World." *The Manchester School of Economic and Social Studies* 56: 119–46.

——. 1999. "Some Notes on National Systems of Innovation and Production, and Their Implications for Economic Analysis." In *Innovation Policy in a Global*

Economy, ed. D. Archibugi, J. Howells, and J. Michie. London: Cambridge University Press.

———. 2007. "Statistical Regularities in the Evolution of Industries. A Guide through Some Evidence and Challenges for the Theory." In *Perspectives on Innovation*, eds. F. Malerba and S. Brusoni. London: Cambridge University Press.

Dosi, G., C. Freeman, and S. Fabiani. 1994. "The Process of Economic Development. Introducing Some Stylized Facts and Theories on Technologies, Firms and Institutions." *Industrial and Corporate Change* 3: 1–45.

Dosi, G., L. Marengo, and C. Pasquali. 2006. "How Much Should Society Fuel the Greed of Innovators? On the Relations Between Appropriability, Opportunities and Rates of Innovation." *Research Policy* 35, no. 8: 1110–21.

Dosi G. and R.R. Nelson, 2010. "Technical Change and Industrial Dynamics as Evolutionary Processes." In *Handbook of the Economics of Innovation*, volume 1, ed. B.H. Hall and N. Rosenberg. Burlington, Vt.: Academic Press, 51–128.

Dosi, G., K. Pavitt, and L. Soete. 1990. *The Economics of Technical Change and International Trade*. London: Harvester Wheatsheaf.

Dosi, G., C. Freeman, R. Nelson, G. Silverberg, and L. Soete, eds. 1988. *Technical Change and Economic Theory*. New York: Columbia University Press.

Freeman, C. 1982. *The Economics of Industrial Innovation*, 2nd ed. London: Pinter.

———. 2004. "Technological Infrastructures and International Competitiveness." *Industrial and Corporate Change* 13, no. 3 541–69.

Freeman, C., and C. Perez. 1988. "Structural Crises of Adjustment, Business Cycles and Investment Behavior." In Dosi et al., *Technical Change and Economic Theory*. London: Pinter, 38–66.

Gerschenkron, A. 1962. *Economic Backwardness in Historical Perspective*. Cambridge, Mass.: Harvard University Press.

Greenwald, B., and J. Stiglitz. 1986. "Externalities in Economics with Imperfect Information and Incomplete Markets." *Quarterly Journal of Economics* 101: 229–64.

Hamilton, A. 1791. "Report on the Subject of Manufactures." In H. C. Syrett et al., 1966, *The Papers of Alexander Hamilton*, vol. 10. New York: Columbia University Press.

Hirschman, A. O. 1958. *The Strategy of Economic Development*. New Haven, Conn.: Yale University Press.

———. 1971. A Bias for Hope. New Haven, Conn.: Yale University Press.

———. 1982. "Rival Interpretations of Market Society: Civilizing, Destructive, or Feeble?" *Journal of Economic Literature* 20: 1463–84.

Hobday, M., and F. Perini. 2009. "Latecomer Entrepreneurship: A Policy Perspective." In Cimoli, Dosi, and Stiglitz, 2009a, 470–505.

Hoff, K. 1996. "Market Failures and the Distribution of Wealth: A Perspective from the Economics of Information." *Politics and Society* 24: 411–32.

Hoff, K., and J. Stiglitz. 2001. "Modern Economic Theory and Development." In Meier and Stiglitz, 2001, 389–459.

ILO. 2004. *A Fair Globalization: Creating Opportunities for All*. Geneva: International Labor Office.

Khan, M. H. 2000a. "Rents, Efficiency and Growth." In *Rents, Rent-Seeking and Economic Development: Theory and Evidence in Asia*, eds. M. H. Khan and J. K. Sundaram. London: Cambridge University Press.

——. 2000b. "Rent-seeking as Process." In Khan, 2000a.

Khan, M. H., and S. Blankenburg. 2009. "The Political Economy of Industrial Policy in Asia and Latin America." In Cimoli, Dosi, and Stiglitz, 2009a, 336–77.

Kim, L. 1993. "National System of Industrial Innovation: Dynamics of Capability Building in Korea." In *National Innovation Systems: A Comparative Analysis*, ed. R. R. Nelson. New York: Oxford University Press.

Kim, L., and R. Nelson. 2000. *Technology, Learning, and Innovation: Experiences of Newly Industrializing Economies*. London: Cambridge University Press.

Krugman, P. R. 1996, *The Self-Organizing Economy*. Cambridge, Mass.: Blackwell.

Lall, S. 2000. *Selective Industrial and Trade Policies in Developing Countries: Theoretical and Empirical Issues*. QEH Working Paper Series, 48.

Landes, D. 1969. *The Unbound Prometheus*. London: Cambridge University Press.

List, F. 1841. *The National System of Political Economy*, trans. S. S. Lloyd. London: Longmans, Green and Co.; first published in English translation in 1885.

Lundvall, B.-Å., ed. 1992. *National Systems of Innovation: Towards a Theory of Innovation and Interactive Learning*. London: Pinter.

Malerba, F. 2002. "Sectoral Systems of Innovation and Production." *Research Policy* 31/2.

Mazzoleni, R., and R. Nelson. 2009. "The Roles of Research at Universities and Public Labs in Economic Catch-Up." In Cimoli, Dosi, and Stiglitz, 2009a, 378–408.

Mazzucato, M. 2013. *The Entrepreneurial State: Debunking Public vs. Private Sector Myths*. London: Anthem.

Meier, G. M., and J. Stiglitz, eds. 2001. *Frontiers of Development Economics* London: Oxford University Press.

Mowery, D. C., and R. R. Nelson. 1999. *Sources of Industrial Leadership: Studies of Seven Industries*. London: Cambridge University Press.

Murphy, K. M., A. Shleifer, and R. W. Vishny. 1989. "Industrialization and the Big Push." *Journal of Political Economy* 97: 1003–26.

Nelson, R. R. 2008. "Economic Development from the Perspective of Evolutionary Economic Theory." *Oxford Development Studies* Volume 36, Issue 1, 9-21

——. 1994. "The Co-evolution of Technology, Industrial Structure and Supporting Institutions." *Industrial and Corporate Change* 3: 47–64.

——. 1959. "The Simple Economics of Basic Scientific Research." *Journal of Political Economy* 67: 297–306.

Nelson, R. R., ed. 2005. *The Limits of Market Organization*. New York: Russell Sage Foundation.

——. 1993. *National Innovation Systems*. London: Oxford University Press.

——. 1982. *Government and Technical Progress*. New York: Pergamon.

Nelson, R. R., and B. Sampat. 2001. "Making Sense of Institutions as a Factor Shaping Economic Performance." *Journal of Economic Behavior & Organization* 44: 31–54.

Nurske, R. 1953. *Problems of Capital Formation in Underdeveloped Countries*. New York: Oxford University Press.

Ocampo, J. A. 2005a. "The Quest for Dynamic Efficiency: Structural Dynamics and Economic Growth in Developing Countries." In Ocampo, 2005b, 3–44.

Ocampo, J. A., ed. 2005b. *Beyond Reforms: Structural Dynamics and Macroeconomic Vulnerability*. Stanford, Calif.: Stanford University Press.

Ocampo, J. A., and L. Taylor. 1998. "Trade Liberalization in Developing Economies: Modest Benefits but Problems with Productivity Growth, Macro Prices, and Income Distribution." *The Economic Journal* 108: 1523–46.

Polanyi, K. 1957. *The Great Transformation.* Boston: Beacon Press.

Reinert, E. S. 2007 *How Rich Countries Got Rich . . . and Why Poor Countries Stay Poor*, London:Constable.

Rodrik, D. 2006. "Goodbye Washington Consensus, Hello Washington Confusion? A Review of the World Bank's Economic Growth in the 1990s: Learning from a Decade of Reform" *Journal of Economic Literature*, vol. 44, no. 4, 973–987.

——. 1997. Has Globalization Gone Too Far? Washington, D.C.: Institute for International Economics.

——. 1995. "Trade and Industrial Policy Reform," In *Handbook of Development Economics*, volume 3, ed. J. Behrman and T. N. Srinivasan. Amsterdam: North Holland, 2925–82.

Rodrik, D., ed. 2003. *In Search of Prosperity: Analytic Narratives on Economic Growth.* Princeton, N.J.: Princeton University Press.

Rodrik D, Hausmann R, and Hwang J. What You Export Matters. 2006. Available at http://j.mp/1JvTrZz.

Rodrik D., and, Hausmann, R. 2006. Doomed to Choose: Industrial Policy as Predicament. Available at http://j.mp/1MnkYCx.

——. 2005. "Growth Strategies." In *Handbook of Economic Growth*, ed. P. Aghion and S. Durlauf, 2005, 967–1014.

Rosenberg, N. 1982. *Inside the Blackbox.* London: Cambridge University Press.

——. 1976. *Perspective on Technology*, London: Cambridge University Press.

Rosenstein-Rodan, P. 1943. "Problems of Industrialization of Eastern and Southeastern Europe." *Economic Journal*, 53: 210–11.

Stiglitz, J. E. 2006. *Making Globalization Work.* New York: Norton.

——. 2002. *Globalization and its Discontents.* New York: Norton.

——. 2001. "More Instruments and Broader Goals Moving toward the Post-Washington Consensus." In *The Rebel Within*, ed. H. Chang. London: Wimbledon Publishing, 17–56. (Originally presented as the 1998 WIDER Annual Lecture, Helsinki, January 1998.)

——. 1996. "Some Lessons from the East Asian Miracle." *World Bank Research Observer* 11: 151–77.

——. 1994. *Whither Socialism?* Cambridge, Mass.: MIT Press.

Stiglitz, J. E., and B. C. Greenwald. 2014. *Creating a Learning Society: A New Approach to Growth, Development, and Social Progress.* New York: Columbia University Press.

Stiglitz, J. E., J. A. Ocampo, S. Spiegel, R. French-Davis, and D. Nayyar. 2006. *Stability with Growth. Macroeconomics, Liberalization and Development.* New York: Oxford University Press.

Teece, D., G. Pisano, and A. Shuen. 1997. "Dynamic Capabilities and Strategic Management." Strategic Management Journal 18–7: 509–33.

Veblen, T. 1915. *Imperial Germany and Industrial Revolution.* London: Macmillan.

Wade, R. 1990. *Governing the Market: Economic Theory and the Role of Government in East Asian Industrialization.* Princeton, N.J.: Princeton University Press.

Wright, G. 1997. 'Toward a More Historical Approach to Technological Change." *The Economic Journal* 107: 1560–66.

CHAPTER 3

Dynamic Efficiency

STRUCTURAL DYNAMICS AND ECONOMIC GROWTH IN DEVELOPING COUNTRIES

José Antonio Ocampo

Debates on economic growth in recent decades have left a legacy of analytical innovations and rich empirical contributions. The explicit recognition of the role of increasing returns and learning processes in economic growth, the related revival of ideas expounded by classical development economics, particularly on the role that external economies play in the development process, and the contribution of neo-Schumpeterian and evolutionary theories, as well as of several brands of neostructuralism and institutional economics, are among the most important analytical innovations.[1]

A large part of this literature focuses on aggregate dynamics, without delving into the dynamics of heterogeneous production structures, particularly those typical of developing countries, in which high-productivity (modern) and low-productivity (informal) sector firms coexist—a phenomenon that has been alternatively called *dualism* or *structural heterogeneity*. In contrast, that heterogeneity is at the heart of classical development economics and structuralist and neostructuralist schools of thought. Other traditional ideas have also received little attention in contemporary debates, particularly the growth-productivity connections associated with the Kaldorian tradition (Kaldor 1978) and the linkages among firms and sectors emphasized by Hirschman (1958).

This chapter argues that economic growth in developing countries is intrinsically tied to the dynamics of production structures and to the specific policies and institutions created to support them. The major focus is on the *dynamic efficiency* of economic structures, defined as their capacity to generate the new waves of structural change that, as argued here, are at the heart of dynamic economic growth.[2] This concept is in sharp contrast with static efficiency, the central focus of traditional microeconomic as well as international trade theories. As argued here, dynamic efficiency may require degrees of state intervention that traditional defendants of static efficiency would consider unacceptable.

In developing countries, the policies and institutions to promote dynamic efficiency include, in particular, those that facilitate the diffusion of innovations generated in the industrialized world (the development of new production sectors and the transfer of technology), encourage the creation of linkages among domestic firms and sectors, and seek to reduce the dualism or structural heterogeneity that characterizes production-sector structures in developing countries. Avoiding macroeconomic instability is also essential, if instability is understood in a broad sense that includes not only high inflation and unsustainable fiscal imbalances, but also sharp business cycles, volatile relative prices, unsustainable current account imbalances, and risky private-sector balance sheets (Ocampo 2008). However, macroeconomic stability is not a sufficient condition for growth. The broader institutional context and the adequate provision of education and infrastructure are what I will call essential *framework conditions*, but generally they do not play a direct role in bringing about changes in the momentum of economic growth.

This chapter makes extensive use of concepts elaborated by the old and the new development and growth literature. The elements on which the analysis is built are well known, but the way they are put together has a number of novel aspects. It is divided into four parts, aside from this introduction. The first takes a look at some methodological issues and growth regularities. The second part focuses on the dynamics of production structures. The third provides a very simple model of the linkages between production and macroeconomic dynamics. The last draws policy implications.

METHODOLOGICAL ISSUES AND STYLIZED FACTS

Time series and cross-section analyses have identified some regularities that characterize growth processes. The role of productivity growth, physical and human capital accumulation, economic policies, institutions and geography, as well as the changes in GDP and employment structures that go along with economic growth, are among the variables that have been extensively researched.

The analysis of the causal links among these variables raises two methodological issues. The first relates to the need to differentiate between factors that play a direct role in generating changes in the momentum of economic growth and those factors that are essential for growth to take place but that do not play a direct role in determining such variations at a specific time. The great historian of world economic growth, Maddison (1991, chap. 1), has referred to this differentiation as that between *proximate* and *ultimate* causality.

Institutions are the best case in point – though there are, of course, large differences of opinion as to what are the appropriate institutions that have to be put in place to guarantee adequate development. In any case, everybody would probably agree that a certain measure of stability in the basic social contract that guarantees smooth business-labor-government relations, a nondiscretionary legal system and patterns of business behavior that guarantee the security of contracts, and an impartial (and ideally efficient) state bureaucracy are crucial to facilitate modern economic growth. Nonetheless, although in some cases they may become proximate causes of growth (or of the lack of it), as in the successful reconstruction (or breakdown) of sociopolitical regimes, they generally play the role of "framework conditions" for economic growth rather than that of direct causes of changes in its momentum. Indeed, an important empirical observation is that some country characteristics, particularly institutional development, are fairly constant over decades, whereas growth is not.[3]

A second methodological issue relates to the fact that a regular feature of economic growth is the simultaneous movement of a series of economic variables: improved technology, human capital accumulation, investment, savings, and systematic changes in production structures.[4] Yet, these variables are, to a large extent, *results* of economic growth. Thus, higher investment ratios have usually been regarded as essential for the acceleration of economic growth, but they may be the result of the accelerator mechanisms generated by dynamic growth. Human capital accumulation is also an essential factor in economic growth, but the accumulation of skills is largely the result of production experience and the expansion of educational systems, largely facilitated, again, by successful economic growth. The same can be argued with respect to productivity growth, if the causal links emphasized by Kaldor are correct, in which case productivity improvements are largely the result of dynamic economic growth—a causal link that is just the opposite to that assumed by neoclassical growth theory since Solow (1956, 2000). This means that disentangling cause and effect or, in empirical analysis, leading and lagging variables, is what growth analysis is all about.[5] Thus, many of the regularities mentioned in the growth literature may be subject to sharply differing interpretations, depending on the interpretation of the causal links involved.

Empirical analysis is obviously the final test of the significance of any theory. In this regard, it is useful to present five sets of regularities or "stylized facts" that are particularly important for understanding growth experiences in the developing world. Some have been seriously overlooked in recent growth debates.

The first one is the persistence of large inequalities in the world economy, which arose quite early in the history of modern economic development and has tended to expand through time. Empirical studies indicate that (absolute) convergence in per capita incomes has been the exception rather than the rule (Rodrik 2014). Indeed, it seems to be a feature only of the more industrialized countries in the post-World War II (WW II) period and, more specifically, in the "golden age" years of 1950 to 1973. The first decade of the twenty-first century is perhaps the only case of fairly broad convergence between developed and developing countries, though at the time of this writing this period of convergence seems to have come to an end. In contrast, convergence was not a characteristic of industrialized countries prior to WW II (Maddison 1991), and the divergence of incomes between developed and developing countries in the nineteenth and twentieth centuries has been aptly characterized by Pritchett (1997) as "divergence, big time."

There have obviously been changes in the world hierarchy, remarkably the rise of Japan to the top group of developed countries in the twentieth century. In the developing world, there have also been some changes: the rise of Latin America in the interwar period and of the Southern Cone countries earlier on (Bértola and Ocampo 2012, chap. 1), or the better known rise of Asian newly industrialized economies (NIEs) since the 1960s and that of China since the 1980s. These episodes of convergence are concentrated at middle-income levels and are associated with the reallocation of labor from low- to high-productivity sectors subject to increasing returns to scale (Ros 2000, 2013). However, on many occasions, such convergence experiences have not endured, and many have ended up in growth collapses (Ros 2000). The mix of rapid and "truncated convergence" and even collapses and, thus, the high variance of growth experiences in both low- and middle-income countries are also a major feature of international growth patterns (Pritchett, 2000). This fact has also been underscored in the recent growing literature on "middle-income traps" (see, e.g., Eichengreen, Park, and Shin 2012, 2013).

In any case, despite changes in the economic landscape, the world economic hierarchy is surprisingly stable. This is reflected in the fact that slightly more than three-fifths of the variance of per capita income levels in the world at the end of the twentieth century could be simply explained by the income differences that already existed in 1914, according to calculations using Maddison's (2001) data. But the world economic hierarchy goes beyond divergence in per capita incomes. It is associated, in particular, with the very high concentration in the generation of core technology in those countries and the equally high concentration of world finance there.

The major implications of this fact are that economic opportunities are largely determined by the position that a particular country occupies within the world hierarchy, which makes climbing the international ladder a rather difficult task. Essential international asymmetries help to explain why the international economy is, in fact, an "unleveled playing field": (1) prohibitive entry costs into technologically dynamic activities and entry costs into mature sectors, which imply that the possibilities open to developing countries may be restricted to the attraction of established multinationals in those sectors; (2) basic financial asymmetries that are reflected in differences in domestic financial development, procyclical access to external financing, and an inability to borrow abroad in the domestic currency; and (3) macroeconomic asymmetries that are reflected in the quite different degrees of freedom to adopt countercyclical macroeconomic policies and even a tendency for developing countries to adopt procyclical policies, owing to their dependence on unstable external financing (Ocampo 2001).

For these reasons, economic development is not a question of going through "stages" within the pattern that industrialized countries followed in the past. It is about increasing per capita income, succeeding in carrying out the associated structural transformations, and employing the appropriate macroeconomic and financial strategies, within the restrictions that each country's position within the world hierarchy creates. This is the essential insight of the Latin American structuralist school (see, e.g., Prebisch 1951; Furtado 1961) and of the literature on late industrialization since Gerschenkron (see Gerschenkron 1962; Amsden 2001).

A second set of regularities is associated with the fact that growth generally comes in spurts rather than as steady flows, and thus entails large elements of discontinuity. This is a basic lesson of historical analysis, one that is stressed by those who view the history of technology as a succession of technological revolutions or waves of innovation that gradually spread through the economic system (Freeman and Soete 1997; Pérez 2002, part I). The view of a growing economy as a sort of "inflating balloon," in which added factors of production and steady flows of technological change smoothly increase aggregate GDP, may be a useful metaphor for some purposes, but it ends up overlooking some of the most essential elements of economic development. An alternative perspective, derived from structuralist economic thinking (broadly defined), views growth as a dynamic process in which some sectors and firms surge ahead and others fall behind as part of a continual transformation of production structures. This process involves a repetitive phenomenon of *creative destruction* (Schumpeter 1962, chap. 8; Aghion and Howitt 1998). Not all sectors have the same ability to inject dynamism into the economy, to "propagate technical progress," to use Prebisch's (1964) concept. The complementarities (externalities) between enterprises and production sectors, together with their macroeconomic and distributive effects, can produce sudden jumps in the growth process or can block it (Rosenstein-Rodan 1943; Taylor 1991; and Ros 2000, 2013) and, in so doing, may generate successive phases of disequilibria (Hirschman 1958). These views imply, in short, that the dynamics of production structures are an active determinant of economic growth, and thus growth cannot be reduced to its aggregate dynamics.

The contrast between the balloon and structural dynamics views of economic growth can be understood in terms of the interpretation of one of the old regularities identified in the growth literature: the tendency of per capita GDP growth to be accompanied by regular changes in the sectoral composition of output and in the patterns of international specialization (see, e.g., Chenery, Robinson, and Syrquin 1986; Balassa 1989). According to the balloon view, these structural changes should be seen as a result of the growth in per capita GDP. In the alternative reading, the ability to constantly generate new dynamic activities is the key to rapid economic growth. In turn, the inability to generate new economic activities will block the development process. Moreover, success in generating new sectors of production may also involve "destruction" of previous activities. In Schumpeterian terms, *creation* is generally matched by *destruction*.

The third set of stylized facts stresses the essential role that elastic factor supplies play in the development process, particularly in facilitating a smooth expansion of dynamic activities. This is reflected, at the aggregate level, in the most successful economies' capacity to attract international capital and, when necessary, labor. Elastic factor supplies also imply that demand, and not only supply factors, plays a role in long-run growth. This is a critical element in Keynesian and Kaleckian theories of economic growth (Kaldor 1978, chaps. 1 and 2; Robinson 1962; Taylor 1991), which have typically been ignored in neoclassical growth analysis and in the new growth literature.

The internal mobility (i.e., reallocation) of capital and labor toward dynamic activities is even more important. Lewis (1954, 1969) provides the essential insight into the role of elastic labor supply in economic development. In a similar fashion, Kaldorian growth-productivity links imply that underutilized labor plays a role in the growth process (Kaldor 1978, chap. 4).[6] Both views imply that economic growth is, to a large extent, the result of improved efficiency in the use of *available* resources, through the reallocation of labor toward activities subject to economies of scale and scope (specialization),[7] as well as the fuller utilization of underemployed labor in some branches of production, particularly agriculture.

The fact that rapid development is the result of the interplay between labor mobility and economies of scale has also been the essential insight of regional economics since its origins, more than a century ago. According to this view, both the interplay between these two factors and their interaction with transport costs are what led to the formation of urban and regional "growth poles," clusters, and urban-rural hierarchies (for a modern version of this interpretation, see Fujita, Krugman, and Venables 1999). This insight can be extended to the analysis of international specialization, as Ohlin (1933) made clear in his seminal work on the subject, a framework that was finally absorbed by trade theory in the 1980s (see Krugman 1990; Grossman and Helpman 1991; and, in relation to developing countries, Ocampo 1986). The "vent for surplus" models of international trade, which go back to Adam Smith, provide an alternative source of elastic factor supplies: the existence of unexploited or underexploited natural resources (Myint 1971, chap. 5).

The fourth set of stylized facts stresses the dependence of long-run growth patterns on the economy's trajectory, i.e., path dependence (Arthur 1994). This is particularly important in economic development because of dynamic economies of scale generated by learning processes, a major implication of which is that the opportunities open to economic agents are largely determined by their production experience. To the extent that economic policies can affect the structure of production, this means that comparative advantages can be created. An interesting historical observation that is relevant in this regard is the evidence that successful experiences of manufacturing export growth in the developing world were generally preceded by periods of import substitution industrialization (Chenery, Robinson, and Syrquin 1986). This implies, in turn, that the loss of production experience may have cumulative effects on growth. This issue was brought forward in the literature on the Dutch disease (Krugman 1990, chap. 7; van Wijnbergen 1984), but it applies equally to the long-term costs of the more recent deindustrialization that several emerging and developing countries experienced as a result of economic liberalization.

In a similar fashion, adverse shocks that affect short-term macroeconomic performance may have cumulative long-term effects in the presence of economies of scale (Easterly 2001, chap. 10). The lasting effects of the debt crises of the 1980s in Africa and Latin America are the most telling example in this regard, and peripheral Europe may be experiencing a similar phenomenon today. Similarly, short-term success may breed long-term growth. There may thus be multiple long-term growth equilibria associated with the macroeconomic trajectories that economies follow. The fact that the formation of macroeconomic expectations involves a significant learning process, particularly in the presence of large macroeconomic shocks, is a basic reason for this (Heymann 2000).

The controversial role of economic policy in growth leads to a fifth set of stylized facts. The traditional emphasis in the orthodox development literature has been on the role of the trade policy regime in economic growth. In this area, the attempt to derive simplistic relationships between trade liberalization and growth, and even between the trade regimes and export growth, has led to misguided conclusions (Rodríguez and Rodrik 2001). An additional stylized fact, derived from comparative analyses of development experiences (see, e.g., the contributions to Helleiner 1994) can be advanced: although trade policy, the private-sector/public-sector mix, and, more broadly, policy-induced incentives do matter, there is no single rule that can be applied to all countries at any time, or to any single country in different time periods. Indeed, successful development experiences have been associated with variable policy packages involving different mixes of orthodox incentives with unorthodox institutional features ("local heresies") (Rodrik 2007, 2014).

Thus, protection has been a source of growth in some periods in specific countries, but has blocked it in others. The same thing can be said of freer trade. Mixed strategies have worked well under many circumstances. The degree of openness in the world economy has obviously been a decisive factor in this regard.[8] The observation, mentioned earlier, that successful experiences of manufacturing export growth in the developing world were generally preceded by periods of import-substitution industrialization, indicates that simplistic generalizations are not very useful. Bairoch (1993, part I) comes to a similar conclusion regarding protection and economic growth in "late industrializers" among what are now developed countries during the pre-WW I period. He also reaches the paradoxical conclusion that the fastest periods of growth in world trade prior to WW I were not those characterized by the most liberal trade regimes.

THE DYNAMICS OF PRODUCTION STRUCTURES

The central theme of this chapter is that the dynamics of production structures are at the root of changes in the momentum of economic growth. These dynamics interact with macroeconomic balances, either generating positive feedback that results in "virtuous" circles of rapid economic growth or, alternatively, generating growth traps. Some measure of macroeconomic stability, broadly defined, is a necessary but not a sufficient condition for dynamic growth. A facilitating institutional environment and an adequate supply of human capital and infrastructure are *framework conditions*, but are not active determinants of the growth momentum.

The ability to constantly generate new dynamic activities is, in this view, the essence of successful development. In this sense, growth is essentially a *meso*economic process, determined by the dynamics of production structures, a concept that summarizes the evolution of the sectoral composition of production, intra- and intersectoral linkages, market structures, the functioning of factor markets, and the institutions that support all of them. Dynamic microeconomic changes are the building blocks, but the *systemwide* processes matter most. Moreover, the characteristics of the structural transformation largely determine macroeconomic dynamics, particularly through its effects on investment and trade balances.

The dynamics of production structures may be visualized as the interaction between two basic, though multidimensional, forces: (1) *innovations,* broadly understood as new activities and new ways of doing previous activities, and the *learning processes* that characterize both the full realization of their potentialities and their diffusion through the economic system; and (2) the *complementarities, linkages,* or *networks* among firms and production activities and the *institutions* required for the full development of such complementarities, whose maturation is also subject to learning. *Elastic factor supplies* are, however, essential to guarantee that these dynamic processes can deploy their full potentialities. The combination of these three factors determines the *dynamic efficiency* of a given production system.

These different mechanisms perform complementary functions: innovations are the basic engine of change; their diffusion and the creation of production linkages are the mechanisms that determine their capacity to transform and generate integrated production systems; the learning that accompanies these processes and the development of complementarities generate dynamic economies of scale and specialization, which are essential to rising productivity; and elastic factor supplies are necessary for innovative activities to operate as the driving force of economic growth.

INNOVATIONS AND ASSOCIATED LEARNING AND DIFFUSION PROCESSES

The best definition of *innovations,* in the broad sense in which this concept is used here, was provided by Schumpeter (1962, chap. 2) a century ago (*new combinations* in his terminology): (1) the introduction of new goods and services or of new qualities of goods and services; (2) the development of new production methods or new marketing strategies; (3) the opening up of new markets; (4) the discovery of new sources of raw materials or the exploitation of previously known resources; and (5) the establishment of new industrial structures in a given sector. Thus, this broad concept includes both the more common use of the concept of innovations in the economic literature (technological innovations) as well as what Hausmann and Rodrik (2003) have called *discovery* (of what one is good at producing) as well as other forms that are usually disregarded today. Innovations, in this broad sense, may arise in established firms and sectors—in a constantly changing world, firms that do not innovate will tend to disappear—but many times they involve the creation of new firms and the development of new sectors of production.

Innovation includes the creation of firms, production activities, and sectors, but also the destruction of others. The particular mix between creation and destruction—or, in Easterly's (2001, chap. 9) terminology, between the substitution and complementary effects of innovations—is critical. The term *creative destruction*, coined by Schumpeter (1962), indicates that there tends to be net creation. This is, of course, essential for innovations to lead to growth, but this may not be the actual outcome in any given location at a certain time. There may be cases of little destruction and, in contrast, cases of large-scale destruction, or a mixed negative case of *destructive creation*. The more localized our focus on the effects of a given innovation, the more likely it is that we will actually see the full typology, as some locations within the world economy may concentrate the creative and others the destructive effects (think, e.g., of the discovery of a synthetic substitute that generates new activities in an industrial center but puts producers of the natural raw material, which is located elsewhere, out of business). Obviously, for growth to take place, net creative forces must prevail.

A common feature of the first four forms of innovation is that they involve the creation of knowledge or, more precisely, the capacity to apply it to production. They thus stress the role of knowledge as a source of market power. Viewed from this perspective, success in economic development can be seen as the ability to create enterprises that are capable of learning and appropriating knowledge and, in the long run, generating new knowledge (Amsden 2001; Lall 2003).

In industrial countries, the major incentive to innovate is provided by the extraordinary profits that can be earned by the pioneering firms that introduce technical, commercial, or organizational changes, or that open new markets or find new sources of raw materials. This incentive is necessary to offset the uncertainties and risks involved in the innovators' decisions, as well as the higher costs that they incur due to the cost of developing the new know-how, the incomplete nature of the knowledge they initially have, the absence of the complementarities that are characteristic of well-developed activities, and the fact that, due to the externalities that the innovating activity has, they may not be able to fully appropriate the benefits of the innovation.

In developing countries, innovations are primarily associated with the spread of new products, technologies, and organizational or commercial strategies previously developed in the industrial centers. The industrial countries' innovations thus represent the "moving targets" that generate the windows of opportunity for developing countries (Pérez 2001). The extraordinary profits of innovators are generally absent and, indeed, production may involve entry into mature activities with thinner profit margins. Thus, in absence of special incentives, there may be a suboptimal rate of search for new economic activities (Hausmann and Rodrik 2003). Entry costs are associated not with the development of new know-how, but instead with the process of acquiring, mastering, and adapting it. Additional entry costs are associated with generating market information, building a reputation in new markets, and, in particular, capitalizing upon opportunities to reduce costs in order to be in a position to successfully break into established production and marketing channels. Entry costs may turn out to be prohibitive for new firms; in this case, the possibilities open to developing countries will be limited to attracting established multinationals that are searching for new places to locate their production activities or linking with them by servicing one of the parts of the value chain they control. Also, the initial decision of the innovator may attract other firms, and, as in the case of innovations in developed countries, these externalities imply that innovators will be unable to capture the full benefits of their actions, again leading to suboptimal investments in innovation.

Viewed in this way, innovations in developing countries are associated much more closely with the transfer of sectors or activities from the industrial world than with technological change as such—or, more precisely, the latter is largely determined by the former. In this view, climbing up the ladder in the world hierarchy entails shortening transfer periods and gradually becoming a more active participant in the generation of technology. Thus, in the past, innovations have included the development of new export staples, as well as import-substitution sectors and their eventual transition to export markets. During the recent liberalization period, innovations have included the development of assembly activities as the result of the disintegration of value chains in the industrialized countries, the growing demand for some international services (e.g., tourism), the increased export orientation of previous import-substitution activities, the privatization processes and the associated restructuring of privatized firms and sectors, and increased access to raw materials (particularly minerals) as the result of strengthened property rights over the associated resources. In turn, in the past the *destruction* of previous production capacities has included the decline of export staples as the result of the development of synthetic substitutes and reduced production of a primary good in a specific location as a consequence of the discovery of new sources of raw materials. In recent years, the destruction has included the disintegration of domestic production chains as the result of international outsourcing and the dismantling of import-substitution activities unable to compete in a more liberal trade environment.

No innovative process is passive, as it requires investment and learning. Innovations are, indeed, intrinsically tied to investment, since they require both physical investments and investments in intangibles, particularly in technological development and learning, as well as in marketing strategies. Moreover, to the extent that innovative activities are the fastest-growing sectors of any economy at any given time, they have high investment requirements.[9] These facts, together with the falling investment needs that characterize established activities, imply that the overall investment rate is directly dependent on the relative weight of innovative activities (and obviously on their capital intensity). High investment is thus associated with a high rate of innovation and structural change.

Innovations also involve learning. Technical know-how must go through a learning and maturing process that is closely linked to the production experience. More generally, to reduce the technology gaps that characterize the international economic hierarchy—to *leapfrog* in the precise sense of the term[10]— an encompassing research and development strategy and an accompanying educational strategy are necessary. Essential insights into learning dynamics have been provided by the evolutionary theories of technical change.[11] These theories emphasize the fact that technology is to a large extent *tacit* in nature, i.e., that detailed "blueprints" cannot be plotted out. This has three major implications.

The first implication is that technology is incompletely available and imperfectly tradable. This is associated with the fact that technology is, to a large extent, composed of intangible human and organizational capital. This implies that, in order to benefit from technical knowledge, even firms that purchase or imitate it must invest in mastering the acquired or imitated technology. Since this is the general case in developing countries, it implies that even though technology is largely transferred from industrialized countries, there is still an active absorption process that must take place. This process involves adaptation and may call for redesigns and other secondary innovations, which will further build up human and organizational capital. The efficiency with which this absorption process takes place will determine, in turn, the productivity of the relevant firms. This explains why firms with similar access to "knowledge" will generally have quite different productivities. Different organizational and marketing strategies will generate further firm-specific features, which are the essential factors behind the selection process that takes place in any sector through time. Existing firms or new entrants could challenge any equilibrium in the resulting industrial structure. According to our definition, major breakups in existing industrial structures are themselves innovations. The entry of developing countries into mature activities also belongs to this category.

The second implication of *tacitness* is that technology proficiency cannot be detached from production experience; i.e., it has a strong "learning by doing" component.[12] Daily production and engineering activities have, in this sense, a research and development component. This link is the specific microeconomic basis of dynamic economies of scale.

A third feature of technical change, unrelated to tacitness, indicates that competition will generate pressures that guarantee the generation and diffusion of innovations. As a result of the latter, innovative firms only imperfectly appropriate the benefits from investments in innovations. Intellectual property rights provide a mechanism for appropriating those benefits more fully in the case of technical innovations or new products and designs, but such a mechanism is not present in other forms of innovations (such as the development of new activities or a new marketing strategy). Innovations have thus mixed private/public good attributes. The rate of innovation depends, then, on the particular balance among costs, risks, and benefits and their appropriability (including their legal protection, in cases where this is possible).

It must be emphasized that these three attributes of technical change—imperfect tradability, close association with production experience, and private/public attributes—are equally characteristic of other forms of knowledge, particularly organizational and commercial knowhow (and, as we will see below, institutional development). Imperfect tradability, due to its "social capital" attributes, and imperfect appropriability are paramount in the case of organizational knowledge. Commercial knowhow plays a crucial role that tends to be overlooked in most analyses, and it certainly plays a pivotal role in international trade (Keesing and Lall 1992). Indeed, one of the most important determinants of the expansion of firms relates to their ability to develop appropriate channels of information and marketing and to build a commercial reputation (goodwill) and a known trademark. Moreover, familiarity with the market enables producers to modify their products and their marketing channels and helps buyers to learn about suppliers, generating clientele relationships that are important to guarantee the stable growth of firms. The crucial role that these factors play is reflected in the fact that marketing departments in larger firms are usually staffed by high-quality personnel. The corresponding capital is organizational in nature and cannot be detached from commercial experience. The dynamic economies of scale are reflected here in reductions in transaction costs, which are associated with the firms' accumulated reputation and trademark recognition. In turn, although the reputation of a particular firm can hardly be copied, its discovery of market opportunities will certainly be imitated. The public-good attributes are thus important and play a vital role in determining the patterns of specialization. As regional economics has recognized for a long time, the agglomeration of producers of certain goods and services in particular locations is largely determined by this factor.

COMPLEMENTARITIES AND ASSOCIATED INSTITUTIONAL DEVELOPMENT

Complementarities are associated with the development of networks of suppliers of goods and specialized services, marketing channels, and organizations and institutions that disseminate information and provide coordination among agents. This concept summarizes the role that backward and forward linkages play in economic growth (Hirschman 1958) but also that of (private, public, or mixed) institutions that are created to reduce information costs (e.g., on technology and markets) and to solve the coordination failures that characterize interdependent investment decisions (Chang 1994). Together they determine how integrated a production system is.

The development of complementarities has both demand and supply effects. The demand effects are part of the Keynesian multiplier mechanism; their absence implies, in turn, that Keynesian leakages may be large, as reflected, e.g., in high propensities to import from abroad such as in assembly activities. Thus, the strength or weakness of the complementarities is the major determinant of macroeconomic multipliers. This, together with the association between the rate of investment and innovations, which has already been explored in the previous section, are two of the essential links between economic structures and macroeconomic performance.

The supply effects of complementarities are associated with the positive externalities that different economic agents generate among themselves through cost reductions made possible by economies of scale in production or lower transport and transaction costs (economies of agglomeration), through the induced provision of more specialized inputs or services (economies of specialization) or through the externalities generated by the sharing of knowledge and the development of human capital that can move among firms (technological or, more broadly, knowledge spillovers). These *strategic complementarities* are the basis of the dynamic economies of scale of a mesoeconomic character that determine the competitiveness—or lack of competitiveness—of production sectors in a given region or country. Under these conditions, competitiveness involves more than microeconomic efficiency: it is essentially a sectoral or even a systemwide feature (Fajnzylber 1990; ECLAC 1990).

In an open economy, demand linkages may be induced by protection. This may facilitate positive supply (agglomeration) effects, but may also generate costs for other production sectors if it involves the protection of intermediate and capital goods. On the other hand, as they cannot be imported, the efficient provision of *nontradable* inputs and specialized services always plays an essential role in guaranteeing systemwide competitiveness. Three nontradable activities are particularly relevant in this regard. The first category is made up of sectors that produce specialized inputs and services, including knowledge, logistic, and marketing services for which closeness to producers who use the inputs or services is a critical factor. The second category is the development of specialized financial services, particularly of long-term and venture capital; due to the asymmetric information that characterizes financial markets, financial services (particularly for small and medium-sized firms) are largely nontradable. The third category is the provision of adequate infrastructure.

Institution building shares the first two features of technological development—imperfect tradability and close association with experience—and, by its very nature, has dominant public-good attributes. As already indicated, the two crucial services that institutions provide are the reduction of information costs and the solution of the coordination failures that characterize interdependent investment decisions. Many of the relevant institutions may be created directly by the private sector: producer organizations which share information that has public-good (or clubgood) attributes, develop joint labor training facilities, and create strategic alliances to penetrate new markets or promotional agencies to encourage complementary investments. However, given their strong public-good attribute, their services tend to be provided in suboptimal quantities. The competitive pressure among firms is quite commonly a major obstacle to the creation and consolidation of such institutions.

ELASTIC FACTOR SUPPLIES

The capacity of innovations and complementarities to generate strong growth effects depends critically on how elastic the supply of factors of production for innovative sectors is. The crucial role played by the ability of innovative activities to attract capital and labor, and to gain access to the natural resources they need to expand, was mentioned earlier as a *stylized fact*. Both the crucial role played by the availability of long-term finance for innovative activities and the fact that financial services have a large nontradable component have also been noted.

Schumpeter (1961) emphasized the elastic supply of capital as essential to facilitate the effects of innovations on economic growth. More broadly, elastic factor supplies play a crucial role in Keynesian and Kaleckian models in which investment—and, thus, aggregate demand—drives not only short-term economic activity, but also long-term growth (Kaldor 1978; Robinson 1962; Taylor 1991). As these models make clear, elastic factor supplies can be guaranteed in several ways: (1) by the existence of unemployed or, more typically, underemployed resources (an issue that was also emphasized earlier); (2) by the endogenous financing of capital accumulation through a redistribution of income toward profits; (3) by interregional and international factor mobility; (4) by social reorganization that allows greater participation in the labor force, particularly by women; and (5) by technical change that breaks factor supply constraints (e.g., increases land productivity or induced capital-intensive technological process to accommodate labor shortages).

In the developing world, an elastic supply of labor is guaranteed by the dualism or structural heterogeneity that characterizes developing countries' production structures, i.e., the coexistence of high- and low-productivity activities.[13] Low-productivity activities, characterized by a considerable element of underemployment (or informality), act as a residual sector that both supplies the labor required by a surge of economic growth and absorbs the excess supply of labor when a dynamic generation of employment in high-productivity sectors is absent. The differentiation made in dualistic models between *traditional* and *modern* sectors is inappropriate to describe this feature of the developing world, as the corresponding structure is certainly more complex; and low-productivity activities are constantly being created anew to absorb excess labor, a fact that makes the label *traditional* entirely inadequate. Indeed, a typical feature of low-growth developing countries over the past decades has been the expansion of low-productivity (informal) sectors to absorb excess labor, including the excess labor generated by restructured sectors. High- and low-productivity sectors are, in turn, heterogeneous in their structure. The term *structural heterogeneity*, coined by Latin American structuralists (Pinto 1970) to describe this phenomenon, is more appropriate and will thus be used in the rest of this chapter.

As educational standards rise, underemployment may increasingly threaten skilled labor. International labor migration provides an additional adjustment mechanism that is probably more important in this case than in that of unskilled labor.[14] This is a reason why rising educational standards, although crucial for successful economic development, may play a passive role in generating variations in the momentum of economic growth.

As discussed by Ros (2000, chap. 3), three features are essential to guarantee an elastic supply of labor for high-productivity activities: (1) low capital requirements in low-productivity activities, which guarantee that they will be largely made up of self-employed workers, whose income is thus determined by average rather than marginal productivities; (2) competition between these activities and high-productivity sectors in the provision of certain goods and services (e.g., in the production or marketing of some consumer goods and in the provision of simple services in general); and (3) a wage premium in high-productivity activities, associated, e.g., with *efficiency wages*.

Structural heterogeneity implies that the dynamism generated by innovative activities and the strength of the linkages they generate determine the efficiency with which the aggregate labor force is used, i.e., the extent of labor underemployment (as well as the underemployment of other factors of production, particularly land). At the aggregate level, this process gives rise to Kaldorian growth-productivity links of similar characteristics, but additional to the microeconomic and mesoeconomic dynamic economies of scales associated with learning and the development of strategic complementarities.

This link is crucial to understanding aggregate productivity growth in developing countries and indicates why it is largely a *result* of dynamic economic growth rather than its cause. Moreover, it implies that there may be a divergence between micro and aggregate productivity trends. Indeed, the fact that some economic agents may be experiencing rapid productivity growth at the firm level, due to the incentives generated by a competitive environment or to their own learning efforts, does not necessarily mean that aggregate productivity will show the same dynamics. The process itself may generate a reduction of employment in innovative activities that, if not counterbalanced by employment growth in other high-productivity sectors, will be reflected in increasing underemployment, thereby adversely affecting aggregate productivity growth. Increased underemployment (and eventually unemployment) may thus swamp the microeconomic gains in efficiency, generating the paradox of a group of highly competitive firms being accompanied by frustrating rates of overall productivity growth. This was, in fact, a feature of Latin America in the 1990s (ECLAC 2000, chap. 1).

The concept of elastic factor supplies can be applied equally to natural resources and infrastructure. The "vent for surplus" models provide a similar adjustment mechanism, in which the increased productivity accompanying economic growth is the result of the exploitation of previously idle or underutilized natural resources. Due to the large indivisibilities characteristic of infrastructure, particularly of transportation networks, major infrastructure projects may spread their benefits over long periods. An interesting implication of this is that the positive effects of infrastructure—as well as investments in education—may reflect not only the externalities they generate, as emphasized in the endogenous growth literature, but also their fixed or quasi-fixed character, which is reflected in variable degrees of utilization, even over long periods of time. Periods of low-productivity growth associated with a "big push" in infrastructure (e.g., during periods of rapid urbanization) may thus be followed by high-productivity growth in later periods. Similarly, a big push in education may not directly lead to faster economic growth; but the rapid absorption of a pool of educated labor into dynamic activities, as the result of an innovation drive, will be reflected in faster productivity growth.

THE INTERPLAY OF INNOVATIONS, COMPLEMENTARITIES, AND ELASTIC FACTOR SUPPLIES

The interplay of these factors provides the essential driving force for structural transformation and the degree of dynamic efficiency that characterizes it. Innovations, if accompanied by strong complementarities, will be reflected in the absorption of an increasing number of workers into dynamic activities. The result will be a virtuous circle of high investment and accelerated technological learning and institutional development. On the other hand, *destructive* forces may predominate, giving rise to a vicious circle of slowdown in productivity and economic growth, decline in investment, increased structural heterogeneity as the surplus workforce is absorbed into low-productivity activities, and a loss of production experience that widens the technology gap vis-à-vis industrialized countries. As we will see in the next section, the positive feedbacks between these structural and macroeconomic factors reinforce one another.

On the basis of previous analysis, table 3.1 provides a typology of processes of structural change. I distinguish first between two polar cases, which I will call *deep* and *shallow* structural transformations. The first are characterized by strong learning (including induced technological innovations) and complementarities (economies of agglomeration and specialization and knowledge spillovers) and, thus, by strong micro- and mesoeconomic dynamic economies of scale, and by the additional productivity effects generated by the reduction in underemployment. This tends to be the case of periods of rapid growth in the developing world. Shallow structural transformations, on the other hand, can be characterized by the weakness of both learning and complementarities. A classic shallow structural transformation is the development of enclave export activities with very limited or even no local contents aside from the labor used in the assembling activities.

The typology also provides two mixed cases. One combines strong learning with weak linkages (e.g., due to high import requirements). This type of process may generate high productivity growth at the firm level in dynamic sectors but also strong structural heterogeneity. Some import-substitution activities of the past were of that sort. This can be called the *short-breath* case, as the initial innovative effect is soon exhausted due to its limited sectoral or systemic effects. Strong linkages but weak learning

Table 3.1   Typology of Processes of Structural Change

Learning process	Complementarities	
	Strong	Weak
Strong	Deep	Short breath
Weak	Labor-absorbing	Shallow

processes, due to the simplicity of the technology involved, characterize the second mixed case. This type of structural transformation will have slow productivity growth at the firm level but will generate significant aggregate productivity effects associated with strategic complementarities and reductions in underemployment. The development of labor-intensive exports is a case in point. This kind of situation will be referred as a *labor-absorbing* case.

This classification is extremely useful in understanding the sources and strength of international competitiveness. Complementarities play the crucial role in this regard. In shallow structural transformation processes, competitiveness does not have any systemic features. Indeed, unless the corresponding activities are associated with the exploitation of natural resources, they are essentially footloose. Even in the case of natural resource development, it can be argued that they are footloose, in the sense that once the resource base is exhausted, the activity will decline, leaving little in the way of development behind. In the short-breath case, where learning is strong but complementarities are weak, competitiveness will be based on firm-specific advantages, which may also generate unstable competitive advantages, as firms can shift their location. However, in the case of deep innovations and, to a lesser extent, labor-absorbing transformations, the essential source of competitiveness is systemic. This gives greater stability to the corresponding patterns of specialization. Even when challenged, the technological and broader development capabilities that have been built up may generate endogenous adaptive innovations.

By leading to the large-scale use of an international network of suppliers and centralized research and development efforts, globalization reduces entry costs into new activities and may facilitate higher productivity growth in a particular multinational firm or sector at the global level. However, it also generates processes of structural change that, from the point of view of each location, are increasingly shallow or at best have a short-breath character.[15] Thus, rapid productivity growth in dynamic firms may not be accompanied by rapid GDP growth in a specific country or location. The corresponding rise in underemployment will lead to low aggregate productivity growth. It must be emphasized that the problem does not lie, in this case, in low productivity growth at the firm level or in a lack of microeconomic efficiency. The problem really lies in the adverse features of the structural transformation process that generates weak links between export and GDP growth.

This interplay between factors also explains another feature of development processes mentioned above—path dependence. As already indicated, learning processes engender patterns of specialization that are largely self-reinforcing. However, to the extent that acquired capabilities are intangible, strong structural shocks (big bangs, as they were called in the 1990s) may have permanent adverse effects, as intangible capital in activities that undergo destruction is lost and it takes time (learning) to develop intangible capital in new activities. This includes institutional processes: old institutions are destroyed, and new ones take time to develop. Defensive restructuring of firms (rationalization of production activities that minimize fixed capital investments) will predominate under these conditions.[16]

Negative macroeconomic shocks could also lead to a significant loss of intangible capital in bankrupt firms, which also generates deadweight losses. In addition, this leads to debt overhangs that weigh upon growth possibilities for a long time. Finally, in periods of rapid structural change and macroeconomic upheaval, uncertainty increases, as old patterns are not a guide of any sort for the formation of expectations as to what the future will look like. Macroeconomic expectations thus become subject to learning, to trial and error, generating strong links between the short- and long-term growth paths (Heymann 2000). This further encourages defensive restructuring as well as speculative behavior on the part of firms. It must be emphasized, however, that this effect is additional to the links discussed in the previous paragraph, which relate to responses to the structural shock per se. Thus, defensive responses may predominate even if macroeconomic instability does not accompany the shock, particularly by firms that see few possibilities of success in the new structural context.

Finally, the classification provided in table 3.1 is useful in understanding some of the social effects of structural transformations. Two particular issues are relevant in this regard: the effects of these transformations on living standards and on the evolution of structural heterogeneity, which will influence, in turn, income distribution. In this regard, *deep* transformations are characterized by a rapid rise in standards of living, whereas the opposite is true of shallow transformations. The evolution of structural heterogeneity will depend, in the first case, on the nature of the innovation, particularly its labor demand features. Thus, deep transformations characterized by a skilled-labor bias (which seems to be a typical feature of technical change today worldwide) may generate a rapid increase in living standards, though accompanied by rising structural heterogeneity and income inequality. On the other hand, the basic differences between short-breath and labor-absorbing structural transformations are their radically different effects on structural heterogeneity: the first leads to increased heterogeneity, whereas the second will clearly have the opposite effect. In this sense, laborabsorbing transformations are the most attractive for low-income countries, as they are based on simple technology, but may have strong convergence effects (through the absorption of labor into higher-productivity sectors) as well as positive effects on equity. Because of their low entry costs, these activities tend to have thin profit margins and may be subject to a deterioration of the terms of trade if international demand fails to expand rapidly (due, among other reasons, to protectionism in the industrialized world, if it slows down the transfer of these branches of production to developing countries).

A SIMPLE FORMALIZATION OF THE LINKS BETWEEN STRUCTURAL AND MACROECONOMIC DYNAMICS

The interrelationships between structural dynamics and macroeconomic performance can be formalized in terms of a dual link between economic growth and productivity.[17] On one hand, economic growth has positive effects on productivity through three channels that have been explored in previous sections: (1) dynamic economies of scale of a microeconomic character, associated with learning and induced innovations;[18] (2) those associated with the exploitation of intra- and intersectoral external economies (economies of agglomeration and specialization and knowledge spillovers); and (3) the positive links generated by variations in underemployment (the attraction of underemployed workers by the expansion of high-productivity activities or, alternatively, the absorption of excess labor by low-productivity activities). Variations in the use of the pool of skilled labor and infrastructure will also generate links of this sort. To use the term employed by Kaldor (1978, chaps. 1 and 2), this link between productivity and production growth will be referred to as the *technical progress function.*[19]

This relationship is shown as TT in figure 3.1. The position of the curve depends on additional determinants of productivity growth. Some of them have been explored in previous sections: (1) the opportunity set associated with the position in the international hierarchy and acquired production and technological capabilities; (2) the reaction of entrepreneurs to these opportunities (which may be called their degree of

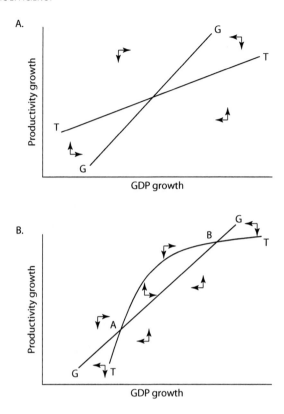

Figure 3.1   Productivity and GDP dynamics.

"innovativeness"); (3) the incentives that firms face (those associated with the competitive environment will be the focus of our attention below); and (4) the quality of relevant institutions.

The second relationship focuses on the reverse causality link: productivity growth increases economic growth. This relationship, shown as GG in figure 3.1, captures the traditional macroeconomic links emphasized in the literature on economic growth. Different schools of economic thought have identified at least four channels. First, technical change increases aggregate supply. Second, it generates new investment opportunities and, through this mechanism, drives aggregate demand; the availability of finance plays a crucial role in facilitating this process. Third, if domestic savings or external financing are not fully endogenous, savings or balance-of-payments gaps will become effective constraints on aggregate demand and will thus determine the shape of the curve.[20]

Fourth, technical change enhances international competitiveness, affecting the trade balance and, thus, aggregate demand; if the economy is foreign-exchange-constrained, the reduction in the trade balance relaxes this constraint and thus also has aggregate supply effects.

It must be emphasized that TT is not an aggregate production function. Rather, its positive slope implies that there is some underutilization of resources at any point in time, and thus growth induces a better allocation of resources (and the lack of growth, a misallocation, particularly through the underemployment of labor). Thus, through the virtuous circle effects that it generates, growth has aggregate *supply* effects, in particular, induced productivity improvements. The aggregate demand effects typical of Keynesian growth models are captured, however, in the GG function. Similarly, it should be emphasized that complementarities have supply (economies of agglomeration and specialization and knowledge spillovers) as well as demand (variations in the Keynesian multiplier) effects. Whereas the former are captured in the TT function, the latter affect the GG curve. If the economy is foreign-exchange-constrained, the corresponding changes in import dependence will also have aggregate supply effects that, in this case, will affect the GG function.

As both curves have positive slopes, the effects that they capture reinforce each other, generating alternating positive feedbacks but also possible negative feedbacks. A stable equilibrium exists when TT is flatter than GG, as shown in figure 3.1A. In Keynesian and foreign-exchange gap models—the two macroeconomic closures I will consider here—the slope of GG will depend on the elasticity of investment, exports, and imports to productivity; if they are relatively inelastic, the corresponding schedule will be steep, and if elasticities are high, it will be flatter. Given the determinants of the technical progress function, TT will be flatter if the following conditions prevail: (1) both micro- and mesoeconomic dynamic economies of scale are not too strong; (2) labor underemployment is moderate; and (3) fixed factors are not very important in the long run.

However, under significant initial (unskilled and/or skilled) labor underemployment or significant underutilization of infrastructure, the slope of TT may be high. Figure 3.1B thus presents a case in which the slope of TT is initially steep but falls at higher rates of economic growth. In this case, there will be a stable equilibrium at B, similar to that shown in figure 3.1A, and an unstable equilibrium at A. Any displacement from saddle point A will lead the economy to a new, higher stable equilibrium at B or, alternatively, to a low-growth trap. Obviously, depending on the position of the curves, other possibilities may exist that can generate explosive virtuous or vicious circles. Also, nothing guarantees that equilibrium will always arise at a positive rate of growth.

It is important to emphasize that the relationships shown here are taken to be of medium- or long-term character.[21] However, since many of the processes we are analyzing are time-bound, the steady-state properties of the model are actually uninteresting. Indeed, innovations may be seen as "spurts" that shift the technical progress function, but tend to weaken through time as innovations spread. Thus, a new wave of innovation shifts the TT function upward and turns it steeper, to T'T' in figure 3.2, accelerating both productivity and income growth. However, as this particular wave of innovations comes to be fully exploited and their structural effects are fully transmitted, the function will shift down and become flatter, to TT in figure 3.2. Productivity and GDP growth will then slow down.[22] If the GG function also shifts leftward (due to weakened "animal spirits"), the slowdown will become even sharper.

A favorable macroeconomic shock—improved access to external financing in a foreign-exchange-constrained economy and improved long-term expectations or long-term investment financing that have a positive effect on investment in a Keynesian model—will shift the GG function rightward to G'G' (figure 3.3). The micro, meso, and macro links summarized in the technical progress function now amplify the favorable macro effects. A negative macroeconomic shock will have the opposite effect. This could include any factor that increases macroeconomic instability. In line with the considerations discussed in the first

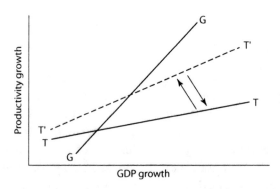

Figure 3.2   Effect of new wave of institutions.

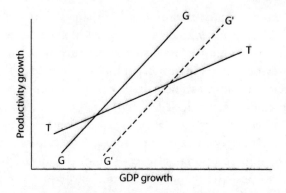

Figure 3.3   Effects of favorable macroeconomic shock.

part of this paper, *any* form of instability matters, including instability in the price level or in major relative prices, an increase in the intensity of the business cycle, or any factor that adversely affects public- or private-sector debt sustainability, among others.

This simple framework may be used to analyze the effects of economic liberalization processes on growth. For that purpose, I have to assume a specific relationship between competition and the rate of innovation. In this regard, a tradition of economic thought, which can be traced to Schumpeter, has emphasized the ability of large firms to internalize the benefits from innovation, a fact that may generate positive links between market concentration and innovations. Contrary to that tradition, the neoclassical defense of liberalization views the lack of competitive pressure as a factor that has adverse effects on productivity.

Another link between reforms and productivity, which was mentioned earlier, has to do with the fact that the uncertainties that characterize structural shocks may lead firms to adopt defensive attitudes. Thus, the initial response to a shock may be rationalization rather a new wave of innovation and investment. The latter may only come with a lag, when uncertainties are reduced. If this is so, the TT curve may not be affected, or indeed may be adversely affected, and the effects of increased competition on productivity will be only transitional.

If the neoclassical assumption about the links between competition and innovation is correct, then opening the economy to competition (including external competition) displaces the TT function upward. Liberalization unleashes, in this case, a degree of innovativeness that the more state interventionist environments of the past repressed. Domestic firms will also have better access to imported inputs and capital goods. However, this is not all that matters. The destruction of domestic linkages and previous technological capabilities would have the opposite effect. Specialization in activities with weaker dynamic economies of scale would tend to make the TT function flatter. If firms shrink, their capacity to cover the fixed costs associated with innovative activities will also decline. One way to express these opposite effects is to say that although the microeconomic effects of competition on productivity growth may be positive, the mesoeconomic (structural) factors may be adverse. The net effects of reforms on TT are thus unclear. On the other hand, through either Keynesian mechanisms or the supply effects characteristic of a foreign-exchange-constrained economy, the increase in the propensity to import generated by trade reform will lead to a leftward shift in the GG function.

Figure 3.4 provides three possible outcomes (there may be others). In case A, the neoclassical effects on TT are strong and prevail over weaker adverse movements of the GG function. Both GDP and productivity growth speed up. In case B, neoclassical effects on TT continue to prevail but are weaker, whereas GG effects are strong. Productivity growth speeds up but overall economic growth slows down. An implication of this is that labor under- and unemployment increase. In case C, adverse structural effects on TT prevail over the positive effects of competition, generating a reduction in both GDP and productivity growth. Under- and unemployment increase sharply. This implies that there is no general presumption that liberalization will accelerate growth, and that the microeconomic links emphasized by defenders of liberalization may be swamped by adverse structural and macroeconomic effects.

POLICY IMPLICATIONS

The previous analysis indicates that institutions that guarantee stability of the basic social contract, the protection of business activities, and an efficient state bureaucracy, as well as the formation of human capital and the development of infrastructure, are certainly important to economic growth, but play the role of framework conditions which, by themselves, are unlikely to affect the growth momentum. The analysis also indicates that the assumption that dynamic productive development and the particular institutions that support it are automatic results of market

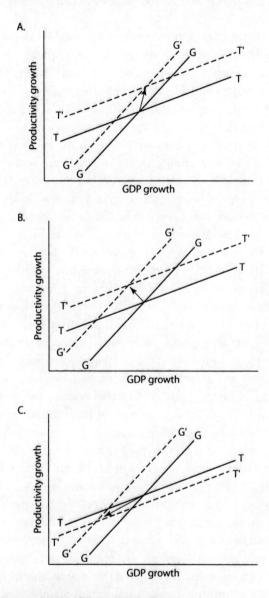

Figure 3.4 Case A: Strong TT, weak GG effects.
Case B: Weak favorable TT, strong GG effects.
Case C: Adverse TT and GG effects.

mechanisms should be abandoned, as it has been demonstrated by the facts to be wrong.

The key to rapid growth in the developing world is the combination of strategies aimed at the dynamic transformation of production structures with appropriate macroeconomic conditions and stability (in the broad sense of the term); to improve the distributive effects of growth, such a strategy must be supplemented with policies aimed at reducing the structural heterogeneity of production structures.

The focus on structural dynamics helps to identify the specific policy areas that authorities should target to accelerate economic growth. Accordingly, efforts should be made to do the following: (1) Encourage innovation, in the broad sense of the term, and the associated learning processes in the areas of technologies, productive organization, and marketing; to the extent that innovations in developing countries are largely associated with the transfer of sectors of production from the industrialized world, a strategy of diversification of the production structure is the key to increased innovations. (2) Encourage the development of complementarities that generate positive demand and, above all, supply effects that result in the development of sectoral and systemwide competitiveness; in the latter case, nontradable inputs and specialized services should be a special focus of attention, particularly in terms of the development of sectors that produce specialized inputs and services (knowledge, logistics, and marketing services), a strong and deep domestic financial system, and adequate infrastructure. (3) Encourage the development of small firms through training, technological diffusion, appropriate financing channels, and the promotion of different forms of associations among small entrepreneurs and of productive, technological, and commercial links between large and small firms.

Under current global conditions, five essential characteristics of the strategies that should serve as the framework for these policies can be identified. First, the emphasis should be on integrating the developing countries into dynamic global markets. Second, there must be a proper balance between individual entrepreneurial initiative, which is decisive for a dynamic process of innovation, and the establishment of institutions aimed at increasing information and coordination among agents. Among the latter, different mixes of public and private institutions should be considered, according to the tradition of each country. Moreover, different mixes of supranational (e.g., within the framework of integration processes), national, and local (decentralized) institutions should also be designed. Third, there should be a mix of horizontal and selective policies.

Indeed, insofar as policies are intended to strengthen competitiveness, a degree of selectivity aimed at reinforcing successful patterns of specialization and helping to breed new sectors (creating comparative advantages) is essential. Furthermore, under budget constraints, any "horizontal" policy must be detailed and hence necessarily becomes selective. Clear cases of these sorts are the allocation of resources from funds for technological development and export promotion. Recognizing that there is an implicit selectivity in horizontal policies will lead to a better allocation of scarce resources than the alternative neutral stance. Fourth, all incentives should be granted on the basis of performance, generating "reciprocal control mechanisms," to borrow Amsden's (2001) term (see also Hausmann and Rodrik 2003). Indeed, the institutional structure itself should be subject to periodic evaluation, within its own learning path. Finally, special attention should be given to the opportunities that small firms provide both for growth and for improving the social outcomes of structural transformations.

A complex issue relates to the framework of international rules, especially those of the World Trade Organization and the wave of bilateral and plurilateral free trade agreements. In this regard, although priority should certainly be given to taking advantage of the maneuvering room provided under existing agreements, there is a strong sense that a larger *policy space* (to borrow the term extensively used in United Nations debates) should be made available to the authorities of developing countries, as policy autonomy has been severely restricted in trade negotiations. In particular, according to the analysis presented in this chapter, they should be allowed to apply selective policies and performance criteria to encourage innovation and create the complementarities that are essential for development.

In the past, national development banks played a crucial role in the developing world in guaranteeing the availability of capital (particularly long-term capital) for new activities, and in many areas they continue to do so. It is unclear whether privatized financial sectors will provide an adequate substitute for them. Private investment banking and venture capital are the best alternatives, but past and recent experience indicates that their expansion in developing countries on an optimal scale is not automatic; indeed, these activities are highly concentrated in a few industrialized countries. Access to international services of this sort may thus be of paramount importance to guarantee finance for innovative activities, but this may generate a strong bias in favor of multinational and large national firms and against small and medium-sized enterprises.

An additional implication of the previous analysis is that structural transformation is not a "once and for all" process, a belief that is implicit in current views of structural reforms. It is rather a persistent task, as the structural transformation process is continuous and may face obstacles at any stage, which may block development. To the extent that, in developing countries, innovative activities are largely the result of the spread of new sectors and technologies previously created in the industrial centers, at any given time these activities may be considered as the new set of *infant sectors* to be promoted (i.e., as infant export activities). This includes the design of instruments to promote the transfer of these sectors to the developing world through trade rules that facilitate and even encourage such transfers, together with appropriate incentives and institutions to further the growth of these infant sectors in developing countries. The instruments developed to promote innovative activities in earlier stages may serve this purpose, but they may have to be readapted or new institutions may have to be created to solve the specific issues involved in guaranteeing the successful development of new sectors in a more interdependent world economy.

The final implication of the analysis is that the process of transformation is not by any means smooth. Destruction is a constant companion of creation, and structural heterogeneity is a persistent feature that can increase at different phases of the development process. Distributive tensions are presumably associated with both factors. There is, in this regard, no unique Kuznets trajectory, as there may be periods of increased structural heterogeneity in the middle stages of the development process as a result of structural transformations or macroeconomic imbalances. Facilitating the transfer of resources from less dynamic to more dynamic activities, avoiding transformation processes that increase structural heterogeneity, and working to upgrade low-productivity activities and generate positive links with high-productivity activities would, in this context, be critical elements in achieving a more equitable development process.

NOTES

This a revised version of the paper published in *Beyond Reforms: Structural Dynamics and Macroeconomic Vulnerability* (Palo Alto, Calif.: Stanford University Press, ECLAC, and World Bank, 2005). ECLAC's copyright for the original version of this article: © 2005 United Nations.

1. The recent literature is extensive. Among the most useful contributions, see Romer (1986), Lucas (1988), Taylor (1991), Nelson (1996), Aghion and Howitt (1998), Rodrik (1999, 2007), Ros (2000, 2013), Barro and Sala-i-Martin (2003), Ocampo, Rada, and Taylor (2009), Lin (2012), and Stiglitz and Greenwald (2014).

2. Note that this concept is entirely different from concepts of dynamic efficiency used in neoclassical optimal growth models.

3. See, e.g., Easterly et al. (1993) and Pritchett (2000).

4. Nonetheless, it has also been argued that there is much less association between some of these variables and economic growth than was traditionally assumed. This has been claimed, in particular, in relation to physical and human capital. See Easterly (2001, part II).

5. There may also be intermediate alternatives: some factors may not "cause" growth in the sense of accelerating the growth momentum, but they can block it. Indeed, this is the case of macroeconomic stability, as has already been pointed out.

6. As Cripps and Tarling (1973) have pointed out, this pattern is confirmed by the growth experience of industrialized countries even as late as during the post-WW II golden years.

7. I will refer below to the phenomenon of increased specialization at the firm level (economies of scope) as *economies of specialization*, as it will be assumed (following, indeed, the line of inquiry pursued by Adam Smith) that the opportunities for such specialization are determined by the size of the market and are thus part of the meso-economic effects to which we will refer below as complementarities.

8. This is generally forgotten when the period of state-led industrialization in Latin America is analyzed. Import substitution obviously made more sense in the closed world economy of the 1930s to 1950s (and in the midst of the protectionist wave that characterized the industrialized world in the late nineteenth and early twentieth centuries) than in the period of gradual but incomplete opening of the industrialized world to the exports of developing countries that started in the mid-1960s (Bértola and Ocampo, 2012).

9. Outsourcing of technology and some features of information and communications technology may have reduced the need for technological followers to invest in learning and adapting technology. However, they have not eliminated the general link between the development of new activities and the investments associated with them.

10. *Leapfrogging* is generally used to refer to the adoption of the latest (e.g., modern information and telecommunications) technologies, even when previous technologies were not used in a given location. However, this is just a necessary condition for the successful development of a specific activity at a particular time. It does not necessarily involve rising up through the international economic hierarchy, which is the appropriate sense in which the term *leapfrogging* should be used.

11. See, in particular, Nelson and Winter (1982), Nelson (1996), and Dosi et al. (1988) and, with respect to developing countries, Katz (1987) and Lall (1990, 2003). Similar concepts have been developed in some versions of the new growth theory in which "knowledge capital" is a form of "human capital," having three specific attributes: it is "embodied" in particular persons, it is capable of generating significant externalities, and it is costly to acquire (Lucas, 1988). However, these theories do not capture a basic corollary of these attributes: firm specificity and the corresponding

coexistence of heterogeneous producers in any given sector of production. This fact turns the concept of "representative producer" into an abstraction that eliminates elements that play an essential role in determining the nature of competition and the divergence in the growth of firms, regions, and nations through time.

12. This may also apply to technology creation. In this sense, the probability of major innovations, even when they are the result of explicit research and development efforts, depends on the accumulated technological knowledge and production experience of firms.

13. As we have pointed out, this factor has not been entirely absent in the industrial world either (see Cripps and Tarling, 1973).

14. This does not mean that the skilled workers who migrate will necessarily be absorbed in high-productivity activities in the receiving countries. There may be, in effect, a net loss of human capital.

15. A particular case of a shallow innovation is the takeover of domestic firms by multinationals, if it weakens domestic demand linkages (by the change in the network of suppliers) and concentrates research and development abroad. Maquila exports may have a similar character, although they can reduce underemployment and may serve as a mechanism for transmitting some organizational and marketing innovations. They may also deepen through time and gradually create domestic linkages, thus becoming a labor-absorbing innovation.

16. This is a central conclusion of an ECLAC project on structural reforms in Latin America, which developed a typology of phases of response to structural reforms. According to this typology, an *offensive* attitude only comes with a lag, particularly when the new institutional environment settles down. See Stallings and Peres (2000) and Katz (2000).

17. For early versions of this model, see Ocampo and Taylor (1998) and Ocampo (2002). A mathematical formulation is provided by Ocampo, Rada, and Taylor (2009, chap. 8).

18. To the extent that new technology is embodied in new equipment, a higher rate of investment induced by faster growth will also increase productivity growth, and should thus be added to the list.

19. Following the literature on the topic, it may also be called the *Kaldor-Verdoorn function*.

20. For a full analysis of gaps in macroeconomic adjustment, see Taylor (1994). As is well known, saving adjusts through variations in economic activity (the Keynesian mechanism), income redistribution between sectors with high and low propensities to save, particularly between capital owners and workers (the Kaleckian mechanism), and variations in the trade balance (external savings). Depending on the source of the rigidity of the mechanism, inflationary gaps, either distributive struggles or external gaps may arise. For a full treatment of these issues, see Taylor (1991).

21. There are also short-run relationships between productivity and economic growth associated with short-term changes in capacity utilization. However, those effects must be seen as deviations from GG.

22. Of course, there is no presumption that TT will return to its original position. This is the case that, for the sake of simplicity, is shown in figure 3.2.

REFERENCES

Aghion, Philippe, and Peter Howitt (1998), *Endogenous Growth Theory*, Cambridge, Mass., MIT Press.

Amsden, Alice (2001), *The Rise of the Rest: Non-Western Economies' Ascent in World Markets*, London, Oxford University Press.

Arthur, W. Brian (1994), *Increasing Returns and Path Dependence in the Economy*, Ann Arbor, University of Michigan Press.

Bairoch, Paul (1993), *Economics and World History: Myths and Paradoxes*, Chicago, University of Chicago Press.

Balassa, Bela (1989), *Comparative Advantage Trade Policy and Economic Development*, New York, New York University Press.

Barro, Robert J., and Xavier Sala-i-Martin (2003), *Economic Growth*, New York, McGraw-Hill.

Bértola, Luis, and José Antonio Ocampo (2012), *The Economic Development of Latin America since Independence*, New York, Oxford University Press.

Chang, Ha-Joon (1994), *The Political Economy of Industrial Policy*, London, Macmillan and St. Martin's Press. Second edition, London, Macmillan Press, 1996.

Chenery, Hollis, Sherman Robinson, and Moshe Syrquin (1986), *Industrialization and Growth: A Comparative Study*, The World Bank, Oxford University Press.

Cripps, T. F., and R. J. Tarling (1973), "Growth in Advanced Capitalist Economies 1950–1970," *Occasional Paper* 40, University of Cambridge, Department of Applied Economics.

Dosi, Giovanni, Christopher Freeman, Richard Nelson, Gerald Silverberg, and Luc Soete eds. (1988), *Technical Change and Economic Theory*, Maastricht Economic Research Institute on Innovation and Technology (MERIT)/The International Federation of Institutes for Advanced Studies (IFIAS), London and New York, Pinter Publishers.

Easterly, William (2001), *The Elusive Quest for Growth: Economists' Adventures and Misadventures in the Tropics*, Cambridge, Mass., MIT Press.

Easterly, William, Michael Kremer, Lant Pritchett, and Lawrence Summers (1993), "Good Policy or Good Luck? Country Growth Performance and Temporary Shocks," *Journal of Monetary Economics*, 32, December.

ECLAC (Economic Commission for Latin America and the Caribbean) (2000), *Equity, Development and Citizenship*, Santiago, Chile.

—— (1990), *Changing Production Patterns with Social Equity*, Santiago, Chile.

Eichengreen, Barry, Donghyun Park, and Kwanho Shin (2012), "When Fast Growing Economies Slow Down: International Evidence and Implications for China," *Asian Economic Papers*, 11, pp. 42–87.

—— (2013), "Growth Slowdowns Redux: New Evidence on the Middle-Income Trap," *NBER Working Paper* no. 18673.

Fajnzylber, Fernando (1990), "Industrialization in Latin America: From the 'Black Box' to the 'Empty Box,' " *Cuadernos de la CEPAL*, no. 60, Santiago, Chile.

Fujita, Masahisa, Paul Krugman, and Anthony J. Venables (1999), *The Spatial Economy: Cities, Regions and International Trade*, Cambridge, Mass., MIT Press.

Freeman, Chris, and Luc Soete (1997), *The Economics of Industrial Innovation*, 3d ed., Cambridge, Mass., MIT Press.

Furtado, Celso (1961), *Desarrollo y Subdesarrollo*, Colección Cuadernos 196, Buenos Aires, Editorial Universitaria.

Gerschenkron, A. (1962), *Economic Backwardness in Historical Perspective*, Cambridge, Mass., Harvard University Press.

Grossman, Gene M., and Elhanan Helpman (1991), *Innovation and Growth in the Global Economy*, Cambridge, Mass., MIT Press.

Hausmann, Ricardo, and Dani Rodrik (2003), "Economic Development as Self-Discovery," *Journal of Development Economics*, 72: 603–633.

Helleiner, Gerald K. ed. (1994), *Trade Policy and Industrialization in Turbulent Times*, New York, Routledge and UNU/WIDER.

Heymann, Daniel (2000), "Major Macroeconomic Upsets, Expectations and Policy Responses," *CEPAL Review*, no. 70 (LC/G.2095-P), Santiago, Chile.

Hirschman, Albert O. (1958), *The Strategy of Economic Development*, New Haven, Conn., Yale University Press.

Kaldor, Nicholas (1978), *Further Essays on Economic Theory*, London, Duckworth.

Katz, Jorge (2000), *Reformas estructurales, productividad y conducta tecnológica*, Santiago, Chile, Economic Commission for Latin America and the Caribbean (ECLAC)/ Fondo de Cultura Económica.

—— (1987) "Domestic Technology Generation in LDCs: A Review of Research Findings," *Technology Generation in Latin American Manufacturing Industries*, Jorge Katz ed., London, Macmillan.

Keesing, Donald B., and Sanjaya Lall (1992), "Marketing Manufactured Exports from Developing Countries: Learning Sequences and Public Support," in Gerald K. Helleiner ed., *Trade Policy, Industrialization, and Development: New Perspectives*, New York, Oxford University Press and WIDER.

Krugman, Paul (1990), *Rethinking International Trade*, Cambridge, Mass., MIT Press.

Lall, Sanjaya (1990), *Building Industrial Competitiveness in Developing Countries*, Paris, OECD Development Center.

—— (2003), "Technology and Industrial Development in an Era of Globalization," in Ha-Joon Chang ed., *Rethinking Development Economics*, London, Anthem Press, chap. 13.

Lewis, W. Arthur (1969), *Aspects of Tropical Trade, 1883–1965*, Stockholm, Almqvist & Wicksell, Wicksell Lectures.

—— (1954), "Economic Development with Unlimited Supplies of Labor," *Manchester School of Economic and Social Studies*, 22, May.

Lin, Justin Yifu (2012), *The Quest for Prosperity: How Developing Countries Can Take Off*, Princeton, N.J., Princeton University Press.

Lucas, Robert E., Jr. (1988), "On the Mechanics of Economic Development," *Journal of Monetary Economics*, 22, 1, July.

Maddison, Angus (2001), *The World Economy —A Millennial Perspective*, Paris, Development Centre Studies, OECD.

—— (1991), *Dynamic Forces in Capitalist Development: A Long-Run Comparative View*, London, Oxford University Press.

Myint, H. (1971), *Economic Theory and the Underdeveloped Countries*, New York, Oxford University Press.

Nelson, Richard R. (1996), *The Sources of Economic Growth*, Cambridge, Mass., Harvard University Press.

Nelson, Richard R. and Sidney G. Winter (1982), *An Evolutionary Theory of Economic Change*, Cambridge, Mass., Belknap Press of Harvard University Press.

Ocampo, José Antonio (2008), "A Broad View of Macroeconomic Stability," in Narcis Serra and Joseph E. Stiglitz eds., *The Washington Consensus Reconsidered*, New York, Oxford University Press, chap. 6.

—— (2005), "The Quest for Dynamic Efficiency: Structural Dynamics and Economic Growth in Developing Countries," in José Antonio Ocampo ed., *Beyond Reforms: Structural Dynamics and Macroeconomic Vulnerability*, Palo Alto, Calif., Stanford University Press, World Bank, and ECLAC, chap. 1.

—— (2002), "Structural Dynamics and Economic Development," in Valpy FitzGerald ed., *Social Institutions and Economic Development: A Tribute to Kurt Martin*, Institute of Social Studies, Dordrecht, Kluwer, chap. 4.

—— (2001), "Raul Prebisch and the Development Agenda at the Dawn of the Twenty-First Century," *CEPAL Review*, no. 75, December.

—— (1986), "New Developments in Trade Theory and LDCs," *Journal of Development Economics*, 22, 1, June.

Ocampo, José Antonio and Lance Taylor (1998), "Trade Liberalisation in Developing Economies: Modest Benefits but Problems with Productivity Growth, Macro Prices, and Income Distribution," *Economic Journal*, 108, 450, September.

Ocampo, José Antonio, Codrina Rada, and Lance Taylor (2009), *Growth and Policy in Developing Countries: A Structuralist Approach*, New York, Columbia University Press.

Ohlin, B. (1933), *Interregional and International Trade*, Cambridge, Mass., Harvard University Press.

Pérez, Carlota (2002), *Technological Revolutions and Financial Capital. The Dynamics of Bubbles and Golden Ages*, Edward Elgar, Cheltenham, UK.

—— (2001), "Technological Change and Opportunities for Development as a Moving Target," *CEPAL Review*, no. 75, Santiago, Chile.

Pinto, Aníbal (1970), "Naturaleza e implicaciones de la 'heterogeneidad estructural' de la América Latina," *El Trimestre Económico*, vol. 37, no. 1, México, D. F., Fondo de Cultura Económica, January–March; reprinted in *Cincuenta años del pensamiento en la CEPAL*, vol. 2, Santiago, Chile, CEPAL/Fondo de Cultura Económica, 1998.

Prebisch, Raúl (1964), *Nueva política comercial para el desarrollo*, Mexico, Fondo de Cultura Económica.

—— (1951), "Theoretical and Practical Problems of Economic Growth" (E/CN.12/221), Mexico City, Economic Commission for Latin America (ECLA).

Pritchett, Lant (1997), "Divergence, Big Time," *Journal of Economic Perspectives*, 11, 3, summer.

—— (2000), "Understanding Patterns of Economic Growth: Searching for Hills among Plateaus, Mountains and Plains," *World Bank Economic Review*, 14, 2.

Robinson, Joan (1962), *Essays in the Theory of Economic Growth*, London, Macmillan.

Rodríguez, Francisco, and Dani Rodrik (2001), "Trade Policy and Economic Growth: A Skeptic's Guide to the Cross-National Evidence," *NBER Macroeconomics Annual*

2000, vol. 15, Ben S. Bernanke and Kenneth Rogoff eds., Cambridge, Mass., MIT Press.

Rodrik, Dani (2014), "The Past, Present and Future of Economic Growth," in Franklin Allen et al., *Toward a Better Global Economy*, London, Oxford University Press, chap. 2.

—— (2007), *One Economics, Many Recipes: Globalization, Institutions and Economic Growth*, Princeton, N.J., Princeton University Press.

—— (1999), *The New Global Economy and Developing Countries: Making Openness Work*, Overseas Development Council, Washington, D.C.

Romer, P. M. (1986), "Increasing Returns and Long-Run Growth," *Journal of Political Economy*, 94.

Ros, Jaime (2013), *Rethinking Economic Development, Growth and Institutions*, London, Oxford University Press.

—— (2000), *Development Theory and the Economics of Growth*, Ann Arbor, University of Michigan Press.

Rosenstein-Rodan, P. N. (1943), "Problems of Industrialization of Eastern and South-Eastern Europe," *The Economic Journal*, 53, June-September.

Schumpeter, Joseph (1962), *Capitalism, Socialism and Democracy*, 3d ed., New York, Harper Torchbooks.

—— (1961), *The Theory of Economic Development*, London, Oxford University Press.

Solow, Robert M. (2000), *Growth Theory: An Exposition*, 2d ed., New York, Oxford University Press.

—— (1956), "A Contribution to the Theory of Economic Growth," *Quarterly Journal of Economics*, 70, 5.

Stallings, Barbara, and Wilson Peres (2000), *Growth, Employment and Equity: The Impact of the Economic Reforms in Latin America and the Caribbean*, Santiago, Chile, Economic Commission for Latin America and the Caribbean (ECLAC)/ Fondo de Cultura Económica.

Stiglitz, Joseph E., and Bruce Greenwald (2014), *Creating a Learning Society: A New Approach to Growth, Development, and Social Progress*, New York, Columbia University Press.

Taylor, Lance (1994), "Gap Models," *Journal of Development Economics*, 45: 17–34.

—— (1991), *Income Distribution, Inflation, and Growth. Lectures on Structuralist Macroeconomic Theory*, Cambridge, Mass., MIT Press.

van Wijnbergen, Sweder (1984), "The Dutch Disease: A Disease After All?" *Economic Journal*, no. 94

PART II

Development Finance

CHAPTER 4

Uncertainty, Investment, and Financing

THE STRATEGIC ROLE OF NATIONAL DEVELOPMENT BANKS

João Carlos Ferraz

DEVELOPMENT BANKS ARE SINGULAR AND USEFUL, NOT EXOTIC, INSTITUTIONS

National development banks (DBs) are often considered "exotic" institutions, typical of developing countries and of incomplete financial markets. Even though their contribution to economic development worldwide has been relevant, especially after World War II, two recent economic phenomena are helping to undermine usually ideologically biased evaluations and to illuminate their strategic role in different economies.

The first phenomenon is the recent financial crisis. In times of serious financial crisis, the importance of national states and public policies is unquestionable. As the experiences of different countries and regions have demonstrated, financial situations of extreme gravity demand immediate and effective actions which, in the recent past, have taken different formats and contents. Expansionary monetary and fiscal policies have been decisive, but also the countercyclical roles played by development banks in different countries have had great importance in offering much needed credit to the economic system, when the supply of resources of private banks receded. A second role, of greater importance from a development perspective, is the engagement of development banks in inducing structural transformation.

This chapter aims at exploring the structural features of national development banks and their role in long-term investment financing. Arguments unfold along three main lines of discussion. First, it is argued that the process of investment and its financing is strongly correlated with different types of uncertainties. Second, the structure, behavior, and performance of development banks must be properly understood in order to appreciate the role that each plays in different economies. Third, development banks have shown a willingness (in the form of resource allocation) to support very challenging investments that are strongly associated with specific and different types of uncertainties. This analysis indicates that development banks are relevant for the economic transformation of countries at different stages of development, in good and bad times. Nevertheless, much remains to be done, and this chapter proposes a research agenda about this singular institution.

This chapter is divided in seven sections, including this introduction and the conclusion. The following one discusses, briefly, the nature of financial markets. From there a discussion on uncertainty and finance is taken up, to provide the analytical basis for the upcoming empirical sections. Section four provides quantitative and qualitative information in an attempt to describe structural organizational features of development banks. In section five a comparative analysis of four prominent international development banks, focusing on core competencies, areas of operation, and financial performance, will be taken up. Section six is dedicated to the analysis of the performance of development banks in facing investment-related uncertainties. The final section summarizes main findings and arguments and proposes a research agenda about development banks.

DO FINANCIAL MARKETS WORK EFFICIENTLY?

The intellectual debate over development banks is scarce, relative to the importance they have held over many decades.

On a more basic level, it is possible to discern two interconnected lines of debate: one that is strongly ideologically biased tries to demonstrate how development banks are unnecessary given the virtues of private financial markets while defendants of development banks try to demonstrate the pitfalls of the latter, thus arguing for a proactive role of the state in investment financing. The second line of debate, which is strongly preferred as the spearhead of attack by critics of development banks, is that politics do affect the efficiency and effectiveness of these institutions. Usually this type of literature is not conducive to the correct understanding of the role played by development banks in given economies since the answer is already known at the point of departure.

Substantive research, however, does exist. As reviewed by Luna-Martínez and Vicente (2012) as well as Ferraz, Além, and Madeira (2013), such research is inserted in a broader investigative program on the role played by financial systems on economic growth. For the purposes of this paper two different approaches are relevant: one that has an historical and/or institutional character and one that is conceptually based. The latter can be subdivided in different theoretical schools: financial repression and credit rationing.

The historical/institutional approach is strongly inspired by Gerschenkron (1973), and the focus is to discern structural features of financial systems in different countries in time. They identify not a single financial structure as a general model but argue that financial systems develop according to the evolving needs of each country and that there is a constant interplay and changing positions between capital market, private bank credit, and public financing.

There are authors, however, who specifically criticize development banks on three main issues: the crowding-out effect in relation to the private industry; the "openness" to political influences on banking decisions; and the discretionary allocation to specific economic groups ("picking winners") (Lazzarini et al. 2015). Mazzucato and Penna (2015), Griffith-Jones (2013), and Rezende (2015) specifically discuss and demonstrate the weaknesses of these arguments.

The "crowding-out" argument is counterposed to the preference of private industry to operate in the short term, where earnings are accrued but with the negative consequence that assets and liabilities just cannot sustain long-run financing. In this sense, development banks with a long balance sheet are structurally prepared to support investment and, even more so, to "inaugurate" new financial market niches that, once well established, can then attract private industry. In this sense, given their developmental role, these institutions can be better described as "crowding in" agencies.

The argument for political influence has two dimensions. First, it is naturally legitimate that, being public institutions of strategic importance, development banks should (and most do) follow policy directives and priorities defined at the political domain, by authorities in power. The importance of political allocation of priorities is even more pronounced in democracies when, by vote, citizens define their preferences for specific development platforms. Second, how can one mitigate the risks of cronyism? In this case, development banks must have explicitly separate functions, impersonal and collegiate decision processes, and independent board members; and from an external perspective, they should be submitted to explicit banking supervision. These are the elements that can constitute proper defenses against political clout.

Finally, much criticism comes from the discretionary allocation of funding. For the defendants of the financial "repression" approach, the competitive market dogma prevails so that market mechanisms—through flexible interest rates—are fully capable of adjusting demand and supply of financial resources toward optimal conditions (Gurley and Shaw 1955; McKinnon 1973). Interventions to control interest rates or by public financial institutions are doomed to fail: intervention would lead to a level of interest rate inferior to the balanced rate, preventing the efficient market adjustment and, in consequence, jeopardizing the development of private financial institutions.

Critics argue that picking winners is not justifiable as bureaucracies do not have the proper means and knowledge to "choose" correctly or, in general, winners can be financed by the market. The most relevant flaw and a structural weakness of these criticisms is that they fail to recognize the possibility of a situation in which, even when agents are willing to pay a higher interest rate to get funds to finance their investments, banks may refuse to offer financing or price financing at levels that would not justify investments given existing opportunity costs (credit rationing). In this case there would be an issue of restricted supply and not of "price" (interest) misfit. The approach of credit rationing then justifies the existence of development banks, which would supply the necessary credit to investment that is unavailable in the private financing system.

But the debate can go even further if one takes into account the role that public institutions may perform not in the interplay between supply and demand for credit but in inducing development. In this direction, Mazzucato and Penna (2015) inspired by Polanyi (2001) defend the role of the state "in shaping and creating markets." By playing such a role, they take risks but also can be rewarded if they adopt a portfolio approach in financing investments, a position also defended by Rodrik (2013) in relation to industrial policies.

When development, understood as structural transformation, is brought into the limelight, the concept of uncertainty becomes of fundamental importance. Structural transformation–based development processes imply the inexistence of probabilistic information about facts that occur in the future. As there is a time lag between the moment a decision is made to allocate resources and the moment when results come about, agents act according to expectations on future earnings. Moreover, decisions on resource allocation, to a great extent, are irreversible. Thus, uncertainty is present in all economic decisions, even though its impact differs according to the nature of resource allocation. For example, production decisions regarding the short term are less complex and therefore are made routinely by taking the past as a good approximation. Investment decisions, in turn, are more complex, as taught by Keynes (1936, 1939).

Investment decisions are based on an array of options for applying capital in different classes of assets, classified according to their expected profitability and liquidity. At one end, holding currency is the decision with the highest level of liquidity but with very low returns. At the other extreme there are long-term investments. Associated with this discussion, Rezende (2015) then calls for a substantive discussion of the role of development banks based not on the notion of market failure but on the theory of financial instability. The association among the nature of investments, different classes of uncertainties, and finance will be taken up next.

IF INVESTMENT INHERENTLY EMBEDS UNCERTAINTIES, THESE MUST BE SPECIFIED!

It is possible to discern, from a logical perspective but still as a preliminary attempt, four types of uncertainty facing development projects leading to structural transformation of economies: the complexity of a project in itself, the time frame of the investment, the prevailing economic conditions, and unexpected development challenges. If these uncertainties are inherently embedded in investment projects, especially those leading to structural transformation of economies, how are they to be financed? Will capital markets and private banks suffice? Alternatively, can development banks be the sole agent behind uncertain related finance? Or, wouldn't a financial industry be more resilient and development prone if public and private partnerships, in different modes, prevailed?

With the goal of structural transformation, development projects have the objective to transform an economy at the local, regional, or national levels. Of special importance are infrastructure and innovation projects, but they can also be related to the strengthening of a particular set of firms, such as small and medium enterprises (SMEs) and/or mergers and acquisitions, to induce technical or firm-level economies of scale and scope and the internationalization of corporations.

The complexity of development projects is particularly high in relation to technological innovations.[1] Uncertainty is very much embedded in technical progress. The process of innovation is increasingly dependent on scientific knowledge and on the convergence of different technologies. As a result, innovations depend on cooperation among firms, scientific institutions, and technology labs and therefore encompass a wide variety of capabilities. Thus, the uncertainties surrounding innovation arise not only because of the pursuit of something that doesn't yet exist, but also because of the need for innovators—firms or research institutions—to bring together partners who have complementary technological capabilities and who can therefore move toward a "convergent process of building up innovations."

A second source of uncertainty has to do with the time dimension of investments. Uncertainty particularly affects investments with long maturation processes, especially in a world dominated by "short-termism" in capital markets. According to Lazonick (2013), time matters because it is directly related to investors having to lock up liabilities with corresponding expectations over future rates of return.

A third source of uncertainty is that associated with unexpected development challenges, which may be forecasted with greater or lesser degree of accuracy. While quantitative population trends (e.g., aging) can be relatively well determined, their consequences, impacts, and especially policy solutions are not foreseeable. Other phenomena, such as climate change, may be specified but without a consensus on either its very existence or potential consequences and remedies. For both cases, it can be expected that new markets will be formed, new companies will emerge, and new investments will occur, all with a high degree of uncertainty in terms of their likely success. Thus, their financing will happen under unknown risk parameters, with high latitude for losses and rewards.

Finally, uncertainties may arise from prevailing economic conditions, especially long-term macroeconomic stability. The "foreseeability" (to the extent that this is possible) over the levels and volatilities of economic growth, long-term interest rates, and the exchange rate will directly affect the propensity of investors to take risks and allocate long-term capital to investment projects. In times of economic crises, uncertainty increases and the propensity of economic agents, especially the financial sector, is to act pro-cyclically. Therefore, credit becomes more expensive, scarce, and concentrated with macroeconomic instability, exactly when refinancing mechanisms and financial support are needed the most.

On the contrary, in the phases of growth, agents tend to allocate resources to riskier assets. This can happen voluntarily as well as involuntarily, for example following a herd behavior guided by collective optimism. As expectations become increasingly less conservative, banks and businesses increasingly assume aggressive financial positions, making their financial stability dependent on the achievement of expected revenue streams. However, this process causes a reduction of the banks' margin of safety, as banks attribute decreasing risk to their borrowers, thus creating a tendency to over-indebtedness and the underestimation of risk (Kregel 1997; Minsky 1982, 1986).

Market failures, information asymmetry, risks, and (especially) the different classes of uncertainty associated with investment projects put in serious check the capacity of capital markets and private banks to finance, all by themselves, investment projects. This is the space for development banks. They may play a fundamental role in minimizing uncertainty in investment projects, through different instruments.

Ferraz, Além, and Madeira (2013), and Coutinho, Ferraz, and Marques (2015) have tried to specify concepts that can be useful for the analysis of development banks. They point out five specific roles that contribute to the understanding of these institutions. First, they are patient institutions when financing new economic activities or the expansion of capacity and capabilities, opening new frontiers, filling gaps, fixing failures, and inducing externalities. Second, they have a role to play in co-developing financial markets. That is, they contribute to the fostering a long-term financing industry when partnering in specific operations or when opening new financial segments. Third, and as it became well known in the recent crisis, development banks contribute to systemic stability especially when taking up a countercyclical role. Fourth, as state institutions, stability matters in terms of sources of funding, assets and liabilities with a long maturity base, well-defined missions, and internal resources (people, technology, processes, and instruments) driven to serve the public interest. Finally, they are *policy supporters*: they have an active role in supporting national or local policy development and long-term planning. Thus, if they are to perform such tasks, nothing is fairer than development banks appropriating and distributing (to society, via the state) the returns of efficient (financial) investment decisions.

Rezende (2015) introduces three roles for development banks, based on the Brazilian experience: the countercyclical one; the promotion of financing for development to induce productivity, infrastructure, and knowledge-based activities; and the development of capital markets.

Mazzucato and Penna (2015) have similar concerns. For them, these institutions (termed *state investment banks*) can induce development of any economy by performing a countercyclical role, a capital development (developmental) role, a new venture support role, and a challenge-led role. The countercyclical role is a permanent feature, that is, not to be activated only during the downside of cycles, and it should be enforced especially to minimize risk aversions and to induce the use of idle capacity. The developmental role is to be played in activities in which a relative consensus exists among different schools, where externalities abound (infrastructure, innovation, SMEs, etc.). But they go further to defend an active role for development banks in strategic trade and in inducing internationally competitive firms (national champions). But it is the venture support role and the development challenge role that the authors emphasize. These institutions support entrepreneurs in their "discovery process," taking risks but benefiting from consequent rewards, very much in a Schumpeterian manner. They are active players in "making things happen" in face of the "blindness of markets." By addressing development challenges these banks induce structural transformation when "shaping and creating markets."

The above-mentioned authors have similar analytical concerns and conceptual propositions. What unites them is the recognition that development banks are mission-oriented institutions in the sense that there are relevant roles to be played in inducing structural transformation of different economies, in different moments of time, not in opposition to but co-partnering with the financial industry. Moreover (and this is an issue that must be stressed), since they are publicly owned, their mission is defined at the political domain. That is, the orientation of the mission of development banks is determined, by administrations in power for a given period of time, aligned with the policy priorities they have put forward for the public.[2]

It is with this understanding that discussions of the source of financing for investments and the relations between market and state-owned institutions must be framed. It is almost impossible to establish definite generalizations (or preferences?) about the role of the state and of the market in financial systems. Of course development banks are a necessary—but not in themselves a sufficient—condition for successful long-term investment in uncertainty-intensive ventures. For development banks to fulfill their mission, societies also need an effective science and technology infrastructure, together with entrepreneurs willing to take chances in the classical Schumpeterian sense. In addition, a risk-prone financial industry willing to partner with development banks in engaging in long-term finance is of vital importance. This is crucial, as investment frontiers may be vast and beyond the means of a sole institution.

WHAT ARE DEVELOPMENT BANKS?

Development banks became an institutional innovation—and a reality in many countries—during the late 1940s, in the wake of the postwar reconstruction. Since then, they have played an important role in supporting not only reconstruction, but also structural transformation, behind the process of economic growth of different nations, including developed ones. Their current economic relevance is not minor. In 2013 the twenty-three members of the International Development Finance Club (IDFC) had a combined asset base of around US$ 2.8 trillion. Obviously the relative importance of each institution in its economy varies. As shown in figure 4.1, the ratio of assets to GDP varies from 0.5 percent in Indonesia to above 14 percent in China, Brazil, and Germany, among others.

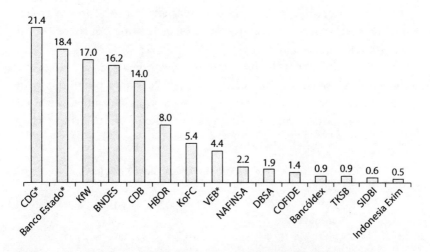

Figure 4.1 IDFC2 associated development banks, assets1/GDP, 2013.

Source: Annual reports of institutions. 1) It wasn't possible remove the assets related to foreign investments/financing; 2) The multilateral banks and institutions for international cooperation weren't included because their investments/financings are related to many countries. *These institutions have other functions besides financing development. Because of this the asset size cannot represent the asset actually related to development.

Development banks also differ in terms of the structure of ownership (wholly or partly public); focus of activity (limited or broad); forms of operation (first- or second-tier); sources of funding; regulatory environment to which they are subject; corporate governance; and size, portfolio, and financial performance.

Luna-Martínez and Vicente (2012) conducted a survey of ninety institutions and classified development banks according to their mandate (as shown in table 4.1). Roughly one-half of them have a wide spectrum of operations while the other half is composed of institutions with mandates over very specific themes or sectors.

Although there is no single format of development banks, it is possible to identify some relevant common features. Usually development banks are placed under planning, industry and trade, or finance ministries. Their mandates are closely associated with goals established in development plans in such a way that it is reasonable to denominate them as mission-oriented institutions.

Along the development processes of different countries, these institutions have been supporting the installation of new activities and/or the expansion of existing economic activities to which the private financial system was not able to provide adequate financing. To a great extent these segments correspond to those potentially contributing to growth and structural transformation of countries, generating positive externalities with relevant social returns.

It is noteworthy that the priorities of development banks change over time, in line with the development of the real economy and of the financial industry of each country. There are also cases in which the institution can play a temporary role, which can be combined with the private sector,

Table 4.1 Scope of the Mandate of Development Banks (*n* = 90)

Wide	47%
Specific, of which,	53%
Agriculture	13%
SME	12%
Foreign Trade	9%
Residential	6%
Infrastructure	4%
Local government	3%
Industry and others	6%

Source: Luna-Martínez and Vicente (2012).

with the aim of developing a credit market niche and creating the basis for the entering and scaling up of the private sector. In this case, development banks assume the role of first mover in credit markets in a specific segment, opening the way for the later entry of the private sector, once these risks and uncertainties have abated.

Several definitions for development banks can be found in the literature (Luna-Martínez and Vicente 2012; UN-DESA 2005). Overall, concepts are relatively close to one another. This study considers development banks as the financial or banking institutions that are controlled by national states and have mandates over market segments or specific sectors and/or over specific regions to induce growth, development, and structural change.

STRUCTURE, BEHAVIOR, AND PERFORMANCE: EXPERIENCES COMPARED

This section analyzes four development banks in detail: China Development Bank (CDB), KfW, BNDES, and Japan Finance Corporation (JFC). They were chosen simply on the basis of size: these are among the largest development banks in the world. Table 4.2 summarizes their structural features.

Table 4.2 Structural Features of Selected Development Banks

Country	China	Germany	Brazil	Japan
Bank name	China Development Bank (CDB)	KfW Bankegruppe (KfW)	BNDES	Japan Finance Corporation (JFC)
Government controls	100%	100%	100%	100%
Sectors and clients	Broad	Broad	Broad	Broad
Lending model	First/second-tier	First/second-tier*	First/second-tier	First/second-tier
Regulation equal to private?	No	No	Yes	No
Council with independent members?	No	No	Yes	No
Year founded	1994	1948	1952	2008

Source: Ferraz, Além, and Madeira (2013) based on CDB, KfW, BNDES, JFC Annual Reports.

* KfW provides direct loans only in international operations.

At this level of analysis, these four banks have very similar structural characteristics: they are 100 percent controlled by the state, they have a broad mission in terms of sectors and clients, they operate directly or through the financial industry, and they have independent members on their boards. In relation to the regime of regulation to which they submit, BNDES is the only one to formally follow rules and to be supervised by the same authority that looks after private banks. KfW and JFC are directly regulated by the ministries to which they respond; and CBD, by the central government. In spite of these differences, they all follow basic prudential rules guiding the private sector, especially those relating to the Basel Accord. The KfW voluntarily applies some rules of the German Banking Act, including those related to capital requirements. CBD has levels of capital requirements based on the Chinese Commercial Banks Capital Adequacy Management Guidelines.

This aspect must be interpreted carefully. To submit these institutions to the regulations and supervision identical to the one of the private-sector banks does induce prudential behavior and positive performance. But these same regulations may bring about negative consequences in terms of the ability and willingness of development banks to allocate capital for long-term financing. An example is the requirement of minimum capital referred to in the Basel Accord for riskier loans, which are generally the niche in which a development bank almost naturally operates. These requirements may induce the institutions to lend more to robust companies, reducing funding for riskier segments and sectors. Therefore, although it is most relevant to maintain an adequate capital base and high levels of security in their operations, to oblige them to very strict rules may limit their ability to finance projects leading to structural transformation.[3]

With respect to funding, CBD and the KfW mostly use proceeds from the issuance of bonds in the market, while JFC and BNDES finance themselves by means of fiscal or para-fiscal resources. JFC and KfW are not subject to corporate taxes, and KfW and CDB, when borrowing, have the explicit backup of soverei gnguarantees.[4]

In terms of behavior, the four development banks support the same segments, with slight differences (table 4.3). The financing of infrastructure, SMEs, innovation, internationalization of firms, and the green economy, in addition to operations in the capital market, is present in all four institutions. Nevertheless, most probably each bank does support these activities differently, in terms of instruments, intensity,

Table 4.3 Segments Supported by Selected Development Banks

	CDB (China)	KfW (Germany)	BNDES (Brazil)	JFC (Japan)
MSME	X	X	X	X
Agriculture	X		X	X
Infrastructure	X	X	X	
Exports		X	X	
Innovation	X	X	X	X
Green Economy	X	X	X	X
Internationalization	X	X	X	X
Capital Market	X	X	X	X
International Financial Cooperation	X	X		

Source: Ferraz, Além, and Madeira (2013) based on CDB, KfW, BNDES, JFC Annual Reports.

and specific destination of resources, depending on the characteristics of the credit market and the degree of economic development in each country.

KfW, BNDES, and JFC (no information was available from CDB) provide loans with different interest rates to different segments or clients, depending on policy or corporate priorities. For the case of Germany, China, and Japan, niches not supported by their main development banks are funded by another institution with specific expertise. Support for exports, for example in China and Japan, is undertaken by specialized agencies. In international operations, KfW and CDB have explicit roles in stimulating international financial cooperation and promoting socioeconomic development in developing countries. In general, as expected, this cooperation may be to the benefit of their national companies.

In terms of performance, few indicators can highlight their relevance in the economy in which they operate. Table 4.4 shows that these four institutions revealed, in 2013, very sound financial performance, each based on a strong asset base.

These four banks (and KDB in Korea) are of fundamental importance to their economies: their credit portfolio to GDP varies from a minimum of 4.4 percent in the Japanese case to 14.5 percent for Germany (figure 4.2). However, when we consider the share of the credit portfolio of the four banks in the total national credit portfolio, the differences are wider: 1.7 percent in Japan, 4.5 percent in Korea, 7.7 percent in China,

Table 4.4 Economic and Financial Performance of Selected Development Banks 2013

	CDB (China)	KfW (Germany)	BNDES (Brazil)	JFC (Japan)
Assets (US$ billions)	1331.3	619.7	363.4	260.4
Loan portfolio (US$ billions)	1162.3	528.8	263.5	222.8
Net profits (US$ billions)	13.0	1.7	3.6	(2.9)
Nonperforming loans ratio (%)	0.48	0.13	0.01	2.98
Return on assests (%)	1.02	0.27	1.01	(1.13)
Return on equity (%)	15.07	6.21	15.34	(6.84)
Number of employees	8468	5374	2859	7361

Sources: CDB, KfW, BNDES, JFC Annual Reports. Figures were calculated using each country's 2013 average exchange rate to the US$. Accounting Standards followed the International Financial Reporting Standard (IFRS). For Japan, which has a different fiscal year, the Annual Report reflects information ending on March 31st, 2014.

12.7 percent in Germany, and 21 percent in the case of Brazil. The most probable explanation for the Japanese and Brazilian extremes is found in the level of development of credit markets in each country: well developed in Japan, underdeveloped in Brazil.

The case of Brazil is worth exploring further: the term structure of interest rates is short and high, inducing economic agents to hold position in Brazilian treasuries which are extremely liquid. Thus banks operate with high spreads and low leverage ratios, thus producing high

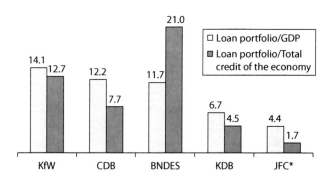

Figure 4.2   Importance of selected development banks in their countries economy (%)

Source: Annual Reports, FMI, Banco Central do Brasil, The Institute of International Finance (IIF), World Bank and German Council of Economic Experts. The Korea Development Bank. The institution was in process of privatization; however, the new government is reviewing the process with the objective of selling only some assets and keeping the KDB as a public development bank.

returns on equity. Based on data from banks, Rezende (2015, 11–12) argues as follows:

> The spread between short-term lending rates and commercial banks' funding costs for business and consumer loans is substantially higher relative to long-term financing activities . . . .The difficulty is the high level and volatility of interest rates and the unattractiveness of low-risk adjusted returns on long-term assets. Hence, domestic private banks have little interest in expanding their long-term loan business portfolios to provide long-term financing.

In sum, this section has demonstrated that the four largest development banks have the structure and the means to play the role of mission-oriented institutions. They also have adequate performance, leading to financial sustainability which, in turn, reinforces the role they play in each economy.

FINANCING (PARTIALLY) THE WAY OUT OF UNCERTAINTIES

In the section "If Investment Inherently Embeds Uncertainties, These Must Be Specified!" it was proposed that development projects may face four types of uncertainty: the prevailing economic conditions; the time frame of an investment project; the complexity of a project in itself; and the political and policy ambiance under which decisions on the allocation of resources are made. This section presents empirical information on the performance of development banks according to each of these sources of uncertainty.[5]

UNCERTAINTIES FROM THE ECONOMIC AMBIANCE

Development banks can contribute to the preservation of economic stability, and this is likely to come about during periods of economic crisis, as the recent period has demonstrated. As credit crunch progressed in the private financial system, countries that had effective and efficient development banks used them to cushion or even to compensate for the fall in the supply of credit, contributing to avoid a greater drop in aggregate demand. Figure 4.3 shows a significant rise in the rate of growth of loans in 2008 and 2009 by BNDES, CDB, and BDB of Canada. KfW's growth in loans came a bit later, in consonance with the European crisis.

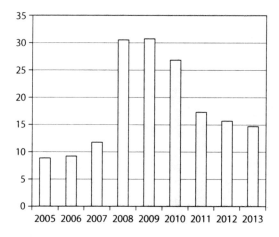

Figure 4.3A Annual growth of loan portfolios of selected development banks (%)
Brazilian Development Bank (BNDES) – Brazil

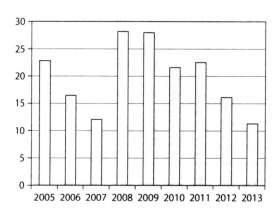

Figure 4.3B China Development Bank (CDB) – China

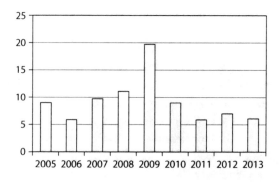

Figure 4.3C Business Development Bank of Canada (BDC) – Canada

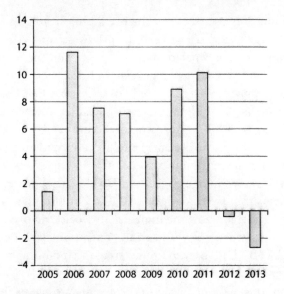

Figure 4.3D KfW – Germany

Source: Annual Reports. Note: In the case of the BDC, the fiscal year is different and covers the period between April this year and March next year. For purposes of comparative analysis, the position at the end of March of the following year was considered.

The importance of a preexisting and effective development bank in promoting economic stability was highlighted by the Conference Board of Canada (2010, 1):

> Once a financial crisis hits, it is too late for governments to create institutional capacity to provide fall-back credit support. The institutions must already exist, with a clear operate mandate, experienced professional staff, and the financial capacity to respond to the financial needs and ramp-up their operations when the private market fails.

The recent crisis demonstrates an important lesson: maintaining an active development bank is not an option, but a necessity for countries willing to maintain a stable and healthy financial system.

UNCERTAINTIES FROM LONG MATURITY

Investments in infrastructure are a good proxy of investments that have a high capital requirement and a long maturity term. These features imply difficulties not only to assess and finance a project, but also to make it economically viable and attractive to the private sector.

Bloomberg (2014) estimated in US$ 509.2 billion the financing from development banks to energy (transmission lines, energy efficiency, and renewable energy) between 2007 and 2013. On that first year financing amounted to US$ 38.7 billion, increasing steadily to reach, the current volume of US$ 90 billion a year. In 2013, national development banks were responsible for 73 percent of the total, and multilateral or regional organizations for the remaining 27 percent.

In Brazil, as shown in figure 4.4, there is a close relation between country investments in infrastructure and BNDES disbursements to the sector. Between 2007 and 2013 medium-size hydroelectric plants expanded capacity from 1.8 to 3.3 GW and wind generation expanded from 247 MW to 2 GW. BNDES backed up investments amounting to 61 percent and 55 percent of the capacity expansion.

Some countries have managed to involve private agents in long-term financing of infrastructure, either through private banks or through the capital market. Others, however, need public institutions to foster adequate financing, either due to institutional, political, historical, and economic difficulties, or even because of the need to create mechanisms that meet the urgent need for growth.

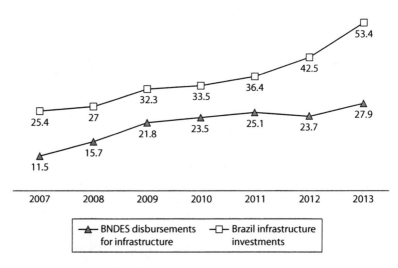

Figure 4.4   Brazil infrastructure investments and BNDES disbursements to infrastructure (US$ billion)

Source: BNDES, ABDIB, ANEEL, EPE, Telebras e SNIS. *2013 estimated.

The Japanese and German cases are quite illuminating given their advanced stage of development. In Japan, the Development Bank of Japan (DBJ), which is aimed at being privatized, had had high importance in the financing of infrastructure; but with the development of the private credit market for this sector, the need for public resources decreased. But even after it is transferred to the private sector, the bank will have provisions allowing it to be a funding provider (through fiscal resources) for extraordinary events (crises or natural disasters) or in specific cases related to the development of sustainable products (Low Carbon Investment Promotion Act), to industrial revitalization and to innovation (Industrial Revitalization Act), with the purpose of increasing the competitiveness of Japan's industry.

In the case of Germany, KfW financing was crucial to the development of the national infrastructure, as in the case of postwar reconstruction and in the modernization of East Germany. However, with the development of the private long-term credit, the use of instruments of public funding for major national infrastructure projects declined. Between 2006 and 2009, public funding for infrastructure accounted for only about 30 percent of total loans (Wagenvoort, Nicola, and Kappeler 2010). This allowed the German bank to refocus its domestic operations in this segment to municipal and social infrastructure (urban structure, energy efficiency of buildings, schools, hospitals, kindergartens, etc.) and to infrastructure for renewable energy.

A study by the LSE Growth Commission (2013, 25) recommended to the British government to set up a bank to fund infrastructure, since investments in this sector were insufficient to meet demand needs.

> There are good theoretical reasons for the creation of such a bank: it can help to overcome key market failures in capital markets in a direct and constructive way. In particular, it can help to reduce policy risk and, through partnerships, to structure finance in a way that mitigates and shares risk efficiently. This will require a whole range of financial instruments including equity and structured guarantees.

UNCERTAINTIES FROM INNOVATION

Development banks stand out in supporting innovation projects. Besides increasing the competitiveness of enterprises, many investments in innovation, such as research in the health sector, transcend specific economic interests and generate positive externalities for the society. The funding of public institutions is crucial since innovation projects are subject to greater uncertainty as to their results impeding, therefore, the interest of the private financial industry.

Figure 4.5 shows the performance of KfW in financing innovation-related projects, broken down in broad categories. The German bank allocates around 24 billion euros per year to activities that are inductive to an innovative economy.

In Brazil the outstanding feature is the high-growth process that BNDES engaged in financing innovation (figure 4.6): from US$ 144 million in 2007 to US$ 3.2 billion in 2013.

UNCERTAINTY FROM UNEXPECTED DEVELOPMENT CHALLENGES

Climate change has been a subject of increasing societal concern. Much debate exists on its veracity, extent, and necessary mitigation actions to be taken up by different actors—developed and developing countries; public, NGOs, private agents; public and private research and financial industries, etc. Regardless of international agreements or local actions, climate change has entered, with force, in the priority agenda of

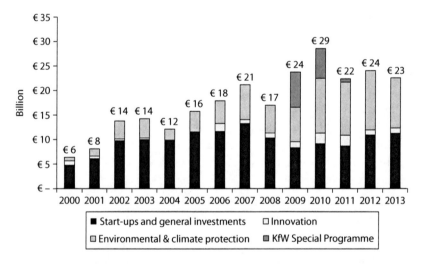

Figure 4.5   KfW Mittelstandsbank: Disbursements to innovation by broad categories, 2000-2013 (Euro billion)

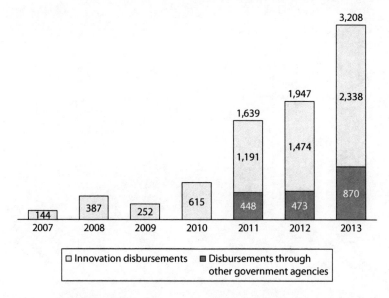

Figure 4.6   BNDES disbursements to innovation projects (current US$ million)

development banks (IDFC 2014). That is, environmentally sustainable projects constitute a segment to which development banks are dedicating increasing attention.[6] Figure 4.7 provides a comparative perspective on the sources of finance for climate change and adaptation in 2012. The strategic role that development finance institutions play in this new and much needed frontier of investments is clear: out of total financing approximately 35 percent or US$ 123 billion of investments were financed by development finance institutions. In this amount, 60 percent were of National Development Banks responsibility.

In these new frontiers, development banks may not only lead the way, but also have a decisive role in fostering the early engagement of the private financial industry. For that they use various instruments, such as participation in long-term funds; and investment in companies through venture capital, securitization, shareholding (in companies and in the fixed-income market), and joint financing to share project risks.

Investments through venture capital are an important means through which development banks can stimulate the capital market and, of course, the development of innovative enterprises. Through private equity, institutions leverage the development of an established company, enabling its

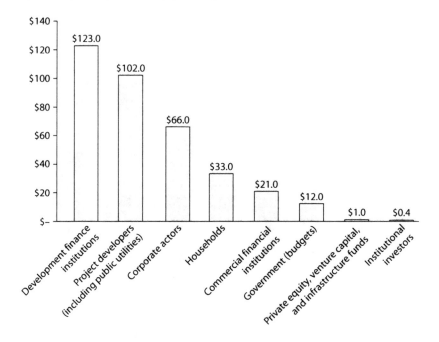

Figure 4.7   Sources of finance for climate change adaptation or mitigation projects in 2012 (US$ billion)

Source: Caetano Penna & Mariana Mazzucato presentation at the Minds Seminar, Rio 28/07/14 based on data from Climate Policy Initiative (2013).

growth and strengthening its capital structure with the subsequent initial public offering (IPO). With venture capital, they reach SMEs and also innovative companies.

CONCLUSION

Development banks are one of the pillars of a resilient financial system, as they are mission-oriented, with long asset and liability base, patiently contributing to fostering structural transformation of economies. They are relevant for countries at all stages of development—at times of stability as well as of crisis. It is in the context of uncertainty that these institutions can best play their role, fostering markets and firms, including financial markets.

In mitigating uncertainties, development banks are capable of mobilizing unique resources and capabilities:

- By offering a wide array of instruments of debt or equity suitable for the different types of uncertainties. These include credit lines with special conditions, grants, credit enhancement mechanisms, direct investment, seed and venture capital or equity funds
- By supporting and fostering coordination among relevant actors
- By participating in the design and support for policy design, implementation, and long-term planning

Of course development banks are a necessary—but not in themselves a sufficient condition for successful long-term investment in risk-intensive ventures. Societies also need entrepreneurs willing to take chances in the classical Schumpeterian sense and a dynamic market. In addition, a risk-prone financial industry willing to engage in long-term finance is of essential importance. These are crucial issues if an investment frontier is vast and beyond the means of a sole institution.

The crisis of 2008–2009 demonstrated how qualified public financial institutions are important to prevent an abrupt decrease in financing investment. Delicate financial situations demand immediate and efficient actions: the success of the performance of development banks in developed and developing countries was due to the fact that they were already competent institutions, with extensive experience. Thus, far from being exotic institutions, these banks are essential public instruments and partners of the private financing system. They are, therefore, key gears in a financial system that seeks a sustainable and dynamic economy to face the challenges that are imposed on each country.

The economic and political science literatures have not made the analysis of these institutions important. It is urgent that efforts be made to substantiate sound assessments according to the role they play in different societies.

The following five areas of research should be developed further:

First, *analytical frameworks must be developed.* It is necessary to build them based on sound concepts. At this level, it is necessary to assess the extent to which concepts such as market failure, credit rationing, financial repression, and investment and financing under uncertainty are functional and adequate to substantiate economics-oriented analytical frameworks. From a political science or political economy perspective, concepts such as mission-oriented practices, bureaucratic insulation, private/public interactions, and the state and market mediations must be examined.

Second, *quantitative exercises with appropriate indicators of economic and financial performance* of a sole institution or comparative exercises should be carried out, based on balance sheets, to reveal, in a systematic way, the recent evolution of these institutions. These exercises could provide benchmarks among them and comparative information in relation to the private industry.

Third, *in-depth analysis or comparative studies of the capabilities and sources of institutional and economic strengths and weaknesses* are essential to define best practices.

Fourth, *the extent to which development banks do play a mission-oriented role* is a central research question which should be tried out in experimental exercises.

Fifth, *the efficiency and effectiveness of development banks must be assessed.* Since they are public institutions, DBs must demonstrate their contribution to society. Also these exercises can be a source of internal learning in order to best fulfill their missions.

NOTES

João Carlos Ferraz is Associate Professor at the Instituto de Economia, Universidade Federal do Rio de Janeiro. Between May 2007 and May 2016, Vice President and Executive Director, BNDES, Brazilian Development Bank. This paper draws on arguments and findings from Ferraz, Além, and Madeira (2013) and from Coutinho, Ferraz, and Marques (2015). It also benefitted from comments made at the IPD/JICA Task Force on Industrial Policy and Transformation Meeting in Jordan, June 5th–6th, 2014 and in New York, February 19–20, 2015. This article is of my own responsibility, and it does not reflect BNDES's positions.

1. Freeman (1982) highlighted technical, market, and general business uncertainties. In Freeman and Soete (1997), the typology was revised to technological, commercial, and organizational uncertainties.

2. Mission-oriented institutions are a concept widely used in the literature on national systems of innovation to define organizations directly related to the generation and diffusion of innovations such as firms, research centers, and universities (Freeman 1987; Nelson ed. 1993).

3. This is a relevant issue requiring much attention from public authorities and a more detailed discussion, which is not part of the scope of this work.

4. Extracts of KfW constitution:

"The Federal Republic guarantees all obligations of KfW in respect of loans extended to and debt securities issued by KfW, fixed forward transactions or options entered into by KfW, and other credits extended to KfW as well as credits extended to third parties inasmuch as they are expressly guaranteed by KfW . . . As a public law institution serving public policy objectives . . . KfW itself is not subject to corporate taxes . . . and as a promotional bank does not seek to maximize profits. KfW does, however, seek to maintain an overall level of profitability that allows it to strengthen its equity base in order to support its promotional activities and to grow the volume of its business. KfW is prohibited from distributing profits, which are instead allocated to statutory and special reserves."

5. This must be considered as an exploratory, unsystematic attempt to investigate whether development banks have had a role to play in minimizing uncertainties in given economies, based on available data, mostly from annual reports.

6. Innovation and environmental sustainability have clear and relevant intersections, since the search for greater energy and environmental efficiency tends to demand and result in innovations of different intensities and types.

REFERENCES

Bloomberg. 2014. "New Energy Finance, Renewables Research Note." September 29.

BNDES (Banco Nacional de Desenvolvimento Econômico e Social). *Annual Reports from 2002 to 2013*. Rio de Janeiro: BNDES.

CDB (China Development Bank). *Annual Reports from 2002 to 2013*. Beijing: China Development Bank.

Climate Policy Initiative. 2014. *The Global Landscape of Climate Financing*. Venice: CPI.

Conference Board of Canada. 2010. *Lessons from the Recession and Financial Crisis*. Ottawa: BDC, Legislative Review.

Coutinho, L., J. C. Ferraz, and F. S. Marques. 2015. "Development, Uncertainty, and the Role of State Investment Banks." In *Mission-Oriented Finance for Innovation: Rethinking Public & Private Risks and Rewards*, M. Mazzucato and C. Penna, 97–104. Science Policy Research Unit, University of Sussex.

Development Bank of Japan. *Annual Report 2012*. Tokyo: Development Bank of Japan.

Ferraz, J. C, A. C. Além, and R. F. Madeira. 2013. "A Contribuição dos Bancos de Desenvolvimento para o Financiamento de Longo Prazo." *Revista do BNDES* (1), 5–42.

Freeman, C. 1987. *Technology Policy and Economic Performance, Lessons from Japan*. London: Pinter.

Freeman, C., and L. Soete. 1997. *The Economics of Industrial Innovation*. London: Pinter.

Gerschenkron, A. 1973. *El atraso economico en su perspectiva histórica*. Barcelona: Ediciones Ariel.

Griffith-Jones, S. 2013. "The European Investment Bank: Lessons for Developing Countries." *WIDER Working Paper*.

Gurley, J. G., and E. S. Shaw. 1955. "Financial Aspects of Economic Development." *American Economic Review* 45: 515–38.

International Development Financial Club (IDFC). 2014. The Club of Experts in Sustainable Development Financing, mimeo. Frankfurt.

Japan Finance Corporation. 2013. *Annual Report 2012*. Tokyo.

Keynes, J. M. 1936. *The General Theory of Employment, Interest and Money*. London: Macmillan.

Keynes, J. M. 1939. The Process of Capital Formation. *The Economic Journal*, September.

KfW Bankengruppe. *Annual Reports from 2002 to 2013*. Frankfurt, KfW.

Korea Development Bank Financial Group. 2013. *Annual Report 2012*. Seoul: KDB.

Kregel, J. A. 1997. "Margins of Safety and Weight of the Argument in Generating Financial Instability." *Journal of Economic Issues* 31(2): 543–8.

Lazonick, W. 2013. "The Financialization of the U.S. Corporation: What Has Been Lost, and How It Can Be Regained." *Seattle University Law Review* 36: 857–909.

Lazzarini, S. G., A. Musacchio, R. Bandeira de Mello, and R. Marconi. 2015. "What Do State Owned Development Banks Do? Evidence from BNDES, 2002–2009." *World Development* 66: 237–53.

LSE Growth Commission. 2013. *Investing for Prosperity: Skills, Infrastructure and Innovation*. London: London School of Economics.

Luna-Martínez, J., and C. L. Vicente. 2012. "Global Survey of Development Banks." *Policy Research Working Paper 5.969*, The World Bank, February.

Mazzucato, M., and C. Penna. 2015. *Beyond Market Failure: The Market Creating and Shaping Roles of State Investment Banks*. Levy Economics Institute, *Working Paper 831*.

McKinnon, R. I. 1973. *Money and Capital in Economic Development*. Washington, D.C.: Brookings Institution.

Minsky, H. 1982. *Can "IT" Happen Again? Essays on Instability and Finance*. New York: M. E. Sharpe.

Minsky, H. 1986. *Stabilizing an Unstable Economy*. New Haven, Conn.: Yale University Press.

Nelson, R. R., ed. 1993. *National Systems of Innovation: A Comparative Analysis*. New York: Oxford University Press.

Polanyi, K. 2001 [1944]. *The Great Transformation: The Political and Economic Origins of Our Time*. Boston, Mass.: Beacon Press.

Rezende, F. 2015. "Why Does Brazil's Banking Sector Need Public Banks? What Should BNDES Do?" Levy Economics Institute, *Working Paper 825*.

Rodrik, D. 2013. "Green Industrial Policy." *Princeton University Working Paper*.

UNDESA (United Nations-Department of Economic and Social Affairs). 2005. "Rethinking the Role of National Development Banks." *Revised Background Document*.

Wagenvoort, R., C. Nicola, and A. Kappeler. 2010. "Infrastructure Finance in Europe: Composition, Evolution and Crisis Impact." *EIB Papers* 15(1): 16–40.

CHAPTER 5

The Roles of Development Banks

HOW THEY CAN PROMOTE INVESTMENT IN EUROPE AND GLOBALLY

Stephany Griffith-Jones and Giovanni Cozzi

The financial sector should help support the real economy. To achieve this key positive role, the financial sector needs to encourage and mobilize savings, intermediate these savings at low cost, ensure savings are channeled into efficient investment (including in innovation and structural change) as well as helping manage the risks for individuals and enterprises. In the context of industrial policy, it should help to fund new sectors and deepen existing ones and to support national and regional development strategies. Ideally, the financial sector could help societies acquire and accumulate learning, valuable for increasing productivity, especially in a dynamic sense (Stiglitz and Greenwald 2014).

Because the financial sector has such important effects throughout the economy it also needs to adhere to a principle of avoiding harming the rest of the economy. Therefore, there should be as few and as small crises that stem from the financial sector, as these have huge costs and are detrimental to economic growth, employment, and investment.

In recent decades, the private financial system generally has not performed any of these functions well.[1] It has created risk, instead of managing it, leading to many major crises. It has been deeply procyclical in that it tends to overlend in boom times and ration credit during and long after crises, limiting both working capital and especially long-term finance crucial for investment. In both tranquil and (even more so) turbulent times, it has not funded sufficiently the long-term investment in innovation and skills that businesses need to grow and create jobs; key sectors such as infrastructure, renewable energy, and energy efficiency have also been insufficiently funded. In the context of industrial policy, the private financial system typically does not want to take too many risks, and—especially in recent times—tends to be unwilling to provide the long-term funding required to develop new sectors and technologies on a sufficient scale.

The problems of the private financial sector have increasingly drawn attention to the positive role that effective public development banks can play. In recent years, the valuable role that national, regional, and multilateral development banks can and often do play is receiving greater recognition in wider and ever-growing circles. These banks played a valuable role by providing countercyclical finance as private credit in and flows to developing countries collapsed during the North Atlantic crisis, which started in 2007. Furthermore, the greater need for instruments to implement more long-term national or regional development strategies has been increasingly recognized. This coincides with growing recognition of the value of a modern "industrial policy" and the importance of an "entrepreneurial and development state" that encourages and leads economic development, providing the vision and the dynamic push for private innovation and structural transformation (Chang 2002; Wade 2003; Mazzucato 2013). Stiglitz and Greenwald (2014) add the very important dimension that successful and sustained growth requires the creation of a learning society and a knowledge economy to increase productivity—and public development banks are an important institutional vehicle for supporting this. Indeed, development banks can help overcome market failures in both financial and knowledge markets simultaneously.

The ability of development banks, at a multilateral, regional, and national level, to help implement and finance development strategies and visions (by funding both the public and private sectors) has thus received greater support. It is also interesting that the role of development banks has been highlighted as important not just in developing and emerging economies but also increasingly in developed ones. Thus the European Investment Bank (EIB)—the bank of the European Union (EU) member states—has played a prominent role in the provision of long-term lending during and after the eurozone debt crisis, as private lending fell. Since its creation in 1956, the EIB and the EU Structural Funds have provided significant funding for the interconnection of national infrastructure on a massive scale, to support the creation of the Common Market and to reduce economic divergence between poorer and richer regions (see Griffith-Jones et al. 2006). More recently, it is engaged in helping fund the creation of a "smart" intra-European electricity grid, to facilitate transmission of renewable energy.

At a national European level, Germany's public development bank, KfW, now the second-largest commercial German bank, has played a very positive role in increasing lending countercyclically (e.g., to small and media enterprises (SMEs)) during the crisis as well as providing significant funding to key sectors, such as investment in renewables and innovation. In Europe, these actions are perceived and highlighted as a valuable model for other countries. For example, France has just created a new public development bank, and the United Kingdom is contemplating the creation of a similar institution. One of the few positive policy responses to the Eurozone debt crises has been the creation of development banks and/or development finance mechanisms, especially for SMEs, in countries such as Ireland, Greece, and Portugal, often with strong support from KfW and the EIB.

The favorable experiences of many development banks in emerging economies, such as BNDES in Brazil and CAF in the Andean region (and spreading increasingly in Latin America) as well as in China, South Korea, and India, are also very important and represent positive lessons for both emerging markets and developed economies. For example, BNDES has taken significant risks in financing important new sectors, such as biotechnology and renewable energy. Furthermore, countries such as Chile have used their development banks for promoting and funding private investment in sectors such as forestry, which generated major exports of paper and cellulose as well as wood. In all these experiences, development banks have pioneered investment in new sectors and technologies, following national or regional priorities as defined by the government, often in consultation with the private sector.

The section "The Analytical Case for Good Development Banks" will elaborate on the analytical reasons why development banks need to play a bigger role in developing, emerging, and developed economies.

The section "From Business as Usual to an Investment-Led Global New Deal" gives a strong illustration of the positive role that development banks can play in helping economies recover after crises as well as grow more generally, by funding investment that will lead to long-term transformation and innovation. Using the global nonequilibrium Cambridge Alphametrics Model (CAM), this chapter presents projections of economic developments that might take place in the period up to 2020 under alternative assumptions about global and European economic governance systems. Three main scenarios are presented: "business as usual," "European investment-led recovery," and "global investment stimulus."

The business-as-usual scenario envisages a world where government initiatives to stimulate growth and employment are constrained as the global investment rate stagnates. The projected macroeconomic outcome for Europe is a long period of low growth due to the harmful effects of austerity policies in the South Eurozone (Italy, Spain, Greece, and Portugal) and lack of significant and effective investment strategies.

Under the European investment-led recovery scenario, the global economy is still struggling to recover due to the absence of a coordinated global investment stimulus. However, the macroeconomic outcome for Europe is more positive as it is assumed that Europe adopts an expansionary fiscal policy stance coupled with a significant boost in private investment to support growth and job creation. An important role in the latter would be played by the use of the European Investment Bank and national development banks, on an ambitious scale, to encourage private investment.

The third scenario, global investment stimulus, demonstrates that a global economic action could lead to significant economic gains. In the spirit of an investment-led "global New Deal," it is assumed that both developed and developing countries significantly boost private investment. This ultimately leads to faster global growth rates and significant employment gains. It is assumed that development banks would play an important role in funding such investment, both in Europe and globally. At the European level, growth and employment objectives are also supported by government spending and investment as well as by private investment. Overall, this scenario assumes that a European investment-led recovery combines with a global investment-led recovery.

In the two alternative investment scenarios presented here, it is assumed that investment rises substantially, on the basis that an expanded role for regional and national development banks will provide the required financing. Simulations for this role will be provided in the European context and globally, especially for developing countries. One important advantage of this approach is that with fairly limited public resources a very large impact can be achieved through leverage. Indeed, in this and other cases, public development banks have the advantage that they can leverage public resources as they fund their loans by bonds issued in the private capital markets, as well as cofinancing with private banks and/or private investors. The contribution of public resources is mainly through an increase in paid-in capital.

European leaders, in a visionary move, already doubled paid-in capital of the EIB by 10 billion euros in 2012, and this facilitated at least an additional EIB lending of 60 billion euros. Furthermore, as the EIB requires 50 percent of cofinance with its loans, the total additional lending since the doubling of paid-in capital was at least 120 billion euros. Our proposal is that they increase paid-in capital by a further 10 billion euros, which will facilitate at least additional similar amounts of lending, resulting in an important increase in private investment. Together with a less austere fiscal policy that does not allow public investment to fall, the simulations show that with the adoption of such policy strategy an additional 5 million much needed jobs can be created in the European Union.

THE ANALYTICAL CASE FOR GOOD DEVELOPMENT BANKS

THEORETICAL FRAMEWORK

Despite development banks' size and importance to economies, surprisingly little academic research has been conducted on the role of and the rationale for these banks. The discussion needs to be placed in the context of the broader debate on the desirable nature and structure of the financial sector.

In the three decades after World War II, it could be argued that the financial sector functioned quite well in both developing and developed countries. National and multilateral development banks were created and performed valuable roles. Private domestic financial sectors were relatively small and fairly tightly regulated.

However, there were policy concerns that "financially repressed" systems, as they were then called, were inefficient. From a theoretical perspective, the idea that financial markets were efficient encouraged financial liberalization, with minimal or no regulation (Gurley and Shaw 1955; McKinnon 1973). This process was followed by frequent and costly crises. Diaz-Alejandro (1985) perceptively synthetized this early on: "Good-bye financial repression, hello financial crisis." Within the efficient financial market school, the existence of public financial institutions, such as development banks, was—almost by definition—seen as negative. As a consequence, development banks were criticized—fairly and unfairly—and their role was reduced sharply in many countries. One of the largest paradoxes was that, during this phase of dominance of the more "neoliberal approach," the World Bank, itself a very important public development bank, played a significant role via policy conditionality attached to its loans in encouraging developing countries to wind down their national development banks.

An alternative theoretical approach emphasized credit rationing, a situation in which, even when agents are willing to pay a higher interest rate to get the funds to finance their investments, banks may refuse financing. In this perspective, the approach of credit rationing justifies the existence of development banks, which would supply the necessary credit to investment that was unavailable in the private financing system.

Another approach is associated with the theory of market failures in financial markets (Stiglitz and Weiss 1981; Stiglitz 1990). Credit rationing occurs due to a malfunction of the financial markets, caused by imperfect information or information asymmetry, which prevents financial markets from functioning efficiently. If borrowers have more information on the expected return of their projects than the lenders do, there is a greater demand for credit than supply, but the adjustment would not be made by increasing interest rates. Furthermore, adverse selection and moral hazard accentuate these market imperfections.

Stiglitz (1994) argues that market failures in financial markets are likely to be endemic as those markets are particularly information-intensive, thus making information imperfections and asymmetries as well as incomplete contracts more important and disruptive than in other economic sectors. Therefore, in important parts of financial markets, market failures tend to be greater than government failures, as Stiglitz (1994) insightfully argues. In such cases government interventions are more desirable than in other sectors if their benefits outweigh their costs. This provides a first robust case for a "visible hand of government," through both effective public development banks and robust regulation of private financial markets.

Stiglitz and Greenwald (2014) further argue that knowledge and information markets also have huge market imperfections, and that knowledge and information are basically public goods. As a consequence, governments have a clear role in promoting a learning society to help achieve increases in productivity. One of the institutional vehicles for helping achieve such a learning society, perhaps more in developing and emerging economies, is good development banks. Besides providing long-term finance, they can offer specific incentives, through their lending, for innovation. Furthermore, because of their long-term perspective, they can help fund, accumulate, and coordinate expertise in specific areas of innovation and in "learning how to learn." Naturally in this task they need to, and do, collaborate with other actors, both public and private. This role in accumulating and promoting knowledge and learning, which has not been sufficiently explored in the literature, cannot be accomplished effectively by most private financial institutions, as they focus mainly or exclusively on short-term profits and tend not to be interested in either past experience or future externalities. Development banks therefore need to help fill the gap.

From a complementary theoretical perspective, several commentators (e.g., Ferraz, Além, and Madeira, 2016; Kregel 1988; Wray 2009) argue there is a preference for liquidity among investors, as well as banks, which is responsible for the limitations on the supply of credit in the economy. There may be a lack of credit for investment even when there are well-developed national and international financial systems. Therefore, as pointed out above, the importance of development banks goes beyond the question of market failure, though it builds on it. Given the uncertainty about the future, depending on the characteristics of the new sectors and projects that require resources, banks often offer no credit or insufficient credit (especially long-term credit) even if the financial system is fully developed.

Therefore, the existence of development banks is justified by the existence of sectors and investment projects that require funding for the future development of the economy, but have high uncertainty as to their future success (Mazzucato 2013). Because of that, they may not be funded by the private financial system which prefers sectors or investment projects whose expected returns are less uncertain. These are often highly complex and expensive sectors and projects, requiring sophisticated expertise in their evaluation that takes account of positive impacts across the economy (positive externalities, e.g., in terms of helping mitigate climate change via lower carbon emissions, as renewable energy does) and/or those in which social returns exceed private returns.

A key market imperfection in the operation of financial markets, basically across the board, is the tendency to "boom-bust," with a feast of finance followed by famine, in both domestic and international finance. Building on the theoretical tradition of Keynes (1936) and Minsky (1977), Kindleberger (1978) developed an historical analysis that considers financial crises as a response to previous excesses. Such excesses seem clearly far greater in financial and banking markets that are more liberalized and not properly regulated. The procyclical nature of private finance implies the need for public development banks to provide both short-term and especially long-term countercyclical finance, as well as the need for countercyclical regulation of banking and financial markets (Griffith-Jones and Ocampo 2014). Griffith-Jones et al. (2012) and Ocampo et al. (2012) provide empirical evidence for the countercyclical response of regional and multilateral development banks, while Brei and Schlarek (2013) and Luna-Martinez and Vicente (2012) provide important empirical evidence for the countercyclical role that national development banks play.

DESIRABLE FUNCTIONS AND CHARACTERISTICS OF DEVELOPMENT BANKS

The above theoretical context and empirical evidence help define the role that development banks do play and need to play.

Four valuable functions seem crucial for national, regional, and multilateral development banks to perform: (1) provision of countercyclical finance, especially for supporting investment; (2) support, through funding, for a dynamic vision and strategy of growth, structural transformation, and increased learning; (3) mobilization of broader financial resources, e.g., by leverage and targeted subsidies; and (4) financing of public goods (Culpeper, Griffith-Jones, and Titelman, forthcoming).

As regards the second function, emphasis is on the especially valuable role that development banks can play to fund investment in the beginning of new sectors or the deepening of existing sectors, where private investment on its own would not invest, as it is too uncertainty-averse. In those cases, development banks can provide the vision—and part of the resources, through either loans or equity—to do those things that at present are not done at all (Mazzucato 2013). This requires development banks to have the expertise and the strategic vision to fund new sectors and technologies.

The fact that development banks can provide long-term loans, have a long-term development perspective, and require lower returns further facilitates this. Development banks can also accumulate their own expertise, which they can transmit to investors and borrowers, as well as promote its development. Thus, development banks can combine, helping to fill gaps in knowledge and in resources. This is the most challenging, but also probably the most valuable role for development banks. For example, the EIB is engaged in helping fund the creation of a "smart" intra-European electricity grid, to facilitate transmission of renewable energy.

However, development banks are also needed to fund sectors or activities where important externalities exist, which implies that social returns are higher than market returns; this is typically the case with environmental externalities. It is interesting that public development banks, and notably the EIB, evaluate projects both on a purely commercial basis and in an environmental way, incorporating a "shadow" (higher than market) price for carbon. This may require the provision of targeted and time-limited subsidies for certain projects to go ahead; in the case of the EU, this can be and is provided from European Commission resources. Finally, the countercyclical role is crucial to help sustain investment, innovation, job creation, and growth in the long periods when private lending falls or, worse, dries up. Uncertainty of funding, accompanied by lower demand, can be a major discouragement for private investment, unnecessarily prolonging stagnation or low growth. Development banks can step in to help with both.

More broadly, there is a different case in favor of development banks, in the sense of the benefits of diversification. Having a more diversified financial structure than one just focused mainly in private (often large) banks may have several advantages. First, it may encourage competition between different types of financial institutions, which could lead to their being more efficient, e.g., in the spreads they charge. Second, a more diversified financial system (especially if it does not have interconnected risks) could lead to less systemic risk and therefore could contribute to financial stability. Third, if different varieties of financial institutions have different strengths,[2] then having a more diverse financial system—vis-à-vis one where the structure of the financial sector is determined spontaneously or is dominated by one type of financial institution—could enhance those financial sector functions needed to help achieve inclusive and dynamic growth.

Indeed, given that financial sectors (particularly liberalized, very lightly regulated ones) can be problematic for growth, the need to pursue pragmatic policies in financial sector development—and not be driven by pure free market ideologies or conditioned too much by the interest of agents in the financial sector—is especially important. It is key not to adopt an either/or attitude, but to look at the best ways of building synergies among institutions of different types (e.g., private and public) as well as encourage best practices within them. For the more dynamic sectors, the initial catalytic role of development banks may be crucial. Public development banks cofinance, and increasingly lend, via private banks, especially in the case of small and medium enterprises. Furthermore, much of their lending is done to private firms. The ability to combine private and public creatively, ideally working constructively together, is an essential feature of a financial system if it is to serve the needs of inclusive and environmentally sustainable growth. In this sense, although it is by no means perfect, the way that German financial sector has developed and operated, e.g., to successfully help fund renewable energy via public and private banks (as well as cooperative banks) and private investors acting together, provides a very good example.

It is indeed valuable for public and private sector banks to collaborate and build on mutual positive synergies. However, it is also important that the vices of one sector (e.g., the excessive financial risk taking of private investment banks and hedge funds, or the use of excessively sophisticated and opaque instruments) not be transmitted to the public development banks, as these can generate future risks. While public development banks can and should assume economic risks related to the uncertainty of going into new sectors, new technologies, new markets, etc., they should not assume purely financial risks by copying or buying from the private financial sector instruments that may offer short-term high financial returns but imply potentially high risks. A preference for simple and transparent instruments, like "plain vanilla loans" or simple equity contributions, seems justified for development banks, especially in the light of the North Atlantic financial crisis. Equity or equitylike instruments have the advantage that they can allow development banks to compensate the higher risks they assume, e.g., in helping develop and fund new sectors and/or technologies by receiving a part of the "upside" if profits are high; such capturing of part of the upside of profitable projects can generate profits, which the development bank can plough into new future activities via, e.g., increasing its capital.

Another important consideration is the scale of development bank lending, in proportion to total lending. There seems to be an important case for a significant scale so they can fulfill their functions well, especially in terms of funding key investments to make a meaningful impact on innovation and structural change and to play a strong countercyclical role when this is necessary, as was clearly the case in the period during and after the North Atlantic crisis, and for financing public goods, such as investment in renewable energy. It is interesting to note that KfW is the second-largest commercial bank in Germany and represents 12.7 percent of total bank credit in the German economy. If the role of regional and other development banks is added, the share of public banks in Germany represents about one-quarter of total bank credit. This is particularly relevant because the German economy is the most dynamic in Europe, having a large ability to innovate and compete internationally, including in advanced industrial goods. The role that KfW has played in helping such innovation, growth, and employment generation is a very understudied but important subject. In the case of Brazil, BNDES represents an even higher proportion of total credit (21 percent) and a particularly high proportion of long-term finance, making it a major instrument for innovation and industrial policy (see Ferraz, Além, and Madeira 2016).

A final desirable feature of effective development banks is that they should have a close dialogue with the private sector in order to develop a joint vision and expertise for funding good projects in strategic sectors. However, development banks should not be captured by narrow private or political interests, because it would misuse resources and distract the development bank from its important roles. Good governance of development banks is therefore essential.

FROM BUSINESS AS USUAL TO AN INVESTMENT-LED GLOBAL NEW DEAL

This section examines three possible alternatives for the global economy and Europe for the period 2015 to 2020. The first is a business as usual scenario in which austerity policies in Europe are maintained in an attempt to reduce fiscal deficits to 3 percent of GDP and debt-to-GDP ratios to 60 percent. In other words, European governments will continue to cut their expenditures to reduce government debt and contain increases in government revenue. This is particularly the case for the South Eurozone where government spending is assumed to reduce from 23 percent of GDP in 2014 to 21 percent by 2020 and in the United Kingdom where government spending decreases from 23 percent in 2014 to 22 percent in 2020.

This scenario pays particular attention to the new 315 billion euro Investment Plan for Europe, widely known as the Juncker Plan (European Commission 2014). As a result, investment as a percentage of GDP in the European Union has increased from 15 percent of GDP in 2015 to 17 percent of GDP by 2020. Thus, in this scenario, it is assumed that within the next 5 years, 85 percent of the resources allocated under the Investment Plan for Europe will feed into higher investment rates across the European Union. If anything, this may be a somewhat optimistic assumption, given that there are concerns that the resources devoted to this plan may not be sufficient to catalyze such large investment.

At the global level, the business as usual scenario envisages a world in which private investment remains subdued in the face of depressed expectations of profitability, continued austerity in some highly indebted countries, and the relatively low-growth environment. As such, the global investment rate as a percentage of world GDP would only marginally increase from 21.4 percent of world GDP in 2014 to 22 percent of world GDP in 2020.

Contrasted to the business as usual scenario are two alternative sets of projections in which significant increases in public and private investment form the basis of sustainable economic recovery. In the first alternative scenario, European investment-led recovery, private investment in the European Union significantly increases from 15 percent of GDP in 2014 to 20 percent of GDP in 2020. In nominal terms, this would imply additional resources for investment, compared to the business as usual scenario, of approximately 530 billion euros by 2020 for the European Union. This sizable increase in investment is based on the recent proposal of the Polish Finance Minister Mateusz Szczurek calling for an EU-wide investment program of 700 billion euros (equivalent to 5.5 percent of EU GDP) (Szczurek 2014a).

With respect to the financing of this investment, EU member states and European institutions have a role to play in providing capital to lending institutions so that credit expansion can support the growth of private investment. There are a number of current proposals in this direction. For instance, a recent study by Cozzi and Griffith-Jones (2014) highlights two promising paths to use limited public resources to achieve important multiplier effects. The first is to increase paid-in capital of the European Investment Bank (EIB). They suggest a further increase of 10 billion euros of the paid-in capital of the EIB, building on the successful experience of a 10 billion euro increase of paid-in capital undertaken in 2012. The capital increase in 2012 facilitated at least an additional EIB lending of 80 billion euros and a total additional lending of 160 billion euros.

The second route to achieve leverage is via the EU budget. Large projects can be cofinanced by the EIB along with private capital from pension funds and insurance companies that currently do not fund large investment projects because of the high risk. Before the crisis, these risks were absorbed by mono-line insurers such as ING. However, after the crisis, it has become more difficult for mono-line insurers to take on this task. To this end, we propose that a very small amount (as a proportion of the EU budget) equal to 5 billion euros a year could be allocated as a risk buffer. Such resources would come from the existing EU budget and could imply some small restructuring of the EU budget. These 5 billion euros a year would allow the EIB to lend an additional 10 billion euros annually, leading to investment up to 20 billion euros annually (Cozzi and Griffith-Jones 2014; Griffith-Jones and Cozzi 2016).

Other viable proposals for financing investment include the institution of a European Fund for Investment (EFI) for 700 billion euros. This fund would be financed by injections of paid-in capital and guarantees by all EU member states, for a total of 105 billion euros, which would then be leveraged by borrowing in the financial markets (Szczurek 2014b). This could be a viable parallel initiative, but it is crucial that contributions from EU member states not be taken into account in defining the fiscal adjustment targets under the Stability and Growth Pact. National development banks could play an important role in cofunding private investment in those countries where they exist. An interesting model is the new public investment vehicle recently created for financing SMEs in Ireland, which has credit lines from the EIB and German KfW, while being capitalized by the Irish public pension fund.

The second important aspect of the European investment-led recovery scenario is the implementation of a more expansionary (or in some cases, less contractionary) fiscal policy stance at the EU level. In this respect, under this scenario European governments either maintain or increase expenditures as a share of GDP in an attempt to create the economic momentum required to substantially increase investment, employment, and economic growth. The more significant increase in government expenditure will occur in the South Eurozone, where it is assumed that government expenditure as a percentage of GDP increases from 22.8 percent in 2014 to 23.8 percent by 2020. The North Eurozone would experience a more marginal increase in government expenditure, from 23 percent of GDP in 2014 to 23.5 percent of GDP in 2020, whereas in the United Kingdom government expenditure will be maintained at 2014 levels (23 percent of GDP) through the period.

Increases in government expenditure in this scenario will be mainly covered by the higher tax revenues, resulting from additional economic output generated under the European investment-led strategy. In addition, to offset any budget deficit pressure that an increase in expenditure could generate, it is assumed that government revenue increases as a result of increases in direct taxation, particularly for the high earners, and as a result of stronger actions to curb tax fraud and tax evasion. In the South Eurozone government, income increases from 16.3 percent of GDP in 2014 to 19 percent in 2020; in the North Eurozone from 12 percent of GDP in 2014 to 22 percent of GDP, and in the United Kingdom from 17 percent of GDP to 19 percent of GDP over the same period.

The final, and most promising, scenario for global recovery is a global investment stimulus scenario. Here, the objective is to evolve the European investment-led recovery scenario in a global context where promoting investment and sustainable economic growth is done on a global scale. In particular, this scenario assumes that both developed and developing countries will put forward initiatives to stimulate private investment. In this context, national and regional development banks can play a fundamental role in developing countries in closing market gaps, supporting the funding of infrastructure projects and technological development, and providing countercyclical financing (Griffith-Jones and Tyson 2013). As discussed above, countries such as Brazil, India, China, and others have had successful development banks, which play a major role in funding and catalyzing private and public investment; it may be desirable to create or expand existing development banks in other emerging and developing economies, as well as in developed economies. This national development bank activity could be complemented by increased loans and equity by existing regional and multilateral development banks; furthermore, the creation of a New Development Bank, under the leadership of the BRICS (see, e.g., Griffith-Jones 2014) as well as the new Asian Infrastructure Fund can give further important support to increased investment in developing and emerging economies.

In the global investment stimulus scenario, global private investment as a percentage of world GDP increases from 21.4 percent to 23.8 percent in 2020. This represents a significant, but realistic, increase compared to the business as usual scenario, where global private investment increases less and reaches 22 percent of world GDP by 2020.

Given the current structure of the CAM model (see box for more information about the model), which divides the world into regions (e.g., low-income Africa, South America, European Union, South Eurozone, and North Eurozone) and large countries (e.g., United States, Brazil, China, India), increases in private investment are programmed at either the country or regional level. For instance, for the region of low-income Africa, private investment in the global investment stimulus scenario increases from 16.4 percent in 2014 to 17.8 percent in 2020. This projection is in sharp contrast with the business-as-usual scenario, where no

The Cambridge Alphametrics Model (CAM)

The Cambridge-Alphametrics Model (CAM) of the world economy is a nonconventional macroeconomic model that is primarily used to make medium- to long-term projections of historical trends of the global economy, blocs of countries, and major individual countries. This macro-model does not have any single, well-defined equilibrium path to which the economy tends to return in the medium- or long-term. Being an open disequilibrium system, a wide variety of outcomes may be simulated with different growth rates and end points (Cripps 2014).

CAM projections draw on continuous historical data from 1970 to the most current year available for model variables (2014 for this exercise). The databank holds series in U.S. dollar values and other units disseminated by UN organizations.

In CAM, the world economy is regarded as an integrated system in which the behavior of different countries and blocs differs and changes progressively through time because of their specific situation in terms of geography, level of development, financial position, and so forth. The macro-model has a common set of identities and behavioral equations for all blocs to reflect the notion that they are part of the same world economy. This common schema allows for panel estimation methods (Cripps 2014).

In the model, aggregate demand and technical progress are the principal drivers unless other important behavioral constrains are introduced into the model. Thus, long-term growth rate is best understood as reflecting growth of aggregate investment and government spending in the world as a whole. These variables in turn reflect confidence, expectations, and policy (Cripps 2014).

specific assumption on private investment is made and historical trends are projected to 2020. Under the business-as-usual scenario, this region would see the private investment rate sharply decline to 14.4 percent by 2020. For Brazil, private investment increases from 16.3 percent of GDP in 2014 to 17.8 percent in 2020 in the global investment stimulus scenario, whereas in the business-as-usual scenario, private investment would decline to 15.4 percent of GDP by 2020.

In developed countries, this scenario also assumes significant increases in investment. For the European Union, the assumptions made on investment, government spending, and income under the European investment-led recovery scenario are brought forward in this global scenario. For the United States the global investment stimulus scenario assumes that private investment increases from 15.8 percent of GDP in 2014 to 19.5 percent in 2020. Greater public investment and/or possible creation of public institutions or mechanisms to help fund private investment could be channels for such investment. This increase would bring investment in the United States to the levels of the early 2000s and represents a significant jump compared to the business as usual scenario, where investment would only reach 17.2 percent of GDP by 2020 (see table 5.1 for a more complete list of historical and projected results of investment as percentage of GDP under both the business as usual and global investment stimulus scenarios).

SCENARIO OUTCOMES

This section presents the projections produced by the CAM under the assumptions and specifications described for the three scenarios. Table 5.2 shows historical and projected average GDP growth rates for each scenario. World growth is faster under the global investment stimulus scenario as benefits of higher investment rates are achieved in most parts of the world.

Under the business-as-usual scenarios, the lack of a coordinated investment stimulus coupled with a continuation of austerity policies in the European Union translates to further decline of the average world GDP growth rate to 2.7 percent for the period 2015–2020.

Under business as usual in the European Union, average GDP growth for the period 2015-2020 reaches only 1.8 percent, which is still well below the levels of the early 2000s. As hoped, private investment in the European Union increases from 15 percent of GDP to almost 18 percent

Table 5.1 Investment as percentage of GDP, selected world blocs and countries, historical data (1990–2014) and projections (2015–2020)

		Historical						Projections					
		1990	1995	2000	2005	2010	2014	2015	2016	2017	2018	2019	2020
European Union*	Business as usual	18.7	16.6	18.6	17.9	16.0	15.3	15.8	16.3	16.8	17.2	17.6	17.7
	Global Investment stimulus							16.0	16.8	17.7	18.5	19.2	19.7
United States	Business as usual	18.8	18.4	20.5	20.3	15.5	15.8	16.2	16.5	16.8	17.0	17.1	17.2
	Global investment stimulus							17.1	18.0	18.6	19.0	19.3	19.5
Brazil	Business as usual	18.0	15.9	15.0	14.2	16.5	16.3	16.2	16.1	15.9	15.7	15.5	15.4
	Global investment stimulus							16.8	17.2	17.4	17.6	17.7	17.8
South America (excluding Brazil)	Business as usual	11.6	18.5	15.7	17.2	18.6	20.7	20.4	20.1	19.8	19.5	19.3	19.1
	Global investment stimulus							20.8	20.8	20.9	20.9	20.9	21.0
India	Business as usual	21.6	22.8	21.0	27.1	28.9	25.4	24.5	24.5	24.3	24.2	24.1	23.9
	Global investment stimulus							25.6	26.2	26.0	26.0	26.0	26.0
China	Business as usual	22.0	29.5	31.1	34.6	40.3	37.9	35.8	35.7	35.4	35.1	34.9	34.7
	Global investment stimulus							35.5	35.8	36.2	36.4	36.6	36.8
South Africa	Business as usual	16.3	13.2	12.7	14.4	16.4	16.7	16.8	16.7	16.4	16.1	15.7	15.4
	Global investment stimulus							17.1	17.4	17.6	17.7	17.8	17.8
Africa low income	Business as usual	11.7	12.0	11.4	11.7	15.2	16.4	17.2	16.6	16.0	15.3	14.8	14.4
	Global investment stimulus							16.9	17.2	17.5	17.6	17.7	17.8
World total	Business as usual	20.3	19.5	19.8	20.5	21.1	21.4	21.4	21.6	21.8	21.9	22.0	22.0
	Global investment stimulus							21.7	22.3	22.8	23.2	23.5	23.8

*Assumptions made on investment for the European Union under the Global Investment Scenario are the same assumptions made under the European Investment-led Recovery scenario.

by 2020 (see table 5.1) due to greater resources availability under the proposed Investment Plan for Europe. However, it is clear that this plan is not sufficiently big to stimulate the European economy. This plan's potential positive effects are further undermined by continued cuts in government spending, which ultimately depress aggregate demand and economic output.

Indeed, the European investment-led recovery scenario demonstrates how the combination of a greater investment plan for Europe (in the

Table 5.2 Historical and projected average GDP growth (%)

	Historical			Business as usual	European investment led recovery	Global investment Stimulus
	2000–2004	2005–2009	2010–2014	2015–2020	2015–2020	2015–2020
World	3.0	2.2	2.9	2.7	3.1	4.3
European Union	2.3	1.0	1.0	1.8	3.0	4.1
United States	2.7	0.9	2.4	1.3	1.4	2.5
Brazil	3.0	3.6	3.1	3.0	3.2	4.7
Other South America	2.3	5.5	4.5	2.8	3.0	4.3
India	5.9	8.1	6.0	6.0	6.2	7.5
China	9.2	11.4	8.6	8.9	9.1	11.4
South Africa	3.6	3.7	2.7	0.8	1.0	2.4
Africa Low income	6.0	6.4	6.0	3.1	3.3	4.8

region of 750 billion euros for the next 5 years), where both the European Investment Bank and national development banks could play an important role, and a more expansionary fiscal stance leads to a much more positive growth performance, as average GDP growth for the period 2015–2020 reaches 3 percent. This is particularly beneficial for the South Eurozone, as average GDP growth for the period 2015–2020 would increase from 1.6 percent under the business as usual scenario to 3.3 percent under the European investment-led recovery scenario. Further, this alternative policy stance in Europe would also have a beneficial effect on world economic output, given the weight of the European economy vis-à-vis the rest of the world.

The global investment stimulus scenario presents a much more optimistic global context where different regions across the globe put in place action to increase investment rates, both through higher public investment and through a greater role of national and regional development banks. In this scenario, for the period 2015–2020, average growth rate of global private investment is 7 percent, which is significantly higher than the average growth rate under the business-as-usual scenario. Higher investment rates translate into higher GDP growth across the world. In South Africa, for instance, average GDP growth for the period 2015–2020 reaches 2.4 percent, whereas under the business-as-usual scenario it only reaches 0.8 percent over the same period. In the region of low income, Africa's average GDP growth is 4.8 percent under the global investment stimulus scenario while, under the business-as-usual scenario, average GDP growth for this region stands at 3.1 percent. Overall, global economic output significantly benefits from a higher global investment at a global level, as average world GDP growth for the period 2015–2020 reaches 4.3 percent.

It is also important to look at the impact of the alternative policy strategies on the European Union and their implication for employment, government debt, and fiscal deficits. This is particularly important given that alternatives to austerity are often discounted by mainstream commentators as not being economically viable because they would lead to higher government debt and greater fiscal deficits.

Figure 5.1 presents the outcomes in terms of government debt to GDP for the South Eurozone and for the United Kingdom. The alternative, investment-led scenarios lead to more favorable results in terms of debt-to-GDP ratios compared to the business-as-usual scenario. While debt levels for all the three scenarios are projected to remain above 60 percent of the debt-to-GDP ratios prescribed by the Stability and Growth Pact, the important gains to GDP achieved in the investment-led scenarios lead to lower levels. In the South Eurozone, under the global investment stimulus scenario, the debt-to-GDP ratio levels off at 135 percent

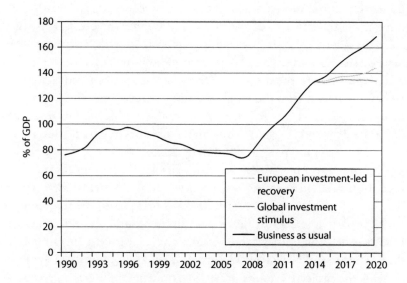

Figure 5.1A   Debt-to-GDP ratio, South Eurozone

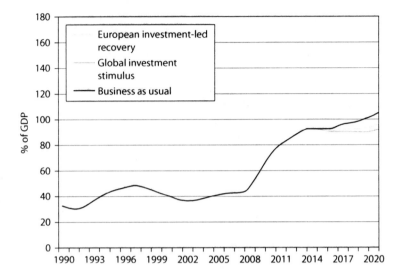

Figure 5.1B   Debt-to-GDP ratio, United Kingdom

of GDP by 2020, while it moderately increases to 144 percent of GDP under the European investment-led recovery scenario. Particularly worrying is the trajectory of debt-to-GDP ratio under the business-as-usual scenario where, as a result of poor economic growth, it continues to increase sharply and reaches 168 percent of GDP by 2020. In the United Kingdom, by 2020 the debt-to-GDP ratio reaches 93 percent under the global investment stimulus scenario and 98 percent under the European investment-led recovery scenario, while under the business-as-usual scenario the debt-to-GDP ratio continues its historically increasing trajectory and reaches 107 percent of GDP by 2020.

The alternative investment scenarios also lead to significant improvement in fiscal deficits in the European Union, in particular vis-à-vis the business-as-usual scenario. Again here the role played by development banks is particularly valuable, as with limited public resources used to fund paid-in capital, they can leverage significant private investment, as they cofinance and co-invest with private banks and investors. Table 5.3 presents the projected results of net government lending as a percentage of GDP for the South Eurozone and the United Kingdom. These two areas of the European Union present the highest fiscal deficits since the onset of the North Atlantic financial crisis.

Table 5.3 Net Government Lending as Percentage of GDP, South Eurozone and United Kingdom

		Historical			Projection	
		2000	2008	2012	2015	2020
South Eurozone	Business as usual				−5.9	−5.1
	European investment-led recovery	−1.0	−4.0	−6.1	−4.9	−4.0
	Global investment stimulus				−4.9	−3.6
United Kingdom	Business as usual	3.5	−4.9	−7.9	−4.7	−4.3
	European investment-led recovery				−4.6	−3.9
	Global investment stimulus				−4.5	−3.9

In the South Eurozone, the more positive results in terms of fiscal deficit reduction are achieved under the global investment stimulus scenario. By 2020, under this scenario, net government lending as percentage of GDP decreases from -6.1 percent in 2012 to -3.6 percent in 2020. The results of the European investment-led recovery scenario are also more favorable than the business-as-usual scenario, as by 2020 net government lending reduces to -4 percent of GPD while in the business-as-usual scenario net government lending as percentage of GDP still remains at −5 percent in 2020. In the United Kingdom the two alternative investment scenarios produce similar results in terms of deficit reduction. Under both scenarios, net government lending as a percentage of GDP reaches −3.9 percent of GDP by 2020. This represents an improvement when compared to the business-as-usual scenario where fiscal deficit in the United Kingdom reduces to −4.3 percent of GDP by 2030.

The analysis of debt-to-GDP ratios and fiscal deficits under the three scenarios shows that an investment-led strategy at the European and global level will bring important gains in Europe in terms of not only higher economic output but also government-debt reduction and improvements in fiscal deficits. Furthermore, the alternative investment scenarios achieve important gains in terms of reduction in unemployment in the European Union. Table 5.4 contrasts unemployment as percentage of labor force for the North and South Eurozone under the three alternative scenarios.

In the South Eurozone, under all three scenarios, the unemployment rate will reduce significantly, as this benefits from additional

Table 5.4 Unemployment as Percentage of Labor Force, North and South Eurozone

		Historical			Projection	
		2000	2008	2012	2015	2020
South Eurozone	Business as usual				19.0	15.5
	European investment-led recovery	11.1	8.8	17.8	18.8	14.2
	Global investment stimulus				18.7	13.3
United Kingdom	Business as usual				6.0	6.7
	European investment-led recovery	6.9	6.8	5.7	5.9	6.1
	Global investment stimulus				5.7	5.3

resources allocated to investment, via the Juncker Plan. However, for the South Eurozone, the global investment stimulus scenario is the one that leads to the lowest unemployment, as unemployment as a percentage of labor force decreases from 17.8 percent in 2012 to 13.3 percent in 2020. The North Eurozone did not experience a surge in unemployment during the period of economic crisis. The unemployment rate for this bloc will also experience a greater improvement under the alternative investment-led scenarios.

CONCLUSION

In recent years, the valuable role that national, regional, and multilateral development banks can and often do play is becoming widely recognized. The positive role these banks have played in providing countercyclical finance as private credit dried up and flows to developing countries collapsed during the North Atlantic crisis, which started in 2007, is widely seen as valuable. Furthermore, the greater need for instruments to implement more long-term national or regional development strategies has been increasingly recognized. This coincides with growing recognition of the value of a modern industrial policy and the importance of an "entrepreneurial" and development state, which encourages and leads economic development, providing the vision and the dynamic push for private innovation and structural transformation. Stiglitz and Greenwald (2014) add the very important dimension that successful and sustained growth requires the creation of a learning society and a knowledge economy to increase productivity; public development banks are an important institutional vehicle for supporting this. Indeed, development banks can help overcome market failures in both financial and knowledge markets simultaneously.

After analyzing the roles that development banks can play, as well as exploring the theoretical underpinnings for this, we have simulated three alternative scenarios, which illustrate the very positive impact that a greater role of development banks—together with a slowing down of the excessive fiscal consolidation that has occurred in recent years—can have on investment, growth, and employment as well as on reducing debt-to-GDP ratios. These simulations, which have looked at both the European level and a global level via a global investment stimulus scenario, show even higher impacts on investment, growth, and jobs. Overall, the analysis presented in this chapter gives a strong and positive illustration of the need to adopt a set of alternative economic policies for economic recovery and sustainable development and of the crucial role that development banks can play in promoting a sustainable and employment-led investment strategy.

NOTES

We thank Akbar Noman and Joseph Stiglitz for inviting us to write this paper, and JICA for the opportunity to present a first draft at the June 2014 Jordan workshop. We thank Edward Griffith-Jones for excellent research assistance.

1. The most notable exceptions are possibly in some of the highly successful East Asian economies.

2. To include some stylized facts, development banks are good at countercyclical lending and at providing long-term finance for private investment in infrastructure, as well as supporting investment and innovation in new sectors; private banks are good at providing international trade credit as well as financing the needs of large companies.

REFERENCES

Brei, M., and A. Schlarek. 2013. "Public Lending in Crisis Times." *Journal of Financial Stability* (9-4): 820–30.

Chang, H. 2002. *Kicking Away the Ladder: Development Strategy in Historical Perspective: Policies and Institutions for Economic Development in Historical Perspective.* London: Anthem Press.

Cozzi, G., and S. Griffith-Jones. 2014. Recovering Investment, Jobs and Growth in Europe. A Proposal. FEPS Policy Viewpoint No. 9. November.

Cripps, F. 2014. "Macro-model Scenarios and Implications for European Policy. Technical Appendix." In *Challenged for Europe in the World 2030*, eds. J. Eatwell, T. McKinley, and P. Petit, 351–368. Farnum: Ashgate.

Culpeper, R., S. Griffith-Jones, and D. Titelman. Forthcoming. "Multilateral Development Banks." In *Global Governance and Development*, eds. J. A. Alonso and J. A. Ocampo. London: Oxford University Press.

Diaz-Alejandro, C. 1985. "Good-Bye Financial Repression, Hello Financial Crash." *Journal of Development Economics* 19(1-2): 1–24.

European Commission. 2014. "An Investment Plan for Europe." Communication from the Commission to the European Parliament, the Council, the European Central Bank, the European Economic and Social Committee, and the Committee of the Regions and the European Investment Bank. Communication Number: Com 903 final.

Ferraz, J. C., A. C. Além, and R. F. Madeira. 2016. "Development Banks Contribution to Long Term Financing." Paper for UN-DESA. Available at *https://web.bndes.gov.br/bib/jspui/handle/1408/7522*. Access date 25 February 2016.

Griffith-Jones, S. 2014. "A BRICS Development Bank: A Dream Coming True?" UNCTAD Discussion Paper No. 215.

Griffith-Jones, S. and G. Cozzi. 2016. "Investment-Led Growth: A Solution to the European Crisis." In *Rethinking Capitalism: Economics and Policy for Sustainable and Inclusive Growth*, ed. M. Mazzucato and M. Jacobs. London: Wiley-Blackwell.

Griffith-Jones, S., A. Steinherr, and A. T. Fuzzo De Lima. 2006. "European Financial Institutions: A Useful Inspiration for Developing Countries?" In *Regional Financial Cooperation*, ed. J. A. Ocampo, 136–63. Baltimore, Md.: Brookings Institute Press.

Griffith-Jones, S., M. Kollatz-Ahnen, L. Andersen, and S. Hansen. 2012. "Shifting Europe from Austerity to Growth: A Proposed Investment Programme for 2012–2015 FEPS." Initiative for Policy Dialogue, Columbia University & ECLM (Economic Council of Labour Movement, Denmark) Policy Brief.

Griffith-Jones, S., and J. A. Ocampo. 2014. "Helping Control Boom-Bust in Finance through Countercyclical Regulation." In *Towards Human Development: New Approaches to Macroeconomics and Inequality*, eds. G. A. Cornia and F. Stewart. London: Oxford University Press.

Gurley, J. G., and E. S. Shaw. 1955. "Financial Aspects of Economic Development." *American Economic Review* 45: 515–38.

Griffith-Jones, S., and J. Tyson. 2013. "The European Investment Bank. Lessons for Developing Countries." WIDER Working Paper No. 2013/019, UNU-WIDER.

Keynes, J. M. 1936. *The General Theory of Employment, Interest and Money*. UK: Macmillan.

Kindleberger, C. P. 1978. *Manias, Panics, and Crashes: A History of Financial Crises*. New York: Basic.

Kregel, J. A. 1988. "The Multiplier and Liquidity Preference: Two Sides of the Theory of Effective Demand." In *The Foundations of Keynesian Analysis*, by A. Barriere. London: Macmillan.

Luna-Martinez, J., and C. L. Vicente. 2012. "Global Survey of Development Banks." Policy Research Working Paper 5.969. The World Bank. February.

Mazzucato, M. 2013. *The Entrepreneurial State*. London: Anthem Press.

McKinnon, R. I. 1973. *Money and Capital in Economic Development*. Washington, D.C.: Brookings Institute.

Minsky, H. P. 1977. "A Theory of Systemic Fragility." In *Financial Crises,* eds. E. Altman and A. Sametz. New York: Wiley.

Ocampo, J. A., S. Griffith-Jones, A. Noman, A. Ortiz, J. Vallejo, and J. Tyson. 2012. "The Great Recession and the Developing World." In *Development Cooperation in Times of Crisis,* eds. J. A. Alonso and J. A. Ocampo, 17–81. New York: Columbia University Press.

Stiglitz, J. E. 1990. "Financial Markets and Development." *Oxford Review of Economic Policy* 5(4): 55–68.

Stiglitz, J. 1994. *Whither Socialism?* Cambridge, Mass.: MIT Press.

Stiglitz, J., and B. C. Greenwald. 2014. *Creating a Learning Society: A New Approach to Growth, Development, and Social Progress.* New York: Columbia University Press.

Stiglitz, J., and A. Weiss. 1981. "Credit Rationing in Markets with Imperfect Information." *The American Economic Review* 71(3): 393–410.

Szczurek, M. 2014a. "Investing for Europe's Future." Vox, CEPR Policy Portal. Available at http://www.voxeu.org/article/investing-europe-s-future. Access date 24 February 2015.

Szczurek, M. 2014b. "Quantifying the Macroeconomic Impact of the European Fund for Investment." Analytical Note. 2014 Annual Meeting. Bruegel Institute. Available at. Accessed: 25 February 2015.

Wade, R. 2003. *Governing the Market.* Princeton, N.J.: Princeton University Press.

Wray, L. R. 2009. "An Alternative View of Finance, Saving, Deficits, and Liquidity." Working Paper 580, Levy Economics Institute of Bard College.

CHAPTER 6

Inside the Black Box of Japan's Institution for Industrial Policy

AN INSTITUTIONAL ANALYSIS OF THE DEVELOPMENT BANK, PRIVATE SECTOR, AND LABOR

Go Shimada

INSTITUTION AS A FACTOR OF SUCCESS, BUT WHAT IS INSIDE?

The creation of the New Development Bank, formerly referred to as the BRICS (Brazil, Russia, India, China, South Africa) Development Bank, reflects a renewed emphasis on the important role of public development banks.[1] The private financial system has not adequately performed its roles in recent decades. The rationale of public development banks is that they supply necessary long-term credit to agents in need, credit that is unavailable in the private financial market (Griffith-Jones 2014).[2] There is little consensus, however, on the efficiency of the financial market, especially in regard to the role of development banks. For instance, the World Bank (1989) discussed the consequences of development banks and policy-based finance in many countries, and it found they were not satisfactory and wasted scarce resources.

Even though negative assessments of development banks have been made, this is contradicted by what we know from successful cases in East Asia, such as Japan and Korea (Vittas and Cho 1996), and more recent examples in emerging economies, such as China and Brazil. A number of scholars question whether these countries' cases are too unique to be replicated. Calomiris and Himmelberg (1995) studied Japan's machine tool industry from 1963 to 1991, and they found that the government's financial intermediation helped to promote investment in Japan. At the same time, they claim that Japan is "an unrepresentative case," pointing to the risk of political capture (Calomiris and Himmelberg 1995, 27).[3] If this claim is true, we should not replicate this model in other countries.

This paper will consider which universal lessons we can learn from the case of Japan and apply to emerging economies and less developed countries. Many authors have lauded institutional factors as contributing to the success of Japan's development banks, such as the extensive use of public-private partnerships (PPPs), the creation of effective monitoring system, and the development of and propagation of credible visions (Vittas and Cho 1996, 292; World Bank 1993). If institution building is the main factor, how can we construct or transform an institutional setup in a given country to be effective? There is no literature to analyze the development bank system from within an institutional change framework (Mahoney and Thelen 2010; Matsuoka 2011). This paper aims to address this research gap by examining Japan's case and focusing on the development bank of Japan, but as a part of the institutional setup for industrial policy.

The rest of the paper is organized as follows. In the next section, we will begin to examine the pros and cons of development banks. In the section following that we will examine the case of Japan, with particular focus on the Reconstruction Finance Bank (RFB, or *Fukko Kinyu Kinko*) and the Japan Development Bank (JDB). In the final section, we will analyze Japan's development banking as part of the institutional framework for industrial policy.

THE PROS AND CONS OF DEVELOPMENT BANKS

Public development banks have been criticized, first, because they and the associated more tightly regulated domestic financial environment kept nominal interest rates lower than they would have been in more competitive markets (distorting economic incentives among both lenders and borrowers), which made the financial market inefficient.[4] Second, it is argued that this type of intervention often results in rent seeking, corruption, and crowding out. Third, development bank programs are frequently used for nonpriority purposes, eventually leading to nonperforming loans. Moreover, lending is difficult to withdraw from development banks once they have been introduced. This issue is known as *political capture*.[5] Ultimately, one must ask: what are the justifications for development banks?

MARKET FAILURE: ASYMMETRY OF INFORMATION

The theory of market failure provides a theoretical background in defense of the public development bank. One example of market failures is imperfect information or information asymmetry (Stiglitz and Weiss 1981; Stiglitz 1994; OECF 1991).[6] This is particularly important in developing countries, where information disclosure on private companies is limited, which causes "adverse selection (fund unviable applicants)," "moral hazard (fund irresponsible borrowers)," and "credit rationing" (Jaffee and Stiglitz 1990). It is difficult to know the risk of lending. Therefore, private banks cannot afford to lend their money to developing countries. To compensate, the interest rate becomes too high for the borrower.[7] The funding cost for private companies is extremely high, and the amount of funds available is much lower than would be appropriate. Lenders become risk-averse because it is difficult for financial institutions to know the current situation of the companies, examine the risk, and lend to them. Under such conditions, financial supply and demand fails to reach an optimum level. For instance, new sectors and new technology tend to be underfunded, as a result of which learning is discouraged.[8] This is a direct result of uncertainties over investment.

In this situation, if there is a bank to finance a new firm, then other banks can learn by observing the credit history of the firm. This will significantly reduce the risk of lending. But by allowing a "free ride" for other banks, the initial bank cannot recover all the risk-adjusted costs it has incurred. This prevents banks from taking on this initial role (Calomiris and Himmelberg 1995). Government development banks have an important role to play to correct market failures, by providing loan guarantees and/or rediscount loans and facilitating innovation and structural transformation, which provide both long-term and short-term finance on "appropriate" terms (that have often implied a subsidy).

In the case of Japan, public financial intermediaries, such as the JDB and Export-Import (EXIM) bank, join private bank-managed syndicates to succeed (with small shares, but as a government guarantee). For companies that face difficulty in accessing finance; such lending is essential for them to grow.[9]

MARKET FAILURE: EXTERNALITIES

Another example of market failure is externalities. For instance, environmental pollution is a typical case of externality. The market does not work to internalize the cost of environmental pollution (there is a significant discrepancy between private and social benefits). It would be necessary for government to promote investment to prevent environmental pollution and its hazards. In this case, to balance the externalities, the government would need to introduce a tax, such as an environment (or pollution) tax, to internalize it. However, it may be politically difficult for a government to introduce such a tax.

Alternatively, government can provide long- and short-term low–interest rate financing as a subsidy. Once this type of loan or subsidy has been introduced, private companies will compete against one another to get it. If there are government banks that have continuous and long-term transactions with those private companies, they can effectively assess the need to provide such subsidies or loans. This is another justification for having government banks (OECF 1991; Okuda and Kuroyanagi 1998).

Externalities are not always negative; considering economic development, there are positive externalities as well. For instance, there is the "cost of discovery" that pioneer firms bear that can benefit imitators; investment in rural areas could benefit society as a whole, and not just private companies, by creating job opportunities and balancing the over-concentration of economic activities in an urban area. Positive externalities could be key to making industrial policy work for economic development.

RISK, ECONOMY OF SCALE, AND OTHERS

Other than asymmetry of information and externalities, risk is another area in which the government needs to intervene. If the investment risk of particular activities is too high, government intermediaries can be effective tools to pool, socialize, and diversity risks (OECF 1991). The high-risk cases include a longer gestation period for industries (private companies cannot patiently wait to recover their costs); innovation (unknown technology, but it might be beneficial); and economy of scale (if investment is small, then the return is small and cannot be profitable). In developing countries, the market for long-term loans does not exist, so it is difficult for private companies to invest even in highly profitable ventures. In this case, government needs to intervene to establish a market and to provide loans to promote business or investment (Okuda and Kuroyanagi 1998).

Finally, in developing countries the financial market tends to be an oligopolistic market, and banks get excess profits. Ideally, governments need to intervene to remove the cartel and promote the entry of a new financial institution. However, this kind of policy is politically difficult for developing countries' governments, as existing banks would oppose such moves. Instead of removing the cartel in order to bypass the oligopolistic market, a development bank could be an effective tool to promote the efficacy of competition in the market (Okuda and Kuroyanagi 1998).[10]

Because of these justifications, development banks actually play an important role in various economies. For instance, according to Griffith-Jones (2014), the KfW, a German government-owned development bank, represents 12.7 percent of total bank credit in that German economy; in Brazil, it is 21 percent for the BNDES. Especially in East Asia, government policy in the financial sector has encouraged investment and led to a stable banking system that encourages saving. This improves financial access in the region, and it has been a major instrument for industrial policy and structural transformation by providing long-term finance, especially to the learning-intensive sectors (Stiglitz and Uy 1996; Stiglitz and Greenwald 2014).[11]

However, in spite of these justifications, there have been difficulties as well (Okuda and Kuroyanagi 1998). One of the difficulties is that it is complicated and costly to assess loan applications, especially those that the private banks refuse. Those include applications from micro, small, and social enterprises, among others. Loans to these companies are not always financially successful, and this puts pressure on the development banks. Typically, we expect development banks to be financially healthy and profitable. However, the nature of their work is risky and complex.

Rather than examining financial profitability, we need to focus on economic and social benefits, which are difficult to measure quantitatively. In other words, it is difficult to objectively measure and assess the impacts of development banks, which leaves them in a politically vulnerable position. Further, if the government needs to finance the development banks, it could worsen the budget deficit of the government and add to inflationary pressures (Okuda and Kuroyanagi 1998).

Another difficulty is rent seeking. For instance, in Japan there was the 1948 Showa Denko scandal, and in Indonesia there was an unjust credit guarantee scandal of the state-owned development bank BAPINDO in 1994.[12]

THE CASE OF JAPAN: DEVELOPMENT BANK
AS A PART OF INDUSTRIAL POLICY

As we have seen, development banking is challenging and has pros and cons. How, then, can we assess the case of Japan? Japan was known for its industrial policy after the war in which development banks played a vital role. The government undertook the task of being an "initial bank," providing credit and promoting businesses, through the JDB, the EXIM Bank, and others.[13] These two banks complemented each other.[14]

However, there was also a financial intermediary to collect deposits. The primary collector was the postal-savings system. That is, the Japanese government played important roles both in collecting deposits and in allocating finance to industrial development. The postal banking system had 22,000 offices and held about 20 percent of the total deposits in Japan in the 1980s (Sakakibara and Feldman 1983).[15] The Japan post is also the largest financial institution with more than 300 trillion yen in assets. It traditionally allocates around 75 percent of its assets to Japanese government bonds. However, the Japan post is not an investor. The fund is entrusted to the Portfolio Management Department (PMD, *Shikin Unyo Bu*) of the Ministry of Finance.[16] According to Sakakibara and Feldman, the PMD mostly supported central and local governments until the early 1950s. After the balanced budget rule of the Dodge plan line in 1949, the PMD started to allocate funds to development banks through the Fiscal Investment and Loan Program (FILP, *Zaiseitoyushi*), and the allocated fund became "off-budget."[17]

To consider the role of the development bank, rather than focusing only on the JDB, it is necessary for us to include other stakeholders as well. We should examine the development bank as a part of the institution for industrial development. Much of the available literature also singles out the importance of institutions in East Asia (e.g., Vittas and Cho 1996).[18] For instance, the World Bank (1993, 358) states the following:

> [Rapid growth economies such as Japan, Korea, Taiwan and China] had competent and insulated bureaucracies and banks to select and monitor projects, and each applied export performance as the main yardstick for credit allocation . . . . Few developing economies today have the institutional resources to consistently impose performance-based criteria for credit allocation.

In other words, their view is that institutional quality uniquely differentiates highly successful East Asia countries from other developing economies. Therefore, it would be useful to more closely examine the institutional aspect of development banks and related stakeholders.

Institutions include a variety of actors that form a society by interacting with one another through formal (e.g., legal) and informal (e.g., traditional rules and social norms) structures (Shimada, 2015a; Matsuoka 2009; North 1990; Olson 1982).[19] Ostrom (2005) defines institutions as rule-structured situations, which enable individuals to act collectively as communities or networks to tackle the problems they face. If properly enforced, the rule of law and a court system reduce uncertainty and transaction costs.

In the context of development banks, those actors include the policy regime (policy makers); ministries (bureaucrats), such as MITI (Ministry of International Trade and Industry) and MOF (Ministry of Finance); development banks, such as RFB and JDB; and the private sector (industrial associations and private companies). In addition to these, this chapter will include labor organizations. As we will see later, the labor-management relationship and productivity movement complement the work of the development banks in postwar Japan.

The role of institutional factors in economic performance has been examined by North (1990), Olson (1982), Aoki (2010), and Ostrom (2005) among others. North and Olson have stated that per capita distribution of "traditional" productive factors (e.g., land, financial capital, natural resources, and technology) cannot fully explain the inequality in per capita incomes. In their view, institutions and social capital mainly determine the differences (Shimada 2014, 2015b).

If institutions are strengthened, then the capacity of an economy or society will also be improved (Shimada 2009). As an institution becomes stronger, its capacity is also strengthened (Matsuoka 2009).[20] The institutional framework for industrial development in Japan can be summarized in figure 6.1. As this entire set of institutions—which we can think of as an institution—became stronger, Japan's capacity to grow was strengthened.

How, then, has this institution been established and changed in Japan? In the next section, we will examine the genesis of the development bank in the postwar period. We do this because the period immediately after the war was very important to defining the nature of the institution (path-dependence).

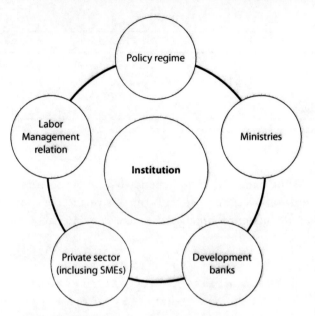

Figure 6.1   **The institution for industrial policy in Japan**

Source: Author.

As Sydow and Koch (2009) have discussed, the path dependence of an institution can be categorized into three phases: (1) preformation period (including "critical juncture"), (2) formation period, and (3) lock-in phase (see table 6.1). The critical juncture occurs when the path forward is chosen. In the formation period, the selected path forms the institution; in this period, the institution is designed to maximize social or economic benefits. In the lock-in phase, all choices are made based on a previous pattern, and no flexibility is allowed. When this is the case, the institution can no longer work effectively. One famous example is the QWERTY keyboard layout: the ABC layout may be more convenient, but the QWERTY layout persists because the technology is locked in and everybody has already learned it (David 1985).

Using this framework, as we will see in the next section, the period between World War II and the establishment of the JDB was a critical juncture. Therefore, we start the next section by examining the genesis of Japan's institution, with special attention paid to the establishment of the development bank. We will see the institution from the following six key aspects: (1) autonomy of the development bank; (2) high appraisal

Table 6.1

	Phase I	Phase II	Phase III
Preformation Period		Formation Period	Lock-in Phase
Until the end of WW II and critical juncture between WW II and the establishment of JDB		1952–1970s	Since 1980s

Source: Modified by the author based on Sydow and Koch (2009, 692).

capacity of the bank; (3) complementarity among sectors (horizontal and vertical spillover) and banks; (4) inclusive and decentralized PPP; (5) long-term transaction among stakeholders; and (6) labor-management relationship.

THE GENESIS: A CRITICAL JUNCTURE
FOR THE FORMATION PERIOD

RECONSTRUCTION FINANCE BANK (RFB)
OR FUKKO KINYU KINKO

After World War II, the RFB, which provided funds to key industries from 1947 to 1949, was established.[21] At that time, the Japanese economy was stagnating, especially in regard to industrial production.[22] The production of coal in 1946 was just 39.1 percent of during the previous year, because of the decisions made by the U.S. General Headquarters (GHQ) in Japan. These decisions were to limit import quantity, which resulted in a lack of raw materials (and higher production cost), and to dissolve big conglomerates (known as *Zaibatsu* in Japan).

These two decisions were important, considering the development of an institution for industrial development in the later stage. Because of the lack of raw materials, the government needed to work closely with the private sector. Further, to make effective use of scarce resources, improved productivity also became a policy issue. The dissolution of the big conglomerate changed the nature of the government–private sector relation. We will examine these changes step by step.

At that time, it was difficult for financial institutions to supply funds for reconstruction because of accumulated bad loans. Combined with these limitations, the mismanagement of economic policy (such as price control) and an electricity shortage caused the Japanese economy to be in a terrible slump. As goods of every description were in short supply, the underlying recognition by the government of Japan of what to do regarding the state of the economy was twofold.

An increase in production was the first priority to tackle. At that time, there was an argument whether increasing production or curbing inflation was a greater priority, but politicians such as Tanzan Ishibashi, who became prime minister in 1956, strongly supported production increase (Okita 1990).[23] To increase production, the government needed to fund production, but the finance was predicted to cause inflation. Contrary to that argument, it was proposed that as production increased, the goods market would eventually balance and inflationary symptoms would gradually settle.

The second priority to tackle was an increase in coal production. At the time, almost all coal was used by the occupation army for the railways and for heating purposes. There was no coal available for industrial production, especially for the export-oriented machinery industry.[24] To tackle the issue, a government coal committee was established under the leadership of Hiromi Arisawa. He was a professor at the University of Tokyo and a planner of the well-known priority production system (*keisha Seisan Hoshiki*). In this system, all the necessary resources were allocated to the coal sector to increase production. As a result of increased coal production, basic goods such as iron, fertilizer, and electricity were also supplied. The increased productions of these basic goods created a feedback loop, which further enhanced the production of coal as well as rice and wheat.

At that time, private companies that produced coal were also in short supply of money and needed to be financed. To tackle a dearth of resources and money, the Priority Production System was created, and the RFB played a central role in this system. The priority sectors of this policy were the following four: coal, electricity, chemical fertilizer, and transportation (in 1948, 70 percent of RFB finance went to these sectors) (Okazaki and Ueda 1995). As Okazaki and Ueda have described, it was impossible for the Japanese government to subsidize industries due to the lack of tax revenue, so the RFB's finances were used as implicit subsidies to firms. The financial support from RFB continued until the Dodge plan (financial and monetary austerity) was implemented in April 1949.[25]

There were different views on the RFB's contribution. On one hand, their financial assistance to coal and steel was considered to be a crucial contributing factor for Japan's reconstruction. On the other hand, the bank was regarded as the prime source of inflation because the RFB was not financed by savings, but by the BOJ (Bank of Japan). The BOJ purchased most of the RFB bonds and increased money supply to the market, which resulted in inflation.[26] This inflation is called *RFB inflation* or *Fukkin inflation*, but it was also an intended consequence of the government's plan (Tanimura 1981). Despite inflation, production made a remarkable recovery; in turn, the government's main policy priority shifted from production recovery to how to curb inflation. With the encouragement of the GHQ, the government imposed strong deflationary measures. Monetary contraction measures included stopping new credit from the RFB.[27]

Furthermore, the RFB was thought to be a hub of rent-seeking activities (bribery, political influence, and financial assistance to unhealthy firms). This criticism increased after the Showa Denko scandal in June 1948.[28] Mr. Hiroshi Tanimura, who became vice minister years later, was the director of the Ministry of Finance and in charge of the RFB at that time. He mentioned during a lecture in China that "The work of the RFB was extremely busy and difficult, and there is a lot of danger of temptation" (Tanimura 1981, 4, translated from Japanese).[29] As we will see later, this scandal had a serious impact on the institutional setup of the JDB itself, and on surrounding stakeholders as well.

The RFB had weak autonomy because of its decision mechanism, which allowed outside organizations to intervene in the decision process. These organizations included the Economic Stabilization Agency (*Anpon*) and the Committee for Reconstruction Fund (*Fukko kinyu iinkai*) among others. The responsibility of loan decisions was dispersed among those organizations. When the RFB was abolished (RFB 1950), it was also revealed that the RFB had dual characters, as a financial institution and a policy implementation organization, and the latter character had greater emphasis. Recognizing this weakness, the JDB had been established with stronger autonomy from outside forces (importance of the independence of public financial institutions).[30]

ESTABLISHMENT OF THE JAPAN DEVELOPMENT BANK (JDB): AUTONOMY AND APPRAISAL CAPACITY

The JDB was established in 1951, taking over the activities of the RFB but with greater independence from political forces to promote industrial development. The JDB had autonomy to decide its lending based on its own appraisal, and without political bias. This political independence is very important to the appropriate institutional design of a development bank. One of the risks of development banking is unproductive rent seeking and political capture. Because of the JDB's autonomy, the relationship between politician and government/development bank was more appropriate, and it had enabled the JDB to avoid rent seeking. To be more precise, because of the failure of the RFB, the principle of self-finance (*Syushisosho*) was installed. The JDB had two important principles in place (Takeda 2009). One was self-finance; the other was complementarity with private banks. We will see this in the next section.

This independence was facilitated by the JDB's high quality of loan appraisal and project oversight on the ground.[31] This capacity and financial independence allowed their loan default rate to remain very low.[32] Adhering to the self-financing principle and maintaining a low default record made the JDB earn a reputation as a reliable and high-capacity bank. Because of its reputation, financing by the JDB became a "signal" for private banks. The default record of JDB was 0.01 percent for the high lending period of 1956–1965. This is much lower than that of the private banks.[33] The high capacity of JDB and its autonomy are important aspects of the institution.

JDB LOAN AS A PART OF INDUSTRIAL POLICY: COMPLEMENTARITY AND POSITIVE EXTERNALITIES

Another very important aspect of the JDB lending was that it was embedded in the government's industrial policies, such as the productivity movement, taxes, subsidies, and others.[34] The national five-year plan gives broad guidelines. Then the lending agencies, including the JDB, decided their lending policies and also to which borrowers to extend credit. Those decisions were made independently.

COMPLEMENTARITY: HORIZONTAL AND VERTICAL SPILLOVER

JDB loans initially mainly financed basic industries at special interest rates that were substantially lower than market rates (Ogura and Yoshino 1984). Basic industries included electricity, iron and steel, shipbuilding, and coal mining. These industries have complementarity with one another. There are mutual benefits (or positive externalities) to collaborate among sectors; we will come back to this point soon. Because of the complementarity among industrial sectors, the loans were used as a kind of subsidy to the target industries with "crowding-in effects" in mind.[35]

After basic industries were developed, the target industries became manufacturing industries such as machine tools and automobile parts.[36] These industries were selected because spillover effects to other industries were considered to be high (Calomiris and Himmelberg 1995). Therefore, this was not an unadulterated picking the winner out of thin air type of intervention. Because of the complementarity among industrial sectors, there was flexibility to change the target industry depending on the situation. The complementarity or spillover effects among sectors are one of the important characteristics of the JDB loan when we think of the bank as a part of an institution.

There are two types of positive externalities; one is horizontal, and the other is vertical. The former is externality from one sector to other sectors (among industrial sectors) (figure 6.2). The latter is externality from big companies to supporting industries, which are mainly small and medium enterprises (SMEs).

This pursuit of vertical externality is one characteristic of the institution. More than 99 percent of the employment has been generated by SMEs in Japan. The SMEs are important not only to make the Japanese economy competitive, but also to raise the living standard of the people.

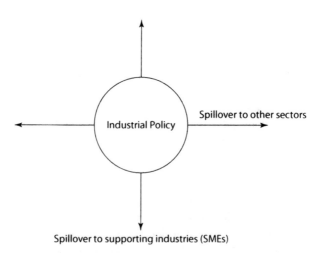

Figure 6.2   Positive externalities

Source: Author.

To support the vertical externality, with guidance from the GHQ, the Small and Medium Enterprise Agency was created in 1948 under the Ministry of Commerce and Industry (later it was reorganized into the MITI).

GHQ purported that the big conglomerates (*Zaibatsu*) institutionally supported Japan's militarism before and during WW II. Therefore, from the beginning of the occupation, the dissolution of conglomerates was one of the first priorities for the GHQ to implement. In 1947, a year before the start of the SME agency, the antimonopoly law was established. GHQ's aim was to prevent the concentration of economic power and to give equal opportunities to everybody who wished to start a business.

To support these movements, other financial institutions were also established, since these companies were too small for a JDB loan. In 1949, the National Finance Corporation (*Kokumin Kinyu Kouko*) was created to support the needs of small enterprises. To supply long-term credit to SMEs, Japan Finance Corporation for Small and Medium Enterprise (JASME, *Chusho kigyo kinyu kouko*) was also established in 1953, as a government financial institution. In this respect, the spillover effects to SMEs were built into Japan's new institutions immediately following the war. This is related to the labor-management relationship, which we discuss later.

COMPLEMENTARITY AMONG BANKS

There is another side of complementarity: complementarity among banks. This was another important operational principle of the JDB. Regarding the JDB loan, the amount of the loan did not matter as much as the announcement that a specific company can borrow from the JDB. This sent an important signal to private banks (the *signaling effect* of the government's industrial policy) to provide loans (reducing agency cost) (Horiuchi and Otaki 1987; Horiuchi and Sui 1993; Ueno 1978). The JDB loans catalyzed loans from private banks by lowering the risk.

In the case of Japan, asymmetry of information in the financial market was an important issue, because private companies mainly borrow from a particular bank, the so-called main bank.[37] The tie between a company and a main bank was cultivated through long-term transaction history. This main bank system is another way for many companies to fill the information gap. However, with the exception of main banks, other private banks are left out. The JDB loans provide important information for those banks on the outside. In other words, the JDB played the role of filling the gap due to the asymmetry of information in the financial market.

In addition, the stock market was still underdeveloped during this period, so the role of equity capital in corporate financing was small.

This was particularly important at the start of reconstruction after the war (Shimada 2015c). Many small or medium enterprises had only a brief history and no record of bank transactions, which made it difficult to assess the risk of lending to those companies. The JDB loans lowered the risk, signaling that there is government backing to this particular sector and these companies. The information was also considered unbiased (or reliable) because JDB's lending had broader aims than profit maximization. In this regard, Horiuchi and Sui (1993) found that JDB loans positively influenced the borrowers' investment expenditure through the information effect.[38]

TRANSITION TO PRIVATE BANKS

Horiuchi and Sui also argue that as banking became more efficient, the importance of the JDB decreased, except in its role providing credit to emerging firms that had not yet established long-term relationships. The JDB regarded itself as an initial lender to new firms, but it also stepped aside once private funds were ready to finance them.[39] This process requires substantial monitoring. Calomiris and Himmelberg (1995) argue that unlike other countries, Japan's credit programs did not cause high social costs. Calomiris and Himmelberg surveyed Japanese banks' lending to the machine tool industry, compared the lending of the EXIM bank and the JDB with Long-Term Credit Bank (LTCB) and Industrial Bank of Japan (IBJ), and concluded that there was no long-term capture of government funds. The EXIM bank and the JDB lent to the same companies less frequently than private banks and for shorter periods.

PPP: INCLUSIVE AND DECENTRALIZED BUREAU PLURALISM

INCLUSIVE

Regarding the risk of rent seeking and political capture, many authors who study Japan point to the role of government and private interaction to avoid these issues (Calomiris and Himmelberg 1995; Vittas and Cho 1996). An interaction that was very extensive and frequent in Japan has been adopted elsewhere and is now called the *public-private partnership* (PPP).

In the mid-1950s, Japan's economic recovery was impeded because of a shortage of steel. This problem was solved through a "deliberative council system," a forum of PPP to coordinate among stakeholders. The members of the councils were industry representatives, bureaucrats, academics, and others. These councils made all the important industrial policy decisions.

The MITI and the related industrial associations established a Screening Committee of Steel for Exporting Machinery. They worked together to secure the necessity supply of 25,000 tons of steel (Okazaki 2001). The MITI also worked with other related ministries, such as the Ministry of Transport, to build necessary infrastructure and to resolve several issues between industries (e.g., between industrial associations of the steel and shipping industries).[40] These arrangements allowed Japanese companies to be competitive. For instance, because of these plans, the price of iron and steel declined to a level to compete with the United States. This also helped to make the Japanese machine industry competitive. In other words, the PPPs were used to resolve bottlenecks impeding Japan's economic growth.

The interaction is not only active, but also inclusive. It involves various stakeholders, such as industrialists (entire industrial sectors), workers, academics, bankers, politicians, and bureaucrats. Interest groups needed to compete to be recognized as national priorities. Horiuchi and Sui (1993) called this an *information effect* of the JDB intermediating the information exchange between MITI and private companies.[41] This was especially true when the MITI started its industrial policy in the late 1950s.[42] Horiuchi and Sui mentioned that the information exchanges went both ways between the MITI and the JDB. The MITI recommended individual firms to the JDB based on its monitoring and investigation, and the JDB was also, according to Horiuchi and Sui, an active provider of information regarding private firms to the MITI, as well as the possibilities of industrial development to help the MITI formulate industrial policy.[43]

BUREAU PLURALISM

Aoki (1988) called this PPP system *bureau pluralism* or *compartmentalized pluralism*.[44] At that time labor mobility among organizations was low, so the sense of belonging (or loyalty) to each organization was very high. In Japan's labor market, unlike in other countries, lifetime employment used to be common practice. Each member of an organization (especially leaders) had a strong incentive to maximize her or his organization's efficacy.

The interests of each private company were aggregated into an economic and industrial association, such as the Japan Iron and Steel Association.[45] Then the counterpart bureau of the industry at the powerful MITI negotiated and coordinated inside the government. Okazaki (2001) characterized this system as pluralistic as well as bureaucratic.[46] It is pluralistic because the bureau in charge coordinates all the stakeholders and bureaucratic because the ministry moves based on the will of economic associations.[47] In this regard, Okazaki pointed out an interesting fact: bureau pluralism and the PPP were innovative phenomena in Japan.

Even though there were similar setups in the prewar period, in Okazaki's analysis there were three differences. First, in the prewar period there were few representatives from industrial associations at government-organized meetings. Second, most members were from *Zaibatsu* (conglomerate) and the chamber of commerce. In other words, they did not aggregate industry-specific interest. Rather, it was a machine based on selected big business owners and geographical representation (chamber of commerce). Third, many members were politicians because, unlike in the postwar period, most of the coordinating role was carried out by politicians rather than bureaucrats. In sum, in the prewar period, the government-firm relationship was very different from postwar bureau pluralism. In terms of the institutional change framework (as shown in table 6.1), this phase can be considered a preformation period.

The change, which was a critical juncture, came in the period between World War II and the establishment of the JDB. This is so because during the war the government needed huge resources to produce aircrafts and ships, and an industrial association to mobilize these resources, such as the Iron and Steel Control Association, was used to that end (Okazaki 2001; Okazaki and Okuno-Fujiwara 1999). According to Okazaki (2001), during the war the position of industrial associations rose substantially as they gained experience working with the government, and it became an important foundation of the postwar economic system.[48] One of the major examples was the *priority production policy*, which we saw earlier.

The PPP is the core of Japan's institution for industrial development. With the PPP in place, the government's industrial policy became feasible and practical. The PPP also made the JDB loan work as a key driver of complementarities among industries (vertical and horizontal) and among banks. However, there is a missing piece in this picture. It is the role of labor-management relations or productivity movement.

LABOR-MANAGEMENT RELATION: PRODUCTIVITY
AND SHARED GROWTH

Soon after WW II, the GHQ released political prisoners such as Tokuda Kyuichi and Shiga Yoshio, who were leaders of the Japan Communist Party, as part of liberating Japan. More precisely, the aim of GHQ was to make Japan a nonautocratic and nonmilitary country. This is a strange decision, judging from today's eyes, but at the beginning of the occupation, GHQ and communist leaders collaborated closely. Following the GHQ policy, various laws and regulations pertaining to workers' rights were passed in 1945 and 1946.

However, this collaboration did not last long. The labor movement became too active and radical. In 1946, soon after the first May Day held in the postwar period, some of the group started to demonstrate, demanding food. The demonstration spread everywhere in Japan and even surged against the Imperial Palace. On May 20, 1946, General Douglas MacArthur issued a statement warning against demonstrations and mass disorder.

Even as the GHQ policy changed, the labor movement continued to spread all over Japan. In October 1946, more than 300,000 private sector workers joined strikes and won higher wages and shorter working hours. As the labor movement became stronger, the conflict between the government and the labor movement grew. Labor called for a general strike for February 1, 1946. The situation became very tense and a solution seemed impossible. A labor movement leader was even injured during a conflict. Ultimately, the GHQ prohibited the general strike with one day remaining. This represented a turning point for the GHQ.

The GHQ policy on labor was also influenced by the international situation, such as the establishment of the People's Republic of China in 1949 and the Cold War between the United States and the Soviet Union. Even as the GHQ tried to repress the labor movement, the conflict got worse in 1949 with the Shimoyama incident (in July), the Mitaka indent (in July), and the Matsukawa incident (in August). The truth remains unknown, but the involvement of the labor movement is widely suspected. In 1950, the GHQ started a red purge, not only of government and journalism but of private companies as well.

This is the period when Japan embarked on efforts to increase production capacity and form the institutions for industrial policy. Therefore, it was critically important that the government and private companies manage labor-management relations to increase production. Furthermore, resources were in short supply, so it was natural for them to consider increasing productivity to maximize output with fewer resources needed.

For instance, in the case of Toyota, production was sharply decreased by an anti-inflationary measure implemented by GHQ in 1949. In 1950, after a long, bitter battle with the union and numerous strikes, Toyota laid off around 2,000 workers and Toyota founder Kiichiro Toyota resigned. This layoff went against an earlier agreement with the union, so the situation got worse. In the same year, however, the Korean War started and the United States began to order a huge amount of trucks. An increase in production was necessary with fewer workers than before (van Driel and Dolfsma 2009, 62). Under these conditions, there was a huge demand for productivity improvements, and that in turn required management to work constructively with labor.

U.S. AID POLICY AFTER WW II

In 1951, the deliberative council of industrial rationalization proposed the establishment of a productivity organization to the government. This movement was supported by the FOA (Foreign Operation Administration) of the U.S. government. This was a precursor organization to USAID (United States Agency for International Development).

During this period, the United States was very actively supporting the productivity movement as a part of the Marshall Plan and the Point Four Program. With help from the United States, the Anglo-American Council on Productivity (AACP) was created in the United Kingdom. From 1948 to 1952, some 66 missions and 900 people from the United Kingdom were received by the United States with most of the costs being borne by the U.S. government. Following the AACP, similar productivity centers were established in Europe: Denmark (1949), Turkey (1949), Austria (1950), West Germany (1950), Netherland (1950), Trieste (1950), Belgium (1951), Italy (1951), Switzerland (1951), Greece (1953), Sweden (1953), and France (1954), among others. As the center of these productivity movements, the EPA (European Productivity Agency) was also established.

Actually, it was the U.S. government that suggested that Japan establish a tripartite combination of government, private sectors, and labor to set up the Japan Productivity Center (JPC), because it was a standard practice in European countries (JPC 2005). A meeting was held in 1954 between Japan and the U.S. government to conclude the aid agreement to Japan on productivity. Shortly after the meeting, the MITI decided to create the JPC as a semipublic foundation, and the Japanese Cabinet also agreed to receive aid from the United States.[49]

However, the labor side (*Sohyo* or General Council of Trade Unions of Japan) objected to this movement. They considered the productivity movement to be a tool for labor subjugation. When the JPC was established in 1955, the General Council of Trade Unions of Japan did not participate. In the same year, trying to work with the labor side, the JPC declared three guiding principles of the productivity movement.[50] This was a kind of promise from management to labor to work constructively. The principles are as follows:

1. *Expansion of employment.* In the long term, improving productivity should lead to expanding employment. However, from the standpoint of the national economy, a public-private partnership is essential in formulating valid policies to prevent the unemployment of surplus personnel through job relocation or other measures.

2. *Cooperation between labor and management.* Labor and management must cooperate in researching and discussing specific methods to improve productivity in consideration of specific corporate circumstances.

3. *Fair distribution of the fruits of productivity.* The fruits of productivity should be distributed fairly among labor, management, and consumers in line with the state of the national economy (JPC 2005, 38).

As one can see, the principles aimed to boost employment, enhance real wages, and raise the standard of living, rather than simply increase competitiveness. This point is very important in understanding the nature of the productivity movement in Japan.

In June 1955, the labor side responded to this principle by issuing eight principles of the productivity movement. They emphasized the importance of *industrial democracy*. Basically, labor's principles were in line with the three guiding principles of the JPC; and in September, they reached an agreement to work together. This changed the nature of the labor-management relation from combative to collaborative.

U.S. aid started in 1955 and continued until 1961. This aid was administrated by the ICA (International Cooperation Administration), which was reorganized from the FOA. During these seven years, the United States invited 393 teams (3,986 people) from Japan. Each team represented an industrial sector, such as steel, electricity, shoe making, and auto parts, among others. Even after U.S. aid ceased, Japan continued to send missions to the United States. In 1965, that number reached 568 teams and 6,072 people (JPC 2005).

SHARED GROWTH

With the help of the United States, many bureaucrats and business personnel studied productivity improvement. This had a significant impact on Japan's manufacturing sector. Toyota Production System (TPS), or *Kaizen*, was born from the productivity movement and spread all over Japan. It dramatically increased Japanese productivity. Beyond that, as echoed by the three guiding principles of the productivity movement, the growth was inclusive (Shimada et al. 2013).

The history of economic growth in Japan is characterized by its remarkable record and more importantly by fairly egalitarian income distributions (Birdsall and Sabot 1993; World Bank 1993).[51] The Gini coefficient very rapidly improved, especially in the 1960s. The coefficient was 0.31 in 1963 and fell to 0.25 in 1971 (Otake 2003).

Without the collaborative partnership between labor and management, the impact of industrial policy including the development bank intervention would have differed. This entire institutional framework drove Japan to very high economic growth in the 1960s and 1970s.

JAPANESE INSTITUTION: DECENTRALIZED STRUCTURE AND SHARED PROSPERITY

So far, we have examined how stakeholders of Japan's institution for industrial policy worked to contextualize the JDB. To summarize, institution's characteristics comprised the following key concepts: (1) autonomy of the development bank; (2) high appraisal capacity of the bank; (3) complementarity among sectors (horizontal and vertical spillover) and banks; (4) inclusive and decentralized PPP; (5) long-term transactions among stakeholders; and (6) collaborative labor-management relationship.

Underlying these characteristics were two vital considerations. One was the decentralized structure and the other was shared prosperity. As we have seen, the institution was decentralized, not top-down. First, the JDB's autonomy meant that it could have its own exit policy and choose when to pass the buck, so to speak, to the private banks. That helped the JDB to avoid political capture and rent seeking. Second, even in the ministry, the power was not concentrated at the top. In practice, each ministerial bureau had a free hand to decide and coordinate policies. Third, throughout the institution, the decentralized mechanism was built in by various policy interventions, productivity movement (bottom-up approach to management), and law (e.g., antimonopoly, labor rights).

Shared prosperity was the opposite side of the coin to the decentralized nature of the institution. There were mutual benefits among industrial sectors through positive externalities. As there were mutual benefits among industrial sectors, other sectors also gained a benefit from industrial policy. And as noted above, this benefit was shared with SMEs, with government support in finance (including providing long-term credit). The SMEs even benefited from having long-term transaction (which is called *Keiretsu*) with large companies. With this long-term connection in place, large companies in many cases offered technological training to SMEs, which had a significant impact on the development of the SMEs. Finally, as we saw, the mechanism for fair distribution of benefit between labor and management was built in at the start of the productivity movement. Arguably, these two built-in features of the institutions were the drivers to move Japan to rapid economic growth.

Before we analyze the policy implications for developing countries, it would be apposite to briefly touch on the lock-in phase.

LOCK-IN PHASE

After the late 1980s, the institutional setup, which worked so well in the past, could not respond to the changing economic environment. According to our institutional framework (as shown in figure 6.1), the institution entered the locked-in phase.

This phase is related to the structural changes of the Japanese economy. In the postwar period, there were mutual benefits or positive externalities (no conflict of interest) among industries (e.g., heavy industry and the rest of the manufacturing sector). A benefit to the coal industry was a long-term benefit to the steel industry and construction industry as well.[52] Under this condition, the Japanese PPP was a very efficient decision-making system with decentralized structure. When industrial development was the priority of the nation, this system worked very effectively. However, decades later, after rapid economic growth and structural transformation, the national policy agenda widened from just industrial development to other issues, including pollution and quality of growth.

The same system worked during the time of complementarity among industries and businesses. The government's industrial policy had been adjusted over time to meet the changing economic needs and goals when there was mutual benefit. However, once that connection became too strong, it became resistant to change, and the same system became a burden to the economy. In other words, the vested interests of ministries and existing companies hampered the necessary reform because they protested change. The need for JDB finance also decreased, and a revised role for the JDB was envisioned.

This lock-in phase is inevitable for any institution. Once trapped, institutions need to work to regain their dynamic nature. However, this issue is beyond the scope of this paper. We now consider how to build an institution that works for economic growth.

DOS AND DON'TS OF DEVELOPMENT BANKS

There are a number of successful development banks in countries' rapidly developing emerging economies such as in Brazil, China, and Malaysia, as there were in economies such as in Korea and Taiwan during their rapid transformation. Each development bank works in its own way to overcome issues such as rent seeking and political capture, and to complement the work of markets. The recent revival of interest in industrial policy raises the issue of the role that development banks can play. So, in revitalizing development banking, what lessons can we learn from Japan's institutions?

AUTONOMY AND HIGH CAPACITY

As this case study of Japan shows, rent seeking can happen in any country and in any context. The question is how the country or the bank can sort out the problem after an incident occurs. If the country is able to respond to the issue, then the system to avoid rent seeking and political capture is more likely to remain in place. As we saw with the JDB, autonomy is the foundation of the bank as well as the entire institution. Because of its autonomous nature, private banks highly regarded the JDB's loan appraisal (signaling effect). Without such autonomy, it could easily succumb to rent seeking and political capture.

There could be a number of paths to secure autonomy for an existing institution. Mahoney and Thelen (2010, 15) divided these paths into four broad types of institutional change: (1) displacement, (2) layering, (3) drift, and (4) conversion.

1. *Displacement*: the removal of existing institutions and/or rules, and the introduction of new ones
2. *Layering*: the introduction of new institutions and/or rules on top of existing ones
3. *Drift*: the change of meaning and impacts of the existing institution and/or rules due to the change in environments
4. *Conversion*: the changed enactment of existing rules due to their strategic redeployment

Their framework can be further classified by strengths and weaknesses of (1) status quo orientation in the politics and (2) resistance to change of the institution (Matsuoka 2011; Kitayama 2011) (table 6.2).

In the case of the JDB, the institution was established through "displacement" in this framework, to overcome the malfunction of the RFB. That is how the JDB gained autonomy for its lending decisions. Depending on a country's situation, there are various ways to secure autonomy, such as layering and conversion. When one is establishing or running a development bank, it is critically important to give it autonomy.

Building capacity for loan appraisal was also a foundation of the success of the development bank, which was actually built on the existing banking institutions. This is the *layering* in our framework. When the RFB was established, only 10.6 percent of people were newly recruited. The JDB basically retained all the staff members of the RFB who wished to stay, but this was not the case for the senior management team. All senior staff members (above the level of directors of divisions, *Kacho*) of the JDB were newly installed from outside the RFB (Okazaki 2009). They came from the Bank of Japan, the Hypothec Bank (*Kangyo Ginko*),

Table 6.2

		Resistance to change of the institution	
		Strong	Weak
Status quo orientation	Strong	Drift	Conversion
in the politics	Weak	Layering	Displacement

Source: Modified by the author based on Kitayama (2011:54).

and the Industrial Bank of Japan. This was done because of discussions that it is not appropriate to operate the JDB with the same staff members from the RFB. No institution can be suddenly established based on nothing. Therefore, the JDB did very well to displace senior management by layering capable, experienced staff members. Without the accumulated knowledge and experience of staff members (human capital), it would have been difficult for the JDB to maintain its quality of loan appraisal.

NETWORK

As an institution, one success of the JDB was to have a strong network among the institution's stakeholders. The JDB had a good division of labor with other private banks; because of it, the JDB gained the trust of private companies. The vertical and horizontal externalities also contributed to strengthen such networks. Inside the institution, labor was constructive. All the players had long-term views, and because of the long-term transaction, their transaction cost was considered to be very low.

Hence, a robust network seems to be another ingredient for a successful institution for industrial policy. To make an institutional network strong, expected gains need to be shared among members. If such an expectation exists, then all stakeholders will be eager to work together collectively. Industrial policy needs to look at how this kind of broad base can be built.

DECENTRALIZED SYSTEM: A UNIQUE ASPECT

When we apply policy implications from Japan's history to other countries, certain aspects remain specific to Japan. Without acknowledging this fact, it would be dangerous to automatically apply Japan's model to other countries. One unique aspect is low labor mobility among organizations. Japan is known for its lifetime employment system. Once people get a job after graduating from a university, they normally stay in the same organization for the rest of their lives. In the short term, the wage is not very high; but the longer the term works for a company or an organization, the better the wage becomes. Therefore, there is an incentive structure for workers to remain in the same organization. This is the same even for senior management.

Under this lifetime employment system, people can have a long-term perspective on how they work in a company or an organization to which they belong. There is also a very strong incentive to maximize organizational benefit rather than short-term individual gains.

In other countries, people's mobility tends to be higher than that of Japan. There, the network structure among stakeholders in the institution would be different. In any case, the long-term transaction itself would be useful to minimize the asymmetry of information. Hence, the way to strengthen the network needs to be considered according to the context of the country and the institution.

Compared with other countries, Japan is also more decentralized in terms of decision making, starting from bureau pluralism, to the bottom-up approach, to the factory floor management (such as the quality control circle). This is also another unique aspect of Japan's institution. In a country with a top-down approach, it would be necessary to think about the path to make the institution strong. Even in this case, shared prosperity would remain a key because of its capacity to enable stakeholders to unite.

CONCLUSION

As we have seen in Japan, two fundamental factors account for an effective development bank and institution: autonomy of the development bank and high capacity. There are several ways to establish these foundations. In case of the JDB, it started with a bribery incident that led to autonomy and a capacity for layering.

Even if the capacity of the development bank is high, there is a limit to what an organization can handle with its human resources, such as finance to SMEs, in the case of JDB. If the workload is too hard for them, it will be difficult for development banks to maintain the quality of appraisal. Therefore, division of labor inside the institutional framework is important for the efficacy of industrial policy. If demarcation among stakeholders is clear, it is easier for them to collectively work together, reducing transaction costs and cosharing risks. Through this process, the institution would become stronger. Even if Japan's case is somehow unique in terms of low human mobility and a decentralized decision-making process, the above points still remain as universal lessons to make institutions work for an economy as well as society.

Finally, a lock-in phase when an institution stagnates is inevitable. How quickly a country can transform its institution is the key to maintaining the dynamic nature of the institution. Taking these considerations into account when establishing or reforming an institution should greatly enhance the chances of success.

NOTES

Go Shimada is Associate Professor, University of Shizuoka, Visiting Scholar, Columbia University, Visiting Scholar, JICA Research Institute, and an Adjunct Researcher, Waseda University.

1. The public development banks include the European Investment Bank of the European Union, KfW (Kreditanstalt für Wiederaufbau) of Germany, and BNDES (Banco Nacional de Desenvolvimento Econômico e Social) of Brazil among others.

2. The role of the financial sector is to catalyze saving and investment in the economy to achieve sustained and inclusive growth, promoting innovation and structural changes.

3. " . . . it is worth noting that the effective operation of industrial direct credit in Japan seems to be an unrepresentative case. In many countries, government interventions have produced large costs through the funding of inefficient borrowers and the capture of public funds by special interests" (p. 27).

4. This is, in other words, *financial repression* (McKinnon 1973; Reinhart, Kirkegaard, and Sbrancia 2011).

5. Because of these concerns, "Western governments (directly, and through the international financial institutions) have strongly pushed developing countries to deregulate and liberalize their financial markets" (Stiglitz and Greenwald 2014, 402).

6. The Overseas Economic Cooperation Fund (OECF 1991), which has been reorganized into the JICA (Japan International Cooperation Agency) since 2008, discussed that government intervention is warranted in the following case: "(1) when investment risk is too high regarding a particular activity (owing to the need for large scale. long gestation period, high technology and market development); (2) when there is significant discrepancy between private and social benefits (e.g., in the case of rural industries that increase job opportunities in rural areas and prevent over-concentration in urban regions); (3) in the case of industries that may save foreign exchange and thus relieve the balance of payments constraint on other growth industries; (4) in the case of investment for pollution control and environment protection; (5) when infant industries face large social set-up costs; and (6)when information problems discourage lending to small and medium scale industries (as quoted by Calomiris and Himmelberg 1995, 3–4)."

7. On the other hand, that is also the reason why microfinance is needed for the poor. Without microfinancial institutions, there is no way for the poor to borrow.

8. Stiglitz and Greenwald (2014) also emphasized the importance of externalities of learning. With the existence of externalities, private returns are very much different from social return. This is another example of market failure.

9. In addition to this, Stiglitz and Greenwald (2014) argue that domestic banks can promote local investment, but foreign banks do not. They attract funds away from local financial institutions, invest out of the country, and impede the creation of a learning society. Even if they invest domestically, foreign financial institutions provide less money to small and medium enterprises because foreign banks have less information on them. Therefore, Stiglitz and Greenwald argue that access to domestic capital is a key instrument of industrial policy.

10. Based on historical perspective, Kindleberger (1978) suggests that financial crisis is created by previous excess. Private finance follows an economic cycle, and the market is not well regulated. This provides yet another justification for short- and long-term countercyclical finance (Griffith-Jones and Ocampo 2014; Ocampo et al. 2012).

11. Stiglitz and Greenwald (2014) posit that it is financial restraint (mildly restricting both entry into banking and the deposit rate).

12. A $430 million letter of credit issued to an Indonesian conglomerate named Golden Key. The letter was issued to equip a petrochemical plant in West Java. The Golden Key drew on the letter, and no equipment was provided. The company was also involved in other fraud allegations.

13. In the case of Japan, private companies mainly borrow from private banks (during the 1959–1963 period, 29.4 percent of the money borrowed was from private banks and 2.7 percent from government credit). The government credit figures in other countries are 0.1 percent in the United States (1959–1963) and 1 percent in the United Kingdom (1964–1968). Comparing these figures, one could say that in Japan government credit plays a relatively greater role than in those countries (Horiuchi and Otaki 1987).

14. Calomiris and Himmelberg (1995) found, while surveying the machine tool industry, that the role of the EXIM bank increased as that of the JDB decreased.

15. With branch offices all around the nation, it made deposit collection easier in rural areas. Sakakibara and Feldman (1983, 20) also mention that the system forced other institutions to compete to collect deposits.

16. The PMD also received funding from national pensions.

17. According to Sakakibara and Feldman (1983, 21), the fund went to the main direct government investor, the FILP, with one-half of the fund earmarked for government financial intermediaries, such as the JDB and Housing Finance Corporation. The target of FILP was large-scale industrial projects, foreign trade finance, and SME finance in the 1950s and 1960s, and it moved to mortgage finance in the 1970s.

18. Vittas and Cho (1996, 292) analyze the factors of success in Japan and Korea, including the presence of specific economic and institutional factors. Economic factors are the maintenance of price stability; an orientation toward export production; encouragement of domestic competition; reliance on the private sector; and a bias toward industrialization. Institutional factors are the use of extensive PPP; the creation of an effective monitoring system; and above all the development and propagation of credible visions.

19. North (1990) views institutions as "the rules of the game" (1990, 3) in a society that forms the way people behave.

20. Matsuoka (2009) categorized the steps of institutional change into three stages: system-making stage; system-working stage; and self-management stage.

21. The RFB was established in 1947 to reconstruct the Japanese economy and was funded by the issuance of bonds which were bought by the Bank of Japan.

22. One important aspect of the postwar period was that all politicians and government officials shared a sense of crisis. Syuzo Inaba, who served the Economic Stabilization Agency (or Anpon) as Deputy Director General, mentioned that "The underlining sense of making the first Economic Recovery Plan from 1947–48 was that . . . without economic independence, there is no possibility to be politically independent. That is, if we can recover prewar economic standards and balance the trade, then Japan can be an independent country" (Inaba 1990).

23. Former President of the Industrial Bank of Japan, Nakayama (1990), also mentioned that in spite of the issues of overborrowing and overlending, the priority was a production increase. Soon after the war, and before the RFB establishment, the Industrial Bank of Japan established the Recovery Funding Bureau, of which Sohei was the managing director.

24. The export-oriented machinery industry was considered to be a driving force in Japan's recovery. The industry was expected to absorb redundant labor that resulted from the decline of the textile industry, as it lagged behind other Asian countries (Okazaki 2001).

25. Most of the RFB loan was a deficit-financing loan (*akaji yushi*), which aimed to compensate private companies' deficits in order to make their operation possible. The Dodge plan banned the flotation of national bonds to cover current deficits. The government could not borrow from the financial market; however, the government borrowed money from postal savings deposits (Sakakibara and Feldman 1983).

26. The amount of bonds issued by the RFB was 109 billion Yen during their operation from 1947 to 1949. The BOJ underwrote 70 percent of them, and increased 38 percent of bank notes (Horiuchi and Sui 1993).

27. Using individual firm-level data, Okazaki and Ueda (1995) found that the loans made by the RFB were to ill-performing firms, but the JDB-financed firms performed much better than other firms. With these results, Okazaki and Ueda conclude that the RFB's lending policy change had a positive impact, and eventually played a large role in the transition from a wartime command economy to a market-oriented system.

28. The president of Showa Denko bribed former Prime Minister (Hitoshi Ashida), then Vice Prime Minister (Suehiro Nihio), to get an RFB loan.

29. Due to these, the lending policy of the RFB changed, abandoning the deficit-financing loans to support only essential equipment purchases "on immediate measures on the industrial finance accompanying revision of prices" (*Kakaku hosei nitomonau tomen no sangyokinyu taisaku*). The "Three Principles of Economic Stabilization" (*Kigyo san gensoku*), by GHQ/SCAP, also influenced the policy change.

30. It is well documented by Okazaki (2009, 36–41) how to make the JDB autonomous.

31. As Calomiris and Himmelberg (1995, 4) emphasized, "[The JDB] prides itself on its success in priming the pumps for private creditors."

32. The funding source is not from issuing bonds, but from postal savings. Together with the Export-Import Bank of Japan and Small Business Finance (SBFC), the JDB played an important role in providing necessary credit to industries. Through the "window" policies, the Bank of Japan (BOJ) also encouraged private banks to lend (Calomiris and Himmelberg 1995).

33. The interest rate of the JDB was 1 or 2 percent less than private rates.

34. Vittas and Cho (1996, 282) summarized the objectives of the industrial policy of Japan into the four following points: to pick winning industries in terms of dynamic comparative advantage; to support smooth transition of phase-out industries; to support SMEs; and to provide infrastructure necessary for growing industries.

35. Some authors called this effect the *information effect* (Horiuchi and Sui 1993), *cowbell effect* (Higano 1986), *focal point* (Ito et al. 1988), and *pump primer* (Calomiris and Himmelberg 1995). They provide two types of credit: special interest rate (*Tokubetsu kinri*) and standard rate (*kijun kinri*). Horiuchi and Sui (1993) emphasized that the amount of credit supplied to an individual firm is very small compared to that from private banks. The share of the JDB loan was 3.5 percent in the first half of the 1950s, and it decreased to less than 2.0 percent in the latter half of the 1950s.

36. However, interestingly, Horiuchi and Sui (1993) argue that the target industries are not rapidly growing industries; rather those industries (e.g., electricity, shipping, and coal) are stagnant and declining industries. Calomiris and Himmelberg (1995) also mention this point. Coal mining received assistance for its spillover potential, but later it was supported to oversee the smooth exit of workers from the sector.

37. When we consider the relationship between the JDB and crowding in private finance, we also need to give some thought to the main bank system. Without considering the banking system as a whole, the lessons learned by emerging economics and less developed countries may be misleading. Some authors, such as Sheard (1989), argue that the main bank is a system that internalizes externalities among main banks through its interbank coordination to share benefits and costs of lending (no free ride on monitoring costs).

38. Horiuchi and Sui (1993) compared the investment made by the JDB-assisted SMEs (treatment group) and nonassisted SMEs (control group) during the period of 1964–1988. In this study, they found that the JDB lending increased investment in the treatment group, as compared to the control group. They also found that the treatment group SMEs gained private financial access after 3years of assistance from the JDB. This indicates that the JDB's assistance had the information effect. Their study also found the information effect is greater if there is no main bank for the SMEs. Based on this result, they argue that the JDB and the main banks are duplicating one another's role.

39. Vittas and Cho (1996, 286) compare lending to general machinery producers. They found that the JDB lending declined overtime. The lending in the late 1960s was between 3.7 and 5.3 percent, and it fell to 0.8 to 2.6 percent in the 1980s. On the other hand, in the same years, the private Industrial Bank of Japan did not experience the same drop; its lending remained the same.

In other words, the response of the JDB to the structural changes of the economy was flexible.

40. Okazaki (2001) described the details of the coordination.

41. Higano (1986) called this a *cowbell effect*.

42. One example is "the extraordinary measures law for the promotion of the machine industry" (*Kikai-kogyo Sinko Rinji Sochi Hou*) in 1956.

43. According to Horiuchi and Sui (1993), the information the JDB possesses is considered to be an insider view of both policymakers and individual firms, and thus it signaled meaning for private banks.

44. Calomiris and Himmelberg (1995) compared this process to the political system of the United States. In the United States, it is special lobbying groups that influence congressional committees.

45. According to Okazaki (2001), there were as many as 528 industrial associations in Japan in the 1970s.

46. Okazaki (2001) examined the Industrial Structure Council, which was established under the MITI (Ministry of International Trade and Industry) to look into the organizational aspects and historical origins of bureau pluralism.

47. Okazaki (2001, 336) mentioned this system as "a highly decentralized system." In his analysis, the system does not have any powerful center to coordinate lower-level work.

48. In 1948, the Japanese government established the Committee for the Economic Recovery Plan to make a long-term strategy for economic recovery. In this committee, there were four branches organized by industry: mining and manufacturing; food and necessities; international trade; and transportation. These branches were mostly chaired by presidents of industrial associations, such as the Japan Coal Association, Japan Iron and Steel Association, Japan Cotton Spinning Association, and Japan Chemical Industries Association.

49. When Tokunaga Hisatsugu joined MITI from Anpon (Economic Stabilization Agency), he received an invitation from the United States to study the productivity improvement movement (the United States bore all the transportation costs as well). Years later he became Vice Minister of MITI. The basic idea behind the productivity improvement movement was to share the fruit of profits among shareholders, labor, and consumers. When he looked back, Tokunaga mentioned, "I thought this is a good instrument to improve labor-management relationship, and promote its dissemination among private companies" (Tokunaga 1990, 1, translated from Japanese). He then established the JPC (Japan Productivity Center). The government assisted this movement for 3 years, spending 3 million Japanese yen every year.

50. This declaration was influenced by the Philadelphia declaration of ILO (International Labor Organization) in 1944.

51. As the World Bank (1993) discussed, the main player for inclusive growth in the region in the 1970s and 1980s was the manufacturing industry. The industrial sector provided employment opportunities and utilized rural unskilled labor in its production. During that period of rapid industrialization, industries in major cities attracted migrant workers.

52. On the flip side, one could say that this was a collective risk-sharing framework enjoyed by governments and private companies.

REFERENCES

Aoki, M. 2010. "'Individual' Social Capital, 'Social' Networks, and Their Linkages to Economic Game." *Annual World Bank Conference on Development Economics 2010, Global Lessons from East Asia and the Global Financial Crisis.* Washington, D.C.: World Bank.

——. 1988. *Information, Incentives, and Bargaining in the Japanese Economy.* New York: Cambridge University Press.

Birdsall, N., and R. H. Sabot. 1993. "Virtuous Circles: Human Capital Growth and Equity in East Asia." *Background Paper for The East Asian Miracle.* Washington, D.C.: World Bank. Policy Research Department.

Calomiris, Charles W., and Charles P. Himmelberg. 1995. "Government Credit Policy and Industrial Performance." *Policy Research Working Paper,* No. 1434. Washington D.C.: World Bank.

David, P. 1985. "Clio and the Economics of QWERTY." *American Economic Review* 75(2): 332–7.

Griffith-Jones, Stephany. 2014. *The Case and Role for Development Banks: The European Example.* Mimeo. Submitted to the IPD (Initiative of Policy Dialogue) taskforce meeting in Jordan.

Griffith-Jones, Stephany, and Jose Antonio Ocampo. 2014. "Helping Control Boom-Bust in Finance through Countercyclical Regulation." In *Towards Human Development: New Approaches to Macroeconomics and Inequality,* eds. Giovanni Andrea Cornia and Francis Stewart. Oxford: Oxford University Press.

Higano, Mikiya. 1986. "The Examination Power of Financial Institution (*Kinyu kikan no Shinsa Noryoku*)." Tokyo: University of Tokyo Press (in Japanese).

Horiuchi, Akiyoshi, and Masayuki Otaki. 1987. "Finance: Government Intervention and the Importance of Bank Lending". In *The Macroeconomic Analysis of the Japanese Economy,* eds. K. Hamada, M. Kuroda, and A. Horiuchi. Tokyo: University of Tokyo Press (in Japanese).

Horiuchi, Akiyoshi, and Qing-Yuan Sui. 1993. "Influence of the Japan Development Bank Loans on Corporate Investment Behaviour." *Journal of the Japanese and International Economies,* 7: 441–65.

Inaba, Syuzo. 1990. Minutes from the Fourth Seminar on Learning from Post-War Japan. Unpublished minutes of internal study meeting. Tokyo: Japan Development Bank. May 10. 1990 (in Japanese).

Ito. M., K. Kiyono, M. Okuno and K. Suzumura. 1988. Economic Analysis of Industrial Policies (Sangyo Seisaku no Keizai Bunseki). Tokyo: University of Tokyo Press (in Japanese).

Jaffee, Dwight, and J. E. Stiglitz. 1990. "Credit Rationing." *Handbook of Monetary Economics,* vol. 2, chap. 16, eds. B. M. Friedman and F. H. Hahn. Vancouver, B.C.: Elsevier.

JPC (Japan Productivity Center, *Syakai Keizai Seisansei Honbu*). 2005. *The 50 Years History of Productivity Movement.* Tokyo: JPC (in Japanese).

Kindleberger, C. P. 1978. Manias, Panics, and Crashes: A History of Financial Crises, New York: Basic Books, revised and enlarged, 1989, 3rd ed. 1996.

Kitayama, Toshiya. 2011. Institutional Development of Welfare State and Local Government. Tokyo: Yuhikaku (in Japanese).

Mahoney, J., and K. Thelen, eds. 2010. *Explaining Institutional Change: Ambiguity, Agency, and Power.* Cambridge: Cambridge University Press.

Matsuoka, Shunji. 2011. "Institutional Approach to Asian Regional Integration." In *The Development of Asian Regional Integration*, eds. S. Matsuoka and Hiroshi Katsumada. Tokyo: Keiso-shobo (In Japanese) .

——. 2009. "Capacity Development and Institutional Change in International Development Cooperation." *Journal of Asia Pacific Studies* 12: 43–73.

McKinnon, Ronald I. 1973. *Money and Capital in Economic Development.* Washington D.C.: Brookings Institution Press.

Nakayama, Sohei. 1990. Minutes from the Sixth Seminar on Learning from Post-War Japan. Unpublished minutes of internal study meeting. Tokyo: Japan Development Bank. October 1 (in Japanese).

North, D. C. 1990. *Institutions, Institutional Change and Economic Performance.* Cambridge: Cambridge University Press.

Ocampo, Jose Antonio, et al. 2012. "The Great Recession and the Developing World." *Development Cooperation in Times of Crisis.* New York: Columbia University Press.

OECF (Overseas Economic Cooperation Fund). 1991. "Issues Related to the World Bank's Approach to Structural Adjustment—Proposal from a Major Partner." *OECF Occasional Paper No. 1.* October. Tokyo.

Ogura, Seiritsu, and Naoyuki Yoshino. 1984. "Taxation and Fiscal Investment and Loan Program". In *The Japanese Industrial Policy*, eds. R. Komiya, M. Okuno, and K. Suzumura. Tokyo: University of Tokyo Press (in Japanese).

Okazaki, Tetsuji. 2001. "The Government-Firm Relationship in Postwar Japan: The Success and Failure of Bureau Pluralism." In *Rethinking of the East Asia Miracle*, eds. J. Stiglitz and S. Yusuf. New York: Oxford University Press.

——. 2009. "The Role of the Reconstruction Finance Bank (RFB)." In *Policy Finance in Japan*, vol. 1, eds. Hirofumi Uzawa and Takeda Haruhito. Tokyo: University of Tokyo Press (in Japanese).

Okazaki, Tetsuji, and Kazuo Ueda. 1995. "The Performance of Development Banks: The Case of the Reconstruction Finance Bank." *Journal of the Japanese and International Economies* 9(4): 486–504.

Okazaki, Tetsuji, and M. Okuno-Fujiwara. 1999. "Japan's Present-Day Economic System and Its Historical Origins." In *The Japanese Economic System and Its Historical Origins*, eds. T. Okazaki and M. Okuno-Fujiwara. New York: Oxford University Press.

Okita, Saburo. 1990. Minutes from the Fifth Seminar on Learning from Post-War Japan. Unpublished minutes of internal study meeting. Tokyo: Japan Development Bank. July 18. 1990 (in Japanese).

Okuda, Hidenobu, and Masaaki Kuroyanagi. 1998. *Development and Finance* (in Japanese). Tokyo: Nihonhyoronsha (in Japanese).

Olson, Mancur. 1982. *The Rise and Decline of Nations: Economic Growth, Stagflation, and Social Rigidities.* New Haven, Conn.: Yale University Press.

Ostrom, Elinor. 2005. *Understanding Institutional Diversity.* Princeton, N.J.: Princeton University Press.

Otake, Fumio. 2003. "Was There the Expansion of Income Inequality?" In *Income Inequality and Social Hierarchy in Japan* (in Japanese), eds. Y. Higuchi and the Ministry of Finance. Tokyo: Nihon Hyoronsha.

Reinhart, Carmen, Jacob Kirkegaard, and Belen Sbrancia. 2011. "Financial Repression Redux." *Finance and Development* 48:22–26.

RFB (Reconstruction Finance Bank, Fukko Kinyu Koko). 1950. *Retrospective of the RFB Loan* (in Japanese). Tokyo: RFB.

Sakakibara, Eisuke, and Robert A. Feldman. 1983. "The Japanese Financial System in Comparative Perspective." *Journal of Comparative Economics* 7: 1–24.

Sheard, Paul. 1989. "The Main Bank System and Corporate Monitoring and Control in Japan." *Journal of Economic Behavior and Organization* 11: 399–422.

Shimada, Go. 2015a. "Towards Community Resilience—The Role of Social Capital after Disasters." In *The Last Mile in Ending Extreme Poverty*, eds. Laurence Chandy, Hiroshi Kato, and Homi Kharas., Washington, D.C.: Brookings Institution.

——. 2015b. "The Economic Implications of Comprehensive Approach to Learning on Industrial Development (Policy and Managerial Capability Learning): A Case of Ethiopia." In *Industrial Policy and Economic Transformation in Africa*, eds. Akbar Noman and Joseph Stiglitz. New York: Columbia University Press.

——. 2015c. "What Are the Macroeconomic Impacts of Natural Disasters? The Impacts of Natural Disasters on the Growth Rate of Gross Prefectural Domestic Product in Japan." In *Growth Is Dead, Long Live Growth: The Quality of Economic Growth and Why It Matters*, eds. Lawrence Haddard, Hiroshi Kato, and Nicolas Miesel. Tokyo: JICA.

——. 2014. "A Quantitative Study of Social Capital in the Tertiary Sector of Kobe: Has Social Capital Promoted Economic Reconstruction since the Great Hanshin Awaji Earthquake?" JICA Research Institute Working Paper, No. 68.

——. 2009. "The Political Economy of the United Nations Development System: UN Reform Debates the 1969 Jackson Report to the Coherence Panel Report of 2006, and the Possibilities of Future UN Reform." *The United Nations Studies*, No. 10 (June 2009). Tokyo: The Japan Association for United Nations Study.

Shimada, Go, Toru Homma, and Hiromichi Murakami. 2013. "Industrial Development of Africa." In *Inclusive and Dynamic Development of Africa*, ed. Hiroshi Kato., JICA. Tokyo: JICA.

Stiglitz, Joseph E. 1994. *Whither Socialism?* Cambridge, Mass.: MIT Press.

Stiglitz, Joseph E., and Andrew Weiss. 1981. "Credit Rationing in Markets with Imperfect Information." *The American Economic Review* 71(3): 393–410.

Stiglitz, Joseph E., and Bruce Greenwald. 2014. *Creating Learning Society—A New Approach to Growth, Development and Social Progress*. New York: Columbia University Press.

Stiglitz, Joseph E., and Marilou Uy. 1996. "Financial Markets, Public Policy, and the East Asian Miracle." *The World Bank Research Observer* 11(2): 249–76.

Sydow, J., and J. Koch. 2009. "Organizational Path Dependence: Opening the Black Box." *Academy of Management Review* 34(4): 689–709.

Takeda, Haruhito. 2009. "Introduction." In *Policy Finance in Japan*, vol. 1, eds. Hirofumi Uzawa and Takeda Haruhito. Tokyo: University of Tokyo Press (in Japanese).

Tanimura, Yutaka. 1981. 'The Development of Japanese Economy and the Roles of Financial and Monetary Policies." Abstract from Seminar in China held in May. unpublished minutes from the the Seminar on Learning from Post-War Japan. Tokyo: Japan Development Bank (in Japanese).

Tokunaga, Hisatsugu. 1990. Minutes from the Third Seminar on Learning from Post-War Japan. Unpublished minutes of internal study meeting. Tokyo: Japan Development Bank. April 6. (in Japanese).

Ueno, Hiroya. 1978. *Economic System in Japan* ("Nihon no keizai seido"). Tokyo: Nihon Keizai Shinbunsha (in Japanese).

Van Driel, Hugo, and Wilfred Dolfsma. 2009. "Path Dependence, Initial Conditions, and Routines in Organizations: The Toyota Production System Re-examined." *Journal of Organizational Change Management* 22(1): 49–72.

Vittas, Dimitri, and Yoon Je Cho. 1996. "Credit Policies: Lessons from Japan and Korea." *The World Bank Research Observer* 11(2): 277–98.

World Bank. 1989. *World Development Report 1989*. New York: Oxford University Press.

——. 1993. *The East Asian Miracle: Economic Growth and Public Policy*. Oxford: Oxford University Press.

CHAPTER 7

Development Banks and Industrial Finance

THE INDIAN EXPERIENCE AND ITS LESSONS

Deepak Nayyar

The object of this chapter is to analyze the role of development finance institutions in the industrialization of the developing world since 1950, but with a focus on India to outline the story, evaluate the experience, and draw lessons that might be valuable for other countries that are latecomers to industrialization. Section I situates the discussion in its wider context, to sketch a picture of the catch-up in industrialization on the part of developing countries, in which the supportive role of governments, even if in different forms, was necessary if not critical everywhere. Section II considers the logic of industrial policy in terms of means and ends, at the macro, meso, and micro level, to explain the rationale for development banks. Section III outlines the evolution of development finance institutions in India, from the late 1940s to the early 2000s, and their striking downsizing thereafter. Section IV discusses the macroeconomic significance of these institutions in the financing of industrialization in India, the factors underlying their recent decline, and the alternative sources of industrial finance that emerged. Section V assesses the performance of India's development finance institutions to highlight the lessons that can be learned from their successes and failures. Section VI provides an international perspective to compare this Indian experience with that of other late industrializers.

I. CATCH-UP IN INDUSTRIALIZATION

The second half of the twentieth century and the first decade of the twenty-first century witnessed rapid industrialization in the developing world, although its spread was uneven between regions and countries.

This catch-up in industrialization began in the early 1950s and gathered momentum in the early 1970s. Structural changes in the composition of output and employment, which led to a decline in the share of agriculture with an increase in the share of industry and services, were an important factor underlying the process.

There was a dramatic transformation in just four decades from 1970 to 2010 (Nayyar 2013). The share of developing countries in world manufacturing value added jumped from one-twelfth to one-third in constant prices and from one-eighth to two-fifths in current prices. Similarly, their share in world exports of manufactures rose from one-twelfth to two-fifths. Industrialization also led to pronounced changes in the composition of their trade as the share of primary commodities and resource-based products fell while the share of manufactures, particularly medium-technology and high-technology goods, rose in both exports and imports.

This industrialization was, however, very uneven between regions: much of it was concentrated in Asia while Latin America stayed roughly where it was and Africa fell further behind. The spread of industrialization was even more unequal between countries within regions. There was a high degree of concentration among a few: Argentina, Brazil, Chile, and Mexico in Latin America; China, India, Indonesia, Korea, Malaysia, Taiwan, Thailand, and Turkey in Asia; and Egypt and South Africa in Africa. In fact, the economic significance of these countries, termed the *Next-14,* was overwhelming in terms of their size (reflected in GDP and population), their engagement with the world economy (reflected in trade, investment, and migration), and industrialization (reflected in manufactured exports and industrial production), as a proportion of aggregates for the developing world (Nayyar 2013). There was also enormous economic diversity within the Next-14. Despite their apparent diversity, it is possible to group them into clusters based on similarities in terms of geography, size, economic characteristics, and development models. They had even more in common across clusters in three factors that put them on the path to industrialization: initial conditions, enabling institutions, and supportive governments. It needs to be said that these factors were just as important for the earlier latecomers to industrialization that are now industrialized countries, whether Japan in Asia or Finland in Europe.

The observed outcomes in terms of manufacturing output and industrial production were significantly attributable to development strategies and economic policies in the postcolonial era that laid the essential foundations for industrialization in countries that were latecomers. In retrospect, it is clear that the role of the state in creating initial conditions, developing institutions, and making strategic interventions was central to the process in the Next-14 (Nayyar 2013). Indeed, in the pursuit of industrialization, the role of government was critical almost everywhere in the developing world (Evans 1995; Wade 1990; Lall 1997; Amsden 2001), although there were differences in the nature and purpose of the role. For countries that stressed markets and openness, it was about minimizing market failure. The emphasis was on getting prices right and buying the skills or technologies needed for industrialization. For countries that stressed state intervention with moderated, calibrated, or controlled openness, it was about minimizing government failure. The emphasis was on getting institutions right and building the skills or technologies needed for industrialization. Of course, this role was not defined once and for all but evolved with industrialization and development (Bhaduri and Nayyar 1996; Nayyar 1997).

In the earlier stages, it was about creating the initial conditions by building a physical infrastructure with government investment in energy, transportation, and communications and in the development of human resources through education. In the later stages of industrialization, there was a change in the nature and degree of this role, which had three dimensions: functional, institutional, and strategic. Functional intervention sought to correct for market failure, whether specific or general. Institutional intervention sought to govern the market by setting the rules of the game for players in the market, to create frameworks for regulating markets and institutions to monitor the functioning of markets. Strategic intervention sought to guide the market interlinked across sectors, not only through industrial policy and technology policy but also through the use of exchange rates and interest rates to attain the long-term objectives of industrialization.

The enabling framework to support or foster industrialization in these countries was built around the late 1950s or early 1960s. The timing was not a coincidence. It was the beginning of the postcolonial era in Asia and Africa, and the rise of development planning as an ideology surfaced almost everywhere, including Latin America. In the quest for catch-up, industrialization was the common aspiration. The foundations of the institutional framework were put in place by proactive governments not only in China and India, but also in Argentina, Brazil, Chile, and Mexico as well as Indonesia, Malaysia, South Korea, Taiwan, Thailand, and

Turkey, with Egypt doing much the same (Amsden 2001). Such frameworks were all about industrial promotion and industrial investment, whether through the use of industrial policy, trade policy, and technology policy or through the establishment of planning offices, industrial boards, and financial institutions. In this spectrum, development banks that provided long-term financing for investment in the industrial sector were particularly important. The object was to create production capabilities, investment capabilities, and innovation capabilities in domestic firms with countries opting for different emphases on the public sector and the private sector (Lall 1990). The creation and evolution of such institutions were integral parts of the process of industrialization and development (Chang 2007). Enabling institutions were not simply about secure property rights and low transaction costs as orthodoxy suggests (North 1990). Obviously, it was not about policy regimes alone. In the early stages, the role of the state was critical in creating enabling institutions that supported the process of industrialization among these latecomers, even if future transition paths turned out to be different.

II. INDUSTRIAL POLICY AND DEVELOPMENT FINANCE

Industrial policy means different things to different people. For some, it includes a wide range of interventions: from industrial promotion, tariff protection, public investment, and R&D support, through regional policies and government procurement, to favoring promising industries or creating skilled workforces, and so on (Reich 1982; Pinder 1982). For others, it is a summary term for interventions by governments that are meant to develop, or retrench, particular industries in a national economy in order to maintain global competitiveness (Johnson 1984). For yet others, it is forms of intervention that are selective or discriminatory, directed toward specific regions, industries, or firms (Lindbeck 1981; Landesmann 1992). In such a continuing spectrum, it can also be more precisely defined as policy aimed at particular industries, or firms, to achieve outcomes that are perceived by the state to be efficient for the economy as a whole (Chang 1996). It would serve little purpose to enter into a discussion on what is meant by industrial policy. In any case, there exists an extensive literature on the subject, which extends to the related domains of strategic trade policy in the world of economic theory and strategic technology policy in the world of economic practice. But it is important to recognize that the conception and design of industrial policy are characterized by specificities in space and in time, because it is shaped both by the context and by the conjuncture. Hence, the means can differ across space and over time. However, the ends are always about outcomes in industrialization that would not be possible through a reliance on markets alone and require state intervention.

Industrial policy, in some form or other, is an integral part of starting, and also sustaining, the process of industrialization in countries that are latecomers to development. It is essential for creating some initial conditions, and it is necessary for creating enabling institutions. Industrial policy is the basic foundation for the supportive role of governments, whether as leaders or catalysts. Such intervention can and does come in different forms at different stages of development. But industrial policy always matters, because industrialization is about learning by doing. The counterfactual validates this proposition. For some countries, in the past, deindustrialization was about unlearning by not doing. For many countries, in the present, the absence of industrialization might have long-term consequences through hysteresis.

Success or failure, in terms of outcomes, depends upon the nature and the quality of intervention. Thus, industrial policy is no panacea: there are benefits and there are costs. In countries that are success stories, the benefits are far greater than the costs, while in countries that are disaster stories the costs are far greater than the benefits. However, outcomes are not binary, and often outcomes are a mix of success and failure that changes over time. Moreover, in the process of learning to industrialize, the costs surface earlier while the benefits accrue after a time lag. It follows that industrial policy must be assessed not at a specific time but over a period of time. Of course, the logic of industrial policy has both static and dynamic aspects, but the critical importance of intertemporal considerations in industrialization makes the latter much more significant. The real question, then, is how to make industrial policy more effective for intended outcomes. At the same time, the risks associated with industrial policy must be balanced against the risks associated with no industrial policy. After all, both government failure and market failure are facts of life.

By setting aside the discourse on the meaning, it is possible to think of industrial policy at the macro level, meso level, and micro level. This blurs the distinction between *general* and *selective* interventions, but it reflects observed realities in practice.

At a macro level, for the economy as a whole, governments seek to foster industrialization through industrial protection and import substitution to manufacture for the domestic market or industrial promotion through export orientation to manufacture for the world market. The stress on the former in large countries is motivated by the object of learning to industrialize, not only in consumer goods but also in intermediate goods and capital goods so that exports are the end of the market expansion path for firms. The emphasis on the latter in small countries is also motivated by the object of learning to industrialize, but with a focus on labor-intensive manufactured consumer goods, so that exports are the beginning of the market expansion path for firms. In both groups, some late industrializers use a mix of trade policies and exchange rates for strategic purposes. Trade policy is characterized by an asymmetry, as it is open for the export sector but restrictive for other sectors, while the exchange rate is undervalued for long periods, so that domestic industry becomes competitive in the world market for manufactured goods.

At a meso level, for particular industries, government intervention seeks to develop sunrise industries or retrench sunset industries. In doing so, some late industrializers use monetary policy in a strategic manner, with differential interest rates for different industries to influence the allocation of scarce investible resources. This practice was perfected in Japan and South Korea. However, such a strategic use of interest rates is far more difficult, if not impossible, in countries that are integrated into international financial markets through capital account liberalization, but remains feasible for countries that retain capital controls. Of course, strategic government support for selected industries is possible through other policy instruments, provided these are not incompatible with World Trade Organization (WTO) obligations or rules. Multilateral rules have certainly diminished this policy space, though some degrees of freedom remain.

At a micro level, for selected firms, government support in the domestic market, or in the world market, seeks to nurture their managerial or technological capabilities, or encourage their horizontal and vertical expansion, so that they are able to realize scale economies not only in production but also in marketing to develop global brand names and create large international firms. The underlying objective is to pick winners and create champions, as Japan and South Korea did, or as China and Brazil are attempting to do. Reality is far more complex, and it could slip into rents and patronage. Its success depends upon the nature of the state and the effectiveness of administrative systems. This, in turn, requires institutionalized control mechanisms.

The economic logic of development banks is simple: in countries that are latecomers to industrialization, capital markets are imperfect. Therefore, new firms, which seek to enter the industrial sector, find it exceedingly difficult to obtain finance for their initial investment, let alone to cover their losses of the learning period, at interest rates that are roughly comparable with the social rate of discount. The problem is exacerbated when such investments are characterized by lumpiness and returns accrue only after a gestation lag. In these circumstances, firms might underinvest, or fail to invest, in the creation of manufacturing capacities that require learning capital. Where capital markets are fragmented, most financing is self-financing, because new entrepreneurs or firms simply do not have access to capital at any price—and even when they do, the interest rates may be too high to make the investment worthwhile. The problem is far more acute for long-term finance where there are indivisibilities in the capital needed by new firms, as the initial losses are high and the learning period is long. It needs to be said that this set of constraints is an essential part of the rationale underlying the infant industry argument (Corden 1974; Chang 2002).

Latecomers to industrialization create development banks essentially to meet these financing needs of pioneering firms in a nonexistent or infant manufacturing sector, which are not met by capital markets or commercial banks because, in their calculus, the risk is too great. In effect, development banks represent a socialization of risk, where the risks associated with financing industrialization in its early stages are borne by society rather than by individuals. Insofar as social objectives diverge from private objectives, it is clearly justifiable to accept lower rates of return for development banks in the short run or medium term, because these rates of return are much higher in the long term for patient capital with the benefit of inside information. In fact, it is plausible to suggest that development finance institutions could compensate society for costs incurred in the learning period by using their influence in governments to appropriate rents and solving coordination failures that are characteristic of markets.

III. EVOLUTION OF DEVELOPMENT FINANCE IN INDIA

The rationale for development finance in India was much the same as it was in other countries that were latecomers to development, shaped by the aspiration to catch up through industrialization. The colonial era, characterized by open economies and unregulated markets, had led to deindustrialization and underdevelopment. Thus, at the time of independence, the situation was simply not conducive: the rate of domestic savings and the level of investment were both very low, the financial sector was underdeveloped, and the central bank accounted for almost one-half of the financial assets in the economy (Goldsmith 1983). The corresponding share of commercial banks was about one-third, but they could not perform any significant role in financing industrialization, because of the lumpiness, risks, and gestation lags associated with investment in manufacturing or infrastructure at the time. The problem was compounded by the mismatches in liquidity and maturity that were inevitable if banks were to provide industrial finance. The accumulation of their own capital among domestic industrialists was just not enough, while there was almost no market for long-term finance, such as debt (let alone equity), that could have been a source of finance for firms. Hence, the creation of institutions to provide long-term development finance for manufacturing firms, or the industrial sector, was almost an imperative.

In retrospect, it is possible to discern three phases in the evolution of these institutions in India: from the late 1940s to the mid-1960s, during the 1980s, and from the late 1990s to the early 2000s.

The first phase, which kick-started industrialization, was the most significant. It had three components: long-term lending institutions that were nationwide, institutions for the states, and what came to be described as investment institutions.

The term-lending financial institutions were created at different times. The Industrial Finance Corporation of India (IFCI) was established in 1948, through a legislative act of parliament, to provide long-term credit for medium and large industrial enterprises in the corporate and cooperative sectors. The Industrial Credit and Investment Corporation of India (ICICI) was established in 1955, under the then Companies Act of 1913, to promote industries in the private sector and meet their foreign exchange needs in investment, with support from the World Bank. The Industrial Development Bank of India (IDBI) was established in 1964, through a legislative act of parliament, as the nodal financial institution to provide long-term finance for industrial development and coordinate such lending activities in conformity with national priorities. Its stipulated role extended beyond finance to refinancing loans, technology development, and banking services, with an advisory role on projects, management, and restructuring. The essential objective of these three national institutions was to provide long-term finance for private investment in the industrial sector. In turn, their primary sources of funds were financing from the Reserve Bank of India on concessional terms and bonds guaranteed by the government at lower-than-market interest rates that could be held by commercial banks to meet their statutory liquidity-ratio requirements.

During the same period, institutions were also created to meet the needs of states in a federal system. State Financial Corporations (SFCs) were established in the 1950s, by creating an enabling institutional framework through an act of national parliament in 1951, to provide long-term finance for small and medium enterprises in the manufacturing sector of respective states that could catalyze investment, generate employment, and spread industry. In pursuit of the same objectives, State Industrial Development Corporations (SIDCs) were established in states, under the national Companies Act of 1956, to promote small and medium-size manufacturing firms, with assistance in the form of rupee loans, debenture subscriptions, underwriting shares, venture capital, equipment leasing, and merchant banking. The primary object of both sets of institutions was to make industrial finance accessible for small and medium enterprises and to foster the geographical spread of industrialization. In turn, these institutions received funds from their respective governments on concessional terms. In fact, state governments were the sole owners of the SIDCs.

The third component, investment institutions, was unusual in this role. It began with the nationalization of insurance businesses in 1956, which led to the creation of the Life Insurance Corporation of India (LIC) that was wholly owned by the government. The object was to make life insurance accessible to rural areas and poor people across the country. The Unit Trust of India (UTI) came next, established in 1964 through a legislative act of parliament as a mutual fund. The object was to provide small savers with investment opportunities. The General Insurance Corporation (GIC) was the last addition to this cluster in 1973, when it was formed as a holding company with four subsidiaries in specific insurance businesses that were already nationalized. The object was to enlarge access to different forms of insurance. These institutions raised finances by mobilizing savings of households, spreading insurance habits, and opening up avenues for higher returns on the financial savings of individuals. Obviously, their sources of finance, either households or individuals, were mostly small savers. The provision of long-term development finance, in the form of loans or equity, emerged as a secondary objective for these institutions, almost as a corollary. For investment institutions, the nature of their business resolved the problem of maturity mismatches, while their ownership by the government made it a potential source of industrial finance.

The second phase was concentrated in the 1980s. It was characterized by the creation of refinancing institutions and sector-specific or specialized institutions. Their object extended beyond finance for the industrial sector and beyond long-term lending to manufacturing firms to address needs that were not recognized earlier or surfaced at later stages of development. The refinancing institutions created were few. The National Bank for Agriculture and Rural Development (NABARD) was established in 1981, through a legislative act of parliament, as an apex institution at the national level that would provide credit for agriculture, rural industrialization, village industries, handicrafts, and other economic activities to promote development in rural areas. Until then, the Reserve Bank of India and the Agriculture Refinance Corporation had performed this role. The National Housing Bank (NHB) was established in 1988, through a legislative act of parliament, as a wholly owned subsidiary of the Reserve Bank of India, to promote specialized housing finance institutions and to mobilize resources for housing loans. Apart from its refinancing role, it was also the regulator of housing finance companies. The Small Industries Development Bank of India (SIDBI) was established in 1989, through a legislative act of parliament, as a wholly owned subsidiary of IDBI, to provide finance for small-scale firms in the industrial sector and for coordinating the functions of institutions engaged in similar activities (Reserve Bank of India 2004).

However, the sector-specific, specialized institutions created were many more. The Housing and Urban Development Corporation (HUDCO) was created in 1970 to finance public-sector housing but soon diversified into financing cooperative and corporate projects. The Rural Electrification Corporation (REC) was also created in 1970 to finance projects for electricity in rural and semiurban India. However, most such institutions began life in the 1980s. The Export-Import Bank of India (EXIM Bank) was set up in 1981, through a legislative act of parliament, wholly owned by the government, to provide credit for the export sector and promote international trade. In 1986, the Shipping Credit and Investment Corporation of India (SCICI), the Power Finance Corporation (PFC), and the Indian Railways Finance Corporation (IRFC) were created to provide institutional finance dedicated to the shipping, power, and railway sectors, respectively. Development finance institutions were also created for renewable energy in 1987 and tourism in 1989 (Reserve Bank of India 2004).

The third phase, from the early 1990s to the mid-2000s, which coincided with reform and deregulation in the financial sector, witnessed a profound transformation of development finance institutions in India. Consequently, a decade later, in the mid-2010s, the picture is strikingly different.

This change is attributable, in large part, to financial sector reforms that began in the late 1990s and gathered momentum thereafter. Except for IFCI, development banks were turned into commercial banks. ICICI made the transition with success, but IDBI did not. Investment institutions also progressively withdrew from this domain. Thus, long-term lending to the industrial sector was stopped by ICICI in 2001–02, IDBI in 2004–05, and UTI in 2003–04. Such lending by IFCI and GIC dropped to very low levels from 2003 to 2004. SFCs and SIDCs also stopped disbursements in 2003–04.

It is not as if alternative mechanisms were created to fill this void. The two new institutions created were dedicated to infrastructure. The Infrastructure Development Finance Company (IDFC) was incorporated in 1997 as a private company to foster the growth of private capital flows for infrastructure financing, on a commercially viable basis, with a mandate to lead such capital into infrastructural sectors. The India Infrastructure Financing Company Limited (IIFCL) was incorporated in 2006, as a wholly owned government company, to provide long-term finance for viable infrastructure projects in transportation, energy, water, sanitation, communication, and commercial infrastructure. Its resources come from borrowing in the domestic capital market, with some access to lower-cost funds in the form of government-guaranteed bonds on which interest is tax-free for bondholders, and it accords priority to public-private-partnership projects. This downsizing has led to a sharp reduction in the role of development banking. The only remaining term lending financial institution is SIDBI, and the only investment institution that still lends to the industrial sector is LIC. Interestingly enough, their lending activities are profitable. The refinancing institutions— NABARD, NHB, and SIDBI—continue in business and are profitable. Among the sector-specific institutions, EXIM Bank, REC, PFC, IRFC, and HUDCO are active and profitable, but the others are less active and less profitable (Reserve Bank of India 2004).

IV. FINANCING OF INDUSTRIALIZATION

The evolution of development finance is reflected in the changing role of these government-led institutions in financing industrialization. Table 7.1 presents evidence on total disbursements, disaggregated into term lending institutions, investment institutions, and state institutions, during the period from 1970–71 to 2012–13. Of course, such lending began much earlier, but total disbursements were modest at Rs. 0.8 billion per annum during the second half of the 1960s. These total disbursements increased from Rs. 2 billion in 1970–71 to Rs. 14 billion in 1980–81, Rs. 146 billion in 1990–91, and Rs. 742 billion in 2000–01, but dropped to Rs. 211 billion in 2005–06 and recovered to Rs. 888 billion in 2012–13. The trends emerge more clearly from figure 7.1, which plots the time-series data on total disbursements and their disaggregated components. It also shows that total disbursements experienced a modest increase during the 1970s, a rapid expansion during the 1980s, and a phenomenal growth during the 1990s, followed by a sharp decline during the first half of the 2000s, to recover thereafter and exceed their earlier peak level but in nominal terms.

The relative importance of different institutions changed over time. During the three decades from 1970–71 to 2000–01, the term lending institutions (IFCI, IDBI, and ICICI) accounted for about two-thirds to three-fourths of total disbursements. Until 1989–90, the state institutions (SFCs and SIDCs) and the investment institutions (LIC, GIC, and UTI) had roughly equal shares in the remaining disbursements, but the share of the former declined rapidly thereafter, as disbursements by SIDBI, which started lending in 1990–91, rose steadily. The precipitous decline of term lending institutions, which began in 2001–02, was complete by 2005–06, as their disbursements came down to negligible levels. Total disbursements recovered starting in 2006–07 and were somewhat above their earlier peak levels by 2008–09, but this recovery was attributable almost entirely to disbursements by SIDBI and LIC.

Trends in total disbursements at current prices might exaggerate the growth in such lending by development finance institutions. But it is difficult to find an appropriate deflator to construct a time series at constant prices. However, it is far simpler to normalize the absolute numbers through a comparison with appropriate macroeconomic variables. Table 7.2 outlines the trends in total disbursements, during the period from 1970–71 to 2012–13, as a percentage of gross domestic fixed capital

Table 7.1A Trends in Disbursements by Development Finance Institutions in India (Rs. Billions): 1970–71 to 2000–2001

Year	IFCI	ICICI	IDBI	SIDBI	LIC, GIC, and UTI	SFCs and SIDCs	Total
1970–71	0.2	0.3	0.6	—	0.1	0.4	1.6
1971–72	0.2	0.3	0.8	—	0.1	0.5	1.9
1972–73	0.3	0.4	0.8	—	0.2	0.6	2.3
1973–74	0.3	0.4	1.4	—	0.3	0.8	3.2
1974–75	0.4	0.5	2.0	—	0.6	1.1	4.6
1975–76	0.3	0.6	2.2	—	0.3	1.3	4.7
1976–77	0.5	0.7	3.4	—	0.5	1.4	6.5
1977–78	0.6	0.9	4.1	—	0.6	1.5	7.7
1978–79	0.7	1.1	6.2	—	0.5	2.0	10.5
1979–80	0.9	1.4	7.5	—	1.9	2.7	14.4
1980–81	1.1	1.9	12.6	—	1.6	3.7	20.9
1981–82	1.7	2.6	15.0	—	2.3	5.1	26.7
1982–83	2.0	2.8	16.0	—	2.0	6.1	28.9
1983–84	2.2	3.3	19.8	—	3.6	6.7	35.6
1984–85	2.7	3.9	22.0	—	5.1	8.0	41.7
1985–86	4.0	4.8	28.0	—	9.0	9.7	55.5
1986–87	4.5	7.0	32.6	—	9.4	12.2	65.7
1987–88	6.6	7.7	40.0	—	11.5	13.9	79.7
1988–89	10.0	10.9	33.8	—	16.1	15.3	86.1
1989–90	11.2	13.6	51.2	—	16.5	17.0	109.5
1990–91	15.7	19.7	45.0	18.4	28.4	18.7	145.9
1991–92	16.0	23.5	57.7	20.3	42.1	22.2	181.8
1992–93	17.3	33.2	67.1	21.5	94.0	22.5	255.6
1993–94	21.6	44.1	81.0	26.7	78.8	22.6	274.8
1994–95	28.4	68.8	106.7	33.9	65.1	29.3	332.2
1995–96	45.6	71.2	107.0	48.0	65.0	41.5	378.3
1996–97	51.6	111.8	114.7	45.8	71.2	42.8	437.9
1997–98	56.5	158.1	151.7	52.4	86.1	35.3	540.1
1998–99	48.2	192.3	144.7	62.9	96.5	38.0	582.6
1999–2000	32.7	258.4	170.6	69.6	127.6	35.8	694.7
2000–01	21.6	316.6	174.8	64.4	127.9	36.4	741.7

formation and value added in the manufacturing sector. It shows that the macroeconomic significance of lending by development finance institutions increased rapidly over time. As a proportion of gross fixed capital formation in the manufacturing sector, total disbursements rose from 10 percent in 1970–71 to 30 percent in 1980–81, 36 percent in 1990–91, and 49 percent in 2000–01, but fell sharply to 6 percent in 2005–06 and

Table 7.1B Trends in Disbursements by Development Finance Institutions in India (Rs. Billions): 2001–02 to 2012–13

Year	IFCI	ICICI	IDBI	SIDBI	LIC, GIC, and UTI	SFCs and SIDCs	Total
2001–02	10.7	258.3	110.1	59.2	116.5	17.5	572.3
2002–03	17.8	—	66.1	67.9	79.0	27.0	257.8
2003–04	2.8	—	49.9	44.1	169.9	8.6	275.3
2004–05	0.9	—	61.8	61.9	89.7	—	214.3
2005–06	1.9	—	—	91.0	117.7	—	210.6
2006–07	5.5	—	—	102.3	277.6	—	385.4
2007–08	22.8	—	—	151.0	284.6	—	458.4
2008–09	33.1	—	—	283.2	623.6	—	939.9
2009–10	60.5	—	—	319.4	537.6	—	917.5
2010–11	84.0	—	—	388.0	401.4	—	873.4
2011–12	56.8	—	—	418.1	519.7	—	994.6
2012–13	15.0	—	—	406.8	466.5	—	888.3

Source: Reserve Bank of India, *Handbook of Statistics on the Indian Economy* and *Report on Currency and Finance*, various annual issues.

Note: The figures in the rightmost column are the sum total of actual disbursements by IFCI, ICICI, IDBI, SIDBI, LIC, GIC, UTI, SFCs, and SIDCs. Prior to 1990–91, SIDBI was part of IDBI. In the period from 2003–04 to 2012–13, an overwhelming proportion of the lending of LIC, GIC, and UTI was accounted for by LIC. It is worth noting that GIC's disbursements from 2003–04 to 2012–13, on average, were only 4 percent of the disbursements by LIC.

recovered just a little to reach 14 percent by 2012–13. It is worth noting that these levels were much higher as a proportion of gross fixed capital formation in manufacturing in the private sector and jumped from about 25 percent in 1970–71 to 75 percent in 2000–01. As a proportion of value added in manufacturing, total disbursements rose from 3 percent in 1970–71 to 9 percent in 1980–81, 20 percent in 1990–91, and 24 percent in 2000–01, but fell sharply to 4 percent in 2005–06 and recovered only a little to 7 percent in 2012–13. Of course, observations at 10-year intervals might conceal as much as they reveal.

The trends emerge more clearly from figure 7.2, which plots the same time-series data. It shows that total disbursements as a percentage of gross fixed capital formation in the manufacturing sector rose continuously from the early 1970s to the mid-1990s, with short dips in the mid-1970s and early 1980s, but dropped significantly in the late 1990s to reach their peak level in 2000–01, and plummeted thereafter to their lowest level in 2005–06, with a modest recovery in subsequent years to far lower levels at par with those in the mid-1970s. Total disbursements as a percentage of value added in manufacturing reveal an almost identical trend over

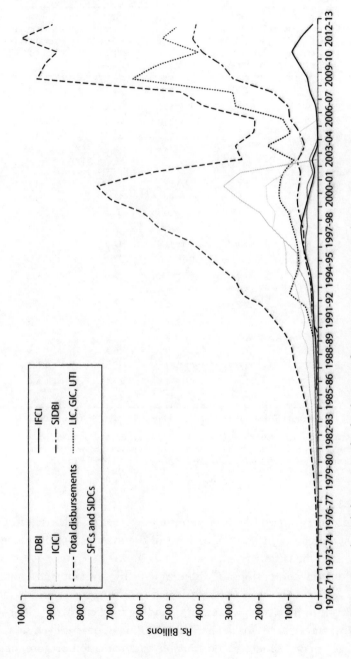

Figure 7.1 Trends in disbursements by development finance institutions in India: 1970–71 to 2012–13

Source: Table 7.1.

Table 7.2 Macroeconomic Significance of Lending by Development Finance Institutions, 1970–71 to 2012–13

Year	Total Disbursements to GFCF in Manufacturing Sector (%)	Total Disbursements to Value Added in Manufacturing Sector (%)	Year	Total Disbursements to GFCF in Manufacturing Sector (%)	Total Disbursements to Value Added in Manufacturing Sector (%)
1970–71	9.4	2.6	1991–92	36.6	19.5
1971–72	10.9	2.8	1992–93	44.3	23.6
1972–73	11.0	3.1	1993–94	43.7	21.9
1973–74	14.5	3.5	1994–95	46.6	21.5
1974–75	14.1	3.9	1995–96	31.5	19.5
1975–76	11.3	3.9	1996–97	30.4	19.9
1976–77	16.0	4.8	1997–98	34.1	23.5
1977–78	16.5	5.1	1998–99	34.8	23.3
1978–79	19.9	6.1	1999–2000	45.2	25.6
1979–80	27.0	7.3	2000–01	48.9	24.2
1980–81	29.8	9.4	2002–03	17.7	7.4
1981–82	26.9	10.3	2003–04	14.5	7.0
1982–83	25.9	10.2	2004–05	7.4	4.7
1983–84	26.4	10.6	2005–06	6.1	4.0
1984–85	25.0	11.0	2006–07	8.6	6.1
1985–86	29.2	13.2	2007–08	8.3	6.3
1986–87	31.3	14.2	2008–09	20.7	11.5
1987–88	35.5	15.1	2009–10	16.2	9.9
1988–89	30.8	13.9	2010–11	12.8	8.1
1989–90	31.9	14.6	2011–12	14.7	8.0
1990–91	35.8	17.0	2012–13	14.0	6.7

Source: Table 1 and Central Statistical Organisation, *National Accounts Statistics*, India.

Note: The percentages have been calculated from figures on total disbursements in Table 1 with figures on gross fixed capital formation and value added in manufacturing at current prices from Central Statistical Organisation, *National Accounts Statistics*, India, annual issues.

the four decades. Indeed, the two graphs follow a very similar trajectory, but for the difference in levels of each set of proportions and dampened fluctuations in the latter.

The industrial composition of disbursements by development finance institutions in India also deserves consideration, although evidence available on this is limited to the three term lending financial institutions—IFCI, IDBI, and ICICI—for the period 1980–81 to 2002–03. Even so, the picture that emerges should be a reasonable approximation because these three institutions accounted for almost two-thirds of total disbursements

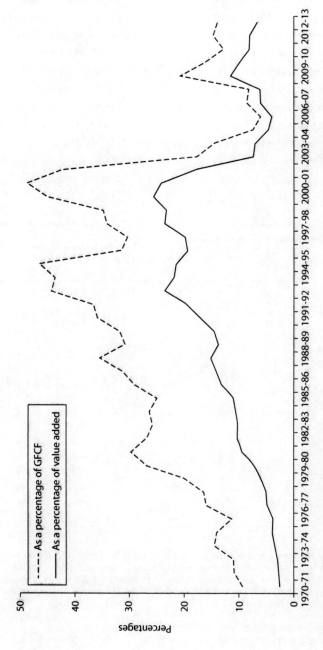

Figure 7.2 **Total disbursements of development finance institutions as a percentage of gross fixed capital formation and value added in manufacturing; 1970-71 to 2012-13**

Source: Table 7.2.

during the 1980s and 1990s, while total disbursements peaked in 2000–01. This evidence is presented in table 7.3 for the major industrial sectors, as annual averages for 5-year periods so that the statistics are kept within manageable proportions. It shows a steady decline in the share of resource-based manufacturing and cement from more than one-fourth in the first half of the 1980s to one-tenth in the early 2000s. The share of metals and metal manufacturing registered an increase from one-sixth in the 1980s to one-eighth in the 1990s, except for the decline in the early 2000s. There was little change in the share of machinery and transport equipment, broadly the capital goods sector, at about one-eighth, although it dropped in the early 2000s. The trend in the share of chemicals, fertilizers, and pharmaceuticals was an inverted U with a peak level around one-fifth in

Table 7.3 Composition of Disbursements by Development Finance Institutions in India: 1980–81 to 2002–03 (Annual averages in percent)

	Industry	1980-81 to 1984-85	1985-86 to 1989-90	1990-91 to 1994-95	1995-96 to 1999-00	2000-01 to 2002-03
1	Resource base manufacturing*	27.6	18.3	21.2	14.7	10.6
2	Chemicals, fertilizers and pharmaceuticals	13.6	17.2	20.4	16.1	11.7
3	Refineries and oil	0.0	0.0	0.8	9.0	7.7
4	Cement	6.4	5.9	5.8	4.3	3.4
5	Metal and metal manufacturing	7.6	9.4	13.3	12.8	9.4
6	Machinery and transport equipment	11.8	11.1	12.4	12.4	8.3
7	Infrastructure†	6.7	9.8	8.0	14.1	15.9
8	Services‡	15.5	16.1	8.0	9.8	23.7
9	Other industries	10.8	12.2	10.1	6.8	9.3
10	Total above	100.0	100.0	100.0	100.0	100.0
11	Total disbursements in Rs. billion	(95.5)	(247.9)	(619.3)	(1704.8)	(701.5)

Source: IDBI, Report on Development Banking in India, various years.

Note: Development finance institutions refer to IFCI, ICICI, and IDBI. The annual averages for the 5-year periods have been calculated from the annual figures on disbursements by sector. However, for the period from 2000–01 to 2002–03, the annual averages have been calculated for the triennium. The total disbursement figures in this table do not correspond to total disbursement figures in the other tables and graphs because the sources are different and the figures in this table relate only to the three term lending institutions.
*Resource base manufacturing includes food, paper, rubber, textiles and jute.
†Infrastructure includes electricity generation, telecommunication, roads/ports/bridges, and industrial estates.
‡Services includes hotels, hospitals, road transport, entertainment. and others.

the first half of the 1990s. The U-shaped trend in the share of services was just the opposite with a peak level that was almost one-fourth in the early 2000s. The share of the infrastructure sector did increase over time but was less than one-sixth even at its peak in the early 2000s. In addition, the sector-specific institutions did provide some resources for infrastructure, at modest levels, in rural electrification, power, and railways. Hence, financing of investment in infrastructure was largely dependent upon resources allocated by the national and state governments.

The decline and fall of the term lending financial institutions, at the national and state levels, which coincided with the withdrawal of most investment institutions from their role in providing industrial finance, in such a short span of time during the early 2000s, might seem puzzling. However, this was neither an accident nor a coincidence. Rather, it was directly and indirectly attributable to financial sector reform beginning in the mid-1990s, which was influenced (if not driven) by the World Bank, as a critical element in the conditions for its structural adjustment loans. In this process, there was direct pressure to reduce such lending and phase out the development finance institutions. It was reinforced indirectly by other components of reform. The cost of borrowing for these institutions rose significantly, as there was a sharp reduction in funds provided on concessional terms by the Reserve Bank of India and government-guaranteed bonds. At the same time, there was increased competition from commercial banks that were allowed to undertake project financing. Eroding profitability was a self-fulfilling prophecy. The problems of development finance institutions were compounded by their past sins which led to an accumulation of nonperforming assets. These were accentuated further by a contagion effect because development finance institutions held one another's shares. Several observers and analysts also highlighted these problems in their critiques at the time (Mathur 2003; Bajpai 2004; Karunagaran 2005). However, most critics argued for correctives and did not suggest closure as a solution for the problems. In fact, the substantive decision had already been made by the government, but the last nail in the coffin came from the report of a committee constituted by the Reserve Bank of India. It came to the conclusion that the business model of development finance institutions was not sustainable without government support, which would no longer be available, and that their role could be performed just as well as, if not better than, by commercial banks and capital markets. Therefore, the committee recommended that state-level term lending institutions be closed down, while national term lending institutions should be converted into banks or nonbanking financial companies. Indeed, the Reserve Bank of India committee explicitly proposed that, of the development finance institutions established by acts of parliament, only the refinancing institutions—NABARD, NHB, and SIDBI—plus the EXIM Bank would continue (Reserve Bank of India 2004). All recommendations were accepted and implemented. The voices of dissent were few (EPW Research Foundation 2004). Of course, the investment institutions never had this formal mandate and, except for LIC, simply withdrew from such lending. It did not require a formal directive from the government as their owner.

This policy induced downsizing of development finance institutions, which were a critical provider of investible resources for the industrial sector until then, and obviously created a void that required alternative sources of financing. To begin, the situation was rescued by internal funds of corporates such as retained profits and existing reserves. The share of internal sources in total corporate financing rose from about 33 percent during 1985–86 to 1999–2000 to more than 60 percent during 2000–01 to 2004–05 (Reserve Bank of India 2006, 268). Some underlying factors that pushed up profits made this possible: the economic boom boosted sales; productivity rose but real wages stagnated; there was a sharp decline in nominal interest rates; and tax concessions reduced taxes on corporate profits. The share of the residual, external sources in total corporate financing witnessed a corresponding decline from about 66 percent to less than 40 percent. In this, the share of development finance institutions dropped from about 10 percent during the 1990s to 2 percent in the first half of the 2000s as interest and amortization payments exceeded gross disbursements. But borrowing from commercial banks did emerge as an alternative source, borne out by an increase in its share of corporate financing from 8 percent in the first half of the 1990s to 12 percent in the second half of the 1990s and 18 percent in the first half of the 2000s. Surprisingly enough, despite a booming stock market, the share of equity capital dropped from 19 percent during the first half of the 1990s to 10 percent in the first half of the 2000s, while the share of debentures dropped from 7 percent to -1 percent (Reserve Bank of India 2006, 268).

Even so, mobilization of capital through equity issues trebled from Rs. 43 billion in 1990–91 to Rs. 131 billion in 2004–05. This mobilization of external resources through equity issues rose further to its peak level of Rs. 636 billion in 2007–08 but dropped sharply following the global financial crisis to Rs. 161 billion in 2008–09 and was at the same level of

Rs. 161 billion in 2012–13 (Reserve Bank of India 2013, 146). It is worth noting that an overwhelmingly large proportion of this was in the form of private placement rather than public issue.

In this context, it is worth noting that two new significant sources of industrial finance for corporates surfaced. The domestic bond market emerged as a significant provider through the private placement route. However, the hike in interest rates at home following the financial crisis, combined with capital account liberalization, and juxtaposed with low interest rates abroad, made external commercial borrowing an increasingly important source of finance. This had two consequences. For the borrowing firms, over time, the interest rate differential was more than neutralized by exchange rate depreciation. For the economy, external debt jumped from $101 billion at the end of March 2001 to $172 billion at the end of March 2007 and $390 billion in the end of March 2013. Of these totals, government debt rose from $40 billion to $46 billion and $68 billion, respectively, while nongovernment debt rose $61 billion to $126 billion and $322 billion, respectively. In the latter, external commercial borrowing, which was essentially corporate borrowing, rose from $24 billion to $41 billion and $121, billion respectively (Reserve Bank of India 2013, 243–6). Clearly, this mode of financing investment in the industrial sector has created a large external debt service burden not only for the corporate sector but also for the economy.

V. ASSESSMENT OF PERFORMANCE AND LESSONS FROM EXPERIENCE

The preceding discussion has attempted to outline the broad contours of the evolution of development finance and its role in the financing of industrialization in India. The next logical step is to assess the performance of development finance institutions in India, which would also make it possible to draw lessons from the Indian experience for countries that are latecomers to industrialization. Interestingly enough, there is something to learn both from its successes and its failures.

In retrospect, it is clear that the development finance institutions made a significant contribution to the provision of industrial finance in independent India. Their total disbursements financed just one-tenth of the modest gross fixed capital formation in India's manufacturing sector in 1950–51, but this proportion multiplied by five to reach almost one-half of a big magnitude in 2000–01. The public sector, which relied on resources allocated by the government to finance its investment, received a negligible proportion of these disbursements, so that this lending was almost entirely to the private sector. Hence, its significance was even greater. Total disbursements, as a proportion of gross fixed capital formation in the private sector, rose from about one-fourth in 1950–51 to three-fourths in 2000–01. It follows that, in the absence of these institutions, such levels of private investment in the industrial sector would have been difficult to finance from alternative sources. The counterfactual is important.

It is also worth noting that the wide range of development finance institutions created a structure that was complex. There were term lending institutions at the national and state levels, which were conventional and not different from those elsewhere but for the multiplicity in numbers. This was the most important source of financing industrialization in India for more than two decades, although their relative importance declined in the 1990s and dropped rapidly in the early 2000s. There were also the investment institutions that mobilized household savings through government-owned insurance firms, or a mutual fund for small savers, functioning as significant long-term lenders to the industrial sector, which were unconventional and different from elsewhere. It was a novel method of transforming savings by households into investment by firms without creating problems arising from maturity mismatches. And their relative importance increased during the 1990s and more so in the 2000s, but that was because the term-lending institutions vanished. The refinancing institutions for agriculture or rural development, housing, and small-scale industries did have multiple functions as lenders, catalysts, and regulators (which was unusual), but were effective in their considerable impact and significant in their multiplier effects. In addition, there were specialized, sector-specific institutions. Of these, some such as the export-import bank were common enough and existed in most countries, but others were uncommon and specific to India, all of which performed useful roles but were limited in their impact because neither the scale nor the spread was large enough, while their problems were accentuated with the dwindling access to concessional finance that was provided by the government.

Surprisingly enough, the allocation of development finance across sectors does not reveal any underlying rationale or systematic approach. It would seem that the distribution of disbursements by the national term lending institutions, between industrial subsectors in manufacturing, was not connected with, let alone driven by, industrial policy at either meso or micro levels. It is striking that there was no focus even on the pharmaceuticals sector. After all, the Patents Act of 1970, which allowed process patents but not product patents, was essentially a strategic industrial policy that transformed the pharmaceutical industry in India into a pharmacy for the developing world. Yet, its relative importance in industrial finance disbursements declined after the mid-1990s. The fate of the textiles and clothing sectors, engaged in manufacturing for export on a large scale, was no different. Similarly, firms manufacturing two-wheelers, commercial vehicles, or auto components had no special or preferential access to industrial finance. In this situation, it is no surprise that information technology was not quite on the horizon. It is plausible to suggest that the allocation of resources between sectors was shaped by the borrowers rather than the lenders. Indeed, the preferential access that some entrepreneurs, firms, or business houses had to development finance institutions was probably an important determinant of outcomes in lending. Government patronage obviously exercised a significant influence. The rising share of nonperforming assets in the portfolio of these institutions was almost an inevitable consequence.

In this context, it is also worth noting that engagement of development finance institutions with the borrowing firms seldom extended beyond lending. Sometimes the process of due diligence for extending loans was limited or incomplete. On occasion, even the debt servicing capacity of the borrower was not reviewed or monitored after the loan had been provided. Similarly, where the lending or investment institutions acquired equity in manufacturing firms, which entitled them to place their nominees on boards of directors, often their role was that of silent partners. It would be no exaggeration to state that their nominated directors seldom functioned independently of the promoters or major shareholders, essentially preserving status quo rather than protecting the interests of the institutions they represented, let alone the interests of minority shareholders.

There are some obvious lessons that emerge from the Indian experience in this sphere. The basic lesson is simple. In the early stages of industrialization, development finance is essential, indeed almost a necessary condition to kick-start the process. Of course, such institutions must strike a balance between commercial norms and developmental needs. But it is clear that, in the absence of such finance, where both access and price matter, private investment in an infant manufacturing sector is exceedingly difficult and simply might not materialize.

The complex structure of development finance institutions in India also carries some positive lessons. For one, the diversity of these institutions served a strategic purpose. The term lending institutions provided long-term development finance to manufacturing firms in the private sector. At the same time, there was some devolution to state-level institutions that ensured access to long-term development finance for small-scale industries in the different regions of this large country. In addition, a development bank for small industries that operated nationwide strengthened the focus on small and medium enterprises. The refinancing institutions in critical areas such as agriculture, rural development, and housing, supported by concessional finance, generated multiplier effects and fostered geographical spread. The specialized, sector-specific institutions served a valuable purpose by providing development finance for sectors where it might not have been adequate from other sources so that it was a useful complement. For another, the nature of support from and to development finance institutions made a difference. Their lending provided financial resources to the firms in the industrial sector, which might not otherwise have had sufficient access to credit for their investments and did so on concessional terms. This was possible essentially because the government or the central bank provided these institutions with access to finance on concessional terms or helped them get preferential access to domestic capital markets through government-guaranteed or tax-free bonds.

The Indian experience also reveals some errors of omission and commission. It is important to learn from these mistakes, and the necessary correctives are clear enough. Unlike most latecomers to industrialization, development finance institutions in India did not lend for infrastructure. By the time this was corrected, it was too little too late. Total dependence on the national government and state governments to finance infrastructural investments was a mistake. At later stages, it was as much of a mistake to hope that private investment, whether domestic or foreign, would provide development finance for infrastructure. At best, it could have been a useful complement, but it could never have been a substitute. The other error of omission was the absence of any coordination between lending by development finance institutions and industrial policy objectives or priorities in terms of sectoral allocations. Even if this was difficult at the micro level in the milieu, some strategic purposes could have been woven in at the meso or macro levels. In fact, some strategic selection of industrial sectors, which would have preferred access to industrial finance (e.g., pharmaceuticals) would have been both feasible and desirable. The serious error of commission was the premature winding down and closure of development banks. It was much too early in India. In fact, their counterparts continue to flourish in several countries of the developing world such as Brazil, China, and Korea as well as in some industrialized countries such as Germany and Japan.

It is important to recognize that, in India, lending and investment institutions provided a means of financing investment for industrialization, but could not have been an instrument of industrial policy because the necessary control mechanisms were missing. Two attributes were essential for the latter, which were simply absent in India. First, it was necessary to strike a balance between incentives and disincentives that would reward performance and penalize nonperformance, not only through the price of credit but also through access to credit. Second, there was need for an institutionalized system of checks and balances that could have prevented collusion between governments and firms, or between development banks and firms, to capture rents, without which the accumulation of nonperforming assets was an inevitable outcome. The institutionalization of such processes over time would have led to the evolution of control mechanisms in which each of the stakeholders exercised some influence in the pursuit of their interests; but such institutionalized processes imposed a discipline on the economic behavior of not only firms but also development banks and the government, which limited excesses in self-seeking behavior on the part of any one stakeholder or even two stakeholders who wished to collude. However, these structural flaws were embedded in the conception and design of the system of development finance in India, for which correctives would have been difficult to introduce. This failure, too, carries important lessons.

VI. AN INTERNATIONAL PERSPECTIVE

The historical origins of development banking can be traced to countries in Western Europe, which developed bank-centered financial systems to finance industrialization, in sharp contrast with the stock market–centered financial markets in Britain and the United States. In France, long-term finance institutions were created in the late 1840s to provide for industrial and infrastructural development. In Germany, *Kreditbanken* were born in the 1870s to finance investments in an infant manufacturing sector (Gerschenkron 1962). These were role models for the provision of industrial finance in Germany and Japan at the end of World War II to support their reconstruction and industrialization. The *Kreditanstalt für Wiederaufbau* (KfW) was established in 1948 as a government-owned bank in Germany, to start with as part of the Marshall Plan. Similarly, the Japan Development Bank was established in 1951 by the Japanese government.

The experience of latecomers to industrialization in Latin America and Asia, during the second half of the twentieth century, also underlines the critical importance of development banks. It is worth citing some examples that are illustrative rather than exhaustive. The early birds were the *Nacional Financiera* (NAFINSA), Mexico, in 1934, and *Corporacion de Fomento de la Produccion* (CORFO), Chile, in 1939. But most development finance institutions elsewhere were established in the 1950s: IFCI in 1948, ICICI in 1955, and IDBI in 1964 in India; *Banco Nacional de Desenvolvomento Economico* (BNDES) in 1952 in Brazil; Korean Development Bank (KDB) in 1953 in South Korea; Industrial Development Bank of Turkey (TSKB) in 1950 in Turkey; and Industrial Finance Corporation of Thailand (IFCT) in 1959 in Thailand. In Malaysia and Taiwan, commercial banks with financial support from governments performed exactly the same function as surrogate development banks. The Development Bank of Singapore (DBS), listed as a public company with foreign capital participation, was set up later in 1968, while the China Development Bank (CDB), entirely government-owned, was established in 1994. The common objective of these diverse institutions was to finance investment through long-term lending and promote industrial development.

In the earlier stages of industrialization, during the period from 1950 to 1980, lending for investment in infrastructure constituted a significant proportion of the total disbursements of development banks in Latin America and Asia, ranging from one-fourth to one-half in Brazil, Mexico, and Korea but tapering off in subsequent decades as the financing needs of infrastructure were progressively met. The solitary exception was development banks in India, where infrastructure accounted for less than one-twentieth of their lending (Amsden 2001). In the later stages of industrialization, development banks lent to domestic firms in the private sector, as also the public sector, to finance investments in manufacturing. In fact, the share of development banks in total investment in the manufacturing sector in countries such as Brazil, India, Korea, Mexico, Thailand, and Turkey, during the 1980s, ranged from one-fifth to two-fifths (Amsden 2001). In Brazil and India, this proportion stayed at high levels in the 1990s. In most of these countries, such provision of development finance was associated with an increase in the share of the manufacturing sector in total gross fixed capital formation, even if sources of financing became more diverse with the passage of time.

The sources of funding for development banks were characterized by diversity as the mix varied across countries and changed over time. To begin, the financing came directly or indirectly from governments, as grants from the exchequer or long-term interest-free loans from the government, in some instances supported by foreign loans from bilateral donors or multilateral institutions such as the World Bank and the regional development banks. Increasingly, however, this support came through off-budget transactions that relied upon public deposits in state-owned banks, post offices, and pension funds. These transactions were typically outside the general government budget, hence beyond parliamentary scrutiny and political processes. Yet, governments exercised enormous influence over the allocation of resources.

The success of development banks as an instrument of industrial policy was shaped by the context and the milieu. In South Korea, the KDB was a phenomenal success. In Brazil, the BNDES performed a critical role. In a few countries, rent-seeking may have created nonperforming assets. This proportion obviously varied across countries and over time. Yet, there can be little doubt that development banks provided essential support for financing industrialization in Brazil, Chile, India, Mexico, Singapore, Thailand, and Turkey, as did their surrogates in Malaysia and Taiwan. Argentina never developed these institutions, which had its consequences. Much later, in China, the CDB performed an effective and valuable role in the industrialization surge that began in the early 1990s.

In retrospect, it is clear that development banks performed multiple functions and were an essential part in each of the three factors common to countries in Asia and Latin America, which carved out their paths as latecomers to industrialization. First, they financed investments in infrastructure, which helped create the initial conditions to kick-start industrialization. Second, they were an important part of the enabling institutions, which did what markets alone would not have to finance investments in the manufacturing sector. Third, they were a vital instrument of industrial policy for governments at the meso level and micro level, which allocated scarce investible resources to selected industries or selected firms.

The importance of development banks as sources of industrial finance diminished after the turn of the century not only in India but also elsewhere. In 2003, Singapore converted DBS into a commercial bank renamed as DBS Bank. In 2004, IFCT in Thailand was sold to the Thai Military Bank and absorbed into commercial banking. In Turkey, TSKB is now a privately owned investment bank in which the largest Turkish commercial bank has a majority share. It is worth noting that Japan was different from these countries. The Japan Development Bank (JDB) was dissolved in 1999 after almost fifty years but replaced by the Development Bank of Japan (DBJ) with a new mandate to focus on regional development. In addition, the Japan Finance Corporation (JFC), wholly owned by the government, was established in 2008 following the merger of four policy-based financing institutions.

It would seem that the role of development banks was diluted during the early 2000s, not only in India but also in several developing countries. This was attributable to the progressive withdrawal of concessional funds made available by governments, which in turn was an integral part of deregulation and reform in the financial sector almost everywhere. Over time, the evolution of domestic capital markets in late industrializing countries might also have diminished the relative importance of development banks, as commercial banks, both in the private sector and in the public sector, entered into long-term financing of investment in the industrial sector. However, such options became available only after some time when domestic capital markets were sufficiently developed. But even development banks, wherever they continued, derived benefits from the emergence of domestic capital markets, which opened up possibilities of borrowing without direct support from the government.

It is hardly surprising that there was a decline in the macroeconomic significance of development banks in countries that followed this sequence of developments. But it is important to recognize that this did not happen everywhere. International comparisons are difficult, since statistics on disbursements are not available for most countries. Table 7.4 presents the available evidence on outstanding loans of development finance institutions as a percentage of GDP in selected countries at the end of 2000, 2005, and 2010. It shows that this proportion dropped steadily during the 2000s to very low levels in some countries such as Mexico and Turkey, where it was less than 1 percent by 2010. In India, this proportion declined far more sharply from 7.4 percent in 2000 to

Table 7.4 Outstanding Loans of Development Finance Institutions as a Percentage of GDP: An International Comparison

	2000	2005	2010
Brazil (BNDES)	6.4	6.5	9.7
China (CDB)	6.8	9.4	11.2
India (ICICI, IFCI, IDBI and SIDBI)	7.4	2.2	0.8
Korea (KDB)	8.6	6.2	6.8
Mexico (NAFINSA)	2.7	1.7	0.9
Turkey (TSKB)	NA	0.04	0.1
Germany (KfW)	8.5	11.5	14.9
Japan (DBJ + JFC)	3.2	2.8	7.2

Source: Annual reports of BNDES, CDB, ICICI, IFCI, IDBI, SIDBI, KDB, NAFINSA, TSKB, KfW, DBJ, and JFC.

Note: For Development Bank of Japan (DBJ), data for 2000 are not available and 3.2 percent is the outstanding loans/GDP ratio for 2002, used here as an approximation. The figure for Japan in 2010 is the sum of DBJ and JFC, of which the latter accounted for 4.4 percent.

2.2 percent in 2005 and 0.8 percent in 2010.[1] However, the decline in this proportion was much less in Korea from 8.6 in 2000 to 6.8 percent in 2010. In Brazil and China, the trend was the opposite. Between 2000 and 2010, this proportion rose from 6.4 percent to 9.7 percent in Brazil and from 6.8 percent to 11.2 percent in China. The industrialized countries, Germany and Japan, provide an even more striking contrast. Between 2000 and 2010, this proportion rose from 8.5 percent to 15.9 percent in Germany, while it rose from a low of around 3 percent, following the closure of JDB, to 7.2 percent, for DBJ and JFC together, in Japan. The reasons why Brazil and China did much better in terms of industrialization during this period than Mexico and India are manifold and complex. Yet, the fact that development finance institutions had a strong presence in the former and a marginal if not vanishing presence in the latter must be a part of the explanation.

NOTES

I would like to thank participants at the IPD-JICA Workshops in Jordan on June 5–6, 2014, and at Columbia University, New York, on February 19 -20, 2015, for perceptive questions and helpful comments on my presentations. I would also like to thank Atul Sanganeria for valuable research assistance.

1. During the 2000s, LIC continued long-term lending to the industrial sector. The evidence on this is presented in table 7.1 in terms of annual disbursements. However, data on outstanding loans of LIC provide figures on total loans, which include loans

against insurance policies and all other loans, taken together, so that there are no separate statistics on outstanding loans of long-term lending to the industrial sector at the end of every year. Hence, the proportions cited above, which relate to IFCI, ICICI, IDBI, and SIDBI, do not include LICs.

REFERENCES

Amsden, Alice H. 2001. *The Rise of the Rest: Challenges to the West from Late Industrializing Economies.* New York: Oxford University Press.

Bajpai, G. N. 2004. "Development Financing in a Changing Environment." *Economic and Political Weekly.* 29 May: 2212–15.

Bhaduri, Amit, and Deepak Nayyar. 1996. *The Intelligent Person's Guide to Liberalization.* New Delhi: Penguin.

Chang, Ha-Joon. 1996. *The Political Economy of Industrial Policy.* London: Macmillan.

———. 2002. *Kicking Away the Ladder: Development Strategy in Historical Perspective.* London: Anthem.

———. 2007. *Institutional Change and Economic Development.* London: Anthem.

Corden, W. M. 1974. *Trade Policy and Economic Welfare.* Oxford: Clarendon Press.

EPW Research Foundation. 2004. "Reviving DFIs: An Urgent Need." *Economic and Political Weekly.* 19 June: 2544–50.

Evans, Peter. 1995. *Embedded Autonomy: States and Industrial Transformation.* Princeton, N.J.: Princeton University Press.

Gerschenkron, Alexander. 1962. *Economic Backwardness in Historical Perspective.* Cambridge, Mass.: Harvard University Press.

Goldsmith, Raymond W. 1983. *Financial Development of India: 1860–1977.* Delhi: Oxford University Press.

Johnson, C. 1984. "The Idea of Industrial Policy," in *The Industrial Policy Debate*, ed. C. Johnson. San Francisco: Institute of Contemporary Studies.

Karunagaran, A. 2005. "Should DFIs be Revived?" *Economic and Political Weekly.* 19 March: 1247–52.

Lall, Sanjaya. 1990. *Building Industrial Competitiveness in Developing Countries.* Paris: OECD Development Centre.

———. 1997. "Imperfect Markets and Fallible Governments: The Role of the State in Industrial Development." In *Trade and Industrialization*, ed. Deepak Nayyar, 43–87. Delhi: Oxford University Press.

Landesmann, M. 1992. "Industrial Policies and Social Corporatism." In *Social Corporatism*, eds. J. Pekkarenin, M. Pohjola, and R. Rowthorn, 242–79. Oxford: Clarendon Press.

Lindbeck, A. 1981. "Industrial Policy as an Issue of the Economic Environment." *The World Economy* 4(4): 391–406.

Mathur, K. B. L. 2003. "Development Financial Institutions at the Crossroads." *Economic and Political Weekly.* 22 February: 799–806.

Nayyar, Deepak. 1997. "Themes in Trade and Industrialization." In *Trade and Industrialization*, ed. Deepak Nayyar, 1–42. Delhi: Oxford University Press.

———. 2013. *Catch Up: Developing Countries in the World Economy*. London: Oxford University Press.

North, Douglass C. 1990. *Institutions, Institutional Change and Economic Performance*. London: Cambridge University Press.

Pinder, J. 1982. "Causes and Kinds of Industrial Policy," in *National Industrial Strategies in the World Economy*, ed. J. Pinder. London: Croom Helm.

Reich, R. 1982. "Why the U.S. Needs an Industrial Policy," *Harvard Business Review*, January-February. https://hbr.org/1982/01/why-the-us-needs-an-industrial-policy.

Reserve Bank of India. 2004. *Report of the Working Group on Development Financial Institutions*. Mumbai: Reserve Bank of India.

———. 2006. *Report on Currency and Finance 2005–06*. Mumbai: Reserve Bank of India.

———. 2013. *Handbook of Statistics on the Indian Economy 2012–13*. Mumbai: Reserve Bank of India.

Wade, Robert. 1990. *Governing the Market: Economic Theory and the Role of Government in East Asian Industrialization*. Princeton, N.J.: Princeton University Press.

PART III

Practice and Proposals

CHAPTER 8

Industrial Policy Revisited

A NEW STRUCTURAL ECONOMICS PERSPECTIVE

Justin Yifu Lin

I. INTRODUCTION

How to promote economic growth has been a topic for economic discourse and research at least since the publication of Adam Smith's *The Wealth of Nations* in 1776. Although past theories have studied how markets and governments play roles in promoting (or repressing) economic development, the growth research still faces significant methodological difficulties and challenges in identifying actionable policy levers to sustain and accelerate growth in specific countries. In particular, the role of government in development is debatable and contentious. Mainstream economists agree that market mechanisms are essential for getting relative prices right and thereby facilitating efficient resource allocation. However, the experiences of successful countries also show that governments often play a crucial role in facilitating industrial transformation.

Industrial policy is an important instrument that is actively used by governments to promote economic development, both in history and in the present. Historical evidence shows that all countries that have successfully transformed from agrarian to modern and advanced economies, including both the old industrial powers of Western Europe and North America and the newly industrialized economies of East Asia, have had governments that played a proactive role in assisting individual firms in overcoming the inevitable coordination and externality problems. In fact, the governments in high-income countries today continue to do so. However, the sad fact is that almost every government in the developing world has attempted, at some point, to play that facilitating role, but most have failed.

In most socialist and developing countries, after World War II, governments tried to build up the capital-intensive industries that prevailed in advanced countries (Lin 2011). Such a *comparative advantage defying* (CAD) strategy was typically advocated by structuralism, the dominant development thinking in the 1950s and 1960s (Lin 2003 and 2009). Under a CAD strategy, the government protected firms in prioritized industries by various industrial policies, such as granting the prioritized enterprises a market monopoly, suppressing interest rates, overvaluing domestic currency, and controlling prices for raw materials, to reduce the costs of investment in and operation of these enterprises.

Government interventions under the CAD strategy, including national planning in the socialist countries and credit rationing, investment, and entry licensing in nonsocialist developing countries, inevitably caused widespread shortages in funds, foreign exchange, and raw materials. Consequently, although the adoption of a CAD industrial policy could establish some advanced industries in socialist and developing countries, it inevitably led to inefficient resource allocation, suppressed working incentives, rampant rent-seeking behavior, deteriorating income distribution, and poor economic performance. If the goal of industrial policies is to narrow the gap between developing and developed countries, then, in almost all cases, the first-generation industrial policy was a failure.

Despite these failures in terms of the effectiveness of industrial policies, all countries continue to adopt industrial policies to promote economic development. Fortunately, there have been a few successful cases of catching up with or significantly narrowing the gap between themselves and advanced industrialized economies by actively implementing industrial policy. For example, Japan was able to shift from a developing country in 1950 with a per capita income one-fifth that of the United States and ultimately became a high-income country and the world's second-largest economy. Japan's rise was the result of an impressive annual growth performance of 9.6 percent during the 1950s and 1960s, driven by the transformation from an agrarian to an industrialized economy. Using an outward-oriented, market-friendly development strategy, the Asian Tigers—Hong Kong SAR, China; the Republic of Korea; Singapore; and Taiwan, China—grew in excess of 7 percent annually between the early 1960s and the early 1990s, demonstrating that it is possible to maintain impressive growth rates and close the gap with advanced economies.

More recently, growth in several large economies, such as China, Brazil, and India, has taken off, turning them into new global growth poles (World Bank 2011). These high growth rates have led to a significant reduction in poverty. Between 1981 and 2005, the percentage of people living below US$ 1.25 a day was halved, falling from 52 percent to 26 percent. This drop in poverty has been most apparent in China. In 1981, a staggering 84 percent of the Chinese lived in poverty. By 2005, this proportion had fallen to 16 percent—well below the average for the developing world. As the Growth Report identified, all countries that have experienced rapid growth have a committed, credible, and capable government (Growth Commission 2008). Without a doubt, implementing industrial policy effectively is only one characteristic of a capable government.

But why have some industrial policy implementations succeeded while others have failed? Is government action really needed in the process of economic development? If so, how can the government identify the right strategy and facilitate economic development through appropriate industrial policy? If we can learn from the failed development attempts as well as the few successes, explore the nature and determinants of economic growth, and provide policymakers with the tools to unleash their country's growth potential, then poverty could become a memory of the past within a generation or two.

In this chapter, I will provide a new structural economic analysis of the reasons for the failure of using industrial policy as an instrument for economic development. I argue that the pervasive failures are mostly due to the government's inability to come up with good criteria for identifying industries appropriate for a given country's endowment structure and level of development. This chapter is organized as follows: Section II introduces the main ideas of new structural economics. Section III explains the rationale for a facilitating state in the process of dynamic economic growth, briefly reviews some important lessons from early industrial development strategies around the world, and analyzes the role of the state in the process of structural change in today's advanced economies. It also examines similar attempts by developing-country governments to adopt policy interventions to facilitate industrial upgrading and economic diversification and analyzes the reasons for their success or failure. Building on the foundations of new structural economics (Lin 2011), Section IV provides a framework for formulating industrial policy based on a new approach called *growth identification and facilitation* (Lin and Monga 2011). Section V concludes.

II. THE NEW STRUCTURAL ECONOMICS

Economic development and transition are among the most challenging issues in modern economic study. The current global crisis, the most serious one since the Great Depression, calls for a rethinking of economic theories. It is therefore a good time for economists to reexamine development theories as well.

New structural economics (NSE) (Lin 2011 and 2012), which is based on analysis of the nature of modern economic growth, proposes a framework for rethinking economic development and industrial policy. It starts with the observation that the main features of modern economic development are continuous technological innovation, industrial upgrading, and economic diversification, which make possible continuous increases in labor productivity and thus per capita income in an economy.

NSE proposes the starting point for the analysis of modern economic development to be an economy's factor endowments, that is, the availability of labor, capital, and natural resources. Factor endowments are given in an economy at any specific time and are changeable over time. The optimal industrial structure in an economy, that is, the industrial structure that will make the economy most competitive domestically and internationally at any specific time, is endogenous to its comparative advantages, which in turn are determined by the given endowment structure of the economy at that time.[1] Economies that try to deviate from their comparative advantages are likely to perform poorly.

With capital accumulation, the economy's factor endowment structure evolves, pushing its industrial structure to deviate from the optimal determined by its previous level. If they try to grow simply by adding more and more physical capital or labor to the existing industries, economies eventually run into diminishing returns. Firms then need to upgrade their industries and technologies accordingly in order to maintain market competitiveness.

If an economy follows its comparative advantage in the development of its industries, they will be most competitive in the domestic and world markets. As a result, they will gain the largest possible market share and generate potentially the largest surplus. Capital investment will also have the largest returns. Consequently, households will have the highest savings propensity, resulting in an even faster upgrade of the country's endowment structure.

A developing country that follows its comparative advantage to build up its industries can also benefit from the advantage of its backwardness in the upgrading process and grow faster than advanced countries. Enterprises in developing countries can benefit from the industrial and technological gap with developed countries by acquiring industrial and technological innovations that are consistent with their new comparative advantage through learning and borrowing from developed countries.

The main question, then, is how to ensure that the economy grows in a manner that is consistent with its comparative advantage. Once the relative prices of capital, labor, and natural resources reflect the relative scarcity of these production factors in the endowment structure, most firms, with the goal of maximizing profit, will be induced to enter the industries consistent with their comparative advantage, because that is the way to minimize their costs of production and maintain competitiveness in the market. Such a relative price system exists only in a competitive market system. In developing countries where this is usually not the case, it is necessary that government action be taken to improve various market institutions so as to create and protect effective competition in the product and factor markets.

However, some costs and benefits of continuous industrial upgrading cannot be internalized by individual firms. First, to enter a new industry, firms need to have information about production technologies and product markets. If such information is not freely available, each firm will have to invest resources to search for, collect, and analyze it. First-movers who attempt to enter new industries can either fail—because they target the wrong industries—or succeed—because the industries are consistent with the country's new comparative advantage. In the case of success, their experience offers valuable and free information to other prospective entrants. They will not have monopoly rent because of competition from new entry. Moreover, the first-movers often need to devote resources to train workers on the new business processes and techniques, and then those workers may be hired by the first-movers' competitors. Even in situations where first-movers fail, their bad experience also provides useful knowledge to other firms. Yet, they must bear the costs of failure themselves. In other words, the social value of the first-movers' investment is usually much larger than the private value, and there is an asymmetry between the first-movers' gains from success and the cost of failure. All these externality issues will make individual firms reluctant to upgrade industrial structure by themselves.

Second, as a country climbs up the industrial and technological ladder, many other changes are required: the technology used by its firms becomes more sophisticated, capital requirements increase, and the scale of production and size of markets also increase. Market transactions increasingly take place at arm's length. A flexible and smooth industrial and technological upgrading process therefore requires simultaneous improvements in soft infrastructure, including educational, financial, and legal institutions, and in hard infrastructure, such as roads, highways, port facilities, and power supplies, so that firms in the newly upgraded industries can reduce transaction costs and reach the production possibility frontier (Harrison and Rodríguez-Clare 2010). Improvement of the hard and soft infrastructure requires coordination beyond individual firms' decisions.

Economic development is therefore a dynamic process marked with externalities and requiring coordination. Undoubtedly, the market is a necessary basic mechanism for effective resource allocation at each given stage of development, but dynamic economic growth requires the government to play a proactive, facilitating role to overcome externality and coordination issues for an economy to move from one stage to another. The government can do so by (1) providing information about new industries consistent with the new comparative advantage determined by the change in endowment structure; (2) coordinating investments in related industries and the required improvements in infrastructure; (3) subsidizing activities with externalities in the starting phase of introducing new industries and new technologies; and (4) catalyzing the development of new industries by incubation or by attracting foreign direct investment to overcome the deficits in social capital and other intangible constraints.

In sum, the NSE framework is three-pronged: it includes an understanding of the country's comparative advantage, defined as the evolving potential of its endowment structure; reliance on the market as the optimal resource allocation mechanism at any given stage of development; and recognition of the facilitating role of the state in the process of industrial upgrading. NSE helps in explaining the economic performance of the most successful developing countries.

III. STRUCTURAL CHANGE, EFFICIENT MARKETS, AND A FACILITATING STATE

Based on the principles of NSE, it is clear why industrial policy is indispensable to economic development: although markets provide incentives for efficiently allocating resources, the incentives are insufficient, because economic development involves industrial upgrading and corresponding improvements in hard and soft infrastructure. Such upgrading and improvements require inherent coordination, with large externalities to firms' transaction costs and returns to capital investment. Thus, in addition to an effective market mechanism, the government should play an active role in facilitating structural changes.

Compared with developed countries whose industries are located on the global frontier and whose industrial upgrading and diversification rely on their own generation of new knowledge through a process of trial and error, developing countries in the catch-up process move within the global industrial frontier and have the advantage of backwardness. In other words, they can rely on borrowing the existing technology and industrial ideas from the advanced countries. This method of acquiring innovation has a lower cost and is less risky than the one used by firms in developed countries (Krugman 1979). Therefore, in a developing country committed to the market system, if firms know how to tap into the potential of the advantage of backwardness and the government proactively provides information, coordination, and externality compensation in the process of industrial upgrading and diversification, then the country can grow much faster than a developed country and achieve the goal of converging with high-income countries (Lin 2009). After all, this was the case for Britain before the eighteenth century; for Germany, France, and the United States in the nineteenth century; and for the Nordic countries, Japan, Korea, Taiwan-China, Singapore, Malaysia, and other East Asian economies in the twentieth century (Amsden 1989; Chang 2003; Gerschenkron 1962; Wade 1990).

Reviewing the historical and contemporary experiences of state intervention, including many failures and a few successes, is helpful for understanding two additional practical reasons why industrial policy is a useful instrument for a facilitating state: (1) the contents of coordination may be different, depending on the industries, and (2) the government's resources and capacity are limited. The government needs to use them strategically.

There is ample historical evidence that today's most advanced economies once relied heavily on government intervention to ignite and facilitate their takeoff and catch-up processes. Government intervention allowed them to build strong industrial bases and sustain the momentum of their growth over long periods. In his well-known survey of trade and industrial policies leading to early economic transformations in the Western world, List (1841) documented various policy instruments through which governments protected domestic industries or even intervened to support the development of specific industries—many of which became successful and provided the bedrock for national industrial development.

Likewise, Chang (2003) has reviewed economic developments during the period when most of the currently advanced economies went through their industrial revolutions (between the end of the Napoleonic Wars in 1815 and the beginning of World War I in 1914). He has documented various patterns of state intervention that have allowed these countries to successfully implement their catch-up strategies. Contrary to conventional wisdom that often attributes the Western industrial successes to laissez-faire and free-market policies, the historical evidence shows that the use of industrial, trade, and technology policies was the main ingredient for their successful structural transformation. This ranged from the frequent use of import duties or even import bans for infant-industry protection to industrial promotion through monopoly grants and cheap supplies from government factories, various subsidies, public-private partnerships, and direct state investment, especially in Britain and the United States (Trebilcok 1981). All European countries trying to catch up with Britain devoted efforts to technology policy. Up to the middle of the first Industrial Revolution, the main channel for technological transfer was the movement of skilled workers who embodied new knowledge. Latecomers to the industrialization process, such as France, attempted to acquire them on a large scale from Britain, but the British government banned the emigration of skilled workers for more than a century, starting in 1719. When new technologies became embodied in machines, they too were put under government control: various laws were adopted throughout the eighteenth and nineteenth centuries to ban the export of "tools and utensils."

Government intervention took many forms in the early experiences of industrialization. In Japan, the government created many factories ("pilot plants") in shipbuilding, mining, textiles, etc., most of which were subsequently sold to the private sector at very low prices and further subsidized. This helped launch the process of industrialization and diversification. Even when government-run enterprises performed poorly, there were many cases of failures that generated a burgeoning private sector. This was most notably the case in Japan during the Meiji Restoration when a vibrant textile industry emerged from the failure of the poorly managed state-owned enterprise. Private firms were successful because they learned skills and management from state-owned firms and introduced various process innovations to replace expensive equipment with inexpensive labor, which was Japan's comparative advantage at the time (Otsuka, Ranis, and Saxonhouse 1988).

Developed-country governments continue to adopt various measures to support industrial upgrading and diversification, although these policies may not be announced under the formal label *industrial policy*. Such measures typically include support for basic research, mandates, allocation of defense contracts, and large public procurements. Local governments also often provide all kinds of incentives to private firms to attract them to particular geographic areas and induce new investments. The application of all these measures needs to identify specific industries or products and amounts to "picking winners."

Almost all developing countries have tried to replicate the earlier models of state-led structural change, especially after World War II. From the planned economies of Eastern Europe and Asia to left-leaning or even liberal regimes in Latin America, Asia, Africa, and throughout the Arab world, many governments have adopted various policy measures to promote industrial development and industrial upgrading (Chenery 1961). While there have been a few successes in East Asia, most of these attempts have failed to deliver the expected results (Krueger and Tuncer 1982; Lal 1994; Pack and Saggi 2006).

A good example is Egypt's industrialization program in the 1950s, which featured heavy industries such as iron, steel, and chemicals. The country's per capita income was about 5 percent of that of the United States, the world's most important steel producer at the time. Unless the government continuously provided costly subsidies and/or protection, Egyptian firms could not attract private investment. I refer to these firms as *nonviable*.[2] In other words, these nonviable enterprises are unable to survive in an open, competitive market even if they are well managed; and unless the government provides subsidies and/or protection, no one will invest in or continue to operate such firms. The lack of capital-intensive industries in developing countries is not, therefore, caused by market rigidity, as structuralism argued, but by the nonviability of the firms in an undistorted, open, competitive market.[3]

The limited fiscal resource capacities of the state made the large-scale protection for and subsidies to these nonviable firms unsustainable. In such situations, governments have had to resort to administrative measures—granting market monopolies to firms in the so-called priority sectors, suppressing interest rates, overvaluing domestic currencies, and controlling the prices of raw materials—to reduce the costs of investment and continuous operation of their nonviable public enterprises (Lin 2009). In such circumstances, government-supported firms cannot be viable in open, competitive markets. Their survival depends on heavy protection and large subsidies through various means such as high tariffs, quota restrictions, and subsidized credit. The large rents embedded in these measures easily become the targets of political capture and create difficult governance problems (Lin 2011).

By contrast, Mauritius, one of the most successful African economies, took off in the 1970s by targeting labor-intensive industries such as textiles and garments. These industries were mature in Hong Kong-China, its "compass economy." Both economies share the same endowment structure, and the per capita income in Mauritius was about one-half that in Hong Kong-China in the 1970s. The Mauritius Industrial Development Authority and Export Processing Zones Development Authority were created by the government to attract Hong Kong-China's investment in its export processing zone. The vision was to position Mauritius as a world-class export hub on the Hong Kong-China model. Together, they have contributed to the country's emergence as an economic powerhouse.

Historical evidence shows that successful countries in their catch-up stage all used industrial policies to facilitate their industrial upgrading, and their industrial policies targeted industries existing in dynamically growing countries with a similar endowment structure and moderately higher per capita income: (1) Britain targeted the Netherlands' industries in the sixteenth and seventeenth centuries; its per capita GDP was about 70 percent of that of the Netherlands. (2) Germany, France, and the United States targeted Britain's industries in the late nineteenth century; their per capita incomes were about 60 percent to 75 percent of Britain's. (3) In the Meiji Restoration, Japan targeted Prussia's industries; its per capita GDP was about 40 percent of Prussia's. In the 1960s, Japan targeted the industries in the United States; Japan's per capita GDP was about 40 percent of that of the United States. (4) In the 1960s to 1980s, Korea, Taiwan-China, Hong Kong-China, and Singapore targeted Japan's industries; their per capita incomes were about 30 percent of Japan's. (5) In the 1970s, Mauritius targeted Hong Kong-China's textile and garment industries; its per capita income was about 50 percent of Hong Kong's. (6) In the 1980s, Ireland targeted the information, electronic, chemical, and pharmaceutical industries in the United States; its per capita income was about 45 percent of that of the United States. (7) In the 1990s, Costa Rica targeted the memory chip packaging and testing industry; its per capita GDP was about 40 percent of Taiwan-China's, which was the main economy in this sector.

Thus, for an industrial policy to be successful, it should target sectors that conform to the economy's latent comparative advantage. The *latent comparative advantage* refers to an industry in which the economy has low factor costs of production, but the transaction costs are too high to be competitive in domestic and international markets. Firms will be viable and the sectors will be competitive once the government helps the firms overcome coordination and externality issues to reduce the risk and transaction costs. But the question is, How are governments able to pick the sectors that are in line with the economy's latent comparative advantages?

A short answer is to target industries in dynamically growing countries with a similar endowment structure and somewhat higher income. Based on the principles of NSE, industrial upgrading is based on changes in comparative advantages due to changes in endowment structure. Countries that have a similar endowment structure should have similar comparative advantages. A dynamically growing country's industries should be consistent with the country's comparative advantages. Some of its industries will lose comparative advantage as the country grows and its endowment structure upgrades. Those "sunset" industries will become the latent comparative advantage of the latecomers. For countries with a similar endowment structure, the forerunners' successful and dynamic industrial development provides a blueprint for the latecomers' industrial policies. Section V proposes a more detailed guide for identifying and facilitating the industries with comparative advantage.

IV. THE GROWTH IDENTIFICATION AND FACILITATION FRAMEWORK

Although the historical and contemporary evidence shows that governments always play an important role in facilitating industrial upgrading and diversification in all successful countries, it may not be enough to validate an idea that has been mired in controversy for so long. Many economists who agree with the general notion that government intervention is an indispensable ingredient of structural transformation have maintained their opposition to industrial policy because of the lack of a general framework that can be used to guide policy making.

To justify that industrial policy is essential to promote economic development, this chapter codifies some basic principles that can guide the formation of successful industrial policy. The first step is to identify new industries in which a country may have latent comparative advantage, and the second is to remove the constraints that impede the emergence of industries with such advantage and create the conditions to allow them to become the country's competitive advantage. Specifically, I propose a six-step process:

(1) The government in a developing country can identify the list of tradable goods and services that have been produced for about 20 years in dynamically growing countries with similar endowment structures and per capita income about 100 percent higher than its own or 20 years ago the country's per capita income level was similar to that of the dynamically growing countries. This step could prevent the government from doing the wrong things or being captured by vested groups for rent seeking.

(2) Among the industries in that list, the government may give priority to those that some domestic private firms have already entered spontaneously and may try to identify the following: (a) the obstacles that are preventing these firms from upgrading the quality of their products or (b) the barriers that limit entry to those industries by other private firms. This could be done through a combination of various methods such as value-chain analysis or the growth diagnostic framework suggested by Hausmann, Rodrik and Velasco (2008). The government can then implement policy to remove these binding constraints and use randomized controlled experiments to test the effects so as to ensure the effectiveness of scaling up these policies at the national level (Duflo 2004). This step takes advantage of tacit knowledge owned by existing domestic firms.

(3) Some of the industries in the list may be completely new to domestic firms, or only a few domestic firms are doing exports. In such cases, the government could adopt specific measures to encourage firms in the higher-income countries identified in the first step to invest in these industries, so as to take advantage of the lower labor costs. The government may also set up incubation programs to catalyze the entry of private domestic firms into these industries. When the tacit knowledge has not existed, the government can help import or cultivate it.

(4) In addition to the industries identified in the list of potential opportunities for tradable goods and services in step 1, developing-country governments should pay close attention to successful self-discoveries by private

enterprises and provide support to scale up these industries. Consequently, an economy will not miss opportunities arising from new technologies or unique local advantages that are not identified by the preceding steps.

(5) In developing countries with poor infrastructure and an unfriendly business environment, the government can invest in industrial parks or export processing zones and make the necessary improvements to attract domestic private firms and/or foreign firms that may be willing to invest in the targeted industries. Improvements in infrastructure and the business environment can reduce transaction costs and facilitate industrial development. However, because of budget and capacity constraints, most governments will not be able to make the desirable improvements for the whole economy within a reasonable time frame. Focusing on improving the infrastructure and business environment in industrial parks or export processing zones is, therefore, a more manageable alternative. Industrial parks and export processing zones also have the benefit of encouraging industrial clustering. This step ensures that the government plays the coordination function in a pragmatic way.

(6) The government may also provide incentives to domestic pioneer firms or foreign investors working within the list of industries identified in step 1, to compensate for the nonrival public knowledge created by their investments. These incentives should be limited in both time and financial cost. They may take the form of a corporate income-tax holiday for a limited number of years, direct credits to cofinance investments, or priority access to foreign reserves to import key equipment. The incentives should not and need not be in the form of monopoly rent, high tariffs, or other distortions. The risk of rent seeking and political capture can therefore be avoided. For firms in step 4 that discovered new industries successfully by themselves, the government may award them special recognition for their contribution to the country's economic development. This step addresses the externality issue.

The industries identified through the above process should be consistent with the country's latent comparative advantage. Once the pioneer firms come in successfully, many other firms will enter these industries as well. The government's facilitating role is mainly restricted to provision of information, coordination of hard and soft infrastructure improvement, and compensation for externalities. Government facilitation through the above approach is likely to help developing countries tap into the potential of the advantage of backwardness and realize dynamic and sustained growth.

In the explanation of the six-step procedure, several other ways of identifying binding constraints are mentioned. In the following, I explain how the growth identification and facilitation framework complements and adds new knowledge to the existing methods.

(1) *Business and investment environment.* There is robust empirical knowledge based on quantitative data on firm performance and perception-based data on the severity of a number of potential constraints facing firms in the developing world. However, this idea is based on the Washington Consensus, and its goal is to introduce a whole set of first-best institutions (in which all the optimality conditions are met). For example, it points out that in most of Sub-Saharan Africa, firms tend to consider many areas of the investment climate to be major obstacles to business development and the adoption of more sophisticated technology. Finance and access to land seem to be areas of particular concern to smaller firms; larger firms tend to perceive labor regulations and the availability of skilled labor as the main constraints to their activity; and firms across the board are concerned about corruption and infrastructure—especially network utilities such as electricity, telecommunications, transportation, and water (Gelb, Ramachadran, Shah, and Turner 2007).

Despite their usefulness, investment climate surveys, which try to capture the policy and institutional environment within which firms operate, can be misused or misinterpreted. First, the government may not have the capacity to introduce all those changes. Economic policies have to reflect the capacity of the state to implement them. In fact, identification of new industries and prioritization of government's limited resources to facilitate the development of those industries are both essential for successful growth strategies in developing countries. Because fiscal resources and implementation capacity are limited, the government in each of those countries has to prioritize and decide which particular efforts and facilities it should improve or where optimally to locate the public services to make those success stories happen. Deng Xiaoping explained that pragmatic wisdom at the beginning of China's transition to a market economy when he advocated for allowing a few regions and people to get rich first so as to achieve common prosperity for all people in the nation. The dynamic growth in those regions and industries would increase fiscal revenues, giving the government more resources to improve infrastructure for other regions in the nation later.

Second, another concern about investment climate surveys is that the first-best institutions may be different at different stages of development.

Countries at different levels of development tend to have different economic structures because of the differences in their endowments. The production activities of countries in the early levels of development tend to be labor-intensive or resource-intensive and usually rely on conventional, mature technologies and produce "mature," well-established products. Except for mining and plantations, this labor- and resource-intensive production has limited economies of scale. Their firm sizes are usually relatively small, and market transactions are often informal, limited to local markets with familiar people. The hard and soft infrastructure required for facilitating that type of production and market transactions is limited and relatively simple and rudimentary. At the other extreme of the development spectrum, high-income countries display a completely different endowment structure. The relatively abundant factor in their endowments is typically capital, not natural resources or labor. They tend to have comparative advantage in capital-intensive industries with economies of scale in production. The various types of hard infrastructure (power, telecommunications, roads, port facilities, etc.) and soft infrastructure (regulatory and legal frameworks, cultural value systems, etc.) that are needed must comply with the necessities of national and global markets where business transactions are long distance and large in quantity and value.

So the optimal institutions may be changing with levels of development. And it is, more or less, irrelevant to list the first-best institutions for developing countries at various stages of development.

Investment climate surveys have two more limitations. First, they do not provide information about industries that do not yet exist, but in which a country has latent comparative advantage. And the existing industries that are surveyed may not be consistent with the country's comparative advantage, either because they are too advanced (as a legacy of a development strategy that defied comparative advantage) or because they have become fundamentally uncompetitive (as a result of a general wage increase that accompanied the country's development). Second, such surveys will not suggest any compensation for the first-movers or ameliorate the external effects associated with the messages conveyed by first-movers.

(2) *Growth diagnostics.* Compared with the laundry list of needed reforms, the growth identification and facilitation framework focuses on binding constraints instead of the whole set of first-best institutions

(Hausmann et al. 2008). The growth diagnostics approach provides a decision-tree methodology to help identify the relevant binding constraints for any given country. It starts with a taxonomy of possible causes of low growth in developing countries, which generally suffer from either the high cost of finance (because of either low economic and social returns or a large gap between social and private returns) or low private returns on investment. The main step in the diagnostic analysis is to figure out which of these conditions more accurately characterizes the economy in question.

Although the growth diagnostics framework attempts to take the policy discussion of growth forward, its focus and the specification of its model remain quite macroeconomic. This is understandable; after all, growth is a macroeconomic concept, and taking the analysis to a sector level would raise issues of sector interactions and trade-offs.

The main concern about the growth diagnostics framework is still the fact that it relies on information based on existing production activities. These activities may be in industries where the country has no comparative advantages. There may be no firms in the new industries in which the countries have latent comparative advantage. It is quite cumbersome to use the growth diagnostics framework to find the industries with potential comparative advantage.

(3) *Product space.* Hausmann and Klinger (2006) investigated the evolution of a country's level of sophistication in exports and found that the industry upgrading process was easier when the move was to "nearby" products in the product space. This is so because every industry requires highly specific inputs such as knowledge, physical assets, intermediate inputs, labor skills, infrastructure, property rights, regulatory requirements, or other public goods. Established industries somehow have sorted out the many potential failures involved in ensuring the presence of all these inputs. The barriers preventing the emergence of new industries are less binding for nearby industries, which require only slight adaptations of existing inputs.

This idea is based on the fact that firms in existing sectors own tacit knowledge that is helpful for successful upgrading and diversification to nearby sectors in the product space. However, from the NSE perspective, the existing sectors may be the wrong sectors because of the wrong interventions in the past. Some sectors in which the country has latent comparative advantage may be totally new to the country, and the tacit knowledge can be brought in with foreign direct investment. In spirit, the comparative advantage and growth identification and facilitation idea is similar to that of monkeys jumping to nearby trees, but the step proposed here is much easier to implement than the product-space analysis proposed by them.

(4) *Randomized control trials.* This concept was adopted by researchers at the MIT Poverty Lab, who suggest that the quest for growth be recentered on assessing the impact of a development project or program (against explicit counterfactual outcomes). Starting with the idea that credible impact evaluations are needed to ensure that the most effective programs are scaled up at the national or international level, they design randomized control trials (RCTs) or social experiments that can be used to leverage the benefits of knowing which programs work and which do not (Duflo and Kremer 2003). Their approach is based on the notion that the standard aggregate growth paradigm relies, to a large extent and mistakenly, on the assumption of a rational representative agent. Stressing heterogeneity in country circumstances and among micro agents, this new wave of research attempts explicitly to account for the heterogeneity of individual households and firms in development analysis and policy. It has produced some useful tools for understanding the effectiveness of some specific microprojects. But even assuming that they can actually transfer lessons from localized development experiences to different geographic or cultural areas, RCTs still fall short in providing useful overall guidance to policymakers confronted with the design of development strategies. In sum, they search for ingredients instead of a recipe.

V. CONCLUDING REMARKS

In this chapter, I provide an NSE perspective on industrial policy, especially in developing countries. Economic development, which reflects ever-increasing average labor productivity and per capita income, is a process of continuous structural changes in technology, industries, and hard and soft infrastructure. The differences in economic structure for countries at different levels of economic development are a result of the differences in their endowment structure. Firms in an industry will be viable in an open, competitive market only if the industry is consistent with the comparative advantage determined by the economy's endowment structure. In the past, development thinking used the advanced countries as references and advised the developing countries to build up what the advanced countries had but they did not have (modern, large-scale, capital-intensive industries in structuralism) or to do what the advanced countries could do relatively well but the developing countries could not (business environment and governance in the neoliberal Washington Consensus). A third wave of new development thinking, NSE, advises developing countries to scale up what they could do well (their comparative advantages) based on what they have now (their endowments).

Every developing country has the potential to grow dynamically for decades, and to become a middle-income or even a high-income country in one or two generations, as long as its government has the right industrial policy to facilitate the development of the private sector along the lines of the country's comparative advantages and tap into the latecomer advantages. For the government's industrial policy to achieve that desirable result, a change in development thinking is necessary.

NOTES

Originally published in *China Economic Journal* 2014; 7: 382.

1. A country's *competitive advantage* refers to a situation in which domestic industries fulfill the following four conditions: (1) They intensively use the nation's abundant and relatively inexpensive factors of production. (2) Their products have large domestic markets. (3) Each industry forms a cluster. (4) The domestic market for each industry is competitive (Porter 1990). A country's *comparative advantage* is the situation in which it produces a good or service at a lower opportunity cost than that of its competitors. The first condition for competitive advantage listed by Porter suggests that the industries should be the economy's comparative advantage determined by the nations' endowments. The third and the fourth conditions will hold only if the industries are consistent with the nation's competitive advantage. Therefore, the four conditions can be reduced to two independent conditions: comparative advantage and domestic market size. Of these two independent conditions, comparative advantage is the more important because if an industry corresponds to the country's comparative advantage, then the industry's product will have a global market. That is why many of the richest countries of the world are very small (Lin and Ren 2007).

2. If a normally managed firm is expected to earn a socially acceptable profit in a free, competitive market without government protection or subsidies, the firm is viable. There could be many factors that affect the viability of a firm. I use the term *nonviability* to describe the inability of normally managed firms to earn socially acceptable profits because of the firms' choices of industry, product, and technology away from those deemed optimal by the economy's endowment structure.

3. The models based on increasing returns, such as Krugman (1981, 1987, 1991) and Matsuyama (1991), and coordination of investments, such as Murphy, Shleifer, and Vishny (1989), assume that the endowment structure of each country is identical and, therefore, that firms will be viable in an undistorted, open, competitive market once the government helps the firms overcome market failure and escape

the poor-equilibrium trap. Such models could be appropriate for considering the government's role in assisting firms to compete with those in other countries at a similar stage of development. Such models are, however, inappropriate as policy guidance for developing countries that are attempting to catch up with developed countries because the endowment structures in developing and developed countries are different. With government help, a developing country might be able to set up firms in advanced capital-intensive industries that have economies of scale; however, because of the scarcity of human and physical capital, the comparative cost of production of firms in the industry in the developing country will be higher than that for firms in a developed country in the same industry. The firms will, therefore, still be nonviable in an undistorted, open, competitive market. As such, the government needs to support and protect the firms continuously after they have been set up.

REFERENCES

Amsden, A. H. 1989. *Asia's Next Giant*. New York: Oxford University Press.

Chang, H.-J. 2003. *Kicking Away the Ladder: Development Strategy in Historical Perspective*. London: Anthem.

Chenery, Hollis B. 1961. "Comparative Advantage and Development Policy." *American Economic Review* 51(March): 18–51.

Duflo, E. 2004. "Scaling Up and Evaluation." In *Annual World Bank Conference on Development Economics 2004*, ed. F. Bourguignon and B. Pleskovic. Washington, D.C.: World Bank.

Duflo, E., and M. Kremer. 2003. "Use of Randomization in the Evaluation of Development Effectiveness." Paper prepared for the World Bank Operations Evaluation Department, July.

Gelb, A., V. Ramachadran, M.K. Shah, and G. Turner. 2007. "What Matters to African Firms? The Relevance of Perception Data." Policy Research Working Paper No. 4446. Washington, D.C.: World Bank.

Gerschenkron, A. 1962. *Economic Backwardness in Historical Perspective: A Book of Essays*. Cambridge, Mass.: Belknap.

Growth Commission. 2008. *The Growth Report: Strategies for Sustained Growth and Inclusive Development*. Washington, D.C.

Harrison, A., and A. Rodríguez-Clare. 2010. "Trade, Foreign Investment, and Industrial Policy for Developing Countries." In *Handbook of Economic Growth*, vol. 5, ed. D. Rodrik, 4039–213. Amsterdam: North-Holland.

Hausmann, R., and B. Klinger. 2006. "Structural Transformation and Patterns of Comparative Advantage in the Product Space." Working Paper No. 128. Cambridge, Mass.: Harvard University Center for International Development.

Hausmann, R., D. Rodrik, and A. Velasco. 2008. "Growth Diagnostics." In *The Washington Consensus Reconsidered: Towards a New Global Governance*, ed. N. Serra and J. E. Stiglitz, 324–54. New York: Oxford University Press.

Krueger, A. O., and B. Tuncer. 1982. "An Empirical Test of the Infant Industry Argument." *American Economic Review* 72: 1142–52.

Krugman, P. 1979. "A Model of Innovation, Technology Transfer, and the World Distribution of Income." *Journal of Political Economy* 87(2): 253–66.

——. 1981. "Trade, Accumulation and Uneven Development." *Journal of Development Economics* 8(2): 149–61.

——. 1987. "The Narrow Moving Band, the Dutch Disease, and the Competitive Consequences of Mrs. Thatcher." *Journal of Development Economics* 27(1/2): 41–55.

——. 1991. "History versus Expectations." *Quarterly Journal of Economics* 106(2): 651–67.

Lal, D. 1994. *Against Dirigisme: The Case for Unshackling Economic Markets.* San Francisco: International Center for Economic Growth, ICS.

Lin, Justin Yifu. 2003. "Development Strategy, Viability and Economic Convergence." *Economic Development and Cultural Change* 53: 277–308.

——. 2009. *Economic Development and Transition.* Cambridge: Cambridge University Press.

——. 2011. "New Structural Economics: A Framework for Rethinking Development." *The World Bank Economic Research Observer* 26(2): 193–221.

——. 2012. *New Structural Economics: A Framework for Rethinking Development and Policy.* Washington, D.C.: World Bank.

Lin, Justin Yifu, and C. Monga. 2011. "Growth Identification and Facilitation: The Role of the State in the Process of Dynamic Growth." *Development Policy Review* 29(3): 264–90.

Lin, Justin Yifu, and Ruoen Ren. 2007. "East Asian Miracle Debate Revisited" (in Chinese) *Jingji Yanjiu* (*Economic Research Journal*) 42(8): 4–12.

List, F. 1841 [1930]. *Das Nationale System der Politischen Ökonomie* (*The National System of Political Economy*), vol. 6, *Schriften, Reden, Briefe.* A. Sommer (ed.). Berlin: Reinmar Hobbing.

Matsuyama, K. 1991. "Increasing Returns, Industrialization and Indeterminacy of Equilibrium." *Quarterly Journal of Economics* 106(2): 616–50.

Murphy, Kevin M., Andrei Shleifer, and Robert W. Vishny. 1989. "Industrialization and Big Push." *Journal of Political Economy* 97: 1003–26.

Otsuka, K., G. Ranis, and G. Saxonhouse. 1988. *Comparative Technology Choice in Development: The Indian and Japanese Cotton Textile Industries.* London: Macmillan.

Pack, H., and K. Saggi. 2006. "Is There a Case for Industrial Policy? A Critical Survey." *World Bank Research Observer* 21(2): 267–97.

Porter, M. E. 1990. *The Competitive Advantage of Nations.* New York: Free Press.

Trebilcok, C. 1981. *The Industrialization of Continental Powers, 1780–1914.* London: Longman.

Wade, R. 1990. *Governing the Market.* Princeton, N.J.: Princeton University Press.

World Bank. 2011. *Global Development Horizons: Multipolarity: The New Global Economy.* Washington, D.C.: World Bank.

CHAPTER 9

Varieties of Industrial Policy

MODELS, PACKAGES, AND TRANSFORMATION CYCLES

Antonio Andreoni

INTRODUCTION

Over the past two decades the global manufacturing landscape has been reshaped by profound structural transformations. These structural dynamics have been mainly driven by changes *within* and increasing interdependences *across* national manufacturing systems as well as alterations to their underpinning sectors and technologies. In this respect the global financial crisis has been accelerating ongoing structural trends, e.g., in terms of redistribution and polarization of manufacturing production across countries and regions. Deindustrialization (the loss of strategic manufacturing industries), increasing trade imbalances, and decreasing technological dynamism have all been major concerns in advanced industrial economies. Meanwhile in middle-income countries, governments have been increasingly threatened by emerging giants that are capturing global manufacturing production and export shares, aggressively pulling ahead in the global technological race. Finally, developing countries have been increasingly questioning the sustainability of a growth model focused mainly on natural resource extraction and, thus, have attempted intra- and intersectoral upgrading measures.

This chapter analyzes and contrasts the variety of industrial policies that a number of major industrial economies have designed and implemented in the recent past in order to govern these transformations and respond to the different challenges they create. In particular, this chapter focuses on three major advanced economies, namely, the United States, Japan, and Germany, whose industrial policies have historically constituted "learning benchmarks" in their respective continental regions. Furthermore, three major economies in the catch-up phase are considered—Brazil, China, and South Africa—which, despite their varying sizes and other fundamental differences, are key reference points and loci for industrial policy experimentation and innovation.

The variation in countries' industrial policy experiences is driven by their contextual—institutional and structural—and political economy differences as well as by the different policy space and rationales for government action. Based on a taxonomic and comparative stylization of countries' industrial policy, this chapter reveals and contrasts emerging patterns and trends in industrial policy practices, as revealed by official government policy documents. These patterns and trends are discussed by providing detailed references to particular institutional solutions and policy instruments. In particular, the chapter focuses on the different industrial policy *governance models* and *packages of measures* adopted by the selected countries over time, i.e., along different *transformation cycles*.

With respect to the industrial policy governance model, this chapter accounts for the existence of multilayered models combining top-down and bottom-up policy interventions. These are managed by different local, regional, national, or federal governments. A multilayered governance model offers greater flexibility in the composition of an industrial policy package, and it often allows for more selectivity in policy design, better monitoring, and policy enforcement. However, it also requires building an articulated institutional infrastructure and achieving an *industrial policy governance coordination* among all the government actors.

Individual policy measures can, of course, target different factor inputs of a country's manufacturing system such as technologies, finance, and infrastructure and act upon different levels of the system (firms, sectors, manufacturing and industrial systems, macroeconomic framework) with varying effectiveness. However, the chapter highlights how the composition and management of overall *industrial policy packages* are increasingly a major source of countries' advantage. Policy measures are intrinsically interdependent and are linked by circular and cumulative relationships. *Industrial policy measures alignment* within policy packages is a response to a fundamental need, namely, managing interdependencies among different policy measures and their cumulative effects. Interdependencies among different policy measures are determined by many factors, including size, "close policy complementarity" (e.g., between technology and sectoral policies), and time horizon or span.

Policy measures tend to operate with different time horizons according to the specific target or challenge they are addressing. Their success depends on two factors: the extent to which the government is able to manage the policy time frame (sometimes by guaranteeing long-term support, in other circumstances by removing the policy when it becomes counterproductive or generates unproductive rents) and the synchronization of policy measures along subsequent *transformation cycles*. Going beyond the standard idea that the policy cycle is linked to one specific government action, this concept is evoked here to identify a cycle of industrial policy action including the government industrial policy measures at a certain time but also those still active measures and institutions introduced by previous governments. Taken all together, these measures constitute the relevant industrial policy package acting upon the national manufacturing system.

This chapter has five main sections. Following the "Introduction," the second section, "Drivers of Industrial Policy Variety," introduces the main drivers of industrial policy variety, namely, differences in the industrial policy context and policy space. According to countries' industrial structures, governments face not only different policy problems (e.g., structural transformation of certain sectors, technological upgrading, and integration in global value chains) but also policy opportunities (e.g., distinctive technological competencies, market access, institutional strengths). The way in which governments address these problems and capture certain opportunities depends on the specific institutional settings characterizing their countries, both their institutional architectures and political settlements. The industrial policy space will also depend, among other things, on the set of policy rationales that are dominant in a certain historical moment.

The third section, "The Industrial Policy Context: Industrial Structures and Institutional Settings," develops the main methodology adopted for analyzing the variety of industrial policy models and the different sets of industrial policy measures constituting the country's policy package. Different transformation cycles are also distinguished based on the time horizon or span of different measures within each policy package. Building on a number of contributions, the chapter presents an advanced taxonomic approach for industrial policy analysis.

The fourth section, "Varieties of Industrial Policy," applies the methodology presented to the six country cases selected, namely, the United States, Japan, Germany, Brazil, China, and South Africa. For each we provide a detailed account of the industrial policy trajectory followed and its current industrial policy model, package, and transformation cycle. Within the plurality of policy measures and institutions identified, this chapter focuses on the most distinctive measures, tools, or institutions adopted in each country. These measures, tools, or institutions are at the frontier of today's industrial policy action. The final section of the chapter, "The New Industrial Policy Frontier: Emerging Global Trends and Practices," takes stock of the multicountry comparative analysis to extract the emerging trends, variety, and convergence of industrial policies in major industrial economies.

DRIVERS OF INDUSTRIAL POLICY VARIETY

Over the last two centuries all those countries that managed to reach a certain level of industrialization and development have implemented a wide spectrum of industrial, technology, and manufacturing policies. Despite a number of similarities in countries' industrial policy experiences and their common fundamental goals (such as the transformation of industrial structures and technological infrastructure), there is significant historical evidence testifying to the extraordinary *variety of industrial policy pathways* (Johnson 1982; Hall 1986; Dore 1986; Okimoto, 1989; Amsden 1989; Wade 1990; Stiglitz 1996; Evans 1995; Chang 2002; Cimoli, Dosi, and Stiglitz 2009; Stiglitz and Lin 2013; Noman et al. 2011; Mazzucato 2014; Salazar-Xirinachs, Nubler, and Kozul-Wright 2014).

Such variety follows from the fact that, at each point in time, a country's industrial policy (i.e., its specific targets, instruments, and mix of measures) will result from a historical and contextual tension. Specifically, this policy-generating tension is between a country's past (its inherited industrial structure and institutional setting) and its envisioned future (its government's industrial vision). It is critical to understand the *policy context* in which industrial policies are designed, implemented, and enforced in each country along its development trajectory in order to disentangle the variety of industrial policies we observe today. Moreover, given that in developing its industrial vision and policies the government will be enabled (or constrained) by the dominant set of industrial policy rationales, it is important to identify what "policy space" different rationales open (or close) in different historical phases. In other words, the room to maneuver available to policymakers reflects the way in which governments understand their relationship and role in the development and transformation of their economies.

THE INDUSTRIAL POLICY CONTEXT: INDUSTRIAL STRUCTURES AND INSTITUTIONAL SETTINGS

The industrial policy context is mainly defined by the country's industrial structure (particularly in relation to its main competitors in the global market) and its institutional setting wherein industrial policy measures are designed, implemented, and enforced, both directly and indirectly. At different stages of development, countries are characterized by different industrial structures, i.e., by a different sectoral and export-basket composition, technological infrastructure, manufacturing systems organization, and degree of market concentration. The industrial diagnostics presented in table 9.1 provide a first snapshot of these differences for the selected countries.

As a result of these structural differences, industrial policies in developing countries such as China, Brazil, and South Africa have faced a number of challenges, including the creation of completely new sectors (e.g., sectoral policies), the absorption and development of technologies, and the achievement of certain product quality standards (e.g., technology, trade, and standardization policies). In contrast, industrialized economies have relied on different policy measures in response to the dramatic transformations in the global manufacturing landscape beginning in the mid-1990s and the "manufacturing loss" experienced during the global financial crisis (Andreoni 2015a). Specifically, they have increasingly come to depend on a combination of policies aimed at (1) rebuilding their manufacturing basis (e.g., incentives, subsidies, and public investment in advanced manufacturing to increase internal production capacity) and (2) winning the global race at the technological frontier (e.g., mission-oriented policies and high-tech strategies).

Even within the group of industrialized economies such as the United States, Germany, and Japan remarkable differences in industrial structures (e.g., their sectoral and technological strengths) have triggered different lines of industrial policy intervention. Japan, whose export performance has been traditionally dependent on two sectors (automotive and electronics), implemented measures aimed at diversifying and increasing the resilience of its industrial base. Germany, in contrast, thanks to its diversified and well-organized manufacturing system, was able to focus

Table 9.1 Industrial Structures in Selected Countries (constant 2000 US$)

	Mfg Value Added (MVA) per Capita	Mfg Export per Capita	Medium-High Tech MVA as Percent of Total MVA	MVA as a Percent of GDP	Medium-High Tech Mfg Export as Percent of Total Mfg Export	MVA as Percent of Total Export	MVA as Percent of World MVA	Mfg Export as Percent of World Mfg Trade
Japan	7,993.99	5,521.02	53.70	20.39	79.75	91.62	14.13	6.53
United States	5,522.09	2,736.13	51.52	14.85	64.74	76.76	24.04	7.97
Germany	4,666.91	13,397.43	56.76	18.57	72.34	86.81	5.32	10.22
China	820.02	1,123.62	40.70	34.16	60.52	96.25	15.33	14.06
Brazil	622.10	667.55	34.97	13.51	36.30	67.30	1.71	1.23
South Africa	567.27	991.15	21.24	14.93	45.66	68.32	0.39	0.45

Source: UNIDO INDSTAT & UNCOMTRADE.

on a technological transition driven by a national green agenda. Finally, the United States, whose manufacturing base has shrunk over the years (reaching a share to GDP ratio below 15 percent) with national champions such as DuPont and IBM having sent production and R&D activities offshore, took a different approach again. The federal government has boosted investment in rebuilding critical production and manufacturing scale-up competencies (O'Sullivan et al. 2013).

The way in which these different policy measures (triggered by different industrial structures) are designed, implemented, and enforced critically depends on the countries' institutional setting. Indeed, to a certain extent, a country's institutional setting develops alongside its industrial structure. This is why countries at initial stages of industrialization, such as the least developed countries (LDCs), or countries such as the United Kingdom that have been experiencing rapid processes of deindustrialization, do not simply face a structural problem of rebuilding their manufacturing basis. Rather, they also face an institutional problem in terms of rebuilding local, regional, and national institutions capable of supporting their industrial sector and their governments' policy action toward that sector.

Within a country's institutional setting we can observe a variety of institutions such as government agencies and departments, development banks, intermediate R&D institutions, industry associations, and chambers of commerce. Each of these can take different forms and perform a plurality of functions affecting industries. The importance of maintaining a distinction between institutional forms and institutional functions has been stressed by Chang (2007, 23) when he highlights the following: "At the very general level, we may say that there are certain functions that institutions have to serve if they are to promote economic development, and that there are certain forms of institutions that serve these functions the best. However, the difficulty is that we cannot come up with an agreed list of the 'essential' functions nor an obvious match between these functions and particular forms of institutions."

In fact, the same institutional functions may be fulfilled by different institutions, and these institutions may take different forms. Moreover, institutions do not work in isolation. They are linked by both diachronic and synchronic relationships of complementarity (Aoki 2001). For example, the "thick" institutional setting underpinning the German manufacturing system includes both a financial infrastructure (development banks and production-focused local banks) and a technological infrastructure (intermediate institutions such as Fraunhofers and industry associations). Crucially, these two infrastructures have codeveloped over time and provide *combined* support to manufacturing companies. Given the prevalence of these kinds of complex interrelationships linking institutions and distributing functions within a certain institutional setting, countries that attempt to import certain institutions are often unsuccessful.

Regulation theory and the literature on the varieties of capitalism have pointed to the relevance of different institutional settings that result from interest-group conflict as a way of understanding this context. Various contributions identified stylized types of capitalist systems and provided insights into the variety of labor-market relationships, natural resource management systems, corporate governance models, and innovation systems (Boyer 1990; Hall and Soskice 2001; Hancke, Rhodes, and Thatcher 2007; Stortz et al. 2013; Walker, Brewster, and Wood 2014). Less attention has been paid to the variety of industrial policy practices and the way in which countries' industrial policy pathways unfold from the interaction between the transformation of industrial structures and changes in their institutional settings (Chang and Rowthorn 1995; Andreoni and Scazzieri 2013; Chang, Andreoni, and Kuan 2013; Akram and Andreoni 2015). Industrial structures and institutional settings are embedded in (and an expression of) the contested domain of interactions and conflicts among different interest groups, both within and beyond national boundaries (Khan and Jomo 2001).

Institutional settings are a fundamental source of industrial policy variety because they are an expression of the distribution of interests and relative power among different groups in a certain country. Distribution of interests and power relationships are also embedded into the same industrial structure and reflect the degree of influence of certain sectors (e.g., finance versus industry, advanced manufacturing industries versus traditional industries or agriculture). They also reflect the influence of different groups within the same sectors (e.g., export-oriented versus inward-looking companies; high-tech versus low-tech companies; companies downstream or upstream in sectoral value chains; domestic versus foreign companies). Thus a country's political settlement determines both "the holding power of firms of different types" and "the effectiveness of particular governance agencies [and] their choices of policy instruments," in particular their management of learning rents (Khan 2013, 274).

To summarize, the variety of industrial policy pathways we observe in today's developed and developing countries and their varying success rates are determined by the circular and cumulative relationship linking industrial structures, institutional settings, and political settlements. For this reason, the comparative analysis of industrial policy variety we present here specifically focuses on a selected number of structural, institutional, and political economy dimensions for each country considered.

THE INDUSTRIAL POLICY SPACE:
CHANGING POLICY RATIONALES

Since World War II countries have gone through three main waves of industrial policies (1940–1970; 1990s to early 2000; 2005 onwards). This was only interrupted by a phase (1970–1990) dominated by the idea that the best industrial policy is no industrial policy. Throughout the first two industrial policy waves, the industrial policy space was defined by two main sets of policy rationales. These were *structural coordination problems* related to demand and technological complementarities; resource scarcity and production factors specificity; and *market failures* determined by information asymmetries, externalities, and public goods (for a review see Pack and Saggi 2006; Rodrik 2007; Chang et al. 2013; Andreoni and Chang 2016).

All these failures have both static and dynamic implications and thus imply trade-offs between "allocative" and "growth" efficiency. As a result of the intertwining of the industrial and innovation policy debates, over the last decade (2005 onward), a new set of *systemic failures* has been increasingly recognized. Relatively less emphasis has been given to sectoral explanations of technology push and demand pull dynamics, at least in the context of the most advanced economies (Soete 2007; Laranya, Uyarra, and Flanagan 2008). In this subsection we analyze these three types of policy rationale in greater detail.

Structural coordination problems tend to arise as dynamic market failures, especially as a result of *strategic uncertainty* (Chang 1994; Lin and Chang 2009; Aghion et al. 2012; Lin 2012). The first problem of coordination is related to the existence of demand complementarities and increasing returns to scale in manufacturing industries (Roseinstein-Rodan 1957; Nurkse 1952). Many sectors and industries require a series of complementary investments in interconnected activities in the early phases of their development. This is so because their returns, and sometimes even existence, depend on their being all structurally connected through a web of forward and backward linkages (Hirschman 1958).

This argument applies not only to developing economies but also to countries at the technological and production frontiers which might also require complementary investments in sets of interrelated new key enabling technologies or production activities. This is increasingly the case given the systemic (and cross-sectoral) nature of manufacturing production and technologies (Tassey 2007). Governments can act to overcome structural bottlenecks along countries' transformation trajectories, facilitating the alignment over time of strategic investments (Andreoni and Scazzieri 2013). Specifically, they can adopt a series of specific subsidies and incentives that do not even have to imply any money transfer, such as ex ante guarantee schemes (Rodrik 2004, 14).

A second problem of structural coordination occurs in the presence of "competing investments." In modern industries, large firms sustain initial huge investments in machinery and productive capacity in order to achieve efficient scale of production. As these initial costs are generally specific and "sunk," oligopolistic competition in these sectors may lead to price wars that may destroy parts of firms' assets or may lead them to bankruptcy. The state can intervene ex ante in many ways to prevent this loss of specific capital. For example, in Japan the state adopted a system of "entry licenses" and in South Korea a "conditional entry system" that artificially tried to "clear" the market by adjusting the supply to the evolution of demand (Chang 1994).

However, collective-action problems may be related not only to investment but also to situations of temporary disinvestment or structural change in the industrial sector. Recession cartels and mechanisms of negotiated exit have been widely used to face periods of economic crisis or accompany structural transformation to reduce losses in the face of limited factor mobility. In these situations, industrial policies introduce "a 'protective' element—that is 'helping losers' by temporarily shielding them from the full forces of the market" (Chang 2003, 262). More generally, the state can introduce mechanisms of socialization of risk to encourage and sustain the process of structural change, economic diversification, and overall productivity growth.

Market failure rationales build on the idea of information problems, namely, insufficient information and lack of price signals, leading to underinvestment (Greenwald and Stiglitz 1986; Stiglitz and Greenwald 2014). Investment in new nontraditional industrial sectors might be strictly limited by capital market failures, lack of effective equity markets, or insufficient financing resources internal to the firm. Moreover, the price mechanism does "not provide clear enough indication of the profitability of resources that do not actually exist (e.g., new skills and technology)" (Ul-Haque 2007, 3).

To deal with these market failures, governments can become a direct surrogate for the capital market through development banks focusing on long-term loans, venture-capital schemes, and alternative forms of risk sharing through bailouts (Stiglitz and Yusuf 2001). They can also nurture infant industries by providing subsidies for a limited time balanced with strong performance requirements, e.g., export market requirements (Chang 1994). Some of these policies can also address problems related to *informational externalities* and "appropriability" in the process of "self-discovery" which drastically affect investment in new activities and technologies (Hausmann and Rodrik 2004; Rodrik 2004). Problems of returns appropriability, and thus underinvestment, also become severe when we deal with highly specific public goods (Tassey 2007) and commonly available manufacturing capabilities (Pisano and Shih 2012).

In recent years, the structural coordination and market failure rationales have been enriched and partially reformulated within a new understanding of techno-innovation dynamics as well as the increasing systemic nature of the modern global economy structured around multisupply chains (Milberg and Winkler 2013). The Systems of Innovation literature pioneered by Freeman (1987), Lundvall (1992), and Nelson (1993) gave way to the identification of new innovation policy rationales. These include infrastructural and institutional problems; technological lock-in, path dependency, and transition failures; quality of linkages and networks configuration failures; and issues related to learning dynamics at the firm, local network, and system levels (Lall 1992; Metcalfe 1995; Edquist 1997; Malerba 2002; Klein Woolthuis, Lankhuizen, and Gilsing 2005).

Some of these policy rationales have also been gradually adopted in the industrial policy debate under the heading of *systemic or network failures* (Chaminade and Edquist 2006; Coe, Dicken, and Hess 2008; Cimoli, Dosi, and Stiglitz 2009; Dodgson, Hughes, Foster, and Metcalfe 2011; Kuznetsov and Sabel 2011; Wade 2012; Stiglitz and Greenwald 2014). These contributions share a holistic conception of the innovation process. More distinctively they also have a multilayered representation of industrial systems whereby agents (i.e., firms, research centers, intermediaries, etc.) are embedded in a network of horizontal and vertical interdependencies that determine their production and innovation performances. Systemic failures may unfold both within and across regional and national industrial systems, all of them being interconnected through global supply chains.

In developing their vision and policy, governments in both developed and developing countries are increasingly relying on a new *policy rationale synthesis*. This combines classical market failures and structural coordination rationales with the new learning and systemic failures arguments developed in innovation and manufacturing systems studies. Modern manufacturing companies orchestrate production processes through complex producer networks spanning across countries as well as different industrial sectors. Modern manufacturing systems consist of complex interdependencies, often across a range of industries, which contribute a variety of components, materials, production systems and subsystems, producer services, and product-related service systems (Tassey 2007 and 2014; Berger 2013; Milberg and Winkler 2013; Locke and Wellhausen 2014).

The taxonomic approach we will now develop to analyze the varieties of recent industrial policy packages is specifically designed to distinguish and draw attention to the policies that work on this systemic level. Indeed, as we will discuss in the sections "Varieties of Industrial Policy" and "The New Industrial Policy Frontier: Emerging Global Trends and Practices," one of the main manifestations of this new policy rationale synthesis is the governments' increasing reliance on policy measures operating at the level of the manufacturing system, beyond classical sectoral boundaries.

INDUSTRIAL POLICY VARIETY AND CHALLENGES: A TAXONOMIC FRAMEWORK

Market, structural, and systemic failures provide governments with an articulated set of policy rationales reflecting the changing conditions of the global industrial system. They also expand the industrial policy space and force a rethinking of the role of regional, national, and supranational governments. Industrial policy definitions have been shaped by these rationales and articulated along the distinction between *selective* (also called *vertical*) and *horizontal* policies, the former being firm- or sector-based while the latter are mainly macroeconomic.

Often comparative analyses of countries' industrial policy packages have relied upon policy rationales and degrees of selectivity of different policy measures. For example, Weiss (2011) proposes a taxonomy listing "market-based measures" according to the policy rationale and their coverage (i.e., degree of selectivity). Kuznetsov and Sabel (2011) build on the distinction between vertical and horizontal policies, comparing different generations of industrial policies across countries. Benhassine and Raballand (2009) consider different degrees of selectivity against the extent of subsidization. Cimoli et al. (2006) propose an exploratory taxonomy distinguishing domains of policy intervention and for each of them policy measures underpinned by different policy rationales. Finally, Warwick (2013) proposes a "typology of industrial policy instruments" structured by policy domains and their horizontal versus selective nature.

Within the national innovation and manufacturing system literature, these types of taxonomy have been also used. For example, the System of Innovationpolicy framework developed by Klein Woolthuis, Lankhuizen, and Gilsing (2005) contrasts "rules" (different system failures) and "actors" (missing actors). Dodgson et al. (2011) develop a policy approach schema comparing countries' trajectories according to their mix of market and coordination logics. To investigate the emerging industrial policies across a selected number of OECD countries, O'Sullivan et al. (2013) present another industrial policy matrix. This maps countries' industrial policy mixes against different "levels of policy intervention" and various "factor inputs" of the national manufacturing system.

In our comparative analysis we build on these contributions to analyze industrial policy varieties. The taxonomic approach we develop here for the comparative analysis maps each country's policy measure i, with $i = 1, 2, \ldots, n$ against two main composite dimensions (policy models and industrial policy packages) and a time dimension (transformation cycle). Figure 9.1 sketches the overall taxonomy as well as the three main policy challenges that governments face in industrial policy making. First is the coordination of the different policy agents within a multilayered industrial policy governance model (*policy governance model and coordination*). The second problem is related to the existence of cumulative interdependencies between the different policy measures within the industrial policy package (*policy packages and measures alignment*). The third problem is the challenge associated with synchronizing policy measures and packages over time (*policy synchronization along transformation cycles*).

POLICY GOVERNANCE MODELS AND COORDINATION

With the first dimension we account for the possibility of different policy governance models. The policy model is defined according to the way

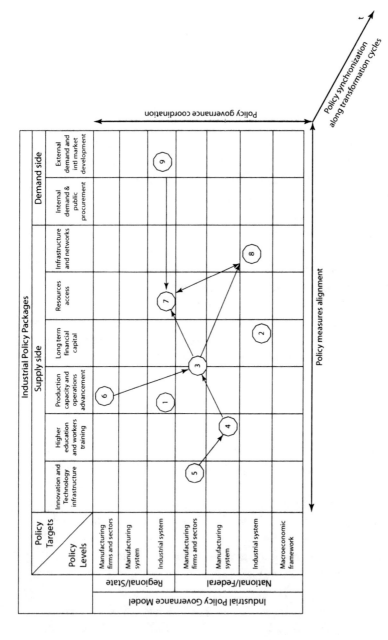

Figure 9.1 Policy package matrix and the industrial policy challenges

Note: In this explanatory policy package matrix, the country has nine main policy measures (two of them—numbers 1 and 2—are new, not having been active in previous transformation cycles). The arrow highlights the existence of interdependencies between different policy measures. In the country cases in section 4 we will report only the measures in the matrix, while the transformation cycles are reported in separate tables. The policy linkages are discussed in the country policy variety analysis.

in which a country frames its industrial policy and the different actors involved in its design, implementation, and enforcement. Countries may frame their industrial policies either within *central plan-based strategies* or within multiple *decentralized initiative-based measures*. In the former case, the policy model tends to be top-down i.e., the national or federal government designs, implements, and enforces the policies. In the latter, the policy model is bottom-up, which means that a plurality of regional or state actors within nations and federations orchestrate multiple industrial policies.

Although this bottom-up model allows for more selective interventions and introduces a certain degree of flexibility in policy action, countries without diffused institutions and distributed government capabilities cannot afford it. Also multiple decentralized initiative-based measures may lack coherence or might conflict and overlap. To avoid this industrial policy coordination problem, governments that could rely on well-developed institutional settings adopted a multilayered policy model combining top-down and bottom-up policy measures.

In the top-down model, targets, objectives, and lines of policy action are formalized in national plans or strategies (as in the East Asian economies as well as in Brazil, India, and South Africa). Countries adopting a more multilayered policy model rely on several specific policy actions and initiatives. These are then reconnected within broader policy strategies whose function is mainly to ensure coherence when these policies reach a scale whereby policy actions require high-level investment or affect broader national or federal interests. This is what has occurred typically in the United States and Germany and to a lesser extent in Japan.

POLICY PACKAGES AND MEASURES ALIGNMENT: TARGETS AND LEVELS OF POLICY INTERVENTION

The second dimension considered in our taxonomy includes two sets of policy measures within industrial policy packages: supply-side and demand-side measures. Supply-side measures are then subdivided into specific factor-inputs policies. The supply-side list starts with policies affecting the innovation and technology infrastructure (typically innovation and technology policies, including precommercial procurement). Then there is higher education and workers' training (typically education policies) followed by production capacity and advanced manufacturing operations (typically manufacturing policies, conditional subsidies and incentives, matching grant schemes, etc.). The list moves on to long-term capital access (typically bank and finance regulations, SMEs' finance policies, development banks, and interest rate macropolicies), resource access (typically energy and technology policies), and finally infrastructure and networks (typically infrastructural and standardization policies). The demand-side measures include standard forms of public procurement (more or less strategically oriented) as well as measures aimed at both giving national companies access to existing external markets and developing new markets.

For both national/federal and regional/state policies and for both supply-side and demand-side measures, we consider three possible *levels of policy action*: individual manufacturing sectors, the manufacturing system, and the industrial system. The dramatic changes in the global manufacturing system (Tassey 2007; Andreoni and Gregory 2013) have necessitated going beyond the standard levels of policy actions, namely, *sectors* (and specific firms when the sector is highly concentrated) and the *macroeconomic framework*. Hence we also identify measures acting upon the *manufacturing system* (thus, across manufacturing sectors) and the *industrial system* as a whole (including the construction, energy, and agroindustry activities).

For each country, each identified policy measure has been mapped against the two main dimensions (as in figure 9.1), and information has been provided in separate tables (tables 9.2, 9.3, 9.4, 9.5, 9.6, 9.7) on the amounts allocated and the government agency managing the policy. Going beyond conventional comparative analyses of countries' industrial policies, where the main emphasis is on the selectivity or effectiveness of single policy measures, our taxonomic approach links individual policy measures and analyzes them as part of an *industrial policy package*.

There are two main reasons that justify this approach. First, the effectiveness of a single policy measure depends on its linkages with other policy measures acting upon the same companies, sectors, and specific institutions of the manufacturing system. Since policies do not work in isolation, their effectiveness might improve by changing or introducing other complementary measures. Also, as is increasingly recognized in the literature (Aiginger and Sieber 2006; Chang 2010), horizontal measures tend to have unintended vertical effects. Thus even at the same level of policy intervention, policy measures might be more or less selective according to the way in which they affect both factor input productivity and the different role that each factor input plays in different manufacturing sectors and along different value chains (Okimoto 1989, 9). In other words, we need to examine the policy complementarities within an overall industrial policy package to capture the degree of selectivity as well as the effectiveness of each individual measure.

Second, the combined effect of different policies (e.g., technology, education, and public procurement policies) tends to be different from the one that the government can achieve by the independent implementation of the same policy measures at different times. An important consequence is that the government can in fact change an incentive system, firms' behavior, or the distribution of rents with combined policies, even with policies that seem, at first sight, to conflict with one another.

In his account of the lessons learned from East Asia, Stiglitz (1996) emphasizes how these countries can be understood only by analyzing their "packages of interactive measures" whereby companies were exposed to different types of internal and external competitive pressures. This policy option is also stressed by Chang (2010, 100) when he writes the following: "In East Asia, free trade, export promotion (which is, of course, not free trade), and infant industry protection were organically integrated, both in cross-section terms (so there always will be some industries subject to each category of policy, sometimes more than one at the same time) and over time (so, the same industry may be subject to more than one of the three over time)." Finally, in the context of Scandinavian countries, Landesmann (1992, 242) stresses how these countries adopted an "interesting mix of both defensive and constructive policies." Our taxonomic approach is able to organize these kinds of policy combinations and study their system-level industrial effects.

POLICY SYNCHRONIZATION AND TRANSFORMATION CYCLES

Policy measures have different time horizons. To recompose the industrial policy package characterizing a given country at each point in time, we introduce the idea of the transformation cycle (T-cycle). While the concept of a policy cycle is generally linked to one specific government action, the *transformation* cycle is defined by starting with the set of policy measures that are active during a certain time and that, within that time frame, constitute a comprehensive policy package. This is defined independently from the government in power and the policy measures it introduces during its policy cycle. Countries' difficulties in *synchronizing policies over time* within each transformation cycle as well as transitioning from one transformation cycle to another (thus from one coherent policy package to another) help explain discontinuities in their industrialization paths.

In the comparative analysis of our country case studies, we have scanned industrial policy measures starting from their last transformation cycle. Each time the identified policy measures appeared to be linked with active policies adopted in previous transformation cycles, they were included in the current industrial policy package. The consideration of transformation cycles allows us to avoid a typical problem in industrial policy analysis, namely, understanding the full package of industrial policy measures that companies face independently from the policies implemented (or simply rebranded) by the current government. For the same reason, governments often find it difficult to recompose the full picture of active industrial policy measures in order to address their potential overlaps or incoherencies, so this analysis can help at the policy-making level as well (Andreoni, Frattini and Prodi, 2016).

The following country sections will mainly focus on the most recent transformation cycles, given that we are aiming at identifying emerging trends, common themes, and policy practices. However, for each country the list of policy measures, together with the allocated amounts and government agencies involved, will report the specific transformation cycle of each policy measure, while they will be visually clustered within the matrix as in figure 9.1. Finally, given the exponential variety and difficulties in reporting regional/state level policy measures, only a selection of representative ones has been discussed.

VARIETIES OF INDUSTRIAL POLICY

The following sections detail the industrial policy varieties for three major industrialized and three major catch-up economies. Within the plurality of policy measures and institutions identified, this chapter focuses on a number of distinctive measures, tools, and institutions adopted in each country. These measures, tools, and institutions are at the frontier of today's industrial policy action. The final section, "The New Industrial Policy Frontier" identifies the emerging focal policy domains.

UNITED STATES: REBUILDING THE MANUFACTURING FOUNDATIONS

Since Alexander Hamilton's *Report on the Subject of Manufactures*, the U.S. government has played a major developmental and entrepreneurial role by adopting and refining various industrial, trade, and technology policies (Chang 2002; Chang et al. 2013). During WW II and the subsequent Cold War, the United States implemented industrial policy packages including long-term procurement contracts, subsidies, investment guarantees, and strategic bailout measures (Markusen 1996). More crucially, the federal government founded and developed an industrial policy institutional infrastructure that conducted basic research and development (R&D) (e.g., national laboratories) as well as managed and financed major industrial initiatives and technological innovations (Block 2008; Tassey 2010; Mazzucato 2014). Today's major players include the Department of Defense, the National Institutes of Health, the National Science Foundation (NSF), the National Institute for Standards and Technology (NIST), the Departments of Energy and Agriculture, and the National Aeronautics and Space Administration (NASA).

Some of today's most successful industrial policy measures in the United States have been introduced and continuously supported along various transformation cycles (see figure 9.2). This is the case of two programs run by the Small Business Administration (SBA), namely, the Small Business Investment Company (SBIC) and the Small Business Innovation Research (SBIR) and Small Business Technology Transfer (STTR). These programs combine loans, R&D grants, and precommercial public procurement to support small businesses, original equipment manufacturers (OEMs), and specialist manufacturing contractors engaged in the development and scale-up of technological systems or components (sometimes for niche segments). With the SBIR Enhancement Act in 2011, the operational and financial capacity of the SBIR was expanded to fuel the economy with $2.5–3 billion in financial capital (Wessner and Wolff 2012). The Manufacturing Extension Partnership (MEP) is another program started in the 1980s, relaunched during the Bush administration, and more recently boosted by a 100 percent budget increase. Today the MEP includes 60 states and regional centers with around 1,300 staff (Ezell and Atkinson, 2011).

Since 2000, the U.S. federal and state governments have gone through three main transformation cycles. The first cycle (2000–2008) under the Bush administration (*American Competitiveness Initiative*) was mainly focused on the traditional pillars of U.S. industrial policies. Specifically, during this cycle the aims were to (1) improve the competitiveness of the industrial system by providing skills, finance, and a tax-friendly business environment, (2) ensure access to international markets through bilateral

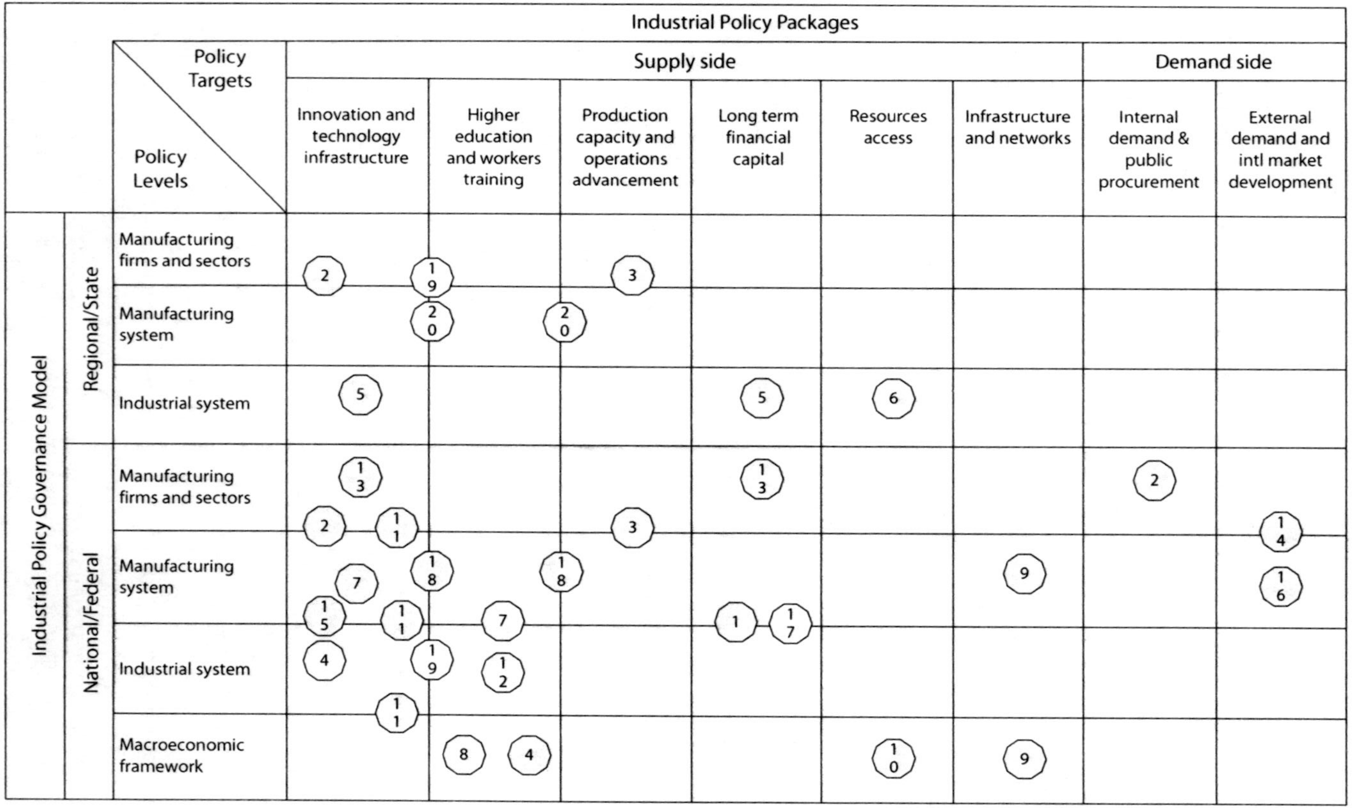

Industrial Policy Packages

Industrial Policy Governance Model	Policy Levels	Policy Targets	Supply side — Innovation and technology infrastructure	Higher education and workers training	Production capacity and operations advancement	Long term financial capital	Resources access	Infrastructure and networks	Demand side — Internal demand & public procurement	External demand and intl market development
Regional/State		Manufacturing firms and sectors	2	19	3					
Regional/State		Manufacturing system		20	20					
Regional/State		Industrial system	5			5	6			
National/Federal		Manufacturing firms and sectors	13, 2, 11	18	3	13				14, 16
National/Federal		Manufacturing system	7, 15, 11, 18	7, 12		17, 1			2	
National/Federal		Industrial system	19					9		
National/Federal		Macroeconomic framework	4, 11	8, 4			10	9		

Figure 9.2 The policy package matrix in the United States

and multilateral agreements, and (3) boost various initiative-based and mission-oriented technology policies. Federal-level initiatives were also complemented by state-level sectoral policies reflecting different states' manufacturing specializations. These initiatives included the setting up of *economic opportunity zones* as well as various energy policy and initiatives connected to new fracking technologies for shale gas (O'Sullivan et al. 2013).

The 2007–8 financial crisis and the subsequent sharp manufacturing loss and employment crisis opened a new industrial policy transformation cycle with an unprecedented one-time US$ 787 billion stimulus package. The American Recovery and Reinvestment Act (ARRA) of 2009 is an extremely articulated policy package covering almost the totality of policy domains. In table 9.2, we focus on a subset of ARRA initiatives more strictly related to industries. Some measures addressed immediate national priorities such as the ad hoc bailouts of entire industrial blocks in the automotive sector (e.g., General Motors and Chrysler). Other policies addressed emerging weaknesses in the U.S. economy.

To confront these weaknesses, the Obama administration first addressed the dramatic shortage of science, technology, engineering, and mathematics graduates and skilled workers via almost $100 billion of federal investment coupled with state-level initiatives. The health sector (and its industries) received another massive boost of more than $100 billion, while an ambitious infrastructural program was launched to address communication, energy, and transportation infrastructure (e.g., roads, grids, and networks). Finally, the possibility of inducing a techno-paradigmatic shift in the energy sector was taken up as a new pathway for systemic structural change and sustained growth. Clean-energy initiatives, mixing loan guarantees for renewable energies, electricity transmission projects, and smart grids, as well as grants for batteries and advanced materials were financed. In addition the Advanced Research Projects Agency—Energy (ARPA-E) coordinated a new mission-oriented research venture in energy.

The financial crisis did not simply reveal fundamental problems in the financial sector. It also made evident how the United States' engine of growth and innovation—its national manufacturing system—was afflicted by a number of structural problems. Persistent trade imbalances, offshoring of production and R&D centers of national champions such as IBM and Du Pont, the relatively slow technological dynamism, and the increasing loss of critical industrial competencies were all manifestations of these problems (Pisano and Shih 2012; Berger 2013; Andreoni 2015a).

Table 9.2 Policy Measures, Model, Governance, Transformation Cycle, and Budgets in the United States

Code	Name	R/N	Transformation Cycle		Agency/ Ministry Name	BLN Dollars
1	Small Business Investment Company (SBIC)	N	1958	Cont.	SBA	23
2	Small Business Innovation Research (SBIR) (from 1992, SBIR/STTR)	N	1982	Cont./Ren	SBA and 11 federal departments	Not avail.
3	Manufacturing Extension Partnership	R	1988	Cont./Ren	NIST	Not avail.
4	American Competitiveness Initiative (ACI)	N	2006	2008	U.S. Congress (108)	5.9
5	Economic opportunity zones	R	2006	2016	Federal and States U.S. Congress (108)	10
6	Fracking and shale gas initiatives	R	2005	Cont.	States	Not avail.
7	Government financing of nanomanufacturing, hydrogen technologies, intelligent and integrated manufacturing	N	2008	Cont.	The National Science and Technology Council	128
8	American Recovery and Reinvestment Act (ARRA) education	N	2009	Cont.	Department of Housing and Department of Education (ED)	94
9	ARRA transportation	N	2009	Cont.	Federal Transit Administration, Department of Transportation (DOT), EPA Office of Transportation and Air Quality (OTAQ), Department of Energy (DOE)	40
9	ARRA infrastructure	N	2009	Cont.	Federal departments	34
10	ARRA energy and environment	N	2009	Cont.	Energy efficiency and renewable energy (EERE), U.S. Department of Energy (DOE)	51
11	ARRA R&D	N	2009	Cont.	Federal departments	16
12	ARRA training	N	2009	Cont.	Federal departments	5

Table 9.2 (Continued)

Code	Name	R/N	Transformation Cycle		Agency/ Ministry Name	BLN Dollars
13	ARRA agriculture	N	2009	Cont.	Department of Agriculture (USDA)	1
13	ARRA Medicaid Medicare	N	2009	Cont.	Centers for Medicare & Medicaid Services (CMS)	105
13	ARRA manufacturing	N	2009	Cont.	U.S. Congress (III), DOE	7.3
14	National Export Initiative (NEI)	N	2010	2014	International Trade Agency	6
15	Race to the top	N	2010	2015	Federal departments	6.9
16	Import/Export Bank	N	2010	Cont.	U.S. Congress (III)	Not avail.
17	Small Business Jobs Act	N	2010	2010	U.S. Congress (III)	30
18	Advanced manufacturing partnership (AMP) (robotics, advanced materials, process efficiency, IT)	N	2011	Cont.	PCAST (Council of Advisors of Science and Technology)	1
19	National Network for Manufacturing Innovation (NNMI)	N	2011	2015	PCAST (Council of Advisors of Science and Technology)	1
20	AMP continuation clusterization (fostering regional initiatives, additional investments in nanotechnology, materials, etc.)	R	2012	Cont.	National Science and Technology Council (NSTC)	Not avail.

This is why, together with the implementation of the ARRA policy package and the continuity ensured to competitiveness strategies (such as the COMPETES and Small Business Jobs Act), the Obama administration also entered a third transformation cycle from 2010. The new industrial policy package increasingly targets the manufacturing system and focuses on a number of selective measures aimed at strengthening the domestic manufacturing base as well as its presence in the international market.

A number of measures were implemented to rebuild the U.S. manufacturing and technological bases. Alongside strengthening the MEP, the government focused on a new National Network for Manufacturing Innovation (NNMI). This is a web of regional institutes working on the development and adoption of advanced manufacturing technologies. Moreover, a number of high-tech initiatives around advanced materials (such as the Materials Genome Initiative) and production technologies (such as Robotics Centre and Additive Manufacturing) were launched with the explicit aim of engaging the global technological race. A number of these initiatives received budget allocations by Congress in 2012 and 2013. Finally, a number financial incentives and tax relief schemes were introduced (e.g., a 20 percent income tax credit for insourcing manufacturing production). These aimed to regain production scale and rebuild industrial commons in critical sectors (O'Sullivan et al. 2013).

Two main initiatives have been launched to improve the export performances of the United States. The 2010 National Export Initiative promoted trade missions, bilateral initiatives, and agreements and the creation and financing of an Interagency Trade Enforcement Centre. The operational and financial capacity of the Export-Import Bank was increased, and export-oriented companies received dedicated financial support.

JAPAN: RESTRUCTURING THE INDUSTRIAL AND ENERGY SYSTEMS

The Japanese industrial policy experience from 1950 to the mid-1980s has been documented in great detail in various works (Johnson 1982; Okimoto 1989; see Chang et al. 2013 for a review). Japan implemented (and experimented with) various industrial, trade, and competition policies (e.g., subsidies for export, investment, R&D, and utility bills; preferential tax breaks, foreign exchange rationing, cartels management, etc.).

It also adopted effective governance models around deliberation councils and the Ministry of International Trade and Industry (MITI).

During its golden age, the Japanese industrial system developed around major industrial drivers (initially in heavy and chemical industry, later in the automotive and electronics sectors). It also nurtured a dense network of small and medium enterprises (SMEs) that specialized in mechanics, automation and robotics, material processing, and sophisticated system components. SMEs were integrated with (and nurtured by) the industrial "pyramid" system (known as *keiretsu*) and received financial and technical support from the public sector. Public support to SMEs remains, considering the whole of the last century, one of the most distinctive features of Japanese industrial policies. During the transformation cycle following the stock market crash of 1990, SME development, together with a few other initiatives (such as R&D investments and export credit insurance), accounted for 90 percent of total expenditure (Chang et al. 2013).

As with the German model, the financial infrastructure provided long-term financing through the Japanese Development Bank (JDB) and other public financial institutions, such as the Long-Term Credit Bank of Japan and the Industrial Bank of Japan. The technological infrastructure, known as *Kohsetsushi Centres,* were established in 1902 and modeled after the U.S. network of agricultural extension and engineering experimentation stations (O'Sullivan et al. 2013; Andreoni and Chang 2014; Andreoni 2015b). These centers are run by regional prefectures and support local SMEs with a variety of quasi-public good technologies for testing, trial production, and scale-up, as well as training services. A number of sector-focused centers also support SMEs in the adoption of new advanced technologies and conduct joint applied research. Both the financial and technological infrastructures are, even today, the backbone of the Japanese industrial policy scheme. Kohsetsushi Centres, for example, have some 262 offices (182 centers) and are complemented by cutting-edge research institutes, such as the National Institute of Advanced Industrial Science and Technology (AIST) (Ezell and Atkinson 2011; O'Sullivan 2011) (see figure 9.3).

From the mid-1990s, the deregulation agenda became dominant in Japan, and its industrial policy was significantly downsized. The newly established Ministry of Economy, Trade and Industry (METI) started adopting 5-year Science and Technology Plans (STPs). These were mainly focused on strengthening the country's knowledge base (with a government verticalization of funding allocation in higher education using a

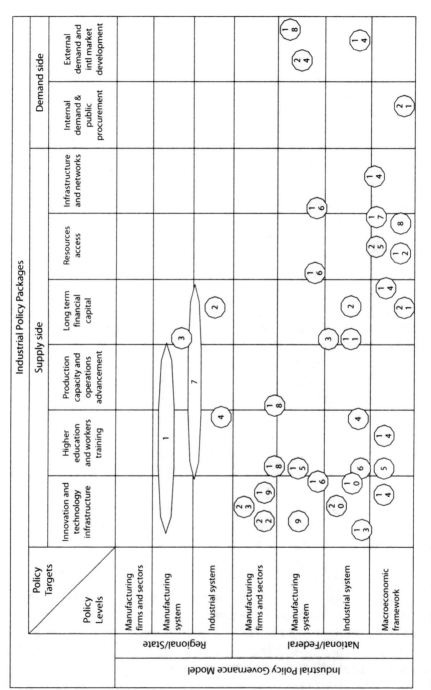

Figure 9.3 The policy package matrix in Japan

"Control Tower" model) and investing in a number of technological domains (life science technologies, information and communications technology (ICT), environment, and nanotechnology materials). The third STP, in particular, promoted a shift from a "hard" economy to a "soft" economy mainly rooted in services, digitalization, digital consumer electronics, robots, and fuel cells technologies. The other major initiative during the first transformation cycle under investigation (1996–2009) was the Industrial Cluster Plan. This aimed at establishing new regional innovation systems ("vital regions"), i.e., local partnerships and cooperation between regional industries and colocated universities and research centers (Nezu 2007) (see table 9.3).

The return of industrial policies to Japan was mainly triggered by two dramatic events, namely, the global financial crisis and the Great East Japan Earthquake in March 2011. Both events highlighted a number of emerging weaknesses of the Japanese industrial and energy system and the consequent need for restructuring. The current transformation cycle started in 2009 with a comprehensive policy package called *New Growth Strategy*. This was followed by a number of initiatives.

First, there was the constitution of the Innovation Network Corporation of Japan (INCJ). This is a public-private partnership aimed at promoting innovation in various areas (green energy, electronics, information technology, and biotechnology to infrastructure-related sectors such as water supply) and enhancing the value of businesses in Japan. INCJ is capitalized at ¥ 300 billion, of which ¥ 286 billion is from the government and the rest from 26 private corporations. Second, an Industrial Competitiveness Committee (under the Industrial Structure Council) was established to formulate a new industrial vision, later called *Industrial Structure Vision 2010*. The new strategy was articulated around five strategic areas and a large number of cross-cutting policies to support the Japanese industry.

To diversify the Japanese industrial structure (moving from "a single high peak to a mountain range" model), the Industrial Competitiveness Committee identified five promising industries: infrastructure-related industries (nuclear power, water, and railways); environment and energy problem-solving industry (smart community, next-generation vehicles, etc.); medical, nursing, health, and child care services; frontier fields (robots, space, etc.); and finally creative industries. For each, a number of policy measures have been designed and are currently integrated into the broader industrial policy package (see table 9.3).

Table 9.3 Policy Measures, Model, Governance, Transformation Cycle, and Budgets in Japan

Code	Name	R/N	Transformation Cycle		Agency/ Ministry Name	BLN Yen
1	Kohsetsushi Centres	R/N	1902	Cont.	MITI/METI Prefectures	NA
2	Japanese Development Bank (JDB)	N	1951	Cont.	MITI/METI	NA
3	SME Basic Act (Last Rev. 2013)	N	1963	Cont.	MITI/METI	NA
4	SME Universities	R/N	1980	Rev 2001	MEXT/ Prefectures	NA
5	Science & Technology First Basic Plan		1996	2000	MITI	17
6	S&T Second Basic Plan	N	2000	2005	METI and Council for Science and Technology Policy (CSTP)	24
7	Industrial Clusters Plan	R/N	2001	2010	METI	NA
8	Basic Act on Energy Policy	N	2002	2006	METI and CSTP	NA
9	National Institute of Advanced Industrial Science and Technology (AIST)	N	2001	Cont.	METI	NA
10	S&T Third Basic Plan	N	2006	2010	METI and CSTP	25
11	SME Manufacturing Enhancement Act	N/R	2006	Cont.	METI, International Energy Agency (IEA)	NA
12	New National Energy Strategy (NNES)	N	2006	2010	METI, IEA	NA
13	Service industry policies		2007	2007	METI	NA
14	New growth strategy		2009	Cont.	METI	NA
15	Special Measures for Industrial Revitalization and Innovation	N	2009	Cont.	METI	NA
16	Innovation Network Corporation of Japan	N	2009	2025	METI	NA
17	New Basic Energy Plan	N	2010	2013	METI, IEA	NA
18	New Industrial Structure Vision	R/N	2010	Cont.	METI	NA
19	Next-Generation Vehicle Plan	N			METI	NA
20	S&T Fourth Basic Plan	N	2011	2015	MEXT, METI	25
21	Industrial Competitiveness Enhancement Act	N	2013	2013	METI	NA
22	Robotic Devices for Nursing Care	N	2013	2017	METI	NA
23	Information policy	N	2013		METI	NA
24	New framework for supporting SMEs in overseas business (e.g., medical technologies)	N			METI	NA
25	Strategic Energy Plan	N	2014	Cont.	METI, IEA	NA

Among the cross-cutting policies, the government adopted a combination of relatively standard measures (corporate tax reform, promotion of R&D, ICT adoption, and the establishment of a National Vocational Qualification System). It also introduced a number of more selective measures aimed at restructuring the industrial system organization. First, the government aims at transforming Japan into a "high-value industrial hub" for Asia by attracting companies and people through preferential taxation, subsidies, and tailored immigration procedures. Second, the government promotes international standardization and a strategic management of standards and certification for opening new markets. Finally, the government and prefectures support the 4.2 million SMEs expanding their business overseas and capturing global manufacturing niches directly, beyond the "intermediation" of national major players.

While the financial crisis triggered a major plan for restructuring and revitalizing the industrial structure, the disaster at TEPCO's Fukushima nuclear plant so disrupted Japanese strategic value chains (especially in electronics and automobiles) that it also necessitated a new energy plan. Just before the earthquake, Japan adopted the New Basic Energy Plan including a number of ambitious targets in terms of energy independence, development of renewable sources, nuclear power, and reduced CO_2 emission (Duffield and Woodall 2011). The most recent Strategic Energy Plan and the Fourth Science and Technology Basic Plan reflect Japan's major concern for its energy system and the need to increase its resilience, stability, and flexibility. The plan entails a number of major reforms, including the introduction of a "multilayered and diversified flexible energy supply-demand structure," the development of an advanced energy-saving society, and the achievement of grid parity in the medium-long term. Finally, it also includes the reestablishment of a nuclear energy policy.

GERMANY: THE "ADVANTAGE" OF COMPOSITION

During the first two decades after the WW II, Germany's recovery was driven by massive investment in strategic industries (always around 20 percent of national income) as well as increasing exports of capital goods. Companies such as Bayer and BASF in the science-based chemical industry or Siemens in electronics, power engineering, and telecommunications became industrial drivers for the entire manufacturing system. Meanwhile a dense network of high-tech, medium-sized companies and specialized contractors—so called Mittelstand—developed sophisticated production technologies (especially in the machine tools sector). Even when national companies such as Volkswagen and Deutsche Telekom were privatized, either the federal or lander (state) governments retained important shares (Chang et al. 2013).

In 1949 the Fraunhofer-Gesellschaft Institutes—one of today's main pillars of German industrial policy—were created (Andreoni 2015b). They undertake collaborative manufacturing research and address technological challenges for the entire industrial system (big and small companies, public sector included). Over the years, the network has grown to 57 institutes (18,000 staff) and specializes in joint precompetitive research, prototyping, and manufacturing scale-up, as well as product-idea commercialization, bilateral applied research with individual firms, and technology transfer schemes. Cutting-edge research includes various sectors and technology platforms such as optics, photonics, micro-electromechanical systems, advanced and composite materials, advanced machining, etc. Over the years, this network of intermediate R&D institutions was complemented by others such as the Steinbeis Centres (4,600 staff) and other sector-focused programs promoted by industry associations (e.g., Allianz Industrie Forschung, or AIF). Higher education and basic research institutes were also developed (e.g., the Max Planck Society) (Atkinson and Ezell 2012).

The second pillar of what later became famous as the German model (*Modell Deutschland*) was a financial infrastructure composed of public or quasi-public banks specialized in industrial finance. The Bank for Reconstruction (KfW), founded in 1947, increasingly moved away from direct lending and became a long-term refinancing bank specialized in lending to banks working with industries. KfW is still owned by the federal government today (80 percent) as well as by lenders (20 percent). The financial infrastructure also includes the German Bank for Settlements (AG) and an articulated multilayered system of public saving banks and credit cooperatives working with SMEs.

The third pillar of the model consists of the regulation of industrial relations (Vitols 1997). Since the 1950s, the Works Constitution Act and the Collective Bargaining Law introduced a set of legally binding sectoral agreements between employers' associations and unions. Such "rigidities" were counterbalanced by an integrated dual training system (Vocational Training Law), including apprenticeship schemes and certified skills and training standards, as well as the adoption of what can be termed *concerted flexibilities*.

While the Hartz Reform of the labor market promoted in 2003 by Schroeder has been often considered the new main driver of German industrial competitiveness, the reality is more complex. Building on its industrial and institutional infrastructure, industrial relations in Germany underwent a process of increasing "decentralization of the wage-setting process from the industry level to the firm level" before Hartz (Dustmann et al. 2014, 168). Together with this process of decentralization of industrial relations, the first industrial policy transformation cycle (2000–2005) was characterized by an increasing emphasis on environmental sustainability, energy efficiency, and renewable energy (German Renewable Energy Act). As a result of these energy policies, Germany is today the world's biggest photovoltaic market (75 percent of cell and 60 percent module production capacity in Europe). It also has 30 percent of total wind power capacity in Europe (12 percent of world capacity) (O'Sullivan et al. 2013). This transformation has played at least as important a role in German industrial competitiveness as the industrial relations reforms (Storm and Naastepad 2015) (see figure 9.4).

From mid-2000, Germany's industrial system went through two main transformation cycles. In both cases the policy vision and main policy lines were framed within a federal plan, called the *High-Tech Strategy* (HTS). However, the policy translation of this plan into specific programs and measures, as well as their implementation, involved not only various federal government ministries but also the landers. The German model is a truly multilayered policy system, including not only the landers and the Federation, but also landers' municipalities (below) and European level institutions (above). Given the extremely complex articulation of these policies and the variety of types of support (e.g. subsidies, loans, grants, guarantees, and participation), table 9.4 focuses only on the main policy lines.

The transformation cycle from 2006 to 2009–2010 started with the HTS, an ambitious plan aimed at coordinating (and exploiting complementarities across) the full spectrum of technology, innovation, and manufacturing policies and regulations. The strategy was designed to address the new challenges posed by globalization, starting from the fundamental premise that "Germany cannot compete on cost." First, it was designed to exploit the new opportunities in health (medical technology and innovative services), sustainability (resource-efficient and energy-efficient production processes), communication and mobility (including ICT, mechanical technologies, and advanced materials for transportation). Second, the strategy targeted a number of partnerships in cross-cutting

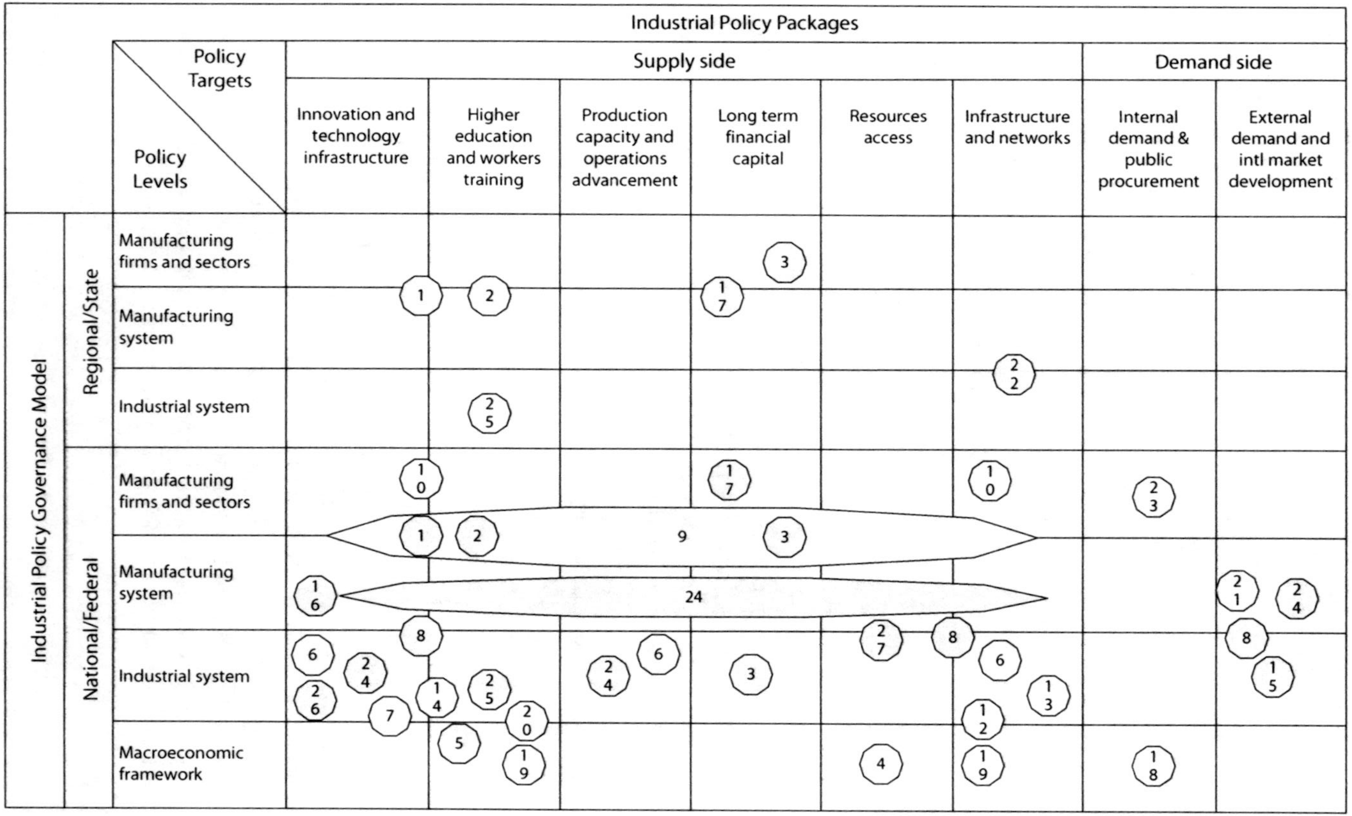

Industrial Policy Packages

Industrial Policy Governance Model	Policy Levels \ Policy Targets	Supply side — Innovation and technology infrastructure	Higher education and workers training	Production capacity and operations advancement	Long term financial capital	Resources access	Infrastructure and networks	Demand side — Internal demand & public procurement	External demand and intl market development
Regional/State	Manufacturing firms and sectors	1	12						
	Manufacturing system		25						
	Industrial system				7 3		22		
National/Federal	Manufacturing firms and sectors	16 10	12		17		10	23	
	Manufacturing system	24 26 8 7 6	25 20 19 5	24 6	3	27	8		21 24 8 15
	Industrial system	14			3	4	9 12 19 13		
	Macroeconomic framework							18	

Figure 9.4 The policy package matrix in Germany

Table 9.4 Policy Measures, Model, Governance, Transformation Cycle, and Budgets in Germany

Code	Name	R/N	Transformation Cycle		Agency/ Ministry Name	BLN Euro
1	Fraunhofers Institutes	N/R	1949	Cont./Ren	Federal Government of Germany plus	Not avail.
2	Vocational Training Law and Steinbeis Centres	N/R	1970s	Cont.	Federal Ministry of Education and Research (BMBF)	Not avail.
3	Long-term financial support (loans and money lending)	N/R	1950–80	Cont.	Federal Economics Ministry and BMBF	Not avail.
4	German Renewable Energy Act	N	2000	2010	Federal Government of Germany plus	Not avail.
5	Agenda 2010	N	2003	Cont.	Federal Government of Germany plus	Not avail.
6	High-Tech Strategy (R&D investments in innovation)	N	2006	2009	BMBF Ministry for Economy and Technology (BMWi)	6
7	High-Tech Strategy (investments in basic research)	N	2006	2009	BMWi, BMBF	13
8	ICT Strategy 2020 (export technologies for renewable energies)	N	2006	2009	BMWi, BMBF	2
9	High-Tech Strategy Nanotechnologies	N	2006	2009	Federal Ministry of the Interior (BMI), BMWi, BMBF Federal Ministry of Labour and Social Affairs (BMAS)	0.64
	High-Tech Strategy Biotechnology	N	2006	2009	Federal Ministry of Food and Agriculture(BMELV), BMWi, BMBF	0.43
	High-Tech Strategy Microsystem technology	N	2006	2009	BMBF	0.22
	High-Tech Strategy Optical Technology	N	2006	2009	BMBF	0.31
	High-Tech Strategy Materials	N	2006	2009	BMI, BMWi, BMBF	0.42
	Production Technologies	N	2006	2009	BMI, BMWi, BMBF	0.25
	Information Technologies	N	2006	2009	BMWi, BMBF	1.2
10	Aerospace	N	2006	2009	BMWi, Federal Ministry of Transport and Digital Infrastructure (BMVBS)	3.9

(Continued)

Table 9.4 (*Continued*)

Code	Name	R/N	Transformation Cycle		Agency/ Ministry Name	BLN Euro
11	Automotive and traffic	N	2006	2009	BMI, BMWi, BMBF	0.77
12	Security and services	N	2006	2009	BMWi, BMBF	0.11
13	Healthcare	N	2006	2009	Federal Ministry of Health (BMG) BMBF	0.8
14	High-Tech Cross-sectoral initiatives (SME, support technology start-ups, create links between industry and science)	N	2006	2010	Federal Government of Germany	2.66
15	International patenting and digital IP law system	N	2007	Cont.	BMU, BMBF	Not avail.
16	Standardization efforts (DIN)	N	2007	Cont.	BMWi	Not avail.
17	ZIM (Zentrales Innovations program Mittelstand)	N/R	2008	Cont.	BMWi	3
18	Konjunkturpakete I e II (economic stimulus)	N	2008	2009	BMWi	20
19	Public infrastructure and education	N	2008	2010	BMVBS, BMBF	14
20	Protection of jobs and modernization of Federal Republic	N	2008	2010	Federal Government of Germany	50
21	Special program for large enterprises	N	2008	2010	BMWi	Not avail.
22	Modernization of local infrastructure	R	2008	2010	BMVBS, BMWi	10
23	Boosting internal demand for new cars	N	2008	2010	BMWi	5
24	High-Tech Strategy 2020	N	2010	2020	BMI, BMWi, BMBF	7.4
25	Excellence Initiative	N/R	2011	2017	BMBF	2.7
26	Pact for Research and Innovation	N	2011	2015	Federal Government of Germany	Not avail.
27	Energy Concept and Energy Policy	N	2011	2050	BMVBS, BMWi, BMB	Not avail.

activities where transversal opportunities emerge (such as new platform technologies and pioneer markets). The strategy also recognized the need to match these new techno-industrial ventures with new regulations in intellectual property, product standards, and the governance of the public procurement system.

With the international financial crisis, a number of countercyclical expansionary measures in public infrastructure, education, and the modernization of the economic system were put in place. Despite the fact that the backbone of the industrial system (Germany's Mittelstand) were receiving significant support from both the technological and financial infrastructure, the government introduced a new program, known as ZIM (Zentrales Innovationsprogramm Mittelstand), to support SMEs' investments, technological innovations, and export market strategies. Large enterprises were also targeted with special programs (e.g., guarantee schemes and loans) coordinated by KfW. Moreover, internal demand was boosted in strategic sectors (e.g., automobiles). Again, the response to the crisis was systemic (the entire system, both industrial drivers, and SMEs were targeted), and the policy measures were aligned with the broader policy package.

The current transformation cycle started in 2010 with the launch of the new High Tech Strategy 2020 and a new Energy Policy Package including more than 120 measures. Although the new HTS mainly builds on the 2006 framework, the federal government further emphasized the importance of research excellence. It also focused more closely on the need to capture future markets with a mix of mission-oriented technology projects (e.g., the new ICT strategy 2020 launched as part of HTS) and export-promotion initiatives (e.g., networks of bilateral chambers of commerce). The systemic and cross-cutting nature of the German industrial policy was recently restated in the new "smart" industrial vision encapsulated in the document *Industry 4.0*. Here *smart* means technological integration across manufacturing industries and beyond, thus including services, smart products, embedded systems, the "internet of things," and a number of other smart applications.

BRAZIL: "AGRI-FACTURING," INDUSTRIAL FINANCE, AND THE NEW INDUSTRIALIZATION PATH

Since the end of the WW II, Brazil underwent three major phases of industrial development with corresponding policy regimes (Ocampo

2006; Chang, et al. 2013). The first wave lasted until 1980 and was characterized by extensive state-indicative planning in the areas of sectoral development (e.g., steel, petrochemical, and renewable fuels policies) and trade protection (e.g., ad valorem tariffs and law of similarities). The state also played a critical role in technological upgrading (e.g., research in agro-technologies within Embrapa and aircraft technologies deployed in Embraer). A number of state-owned enterprises in strategic manufacturing sectors were developed such as Petrobras in 1953, Usiminas in 1956, Eletrobras in 1962, and Embraer in 1969 as well as a public development bank established in 1952.

Some of these companies and institutions are today the pillars of the Brazilian industrial, financial, and agricultural system. For example, the Brazilian Development Bank (BNDES) is the main provider of long-term finance in the country and one of the biggest in the world when measured by assets, equity, and disbursement (Ferraz et al. 2013). Embrapa is today the largest research and development (R&D) agency in Latin America. It includes 47 research centers (15 National Thematic Centers, 16 National Commodity Centers, and 16 Regional Resource Centers) throughout the country. It hosts 9,284 employees and has an annual budget of over US$ 1 billion. Similar to Fraunhofers in Germany, Embrapa plays a critical intermediary role between agricultural and manufacturing R&D, education, markets, and in-farm agricultural production. It also bridges and transfers knowledge, technical solutions, and innovations across different sectors, thus facilitating various forms of inter-sectoral learning (Andreoni 2014; Andreoni and Chang 2014) (see figure 9.5).

During the 1980s and 1990s, the debt crisis forced the Brazilian government to reduce its industrial policy interventions in favor of structural adjustment policies and macroeconomic stabilization (Real Plan). During this second phase, the total number of special trade regimes and tariff rates was reduced, and a significant number of public enterprises were privatized.

The Ministry for Science, Technology, and Innovation (MCTI), which was established in 1985, started promoting a number of innovation policies in only the second part of 1990s. In particular, in 1997, MCTI instituted various sectoral funds in support of the National Fund for Scientific and Technological Development (FNDCT). This is a government budget fund aggregating public and private revenues to support both refundable (loans) and nonrefundable (grants) technology programs (see table 9.5).

The third phase of industrial development and policy started in November 2003 with the first Lula government. Since then Brazilian

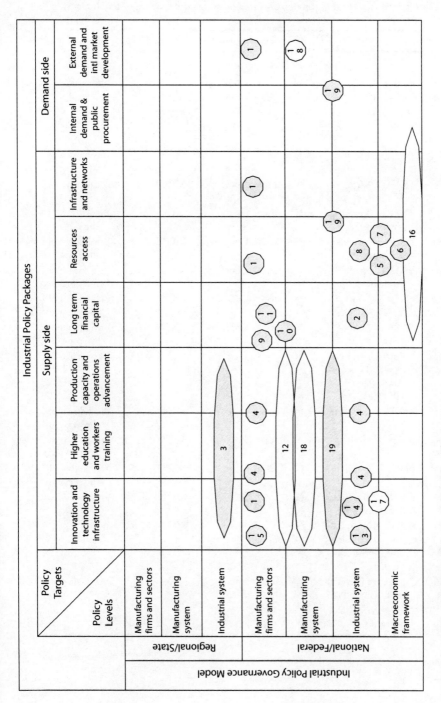

Figure 9.5 The policy package matrix in Brazil

Table 9.5 Policy Measures, Model, Governance, Transformation Cycle, and Budgets in Brazil

Code	Name	R/N	Transformation Cycle		Agency/ Ministry	BN dollar
1	SOEs	N	1950s	Cont.		Not avail.
2	BNDES	N	1952	Cont.		Not avail.
3	Embrapa	R	1972	Cont.	MAPA	Not avail.
4	Plan to support sectorial innovation (FNDCT)	N	1997	2007 Reformed	MCTI	78
5	FNDCT Energy	N	1997	Cont.	MCTI	Breakdown of the previous
6	FNDCT Water Resources	N	1998	Cont.	MCTI	Breakdown of the previous
7	FNDCT Terrestrial Transportation	N	1999	Cont.	MCTI	Breakdown of the previous
8	FNDCT Mineral Resources	N	2000	Cont.	MCTI	Breakdown of the previous
9	FNDCT Spatial Activities	N	2001	Cont.	MCTI	Breakdown of the previous
10	FNDCT Informatics	N	2002	Cont.	MCTI	Breakdown of the previous
11	FNDCT Agribusiness	N	2003	Cont.	MCTI	Breakdown of the previous
12	Industrial, Technology, and Foreign Trade Plan (PITCE)	N	2003	2007	MCTI, MDIC	Not avail.
13	FNDCT Biotechnology	N	2004	Cont.	MCTI	Breakdown of the previous
14	FNDCT Health	N	2005	Cont.	MCTI	Breakdown of the previous
15	FNDCT Aeronautics	N	2006	Cont.	MCTI	Breakdown of the previous
16	Growth Acceleration Program (PAC)	N	2007	2010	MDIC MCT	505
17	Action Plan on Science, Technology, and Innovation (PACTI)	N	2007	2010	MCT MDIC	41
18	Productive Development Policy Plan (PDP)	N	2008	2010	MDIC	Not avail.
19	The Brasil Maior Plan	N	2011	2014	MDIC MCT	571

industrial policies have been through three further transformation cycles, partially in response to the emerging industrial challenges and the transformed global competitive scenario (Kupfer, Ferraz, and Marques 2013). The first transformation cycle during the Lula presidency started in 2003 with the announcement of a new policy package called *Industrial, Technology and Foreign Trade Policy* (PITCE). The Brazilian Industrial Development Agency (ABDI) and the Council for Industrial Development (CNDI), made up of 23 Government Ministers, the BNDES President, and 14 industry representatives, were created to coordinate and implement the new PITCE. These two institutions also sought to facilitate the dialogue between the public and private sectors (private companies, universities and research institutes, government agencies, and labor unions).

PITCE had two main goals. First, it aimed at increasing industrial competitiveness by boosting technological development in key sectors (semiconductors, software, pharmaceuticals and medicines, and capital goods), thus promoting the export of higher value-added products. Second, it sought to develop the scientific and technological systems and legislation (in particular with respect to biotechnology, nanotechnology, and biomass/renewable energies) for capturing value opportunities in industries such as oil and gas, agriculture, and pharmaceuticals. Both industrial and technology policies were coupled with highly specific financing programs, such as the Profarma (pharmaceutical) and the Prosoft (software). There were also two supersectoral programs, called Strong Industry and Innovate Brazil, managed by the Brazilian Development Bank BNDES (for a total investment of R$ 4.4 billion).

Furthermore, a number of reforms started in 2004 "made it possible to integrate a large fraction of investments in funds by transversely bridging them in line with government policies, eliminating duplication and scattershot initiatives" (ABDI 2006, 20). For example, with the enactment of the FNDCT Law in 2007 (and follow-up decree in 2009), the National Fund started aggregating revenues from 15 sectoral funds (and adopting new credit instruments). Among these funds, 13 provide sector-specific support to innovation and start-ups (called *vertical actions*), while two provide support to any sector by promoting university-industry interaction, knowledge transfer, and scientific and technological institutions infrastructure (called *transversal*). These funds play a critical role in financing applied industrial research (including precompetitive research), prototyping, and commercialization of innovation, problem-driven basic research, intellectual property rights (IPR). and public-private partnerships (PPPs).

The second transformation cycle during the Lula period started in May 2008 and was marked by the ambitious industrial policy package called *Productive Development Policy* (PDP) and the countercyclical overall *Growth Acceleration Program* (PAC). The PDP was structured around four challenges. (1) sustain the expansionary cycle by maintaining the rate of growth in gross fixed capital formation (GFCF) ahead of the GDP; (2) upgrade and diversify the export basket; (3) foster technological investment and innovation; and (4) restructure the industrial system and support SMEs as well as national industrial drivers. The PDP is a complex industrial policy package aligned with specific macrotargets and comprising 425 policy measures (organized in 34 programs including both sectoral and systemic actions). The sectoral actions expand the PITCE targets along three main lines: mobilization programs in strategic areas, programs to strengthen competitiveness, and programs to consolidate and expand leadership (Kupfer, Ferraz, and Marques 2013).

During this period, the funding base of BNDES was also substantially expanded to allow the country to reach a GFCF rate of 21 percent by 2010 while the spread for credit lines in trade of capital goods was substantially reduced. BNDES has been also increasingly instrumental in supporting national companies in gaining global market shares (for a comprehensive list of implemented programs and finance schemes, see Ferraz et al. 2013). More critically, the lowering of interest rates has naturally led to the depreciation of national currency and increased the competitiveness of the Brazilian export-oriented firms.

The Brasil Maior Plan (PBM) was launched in 2011 and signaled the beginning of the current (third) industrial policy transformation cycle in Brazil since 2003. The *strategic map* underpinning the PBM identifies four interdependent guiding principles and objectives. First, strengthen critical competencies in terms of production capacity, corporate R&D, and industrial skills; second, enhance value chains by structural upgrading and reorganization of production systems. Third, the PBM sought to expand both domestic and foreign markets beyond specialization in primary goods and finally also sought to expand social and environmental sustainability development. A number of different policy measures have been adopted to implement these guidelines. For example, the PBM strengthens production chains, diversifying/upgrading exports through tax relief, trade remedies (e.g., antidumping measures), financing, and loan guarantees for exporters (especially for SMEs). More short-term measures have been integrated as well as systemic and long-term measures such as infrastructure development and demand-side interventions (e.g., the government procurement policy was updated).

In line with the PDP, the PBM is redesigning policy targets based on production systems concepts. It is trying to identify new instruments to strengthen industrial policy effectiveness and favor public-private collaboration (e.g., by establishing a new public-private governance scheme, including sectoral competitiveness councils) (Kupfer, Ferraz, and Marques 2013). In particular, given the complexity of the policy packages and shortness of the transformation cycles described above, Brazil is currently addressing the institutional problem of aligning the multiple and different policy measures.

CHINA: REACHING JAPANESE QUALITY AT CHINESE PRICES

During the final two decades of the last century, China prepared its gradual transition to a market economy. Industrial policies were an integral part of China's strategic 5-year planning. Many initiatives and policy measures, especially in the early period, were inspired by the successful experiences of Japan and Korea. While the Sixth Plan (1981–1985) marked a more distinctive outward-oriented approach, focusing on importing technologies and developing endogenous capabilities, the Seventh Plan (1986–1990) was the first one to introduce the concept of industrial policy officially. The newly established Industrial Policy Department started revising the overall industrial policy approach which culminated in the strategic plan *Outline of State Industrial Policies for the 1990s* in March 1994 (Chang et al. 2013).

The 1989–1995 transformation cycle was characterized by a combination of sectoral policies and a new set of technology and cluster policies aimed at advancing manufacturing domestic competencies and building integrated industrial systems. The government identified five strategic "industrial pillars," namely, automobiles, electronics, machinery, construction, and petrochemicals. Each targeted sector received a policy package of complementary measures (e.g., tariffs and nontariff barriers, import quotas, local content requirements, licensing systems, tax exemptions, subsidized lands, and subsidized loans from state-owned policy banks) and relied increasingly on state-owned enterprises (SOEs). The automobile and semiconductor industries, e.g., were guaranteed market protection in exchange for technology transfer, while increases in companies' production scale were reached through government-led mergers and acquisitions (Lo and Wu 2014).

The adoption of industrial consolidation policies continued over the most recent transformation cycles (after 2001), until the recent cases of mergers and acquisitions (e.g., China Electronics Corporation's acquisition of Irico Group, a photovoltaic equipment manufacturer). Recent legislation has restated the need to build global champions in the automotive, iron and steel, cement, shipbuilding, aluminum, rare earth metals, electronics, and pharmaceutical industries (MIIT 2013).

State "policy banks" as well as local governments played a critical role in providing targeted financial support (and special conditions) to companies in pillar industries, especially SOEs. The Export-Import (Exim) Bank of China, the Agricultural Development Bank of China (ADBC), and China Development Bank (CDB) are still today critical industrial policy arms for the implementation of industrial policy. The overall financial infrastructure was also given a pro-industrial development vocation by law. This is clear from Chapter IV, Article 34, of the 1995 Law of the People's Republic of China on Commercial Banks. This law specifically states, "A commercial bank shall conduct its loan business in accordance with the need for the development of the national economy and social progress and under the guidance of the state industrial policy" (Chang, Andreoni, and Kuan 2013) (see figure 9.6).

Two of todays' most successful industrial policies in China were introduced during this period as well (Fan and Watanabe 2006). In 1986, the National High Tech Development Plan (also known as the *863 Plan*) introduced the first articulated national technology strategy in China. A number of key technologies were targeted including biotechnology, space, information technology, laser technology, automation, energy, and new materials. Over the years this technology plan was updated to include emerging technologies such as telecommunications (1992) and marine technology (1996). The second program, called the Torch Program, was initiated in 1988. It promoted (1) high-tech clusters development around science and technology industrial parks (STIPs), software parks, and productivity promotion centers (innovation clusters); (2) high-tech business start-up services (technology business incubators); (3) financial services for innovation (InnoFund and Venture Guiding Fund).

The Innovation Clusters program was aligned with the development of national high-tech zones (SHTZs) and special economic zones (SEZs).

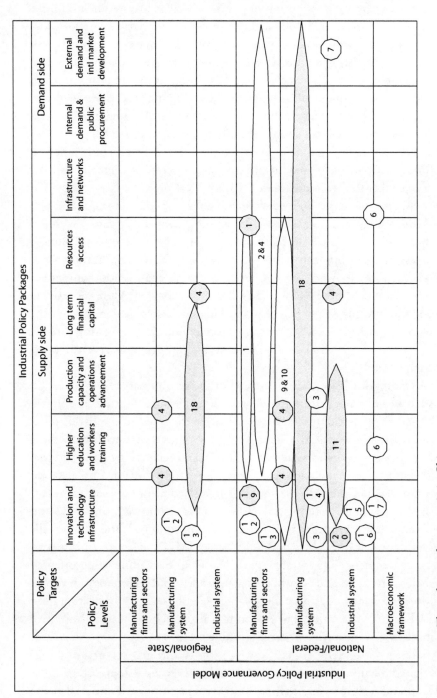

Figure 9.6 **The policy package matrix in China**

The geographical distribution of public as well as private foreign investment was also centrally planned. Coastal areas such as Guangdong and Fujian were prioritized during the early days of the open-door policy, while more recently inland areas have been the main targets of infrastructural investment. Emphasis was placed on developing clusters in different towns and cities with unique pillar industries. (e. g., Shunde specializes in electrical goods while manufacturing towns such as Xiaolan specialize in locks and electronic acoustics and Guzhen in lighting fittings) (Zhang 2013).

Economies of agglomeration in targeted sectors and regions were also boosted by the development of targeted programs of financial support comparable to the United States' SBIR/STTR program (see above). The InnoFund, set up in 1999, offers loan interest subsidies and equity investment to high-tech domestic SMEs (Chinese-owned companies with less than 500 employees, 30 percent of which must be technicians) willing to invest in emerging technologies and product commercialization. Since its creation the InnoFund has financed more than 9,000 companies' projects with almost US$ 1 billion of funds allocated. More recently, in 2007, the Ministries of Sciences and Finance supplemented this scheme with the Venture Guiding Fund, a program aimed at investing directly in VC funds, with coequity investment, grants, and risk subsidies compensations.

The market liberalization agenda in the second part of the 1990s did slightly downsize Chinese industrial policy efforts (agriculture, infrastructure, construction, and services were included in the list of pillar industries). However, the Tenth Five Year Plan (2001–2005) marked the beginning of renewed systemic industrial and technology policy efforts. The most recent industrial policy transformation cycle in China started in 2002 when the 16th National Congress committed itself to pursuing "a new path of industrialization." This vision was confirmed and developed in President Hu Jintao's Medium- to Long-Term Plan for the Development of Science and Technology (MLP) in 2006. In this plan the government aims at transforming China into an "innovation-oriented society" by 2020 and "world leader in science and technology" by 2050. More fundamentally, this plan will complete the country's transition from a labor-intensive industrial system to a high-tech and capital-intensive modern manufacturing system (see table 9.6).

The 15-year MLP signals a shift from traditional sectoral and segmented planning to a more systemic and cross-sectoral approach to structural and technological change. The MLP identifies a number of social

Table 9.6 Policy Measures, Model, Governance, Transformation Cycle, and Budgets in China

Code	Name	Transformation Cycle		Agency/ Ministry Name	BN Dollars
1	Sixth Five Year Plan	1981	1985	State Planning Commission (SPC)	Not avail.
2	Seventh Five Year Plan, Decision on Current Industrial Policy Priorities (1989)	1986	1990	State Planning Commission (SPC)	Not avail.
3	National High-Tech Plan, 863 Plan (7FYP)	1986	2001	State Planning Commission (SPC)	Not avail.
4	Torch Programme (7FYP)	1988	Cont.	State Science and Technology Commission	Not avail.
5	Eighth Five Year Plan, Outline of State Industrial Policies for the 1990s (1994)	1991	1995	State Council	Not avail.
	10-Year Plan for National Economic and Social Development	1991	2000	State Council	Not avail.
6	9th Five Year Plan (Infrastructure, Industry, Education, and Energy Based)	1996	2000	State Council	Not avail.
7	Regulations of Guidance on Foreign Direct Investment	1995–7	2001	State Council	Not avail.
	Long-term target for the year 2010	1996	2010	State Council	Not avail.
9	Tenth Five Year Plan	2001	2005	State Council	Not avail.
	Automobile Industry	2004	2012	State Council	Not avail.
	Adjustment of Industrial Structures	2005	2012	State Council	Not avail.
10	Eleventh Five Year Plan	2006	2010	State Council	Not avail.
11	Medium- to Long-Term Plan for the Development of Science and Technology	2006	2020	State Council	Not avail.
12	Machine-building industries	2006	2012	NDRC	Not avail.
13	Acceleration of Services Sector Development	2007	2012	State Council	Not avail.
14	Industrial Technology Policy	2009	2012	MIIT (Ministry of Innovation and Information Technology)	Not avail.
15	Information Technology industry	2009	2012	State Council	Not avail.

(*Continued*)

Table 9.6 (Continued)

Code	Name	Transformation Cycle		Agency/ Ministry Name	BN Dollars
16	Logistics industry	2009	2012	State Council	Not avail.
17	Culture industry	2009	2012	State Council	Not avail.
18	Twelfth Five Year Plan	2011	2015	State Council	Not avail.
19	Industrial Restructuring and Upgrading (12FYP)	2011	2015	CCP, CC, NPC	Not avail.
20	Fostering 7 Strategic Emerging Industries (12FYP)	2011	2015	State Council	Not avail.

and technological challenges related to agriculture, population and health, public security, water and mineral resources, manufacturing, and energy. The most important challenges identified have been addressed within a two-pillar policy package. First, this consists of sixteen engineering and science megaprojects for developing key technologies. These technologies included core electronic devices, large-scale integrated circuits, wideband-wireless communication technologies, advanced large-scale pressured water reactors, pharmaceutical products, giant airplane technology and avionics, and new transgenic breed varieties. Second, it also consists of eight R&D programs in "cutting-edge technological areas" (advanced energy, advanced manufacturing, aerospace and aeronautics, biotechnology, information, laser, new materials, and oceanic technologies). The MLP policy package relies on a variety of policy measures and tools such as tax incentives, subsidies, development of technological standards and IPRs, coordination of civilian and military research, and technology pre-commercial procurement (Cao, Suttmeier, and Simon 2006).

A number of other policy measures have been introduced since 2005, as part of the Eleventh and Twelfth Five Year Plans. The policy model has relied increasingly on the involvement of provinces and municipalities, especially in the implementation of national plans such as those regarding sectoral policies. This is the case of the automotive sectoral policies (after 2011) as well as other industries such as the photovoltaic sector. Policy coordination is achieved through the National Development and Reform Commission (NDRC) which drafts industrial plans for the State Council, but also collect inputs from the CCP Central Committee, and provincial and municipal governments (Dorn and Cloutier 2013).

This new policy model has also allowed the central government to fully exploit competitive forces in technological upgrading. Alongside traditional export-driven competition, companies from different provinces (and the provinces themselves) have developed strong competitive relationships and, in turn, increased domestic technological dynamism. SOEs have also engaged in the global technological race, and together with public finance, they have become the main drivers of infrastructural investment. The development of infrastructure such as roads and the high-speed railways has, in turn, boosted internal demand for cars and given national champions the opportunity to absorb, adapt, and improve foreign technologies, e.g., the high-speed trains and rail networks. In only three years, the biggest high-speed rail network in the world was constructed and the trains produced, mainly relying on domestic technological capabilities, reached the record speed of 500 km/hr.

The sectoral policies have been also updated in a number of *Priority Investment Catalogues* and new pillar industries identified. The industries were selected according to their strategic role (e.g., defense, coal, electricity generation and distribution, telecommunications, petroleum and petrochemical, civil aviation, and shipping in 2006). They were also chosen for their growth potential (e.g., alternative-fuel cars, biotechnology, environmental and energy-saving technologies, alternative energy, advanced materials, new-generation information technology, and high-end equipment manufacturing in 2007). In particular, the Twelfth Five Year Plan has targeted a number of traditional industries including cotton, textiles and apparel, biochemicals, capital goods, electric appliances, footwear, oil and related equipment, and steel). It has also focused on seven strategic emerging industries (energy conservation and environmental protection, next-generation information technology, bio-industries, high-end assembly and manufacturing industries, new energy sources, new advanced materials, and new energy automobile industries) and thirty-five projects for subindustries (Shih 2011).

As a result of this accelerated process of structural change and the new industrial policy approach, China has entered a path of indigenous innovation (zizhu chuangxin). A recent MIT study (Berger 2013, 145) has shown that until 2005 there was limited evidence of domestic innovation capabilities. However, over the last four years, companies in high-tech sectors have developed scale-up capabilities (increasingly mastering the scale-up of complex system products and processes, translating into advanced product design and advanced manufacturing and reducing the time to the market). Companies have also developed redesign, reverse, and reengineering competencies (reassembling foreign components, changing functions, materials, and product characterization). Thus these companies are increasingly able to produce products with "Japanese [good enough] quality at Chinese prices," making them the most striking example of the success of China's new industrialization policies.

SOUTH AFRICA: A NEW INDUSTRIAL POLICY COURSE?

During the apartheid period (1976–1993), despite some considerable successes in establishing certain upstream industries based on natural resource advantages, South Africa's industrial policy was burdened with many objectives and internal tensions that ultimately undermined its medium-long term viability (Chang 1998). The "minerals energy complex" did not trigger any sectoral diversification, apart from contributing to the development of industries specialized in semiprocessed commodities. Moreover, the privatization of strategic SOEs such as Sasol (petrochemicals) and Iscor (steel) allowed the newly private monopolies to extract rents from downstream manufacturing companies, ultimately undermining their competitiveness (Fine and Rustomjee 1996).

With the end of apartheid, the new South African government tried to develop a new industrial policy framework encapsulated in the industrial strategy project document *Improving Manufacturing Performance in South Africa*. The same commitment to new industrial policy efforts was evident in the DTI's (Department of Trade and Industry) document *Support Measures for the Enhancement of the International Competitiveness of South Africa's Industrial Sector*, issued in 1995. These new industrial policies represented a fundamental shift from demand-side to supply-side industrial promotion. A new array of policy measures were adopted such as investment incentives, human resource development, support for R&D, and provision of information on production methods, international market conditions, etc. (see figure 9.7).

Despite this emphasis on supply-side interventions, these strategies paid relatively limited attention to the much needed increase in physical and infrastructural investment. However, the need for policy coordination and alignment of broader macroeconomic, education, and trade policies was acknowledged in these documents. Unfortunately, until recently, the effort at such coordination remained limited to very broad framework and ad hoc exercises (e.g., *New Growth Path* in 2000).

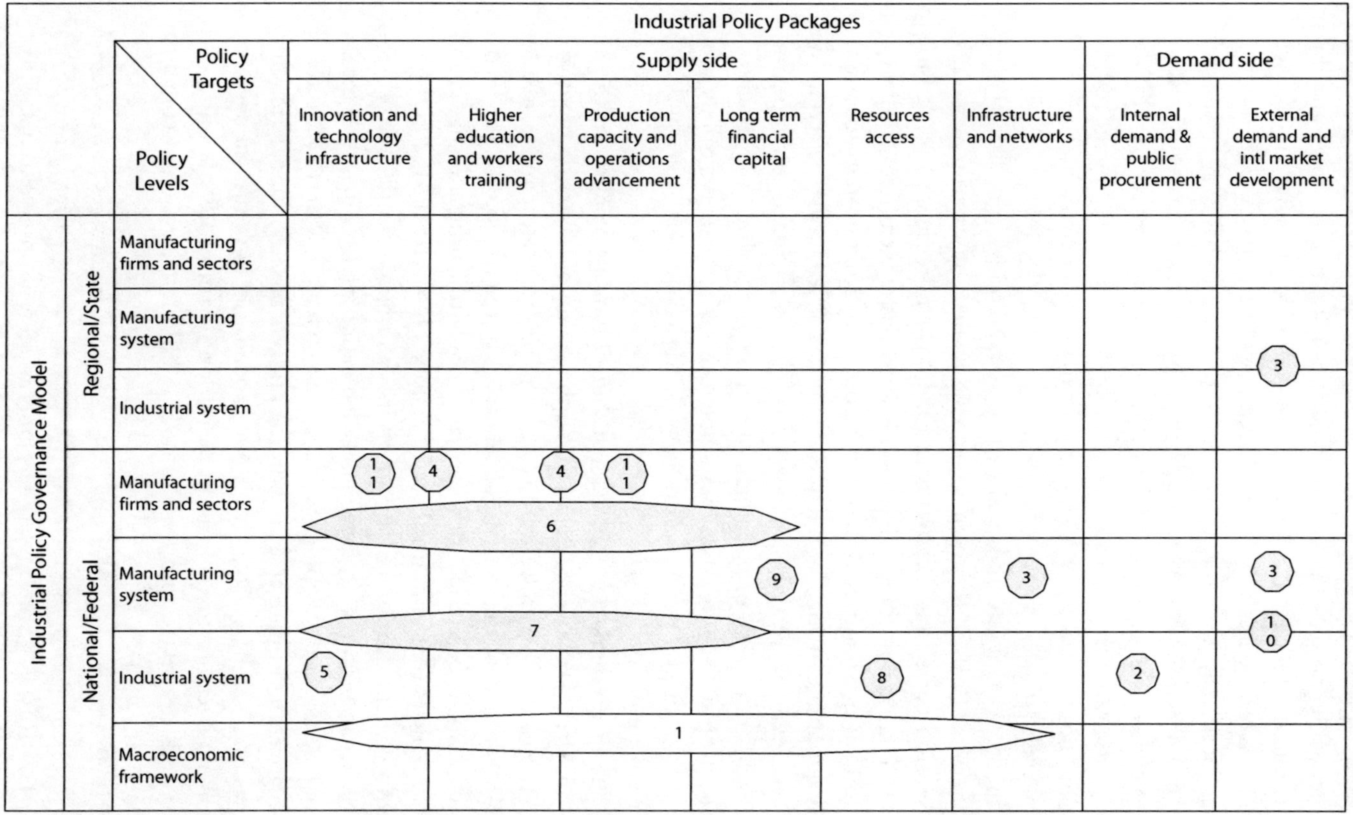

Industrial Policy Packages

Industrial Policy Governance Model	Policy Levels	Policy Targets	Supply side						Demand side	
			Innovation and technology infrastructure	Higher education and workers training	Production capacity and operations advancement	Long term financial capital	Resources access	Infrastructure and networks	Internal demand & public procurement	External demand and intl market development
Regional/State		Manufacturing firms and sectors	1	4	1					
		Manufacturing system								
		Industrial system								3
National/Federal		Manufacturing firms and sectors	6 (span)			9				
		Manufacturing system	7 (span)					3		3
		Industrial system	5				8		2	10
		Macroeconomic framework	1 (span)							

Figure 9.7   The policy package matrix in South Africa

Between 1995 and 2007 laissez-faire economic reforms dominated the scene, while industrial policy interventions remained scattered and discontinuous (Zalk 2014; Mahmood, Andreoni and Chang 2017). Their limited effectiveness was due to a number of persistent contextual factors. Specifically, there were problems with institutional weaknesses, lack of government capabilities, and strong opposition to the policies from powerful economic interest groups. There were also problems with the policy itself, in terms of its limited vision and lack of instrument coordination, not to mention difficulties with the intermediate objectives and implementation.

In 2007, with the approval of the new National Industrial Policy Framework (NIPF), South Africa entered its first industrial policy transformation cycle since the 1990s (Zalk 2014; Andreoni and Neuerburg 2014). Four major industrialization objectives were identified: (1) diversification of nontraditional tradable sectors and strong support for value-added manufacturing; (2) the movement toward a knowledge economy; (3) employment creation via labor-intensive manufacturing development; (4) industrialization of marginalized regions and inclusion of disadvantaged people. The NIPF was then implemented in three-year rolling programs—Industrial Policy Action Plans (IPAPs)— in 2007, 2010, and 2013 (see table 9.7).

The IPAPs marked a fundamental shift in industrial policy making in South Africa for various reasons. First, the design of the action plans was based on extensive consultations with the private sector, and a broader cabinet-level coordination of policies was introduced. Second, the IPAPs have increasingly stressed the importance of coordinating and aligning all those policies that impact industrialization. Third, the IPAPs build on a rigorous identification of key constraints and opportunities for subsectors and accordingly developed detailed action plans. Finally, in recent years, industrial development has received increasing shares of the available government budget. Based on the budgets of the National Treasury, it has been estimated that the public expenditure in industrial development policies increased from R 5.8 billion in 2010 to R 9.4 billion in 2013 and is expected to reach almost R 12 billion in 2016 (Andreoni and Neuerburg 2014).

IPAPs are structured along two different main axes called *IPAP Sectoral Interventions* and *IPAP Transversal Interventions*. The IPAP 2013/14–2015/16 features a large number of sectoral interventions. These are broadly divided between sectors that were already supported in 2007

Table 9.7 Policy Measures, Model, Governance, Transformation Cycle, and Budgets in South Africa

Code	Name	R/N	Transformation Cycle		Agency/ Ministry	BN dollar
1	New Growth Path (NGP)	N	2000	Cont.	DTI	Not avail.
2	Preferential Procurement Policy Framework Act (PPPFA)	N	2000	2011 Reformed	DTI	Not avail.
3	Industrial Development Zone (IDZ), (SEZs from 2013)	N/R	2000	2013 Reformed	DTI	Not avail.
4	CTCP (Clothing and Textiles Competitiveness Programme)	N	2001	Cont.	Industrial Development Corporation (IDC) and DTI	Not avail.
5	SPII (Support Programme for Industrial Innovation)	N	2005	Cont.	Department Trade and Industry (DTI)	0.01
6	Industrial Policy Action Plan 1, 2, and 3 (IPAP) (sectoral programmes)	N/R	2007	2016	DTI	Not avail.
7	Industrial Policy Action Plan 1, 2, and 3 (IPAP) (transversal programmes)	N/R	2007	2016	DTI	Not avail.
8	IPP Renewable Energy Independent Power Producer Programme	N	2010	Cont.	Department of Energy	Not avail.
9	IPAP—Mfg Competitiveness Enhancement Programme (MCEP)	N	2012	2015	DTI and IDC	0.7
10	EMIA Export Marketing Investment Assistance Scheme	N	2012	Cont.	DTI	Not avail.
11	APDP (Automotive Production and Development Programme)— Previous Motor Industry Development Programme	N	2013	2020	DTI Industrial Development Division (IDD)	Not avail.

(cluster 1) and several additional priorities that include qualitatively new areas of intervention (cluster 2). Cluster 2 includes green and energy-saving industries, downstream mineral beneficiation, and shipbuilding. Additionally, there are longer-term targets for the development of capabilities in advanced manufacturing (cluster 3), including nuclear, advanced materials, and aerospace.

Among the cluster 1 sectoral-targeted programs (agro-processing, plastics and pharmaceutics, automobiles, clothing, textiles, footwear and leather, metals fabrication, and business process services), the Automotive Scheme (APDP) awards cash grants to invest in productive assets (machinery, equipment, etc.). Moreover, the Clothing/Textiles scheme (CTCP) provides grants to individual firms to upgrade the skill-level of their labor force or to invest in product and process improvements. And finally, the Agro-processing Fund develops strategies and action plans with selected individual enterprises (DTI 2012).

IPAP Transversal Interventions include eight main areas: public procurement, competition policy, innovation and technology, skills for the economy, special economic zones (SEZs), regional integration, development trade policy, and industrial financing.

As part of the industrial financing the DTI introduced the *Manufacturing Competitiveness Enhancement Programme* (MCEP), a grant-matching scheme to assist local manufacturers to improve shop-floor level competitiveness and job retention (Andreoni and Neuerburg 2014). The MCEP consists of two main subprograms: the Production Incentive Programme (PIP) and the Industrial Financing Loan Facility (IFLF). Companies can apply for one or a combination of different subprograms at company and/or cluster level. Qualifying investment activities include capital equipment for upgrading and expansions; green technology upgrades for cleaner production and resource efficiency activities; enterprise-level competitiveness improvement activities for new or increased market access, product, and process improvement; related skills development; and conducting market and feasibility studies. During the 2012–13 financial year, the MCEP approved 197 projects to assist manufacturing enterprises across all provinces with a total value of R 983 million and a total projected investment of approximately R 4.2 billion.

Another transversal intervention that received significant attention and funding is the development of the SEZs. South Africa established an Industrial Development Zone (IDZ) Program in 2000 with the aim of attracting FDI and promoting the export of value-added commodities. With the Special Economic Zone Bill passed in 2013, the IPAP reformed SEZs by developing a dedicated legislative framework and regulation, explicitly linking them to regional development programs for marginalized regions. To increase industrial policy effectiveness, the Preferential Procurement Policy Framework Act (PPPFA) was amended in 2011, and a number of mechanisms to promote strategic procurement were adopted.

Finally, the IPAP 2013–2014 recognized the existence of intervention gaps and misalignments along the innovation value chain and the need to review and restructure existing SPII and THRIP programs. Sector-specific technology platforms combined with enabling cross-cutting technologies (i.e., advanced materials, nanotechnologies, and

micro- and nano-electronics) were prioritized. However, with the exclusion of business incubators attached to universities or science councils, the majority of these policy interventions rely upon sectoral funds and finance instruments. Less emphasis seems to be given to the development of intermediate institutions and other infrastructure for systemic technological upgrading.

THE NEW INDUSTRIAL POLICY FRONTIER: EMERGING GLOBAL TRENDS AND PRACTICES

Despite the variety of countries' industrial policy pathways, models, and policy packages, a number of focal policy domains and practices are emerging in common. To begin, all countries are adopting a mix of selective sectoral policies and manufacturing system policies. The latter are aimed at supporting the symbiotic development (or restructuring) of complementary groups of industrial sectors. Thus, in manufacturing policies, the selectivity goes beyond sectoral boundaries and focuses on linkages across sectors.

In countries such as the United States, Germany, and Japan, sectoral policies tend to operate at the state, regional, or municipality level while manufacturing system policies are orchestrated at the federal or national level. In these countries, manufacturing system policies mainly consist of picking "enabling" and "platform" technologies, as well as providing selective financial support to new ventures at the technological frontier. Multilayered industrial policy models combining top-down and bottom-up approaches offer greater flexibility in the composition and effective management of industrial policy packages. However, without strong policy enforcement and coordination at the federal or national level, multilayered policy models run the risk of incoherence with different levels undermining one another.

Developing countries such as China and Brazil have been increasingly adopting manufacturing system policies and converging toward a multilayered governance model found in our examples of advanced economies. China in particular has increasingly involved (and arbitrated between) regional governments in selective sectoral policies and local industrial cluster development. Brazil has benefited from increasing government capabilities and institutional capacity (especially a better-functioning legal system). However, its sectoral policies are less selective (almost all sectors are targeted) while its manufacturing system policies are undermined by technological and infrastructural weaknesses. Finally, South Africa is still catching up in the implementation of its full sectoral policy package, and its manufacturing system policies still perpetuate a highly polarized industrial system (a few traditional sectors receive the bulk of the government support).

Despite the documented variety, all selected countries have increasingly strengthened their technological and financial support to the overall manufacturing and industrial system. As discussed, both the technological and financial infrastructures of the selected countries are extremely different in terms of the scope of intervention, functions, and institutional forms. Those countries such as Germany, the United States, and Japan, whose technological infrastructure developed over the last century (aligned alongside the manufacturing system), have managed to build a strong comparative advantage in high-tech activities. The Fraunhofers in Germany, the Kohsetsushi Centers in Japan, and the NNMI institutes in the United States specialize in applied industrial and manufacturing research, scaling up production, and risk reduction, especially for emerging technologies. These "diffused" technological infrastructures are also complemented by "punctual" mission-oriented initiatives aimed at anticipating current and emerging challenges (e.g., environmental, health, and mobility issues).

This increasing emphasis on the *selective learning and industrial knowledge provision* has mainly characterized mature industrial systems. Emerging industrial countries such as China have more recently intensified their support for a diffused system of industrial R&D intermediate institutions, beyond the firms. This reflects increasing Chinese efforts to develop external economies, supply chains, and knowledge-intensive industrial ecosystems around major national and foreign companies. Brazil has successfully developed its agro-technological infrastructure and is currently attempting to replicate the Embrapa model to support manufacturing upgrading. South Africa, meanwhile, is relying mainly on financial support, while less emphasis has been given to intermediate institutions for industrial development and thus public-private technology infrastructure development.

Financial support schemes including loans, long-term financing, matching grants, and financial guarantees, to name but a few, are widely adopted by all the selected countries (e.g., SBIR in the United States, InnoFund in China, FNDCT in Brazil, and MCEP in South Africa). However, the effectiveness of these schemes depends on the degree of selectivity of the financial support provided (i.e., the investment conditionality and technological requirements attached to it). Effectiveness also depends on the existence of a financial infrastructure able to implement, manage, and enforce these financial support schemes. Germany, but also China and Brazil, found in the development banks important operational arms for implementing public financial schemes as well as orienting, coordinating, and supporting companies' long-term strategies.

All the supply-side measures discussed above have been increasingly coupled by a renewed emphasis on demand-side industrial policies. Increasing global competition has pushed all countries to support their internal demand with more strategically focused public procurement policies and their external demand with selective support for export-oriented companies. The latter has been provided through tax benefit or financial support of specialized banks (e.g., United States, Japan, and China).

The selective measures currently adopted in the countries analyzed have been clearly affected (and in certain cases amplified) by the extraordinary countercyclical policies that have been implemented in response to the financial crisis. For example, the ARRA program in the United States has boosted investment in infrastructure upgrading and development as well as education. Similarly, during the recession, Germany's investment in green technologies development, companies' technological transition, and sustainability has been of great significance. China even managed to increase its already extremely high level of internal investment in modern infrastructure (e.g., the massive 3-year effort to build the high-speed train network). Not only do these policies generate increased industrial and infrastructural capabilities (thus, increasing productivity and reducing transaction costs), but also in certain cases they have been used in conjunction with interest rate policies to encourage countercyclical investment and sustain growth.

The new frontier of industrial policies appears increasingly complex. Despite a number of key industrial policy domains characteristic to all countries, variety persists and to a certain extent increases in response to countries' different industrial trajectories and policy pathways. New tensions are also emerging within and across regions. While industrial policies are still acting within the federal or national boundaries, national manufacturing systems are becoming so integrated that the impact of national industrial policies increasingly has consequences across the board. Moreover, the complexity of the new manufacturing systems is making the problem of industrial policy coordination, alignment, and synchronization over time even more urgent than before. Industrial policy packages are increasingly adopted, but the alignment and enforcement of the measures remain fundamental challenges even for those countries adopting more articulated governance models. Indeed, the problem of policy alignment is related not simply to the set of policies within the industrial policy package, but also to the countries' industrial policy packages and their macroeconomic policies as well. While there is no "one size fits all" industrial policy strategy, understanding the variety of countries' industrial policy experiences expands government policy imagination and points to the scope for improving industrial policy package coordination, alignment, and synchronization.

REFERENCES

ABDI (Brazilian Agency for Industrial Development). 2006. *An Industrial Policy for Brazil.* Brasilia: ABDI.

Aghion, P., M. Dewatripont, L. Du, A. Harrison, and P. Legros. 2012. "Industrial Policy and Competition." *NBER Working Paper 18048.*

Aiginger, K., and S. Sieber. 2006. "The Matrix Approach to Industrial Policy." *International Review of Applied Economics* 20(5): 573–601.

Akram, H., and A. Andreoni. 2015. "Welfare State and Industrial Transformations: The Dynamics of Inequality and the Challenge of Policy Alignment." SASE Annual Conference, London School of Economics, July.

Amsden, A. 1989. *Asia's Next Giant: South Korea and Late Industrialization.* New York: Oxford University Press.

Andreoni, A. 2014. "Structural Learning: Embedding Discoveries and the Dynamics of Production." *Structural Change and Economic Dynamics* 29:58–74.

——. 2015a. "The Political Economy of Industrial Policy: After the Crisis, back on the Agenda." In *Handbook of Political Economy and Law*, ed. U. Mattei and J. Haskell. Cheltenham and Northampton: Edward Elgar.

——. 2015b. "The Variety of Public Goods Production, Technologies and Policy: New Insights from Engineering-Economics Twists." IASS mimeo, Potsdam.

Andreoni, A., and H.-J. Chang. 2014. "Agricultural Policy and the Role of Intermediate Institutions in Production Capabilities Transformation: Fundacion Chile and Embrapa in Action." Working paper, DRUID, Copenhagen, 16–18 June.

——. 2016. "Industrial policy and the future of manufacturing: theoretical reflections." *Economia e Politica Industriale. Journal of Industrial and Business Economics*, forthcoming.

Andreoni, A., F. Frattini, F. and G. Prodi, G. 2016. "Structural Cycles and Industrial Policy Alignment: The private-public nexus in the Emilian packaging valley." *Cambridge Journal of Economics*, forthcoming.

Andreoni, A., and M. Gregory. 2013. "Why and How Does Manufacturing Still Matter: Old Rationales, New Realities." *Revue d'Economie Industrielle* 144(4): 17–54.

Andreoni, A., and P. Neuerburg. 2014. "Manufacturing Competitiveness in South Africa: Matching Industrial Systems and Policies." South Africa-EU Strategic Partnership Conference, Johannesburg, 20–21 May.

Andreoni, A., and R. Scazzieri. 2013. "Triggers of Change: Structural Trajectories and Production Dynamics." *Cambridge Journal of Economics* 38: 1391–1408.

Aoki, M. 2001. *Toward a Comparative Institutional Analysis*. Cambridge, Mass.: MIT Press.

Benhassine, N., and G. Raballand. 2009. "Beyond Ideological Cleavages: A Unifying Framework for Industrial Policies and Other Public Interventions." *Economic Systems* 33(4): 293–309.

Berger, S. 2013. *Making in America. From Innovation to Market*. Cambridge, Mass.: MIT Press.

Block, F. 2008. "Swimming Against the Current: The Rise of a Hidden Developmental State in the United States." *Politics & Society* 36: 169–206.

Boyer, R. 1990. *The Regulation School: A Critical Introduction*. New York: Columbia University Press.

Cao, C., R. P. Suttmeier, and D. F. Simon 2006. "China's 15-Year Science and Technology Plan." *Physics Today*, 54: 1–38.

Chaminade, C., and C. Edquist. 2006. "Rationales for Public Policy Intervention from a Systems of Innovation Approach: The Case of VINNOVA." CIRCLE Working Paper, 2006/04, Lund University.

Chang, H. J. 1994. *The Political Economy of Industrial Policy*. Basingstoke, England: Macmillan.

——. 1998. "Evaluating the Current Industrial Policy of South Africa." *Transformation* 36: 51–72.

——. 2002. *Kicking Away the Ladder*. London: Anthem.

——. 2003. "Trade and Industrial Policy Issues." In *Rethinking Development Economics*, 257–76, ed. H-J. Chang. London: Anthem.

——. 2010. "Industrial Policy: Can We Go Beyond an Unproductive Debate?" In *Lessons from East Asia and the Global Financial Crisis*, ed. J. Y. Lin and B. Pleskovic. ABCDE, Annual World Bank Conference on Development Economics, Seoul.

Chang, H. J., ed. 2007. *Institutional Change and Economic Development*. United Nations University Press.

Chang, H. J., A. Andreoni, and M. L. Kuan. 2013. "International Industrial Policy Experiences and the Lessons for the UK." In *The Future of UK Manufacturing: Scenario Analysis, Financial Markets and Industrial Policy*, ed. A. Hughes. E-book. London: UK-IRC.

Chang, H.-J., and B. Rowthorn, eds. 1995. *Role of the State in Economic Change*. Oxford: Oxford University Press.

Cimoli, M., G. Dosi, and J. Stiglitz, eds. 2009. *Industrial Policy and Development. The Political Economy of Capabilities Accumulation*. Oxford: Oxford University Press.

Cimoli, M., M. Holland, G. Porcile, A. Primi, and S. Vergara. 2006. "Growth, Structural Change and Technological Capabilities. Latina America in Comparative Perspective." LEM Working Paper 2006/11.

Coe, N. M., P. Dicken, and M. Hess. 2008. "Global Production Networks: Realizing the Potential." *Journal of Economic Geography* 8(3): 271–95.

Dodgson, M., A. Hughes, J. Foster, and S. Metcalfe. 2011. "System Thinking, Market Failure, and the Development of Innovation Policy: The Case of Australia." *Research Policy* 40: 1145–56.

Dore, R. 1986. *Flexible Rigidities: Industrial Policy and Structural Adjustment in the Japanese Economy 1970–80.* London: Athlone Press.

Dorn, J., and T. Cloutier. 2013. *Report on Chinese Industrial Policies.* Atlanta, Ga.: King & Spalding.

Duffield, J., and B. Woodall. 2011. "Japan's New Basic Energy Plan." *Energy Policy* 39: 3741–9.

Dustmann, C., B. Fitzenberger, U. Schonberg, and A. Spitz-Oener. 2014. "From Sick Man of Europe to Economic Superstar: Germany's Resurgent Economy." *Journal of Economic Perspectives* 28(1): 167–88.

Edquist, C., ed. 1997. *Systems of Innovation: Technologies, Institutions and Organizations.* London: Pinter/Cassell.

Evans, P. 1995. *Embedded Autonomy: State and Industrial Transformation.* Princeton, N.J.: Princeton University Press.

Ezell, S. J., and R .D. Atkinson. 2011. *International Benchmarking of Countries' Policies and Programs. Supporting SME Manufacturers.* Washington, D.C.: Information Technology and Innovation Foundation.

Fan, P., and C. Watanabe. 2006. "Promoting Industrial Development through Technology Policy: Lessons from Japan and China." *Technology in Society* 28: 303–20.

Ferraz, J., C. Figueiredo, C. Leal, F. Marques, and M. Miterhof. 2013. "Financing Development: The Case of BNDES." In *The Industrial Policy Revolution I,* ed. J. Stiglitz and J. Y. Lin, 143–57. Basingstoke, U.K.: Palgrave.

Fine, B., and B. Rustomjee. 1996. *The Political Economy of South Africa: From Minerals-Energy Complex to Industrialisation.* London: Hurst.

Freeman, C. 1987. *Technology Policy and Economic Performance: Lessons from Japan.* London: Pinter.

Greenwald, B., and J. Stiglitz. 1986. "Externalities in Economies with Imperfect Information and Incomplete Markets." *Quarterly Journal of Economics* 101:229–64.

Hall, P. 1986. *Governing the Economy: The Politics of State Intervention in Britain and France.* Oxford: Oxford University Press.

Hall, P. A., and D. Soskice. 2001. *Varieties of Capitalism: The Institutional Foundations of Comparative Advantage.* Oxford: Oxford University Press.

Hancke, B., M. Rhodes, and M. Thatcher. 2007. *Beyond Varieties of Capitalism.* Oxford: Oxford University Press.

Hausmann, R., and D. Rodrik. 2004. "Economic Development as Self-Discovery," *Journal of Development Economics* 72(2), 603–33.

Hirschman, A. 1958. *The Strategy of Economic Development.* New Haven, Conn.: Yale University Press.

Johnson, C. 1982. *MITI and the Japanese Miracle: The Growth of Industrial Policy, 1925–1975*. Stanford, Calif.: Stanford University Press.

Khan, M. H., and K. S. Jomo. 2001. *Rents, Rent-Seeking and Economic Development*. Cambridge: Cambridge University Press.

Khan, M. 2013. "Technology Policies and Learning with Imperfect Governance." In *The Industrial Policy Revolution I*, ed. J. Stiglitz and J. Lin, 79–115, Basingstoke: Palgrave.

Klein Woolthuis, R., M. Lankhuizen, and V. Gilsing. 2005. "A System Failure Framework for Innovation Policy Design." *Technovation* 25: 609–19.

Kupfer, D., J. Ferraz, and F. Marques. 2013. "The Return of Industrial Policy in Brazil." In *The Industrial Policy Revolution I*, ed. J. Stiglitz and J. Lin, 327–40. Basingstoke: Palgrave.

Kuznetsov, Y., and C. Sabel. 2011. "New Open Economy Industrial Policy: Making Choices without Picking Winners." PREM Notes Economic Policy, World Bank, September, p. 116.

Lall, S. 1992. "Technological Capabilities and Industrialization." *World Development* 20(2): 165–86.

Landesmann, M. 1992. "Industrial Policy and Social Corporatism." In *Social Corporatism*, ed. J. Pekkarinen, M. Pohjola, and B. Rowthorn. Oxford: Oxford University Press, 242–79.

Laranja, M., E. Uyarra, and K. Flanagan. 2008. "Policies for Science, Technology and Innovation: Translating Rationales into Regional Policies in a Multi-Level Setting." *Research Policy* 37: 823–35.

Lin, J. 2012. *New Structural Economics—.A Framework for Rethinking Development and Policy*. Washington, D.C.: World Bank.

Lin, J., and H.-J. Chang. 2009. "Should Industrial Policy in Developing Countries Conform to Comparative Advantage or Defy It?" *Development Policy Review* 27(5): 483–502.

Lo, D., and M. Wu. 2014. "The State and Industrial Policy in Chinese Economic Development." In *Transforming Economies*, ed. J. M. Salazar-Xirinachs, I. Nubler, and R. Kozul-Wright. Geneva: ILO.

Locke, R., and R. Wellhausen, eds. 2014. *Production in the Innovation Economy*. Cambridge, Mass.: MIT Press.

Lundvall, B. A., ed. 1992. *National Systems of Innovation: Towards a Theory of Innovation and Interactive Learning*. London: Pinter.

Malerba, F. 2002. "Sectoral System of Innovation and Production." *Research Policy* 31: 247–64.

Markusen, A. 1996. "Interaction between Regional and Industrial Policies: Evidence from Four Countries." *International Regional Science Review*, 19(1/2): 49–77.

Mazzucato, M. 2014. *The Entrepreneurial State*. London: Anthem Press.

Metcalfe, S. 1995. "Technology Systems and Technology Policy in an Evolutionary Framework." *Cambridge Journal of Economics* 19: 25–46.

MIIT (Ministry of Industry and Information Technology of the People's Republic of China). 2013. *Guidance on Corporate Mergers and Acquisitions to Accelerate the Growth of Key Industries*.

Milberg, W., and D. Winkler. 2013. *Outsourcing Economics*. Cambridge: Cambridge University Press.

Mahmood, M., A. Andreoni. and H.-J. Chang. 2017. *Developing with Jobs: Manufacturing growth, productive employment and policies in developing countries*, Basingstoke: Palgrave Macmillan.

Nelson, R., ed. 1993. *National Innovation Systems: A Comparative Analysis*. New York: Oxford University Press.

Nezu, R. 2007. "Industrial Policy in Japan." *Journal of Industry, Competition and Trade* 7(3–4): 229–43.

Noman, A., K. Botchwey, H. Stein, and J. Stiglitz. 2011. *Good Growth and Governance in Africa. Rethinking Development Strategies.* Oxford: Oxford University Press.

Nurkse, R. 1952. "Some International Aspects of the Problem of Economic Development." *The American Economic Review* 42(2): 571–83.

Ocampo, J. A. 2006. "Latin America and the World Economy in the Long Twentieth Century." In *The Great Divergence: Hegemony, Uneven Development and Global Inequality*, ed. K. S. Jomo. New York: Oxford University Press, 44–93.

Okimoto, D. I. 1989. *Between MITI and the Market: Japanese Industrial Policy for High Technology.* Stanford, Calif.: Stanford University Press.

O'Sullivan, E. 2011. *A Review of International Approaches to Manufacturing Research.* Cambridge: University of Cambridge Institute for Manufacturing.

O'Sullivan, E., A. Andreoni, G. Lopez-Gomez, and M. Gregory. 2013. "What Is New in the New Industrial Policy? A Manufacturing System Perspective." *Oxford Review of Economic Policy* 29(2): 432–62.

Pack, H., and K. Saggi. 2006. "Is There a Case for Industrial Policy? A Critical Survey." *World Bank Researcher Observer* 21(2): 267–97.

Pisano, G. P., and W. C. Shih. 2012. *Producing Prosperity: Why America Needs a Manufacturing Renaissance.* Boston: Harvard Business Review Press.

Rodrik, D. 2004. "Industrial Policy for the Twenty-First Century."Mimeo, Harvard University.

———. 2007. "Normalizing Industrial Policy." Working paper. Cambridge, Mass.: John F. Kennedy School of Government.

Roseinstein-Rodan, P. 1957. *Notes on the Theory of the "Big Push."* Cambridge, Mass.: MIT Center for International Studies.

Salazar-Xirinachs, J. M., I. Nubler, and R. Kozul-Wright, eds. 2014. *Transforming Economies.* Geneva: ILO.

Shih, W. 2011. "China's Five Year Plan, Indigenous Innovation and Technology Transfer and Outsourcing." Testimony before the US-China Economic & Security Review Commission, June 15.

Soete, L. 2007. "From Industrial to Innovation Policy." *Journal of Industrial Competitiveness and Trade* 7: 273–84.

Stiglitz, J. 1996. "Some Lessons from the East Asian Miracle." *World Bank Research Observer* 11(2): 151–77.

Stiglitz, J., and B. Greenwald. 2014. *Creating a Learning Society.* New York: Columbia University Press.

Stiglitz, J., and J. Y. Lin, eds. 2013. *The Industrial Policy Revolution I.* Basingstoke: Palgrave.

Stiglitz, J., and S. Yusuf, eds. 2001. *Rethinking the East Asia Miracle.* Washington, D.C.: World Bank.

Storm, S., and C. W. M. Naastepad. 2015. "Crisis and Recovery in the German Economy: The Real Lessons." *Structural Change and Economic Dynamics* 32: 11–14.

Stortz, C., B. Amable, S. Casper, and S. Lechevalier. 2013. "Bringing Asia into the Comparative Capitalism Perspective." *Socio-Economic Review* 11: 217–32.

Tassey, G. 2007. *The Technology Imperative*. Cheltenham and Northampton: Edward Elgar.

——. 2010. "Rationales and Mechanisms for Revitalizing US Manufacturing R&D Strategies." *Journal of Technology Transfer* 35: 283–333.

——. 2014. "Competing in Advanced Manufacturing: The Need for Improved Growth Models and Policies." *Journal of Economic Perspectives* 28(1): 27–48.

Ul-Haque, I. 2007. "Rethinking Industrial Policy." UNCTAD Discussion Papers No. 183.

Vitols, S. 1997. "German Industrial Policy: An Overview." *Industry and Innovation* 4(1): 15–36.

Wade, R. 1990. *Governing the Market: Economic Theory and the Role of Government in East Asian Industrialization*. Princeton, N.J.: Princeton University Press.

——. 2012. "Return of Industrial Policy?" *International Review of Applied Economics* 26(2): 223–39.

Walker, T., C. Brewster, and G. Wood. 2014. "Diversity between and within Varieties of Capitalism: Transnational Survey Evidence." *Industrial and Corporate Change* 23(2): 493–533.

Warwick, K. 2013. "Beyond Industrial Policy. Emerging Issues and New Trends." OECD Science, Technology and Industrial Policy Papers No. 2.

Weiss, J. 2011. "Industrial Policy in the Twenty-First Century." UNU-WIDER Working Paper, 2011/55.

Wessner, C. W., and A. Wolff, eds. 2012. *Rising to the Challenge: US Innovation Policy for Global Economy*. Washington, D.C.: National Academy of Sciences Press.

Zalk, N. 2014. "Industrial Policy in a Harsh Climate: The Case of South Africa." In *Transforming Economies*, ed. J. M. Salazar-Xirinachs, I. Nubler, and R. Kozul-Wright. Geneva: ILO.

Zhang, X. 2013. "Clusters as an Instrument for Industrial Policy: The Case of China." In *The Industrial Policy Revolution I*, ed. J. Stiglitz and J. Lin. Basingstoke: Palgrave.

CHAPTER 10

Industrial Strategies

TOWARD A LEARNING SOCIETY FOR QUALITY GROWTH

Akio Hosono

The critical importance of learning and innovation for growth and development is being increasingly emphasized among scholars, development policy makers, and practitioners. In the academic sphere, Stiglitz and Greenwald published a book in 2014 titled *Creating a Learning Society: A New Approach to Growth, Development, and Social Progress,* with the main message emphasizing the centrality of learning and arguing that there is an important role for government to play in shaping an innovative economy and promoting learning (Stiglitz and Greenwald 2014, 7). In recent policy discussions on quality of growth, innovation has been considered an important attribute. For instance, in the Asian Pacific Economic Cooperation (APEC) growth strategy agreed on in 2010 in Yokohama, innovation is explicitly referred to as one of the five attributes of good quality growth. Likewise, a year later at the Summer Davos meeting—which focused on "mastering quality growth"—in Tailian, China, the Chinese premier pointed out that together, technology and innovation constitute one of the five dimensions for achieving high quality growth.

In this chapter I aim to provide insights into effective approaches to create a learning society for such quality growth. It draws from cases of international development cooperation, looking at (1) inclusive and innovative growth, (2) inclusive, innovative, and sustainable growth, and (3) inclusive and innovative growth accompanied by enhanced resilience. It recognizes that each society or country has its own distinctive development agenda and different combinations of endowments as well as its own particular development challenges.

Hosono (2015a, 2015b, 2015c) analyzed seven outstanding cases of industrial development and transformation: the automobile industry in Thailand, the garment industry in Bangladesh, rice production in Tanzania, agroforestry in semiarid areas of Kenya, Cerrado agriculture and agro-industry development in Brazil, knowledge-intensive industries in Singapore, and aquaculture of salmon and shellfish in Chile. These cases illustrated the mutual causality between transformational development, on one hand, and the constant development of capabilities and knowledge through learning, on the other hand. It was for this purpose that the respective governments facilitated learning and capacity development. In most of these cases, effective institutions fulfilled the role of facilitator.

Bearing in mind that these outstanding cases of transformation were accompanied by a learning process and enabled by learning capacity, in this chapter I discuss effective approaches to initiate and maintain momentum and to scale up the learning process, drawing from cases of international cooperation for capacity development. These cases are analyzed from a "learning perspective." They have not necessarily produced transformation directly, as with the above-mentioned outstanding cases, but have still had a significant impact on the learning process of a society and thereby enabled changes in companies or organizations, local or regional economies, or even national economies.

Based on the above discussion, I pose the following research question: What industrial development strategies and approaches are effective in promoting learning to attain transformation with good growth of quality, given the challenges countries face and the changing endowments they count on?

In the section "Key Issues from an Analytical Perspective," I discuss key issues and provide an analytical perspective. In the sections "Cases of Learning for Specific Capacity," "Cases of Learning to Learn and Enhancing Core Capacity," and "Lessons from Case Studies," I present and discuss some cases illustrating the above-mentioned three categories. In the section "Conclusion," I offer some concluding remarks.

KEY ISSUES FROM AN ANALYTICAL PERSPECTIVE

LEARNING, INNOVATION, AND QUALITY OF GROWTH

In recent policy debates on growth and development, increasing attention is being paid to the *quality* of economic growth, particularly in terms of its relation to jobs and inclusiveness, sustainability, learning, accumulation of skills and capabilities, innovation, and so on.[1] In Asia and the

Pacific region, APEC leaders at Yokohama in 2010 agreed on the *APEC Growth Strategy*.[2] This strategy stressed that "the quality of growth" needs to be improved, so that it will be more balanced, inclusive, sustainable, innovative, and secure (Hosono 2015a). Ten months later, the World Economic Forum held its annual Asian Summer Davos meeting, this time focusing on "Mastering Quality Growth," in which sustainability, inclusion, fairness, balance, and technology and innovation were highlighted (World Economic Forum 2011, 3). More recently, the Asian Development Bank (ADB) issued a report focusing on Asia's economic transformation (ADB 2013). The report noted that development is distinct from aggregate growth, which can occur without significant transformation, such as in some oil-rich economies. This report highlighted key components of structural transformation.[3]

Most recently, at the Twenty-Second APEC Economic Leaders' Declaration, the "Beijing Agenda for an Integrated, Innovative and Interconnected Asia-Pacific" (APEC 2014, 7) stated that "We agree to strengthen macroeconomic policy coordination with a view to forging policy synergy, and creating a sound policy environment for the robust, sustainable, balanced and inclusive economic growth in the region." The declaration emphasized innovative growth in particular: "We recognize innovation as an important lever for economic growth and structural reform . . . We realize that the prospects for the shared prosperity of APEC will depend on innovative development, economic reform and growth in the region, which are complementary and mutually reinforcing."

The shift toward recognizing quality growth has also occurred at the national government level in Asia. The new generation of Chinese leaders and the government set out an ambitious and comprehensive agenda in terms of structural reforms laid out in the *Decision by the Third Plenum Session of the Chinese Communist Party* held in 2013. In addition to rebalancing the economy, mitigating social inequality, protecting the environment, and addressing climate change, the need to address the rural-urban divide and improve the quality of growth has been placed high on the policy agenda (Wang, Wang, and Wang 2014, xi). In Japan, the *Annual Report on the Japanese Economy and Public Finance 2012* featured growth with "quality" (Government of Japan, Cabinet Office 2012, 226). Some other countries within Asia, including Malaysia, Thailand, India, Bhutan, and Vietnam, have been introducing similar concepts. For example, Malaysia launched a "New Economic Model" within the framework of both inclusive and sustainable growth in 2012 (UN-ESCAP 2013, 8).

In 2015, the Japanese government announced the *Charter of Development Cooperation* to replace the *Official Development Assistance (ODA) Charter*. It stated that one of the most important challenges of development is "'quality growth' and poverty eradication through such growth," in which inclusiveness, sustainability, and resilience are stressed (Government of Japan, Cabinet Office 2015, 5–6).

Although the precise definition of what constitutes high quality of growth might differ across the above-mentioned documents, they commonly give a high priority to innovative, inclusive, and sustainable dimensions of growth.

LEARNING CAPACITY AS THE MOST IMPORTANT ENDOWMENT[4]

At the same time as this growing recognition of the importance of innovation in quality growth, discussions on the importance of learning, accumulation of knowledge, and capabilities have deepened. Cimoli, Dosi, and Stiglitz (2009, 2) stated that "great transformation" entails a major process of accumulation of knowledge and capabilities, at the levels of both individuals and organizations. Later, Noman and Stiglitz (2012, 7) emphasized that "Long-term success rests on societies' 'learning'—new technologies, new ways of doing business, new ways of managing the economy and new ways of dealing with other countries."

Most recently, Stiglitz and Greenwald (2014, 26) presented a more systematic and holistic analysis of what constituted a learning society, stating that "the most important 'endowment,' from our perspective, is a society's learning capacities (which in turn is affected by the knowledge that it has; its knowledge about learning itself; and its knowledge about its own learning capacities), which may be specific to learning about some things rather than others." They further state that a country's policies have to be shaped to take advantage of its comparative advantage in knowledge and learning abilities, including its ability to learn and to learn to learn, in relation to its competitors, and to help develop those capacities and capabilities further (Stiglitz and Greenwald 2014, 26).

ENDOWMENTS, INDUSTRIAL TRANSFORMATION, AND QUALITY GROWTH: FOCUS OF INDUSTRIAL STRATEGY

The nexus between changing endowments, industrial transformation, and quality growth needs to be the main focus of an industrial strategy. According to Noman and Stiglitz (2012), the "old" policies focused on improving economic efficiency within a static framework. They argued, however, that "The essence of development is dynamic. What matters, for instance, is not comparative advantage as of today, but dynamic comparative advantage" (Noman and Stiglitz 2012, 7). Lin (2012), while discussing the "changing comparative advantage" argues that "The more effective route for their learning and development is to exploit the advantages of backwardness and upgrade and diversify into new industries according to the changing comparative advantages determined by the changes in their endowment structure" (Lin 2012, 73).

As such, quality of growth needs to be discussed in the context of changing endowments and transformation, because industrial transformation is a driver of growth and could be related to different attributes of growth. Industrial strategy needs to focus on public policies that affect the quality of growth based on changing endowments and industrial transformation.[5] In sum, industrial strategy needs to address enhancement of endowments and, among others, the learning capacity with accumulation of knowledge and capabilities, infrastructure, human capital, social capital, natural capital, financial capital, institutions, and so forth. It needs to catalyze or facilitate industrial transformation, taking full advantage of changing endowments, through creation of new industries, deepening of value chains, diversification, and so on. Industrial strategy needs also to attain the desired attributes of quality growth in the process of industrial transformation, which is the foundation and driving force of economic growth.

LEARNING SOCIETY AND CAPACITY DEVELOPMENT

Also, in recent discussions on aid effectiveness and later development effectiveness, especially among aid practitioners, capacity development has emerged as a central issue. The *Accra Agenda for Action*, adopted in 2008 at the third High-Level Forum on Aid Effectiveness, emphasized *capacity development* (CD) even more strongly than the Paris Declaration, which incorporates CD as a key cross-cutting theme in aid effectiveness.[6] The outcome document of the United Nations summit on its Millennium Development Goals (MDGs) in September 2010 repeatedly asserts the importance of capacity and capacity development. Underlying this trend is a growing recognition among donor organizations, donor governments, and partner countries that lack of capacity has been, and will likely remain, a major obstacle in translating policy into development results (Hosono et al. 2011, 179).

Knowledge and learning in a CD process have increasingly been a feature of recent discussions. Clarke and Oswald (2010) argue that mutual learning might even be considered to be CD. If CD is perceived as a mutual learning process, this demands that we shift our idea of what knowledge is and how it can be generated away from the traditional transfer-of-knowledge model toward a cocreation-of-knowledge model (Hosono et al. 2011, 181). As such, international cooperation for CD processes with a stronger focus on learning and cocreation of knowledge or innovative solutions could be considered one effective approach in creating a learning society within developing countries.[7]

LEARNING FOR SPECIFIC CAPACITY AND LEARNING TO LEARN FOR ENHANCING CORE CAPACITY

Stiglitz and Greenwald (2014) distinguish between learning abilities, stating that "Learning abilities can, of course, be specific or general" and that "We can direct our efforts at enhancing specific abilities. These may serve an economy well if it is pursuing a narrow niche; or efforts can be directed at more general learning abilities that may serve it well in periods of rapid transition and great uncertainty" (Stiglitz and Greenwald 2014, 50). They further mention that "Just as *knowledge* itself is endogenous, so is the ability to *learn*. Some economic activities (conducted in certain ways) not only facilitate learning, they may facilitate *learning to learn*" (Stiglitz and Greenwald 2014, 50; italics in original). Several studies on capacity development also refer to the two types of capacity. Capacity embodies not only specific technical elements, such as specific health care or road construction skills, but also so-called core capacities (Hosono et al. 2011, 180). They include generic and cross-cutting competencies and the ability to commit and engage; to identify needs and key issues; to plan, budget, execute, and monitor actions; and most importantly to acquire knowledge and skills (UNDP 1998; ECDPM 2008; JICA 2006, 2008). Learning for specific capacity could enable learning to learn, while the capacity of learning to learn could facilitate learning for a specific capacity.

DETERMINANTS OF LEARNING

Stiglitz and Greenwald (2014, 56–57) identified the following major determinants of learning: (1) learning capabilities; (2) access to knowledge; (3) the catalysts for learning; (4) creating a creative mind-set—the right cognitive frames; (5) contacts—people with whom one interacts—who can catalyze learning, help create the right cognitive frame, and provide crucial inputs into the learning process; and (6) the context of learning.

An emerging view on CD sees knowledge as the product of continuous human interaction within specific contexts, in which knowledge and innovative solutions are cocreated through a mutual learning process and acquired through practical experiences (Hosono et al. 2011, 182). In this process, five factors are considered essential: stakeholder ownership, specific drivers, mutual learning, pathways to scaling up, and catalyzers (including external actors) (Hosono 2013, 257).

Figure 10.1 roughly illustrates capacity development as a dynamic, endogenous, and continuous process through which learning for both specific capacity and learning to learn (core capacity) take place. The above-mentioned "determinants of learning" are extremely important in this process, although the sequences and relationships among them could be different from those indicated in this figure, depending on different contexts.

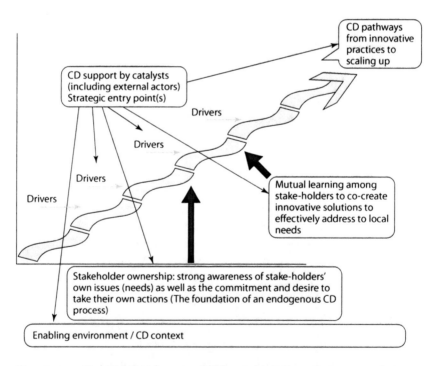

Figure 10.1   Capacity Development (CD) as a dynamic, endogenous, and continuous process

Source: Author, based on Hosono et al. 2011.

INDUSTRIAL STRATEGY AND EFFECTIVE APPROACHES FOR LEARNING: RESEARCH QUESTIONS

So the relevant question for this exercise is, What industrial strategies and approaches are effective in promoting learning to attain the desired quality of growth, given the various challenges countries face and the endowments they count on? I will draw from experiences of international development cooperation to discuss this research question mainly in the following three areas: (1) learning for inclusive and innovative growth; (2) learning for inclusive, innovative, and sustainable growth; and (3) learning for inclusive and innovative growth that strengthens resilience and human security. Cases relevant to the above-mentioned areas have been selected from widely applied approaches in diverse learning contexts. This chapter specially focus on how in practice the determinants of learning interact to initiate, catalyze, and maintain momentum in the process of learning and learning to learn.

LEARNING FOR INCLUSIVE AND INNOVATIVE GROWTH

In recent years, *inclusive development* has attracted increasing attention in the international community. In 2007, the World Bank president declared that contributing to inclusive and sustainable globalization was the vision of the World Bank Group. The Japan International Cooperation Agency (JICA) incorporated the term *inclusive* into its vision statement in 2008. A year later, ADB positioned inclusive growth as one of the three agenda items in its long-term strategic framework of Strategy 2020 (ADB 2009). As mentioned above, the APEC Growth Strategy was agreed upon in 2010, and *inclusive growth* featured in the document as one of the five desired attributes for growth.[8]

In these documents, inclusive growth has two interrelated aspects: With inclusive growth, all people participate in growth, and at the same time all people benefit from growth.[9] But, from a learning society perspective, inclusive growth goes far beyond the above-mentioned aspects and has an intrinsic relationship with innovative growth. Growth could be really inclusive and, at the same time, innovative, when growth takes full advantage of the talents of all. Stiglitz and Greenwald (2014) state that "Our argument for why inclusive growth is so important goes beyond the standard one that it is a waste of a country's most valuable resource, its human talent, to fail to ensure that every one lives up to his or her abilities" (Stiglitz and Greenwald 2014, 468). They suggest that policies that promote more inclusiveness may promote greater learning (Stiglitz and Greenwald 2014, 381).

Table 10.1 highlights some relevant approaches of international cooperation programs, aiming at learning for specific capacities or learning to learn for general or core capacity. From this perspective, these approaches are analyzed below to obtain some indication of how inclusive and innovative growth might be attained through learning. First, I discuss two cases related to learning for specific capacities. One is the case of the Smallholder Horticultural Empowerment Project (SHEP) in Kenya, focusing on individual farmers' learning. The other is the case of the Local Government Engineering Department (LGED) in Bangladesh, which focuses on organizational learning.

Following these two cases, I discuss an additional three cases focusing on learning to learn or general/core capacity. In the first case, I examine livelihood improvement programs that focus on improvements other than those stemming from raising incomes (e.g., improved cooking stoves), because they aim primarily to enable rural women to become aware of the numerous problems that exist in daily life, and address them as problems that need to be solved. As such, the objective of these programs was *learning to learn* through *learning by doing* and making efforts to improve

Table 10.1 Approaches to Learning for Specific Capacity and Learning to Learn

	From Learning for Specific Capacity to Learning to Learn	Focusing Directly on Learning to Learn (Enhancing Core Capacity)
Mainly focusing on individuals' learning	Capacity development for specific purposes, which gradually enables learning to learn (e.g., Smallholder Horticultural Empowerment Project)	Learning to learn for improvement of livelihood
Focusing on both individuals' and groups' learning (associations, cooperatives, and so on)	Capacity development for specific purposes, which enables individuals' and groups' learning to learn	"Learning to learn" for creation and development of inclusive business through One Village One Product (OVOP) initiatives
Mainly focusing on organizations' learning and institution building	Capacity development for specific purposes, which enables the organizations' learning to learn (e.g., local government engineering dept.)	Learning to learn in organizations through kaizen, Just in Time (JIT), TQM, knowledge management, and other initiatives

livelihood in its multiple dimensions. This approach has an advantage because the initiatives of such livelihood improvement are much less risky than initiatives of income improvement through production. But the process of finding solutions to livelihood problems and the uplifting of rural livelihood can lead to learning to learn and later the advancement of production activities. In Oita, Japan, where the One Village One Product (OVOP) initiative was born, women with experiences of livelihood improvement programs later effectively promoted OVOP's production activities. I discuss the OVOP programs in Japan, Thailand, and other countries as the second case. Finally, the third case of learning to learn, or of acquiring core capacity, is a series of approaches such as kaizen, just in time (JIT), Total Quality Management (TQM), knowledge management, and so on normally utilized by enterprises and organizations.

CASES OF LEARNING FOR SPECIFIC CAPACITY

Case 1: Learning for inclusive and innovative growth enabled by capacity development of small-scale farmers with increased responsiveness to market needs: Initiatives of SHEP and SHEP UP in Kenya[10]

Kenya has considerable potential for commercial agricultural diversification thanks to good market access and the empowerment of farmers. Demand for horticultural products has been increasing in Africa. In Kenya, horticultural production has achieved an average annual growth rate of 20 percent since the 2000s. More than 60 percent of horticultural products are produced by small-scale farmers who have benefited from higher incomes from the sale of horticultural products. Compared to grain production in Kenya, horticulture is more labor-intensive, requiring more complex techniques and bigger inputs, including seeds, fertilizer, and pesticides. Land productivity is higher under properly managed horticulture. Based on this premise, the Kenyan government launched the Smallholder Horticultural Empowerment Project (SHEP) in 2006 (Aikawa 2013, 144–5). SHEP aimed mainly at developing the capacity of smallholder horticulture farmer groups.

SHEP and SHEP Unit Project (SHEP UP) started with the premise that horticultural farming is an industry, no matter how small the scale of the market as a whole or how little the output of individual farmers.

Based on that premise, the projects developed a series of activities to encourage farmers to develop behavior to respond to the needs of the market, using these as both the starting point of their strategy and their ultimate goal. Many African countries are encouraging their farmers to transform their current subsistence-oriented agriculture into more explicitly commercially oriented ventures. However, small-scale farmers in Africa did not necessarily know how to achieve this, though they had been implicitly farming based on rational decision making, just as in a business. SHEP and SHEP UP filled this gap (Aikawa 2013, 163–4).

Since the 1990s, many donors have been providing support for value chain development. Their support tended to focus on the downstream part of the supply chain from production through sales, or the portion close to postharvest processing and sales. In contrast, SHEP and SHEP UP provided support to small-scale farmers through every step, from production to sales, covering various aspects of the activities in ways that were adoptable by the farmers. In doing so, the project always put the farmers at the center as it designed its activities and refined its methods (Aikawa 2013, 163–4). As a result, SHEP achieved remarkable results.[11] This approach is now being introduced into ten sub-Saharan African countries as well as Palestine and El Salvador.

Aikawa (2013) explains the learning process of SHEP as follows:

> Various techniques were introduced in the project. They were simple and applicable, using materials easily available to the farmers. In fact, in Kenya, a country where they have reached a certain level of technological know-how at the research station, the issue was not how to develop new technologies, but how to validate existing technologies from the farmers' perspective and put them to practical use. Based on this understanding, the project focused on the introduction of techniques that were immediately usable the moment they were learned, such as the technique for correct planting using twine. The guidance on these techniques was provided jointly by Kenyan experts with abundant experience in horticulture and by Japanese experts who could provide advice from an outsider's point of view. Even when introducing technologies quite new to the farmers, the project made sure that they would be applicable with the materials and techniques already existing locally. Such technologies

included road maintenance using sand bags (Do-no), fermented organic manure (Bokashi), and easy-to-handle weeding tools (154).

Aikawa (2013) further states that farmers' skills improved significantly because farmers' intrinsic motivation was significantly enhanced when they determined, on their own, the target crops to produce based on the result of a market survey they themselves had conducted. This, in turn, increased awareness and motivated the farmers to more thoroughly learn techniques through in-field training. When the farmers succeeded in marketing their products, this successful experience further promoted their sense of competence, leading to even greater motivation. Thus, the whole process can be described as an interaction between enhanced intrinsic motivation and increased skill levels complementing and reinforcing each other, leading to sustained growth (Aikawa 2013, 159).

Case 2: Learning for inclusive and innovative growth through capacity development in rural infrastructure development: Local Government Engineering Department (LGED) of Bangladesh[12]

The development and maintenance of rural infrastructure are a priority of the Bangladesh government, as stated in its National Rural Development Policy (NRDP), formulated in 2001, and in its first (2005) and second Poverty Reduction Strategy Papers (PRSPs) (2008). The semiautonomous Local Government Engineering Department evolved through a series of organizational changes from the Rural Works Cell (the "Cell"), which had inherited the infrastructure components of the famous "Comilla model" of the 1960s.[13] According to Fujita (2011), LGED has displayed remarkable progress in organizational development. During this period, a highly decentralized LGED, with over 10,000 staff, firmly established a reputation for professionalism and excellence in rural infrastructure provision and maintenance (World Bank 2009). LGED has worked closely with local stakeholders (governments and beneficiaries) to ensure broad participation at all stages of projects. It has also adopted labor-based technologies to create employment for the poor and has used local materials in construction and maintenance. As such, LGED has been playing a growing role in the capacity development of local government and local community groups in the context of decentralization of central government functions. Rural infrastructure projects have now been spread nationwide. Today, LGED is one of the largest public sector organizations in Bangladesh, with a budget accounting for 14 percent (FY 2009–10) of the total development budget of the government (Fujita 2011).

LGED's business model is conducive to organizational learning. Rural infrastructure, such as roads, village markets, and communal irrigation, is individually relatively small and can therefore be implemented quickly— in one to two years—and is of low risk to LGED even if some fail. These characteristics have enabled LGED to distinguish project successes and failures within a short time and to adopt new technologies. These elements have contributed to knowledge and experience accumulation. A 2008 report on LGED's assessment exercise pointed out that "The organization has quickly adapted itself to new experiments, technologies," reflecting a process of mutual learning among the agency's staff at various levels (Wilbur Smith Associates 2008). The mutual learning through interaction among stakeholders is vital for a clear understanding and identification of local needs. This enables local knowledge and resources to be identified and innovative solutions to be developed in partnership with local beneficiaries. This case shows that mutual learning and trust are vital to discovering locally appropriate innovative solutions to meet the needs of beneficiaries and stakeholders.

CASES OF LEARNING TO LEARN AND ENHANCING CORE CAPACITY

Case 3: Learning for inclusive and innovative growth through rural livelihood improvement (seikatsu kaizen) programs in Japan and developing countries[14]

Rural life improvement programs were implemented throughout Japan in the post-WW II period for about 20 years. Sato (2003, 34–35) emphasizes that the process of economic and social development in postwar Japan would have been impossible without a scheme for "social development," particularly in terms of the achievements obtained by various life improvements in rural areas. The key word for social development in rural areas of Japan at that time was seikatsu-kaizen (life improvement). Thus, Japan was able to quickly and broadly distribute the fruits of rapid growth because social development programs, referred to as the *rural life improvement movement*, had laid the groundwork over the 20 years prior to the period of rapid growth.

In the summer of 1945, Japan faced the same array of problems faced by many of the developing countries today, such as food shortages, malnutrition, health deterioration, and poor sanitary conditions (Sato 2003, 36). Amid these circumstances, livelihood improvement initiatives were implemented. This involved an approach by which women themselves were encouraged to actively take part in identifying problems in their own living conditions, setting issues, formulating living improvement plans, and applying and monitoring these policies (JICA 2003a, 1). Livelihood improvement extension workers in Japan were expected to play the role of facilitators who enabled rural women to become aware of the numerous problems that existed in their daily life and recognize them as problems.

In fact, many of the problems in rural Japan were rooted in everyday living, for instance, the cooking stove. Rural women used to bend down low to use a kitchen stove located on the floor. They had to stoop while cooking, a physically grueling posture, and because there was no ventilation in the houses, the smoke resulted in eye problems. Such improvements as waist-high stoves and chimneys were introduced countrywide as solutions to everyday problems. Other innovations such as improved work clothes and more nutritious food were also introduced. However, it was not until village women became aware of the problems of the cooking stoves they were using, the inconveniences of their work clothes, and the problems of their daily diet that they started exploring ways for improvement. In other words, the extension workers did not impose the improved cooking stoves from the outset (Sato 2003, 39).

One of the most important factors behind the success of the rural livelihood improvement movement was the dedication of the women who became livelihood extension workers (or "home advisers"). Female home advisers worked together with male farm advisers (agricultural extension workers) in extension programs. According to Mizuno (2003, 24), the purpose of rural life improvement for farm households was to "improve the lives of farm households and foster thinking farmers," through the improvement of livelihood skills of farm households. Behind this was the notion that improvements in both production and livelihood are on equal footing and that solutions to livelihood problems and uplifting of rural livelihood would lead to the advancement of production activities. This can be compared to the production-oriented approach, which argued that improving the existing production would automatically improve the quality of life.

Issue-specific specialists were posted in each prefecture to provide support to livelihood extension workers. This established a system in which specialists in food, clothing, and shelter offered advice to livelihood extension workers. Extension programs were designed by the Ministry of Agriculture, Forestry, and Fisheries, but part of the expense was borne by prefectural governments. For this reason, while unified instructions were issued from the central body, programs unique to each prefecture were also carried out to the extent that the local government budget permitted. Other ministries such as the Ministry of Health and Welfare (nutritional improvement, birth control, and maternal and child health care) and the Ministry of Education (social education, etc.) also supported the rural life improvement movement. While green bicycles were provided as a means of transportation for rural livelihood extension workers, public healthcare nurses rode on white bicycles.

To take a general view of the initial results of rural life improvement programs in postwar Japan, there were 5,461 home living improvement practice groups as of the end of March 1956. The most common target of improvement was cooking stoves, followed by the preparation of preserved foods and the making of improved work clothes. For example, according to the results of the 1956 national survey on cooking stove improvement, 2.2 million households (38 percent of all farm households) had already improved their cooking stoves, 1.58 million households (27 percent) had improved their cooking stoves after the introduction of the rural life improvement movement, and 1.47 million households (25 percent) were planning to improve their cooking stoves within one year (Mizuno 2003, 26).

This approach has been introduced in several developing countries in Latin America and Africa as well as Asia (APO 2003; Instituto de Desarrollo 2013; JICA 2013a). In particular, eight Central American and

Caribbean countries (Costa Rica, Dominican Republic, El Salvador, Guatemala, Honduras, Mexico, Nicaragua, and Panama) assimilated the approach to the extent that they have promoted networking in the region for better dissemination of knowledge. The Dominican Republic has gone so far as to establish a government bureau to promote coordinated efforts for better regional development (JICA 2013a and 2015).

Case 4: Learning for inclusive and innovative growth in incubating inclusive business: One Village One Product (OVOP) initiatives

The One Village One Product movement began in 1979 in the Japanese Prefecture of Oita (population 1.23 million). The area was going through difficult economic times that resulted in many young people leaving. In light of this, OVOP was actively used to promote economic progress.

The original concept was to encourage local areas to create and sell special products in their communities. OVOP was based on the idea of local initiatives, which depend on the energy, creativity, and desire of local citizens using local resources to restore their economies. To achieve global recognition, the quality of local products must meet internal and international market standards. Thanks to the constant efforts of local communities, many new products from Oita have been brought to market, revitalizing the economy there. Rather than award subsidies to local areas (something that had been found to reduce the spirit of independence in other parts of the country), the prefecture's government encourages each community by providing technical assistance (to improve production quality), market research, and advertising. To increase sales, the Oita One Village, One Product Corporation was set up to assist and identify new markets. This type of initiative could be considered as a potential model for incubating and promoting inclusive businesses[15] and clusters.

The three principles of the OVOP movement are (1) the creation of globally acceptable products and services based on local resources, (2) self-reliance and creativity, and (3) human resource development. Kurokawa, Tembo, and Willem te Velde (2010, 7) state that "The feature common to all three is an emphasis on local ownership." They further explain: "The first principle is best expressed through the motto 'think globally, act locally.' Local residents are expected to create globally marketable products and services that embody people's pride in the material and cultural richness of their home areas. The 'story' behind any product or its development helps to attract consumer attention. Such homegrown flavor adds value to local products while the use of local human and material resources helps to make economic activities sustainable." In the OVOP movement, self-reliance and creativity are considered crucial in the development of marketable products and services, since local knowledge and instinct can aid in the discovery of local "buried treasures." Everything local is potentially valuable, but whether that potential becomes a reality depends on the initiative and effort of local people.

As such, learning to learn could be considered one of core elements of OVOP. Haraguchi (2008, 12) emphasizes that the process of interactive learning in their activities makes OVOP an effective and sustainable rural development method. He states that "For OVOP farmers, delivering their products to markets is not the end process of their production activities. It goes beyond, to the extent that it involves having direct interaction with retailers and consumers, obtaining feedback on product quality, prices and production volumes for continuous improvement." This learning dimension appears to be similar to that of SHEP, discussed above.

Haraguchi further states that

> To enhance their learning capabilities, some OVOP farmers have strengthened their ties with consumers by having their own cooperative shops and restaurants, which serve dishes using their products. These venues allow producers to interact with consumers and also provide opportunities to directly receive comments on their products, which helps to increase added value and promote their products by introducing innovative dishes made with their products. The feedback from customers is pooled together and shared within a producer group for joint learning and continuous improvement of products and marketing.

Haraguchi (2008, 14–15) concludes that "In essence, taking part in the multiple stages along a value chain from production of raw materials, processing, selling and servicing, OVOP producers can maximize their learning opportunities . . . . Moreover, such comprehensive information together with their direct experience in different stages of a value chain helps them to generate new ideas. By enhancing learning opportunities in their activities and sharing ideas among members of an OVOP group, they constantly work toward the goal of reaching a better marketing mix."

The Thai government launched the official One Tambon One Product (OTOP) Development Policy in 2001 as a measure to revitalize and diversify the rural economy as a part of its national economic restructuring. OTOP, like OVOP, aims to encourage the development of rural economies through the use of local resources with community members' participation. Although OTOP was a top-down approach compared to OVOP's bottom-up approach, some important impacts have been acknowledged. For example, Wattanasiri (2005) stated that "The benefits of OTOP have not only been economic. Local community leadership and pride have also grown as a result." As knowledge of local conditions is only available at the local level, the role of OTOP subcommittees under the auspices of the Ministry of the Interior in facilitating the process of decentralization has been crucial (Kurokawa, Tembo, and Willem te Velde 2010, 13).

Malawi introduced the OVOP approach in 2003. It was the first country to do so in sub-Saharan Africa. It was expected to support the economic empowerment of rural communities and contribute to attaining the Millennium Development Goals (MDGs) through helping to add value to local raw materials and promote import substitution wherever it could be achieved efficiently (Kurokawa, Tembo, and Willem te Velde 2010, 20). In 10 years, the number of participants in OVOP in Malawi increased to 28,000 (more than 100 groups).[16]

Note that OVOP initiatives are inclusive not only because community members' participation in its activities is overwhelming but also for the significant participation of women. Nearly 90 percent of OTOP members in northeast Thailand were women, and in Malawi and Japan a large number of female members can be observed in many OVOP groups (Kurokawa, Tembo, and Willem te Velde 2010, 38). Based on the experiences of Japan and other countries, OVOP initiatives have been introduced in many Asian, African, and Latin American countries.

Case 5: Learning for inclusive and innovative growth through kaizen, Just in Time (JIT), total quality management (TQM), and beyond, in Japan, the United States, Singapore, and other countries

Experiences in Japan[17]

Most Japanese manufacturing companies implemented quality and productivity initiatives for the first time after Dr. William Edwards Deming, a U.S. statistician and consultant, gave a series of lectures on the statistical process control of production and quality for hundreds of Japanese engineers and managers in 1950. Only a few Japanese companies, such as Toyota, were aware of the importance of the U.S.-derived statistical control of quality before Dr. Deming came to Japan in 1947. He came at the request of the U.S. Armed Forces to assist in the planning of Japan's National Census, to be carried out in 1951. Accordingly, Japanese companies first introduced the statistical quality control (SQC) approach, which was developed from the U.S. practice of sampling and inspecting products in order to eliminate defective ones. Efforts were made to reduce the rate of defective products, or to improve yield rates (known in Japan as budomari). The quality control (QC) processes to attain these goals also improved productivity at the same time.[18]

Quality Control Circles with Kaizen: An Effective Approach to Learning to Learn at the Front Line

The Japanese way of QC was gradually consolidated when it was applied at the factory floor level. Instead of the top-down approach common in the United States and other countries, a bottom-up approach was adopted in Japan. A team commonly known as the *quality control circle* (QCC) is either organized spontaneously or follows the guidance of QC specialists in many Japanese companies. Several workers (normally more than three and up to ten) from the factory floor participate in each QCC. They identify the causes of defective products and possibilities for improving products or production methods. According to Ishikawa (1990),[19] The basic philosophy of QC circle activities carried out as part of companywide quality control activities is (1) to contribute to the improvement and development of the corporate culture, (2) to create cheerful workplaces that make life worthwhile and where humanity is respected, and (3) *to exercise people's capabilities and bring out their limitless potential*" (Ishikawa 1990, 78–79; italics added). Here we find exactly what Stiglitz and Greenwald (2014) emphasized regarding the real meaning of inclusive growth, which is intrinsically innovative growth in the sense that "*it is a waste of a country's most valuable resource, its human talent, to fail to ensure that every one lives up to his or her abilities*" (Stiglitz and Greenwald 2014, 468; italics added).

The number of QCCs registered at the Union of Japanese Scientists and Engineers (JUSE) increased from 50,000 in the mid-1970s to 420,000 in 2001. The number of participants of QCCs increased from 500,000 to 3,200,000 during the same period (DBJ and JERI 2003, 59). Together with QCCs, many Japanese methods of quality and productivity improvement have been developed and continuously improved. One of the most widely implemented in Japan is known as "5S," which consists of seiri, seiton, seiso, seiketsu, and shitsuke; these terms stand for, respectively, structure, systemize, sanitize, standardize, and self-discipline.[20] Today, 5S is considered to be an effective and smooth entry point to kaizen, a Japanese approach of continuous improvement for quality, productivity, and beyond. Kaizen is a Japanese concept that can be translated, literally, as "improvement" or "continuous improvement." It is not easy to define kaizen in a strict sense since it corresponds to evolving initiatives and activities in the quality and productivity areas and can be adapted very flexibly to the context of each factory floor. Several methods, including 5S, are commonly practiced by teams like QCCs.

Total Quality Management: An Effective Approach to Organizational Learning

The Japanese way of QC was gradually scaled up from the factory floor level to the whole company. QC was introduced to cover design, marketing, after-service, purchase of materials and machinery, and other company departments. At the same time, all company employees, including managers, engineers, supervisors, office-workers, and front-line factory workers, participated in QC. This bottom-up holistic approach developed in Japan is called the Japanese-type *companywide quality control* (CWQC) or *total quality control* (TQC).

Total quality management (TQM) is a kind of management system and strategy based on CWQC or TQC, and it was widely promoted in the 1980s. The *Handbook for TQM and QCC,* edited by the Development

Bank of Japan and the Japan Economic Research Institute (DBJ and JERI 2003, vii), explains that "Total Quality Management includes a number of management practices, philosophies and methods to improve the way an organization does business, makes its products, and interacts with its employees and customers. Kaizen (the Japanese word for continuous improvement) is one of those philosophies." According to this handbook, "The success of Japanese business in Canada, Latin America, and the United States as well as in Europe is attributable to TQM, a concept now widely practiced throughout Asia."

Impacts of TQC/TQM and Creation of a Learning Enterprise

One of the significant impacts of Japanese TQC/TQM is often explained through descriptions of the development of the car industry after the oil crises in the 1970s. During this period, TQC was extended to activities for energy conservation and measures for resource maintenance. It greatly impacted various industries and became more securely established as a valuable quality framework for Japanese industrial development.

The Toyota Production System (commonly called TPS) can be considered one of the most systematic and advanced Japanese TQC or TQM systems. As Liker (2004, 4), the author of *The Toyota Way*,[21] stated, "Toyota invented 'lean production'—also known as 'the Toyota Production System' or TPS—which has triggered a global transformation in virtually every industry to Toyota's manufacturing and supply chain philosophy and methods over the last decade." He further states: "TPS is often known as 'lean' or 'lean production,' since these were the terms made popular in two best-selling books: *The Machine That Changed the World: The Story of Lean Production* (Womack, Jones, and Roos 1990) and *Lean Thinking* (Womack and Jones 1996). These authors make it clear that the foundation of their research on lean production is TPS and its development by Toyota" (Womack, Jones, and Roos 1990, 3t4; Liker 2004, 15).

In the 1990s, through the work of the Massachusetts Institute of Technology's (MIT's) International Motor Vehicle Program (IMVP) and the above-mentioned best sellers based on its research, "the world manufacturing community discovered 'lean production'—the authors' term for what Toyota had learned a decade earlier through focusing on speed within its supply chain: *shortening lead time by eliminating waste in each step of a process leads to best quality and lower cost, while improving safety and morale*" (Liker 2004, 25; italics in original). The idea of shortening the lead time by eliminating waste in each step is related to the concept of Just-in-Time (JIT). "Simply put, JIT delivers the right items at the right time in the right amounts. The power of JIT is that it allows you to be responsive to the day-by-day shifts in customer demand, which was exactly what Toyota needed all along" (Liker 2004, 23).

Liker (2004) highlighted the importance of learning in TPS: "I believe Toyota has raised continuous improvement and employee involvement to a unique level, creating one of the few examples of *a genuine learning enterprise in human history*—not a small accomplishment" (Liker 2004, xv; italics added). He further states: "The highest level of the Toyota Way is organizational learning. Identifying root causes of problems and preventing them from occurring is the focus of Toyota's continuous learning system" (Liker 2004, xvi). This concept of learning enterprise is similar to the exploration by Stiglitz and Greenwald (2014, 88) of the learning firm, which together with a learning macro-environment constitutes critical aspects of learning architecture. The importance of the learning firm is emphasized by them "because so much learning occurs within organizations and because so much knowledge resides within firms." Related to this view is that of Nonaka, Toyama, and Hirata (2008, 3), who stated, "We need a theory of the knowledge-based firm that can explain how firms perceive and interpret realities, interact with various players both inside and outside the organization, and synthesize various subjective interpretations into a collective knowledge that becomes objectified and validated as a universal knowledge asset of the firm."

Experiences in the United States

DBJ and JERI (2003, 46–47) summarized the TQM dissemination process in the United States as follows.[22] During World War II, the U.S. Army and Navy actively introduced quality control to maximize their military hardware production. The American National Standards Institute (ANSI) established military standards and conducted seminars to disseminate those ideas. Yet in the 1970s, U.S. industry was losing its competitiveness in the world market.

In 1980, an NBC broadcast coined a famous saying: "If Japan can, why can't we?" The program concluded that Japanese success was attributed to the teachings of Deming and Japanese adherence to his principles (Anschutz 1995, 17). Prior to this broadcast, Deming had not been widely recognized, yet the broadcast provided the springboard to a wider and far more receptive U.S. audience for Deming's ideas. Soon after the broadcast, the U.S. government started its catch-up movement under the Reagan presidency. TQM was introduced by the Ford Motor Company, and many others followed. Later President Reagan established the Malcolm Baldrige National Quality Award in 1987, aiming to expedite quick recovery actions to go beyond the quality level that Japan had achieved by the year 2000.

Late in 1986, MIT convened its first commission on a major national issue since World War II, the Commission on Industrial Productivity. The goals of the study were to address the decline in U.S. industrial performance, then perceived to be so serious as to threaten the nation's economic future (Dertouzos, Lester, and Solow 1989, xiii). The sixteen commissioners were all members of the MIT faculty. The ultimate aim was to formulate a set of recommendations that would help the nation to sustain strong growth in productivity (Dertouzos, Lester, and Solow 1989, 3). The Commission's report, *Made in America: Regaining the Productive Edge*, found that an area in which U.S. firms often lagged behind their overseas competitors was in exploiting the potential for continuous improvement in the quality and reliability of their products and processes (Dertouzos, Lester, and Solow 1989, 74). The report noted that "The cumulative effect of successive incremental improvements and modifications to established products and processes can be very large and may outpace efforts to achieve technological breakthroughs." It further states: "In the long run, technological progress rests on a foundation of both incremental improvements and radical breakthroughs, and finding the right balance between them is a constant challenge. Lewis Branscomb (1987, 74) has suggested that Japanese firms have been more effective in combining the two approaches."[23]

On the other hand, Womack, Jones, and Roos (1990, 3–4) discussed the motivation for engaging in the above-mentioned research of MIT's International Motor Vehicle Program (IMVP):

We concluded that the auto industries of North America and Europe were relying on techniques little changed from Henry Ford's mass production system and that these techniques were simply not competitive with a new set of ideas pioneered by the Japanese companies, methods for which we did not even have a name . . . . [T]he Western companies didn't seem to be able to learn from their Japanese competitors. Instead, they were focusing their energies on erecting trade barriers and other competitive impediments, which we thought simply delayed dealing with the real issue . . . . [W]e feared that North America and Europe would seal themselves off from the Japanese threat and, in the process, reject the opportunity for the prosperity and more rewarding work that these new techniques offer. We felt that the most constructive step we could take to prevent this development from occurring would be to undertake a detailed study of the new Japanese techniques, which we subsequently named "lean production," compared to the older Western mass-production techniques.

However, TQM was not well organized when it first was disseminated in the United States, according to DBJ and JERI (2003, 47):

Dr. J. M. Juran mentioned that only gradually did it become clear to upper-tier managers that the quality leadership could not be achieved by a pecking away—by merely bringing in this or that tool or technique. They learned that, instead, it was necessary to apply the entire array of quality knowhow (the quality disciplines) throughout the entire company, to all functions and at all levels of all departments in a coordinated way. At the outset there was no agreed standardized definition for TQM. As a result, the concept of TQM became a blur among companies and even in the general literature. This confusion has since been reduced by the publication of the criteria used by the National Institute of Standards and Technology, which was used to evaluate the applications for the United States Malcolm Baldrige National Quality Award (Baldrige Award). By the early 1990s, this wide exposure had made the Baldrige Award criteria the most widely accepted definition of what is to be included in TQM.

In this regard, Stiglitz and Greenwald (2014, 38) made an important observation. They discussed what is suggested by the performance of the U.S. manufacturing sector between the 1970s and early 1980s, on one hand, and the late 1980s and 1990s, on the other hand.

Between these two periods, the annual rate of growth of U.S. manufacturing productivity rose by 2.0 percent from 0.9 percent to 2.9 percent. The improvement coincided with a marked rise in the U.S.

real interest rate (normally associated with *less* investment in technology) and government deficits, a decline in U.S. research and development spending, and no detectable improvement in the performance of U.S. education (as measured by standardized tests). At the same time, it cannot be attributed to the availability of new technology. Such technology would have been equally available to other G7 economies. Over the period in question, the U.S. improvement in annual manufacturing productivity growth was 1.9 percent higher than that of the other G7 countries. The improvement was thus a U.S., not a global, phenomenon. What seems to have changed in U.S. manufacturing was an intensified focus on improved operations management through the rigorous implementation of procedures such as benchmarking, total quality management, and reengineering—in our language, an intensified focus on learning. America seemed to have learned how to learn.[24]

These experiences confirm that the learning process has been closely related to approaches such as TQM also in the United States. Together with experiences in Japan, this provides insights into effective approaches to create a learning firms and learning societies, which are the drivers for good growth in quality.[25]

Experiences in Singapore[26]

Singapore was the first country in Southeast Asia to systematically introduce quality and productivity initiatives. According to former Prime Minister Lee Kuan Yew, "The shift to a knowledge-intensive industrial structure with strong international competitiveness is only possible through the human-resource development of 2.6 million people, the only resource Singapore has" (JPC 1990, 1).[27] Lee's concern was how to organize and motivate Singapore's workforce to make best use of the modernization of plants and capacity building. In April 1981, the Committee on Productivity was set up by representatives of enterprises, worker organizations, government officials, and academics.

The committee reviewed the experiences of productivity movements in Japan, another country without natural resources. It then presented a report to the president of the National Productivity Board (NPB) of Singapore, which had been designated as the main body for promoting productivity development in Singapore. In June 1983, the Singapore

Productivity Development Project (SPDP) was launched with the support of the Japanese government.

Some 15,000 Singaporean engineers, managers, and other professionals participated in the project. Two hundred engineers, managers, and other professionals from Singapore took part in training courses in Japan, and more than 200 Japanese experts were dispatched to Singapore. In addition, more than 100 textbooks and other training materials were prepared specifically for the project. During the period of SPDP and beyond, labor productivity in manufacturing industries improved by an annual average rate of 5.7 percent (1981–1986), 3.0 percent (1986–1991), and 4.8 percent (1991-1996). In 1990, when SPDP ended, 90 percent of workers in the country were involved in productivity development activities, compared with 54 percent in 1986. In 2001, 13 percent of the total labor force was participating in quality-control circles (QCCs), in comparison with 0.4 percent in 1983, when SPDP started.

The NPB's activities gathered considerable momentum, progressing from the awareness stage (1982–1985), during which it created widespread awareness of the importance of productivity among companies and workforce, to the action stage (1986–1988), when it translated awareness into specific programs to improve productivity in the workplace, and finally the follow-up stage (1988 to the present), in which it encouraged ownership of the productivity movement (see Ohno and Kitaw 2011; Ohno 2013). The NPB merged with the Singapore Institute of Standards and Industrial Research in 1966 to create the Productivity and Standards Board (PSB), bringing together the soft skills and the technical aspects of productivity. The PSB was later strengthened and reorganized into the Standards, Productivity, and Innovation Board (SPRING) in 2002. NPB, PSB, and now SPRING have played a crucial role in mainstreaming cross-cutting general-purpose technologies (GPTs) in Singapore's industrial development and economic transformation. As such, they catalyzed the process of learning to learn among the country's workers and companies. Thus, the Kaizen Project laid the groundwork for Singapore's growth, contributing to upgrading the country's industrial structure (JICA 2014, 4).

Experiences in Other Developing Countries

JICA's full-fledged assistance in kaizen, quality, and productivity dates back to 1983 when it started the above-mentioned project in Singapore. Over about three decades, different kinds of cooperation activities to introduce kaizen were carried out by JICA in around fifty countries. Activities related to kaizen have been widely developed in Asia through the efforts of the Asian Productivity Organization (APO), Japan Productivity Center (JPC), the Overseas Human Resources and Industry Development Association (HIDA; formerly Association of Overseas Technical Scholarship, AOTS) as well as JICA. In Africa, several kaizen and related initiatives have been implemented (Shimada. 2015). In Latin America, according to Garcia-Alcaraz, Maldonado-Marcias, and Cortes-Robles (2014), nowadays it is very common to see senior management making daily rounds in the production areas, identifying opportunities for improvement, following up, and supporting the implementation of continuous improvement. In particular, lean tools are frequently used in many Mexican companies that manufacture products to be exported mainly to the United States (Garcia-Alcaras, Maldonado-Marcias, and Cortes-Robles, 2014, 3–4).

Through these experiences, it has been demonstrated that kaizen and related initiatives can be put into practice in a variety of cultural and socioeconomic settings, not just some peculiarly Japanese characteristics (Ueda 2009, 63; Hosono 2009b, 29–36; Shimada 2015, 111–13).

LESSONS FROM CASE STUDIES

We can identify several common features from the "learning to learn" perspective in the five cases discussed above, despite their diversity. The common features are, among others: (1) there are easy entry points to commence the learning process; (2) the costs and risks are low; (3) the focus is on learning by doing and mutual learning to cocreate innovative solutions; (4) learning makes an intrinsic contribution to the objective, be it livelihood improvement, inclusive business, quality and productivity improvement, incremental innovation, and so on. Each of these is examined in greater detail below.

EASY ENTRY POINTS COMMENCING THE LEARNING PROCESS

In the case of SHEP, at the research station, a certain level of technological know-how had been already achieved. A preexisting knowledge base was already there—the issue was how to validate existing technologies from the farmers' perspective and put them to practical use. Based on this understanding, SHEP focused on the introduction of techniques that were immediately usable the moment they were learned. The project made sure that the techniques would be applicable and compatible with the materials and techniques already existing locally. In the case of LGED, the characteristics of rural infrastructure, such as its relatively small scale and comparatively low risk, enabled LGED to distinguish project success and failures within a short time and to adopt new technologies, contributing to learning and the further development of the knowledge base. In the case of the livelihood improvement approach, the most typical targets of improvement in Japan and other Asian countries were the construction of simple water supply systems, communal cooking and child care during the peak agricultural season, improvement of cooking stoves and toilets, preparation of preserved foods, and the making of improved work clothes. In OVOP initiatives, local people and their groups have been encouraged to "self-discover" promising local products and to start selling in local markets. In kaizen initiatives, the first activities are normally 5S strategies, which could be performed by any worker.

LOW COST AND LOW RISK

We need to take into account two types of costs. The first aspect is the cost of acquiring knowledge and technology. The second aspect is the cost of implementing activities (running costs) and other costs such as a new investment (start-up costs). In all five cases, knowledge and technology were free public goods. The cost of implementing activities in all five cases was almost nil or very low. The lowest-cost activities among the five cases were those of livelihood improvement, and at the same time almost no risk was implied. In SHEP, the risk was lowered by market research by the farmers themselves. Farmers were able to apply techniques provided for free. OVOP activities were able to be initiated with few substantial investments, and costs were low because only the reasonable costs of production of local goods and services were needed. Kaizen and related initiatives normally do not imply significant investment, because 5S and other activities only require modifications to the organization, work flow, and so on, in spite of significant effects on quality, delivery, and productivity.

LEARNING BY DOING, MUTUAL LEARNING, AND COCREATION OF INNOVATIVE SOLUTIONS, STRENGTHENING COGNITIVE SKILLS AND CAPACITY OF LEARNING TO LEARN

As Stiglitz and Greenwald (2014, 52) state, "we learn by doing." In all five cases, individuals and organizations learned to learn through learning from others, or mutual learning, and they cocreated innovative solutions to issues they needed to address. In the case of SHEP, farmers based their decisions on their own marketing survey, and this may have strengthened farmers' cognitive capacity as well as their motivation. Farmers have been able to learn to learn. In the case of LGED, the mutual learning through interaction among stakeholders was vital for a clear understanding and identification of local needs. At the same time, this enables local knowledge and resources to be identified and innovative solutions to be developed in partnership with local beneficiaries. This case illustrates the importance of mutual learning and trust for discovering locally appropriate innovative solutions to meet the needs of beneficiaries and stakeholders.

In the case of livelihood improvement, rural women themselves were encouraged to actively take part in identifying problems in their own living conditions, setting issues, formulating living improvement plans, and so on. As such this initiative was not just about the improvement of livelihood, but a learning process, particularly to enhance the capacity of learning to learn. In the case of OVOP, participants and their groups, taking part in multiple stages along a value chain, including production of raw materials, processing, marketing, and servicing, can maximize their learning opportunities. Such comprehensive knowledge based on experiences of learning by doing and mutual learning has helped them to generate new ideas and innovative products. By enhancing learning opportunities in their activities and sharing ideas among members of an OVOP group, they work constantly toward reaching a better marketing mix.

In the case of kaizen and related initiatives, quality control circles could be considered an effective approach for front-line workers to contribute to and receive the benefit of mutual learning through kaizen activities and to enhance the learning capacity to learn. Total quality management could be considered an effective approach to organizational learning. These approaches ensure that every one lives up to her or his abilities and enables genuine inclusive and innovative growth.

THE IMPACT OF LEARNING ON INNOVATIVE SOLUTIONS, INCLUSIVE BUSINESS, QUALITY, PRODUCTIVITY, AND BEYOND

In the five cases studied, learning contributed, in diverse ways, to cocreating innovative solutions, starting up new industries through inclusive business, and industrial development through the continuous improvement of quality and productivity as well as incremental innovation. The livelihood improvement initiatives and LGED are cases where mutual learning facilitated creation of innovative solutions to challenges that rural farmers faced. Learning is essential in incubating inclusive business, and enabling innovative and inclusive growth, as we observed in the cases of SHEP and OVOP initiatives.

Learning also contributes to productivity as well as quality and innovation. As the World Bank (2015, 128) states, increasing productivity is central to raising living standards, and productivity growth can arise either from augmenting the factors of production—human capital, physical capital, and technology—or from making better use of existing factors. "Learning" contributes to productivity growth in both ways. First, learning enables new and innovative ways to make more efficient use of existing endowments. Second, learning—especially learning to learn—through enhancement of learning capacity as the most important endowment contributes to changing comparative advantage, thereby enabling industrial transformation. Table 10.2 compares the different approaches mentioned above with the conventional technological transfer approach through the lens of learning.

LEARNING FOR INNOVATIVE, INCLUSIVE, AND SUSTAINABLE GROWTH

A "green economy" could be a pathway to sustainable development and poverty reduction, as highlighted in the report on the green economy prepared for the Rio+20 Conference by the United Nations Environment Program (UNEP 2011) in 2011. UNEP (2010) defined a green economy as one that results in improved human well-being and social equity, while significantly reducing environmental risks and ecological scarcities. As such, the realization of an inclusive green economy requires innovative solutions.

Although sustainability and environmental aspects should be fully taken into account in any process of development, special attention to these aspects is needed in cases of transformation in which *natural capital*

Table 10.2 Comparison of Different Approaches to Enhance Learning Capacity

	Conventional Technology Transfer	Capacity Development (CD) Approach	Livelihood Improvement Initiatives (Individuals)	One Village One Product Initiatives (Groups and Individuals)	Kaizen, QCCs, JIT, TQM, and Related Approaches (Organizations)
Learning	Filling technological gap, without learning	Mutual learning and cocreation of innovative solutions, addressing specific challenges	Mutual learning and cocreation of innovative solutions, achieving livelihood improvement	Mutual learning and cocreation of innovative solutions, incubating and promoting inclusive business	Mutual learning and co-creation of innovative solutions improving quality, productivity, and attaining incremental innovation
Learning to learn	No learning to learn is expected	Not always focusing on learning to learn	Focusing on learning to learn	Focusing on learning to learn	Focusing on learning to learn
Local conditions	Not considered	Fully considered	Fully considered	Fully considered	Fully considered
Inclusiveness and easy application	Not considered	Fully considered	Fully considered	Fully considered	Fully considered
Cost and risk	Relatively high	Relatively low	Very low	Low	Low
Implementing organizations		Donors including JICA	Asia and Latin America by JICA	Asia, Africa, and Latin America by JICA and JETRO	Asia, Africa and Latin America mainly by JICA, APO, JPC, and HIDA

Note: JETRO: Japan External Trade Organization; APO: Asian Productivity Organization; JPC: Japan Productivity Center; HIDA: Overseas Human Resources and Industry Development Association.

Case 6: Toward an Inclusive Green Economy: Agroforestry in Kenya

About 83 percent of the total land surface of Kenya is covered by arid and semiarid lands (ASALs) that are vulnerable to global warming and climate change, and these areas are consequently characterized by a very high incidence of poverty. Therefore, one of the most serious challenges faced by the country is the need to cope with desertification of ASALs, preserving their ecology and environment, while at the same time reducing poverty in these regions. This means that the introduction and consolidation of an "inclusive green economy" will be necessary to sustain these vast areas.

Kenya relies on firewood and charcoal for more than 70 percent of its total energy consumption and around 90 percent of the energy consumption in homes. The increasing demand for firewood and charcoal, caused by a combination of a growing population, overgrazing, and disordered cultivation, has devastated forest areas. This not only has created great difficulty in supplying firewood and charcoal but also has resulted in a decline in the productive capacity of the land and the destruction of the natural environment (JICA 2003b). Moreover, the effects of climate change could aggravate the environment in many ASALs.

Several innovative solutions to address the issues have been developed and brought into the mainstream. One of the most important is *social forestry*, defined as a "form of forestry that aims at both the improvement of the economy and the preservation of forest resources, by entrusting local people with the management and ownership of the forest resources" (JICA 2003b). It is a very similar concept to the inclusive green economy as a pathway to sustainable development and poverty reduction, as discussed above. An effective instrument developed and disseminated to promote social forestry has been the *farm forest*.

A period of more than 20 years has seen the introduction of three consecutive Kenya–Japan projects to strengthen social forestry in semiarid areas of Kenya—with remarkable results. Through these projects, with the Kenya Forestry Research Institute (KEFRI) as an implementing agency, basic tree nurseries and tree-planting technology in arid and semiarid regions have been developed. In conjunction with this, the capacity of core farmers was strengthened as the basis for the extension of the model developed under the Kenya–Japan technical cooperation projects. For the extension of this model, the Farmers

CASE 6, CONTINUED

Field School (FFS) approach, an existing proven extension approach in the agricultural sector, was applied to the forestry sector through innovative adjustments to the methodology. Through the FFS, a range of techniques were disseminated, such as seedling production, fruit tree planting (mango, grevillea, and others), poultry raising, vegetable cultivation, utilization of compost, and the creation of woodlots (JICA 2013c). As a result of all these measures, Kenya Forestry Service (KFS), Kenya Forestry Research Institute, farmer facilitators and farmers, as well as JICA, have developed incrementally appropriate solutions to address the challenges mentioned above. They are based on a series of technological and institutional innovations, and they have produced synergies to take full advantage of social forestry.

The FFS has developed ownership and strengthened communities and farmers' capacity with knowledge about forestry (JICA 2009, 15). Through FFS, individual farmers, farmers' groups, and the surrounding farmers are continuing to raise and produce seedlings and plant trees. They have started to sell social forestry products such as mangoes, seedlings, lumber, and firewood. Through these activities, farmers are increasing their awareness of methods to improve their livelihood. Wider extension activities related to social forestry are expected, as graduate farmers from FFS give advice about agriculture and social forestry to neighboring and surrounding area farmers (JICA 2009, 15–16). The most important achievement is that the growth of trees contributes to the improvement of the livelihood of farmers, attaining the overall goal of social forestry projects toward a green economy.

is the essential endowment that enables the transformation (OECD 2008, 30). Understanding the synergies and trade-offs among critical dimensions of the growth quality, such as inclusive, sustainable, resilient, and innovative aspects, is normally most difficult in the cases where natural capital plays the crucial part of transformation. Analysis of these cases could point the way toward more effective approaches to quality growth in conjunction with sustainability and inclusiveness. Previously I discussed this perspective in relation to the cases of Chile's salmon and Brazil's Cerrado agriculture (Hosono 2015a).

LESSONS FROM THE CASE STUDY

Several aspects of learning discussed in the previous section can be observed in the above case. The easy entry points can also be identified in the Farmers Field School approach, and farmers had access to knowledge on agroforestry as a public good for free. Mutual learning and cocreation of innovative solutions were also relevant. As explained, Kenya Forestry Service, Kenya Forestry Research Institute, farmer facilitators, farmers, and JICA have incrementally developed appropriate solutions to address local challenges. Costs and risks were low, because production activities were introduced incrementally. In the whole process, learning was the key in starting up and consolidating "green growth"—the inclusive and sustainable growth defined by UNEP—through innovative and inclusive business development.

LEARNING FOR INCLUSIVE AND INNOVATIVE GROWTH WITH ENHANCED RESILIENCE

To formulate a comprehensive approach to disaster risk management and enhance resilience in developing countries, the following three aspects appear to be crucial. First is the importance of both risk prevention and risk reduction, as discussed in *Towards Reconstruction: Hope Beyond the Disaster* (Reconstruction Design Council in Response to the Great East Japan Earthquake 2011). Second, it is necessary to take into account changes in risk over time, such as the effects of climate change, urbanization, and so on. Third, especially in the case of developing countries, affordability for governments, communities, and inhabitants should be fully taken into account.

Generally speaking, the main aspects of the standard framework of risk management are risk avoidance or prevention, risk reduction, and risk transfer (insurance). In terms of risk avoidance, in addition to strengthening the capacity of disaster risk management, ensuring quality standards for public works, seismic building codes, and land use regulations is also important. For risk reduction, predisaster investment and seismic reinforcement construction are essential. To enhance resilience in these aspects of disaster risk management, inclusive and innovative approaches are critical, as case 7 confirms.

LESSONS FROM THE CASE STUDY

Determinants of learning discussed in the previous sections can also be observed in the case of integrated disaster risk management. Easy

Case 7: Toward an integrated approach for disaster risk management to enhance resilience: *Bosai, Taishin, Gensai,* and beyond in Central America[28]

Central American countries are known to be among the world's most vulnerable countries to natural disasters. The presidents of member countries of the Central America Integration System (Sistema de la Integración Centroamericana, SICA) adopted, on October 30, 2010, the Central America Policy of Integrated Disaster Risk Management (PCGIR). This was done to respond to the need to update regional commitments designed to reduce and prevent disaster risks and thereby to contribute to an integrated vision of development and security in Central America. PCGIR highlights the importance of developing local capacity to reduce risk and to respond to disasters by strengthening the autonomy and resilience of communities. *Bosai* (disaster prevention) projects in the region, assisted by Japanese cooperation, have constituted an important pillar in the implementation of the PCGIR.

The regional progress report of Hyogo Framework of Action (HFA) on Central America, updated April 2011, established two indicators for HFA priorities in relation to the local disaster risk management: "Sub/regional early warning systems exist" and "Sub/regional information and knowledge sharing mechanism available." Among the most significant achievements of *Bosai* is its contribution to the progress toward achieving these regional indicators. In terms of "risk literacy," *Bosai* focuses on making the residents fully understand the risks of their own community and taking actions on their own by maintaining smooth communication among the community, municipality, and national agencies, while at the same time letting the community implement risk mapping through repeated discussions and site inspections.

Capacity development in the context of *Bosai* aims to let the community prepare risk maps and disaster management plans and improve them on its own. From the perspective of continuous improvement, or kaizen, this helps communities to develop the capacity to cope with ever-changing risks. CD processes both at community and local government levels strengthened their capacity to effectively respond to various disasters including earthquakes, flooding, and landslides and to take various concrete actions such as hazard maps, early warning systems, disaster prevention plans, evacuation routes, and emergency response plans.

In the *Bosai* Project, there have been several cases of cocreation of innovative low-cost solutions to reduce vulnerability to disasters in the target communities and to strengthen the capacity of disaster risk management. Some communities in Panama, Costa Rica, Honduras, and El Salvador have constructed small mitigation works such as used-tire dikes and retaining walls as well as promoting some remarkable involvement and commitment in voluntary labor. Some other outstanding examples include the installation of rainfall equipment or rain gauges (known as *fluviometro*), which include an alarm unit for community-operated flood warnings and a water glass (water level monitor) with automatic warning systems. Through this process of capacity development, effective mutual learning among stakeholders and cocreation of innovative solutions can clearly be recognized.

Based on the experiences of the targeted communities, national scale-up processes have taken place in each country. The installation of rain gauges for early warnings of flood was extended beyond the targeted communities in El Salvador. A plan to set up warning sirens in more than 150 communities is being implemented in Tegucigalpa, Honduras. The Frog Caravan is one such successful activity of the *Bosai* Project in that the practice has been widely extended beyond the target communities.[29] The Frog Caravan has also been conducted by other donors, and in Guatemala there are now plans to incorporate it into the school curriculum. A plan to extend the Frog Caravan nationwide has been implemented in Guatemala and Panama.

The impact of the *Bosai* Project has been recognized following some natural disaster events. When Hurricane Ida slammed into El Salvador in November 2009, it triggered massive flooding and landslides and more than 300 persons were killed or went missing. However, in the coastal village of Las Hojas there were no deaths, and a later investigation attributed this at least partly to the fact that a disaster early warning system had been installed there by JICA. A more comprehensive approach to disaster risk management has now been adopted in El Salvador. The *Gensai* Project was initiated to strengthen the resilience of infrastructure to protect the lifelines of inhabitants, in addition to *Bosai* and *Taishin* (discussed below). These projects are expected to produce synergistic effects with *Gensai*, thereby making a much more integrated and effective capacity to address the risk of natural disasters.

According to a study of the two large earthquakes that hit El Salvador in 2001, of the destroyed houses 60 percent were those of poor people whose income was less than twice the country's minimum wage. It should be emphasized that specific technologically and financially feasible options are essential for developing countries. Fiscal and other constraints of government along with the low incomes of the most vulnerable inhabitants of the country should be fully taken into account.

The low-cost earthquake-resistant housing (*Taishin*) project in El Salvador is a way to address this issue. JICA started a cooperation project with the National Center for Disaster Prevention (CENAPRED), Mexico, after the big earthquake in the central part of Mexico in 1985. The technology and innovative methods developed by CENAPRED have since been used in the *Taishin* Project, with cooperation from Japan from 2003 through 2012, which aimed at furthering earthquake-resistant housing in El Salvador.

Houses made of improved adobe, soil cement, block panels, and concrete blocks were tested with their respective appropriate structures in large structure laboratories at the University of El Salvador and the Jose Simeon Cañas University of Central America. The *Taishin* Project included the establishment of official technological standards for earthquake-resistant houses and institution building for the governmental urban and housing development agency in charge of housing policies and construction permits. Subsequently, the experiences and innovation from the joint *Taishin* Project CENAPRED/JICA/Japan Institute of Construction/El Salvador were shared throughout Central America.

Finally, note that further efforts are necessary to address disaster risks, especially in poor urban districts. One-half of the world's population now lives in urban areas, and urbanization is accelerating in developing countries where urban sprawl, slums, and inadequate infrastructure provision are common outcomes of the process of urbanization. Furthermore, urban slums have been expanding in high-risk areas in the case of many developing countries. Therefore, the international community and donors need to focus on disaster prevention for the urban poor.

Programs of "urban redevelopment" that include land readjustments could provide an effective approach to addressing the problems of urban poverty and slums while at the same time promoting disaster prevention.

After urban areas are subdivided and settled, whether legally or illegally, it is extremely difficult to rearrange property patterns, and it is both difficult and expensive to ensure land for proper public purposes and facilities. Land readjustment is based on a public-private partnership model, in which local governments, residents, and landowners bear the urban development costs and share benefits in places where land use patterns are inadequate and/or risky. Normally every transformed lot will be smaller than the original one because of the need to significantly increase public space, but the lot's value will be higher as a result of better access to additional facilities as well as improved safety and disaster prevention.[30] JICA has been supporting land readjustment initiatives in Brazil, Thailand, and dozens of other developing countries. For better urban land use, taking into account high-risk areas should be one of the most important measures to enhance resilience and reduce disaster risks.

entry points were identified in the *Bosai* Projects. First, *risk literacy* was enhanced, with the focus on making the residents fully understand the risks of their own community and take actions on their own. From the perspective of continuous improvement or kaizen in the context of *Bosai* to cope with ever-changing risks, CD aims to let the community prepare risk maps and disaster management plans, and improve them, on its own. CD processes by both the community and local government levels strengthened their capacity to effectively respond to various disasters and to take various concrete actions. Learning by communities and their members effectively takes place in the *Bosai* Projects. *Bosai* at the community level is effective only when the process is inclusive, in which all members contribute to and get benefits from the *Bosai* activities.

Learning by doing, mutual learning, and cocreation of innovative solutions were also a feature of *Bosai* and related activities. As discussed, major achievements at the community level include the development of organizations, risk maps, evacuation routes, early warning systems, and emergency response plans. Greater levels of involvement and commitment in voluntary labor were also observed. We can recognize clearly that through this process, mutual learning among stakeholders and cocreation of innovative solutions were attained.

In *Taishin* Projects, low-cost earthquake-resistant housing technology established through cutting-edge laboratory experiments was provided for free as a public good. This technology opened up the possibility of a new type of inclusive business for low-income people with the participation of other stakeholders, such as NGOs in El Salvador. The technology has now been shared with some other Central American countries. In both *Taishin* and *Gensai* Projects, organizational learning and institution building took place. As such, learning, including learning to learn, effectively contributed to innovative and inclusive development, enhancing resilience in El Salvador and other Central American countries that belong to the Center of Coordination for the Prevention of Natural Disasters in Central America (CEPREDENAC).

CONCLUSION

The case studies presented here illustrate how learning and the accumulation of knowledge and capabilities play a vital role in attaining inclusive and innovative growth. Several approaches for learning to attain desired attributes of growth were identified above, including those related to specific capacity and those related to core capacity (or specific and general learning abilities). These approaches promote activities that not only promote learning but also facilitate learning to learn.

In these approaches, several common features can be observed: (1) easy entry points are available to initiate the learning process; (2) the costs and risks are low; (3) the focus is on learning by doing and mutual learning to cocreate innovative solutions; and (4) learning makes an intrinsic contribution to the particular objective being pursued: livelihood improvement, inclusive business, quality and productivity improvement, incremental innovation and beyond. Learning and learning to learn are also essential for the green economy, which results in improved human well-being and social equity, while significantly reducing environmental risks and ecological scarcity. To enhance resilience to cope with disaster risks, innovative and inclusive approaches are indispensable, because disaster risk management is possible only with the participation of all residents and other stakeholders who through mutual learning have to find locally specific innovative solutions.

The case studies also show that to catalyze and facilitate the learning process, public policies based on a strategy that addresses learning capacity, endowments, and transformation appear to be essential. The strategy needs to be formulated while keeping in mind changing endowments and continuous transformation, which enable achievement of high growth of quality.

NOTES

1. For a literature review and discussion of the quality of growth, see Haddad, Kato, and Meisel (2015) and Hosono (2015a).

2. The APEC (Asia Pacific Economic Cooperation) Leaders' Growth Strategy was agreed on November 14, 2010. It is referred to as the *APEC Growth Strategy*. APEC comprises 55 percent of real global GDP, 44 percent of global trade, and 40 percent of the global population. The APEC Growth Strategy mentions that APEC senior officials should report to leaders in 2015 for their review on APEC's progress in promoting the APEC Growth Strategy (APEC 2010, 12).

3. The five components are a reallocation of factors of production; diversification, upgrading, and deepening of the production and export baskets; use of new production methods and processes and different inputs; urbanization; and social changes (ADB 2013, 3–5).

4. An endowment is what determines the comparative advantage of a country. For an in-depth discussion of the relationship between endowments and static and dynamic comparative advantage, see, e.g., Stiglitz and Greenwald (2014, 24–25).

5. The author uses the term *industry* very broadly to refer to not only the manufacturing sector but also agro-business, modern agriculture, aquaculture, transport, logistics, tourism, and any other activities that produce goods and services that are new in the country and that require significant human (and social), financial, and natural (and environmental) capital and infrastructure, as well as accumulation of learning (knowledge and capabilities).

6. For a literature review on CD, see Hosono et al. 2011.

7. This perspective is reflected in Japan's development cooperation approach. The *New Charter of Development Cooperation of Japan* states: "In its development cooperation, Japan has maintained the spirit of jointly creating things that suit partner countries while respecting ownership, intentions and intrinsic characteristics of the country concerned based on a field-oriented approach through dialogue and collaboration. It has also maintained the approach of building reciprocal relationships with developing countries in which both sides learn from each other and grow and develop together. These are some of the good traditions of Japan's cooperation which have supported self-help efforts of developing countries and aimed at future self-reliant development" (Government of Japan, Cabinet Office 2015, 4–5)

8. For a definition and recent discussion of inclusive growth, see Kozuka (2014).

9. For a more extensive discussion on transformation and inclusive growth, see Hosono (2015b).

10. This case draws heavily on Aikawa (2013).

11. According to the final monitoring survey carried out in October 2009 just before the termination of SHEP, the average per-group horticulture-related net income among the 114 organizations increased by 67 percent over the baseline survey; while the average per-farmer net income increased by 106 percent over the baseline survey. While incomes increased for both men and women, the gap between them fell from 31 percent at the time of the baseline survey to 15 percent at the final monitoring survey. The survey covered a total of 2,177 individual small-scale farmers belonging to 114 of 122 model farmers' groups from which data could be obtained in a similar manner to the baseline survey (Aikawa 2013, 151).

12. This case draws heavily from Hosono et al. (2011, 188–94) and Fujita (2011).

13. Wilbur Smith Associates (2008); Government of Japan, MOFA (2006).

14. This part draws from Hosono (2009a).

15. UNDP (2010, 3) defined *inclusive business* as models which include poor people into value chains as producers, employees, and consumers.

16. One of the most popular items to come out of Malawi's One Village, One Product initiative was moringa powder. Made from the leaves of the highly nutritious moringa tree, the powder is said to contain twice as much protein as yogurt, seven times more vitamin C than oranges, and four times as much calcium as milk. The powder can be boiled and then applied to the body as a medicine, drunk as tea, or added to food. Another Malawian product is the 100 percent natural *mapanga* honey, which comes from the nectar of mango flowers in the south of the country. Another noteworthy example is the growing lineup of products made from the baobab tree. In Malawi, oil extracted from the fruit of the baobab tree is commonly used as a cooking ingredient. In Japan, the vitamin-rich oil is popularly used as a moisturizing ingredient in cosmetics. A sweet-and-sour jam made from the fruit is also popular (JICA 2013b).

17. This part draws heavily from Hosono (2009b, 23–29) as well as DBJ and JERI (2003). It is also based partly on the author's experiences in some Japanese cooperation projects in the areas of kaizen, quality, and productivity improvement, such as the Chairman of the Advisory Committee for the "Technical Cooperation for Brazilian Institute of Quality and Productivity Project" from 1995 to 2000.

18. The close relationship between quality and productivity was widely recognized in Japan, and the two words *quality* and *productivity* (quality control and improved productivity), have often been referred to together. On one hand, to clearly define the concept of quality, it is necessary to establish industrial norms or standards. This is so because a product is considered defective only when it does not satisfy the quality norm or standard. The Japan Industrial Standard (JIS) and Japan Agricultural Standard (JAS) were introduced by law in Japan in 1949 and 1950, respectively. JIS defines QC as a part of quality management. On the other hand, at the worldwide level, ISO 9000, established by the International Organization for Standardization (ISO), is well known as the international standard relating to quality management systems.

19. Dr. Kaoru Ishikawa, ex-rector of the Musashi Institute of Technology (recently renamed Tokyo City University), is considered the founder of quality control in Japan as well as the father of the QC circle, as a result of the important theoretical and practical contributions he made. His book *Introduction to Quality Control,* first published in 1954 (Ishikawa 1954), is one of the most widely read books in Japan in this field. The third edition (1989) was translated into English and published in 1990 (Ishikawa 1990). There are a large number of well-known engineers and managers who have promoted quality activities in many Japanese companies. One of the most prominent is Taiichi Ohno, ex-vice president of Toyota Motor Company. He is one of those who consolidated the Toyota Production System (TPS). Another prominent Japanese engineer who contributed substantially to quality activities is Dr. Shigeo Shingo, a consultant for Toyota and Panasonic, among others. In recognition of his work, Utah State University created the Shingo Prize. Masaaki Imai, who once worked for Japan Productivity Center in Washington, D.C., founded the Kaizen Institute Consulting Group in 1986 and wrote, in the same year, *Kaizen: The Key to Japan's Competitive Success.*

20. While these five slogans have been translated in various ways, they roughly refer to removing unnecessary things, arranging tools and parts for easy view, keeping the workplace clean, maintaining personal hygiene, and exhibiting disciplined behavior.

21. According to Liker (2004, xi–xii; italics in original):

"The Toyota Way can be briefly summarized through the two pillars that support it: 'Continuous Improvement' and 'Respect for People.' Continuous improvement, often called kaizen, defines Toyota's basic approach to doing business. Challenge everything. More important than the actual improvements that individuals contribute, the true value of continuous improvement lies in creating an atmosphere of continuous *learning* and an environment that not only accepts but actually *embraces* change. Such an environment can only be created where there is respect for people—hence the second pillar of the Toyota Way. Toyota demonstrates this respect by providing employment security and seeking to engage team members through active participation in improving their jobs"

22. This and the following paragraphs draw on DBJ and JERI (2003).

23. In this regard, Imai (1986) compares *kaizen* and *innovation*. The terms correspond, respectively, to "incremental innovation" and "breakthrough" in terms of Dertouzos, Lester, and Solow (1989). According to Imai, while *kaizen* is of long-term and long-lasting effect, with small steps, with involvement of everybody, based on conventional know-how and state-of-the-art practices that require little investment, *innovation* is of short-term but dynamic effect, with big steps, with involvement of a selected few "champions," based on technological breakthroughs, new inventions, and new theories, requiring large investment (Imai 1986, 25).

24. Stiglitz and Greenwald (2014, 528) noted further that, interestingly, some of the learning involved learning from foreign firms, e.g., about quality circles and JIT production.

25. According to a recent study on productivity gaps for Japanese and U.S. industries by Jorgenson, Nomura, and Samuels (2015, 21–26), total factor productivity (TFP) gaps were very large both in manufacturing and nonmanufacturing sectors in 1955. The gap for manufacturing productivity relative to the United States (U.S. = 100) disappeared by 1980, peaked at 103.8 in 1991, and deteriorated afterward, leaving a current gap that is almost negligible. The gap for nonmanufacturing also contracted between 1955 to 1991, when the gap reached 8.9 percent, but expanded afterward. Japanese "motor vehicles," "primary metal," and "other electrical machinery" sectors have higher levels of TFP than their U.S. counterparts. In machinery, computer, and electronics products, U.S. levels of TFP are higher than Japan's. In nonmanufacturing sectors, the U.S. TFP is generally higher, especially in agriculture, forestry, and fishery. However, in medical care and communications, Japan's TFP is higher.

26. This part draw heavily from Hosono (2015c, 89–94) and JICA (2014).

27. Comments made by the prime minister during his visit to Kohei Goshi, honorary president of the Japan Productivity Center (JPC) in June 1981 (JPC 1990, 1).

28. This case study draws heavily from Hosono (2012).

29. Frog Caravan (Caravana de Rana) is an innovative training system to teach natural disaster prevention developed by a Japanese nonprofit organization (NPO),

Plus Arts (+Arts), in 2005. In Japan the frog is considered a friendly symbol, promoting good feelings. Frog caravans tour schools, engaging local officials, teachers, and schoolchildren. They introduce games to teach children, e.g., how to extinguish fires or rescue people trapped under rubble in the wake of an earthquake.

30. With regard to cases of "land readjustment projects" and Japanese cooperation, see, e.g., De Souza (2009; 2012).

REFERENCES

ADB (Asian Development Bank). 2009. *Strategy 2020: Working for an Asia and Pacific Free of Poverty.* Manila: ADB.

——. 2013. *Key Indicators for Asia and the Pacific 2013: Asia's Economic Transformation: Where to, How, and How Fast?* Manila: ADB.

Aikawa, Jiro. 2013. "Initiatives of SHEP and SHEP UP: Capacity Development of Small-Scale Farmers for Increased Responsiveness to Market Needs." In *For Inclusive and Dynamic Development in Sub-Saharan Africa,* 143–69. Tokyo: JICA Research Institute.

Anschutz, Eric E. 1995. *TQM America: How America's Most Successful Companies Profit from Total Quality Management.* Sarasota, Fla.: McGuinn & McGuire.

APEC (Asia Pacific Economic Cooperation). 2010. "The APEC Leaders' Growth Strategy." Yokohama, Japan, 14 November. http://www.apec.org/Meeting-Papers/ Leaders-Declarations/2010/2010_ael m/growth-strategy.aspx.

——. 2014. "Beijing Agenda for an Integrated, Innovative and Interconnected Asia-Pacific." Beijing, November 11. http://www.apec.org/Meeting-Papers/Leaders-Declarations/ 2014/2014_aelm.aspx.

APO (Asian Productivity Organization). 2003. *Rural Life Improvement in Asia.* http:// www.apo-tokyo.org/00e-books/AG-07_RuraLife.htm.

Branscomb, Lewis. 1987. "Towards a National Policy on Research and Development." Conference sponsored by the Council on Research and Technology (CORE-TECH) and the Conference Board, MIT, October 8. (Cited by Dertouzos et al. 1989.)

Cimoli, Mario, Giovanni Dosi, and Joseph E. Stiglitz, eds. 2009. *Industrial Policy and Development: The Political Economy of Capabilities Accumulation.* Toronto: Oxford University Press.

Clarke, Peter, and Katy Oswald. 2010. "Introduction: Why Reflect Collectively on Capacities for Change?" *IDS Bulletin* 41(3): 1–12.

DBJ (Development Bank of Japan) and JERI (Japan Economic Research Institute). 2003. *Handbook for TQM and QCC.* Washington, D.C.: Inter-American Development Bank (IDB).

Dertouzos, Michael, Richard Lester, and Robert Solow. 1989. *Made in America: Regaining the Productive Edge.* Cambridge, Mass.: MIT Press.

De Souza, Felipe Francisco. 2009. *Metodos de Planejamento Urbano: Projetos de Land Readjustment e Redesenvolvimento Urbano.* Sao Paulo: Paulo's Editora.

——. 2012. "Land Readjustment Pilot Projects in Sao Paulo: A Comparative Analysis Between the Periphery and the Urban Center Proposals." Paper presented at the Annual World Bank Conference on Land and Poverty. April 23–26. Washington, D.C.

ECDPM (European Center for Development Policy Management). 2008. "Capacity, Change, and Performance: Study Report." Discussion Paper 59B. April. Maastricht, Holland: ECDPM.

Fujita, Yasuo. 2011. "What Makes the Bangladesh Local Government Engineering Department (LGED) So Effective? Complementarity between LGED Capacity and Donor Capacity Development Support." Working Paper 27. Tokyo: JICA Research Institute.

Garcia-Alcaraz, Aide, Aracely Maldonado-Marcias, and Guillermo Cortes-Robles. 2014. *Lean Manufacturing in the Developing World: Methodology, Case Studies and Trends from Latin America.* New York: Springer.

Government of Japan, Cabinet Office. 2012. *Annual Report on the Japanese Economy and Public Finance 2012.* Tokyo: Cabinet Office.

——. 2015. *Cabinet Decision on the Development Cooperation Charter.* Tokyo: Cabinet Office.

Government of Japan, MOFA (Ministry of Foreign Affairs). 2006. "Government of Bangladesh Programme-Level Evaluation: Japanese Assistance to LGED-Related Sectors." Tokyo: Ministry of Foreign Affairs.

Haddad, Lawrence, Hiroshi Kato, and Nicolas Meisel, eds. 2015. *Growth Is Dead, Long Live Growth: The Quality of Economic Growth and Why It Matters.* Tokyo: JICA Research Institute.

Haraguchi, Nobuya. 2008. "The One Village One Product (OVOP) Movement: What It Is, How It Has Been Replicated, and Recommendations for a UNIDO OVOP Type Project." UNIDO Research and Statistics Branch Working Paper 03/2008. Vienna: UNIDO.

Hosono, Akio. 2009a. "A Memo on Rural Life Improvement Movement." Tokyo: GRIPS Development Forum.

——. 2009b. "*Kaizen:* Quality, Productivity and Beyond," GRIPS Development Forum. *Introducing KAIZEN in Africa.* 23–37. Tokyo: GRIPS.

——. 2012. "Climate Change, Disaster Risk Management, and South-South/Triangular Cooperation." In *Scaling Up South—South and Triangular Cooperation,* ed. Hiroshi Kato 15–41. Tokyo: JICA-RI.

——. 2013. "Scaling Up South—South Cooperation through Triangular Cooperation: The Japanese Experience." In *Getting to Scale: How to Bring Development Solutions to Millions of Poor People,* ed. Laurence Chandy, Akio Hosono, Homi Kharas, and Johannes Linn, 236–61. Washington, D.C.: Brookings Institution.

——. 2015a. "Industrial Transformation and Quality of Growth." In *Growth Is Dead, Long Live Growth: The Quality of Economic Growth and Why It Matters,* ed. Lawrence Haddad, Hiroshi Kato, and Nicolas Meisel, 267–300. Tokyo: JICA Research Institute.

——. 2015b. "Catalyzing Transformation for Inclusive Growth." In *Japan and the Developing World: Sixty Years of Japan's Foreign Aid and the Post-2015 Agenda,* ed. Hiroshi Kato, John Page, and Yasutami Shimomura, 167–87. New York: Palgrave Macmillan.

——. 2015c. "Industrial Strategy and Economic Transformation: Lessons from Five Outstanding Cases." In *Industrial Policy and Economic Transformation in Africa,* ed. Akbar Noman and Joseph Stiglitz, 53–101. New York: Columbia University Press.

Hosono, Akio, Shunichiro Honda, Mine Sato, and Mai Ono. 2011. "Inside the Black Box of Capacity Development." In *Catalyzing Development: A New Vision for Aid*, ed. Homi Kharas, Koji Makino, and Woojin Jung, 179–201. Washington, D.C.: Brookings Institution.

Imai, Masaaki. 1986. *Kaizen: The Key to Japan's Competitive Success*. New York: McGraw-Hill.

Instituto de Desarrollo. 2013. *El Mejoramiento de Vida en Paraguay*. Asuncion and Tokyo: Ministerio de Agricultura y Ganaderia and JICA.

Ishikawa, Kaoru. 1954. *Hinshitsu Kanri Nyumon* [*Introduction to Quality Control Control*] (in Japanese). Tokyo: JUSE Press.

——. 1990. *Introduction to Quality Control*. Tokyo: 3A Corporation.

JICA (Japan International Cooperation Agency). 2003a. *Study on the Livelihood Improvement Programme in Rural Japan and the Prospects for Japan's Rural Development Cooperation*. Tokyo: JICA.

——. 2003b. "Terminal Evaluation on the Social Forestry Extension Model Development Project for Semiarid Areas." Tokyo: JICA.

——. 2006. "Capacity Development: What Is CD? How JICA Understands CD, and How-to Concepts for Improving JICA Projects." Tokyo: JICA.

——. 2008. "Capacity Assessment Handbook: Managing Programs and Projects toward Capacity Development." Tokyo: JICA.

——. 2009. "Summary of Terminal Evaluation on Intensified Social Forestry Project." Tokyo: JICA.

——. 2013a. "Central America and the Caribbean: 'Life Improvement Approach' Helps Farmers Increase Self-Reliance" *JICA News*, April 19. Tokyo: JICA.

——. 2013b. *Focus on African Development*. Press release at Tokyo International Conference on African Development (TICAD).

——. 2013c. "Internal Ex-Post Evaluation for Technical Cooperation Project: Intensified Social Forestry Project in Semi-arid Areas of Kenia." Tokyo: JICA.

——. 2014. "The *Kaizen* Project: Laying the Groundwork for Singapore's Growth." *JICA's World*, January 2014. Tokyo: JICA.

——. 2015. "Chiiki no Shorai wo Kaeru Chiisana Doryoku" ["Small Efforts Which Could Change the Future of the Region"]. *Mundi*, May. Tokyo: JICA.

Jorgenson, Dale W., Koji Nomura, and Jon D. Samuels. 2015. "A Half Century of Trans-Pacific Competition: Price Level Indices and Productivity Gap for Japanese and U.S. Industries, 1955–2012." RIETI Discussion Paper Series 15-E-054. Tokyo: The Research Institute of Economy, Trade and Industry (RIETI).

JPC (Japan Productivity Center). 1990. *Singapore Productivity Improvement Project*. Tokyo: JPC.

Kozuka, Eiji. 2014. "Inclusive Development: Definition and Principles for the Post-2015 Development Agenda." In *Perspectives on the Post-2015 Development Agenda*, ed. Hiroshi Kato, 109–22. Tokyo: JICA Research Institute.

Kurokawa, Kiyoto, Fletcher Tembo, and Dirk Willem te Velde. 2010. "Challenge for the OVOP Movement in Sub-Saharan Africa: Insights from Malawi, Japan, and Thailand." JICA-RI Working Paper 18. Tokyo and London: JICA and ODI.

Liker, Jeffrey K. 2004. *The Toyota Way*. New York: McGraw Hill.

Lin, Justin Yifu. 2012. *New Structural Economics: A Framework for Rethinking Development and Policy*. Washington, D.C.: World Bank.

Mizuno, Masami. 2003. "Rural Life Improvement Movement in Contemporary Japan." *Study on the Livelihood Improvement Programme in Rural Japan and the Prospects for Japan's Rural Development Cooperation*. Tokyo: JICA.

Noman, Akbar, and Joseph E. Stiglitz. 2012. "Strategies for African Development." In *Good Growth and Governance for Africa: Rethinking Development Strategies*, ed. A. Noman, K. Botchwey, H. Stein, and J. E. Stiglitz, 3–47. New York: Oxford University Press.

Nonaka, Ikujiro, Ryoko Toyama, and Toru Hirata. 2008. *Managing Flow: A Process Theory of the Knowledge-Based Firm*. New York: Palgrave Macmillan.

OECD (Organization for Economic Co-operation and Development). 2008. *Natural Resources and Pro-Poor Growth: The Economics and Politics*. Paris: OECD.

Ohno, Izumi, and Daniel Kitaw. 2011. "Productivity Movement in Singapore." In *Kaizen National Movement: A Study of Quality and Productivity Improvement in Asia and Africa*, 49–68. Tokyo: JICA and National Graduate Institute for Policy Studies (GRIPS) Development Forum.

Ohno, Kenichi. 2013. *Learning to Industrialize: From Given Growth to Policy-Aided Value Creation*. New York: Routledge.

Reconstruction Design Council in Response to the Great East Japan Earthquake. 2011. *Towards Reconstruction: Hope Beyond the Disaster*. Tokyo: Ministry of Foreign Affairs (Japan) (provisional translation).

Sato, Hiroshi. 2003. "Rural Life Improvement Experience in Japan for Rural Development in Developing Countries." *Rural Life Improvement in Asia*. Tokyo: Asian Productivity Organization (APO).

Shimada, Go. 2015. "The Economic Implication of a Comprehensive Approach to Learning on Industrial Policy: The Case of Ethiopia." In *Industrial Policy and Economic Transformation in Africa*, ed. Akbar Noman and Joseph Stiglitz, 102–22. New York: Columbia University Press.

Stiglitz, Joseph, and Bruce Greenwald. 2014. *Creating a Learning Society: A New Approach to Growth, Development, and Social Progress*. New York: Columbia University Press.

Ueda, Takafumi. 2009. "Productivity and Quality Improvement: JICA's Assistance in Kaizen." GRIPS Development Forum. *Introducing KAIZEN in Africa*. Tokyo: GRIPS.

UNDP (United Nations Development Program). 1998. "Capacity Assessment and Development in a Systems and Strategic Management Context." MDGB Technical Advisory Paper 3. New York: UNDP.

——. 2010. *The MDGs: Everyone's Business: How Inclusive Business Models Contribute to Development and Who Supports Them*. New York: UNDP.

UNEP (United Nations Environment Program). 2010. *Green Economy: Developing Countries' Success Stories*. Nairobi: UNEP.

——. 2011. *Towards a Green Economy: Pathway to Sustainable Development and Poverty Reduction*. Nairobi: UNEP.

UN-ESCAP (United Nations Economic and Social Commission for Asia and the Pacific). 2013. *Shifting from Quantity to Quality: Growth with Equality, Efficiency, Sustainability and Dynamism*. Bangkok: UN-ESCAP.

Wang, Xiaolin, Limin Wang, and Yan Wang. 2014. *The Quality of Growth and Poverty Reduction in China*. Heidelberg: Springer.

Wattanasiri, Chamnan. 2005. *Strengthening of Thailand's Grassroots Economy of the Royal Thai Government (RTG)*. CD Dept., Ministry of Interior, Thailand.

Wilbur Smith Associates. 2008. "Final Report on the Technical Assistance Services to Support Implementation of the Institutional Strengthening Action Plan (ISAP) of LGED." Dhaka: Wilbur Smith Associates.

Womack, James, and Daniel Jones. 1996. *Lean Thinking: Banish Waste and Create Wealth in Your Corporation*. New York: Free Press.

Womack, James, Daniel Jones, and Daniel Roos. 1990. *The Machine that Changed the World: The Story of Lean Production*. New York: Macmillan.

World Bank. 2009. "Operational Risk Assessment for Local Government Engineering Department in Bangladesh: Final Report." Washington, D.C.: World Bank.

World Bank. 2015. *World Development Report 2015: Mind, Society and Behaviour*. Washington, D.C.: World Bank.

World Economic Forum. 2011. *Annual Meeting of the New Champions 2011: Mastering Quality Growth*. Dalian, China: World Economic Forum Summer Davos in Asia.

CHAPTER 11

Could Technology Make Natural Resources a Platform for Industrialization?

IDENTIFYING A NEW OPPORTUNITY FOR LATIN AMERICA
(AND OTHER RESOURCE-RICH COUNTRIES)

Carlota Perez

Those who doubt the potential dynamism of natural resources (NR) assume that there are truths about certain sectors that do not change over time. This is reflected in much of the literature on development and has filtered into the beliefs of policy makers. Yet evolutionary economists hold that technological change is at the very heart of economic growth, with constant shifts in the relative dynamism of companies, industries, and sectors. Indeed, even a cursory glance at the natural resources sector reveals that the context has significantly changed since the postwar period, when many of the current ideas about development evolved. The character of energy, materials, and food markets has shifted dramatically; the potential for innovation in developing countries is much greater than before; all markets have segmented into niches; global corporations have changed their behavior; and, last but not least, environmental factors have come into play as a challenge and as a growth opportunity for both developed and developing nations.

This chapter examines the implications of such technological changes for resource-endowed countries, building on the notable shift in the level of awareness, in both theory and practice, of the role of innovation in growth and development. In line with the neo-Schumpeterian and evolutionary tradition, the chapter starts from the idea that some industries,[1] in some periods, offer greater opportunities for innovation and dynamism than others. It will argue that the reasons for not seeing the natural resource industries among those with higher opportunities for most of the twentieth century are largely historical and that the context has changed significantly.

The information and communications technologies (ICTs), together with the techno-economic paradigm that has evolved as the optimal way of using their potential to the fullest (Perez 1985 and 2002), are changing the opportunity space for innovation in natural resources, which increases technological dynamism in the whole network of activities upstream and downstream, from initial investment and exploitation to final use. The new opportunity space allows for a more limited type of resource-intensive industrialization strategy than that of the United States between 1880 and 1914, when the country forged ahead to world industrial leadership (Wright 1997). Crucially, though, a resource-intensive industrialization strategy will require innovative economic, financial, and technological policies to promote an institutional arrangement that mitigates the "resource curse" (Stevens and Dietsche 2008; see also Acemoglu, Johnson, and Robinson 2002). The task of this chapter is to identify the opportunity rather than to design the policies that can avoid its shortcomings.

AS TECHNOLOGY CHANGES, SO DO OPPORTUNITIES

Examining the historical record from the British industrial revolution of the 1770s to the present, one can observe that fast growth and catch-up processes tend to cluster in certain regions or countries, which move in similar directions for a certain period. This reflects the fact that, as indicated in table 11.1, technological progress—and accompanying "development"—in capitalism does not occur along a continuous line; rather it has gone through five technological revolutions. Each leads to a new "techno-economic paradigm"—or best-practice common sense—that, together with the spread of new infrastructures, leads to a great surge of development every 50 to 60 years and drives a leap in potential productivity across all industries (Perez 1985 and 2002; Freeman and Perez 1988; Freeman and Louçã 2001).

Such massive transformations are contingent on context and conditions, both regional and technological. The nature and patterns of diffusion of each technological revolution determine the changing context for development and open successive and different scenarios for action, or windows of opportunity, while closing old ones. Each can also change the ranking of countries, when the old leaders remain attached to their traditional knowledge and structures while the new ones can "leap-frog"

Table 11.1 The Industries and Infrastructures of Each Technological Revolution

Technological Revolution	New Technologies and New or Redefined Industries	New or Redefined Infrastructures
First: From 1771 *The industrial revolution* Britain	Mechanized cotton industry Wrought iron Machinery	Canals and waterways Turnpike roads Water power (highly improved waterwheels)
Second: From 1829 *Age of steam and railways* In Britain and spreading to the Continent and the United States	Steam engines and machinery (made in iron; fueled by coal) Iron and coal mining (now playing a central role in growth)* Railway construction Rolling stock production Steam power for many industries (including textiles)	Railways (use of steam engine) Universal postal service Telegraph (mainly nationally along railway lines) Great ports, great depots, and worldwide sailing ships City gas
Third: From 1875 *Age of steel, electricity, and heavy engineering* United States and Germany overtaking Britain	Cheap steel (especially Bessemer) Full development of steam engine for steel ships Heavy chemistry and civil engineering Electrical equipment industry Copper and cables Canned and bottled food Paper and packaging	Worldwide shipping in rapid steel steamships (use of Suez Canal) Worldwide railways (use of cheap steel rails and bolts in standard sizes) Great bridges and tunnels Worldwide telegraph Telephone (mainly nationally) Electric networks (for illumination and industrial use)
Fourth: From 1908 *Age of oil, the automobile, and mass production* In the United States and spreading to Europe	Mass-produced automobiles Cheap oil and oil fuels Petrochemicals (synthetics) Internal combustion engine for automobiles, transport, tractors, airplanes, war tanks, and electricity Home electrical appliances Refrigerated and frozen foods	Networks of roads, highways, ports, and airports Networks of oil ducts Universal electricity (industry and homes) Worldwide analog telecommunications (telephone, telex, and cablegram), wired and wireless
Fifth: From 1971 *Age of information and telecommunications* In the United States and spreading to Europe and Asia	The information revolution: Cheap microelectronics Computers, software Telecommunications Control instruments Computer-aided biotechnology and new materials	World digital telecommunications (cable, fiber optics, radio, and satellite) Internet/electronic mail and other e-services Multiple-source, flexible use electricity networks High-speed physical transport links (by land, air, and water)

Source: Perez 2002, table 2.2, p. 14.

*These traditional industries acquire a new role and a new dynamism when serving as the material and the fuel of the world of railways and machinery.

and jump directly into the new (Perez and Soete 1988; Goldemberg 2011) as long as they have already acquired the social capabilities (Gershenkron 1962; Dore 1989).

For example, in the 1870s the United States and Germany made a huge leap and caught up to industrial Britain, deploying the heavy engineering that emerged in the Age of Steel. At the same time, Australia, New Zealand, Argentina, and others made a leap forward in their development, benefiting from the counterseasonal trade made possible by the steamships and transoceanic telegraph that this engineering produced, as well as from the funding flowing from the City of London. During the next surge, the postwar United States displaced the United Kingdom as the world leader, promoting a new paradigm of mass consumption based on cheap oil, automobiles, and plastics, which was quickly emulated by Western Europe. In the maturity phase of this paradigm (see Perez 2002, 62–67; Perez 2008, 6–9), both Latin America and Asia achieved high rates of growth thanks to protected import substitution industrialization (ISI).[2] Similar observations can be made about the connection between the process of diffusion of the ICT technologies and the recent (and different) leaps forward made, first by Japan, then by the Four Asian Tigers (Hong Kong, Singapore, South Korea, and Taiwan), and subsequently by India and China.

The specific nature of each technological revolution and the successive windows of opportunity that it opens mean that development possibilities are a moving target—and that development strategies are therefore temporary and must be updated and redesigned accordingly. Opportunities change not only with each major shift in technology, but also with the contextual legacy of the previous paradigm and the stage of deployment of the new one (Perez 2001). It is important to underline that the notion of windows of opportunity presented here does not argue on the basis of static comparative advantages. It is rather underpinned by the observation that major surges of technical change radically modify the context and make obsolete not only the old technologies but also the ideas about development that emerged to handle them (Perez 2001). This is why, although here the focus is on the Latin American case, it should equally be of interest to other resource-rich regions.

This is the same basis for arguing that attempting to directly imitate current (or recent) successes is of little use, as these were achieved with past opportunities. Similarly, it is not wise to develop policy theories on the basis of data from recent decades. By contrast, a long view of history can be useful for revealing patterns whose equivalents may be identified in the present. Tomorrow's successes do not depend upon copying what has recently succeeded, but rather on anticipating the future today.

In fact, the current window of opportunity calls for policies that are able to transform *static* comparative advantages in natural resources into *dynamic* advantages, fostering diversification of production in knowledge-intensive activities that are horizontally, vertically, and laterally related to the NR sectors each country chooses to develop (Marin, Navas-Aleman and Perez 2010, 2015). An appropriate policy strategy would promote technical change and would entail the creation of conditions for learning and innovating that would result in new value-adding processes and in more specialized products with higher and more stable prices and markets. This means that the current opportunity opens up the possibility of adding some of the key characteristics of manufacturing to NR industries in a process of resource-intensive industrialization.

THE LESSONS AND LEGACY OF THE RECENT PAST—GROWTH WITH THE ISI MODEL

However, to make the best of an opportunity, it is also necessary to have previously accumulated a certain level of capabilities, both technological and social (Gershenkron 1962). Good timing is therefore essential, together with recognition of the opportunity and the political and entrepreneurial determination to take advantage of it. Thus the outcomes can be very different, and not all advances are irreversible.

From the late 1950s to the late 1970s, Latin America and the Four Asian Tigers used the opportunity of import substitution industrialization. The policy brought together two sets of interests: the mature industries in the advanced world looking for market growth and the then-called "third world" governments looking for paths to development. At this point in the mass production revolution, many of the large corporations in the advanced countries were facing two main limits to growth. On the technological front, they were finding it increasingly difficult to innovate either in processes to raise productivity in their established production lines or in products to revive their saturated markets. The consumer-driven "American way of life" which characterized this paradigm had already been adopted by the workforce of the advanced countries and the narrow elites of most of the developing world. Market growth was primarily being achieved through *planned obsolescence* paired with advertising and credit (consumer debt), inducing and enabling existing consumers to buy new replacement products. At the same time, the nascent developing countries had neither the technology nor the market scale to set up competitive industries and were basically exporting raw materials and importing manufactured products. The price "scissors" between lower-value raw materials and higher-value final products, to which Prebisch (1950) and Singer (1950) called attention, got even worse as corporations faced limits to productivity and markets and tried to squeeze raw material prices and to transfer salary increases to the consumer.

The ISI model offered a dynamic solution. By locating the final assembly stage in potential consumer destinations, it mobilized the economies of the developing countries at the same time as it expanded world markets. In the model applied by the Latin American countries, as shown in figure 11.1, the export of raw materials provided the tax and foreign exchange income to finance foreign investment in a fully protected process of industrialization for the domestic market. In the mid-1970s, when international banks lavishly poured OPEC money into Latin America's public and private companies (Marichal 1988), governments shifted to expanding public investment in basic industries and to subsidizing uncompetitive exports.

Sufficient tariff barriers and the acceptance of low productivity and high prices achieved both growth and employment. Although the assembly of products designed elsewhere, under the supervision of foreign experts or following process manuals, led to little technological learning and left scant space for innovation (Bell and Pavitt 1993), the process did generate demand for complementary activities in which real learning and innovation could take place. Local technological capabilities were required—and acquired—to build, improve, and operate ports, airports, roads, electricity, telephony, and water (usually developed with state funds and under state control), as well as in the accessory industries such as cardboard, printing, packaging, glass, plastics, cement, and building materials (generally developed by the private sector). This aspect of the model is particularly important, given that most of those complementary activities were processing industries (as distinct from fabricating)—precisely the skills that may be required for building dynamic networks around natural resources, as is discussed shortly. Previous learning also continued—and in some cases intensified—in natural resources themselves: mining, oil extraction, agriculture, livestock, and so on. As figure 11.1 indicates, the strategy additionally created demand for a wide professional

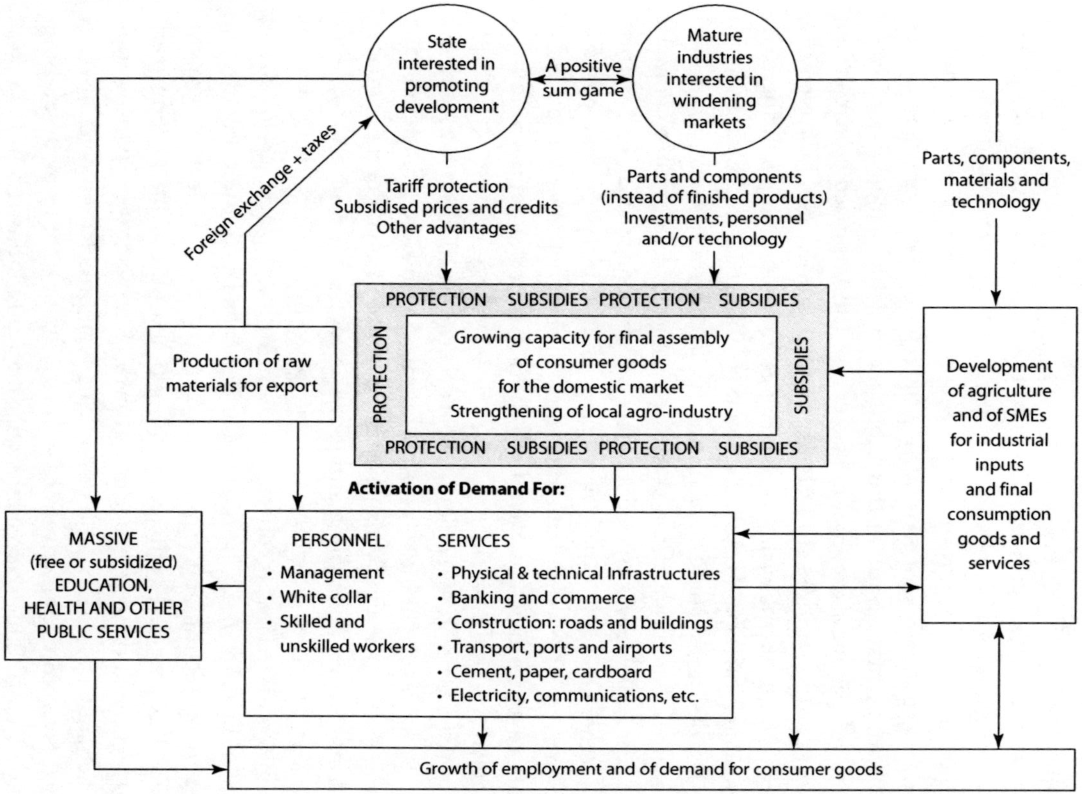
State interested in promoting development
A positive sum game
Mature industries interested in windening markets
Foreign exchange + taxes
Tariff protection
Subsidised prices and credits
Other advantages
Parts and components (instead of finished products)
Investments, personnel and/or technology
Parts, components, materials and technology
Production of raw materials for export
PROTECTION SUBSIDIES PROTECTION SUBSIDIES
PROTECTION
Growing capacity for final assembly of consumer goods for the domestic market
Strengthening of local agro-industry
SUBSIDIES
PROTECTION SUBSIDIES PROTECTION SUBSIDIES
Development of agriculture and of SMEs for industrial inputs and final consumption goods and services
Activation of Demand For:
MASSIVE (free or subsidized) EDUCATION, HEALTH AND OTHER PUBLIC SERVICES
PERSONNEL
• Management
• White collar
• Skilled and unskilled workers
SERVICES
• Physical & technical Infrastructures
• Banking and commerce
• Construction: roads and buildings
• Transport, ports and airports
• Cement, paper, cardboard
• Electricity, communications, etc.
Growth of employment and of demand for consumer goods

Figure 11.1 **The Latin American model of Import Substitution Industrialization (ISI)**

middle class and a trained workforce to run the assembly plants, organize logistics, and manage the business services from banks to distribution. Furthermore, while brands and process technologies were typically
imported, they sometimes had to be adapted to the characteristics of
local produce and consumer preferences, opening some space for local
engineering.

While justifiable criticisms have been leveled at ISI, as implemented
in Latin America it can be seen as an adequate strategy for the context
at the time. The import of parts for assembly, rather than of products,
worked as a starter engine for moving the rest of the economy and created
a developmental culture in the public sector, which made major investment in basic industries and infrastructure and improved or established
mass education and health systems. Larger countries such as Argentina,
Mexico, and Brazil, with a previously established manufacturing base,
went much further in weaving a complete industrial structure, but even
the less developed countries were able to make a substantial leap forward
in growth. For about fifteen years the average growth of most countries
in Latin America was around 4 percent, with periods when one country
or another grew at a 10 percent average. ISI in this region was a positive-
sum strategy, albeit with limited results. However, when world conditions
changed and protection was lifted, the lack of technological autonomy
doomed the model to collapse.

In Asia, the leap to development also began with ISI, in fact, with less
success at the beginning. However, Taiwan, South Korea, Singapore, and
Hong Kong—the Four Asian Tigers—engaged in much deeper, broader,
and more systemic learning and growth processes (Amsden 1989; Wade
1992). It is likely that the lack of an independent source of foreign income
from raw materials (in contrast to Latin America) played an important
role in the difference. The Four Asian Tigers had to devise a way of using
import protection and export subsidies to achieve export-led growth.
They thus provided sheltered learning time to their "infant industries"
and facilitated the emergence and growth of competitive exporting companies and industrial complexes, uniting high productivity with low-cost
labor and producing advanced-country quality goods at developing-
country costs. This was exactly what maturing industries were looking
for in the 1970s and early 1980s. There was arguably an element of luck
in what happened next. Electronics products and components happened to be the core of the next revolution, so their assembly prepared
the required capabilities, whereas the Latin Americans, starting earlier,

mainly assembled cars and home electrical appliances. The Asian countries quickly understood the importance of ICT and the trend toward global markets. They constructed—explicitly or implicitly—clear and nationally shared "visions" for their economic development and worked on building global alliances.

Yet the key to the Asian success was their huge effort in training and education and the process of intensive technological learning, aided by subsidies only while required.[3] In essence, they were able to make the most of the limited opportunities that presented themselves in the 1960s to build a platform for development that allowed them to take much greater advantage of the next window of opportunity. When the ICT revolution came, they were able to make the leap and innovate their way up.

Could the Latin Americans make such a leap now? It would be fruitless to attempt to replicate the Asian route to development. That particular window of opportunity has passed, and the current context is completely different. The ICT revolution is already midway along its diffusion path, and the Asian region is far ahead in its accumulation of knowledge and experience in technology, production, management, and trade. It has also become the most dynamic market, constantly incorporating new industries, new territories, and new consumers.

It would make sense to see whether the Latin American car can be hitched to Asian growth by finding market complementarity. In their catch-up process, the Asians made global alliances and engaged in intense technological learning and training efforts in the *fabricating* industries (electronics, electromechanical goods, and textile clothing) when the advanced countries of the West were becoming import markets. Could Latin America do something similar in the NR-related *processing* industries? Can they take advantage of the vast range of inputs and food required by the advancing Asian economies? Is there enough technological dynamism in the energy industry, in materials (basic and special, natural and synthetic, macro and nano) and in biological products (traditional and advanced, ecological, and biotechnological) to drive a learning and development process?

The remainder of this chapter will argue that the criticisms raised against NR as a basis for development stem from specific historical conditions and from their narrow identification as *raw* materials (or primary commodities); that the technological complexity in potential innovation networks around NR production is high and growing; and that the knowledge accumulation in the materials and life sciences required for advancement in those networks can prepare the continent for making a leap in development in the next technological revolution (which might be some combination of biotechnology, nanotechnology, and new and "green" materials). In other words, the conditions are ripe for a new type of natural resource–intensive industrialization process, whereby exploitation of natural resources and, crucially, their processing are used as the springboard for industrialization and economic development.

HISTORICALLY CHANGING VIEWS ON NATURAL RESOURCES: FROM BLESSING TO CURSE AND BACK?

The prevailing notions about the potential contributions of natural resources to development have changed radically over time, depending on the dominant technologies and the windows of opportunity available. Prior to the era of mass production, during the period that can be recognized as the first globalization (1870s to 1914), natural resources were seen as key to development. The technological revolution then taking place, in the age of steel and heavy engineering, was about chemistry and electricity, transcontinental railways and world-trading steamships, metallurgy, and major engineering projects. Such global infrastructures enabled counterseasonal world markets for meat, wheat, and other agricultural products. Natural resources were considered a blessing, not a curse, with Australia, New Zealand, Canada, Sweden, the United States, and others partly owing their catch-up successes to their resource endowment. Argentina in the 1880s to the 1890s was seen as the next United States. Yet, as Reinert (2004) emphasizes, policy makers in those countries also understood that raw materials alone—without concomitant highly skilled, technology-intensive activities—would not result in development.

It was not until the 1950s, during the successful postwar deployment of the mass production paradigm in the West, that criticism grew toward NR. The neoclassical prescription about taking advantage of resource abundance did not convince the structuralists, preoccupied with the poor economic performance of Latin American and African countries. Prebisch (1950) and Singer (1950) emphasized several types of demand and supply rigidities, which would explain the "price scissors" that increasingly favored manufactured goods over primary commodities. Other scholars, such as Nurkse (1958), noted that prices of commodities were very unstable, thus making NR-reliant countries vulnerable to constant changes in exchange rates, tax revenues, and local investment. A third group emphasized problems arising due to the domination of NR activities in developing countries by multinational corporations (MNCs). Not only were profits repatriated, but local investment and the instigation of backward and forward linkages were very limited, preventing future development (Singer 1950 and 1975). The assumption thus arose that only manufacturing led to development, with natural resources being a dead end (Singer 1949; Prebisch 1951).

This assumption has been compounded since then. The late 1970s brought concerns about the "Dutch disease," whereby a booming resource sector strengthens the currency, disadvantaging other exports, in particular of manufactured goods (*The Economist* 1977). Since the 1990s, a wave of empirical studies (Sachs and Warner 1995 and 2001; Auty 1990 and 1993; Gylfason, Tryggvi, and Gylfi 1999; Torvik 2002) suggest the existence of a "resource curse," which can make development difficult because of the resulting corruption and reduced incentive to invest for wealth creation when the centralized economic rents are generated by these resources. This also has the potential to affect democracy negatively, as government has no need to be accountable to taxpayers.

It is not that those authors were wrong, in either period. It is that the contexts were different—and they therefore provided different conditions for development that led to different views. Today, many manufactured products have become low-cost commodities, and natural resources have experienced very high prices. These phenomena could make both the Dutch disease and the resource curse even more acute. Addressing those obstacles will require institutional innovation to take those conditions into consideration in the formulation of economic development strategies.

HOW HAS THE CONTEXT CHANGED FOR NATURAL RESOURCE PRODUCERS? REVISITING THE POTENTIAL FOR TECHNOLOGICAL CATCH-UP

This chapter rests on the observation that the context around the use of natural resources is now significantly different from that of the postwar era. There are four main dimensions of significant change: price trends, the nature of markets, the conditions for technological dynamism, and the new globalized economy.

A CHANGE IN NATURAL RESOURCE PRICE LEVELS

At the most basic level, the consumer behavior of the previous age and the push toward full global development have led to a fast-growing demand for materials, energy, and food in the emerging countries, which has increased the overall demand for natural resources. This has been leading to the exhaustion of the most easily accessible sources and pushing marginal costs up. Additionally, the impact of climate change will probably intensify that effect. This means that, without losing their customary volatility, raw material prices are likely to oscillate at higher average levels (Dobbs et al. 2011; Farooki and Kaplinsky 2012). This makes them both a valuable advantage and an obstacle. They can be used as a source of funding for the technologization of natural resources or can be lost in corruption.

THE NEW HYPERSEGMENTED NATURE OF ALL MARKETS

Together with the volume and its impact on supply and on prices, the nature of markets has changed. As shown in figure 11.2A, there is now a market hypersegmentation of all products and activities into a wide and varying range, spanning from high-volume, low-price commodities to an array of low-volume, high-price niche products (Anderson 2006). As shown in figure 11.2B, this fracturing of the market applies as much to manufacturers as to services and primary sector products, and it also affects each activity along the value chain. Starting from the raw materials, it is possible, with innovation, to move up to higher-value products or move along to more adaptable products that can be custom-made for specific clients, increasing both the value and stability of prices.

The NR markets, although still primarily based on commodities, are thus seeing an increasing proportion of specialized materials and premium produce for the high-end niche markets. From organic to gourmet, through various dietary products, the food market is segmenting into many specialized niches. The same is happening in the materials sector, where customized alloys, green chemistry, nano-materials, and other products adapted to demand requirements and specifications are proliferating and reaping high rewards. Meanwhile, the realm of tangible products has also experienced a hypersegmentation. On one hand there are the high-end niche products (which often require special materials),

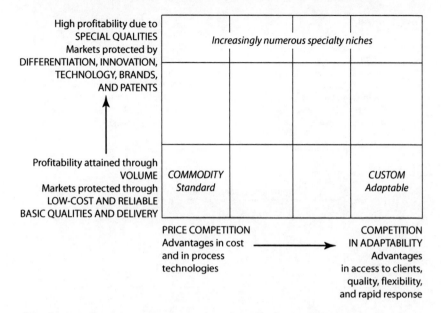

Figure 11.2A   The hyper-segmentation of markets and its differing conditions

but on the other hand, we have witnessed the commoditization of most standard assembled products with very narrow profit margins. This makes it more difficult for Latin America to compete in the fabrication industries—given the extremely low cost of labor in Asia and their accumulated experience—at the same time as it opens spaces in natural resource–related production.

AMPLE PATHWAYS TO INFORMATION AND GLOBAL MARKETS THROUGH ICT

Innovation is now much more accessible to newcomers. ICT makes information more easily available, facilitates design, and enables entry into the hypersegmented product and service markets. Hence, technological dynamism in all sectors, including NR, is higher than ever before, spurred by differentiation in demand and increasingly shaped by environmental and health concerns. In the NR sector, the focus used to be on processes to lower the cost of homogeneous products and to overcome local limits, whereas today we see innovation to be increasingly geared to special materials and food products.

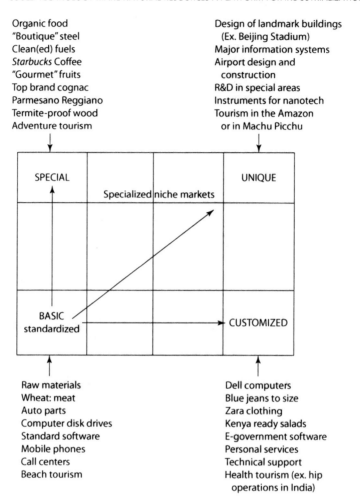

Organic food
"Boutique" steel
Clean(ed) fuels
Starbucks Coffee
"Gourmet" fruits
Top brand cognac
Parmesano Reggiano
Termite-proof wood
Adventure tourism

Design of landmark buildings
(Ex. Beijing Stadium)
Major information systems
Airport design and
construction
R&D in special areas
Instruments for nanotech
Tourism in the Amazon
or in Machu Picchu

SPECIAL

Specialized niche markets

UNIQUE

BASIC
standardized

CUSTOMIZED

Raw materials
Wheat: meat
Auto parts
Computer disk drives
Standard software
Mobile phones
Call centers
Beach tourism

Dell computers
Blue jeans to size
Zara clothing
Kenya ready salads
E-government software
Personal services
Technical support
Health tourism (ex. hip
operations in India)

Figure 11.2B   Some examples of positioning: materials, manufacturers, and services

Source: Perez 2010.

ICT has also enabled the new transport and distribution systems that make it easier for small and medium companies to access markets independently. This new context has led to the development of a much greater variety of distribution outlets (from the narrowly specialized to the hypermarkets) and the concomitant transport systems, allowing producers of different quantities and qualities to trade globally and on affordable terms. The fact that Kenya can provide packaged, ready-washed salads delivered by air every morning to the United Kingdom, to be distributed among the supermarkets across the country according to their orders the previous afternoon (Jaffee and Masakure 2005), is an example of the substantial change that has been occurring in global trade.

A SHIFT IN BEHAVIOR: FROM THE OLD MNC TO THE GLOBAL CORPORATION

Since the 1980s, the behavior of multinational corporations (MNCs) has been changing, as they morph from isolated affiliates acting as foreign enclaves in each country into fully globalized, strongly interacting value networks. Such global corporations (GCs) are now concerned with finding competent and reliable suppliers and partners (Urzúa 2012). Hence, they now have a financial interest in engaging in training and the proper transfer of technology to ensure quality across the whole structure (Ernst and Kim 2002). This presents new problems, of course, especially regarding the uneven distribution of gains among the participants in the value chain (Gereffi, Humphrey, and Sturgeon 2005); but the accumulation of knowledge and experience and the expectation of continuous improvement by all open learning possibilities for later autonomy that were not available with the low-productivity ISI model.

Nor are the GCs able to exhibit the cartel-like behavior that was once the common modus operandi of Western MNCs in developing nations. Such market control is being dislodged by East–West competition for access to resources. This creates conditions for stronger negotiating positions for the producer nations, reinforced by the much greater access to information through ICT.

CAN LATIN AMERICA HITCH ITS CAR TO ASIAN GROWTH?

The conditions of Asia, with its abundance of population and its relative dearth of natural resources, are in contrast with the relatively low population density of most of Latin America and its plentiful endowment in NR. These are the basic facts underlying the potential of a successful complementarity. The possibility of competing with Asia in *fabricated* mass production is unlikely for the foreseeable future, given their much lower labor costs and much greater accumulated experience. By contrast, the experience that Latin American countries have accumulated to a varying degree in NR production (agriculture, mining, and energy) and in the *processing* industries (agro-industry, cement, beer, paper, glass, oil refining, chemistry, metallurgy, etc.) gives them a basic platform for building further capabilities to innovate and improve the export profile. Fabrication of innovative equipment for the NR industries has also been developed in the more advanced countries of the region, as discussed later in this chapter. In addition, the infrastructures for logistical and institutional support are basically in place: from ports, roads, and a construction industry to telecoms and banking.

This complementarity between the two continents has the potential to engender strong trade links for at least a few decades. Engels' (1857) "law" of decreasing consumer expenditure on food as incomes rise, may not kick in for quite a while as the billions of inhabitants of China, India, and other emerging countries gradually join the ranks of the middle class. Demand for both food and materials, standard and special, is not likely to decrease for many years.

In Latin America, the variety in resource endowment can be seen as an advantage both in confronting global markets and for intraregional trade. The similarities may contribute to various forms of collaboration in technology and innovation. The primary limitations, both nationally and across the board, are the traditional power structures accompanied by high levels of corruption, entrenched poverty, and especially poor education outside middle- and upper-class urban centers. But at the same time, social capabilities across the continent mean that there is the potential for an explosion of development in these areas: the organizational and business skills of the long-standing educated middle class are rapidly being revitalized by the return of a globalized younger generation educated abroad.

Yet the key to success in progressing beyond the mere export of raw materials is innovation capacity, and that depends on education and continuous learning (Bell 2006). The lack of such progress is the Achilles heel of any strategy in Latin America, including the one being proposed here. As is seen in the next section, if natural resources are to lead to development, they will have to encompass a very wide network of participants and activities, all with an innovative approach. Without a strong shift toward science and engineering in the educational system and without intense and persistent learning efforts on the part of companies and the public sector, success is simply not possible, whatever the strategy.

THE IMPORTANCE OF NETWORKS AS SYSTEMS OF INNOVATION

Taken in isolation, endowments in resources or capabilities are insufficient. What is crucial to understand in the contemporary context of NR is the importance that networks (and particularly ICT-enabled networks) play in development. It is no longer useful to see natural resources as just the extracting or farming activity on its own; but it is important to embrace and promote the complete network, from capital goods and other investment requirements through the production and various processing activities, all the way to packaging, distribution, and end use. Such a network of actors and activities is what is now understood as a system of innovation (Lundvall 2007). As shown in figure 11.3, such a system includes innovative potential at every step in the NR process, from exploration, research, design, and engineering to transportation, marketing, and distribution, as well as in the universities, research development and engineering (RD&E) institutes, and knowledge-intensive business services (KIBS) (Urzúa 2012; Perez 2010b), supporting each element of the value chain.

Indeed, such is the complex set of interactions among the many activities involved in the exploitation of NRs nowadays—upstream, downstream, and laterally (Morris, Kaplinsky, and Kaplan 2012)—that it is essential for any development strategy to map and identify the technological opportunity space that will allow the flourishing of a dynamic path within any one of these industries. The spectrum of possibilities is very wide: mining, metallurgy, chemicals, petrochemicals, pharmaceuticals, custom materials, livestock, agriculture, agro-industries, aquaculture, forestry, paper, biotechnology, energy, nanotechnology, tourism, etc. (each includes the range from commodities to specialties). Success in the natural resource industries depends on continuous improvement of technologies, companies, products, and human capital, across networks that encompass research, engineering, and design: construction, adaptation, installation, compatibility, and maintenance; software and systems services; equipment and instruments; laboratory services; quality control, evaluation, measurement, and certificates; conservation and packaging; transport, marketing, and distribution; technical service to users; market intelligence; improvements and new products; patent lawyers; contract negotiation; training and education of specialized personnel; financial services; and so on. This is a far cry from raw materials only.

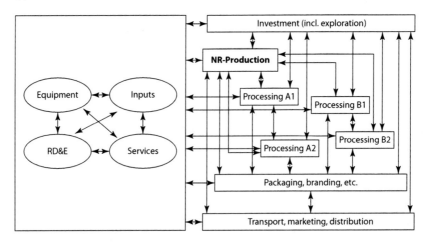

Figure 11.3   Innovative interactions in a natural resource-based network

Source: Perez et al. 2014.

THE FORCES DRIVING INNOVATION IN THE NATURAL RESOURCE NETWORKS

Once it is understood that the unit of analysis for a successful NR strategy is the entire *network*, it becomes important to confirm that there are new conditions making it possible and profitable to innovate in such networks in a developing-country context. Only then can it be seen as realistic to pursue an innovation-intensive path based on the NR endowment of each country or region.

Currently, one can identify several sources of dynamism driving innovation in the natural resource sectors (Perez, Marin, and Navas-Aleman 2014). Some have already come under discussion, as factors in the changing context for development. As shown in figure 11.4, these drivers emerge from four main factors: the growth in market volume, the changes in the market context, the shifts in market requirements, and the advances in ICT and other technologies.

GROWTH IN MARKET VOLUME

Fast-growing global demand for materials and food intensifies the traditional innovation challenges for NR producers. Reaching lower quality and less accessible lands or deposits has always required "remedial"

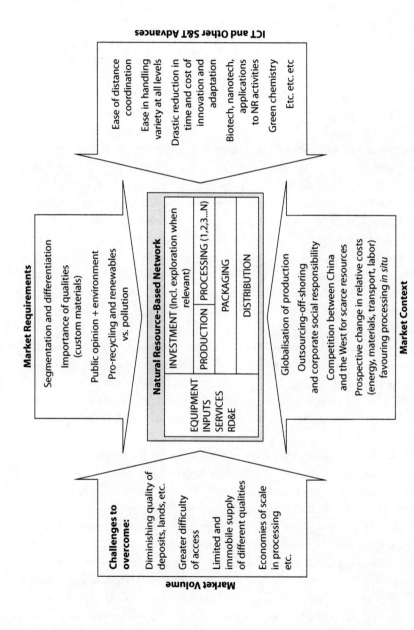

Figure 11.4 The forces driving innovation in the natural resource networks

Source: Perez et al. 2014.

innovation, increasing the cost of marginal supplies and benefiting the better-located ones. Yet, as demand approaches planetary limits, the required innovation effort becomes more complex and usually more costly, tending to raise the average level around which global prices fluctuate[4] (Farooki and Kaplinsky 2012). This has been the case with deep-sea oil and is likely to increasingly characterize food markets as more millions enter the consumption ladder.

Higher prices due to reliable demand growth will stimulate innovation in new production technologies and higher productivity in existing ones. In Argentina and Brazil, the high demand for soya in Asia has led to innovation in production methods such as zero tillage (Ekboir 2003; Bisang 2008) and in seed varieties through biotechnology (Marin and Stubrin 2015). It has also transformed the traditional *chacarero* agriculture of medium-scale farming into a highly technified land rental production system (Bisang 2008). These developments may be as controversial as the "green revolution" in the 1960s, which extended to developing countries the mass production methods of land management, irrigation, mechanization, hybrid seeds, and especially petrochemical fertilizers and pesticides. Social decisions on the balance between the advantages and disadvantages of the new technologies will be on the table, while the new challenges may also lead to environmentally and socially benign alternatives. For instance, Marin, Stubrin, and Van Zwanenberg (2014) discuss the transgenic and cross-breeding approaches as alternatives in terms of both their effectiveness and their implications. Indeed, deciding on the specific *direction* of technical change and economic development will require the participation of a wide range of social actors (Stirling 2008 and 2009).

Once the innovation system moves away from the established practices or usual conditions, it becomes necessary to develop special equipment and inputs. That is indeed what has occurred in both Brazil and Argentina, where equipment for zero-tillage agriculture has encouraged machinery producers to develop specialized seed planters, sprayers, and equipment for residue management and has led to a significant export drive (Garcia 2008). These developments are similar, though on a smaller scale, to the process whereby Norway became a specialized supplier of equipment and services for deep-sea oil production. The Norwegians pioneered such activities after the oil price hike in the 1970s and are now world exporters in the sector (Leskinen, Bekken, Razafinjatovo, et al. 2012).

The context may also be changing in favor of processing locally. Transporting raw materials looks likely to become uneconomical because of rising energy and transport costs, and in any case it may become unacceptable because of environmental policies. Particularly in the case of minerals, raw exports contain a high percentage of waste (in copper, waste is typically 70 percent). Changes in context and relative costs and prices are bound to facilitate negotiations with foreign producers and buyers, in addition to spurring local investment and innovation in processing, perhaps in the direction of more flexible facilities, In essence, although the basic resource exports would continue to be the "bread and butter" income of the country in question, there can be a set of dynamic processes that stimulate innovation, investment, and know-how accumulation upstream and downstream, allowing a greater control of the whole learning network and opening the possibility of lateral innovation, improving other sectors with similar equipment or input requirements (Walker and Jourdan 2003).

CHANGING MARKET REQUIREMENTS

Yet demand is not growing homogeneously. As already discussed, all markets are segmenting into multiple niches, for higher or different qualities as well as in adaptations to specific user requirements. This opens the possibility of innovating to increase the value of the export mix by including a greater proportion of special products. Such premium segments can include special materials and alloys as well as "gourmet" fruit, based on the development of preservation techniques to rescue and export the flavors of nonstandardized products, in addition to the organic products of traditional agriculture.

Lowering the cost of luxury products and raising the quality of standard ones are two of many alternative directions in market differentiation. One of the countries that has taken this route in several sectors is Brazil. The forestry sector, for instance, has developed varieties and treatment of eucalyptus to make it look like and behave as expensive mahogany (Figueiredo 2009) as well as other varieties that boast such improvements in productivity, quality, and environmental protection that the country is now the world quality leader in the production of pulp for paper (Flynn 2003; Figueiredo 2009).

And the opportunities for niche market access enabled by ICT are open to all, large or small, from traditional farmers to the innovative high-technology companies. Producers of niche inputs for production processes can aim at disperse global markets enabled by Internet communication and flexible transport systems. Consumer niche products benefit additionally from the existence of specialized outlets (health food stores, organic markets, gourmet restaurants, luxury product shops, etc.) and from global buyer chains, Fair Trade networks, and so on. The organizational capacities brought by ICT can result in high-volume end users working with small-volume producers in a way that was previously untenable; e.g., the global coffee chain Starbucks, in order to have reliable high-quality supplies of coffee, works with growers in several countries, providing training and guaranteed markets and prices (Duda et al. 2007).

An additional and growing trend that will change the spectrum of market options is the combination of health concerns with social and environmental sustainability. In Brazil, for instance, the organic cosmetics sector is already 10 percent of the market and is exporting and growing (Galvao et al. 2011).

CHANGES IN THE MARKET CONTEXT

The other important feature driving innovation in all sectors is globalization, which has changed not only the location of production but also the character of the global corporation and of the opportunities for potential producers. GCs are taking advantage of doing innovation in the various countries where they operate (Marin 2007) as well as being increasingly willing to contract out tasks requiring technical expertise. The process of outsourcing and offshoring in which most fabricating industries have engaged distinguishes the core competencies that must remain with the GC, the noncore specialized processes that should be outsourced to partners with high capabilities, and the less complex processes that can be outsourced to several suppliers under close monitoring—and most likely accompanied by training—to guarantee quality and reliable delivery. The GC aims to achieve maximum quality at minimum cost, while generating optimum innovation capability and sustained competitiveness across the whole value chain (Prahalad and Hamel 1990). Thus the space and behavior of the global corporations (GCs) are different from the typical enclaves of the old MNCs, providing opportunities for entering and climbing the value ladder, with possibilities of increasing local production and employment upstream and downstream (Ernst and Kim 2002; Gereffi, Humphrey, and Sturgeon 2005; Navas-Aleman 2011).

It is true that the conversion from the old model has not gone as far in the processing- and resource-related industries as in assembly-based ones. But it has begun. De Beers, the traditional giant in diamond production, has been outsourcing successive processing stages to Botswana, contributing to one of Africa's current success stories (Warhurst 2008). BHP Billiton in Chile is engaged in the creation and strengthening of a network of local suppliers, from the simplest services to the most high-tech[5] (Comisión Minería y Desarrollo de Chile 2014). As the trend toward more in situ processing becomes a reality through a shift in the relative costs of energy and transport and/or environmental taxes, foreign companies will be stimulated to increase the links of the value chain to be located at source. Furthermore, the transparency provided by the Internet makes it increasingly difficult for foreign companies to ignore the context in which they operate. Corporate social responsibility (CSR) can be, at a minimum, a form of contributing to the well-being of the community through donations and welfare projects; but at best CSR can elevate local innovation capacities and help to grow the human capital of its own personnel and of the host country.[6]

At the same time, there are increasing possibilities for local companies to globalize, creating regional networks of production and global marketing. Again, this has happened already to a varying extent across Latin America. One of many examples is Cemex, the Mexican cement giant, which now produces in fifty countries around the world, of which about ten are in Latin America; another is the Brazilian steel company Gerdau; still others are evident across the food industry, such as Arcor (Argentina), Bimbo (Mexico), Polar (Venezuela), Noel (Colombia), JBS (Brazil), and so on. Such expansion in the NR processing industries is part of the context changes and has required increasing innovative and adaptive capabilities on the part of erstwhile local companies.

Global and regional geopolitics are also changing, opening opportunities for more effective negotiation. As mentioned before, competition for access to resources between East and West enables innovation capabilities and greater processing to become attainable goals in investment and trade agreements. There may also be greater potential for international agreements such as the new global development pact proposed by Cimoli, Dosi, and Stiglitz (2009) and also in this text. Just as the official recognition of labor unions and subsequent collective bargaining in the age of mass consumption resulted in salaries that increased with productivity and guaranteed growing consumer demand, it could be that advanced countries and GCs would find it to their advantage to have growing markets for sophisticated equipment and goods in a dynamic and advancing developing world (Perez 2013). In the United States at that time, resistance to the required shift was as strong as it is now, and yet the shift did occur and brought the postwar boom.

The environmental challenge is the other shift in market context driving innovation in all sectors, changing the context in which both business and society operate and redefining our concept of the "good life" from one of mass consumption to one that is sustainable. Climate change and other issues of sustainability are resulting in increasing regulation, which is leading to innovation in renewable materials and energy, recyclables, low-energy processing, water-based chemistry, biodegradable materials, and other adaptive capacities. These innovations may also prove an alternative outlet for NR industries facing a backlash against more traditional extractive industries which is due to the danger of resource exhaustion, the threat of increasing air and water pollution and of global warming, and the fear of unpredictable consequences of technological advances (such as genetically modified crops). Such developments will further stimulate efforts to increase productivity and to overcome the limits in supply through innovation.

ADVANCES IN ICT AND OTHER TECHNOLOGIES

While all the above drivers of innovation can be seen as part of the context of the current techno-economic paradigm, many drivers—notably the rise in market volume and the associated environmental concerns—are a consequence of prior surges. However, the direct impacts of ICT technologies on the NR industries are numerous. It is now infinitely easier to establish interactive networks with intense communication for coordination of production and services, logistics, and administration, giving the NR industries the capacity to cooperate in local, regional, and global networks. Distance monitoring—of livestock, oil wells, plantations, fishing areas—is becoming increasingly possible, while intelligent control systems are being developed and used for irrigation, processing, sorting, and distribution. Thus the varieties and peculiarities, in both source and demand, that were problematic in the days of mass production are handled easily with ICT.

Great strides in customization have been made in the life and materials sciences as well as in chemistry, particularly with the use of computerized synthesis. The time and cost of acquiring and processing the necessary information for research and innovation have been drastically reduced. The same can be said about designing experimental prototypes by the user industries and measuring impacts. Innovation can occur in the product mix from research to design to processing to distribution, at which point innovations in transport, distribution, and retail allow for the accommodation of multiple destinies and small quantities.

Biotechnology and nanotechnology are particularly important to the NR industries, which deal after all with biology and materials (Hernandez-Cuevas and Palenzuela 2004). Genetically modified crops, tissue culture as means of plant reproduction, vaccines for cattle and fish, and the use of bacteria for mining (leaching) and for the digestion of oil spills and other polluting agents in water already indicate the many directions in which biotechnology is being applied in NR, while nanotechnology is contributing to innovations in materials and processing, such as the development of energy-saving and pollution-reducing surfaces and of protective coatings for preservation that improve the handling and packaging of natural products.

Currently advances in both biotechnology and nanotechnology are highly dependent on the information-processing capabilities and the accuracy of instruments provided by ICT. Yet they have the potential to unleash a technological revolution of their own. The likelihood is quite high that the breakthroughs which will lead to the next technological paradigm shift may come from these technologies. Participating in their development in these early stages could place the Latin American countries in a good position for a major leap forward when these technologies become all-pervasive, low-cost, and high-growth. This is precisely what the Asians were able to do on the basis of their early involvement with the fabrication of electronic components and products, before the advent of the microprocessor, the personal computer, mobile telecommunications, and the Internet.

Essentially, then, there is no longer a reason to reject natural resources as a possible basis, or springboard, for a dynamic, technologically active strategy based upon them. ICT has allowed the NR-based sector to overcome the conditions which Singer (1950, 476) rightly described when saying that natural resources did not "provide the growing points for increased technological knowledge, urban education, the dynamism and resilience that goes with urban civilization, as well as the direct Marshallian external economies." Yet Singer went on to clarify:

"No doubt under different circumstances commerce, farming, and plantation agriculture have proved capable of being such 'growing points.'" Indeed, the new enabling technologies and the global market context provide a fresh set of possibilities around natural resources that can be used as a springboard for a different direction in industrialization. This takes on an even stronger meaning when one takes into account (1) the difficulty of competing with the Asian nations in the mass fabrication of consumer goods and (2) the growing import demand for basic and specialized industrial inputs and food in those same countries (Kaplinsky 2005). Those export markets can be supplied covering the whole range, from the basic commodities to an increasing proportion of higher value–added products with greater differentiation and adaptability.

A DUAL INTEGRATED STRATEGY

Of immediate concern in considering an NR-based strategy for Latin America is its capacity to create sufficient employment and alleviate poverty, given the income polarization that characterizes the region. The processing industries and innovation activities are not as labor-intensive as assembly production and require increasingly qualified personnel. Thus, while a strategy based on them promises rising incomes and a better quality of life for the participants, it will not be as effective in job creation per unit of investment. Such industries can contribute to economic growth and to the enrichment in human and technical capital—both crucial for catch-up—but they cannot do enough to reduce the gulf between rich and poor, eliminate unemployment, and overcome poverty.

Poverty and unemployment worsened in Latin America during the "lost decade" of the 1980s and have given rise to social discontent, resentment, and an ardent desire for change. Since the "trickle down" effect has not proved its capacity to "raise all boats," the problem needs to be faced directly. Recent improvements in several countries, based more on income redistribution and service or government jobs than on new, good-quality, high-productivity employment, are not sufficient. Policies must be enhanced in any effective strategy for development. Not doing so would be socially unacceptable and politically unstable.

This suggests the need to set up two complementary and simultaneous policies: one is a top-down approach with the goal of economic growth and global positioning, and the other is a bottom-up strategy to ensure full employment and well-being for all, as shown in figure 11.5.

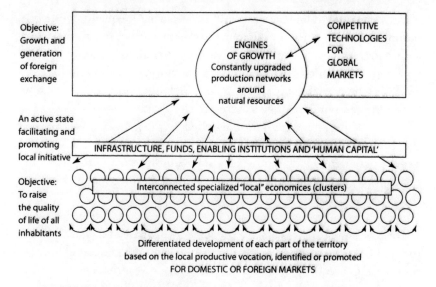

Figure 11.5 A dual integrated strategy: Top-down and bottom-up

This two-pronged approach can be called a *dual integrated model* (Perez 2010a) with both prongs enabled by the new global conditions. The top-down part of the strategy would be oriented toward achieving technological mastery and deep specialization, aiming at global competitiveness. The industries involved—the multifaceted NR networks—would act as the engines of growth of the economy and the main sources of foreign exchange. The bottom-up part of the strategy would involve the promotion of wealth-generating activities in every corner of the territory and differentiated development aimed at whatever market is most suitable: local or regional, national or global. Here the prime objective is to raise the quality of life of all citizens. Yet, since these bottom-up production activities would tend to be in specialized "clusters," targeting niche markets based on local advantages, it would, in turn, feed back into the NR networks, encouraging constantly upgraded production around NR. This type of bottom-up innovation is indeed already occurring on an ad hoc basis, from Fair Trade cooperatives and other localized but networked civil society initiatives to regional developments in bringing technology to poor farmers (Gibson 2005) or advances in modern infrastructure such as mobile banking and distributed energy (Murray 2012). In other words, although in the first area competitiveness is the goal and in the second it is a means, the dual strategy could tackle social inequality while promoting converging processes of growth and innovation. It is through such a dual strategy that a resource-intensive industrialization process would be able to create not only economic growth but also full employment and rising living standards across society, including the rural population, hopefully stemming the flow toward the city slums.

Such a dual strategy cannot be achieved by the market alone, but neither can it effectively be imposed by government, and much less so in the current paradigm which requires constant innovation and the flexibility to adapt to context changes. The model can function properly only as a socially shared vision, with the various agents of change acting autonomously but following a common strategic direction, integrated by an active government that is able to provide an adequate and effective institutional framework. Implementation would require a process of consensus building, involving business, government, universities, and society, as well as subsequent policy measures to induce and facilitate market behavior in the agreed direction(s) (Stirling 2008 and 2009).

The dual model would also require institutional innovations and most likely different agencies providing adequate support for each participant group. The top-down half implies a process of *embedded autonomy* (Evans 1995; Rodrik 2004), in which the top-level public and private actors engage in strategic collaboration to make consensus decisions affecting whole networks that may involve international negotiations, while the bottom-up half would require municipal and local-level agencies, strengthened by the direct support of specialized personnel, able to identify, promote, and facilitate the adequate production and marketing activities, in addition to engaging in training (coaching) and funding. Thus the dual model implies a dual role for government, providing appropriate support on either end, while also engaging in the customary activities relating to infrastructure and human capital which improve the context for all.

CONDITIONS OF VIABILITY: THE CHALLENGES AND THE OBSTACLES

This chapter has endeavored to answer three main questions: Have natural resources become capable of sustaining a dynamic innovative strategy? Are there conditions for the developing countries to innovate in order to take advantage of this opportunity? And if they do so, are there export channels and markets for countries to use them as a springboard for growth and social development? The answer we came to, in all three cases, was positive. The opportunity exists, and it is technologically and economically viable to consider a natural resource–based industrialization strategy. The next question, however, is much more complex and difficult to answer: Are the Latin American countries ready and able to set up such a strategy, and is there a favorable sociopolitical context for them to succeed?

No strategy for development is simple or easy. The challenges presented by the dual development model are major: obstacles that include competition from other potential adopters; the traditional risks associated with NR in addition to many new risks relating to sustainability; conflicts with established power structures; and the difficulty of building political will and consensus around a new strategic direction. Even prior to implementation, technical and social capabilities and courageous institutional innovations are needed to design and build consensus on a common strategic direction, and to design and then implement adequate stimulating and supporting policies.

But none of this is impossible. Indeed, this is a characteristic of every techno-economic paradigm: making what seemed impossible commonsense practice. Establishing adequate institutions and policies is essential to building political will. When setting up ISI, Raul Prebisch (first in CEPAL and then in UNCTAD) initiated a broad program of international negotiations and advisory support, which included the training of a great number of public servants (Dosman 2008). In this instance, a significant amount of accumulated capabilities already exists, especially in top-down activities related to dealing with companies engaged in NR production and export. However, a regional program for the massive training of consultants to aid in the bottom-up part of the strategy would be warranted.

THE NEED FOR ADEQUATE CAPABILITIES AND VISION TO MAKE THE DOUBLE LEAP

Unlike ISI, which was an adequate response to existing conditions but which in Latin America did not create a platform for future growth, the promise of this strategy at this time is that it endows the continent with the potential to make a leap to development in two stages. Because of the nature of technological paradigm shifts, the Latin American countries can achieve growth now by taking advantage of the current window of opportunity for NR producers and can prepare to make a leap in development with the next technological revolution by developing capabilities, companies, and global networks in the sectors of the future (biotechnology, nanotechnology, bioelectronics, new materials, green chemistry, etc.).

Just as the success stories in Asia cannot be repeated because the microelectronics-related opportunity space came and went, the current window of opportunity with the processing industries in relation to natural resources will also pass and a new one will come along.

This is what happened in Asia: it went from ISI and exports in mass production to capitalizing on globalization in the ICT revolution. However, to achieve the equivalent requires intense efforts in training, education, RD&E, and innovative cooperation at all levels and in all stages. This chapter has argued that the context conditions are currently in place, but it remains to be seen whether the Latin American nations already have the social capabilities or would be willing to seriously engage in acquiring them in order to implement these complex efforts.

FACING PROBABLE COMPETITION

The window of opportunity being discussed is open to all resource-rich countries with a certain level of business and technological capabilities. And the dual model strategy is one that could be applied by others. Indeed, it is highly likely that there will be competition on a global scale among producers as well as between the companies and countries that require the resources. In this competitive arena, the advantage will go not only to those possessing the resources with more dynamic demand and higher prices, but also, perhaps more crucially, to those who have already acquired basic technological and social capabilities for producing, negotiating, networking, and innovating. There is a path-dependent character to the "hot spots" of growth in the global economy. In these respects, as this chapter has argued, Latin America has strong foundations on which to build. At the same time, the diversity of resources will result in a variety of competition conditions, and in all these cases it is important not to underestimate the advantage that goes to those who make the first move. The countries that first attract the investors and allies who bring the technologies, and those that more intensively engage in learning and innovating, acquire dynamic advantages that put them in a better competitive position.

TRADITIONAL OBSTACLES AND NEW UNCERTAINTIES

There are, of course, numerous risks involved in embarking on such a strategy. Obstacles and uncertainties abound. Price volatility for both raw materials and processed products will warrant not only national policies to minimize the negative impacts but also possibly concerted international action. The so-called Dutch disease, affecting the potential for investment and export competitiveness, also remains a problem to confront even in the new market conditions. Addressing it might require a well-devised "rent management" policy, together with stemming corruption practices through transparency mechanisms (they, too, perhaps in coalition with the advanced countries).

New uncertainties appear in relation to climate change, which looks likely to negatively affect agricultural resources, even as it opens up space for innovation. Similarly, environmental policies may affect demand in one area while they open up new possibilities in another. The threat of the overexploitation of resources is ever present, while biotechnology and other radical innovations present solutions that could involve new risks. All these sustainability issues might also lead to a backlash against the use of NR, and any resource-based strategy will have to take these valid concerns into account together with the public opinion that they generate.

A POLITICAL AND POLICY CHALLENGE

Any new strategy will encounter political resistance from across the political spectrum, both internally and externally. The strategy recommended here has the added difficulty of requiring a conceptual shift, placing innovation at the *core* of growth and development policy, rather than as a specialized, isolated component of industrial policy (Mazzucato and Perez 2014). In practical terms, this means moving the science and technology agenda from the fringes of the cabinet in marginal ministries or councils to the very center of the strategy to be pursued. Equally, training and educational policy would need to shift from a quantitative effort to a much more complex and "mission-oriented" endeavor (Mazzucato and Penna 2015), with intense collaboration between the public and private sectors and the willingness to take advantage of foreign sources of the required knowledge. If there is a single timeless lesson that can be learned from the success of the Four Asian Tigers, it is their emphasis on learning, both internal (within companies) and external (in public and private education and training systems).

Conflicts of interest will always remain, even without the difficulties presented by the varying levels of corruption across the region, and especially in those countries with a less developed democratic system and a public sector that is more politicized, less stable, and less technical. Winning over the traditional groups who control the natural resource sectors may not be easy in some regions, while not all global corporations are likely to be ready to participate in such a strategy. In the face of these constraints, achieving a positive-sum game between business and society will be a major challenge.

In addition, any specialization strategy, particularly when associated with natural resources, confronts market risks in both volume and prices and requires monitoring of future trends and intelligent hedging.

Nevertheless, all successful strategies involve facing challenges and risks while taking advantage of the opportunities that are also present. The aim of this chapter has been to argue that (1) the possibility of building a platform for development by innovating across the value network around natural resources exists in the new market conditions and (2) while important, the sources of the "natural resource curse" can be addressed through strategic policies. The networks of NR production and their multiple linkages upstream, downstream, and laterally present an innovation space of higher profitability that the probable trends in the global economy will do nothing but expand. The drawbacks and risks involved in any strategy will increase if they are not recognized and if adequate safeguards are not incorporated. But at present, the greatest risk of all is for Latin American countries to miss the boat—to ignore the current window of opportunity and turn their backs on the possibility of making a double leap to development.

NOTES

I want to thank Tamsin Murray-Leach for her excellent support in editing and preparing this manuscript and Caetano Penna for his useful comments.

Centennial Professor at the London School of Economics (LSE), UK, Professor of Technology and Development, Nurkse Institute, Tallinn University of Technology, Estonia, and Honorary Professor, SPRU, University of Sussex, UK

1. Throughout this chapter, the terms *industry* (*industries*) and *industrialization* are broadly conceived, beyond a narrow focus on *manufactures* and *manufacturing* in the sense of fabrication by assembly, to encompass not only the processing industries but also high-tech services and, in general, all activities that involve technological advance in any of their stages.

2. The policy was also implemented in Africa, but too late for those nations to fully benefit.

3. In Latin America, the tariff level during ISI was customarily calculated in relation to the local cost of producing the equivalent product, so there was no incentive for productivity increases, let alone innovation. As the model moved toward export promotion in the mid-1970s, subsidies tended to be calculated in a similar manner and had no expected tapering in time.

4. This effect has to be disentangled from that provoked by financial speculation.

5. This practice of multiplying world-class mining services has now become national strategy in Chile (Corfo 2014).

6. An example is the Alcatraz Project of the Santa Teresa Rum company in Venezuela, which has rescued hundreds of young people in the area from drugs and violence by training them, teaching them to work in construction or in its own plants, creating a rugby team that competes internationally, engaging the women in the community in production activities and several other forms of social integration that have changed the atmosphere in that relatively poor district of the central valleys in the country. The project has been so successful that it has attracted the support of several international and local organizations and continues to grow and expand its activities. See http://www.fundacionsantateresa.org/inicia_pa.php?lang=esp.

REFERENCES

Acemoglu, D., S. Johnson, and J. Robinson. 2002. "Reversal of Fortune: Geography and Institutions in the Making of the Modern World Income Distribution." *The Quarterly Journal of Economics* 117 (4): 1231–94.

Amsden, A. H. 1989. *Asia's Next Giant: South Korea and Late Industrialization*. New York: Oxford University Press

Anderson, C. 2006. *The Long Tail: Why the Future of Business is Selling More of Less*. New York: Hyperion.

Auty, R. 1990. *Resource-Based Industrialization: Sowing the Oil in Eight Developing Countries*. Oxford: Clarendon Press.

———. 1993. *Sustaining Development in Mineral Economies: The Resource Curse Thesis*. London: Routledge.

Bell, M., and K. Pavitt. 1993. "Technological Accumulation and Industrial Growth: Contrasts Between Developed and Developing Countries." *Industrial and Corporate Change* 2(2): 157–211.

Bell, R. Martin. 2006. "How Long Does It Take? How Fast Is It Moving (if at All)? Time and Technological Learning in Industrialising Countries." *International Journal of Technology Management* 36(1/2/3): 25–39.

Bisang, R. 2008. "The Argentine Agricultural Scene: Recent Changes, Future Challenges and Latent Conflict (ARI)." November. Real Instituto Elcano. http://www.realinstitutoelcano.org/wps/portal/rielcano_eng/Content?WCM_GLOBAL_CONTEXT=/Elcano_in/Zonas_in/Latin+America/ARI 111–2008. Accessed on July 7, 2009.

Cimoli, M., G. Dosi, and J. Stiglitz. 2009. "The Future of Industrial Policies in the New Millennium: Toward a Knowledge Centered Development Agenda." In *Industrial Policy and Development*, ed. M. Cimoli, G. Dosi, and J. Stiglitz, 541–60. Oxford: Oxford University Press.

Comisión Minería y Desarrollo de Chile, eds. 2014. "Minería, Una Plataforma de Futuro para Chile." Consejo Nacional de Innovación para el Desarrollo, Gobierno de Chile, Diciembre 2014. http://www.economia.gob.cl/wp-content/uploads/2014/12/Mineri%CC%81a-Una-Plataforma-de-Futuro-para-Chile.pdf.

Corfo. 2014. "Programa Proveedores de Clase Mundial: Catálogo de Proyectos 2013–2014." Corfo, Gobierno de Chile. http://catalogo.corfo.cl/cgi-bin/koha/opac-detail.pl?biblionumber=4223&shelfbrowse_itemnumber=4373#shelfbrowser.

Dobbs, R., J. Oppenheim, F. Thompson, M. Brinkman, and M. Zornes. 2011. *Resource Revolution: Meeting the World's Energy, Materials, Food and Water Needs*. London: McKinsey Global Institute, McKinsey and Co.

Dore, R. 1989. "Latecomers' Problems." *The European Journal of Development Research* 1(1): 100–07.

Dosman, Edgar J. 2008. *The Life and Times of Raúl Prebisch, 1901–1986*. Kingston, Montreal: McGill–Queen's University Press.

Duda, S., L. James, H. Lee, Z. Mackwani, R. Munoz and D. Volk 2007. "Starbucks Corporation: Building a Sustainable Supply Chain." Stanford Graduate School of Business. HBS Case studies.

Ekboir, J. 2003. "Research and Technology Policies in Innovation Systems: Zero Tillage in Brazil." *Research Policy* 32(4): 573–86.

Ernst, D., and L. Kim. 2002. "Global Production Networks, Knowledge Diffusion, and Local Capability Formation." *Research Policy* 14: 1417–29.

Evans, P. 1995. *Embedded Autonomy: States and Industrial Transformation*. Princeton, N.J.: Princeton University Press.

Farooki, M. Z., and R. Kaplinsky. 2012. *The Impact of China on Global Commodity Prices: The Global Reshaping of the Resource Sector*. London: Routledge.

Figueiredo, P. 2009. "Industrial Policy, Innovation Capability Accumulation and Discontinuities." Paper presented at the Copenhagen Business School Summer Conference, June 17–19.

Flynn, B. 2003. "Eucalyptus: Having an Impact on the Global Solid-Wood Industry." *Wood Resources International*. http://www.wri-ltd.com/marketPDFs/Eucalyptus.pdf. Accessed on July 19, 2009.

Freeman, C., and F. Louçã. 2001. *As Time Goes by: From the Industrial Revolutions to the Information Revolution*. New York: Oxford University Press.

Freeman, C., and C. Perez. 1988. "Structural Crises of Adjustment: Business Cycles and Investment Behaviour." In *Technical Change and Economic Theory*, ed. Dosi et al., 38–66. London: Pinter.

Galvão, A., M. Juruá, L. Esteves, and F. Castanheira. 2011. "The Amazon Region and the Use of Its Biodiversity." Sectorial Report for the IDRC project. From *Opening up Natural Resource-Based Industries for Innovation: Exploring New Pathways for Development in Latin America*. https://dl.dropboxusercontent.com/u/29408306/NR%20Project_Sectorial%20Report_Brazil.pdf.

Garcia, G. 2008. "The Agricultural Machinery Industry in Argentina: From Restructuring to Internationalization?" *CEPAL Review* 96: 223–39.

Gereffi, G., J. Humphrey, and T. Sturgeon. 2005. "The Governance of Global Value Chains." *Review of International Political Economy* 12(1): 78–104.

Gerschenkron, A. 1962. "Economic Backwardness in Historical Perspective." In *Economic Backwardness in Historical Perspective*, 5–30. Cambridge, Mass.: Belknap Press.

Gibson, A. 2005. "Bringing Knowledge to Vegetable Farmers: Improving Embedded Information in the Distribution System." *The KATALYST Cases*, Case Study Number 1. http://www.springfieldcentre.com/wp-content/uploads/2012/10/sp0502.pdf.

Goldemberg, J. 2011. "Technological Leapfrogging in the Developing World." *Georgetown Journal of International Affairs*, 12(1): 135–41.

Gylfason, T., T. Tryggvi, and Z. Gylfi. 1999. "A Mixed Blessing: Natural Resources and Economic Growth." *Macroeconomic Dynamics* 3 (June): 204–25.

Hernandez-Cuevas, C., and Pablo Palenzuela. 2004. "Strategies to Capture Biotechnology Opportunities in Chile." *Electronic Journal of Biotechnology* 7(2): 174–90.

Jaffee, S., and O. Masakure. 2005. "Strategic Use of Private Standards to Enhance International Competitiveness: Vegetable Exports from Kenya and Elsewhere." *Food Policy* 30(3): 316–33. http://www.sciencedirect.com/science/article/pii/S0306919205000333 - aff2.

Kaplinsky, R. 2005. *Globalisation, Poverty and Inequality: Between a Rock and a Hard Place*. Cambridge: Polity.

Leskinen, O., P.K. Bekken, H. Razafinjatovo, and M. García. 2012. *Norway Oil and Gas Cluster: A Story of Achieving Success Through Supplier Development*. Boston, Mass.: Harvard Business School.

Lundvall, B.-A. 2007. "National Innovation Systems—Analytical Concept and Development Tool." *Industry and Innovation* 14(1): 95–119.

Marichal, C. 1988. *A Century of Debt Crises in Latin America*. Princeton, N.J.: Princeton University Press.

Marin, A. 2007. "Thinking Locally: New Approaches to Foreign Direct Investment." *SCi-DEV*, 1 January. http://web.scidev.net/en/policy-briefs/thinking-locally-new-approaches-to-foreign-direct-.html.

Marin, A., L. Navas-Aleman, and C. Perez. 2010. "The Possible Dynamic Role of Natural Resource-Based Networks in Latin American Development Strategies." *Globelics Working Paper* 43-1, April. http://umconference.um.edu.my/upload/43-1/papers/292%20AnabelMarin_LizbethNavas-Aleman_CarlotaPerez.pdf.

Marin, A., L. Navas-Aleman, and C. Perez (2015) "Natural Resource Industries as a Platform for the Development of Knowledge Intensive Industries" in *Tijdschrift Voor Economische en Sociale Geografie (Journal of Economic and Social Geography)*, 106 (2):154–68.

Marin, A., and L. Stubrin. 2015. Innovation in Natural Resources: New Opportunities and New Challenges. The Case of the Argentinian Seed Industry. *UNU-Merit Working Paper*, Maastricht. http://www.merit.unu.edu/publications/wppdf/2015/wp2015-015.pdf. Accessed February 2015.

Marin, A., L. Stubrin, and P. Van Zwanenberg. 2014. "Developing Capabilities in the Seed Industry: Which Direction to Follow?" *SPRU Working Paper Series*, SWPS 2014–12, June 2014. https://www.sussex.ac.uk/webteam/gateway/file.php?name=developing -capabilities-in-the-seed-industry.pdf&site=25. Accessed February 2015.

Mazzucato, M., and C. C. R. Penna, eds. 2015. *Mission-Oriented Finance for Innovation: New Ideas for Investment-Led Growth.* London: Policy Network.

Mazzucato, M., and C. Perez. 2014. "Innovation as Growth Policy: The Challenge for Europe." In *The Triple Challenge: Europe in a New Age,* eds. J. Fagerberg, S. Laestadius, and B. Martin. London: Oxford University Press, chap. 9, pp. 227–62 [early version as *SPRU Working Paper Series* SWPS 2014–13, July 2014. https://www .sussex.ac.uk/webteam/gateway/file.php?name=2014-13-swps-mazzucato-perez .pdf&site=25.

Morris, M., R. Kaplinsky, and D. Kaplan. 2012. "'One Thing Leads to Another'— Commodities, Linkages and Industrial Development." *Resources Policy* 37(4): 408–16.

Murray, R. 2012. "Global Civil Society and the Rise of the Civil Economy." In *Global Civil Society 2012,* ed. Helmut Anheier, Marlies Glasius, and Mary Kaldor. London: Palgrave Macmillan.

Navas-Aleman, L. 2011. "The Impact of Operating in Multiple Value Chains for Upgrading: The Case of the Brazilian Furniture and Footwear Industries." *World Development* 39(8): 1386–97.

Nurkse, R. 1958. "The Quest for a Stabilization Policy in Primary Producing Countries." *Kyklos,* 11(2): 139–265.

Perez, C. 1985. "Microelectronics, Long Waves and Structural Change: New Perspectives for Developing Countries." *World Development* 13(3): 441–63.

——. 2001. "Technological Change and Opportunities for Development as a Moving Target." *CEPAL Review* 75 (December): 109–30.

——. 2002. *Technological Revolutions and Financial Capital: The Dynamics of Bubbles and Golden Ages.* Cheltenham: Elgar.

——. 2008. "A Vision for Latin America: A Resource-Based Strategy for Technological Dynamism and Social Inclusion." *Globelics* Working Paper No. 2008–04. http:// dcsh.xoc.uam.mx/eii/globelicswp/wp0804-en.pdf.

——. 2010a. "Dinamismo tecnológico e inclusión social en América Latina: una estrategia de desarrollo productivo basada en los recursos naturales." *Revista CEPAL* 100: 123–45.

——. 2010b. "Hacia la PYME latinoamericana del futuro: Dinamismo Tecnológico e Inclusión Social." In *SELA: PYMES como factor de integración: 35 años de esfuerzo continuo del SELA,* 111–23. Barquisimeto, Venezuela: Editorial Horizonte.

——. 2013. "Unleashing a Golden Age After the Financial Collapse: Drawing Lessons from History." *Environmental Innovation and Societal Transitions* 6: 9–23.

Perez, C., and L. Soete. 1988. "Catching Up in Technology: Entry Barriers and Windows of Opportunity." In *Technical Change and Economic Theory,* eds. G. Dosi et al., 458–79. London: Pinter.

Perez, C., A. Marin, and L. Navas-Aleman. 2014. "The Possible Dynamic Role of Natural Resource Based Networks in Latin American Development Strategies."

In *National Innovation Systems, Social Inclusion and Development*, eds. G. Dutrenit and J. Sutz, 380–412. Cheltenham: Elgar.

Prahalad, C. K., and G. Hamel. 1990. "The Core Competence of the Corporation." *Harvard Business Review*, May-June: 79–91. https://hbr.org/1990/05/the-core-competence-of-the-corporation.

Prebisch, R. 1950. "The Economic Development of Latin America and Its Principal Problems." United Nations Dept. of Economic Affairs.

——. 1951. *Estudio Económico de América Latina 1949*. New York: CEPAL.

Reinert, E. S., ed. 2004. *Globalization, Economic Development and Inequality: An Alternative Perspective*. Cheltenham: Elgar.

Rodrik, D. 2004. "Industrial Policy in the Twenty-First Century." *KSG Working Paper* No. RWP04–047.

Sachs, J., and A. Warner. 1995 (revised 1997 and 1999). "Natural Resource Abundance and Economic Growth." *National Bureau of Economic Research*. Working Paper No. 5398.

——. 2001. "The Curse of Natural Resources." *European Economic Review* 45(4/6): 827–38.

Singer, H. 1949. "Economic Progress in Underdeveloped Countries." *Social Research: An International Quarterly of Political and Social Science* 16(1): 9–11.

——. 1950. "The Distribution of Gains between Investing and Borrowing Countries." *American Economic Review* 44(2): 473–85.

——. 1975. *The Strategy of International Development: Essays in the Economics of Backwardness*. White Plains, N.Y.: International Arts and Sciences Press.

Stevens, P., and E. Dietsche. 2008. "Resource Curse: An Analysis of Causes, Experiences and Possible Ways Forward," *Energy Policy* 36(1): 56–65.

Stirling, A. 2008. "'Opening Up' and 'Closing Down' Power, Participation, and Pluralism in the Social Appraisal of Technology." *Science, Technology & Human Values* 33(2): 262–94.

——. 2009. "Direction, Distribution and Diversity! Pluralising Progress in Innovation, Sustainability and Development." *STEPS Working Paper*, vol. 32.

The Economist. 1977. "The Dutch Disease." November. 26: 82–83.

Torvik, R. 2002. "Natural Resources, Rent Seeking and Welfare." *Journal of Development Economics* 67: 455–70.

Urzúa, O. 2012. "Emergence and Development of Knowledge-Intensive Mining Services (KIMS)." *Working Papers in Technology Governance and Economic Dynamics*, No. 41. The Other Canon Foundation and Tallinn University of Technology.

Wade, R. H. 1992. "East Asia's Economic Success: Conflicting Perspectives, Partial Insights, Shaky Evidence." *World Politics* 44(2): 270–320.

Walker, M., and P. Jourdan. 2003. "Resource-Based Sustainable Development: An Alternative Approach to Industrialisation in South Africa." *Minerals & Energy—Raw Materials Report* 18(3): 25–43.

Warhurst, A. 2008. "How Botswana Leverages Growth." *Business Week*, April 30. http://www.businessweek.com/globalbiz/content/apr2008/gb20080430_874526 .htm. Accessed on July 19, 2009.

Wright, G. 1997. "Toward a More Historical Approach to Technological Change." *The Economic Journal* 107: 1560–66.

CHAPTER 12

Manufacturing Development

THE ROLE OF COMPARATIVE ADVANTAGE, PRODUCTIVITY GROWTH, AND COUNTRY-SPECIFIC CONDITIONS

Nobuya Haraguchi

INTRODUCTION

The chapter examines the trends of productivity changes in manufacturing industries and determines the role of comparative advantage, productivity growth, and country-specific conditions in manufacturing development. Comparative advantage is exemplified by the development potential of different industries at various levels of gross domestic product (GDP) per capita, which, in turn, has strong correlations with a country's human and capital resource endowments and the relative costs of production factors. To indicate the level of a country's technological capability, labor productivity growth is used as a proxy to understand its relation to developments in manufacturing subsectors. Finally, to understand the distinct experiences and potentials of countries' manufacturing development, the chapter investigates country-specific conditions that are both positive and negative deviations from the development patterns.

Early development literature provides evidence of the association between the initial surge of modern economic growth and the sustained shift in the share of economic activities from agriculture to manufacturing (Clark 1957; Kuznets 1966). In turn, authors from the different schools of economics emphasize the significance of structural change within the manufacturing sector, i.e., upgrading the industrial structure to sustain industrialization (Taylor 1969; Chang 2003; Felipe 2009; Lin 2011).

In his proposition for new structural economics, Lin emphasizes the importance of structural change based on the comparative advantages of a country, which are largely shaped by the country's resource endowment structure (Lin and Monga 2011; Lin 2011). He highlights the dynamic and catalytic role of the manufacturing sector in economic development and argues that a country moves from one manufacturing industry to another, given that the development trajectory of each manufacturing industry follows an inverted-U shape. Lin does not seem to concur with the possibility of a country leap-frogging to industries in which it does not have a comparative advantage. He perceives the government's role as priming the pump to facilitate industrial upgrading in relation to changes in comparative advantage, as moving to a new industry involves risks and will not be optimal if left to the market alone.

One school of thought places much greater weight on technological capability and the competitiveness of industries than on the comparative advantages of a country as guiding points for economic development. According to this school, defying comparative advantage (to certain limitations) and building the technological capability required for industries that are more advanced than those based on a country's comparative advantage are crucial for industrialization (Lin and Chang 2009). The government is expected to play a much more active role and to implement industry-specific policies rather than to simply improve infrastructure and correct coordination failures.

In this chapter I do not provide evidence to support one of these representative views on development. Nor do I propose an appropriate level and types of government intervention conducive to a country's development. The aim of this chapter is to discuss the empirical results to better understand how comparative advantage, productivity growth, and country-specific conditions drive industrial development. To illustrate the three factors' respective roles in the path of development, in this chapter I analyze the evolving patterns of manufacturing industries and corresponding changes in productivity.

The starting point of this analysis is to identify the intersection of these two schools of thought. Both acknowledge the manufacturing sector as the engine of economic development as well as the significance of the sector's continuous structural upgrading to sustain that engine. The manufacturing industry may offer more opportunities than other sectors in product diversification (Imbs and Wacziarg 2003), structural upgrading that deepens the industrial structure, and productivity increase. Rodrik points out that unlike the case of the economy as a whole, countries' manufacturing sectors reveal unconditional convergence. The further a country is behind the technological frontier in a manufacturing industry, the faster that industry's labor productivity will grow (Rodrik 2011).

One of the disagreements among economists who believe that the manufacturing industry plays a key role in economic development relates to the given subsector in manufacturing that a country ought to enter or focus its development efforts on at different stages of development. On one hand, those who put weight on comparative advantage recommend to countries to align their development strategies with the signals arising from a country's changing endowment structure, which shifts only gradually. On the other hand, others focus on the prospects and types of technological development that manufacturing industries could generate and their long-term potential contribution to the economy in general. Still others stress the role of government to provide support for long-term investment in human and physical capital (World Bank 1993).

In this chapter I provide evidence of how different development aspects, such as comparative advantage, technological improvements, and country-specific conditions, may relate to manufacturing development. In the next section I discuss the data and methodologies and follow with an analysis of the results.

DATA, VARIABLES, AND ESTIMATIONS

To illustrate the development trajectories of individual manufacturing subsectors (hereafter referred to as *manufacturing industries* or simply *industries*) and to draw policy implications, I examine changes in the real value added per capita in relation to an increase in public-private partnership (PPP) adjusted GDP per capita[1] instead of changes in the value-added share of each industry.[2] An analysis based on changes in value added per capita allows one to gain insights into the development characteristics of each industry; unlike in the case of changes in value-added shares of individual manufacturing industries within the total manufacturing value added, the calculation is not affected by the rise and fall of other industries. However, taking a comparative perspective across industries is important for understanding changes in the relative importance of industries, since the rise of one industry inevitably affects others through the transfer of production factors. The development patterns of the different industries are therefore compared with one another.

The analysis is conducted for the manufacturing industries at the two-digit level of the International Standard Industrial Classification (ISIC) revision 3. There are 23 industrial categories in total. However, as countries often report industries 18 and 19, 29 and 30, 31 and 32, and

34 and 35 together, I combined each pair into one industrial category to have a consistent data set across countries. Furthermore, I dropped industry 37, recycling, as it has been reported by only a very limited number of countries. Table 12.1 presents the industrial classifications used in this study. Ideally, real value added should be calculated as an output in constant price, excluding various purchases from other industries valued in constant prices. However, such price-adjusted data are not available for a large number of countries, in particular for developing countries, to reliably estimate the development patterns of manufacturing industries. Alternatively, to adjust changes in price, I use the *index of industrial production* (IIP) which is available at the two-digit level of the ISIC. Some countries have already begun reporting their industrial data based on the latest ISIC revision (revision 4); however, I use the IIP based on revision 3 of the ISIC, which has been widely used since the mid-1980s. To obtain a longer time series data, UNIDO has combined the IIP of revision 2 of the ISIC, which goes back to the early 1960s, with revision 3 to arrive at an IIP that covers the years 1963 to 2004 based on revision 3 of the ISIC. Multiplying such a series of volume indices by the value added of a given base year—1995 in the case of this study—made it possible to approximate real value added for a time series.[3] However, the IIP is available for only around 70 countries. Hence, when this approach is used, approximately 50 countries that do not have an IIP—but for which the nominal value-added data for their manufacturing industries are available—cannot be included in regressions to estimate manufacturing development patterns. Since many countries without an IIP are developing and emerging nations, it is important to also reflect their development trajectories in the estimations of manufacturing structural change.

The sector wide *manufacturing value added* (MVA) deflators are available for most of the countries without an IIP. However, applying an MVA deflator across manufacturing industries might produce biases, as inflation rates from one industry to another could differ significantly (e.g., between the food and beverages industry and the petrochemical industry) for given years.[4] To reflect the industry-specific inflation trend, I decomposed the respective country's manufacturing-wide deflation, using an inflation structure based on the same year's IIP of another country located in the same region and at a relatively similar development stage. Using this approach, I try to reflect industry-specific inflation trends by equating the sum of the nominal value added divided by the sum of the

Table 12.1 Manufacturing Data Classification Used in This Study

ISIC description	Abbreviation	ISIC Code
Food and beverages	Food and beverages	15
Tobacco products	Tobacco	16
Textiles	Textiles	17
Wearing apparel, fur and leather products, and footwear	Wearing apparel	18 and 19
Wood products (excluding furniture)	Wood products	20
Paper and paper products	Paper	21
Printing and publishing	Printing and publishing	22
Coke, refined petroleum products, and nuclear fuel	Coke and refined petroleum	23
Chemicals and chemical products	Chemicals	24
Rubber and plastic products	Rubber and plastic	25
Nonmetallic mineral products	Nonmetallic minerals	26
Basic metals	Basic metals	27
Fabricated metal products	Fabricated metals	28
Machinery and equipment not elsewhere classified and office, accounting, computing machinery	Machinery and equipment	29 and 30
Electrical machinery and apparatus; radio, television, and communication equipment	Electrical machinery and apparatus	31 and 32
Medical, precision, and optical instruments	Precision instruments	33
Motor vehicles, trailers, semitrailers, and other transport equipment	Motor vehicles	34 and 35
Furniture; manufacturing not elsewhere classified	Furniture, not elsewhere classified	36

real value added of manufacturing industries with the country's MVA deflator. This approach allows me to include around 70 countries with an IIP and 50 countries without an IIP in these estimations. Appendix A explains this procedure in detail.

Past studies acknowledge that country size has an overarching influence on economic structural change (Chenery and Taylor 1968), with effects on both the intercepts and the slope of the estimated patterns. Thus, instead of including population in the equation as an additional explanatory variable, many studies resort to dividing countries into size groups, applying a certain population size as a threshold. The problem related to this approach in past studies has been that this threshold was often arbitrarily used without determining whether such groups differ statistically in terms of their development patterns. To classify countries into three groups of different sizes, I applied thresholds to divide them into small, medium, and large countries, and I examined at which threshold level the maximum number of manufacturing industries is obtained whose development patterns statistically differ from one another. I achieved this by applying the Wald test. Based on the results, I used thresholds of 3 million and 12.5 million to divide countries into small, medium, and large countries. In accordance with these thresholds, medium-sized countries with a population from 3 million to 12.5 million have different development patterns than small-sized countries with populations of less than 3 million for 13 out of 18 manufacturing industries. The development patterns of all industries in large-sized countries with populations over 12.5 million differ from those of medium-sized countries.

It does not suffice to divide countries into three groups by using the above method to unequivocally claim that a distinct pattern emerges for each group. Ideally, countries in the same group should have at least statistically equal coefficients for the slopes, if not for both the intercepts and slopes. To determine whether countries within the same group have similar development patterns, I examined the statistical significance of both the individual country intercepts and the slopes of the explanatory variables used in the estimations. Individual country intercepts are significant across most of the countries and industries, and therefore it can be inferred that countries differ in terms of intercept levels. Individual slopes are statistically insignificant for the majority of countries across all industries, which indicates that countries in different size groups do not significantly differ from one another in terms of slope.

It is assumed that industries undergo three development stages—pre-takeoff, growth, and decline—following the pattern of a cubic function. However, those industries that can sustain growth over a long time may have a more linear development trajectory, while other industries that experience growth from a very early stage of development and decline only at a later stage may indicate a more quadratic pattern. Hence, I included cubic and square terms of GDP per capita in the equation in order for the results to denote possible patterns of manufacturing development, depending on the statistical significance of these GDP per capita terms. The objective of the study is to ascertain how industries in countries of different size groups are likely to develop. It is therefore useful to first consider only the relationship between value added per capita and GDP per capita to tease out the "average" industrial development patterns of the different country size groups. To control for the effect of unobserved country-specific conditions, I apply the fixed effect estimation procedure. For this purpose, equation (12.1) is used for each manufacturing industry in the three groups of countries of different size:

$$\ln RVA^i_{ct} = \alpha_1 + \alpha_2 \times \ln RGDP_{ct} + \alpha_3 \times \ln RGDP^2_{ct}$$
$$+\alpha_4 \ln RGDP^3_{ct} + \alpha_c + e^i_{ct} \tag{12.1}$$

Subsequent analyses address how demographic and geographic conditions shape the groupwide average pattern to demonstrate which other country conditions, aside from a country's development stage, affect the level of manufacturing development. Thus, the regression equation includes variables for population density POPD and natural resource endowment (RPC).[5]

$$\ln RVA^i_{ct} = \alpha_1 + \alpha_2 \times \ln RGDP_{ct} + \alpha_3 \times \ln RGDP^2_{ct} + \alpha_4 \times \ln RGDP^3_{ct}$$
$$+\alpha_5 \times \ln POPD_{ct} + \alpha_6 \times \ln RPC_{ct} + \alpha_c + e^i_{ct} \tag{12.2}$$

The subscripts c and t denote country and year, respectively, whereas i signifies the respective manufacturing industry where RVA is real value added per capita. As for the right-hand side variables:

$RGDP$ = real GDP per capita
$RGDP^2$ = real GDP per capita squared
$RGDP^3$= real GDP per capita cubed
$POPD$ = population density
RPC = natural resource endowment per capitai[6]
α_c = country fixed effect
e^i_{ct} = unexplained residual

Both dependent and explanatory variables are expressed in logarithmic terms to measure the elasticity of each variable. The regression results are presented in appendix B.

RESULTS AND ANALYSIS

In this section, first I identify the development trajectories of industries and how the growth potentials shift from one industry to another along a country's development path to determine whether there are any indications of the existence of comparative advantages at different stages of development. Subsequently, a given industry's development pattern is analyzed together with the patterns of the industry's labor productivity changes to elucidate the role of technological development and gain further insights into the relevance of comparative advantage in industrial development. Finally, I investigate how income levels, demographic and geographic conditions, and other country-specific factors affect the development patterns of manufacturing industries. In view of the limited space in this chapter, only eight industries in the manufacturing sector are analyzed—food and beverages, textiles, wearing apparel, chemicals, basic metals, fabricated metals, electrical machinery and apparatus, and motor vehicles—which are considered representative of the different characteristics of the manufacturing sector in terms of their periods of emergence in a country's general and technological development. For convenience, industries are classified into early, middle, and late industries on the basis of the criteria indicated in the note to table 12.2. The eight industries studied here are shown in bold font in the table.

PATTERNS OF MANUFACTURING DEVELOPMENT

As discussed above, I identified distinct patterns of development for each industry and group. Figure 12.1 illustrates the development patterns of the eight selected industries in large countries with a population of more than 12.5 million.

The food and beverages industry is typically the first to take off, reaching an elasticity of 1 (i.e., the industry starts growing faster than the rate

Table 12.2 Development Stages of Manufacturing Industries

Early	**Food and beverages**, tobacco, **wextiles, wearing apparel**, wood products, publishing, furniture Nonmetallic minerals
Middle	Coke and refined petroleum Paper **Basic metals** **Fabricated metals**
Late	Rubber and plastic **Motor vehicles** **Chemicals**, machinery and equipment, **electrical machinery and apparatus**, precision instruments

Note: Manufacturing subsectors are classified into early, middle, and late industries if an industry's share in GDP is estimated to peak before US$ 6,500 GDP per capita in Purchasing Power Parity (PPP) at constant 2005 price, between US$ 6,500 and US$ 15,000, and after US$ 15,000, respectively. These income ranges correspond to our income classifications—low and lower middle, upper middle, and high incomes—in terms of GDP per capita PPP. In the table, industries are listed from those that peak at lowest income level to those that peak at the highest income level in terms of their value-added shares in GDP. Industries that peak approximately at the same income level are listed horizontally.

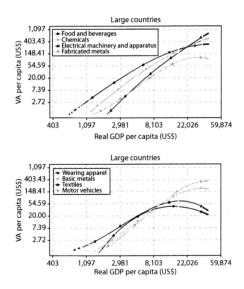

Figure 12.1   Development patterns of manufacturing industries in large countries

Source: Produced by the author based on regression estimations.

of GDP per capita) with less than US$ 100 GDP per capita. Other early industries shown here are the textiles and wearing apparel. Aside from the food and beverages industry, the early industries, including tobacco and wood products (which are not shown in the figure), tend to start slowing down earlier than other industries. It is estimated that the tobacco and wood products industries will start growing slower than the per capita growth rate in large countries when these countries reach around US$ 5,000 GDP per capita. The same slowdown is expected to kick in for the textiles and wearing apparel industries at a GDP per capita level between US$ 7,000 and US$ 10,000. The chemicals industry belongs to the late industry group, but it emerges at a relatively low income owing to the production of some basic chemicals, such as dying materials, and sustains the fast growth over a long income range because of structural changes within the industry.

The electrical machinery and apparatus, motor vehicle, fabricated metal, and basic metal industries start their development later and can sustain their growth rates longer than the early industries, with the exception of the food and beverages industry. Among these sectors, the middle industries, such as basic metals and fabricated metals, begin declining earlier than the others, when countries reach an approximate GDP per capita level between US$ 17,000 and US$ 20,000, respectively. The motor vehicle industry is expected to start growing slower than per capita growth rate at a GDP per capita level of around US$ 25,000. The electrical machinery and apparatus industry is the most sustainable industry and can maintain a fast growth rate for a long time. Though not included in the figure, the rubber and plastic as well as the machinery and equipment industries also maintain a faster-than-the-economy growth rate until the country reaches around US$ 30,000 and US$ 45,000 GDP per capita, respectively.

Next, the manufacturing development patterns of large countries are compared with those of medium and small countries (see figures 12.2 and 12.3). For each industry, the development patterns of the three country groups are shown together in appendix C. The dotted lines, which represent industries at a low and high GDP per capita levels, especially in small countries, signify limited data availability and consequently may be less reliable representations of the development patterns. Generally, the sequence of development among industries in medium and small-sized countries is similar to that in large ones. As is the case in large countries, the food and beverages, textiles, and wearing apparel industries tend to also develop and have a larger share in terms of value added in the manufacturing sector during the early stage of a country's development. Among these, the food and beverages industry is more sustainable.

Some differences are evident among the three country groups. The early industries seem to hold more dominant positions in the manufacturing sector from the low to the middle income stages in medium and small countries in comparison with large ones (see figures 12.2 and 12.3). Furthermore, the early industries in medium and small countries reach their peak points (at which their value added per capita begins to decline) earlier than large countries do.

For example, the textiles industry of medium and small countries is likely to start declining when a country's GDP per capita rises to US$ 7,000 to US$ 10,000, while the decline of that same industry in a large country normally occurs after a GDP per capita level of US$ 15,000 has been reached. In the case of the food and beverages industry, the decline begins at around US$ 20,000 to US$ 30,000 GDP per capita for medium and small countries as opposed to around US$ 45,000 for large countries.

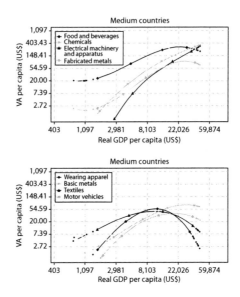

Figure 12.2 Development patterns of manufacturing industries in medium-sized countries

Source: Produced by the author based on regression estimations.

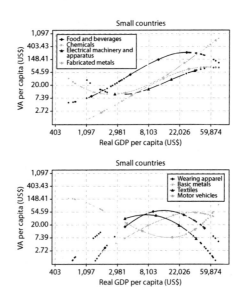

Figure 12.3 Development patterns of manufacturing industries in medium-sized countries

Source: Produced by the author based on regression estimations.

With regard to the middle industries, which predominate over the early industries at a later stage of development, the basic metal and fabricated metal industries of medium and small countries are less sustainable than those of large countries.

The basic metal industries of medium and small countries start growing slower than the economy at a GDP per capita level of approximately US$ 10,000 to US$ 13,000, and the fabricated metal industry reaches that point at around US$ 15,000 to US$ 16,000 of GDP per capita, while the same slowdown becomes evident in large countries at a GDP per capita level that is US$ 5,000 higher than the equivalent in medium and small countries for the basic metal industry and US$ 2,000 higher, respectively, for the fabricated metal industry.

Larger countries, in particular, tend to have an advantage over smaller ones in the basic metal industry. The estimated highest value-added per capita level that the basic metal industry can reach in large, medium, and small countries is US$ 191, US$ 76, and US$ 51, respectively. However, country size does not significantly impact the development of industries based on higher processed products such as the fabricated metal industry.

As figures 12.1, 12.2, and 12.3 indicate, the most notable difference between small countries and other countries is the limited development prospects of the electrical machinery and motor vehicle industries in small countries. The electrical machinery industry of small countries begins to decline before reaching a value added of US$ 100 per capita, while it maintains a fast growth rate in medium and large countries, even at a high income level, and reaches a much higher level of value added per capita. The motor vehicle industry has very limited prospects for successful development in small countries. Economies of scale play a crucial role in the development of this industry, and country size seems to be of relevance. The motor vehicle industry (including parts and accessories) in medium-sized countries may reach a certain level of development, while the industry has a much higher development potential in large countries.

The above analyses on manufacturing development patterns within and across country groups of different sizes indicate that certain patterns exist in the sequence of manufacturing development which correspond with countries' development stages. Furthermore, the development potential of each industry differs among and across countries of different sizes. Thus, through market mechanisms and, if necessary, with government facilitation, countries need to shift resources from one industry to another to foster the development of those industries that offer advantages in a particular stage of a given country's development. Among the industries selected in this study, the chemicals, electrical machinery and apparatus, and fabricated metal industries of medium-sized countries are comparable to those of large countries in terms of the sustainability of their growth. Small countries do not seem to benefit from industries that require economies of scale to produce a large volume of materials for further processing, such as the textiles and basic metal industries. Small countries do not, however, seem to have less of an advantage in processing industries, namely, in the wearing apparel, fabricated metal, and chemical industries, although the emergence of these industries in small countries may be slower than in the other countries.

INDUSTRIAL DEVELOPMENT AND CHANGES IN PRODUCTIVITY

The patterns of industrial development identified above purport the existence of comparative advantages in the sense that a given development period exists in which each manufacturing industry tends to prosper and, consequently, dominant industries change in accordance with a country's development, which proceeds with its changes in endowment structure. However, productivity growth may also be a reason behind the development of an industry. In that case, it is difficult to identify the clear-cut effects of comparative advantage on industrial development or even its existence. To further elucidate this, the patterns of both value-added per capita and labor productivity changes are combined to analyze the role of the latter in industrial development.

Figures 12.4, 12.5, and 12.6 illustrate how value added per capita (industry size in terms of value) and labor productivity change as GDP per capita increases for the eight industries introduced above. Thereby, some interesting attributes of industries are unearthed and provide insights into the question raised in this subsection. For some early industries such as textiles and wearing apparel, labor productivity does not seem to play a significant role in their development. On one hand, during their rapid growth period, labor productivity does not generally increase much, although degrees of difference do exist between the various country size groups. On the other hand, an increase in labor productivity in the later stages of their development does not seem to change the course of the industries' decline in terms of valued added per capita. The results indicate that labor productivity increases once these early industries mature because less competitive firms exit the industries and the remaining

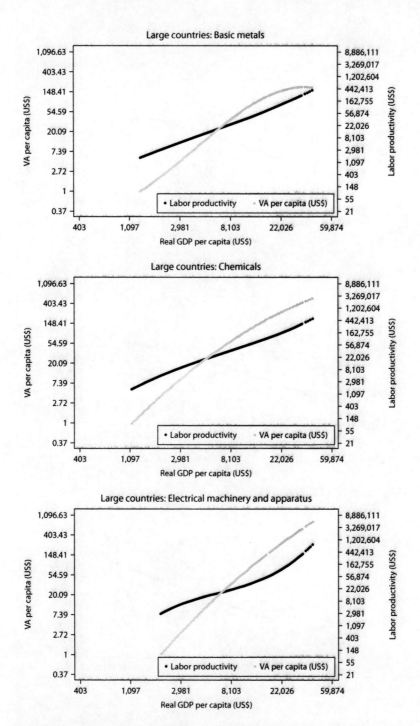

Figure 12.4   Development patterns of value added per capita and labor productivity of manufacturing industries in large countries

Source: Produced by the author based on regression estimations.

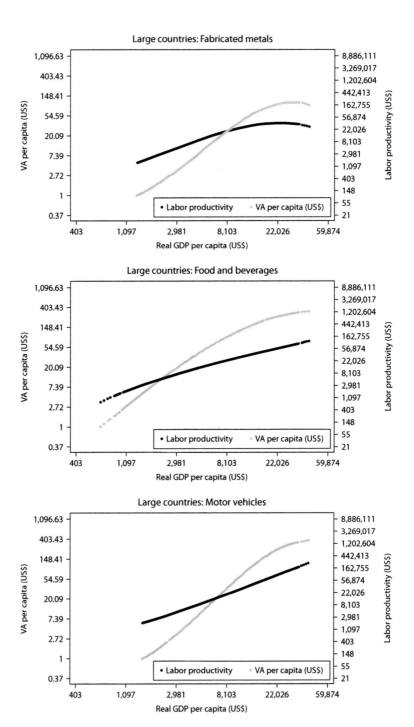

Figure 12.4   (*Continued*)

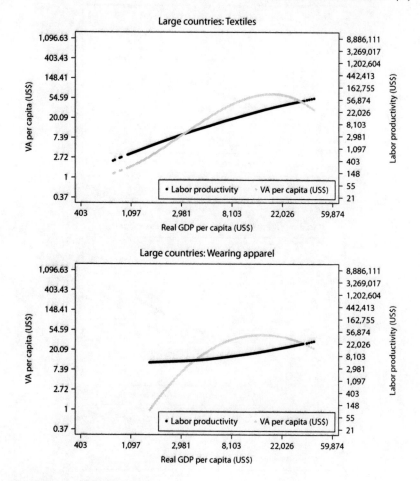

Figure 12.4   (*Continued*)

firms replace labor with capital as the wage rate increases. This represents a strong case for the role of comparative advantage in the growth of these industries, as the stage of development together with the related endowment structure seems to be a major determinant for the industries' development.

The role of comparative advantage in the growth of the other industries may not be as obvious as in the case of the early industries, but the effects of comparative advantage on the growth of each industry becomes visible when one is looking at the points at which industries begin losing this advantage. For example, the value added per capita

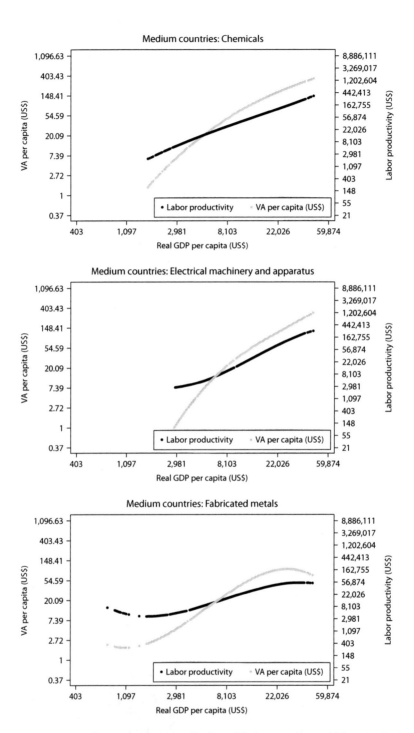

Figure 12.5 Development patterns of value added per capita and labor productivity of manufacturing industries in medium-sized countries

Source: Produced by the author based on regression estimations.

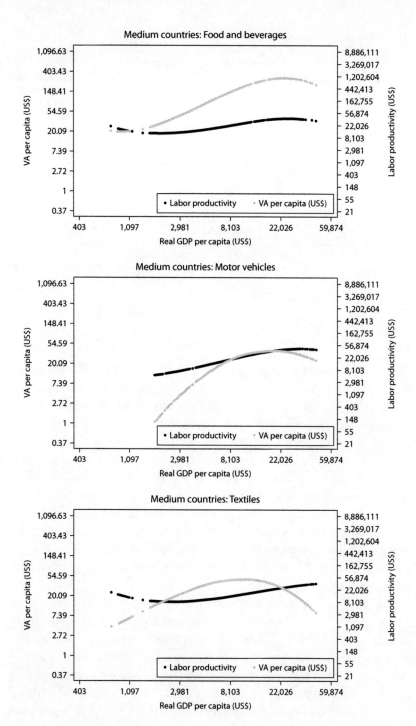

Figure 12.5 (*Continued*)

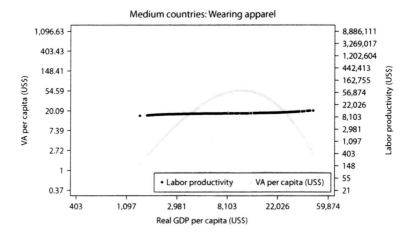

Figure 12.5 (*Continued*)

of the basic metals industry starts slowing down and declining at certain stages of development, even though the growth of labor productivity remains more or less unchanged. It is likely that an industry begins to lose its comparative advantage around the time the growth rate of valued added per capita becomes lower than that of labor productivity. Before reaching this point, the increase in productivity brought higher returns in terms of valued added per capita—higher than the efforts made to increase productivity—seemingly by a dint of the comparative advantage. However, once the growth of value added per capita starts becoming smaller than that of productivity, an increase in the industry's productivity translates to an increasingly smaller rate of the industry's expansion, again due to the onset of the industry's insurmountable comparative disadvantage.

Likewise, the approximate time period of the loss of comparative advantage for each industry can be estimated by dividing the growth rate (slope) of value added per capita by the growth rate (slope) of labor productivity across GDP per capita levels. An elasticity value that is smaller than 1 and signifies the percentage increase in value added per capita for a 1 percent increase in labor productivity implies that the industry is disadvantaged relative to the industries that have a value higher than 1. Figures 12.7, 12.8, and 12.9 illustrate how this elasticity changes on average and when industries lose their comparative advantage.

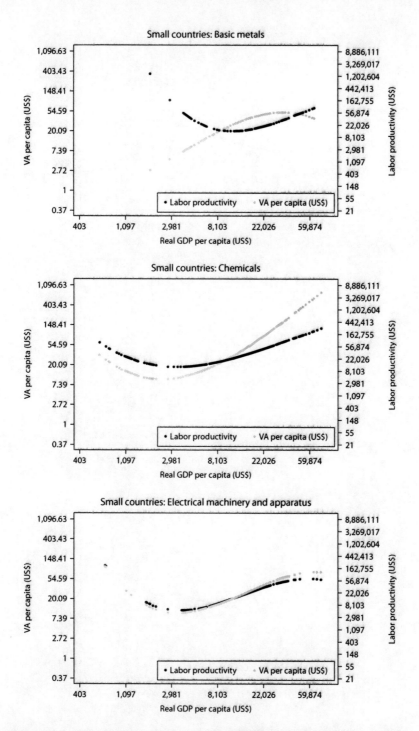

Figure 12.6 Development patterns of value added per capita and labor productivity of manufacturing industries in small countries

Source: Produced by the author based on regression estimations.

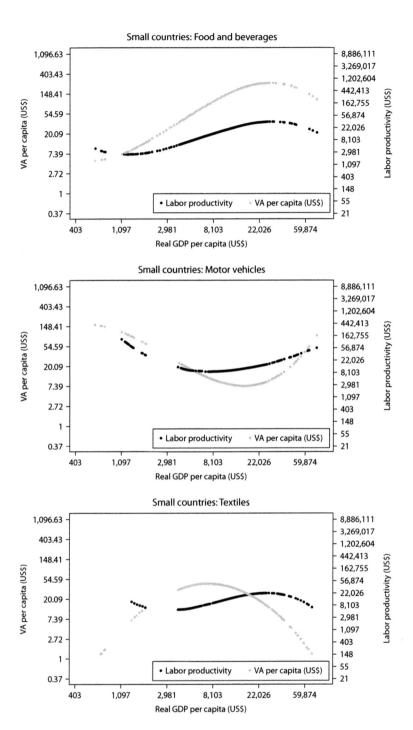

Figure 12.6 (*Continued*)

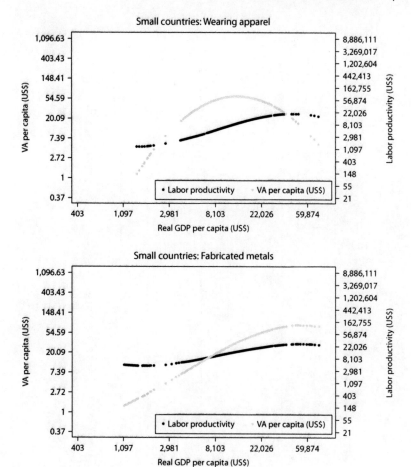

Figure 12.6   (*Continued*)

As figure 12.7 exemplifies, large countries lose comparative advantage in the textiles (S17) and wearing apparel (S18) industries when they reach GDP per capita levels of around US$ 9,000 and US$ 10,000, respectively (which are the levels that fall below an elasticity of 1 in the graph). As expected, advantages in these industries cease earlier than in the other industries included in this analysis. The extreme change in the elasticity of the fabricated metals industry (S28) is attributable to the decline of productivity before the value added per capita begins to fall. However, it can be presumed that this industry's advantage ceases at the latest once the

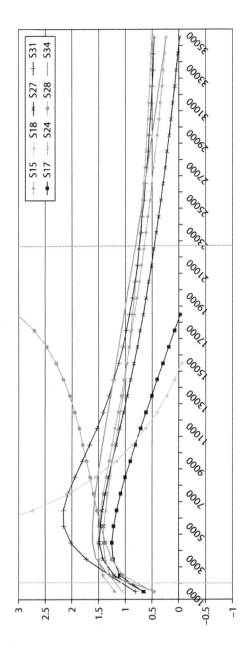

Figure 12.7 Elasticity changes (% change in value added per capita per % change in labor productivity) in accordance with GDP per capita increase for large countries

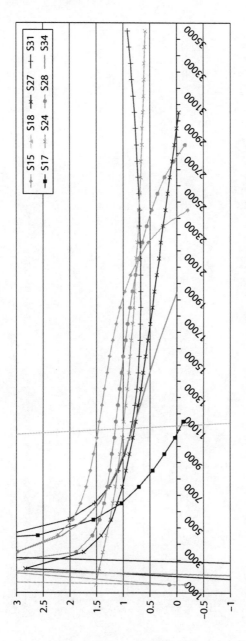

Figure 12.8 Elasticity changes (% change in value added per capita per % change in labor productivity) in accordance with GDP per capita increase for medium-sized countries

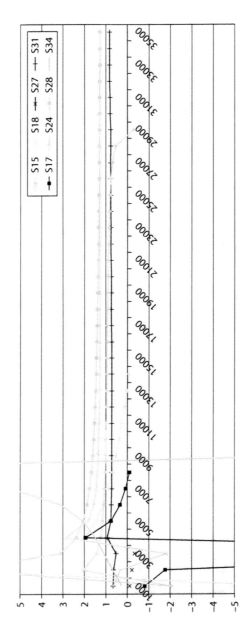

Figure 12.9 Elasticity changes (% change in value added per capita per % change in labor productivity) in accordance with GDP per capita increase for small countries

value added per capita starts declining. Following the textiles and wearing apparel industries, large countries are likely to lose their advantage in basic metals production (S27) at around US$ 13,000 GDP per capita. Next, the chemicals (S24), food and beverages (S15), electrical machinery and apparatus (S31), and motor vehicles (S34) industries lose their advantage (in that order). The difference in the slopes of the descending lines between the early (except for food and beverages) and the other industries is worth noting. In the case of the textiles and wearing apparel industries, advantages decline rapidly despite an increase in labor productivity. Yet for late-emerging industries, such as the electrical machinery and apparatus industry, a rise in productivity is associated with the growth of the given industry much longer than with that of the textiles and wearing apparel industries, even after the advantage has ceased at an elasticity of 1. In other words, a loss of comparative advantage also seems unavoidable for the late industries, but unlike most of the early industries, they can potentially extend the growth through productivity increase.

In the case of medium-sized countries, as illustrated in figure 12.8, there are shorter time lags in the decline of comparative advantage of both the textiles (S17) and the wearing apparel (S18) industries and that of others, excluding the chemicals (S24) and the electrical machinery and apparatus (S31) industries. With the exception of these two industries, it also appears that productivity increase has more limited effects on the sustenance of the growth of the late-emerging industries, as evidenced by their shorter right-hand tails. Their productivity declines either soon after the value added per capita begins to deteriorate or the value added per capita drops despite the continued increase in productivity. The case of the motor vehicle industry (S34) is representative of this difference. Large countries lose their advantage in the motor vehicle industry at a GDP per capita level of around US$ 20,000. Medium-sized countries tend to pass this stage at one-half of that GDP per capita level. There seems little advantage for medium-sized countries in the motor vehicle industry. However, the chemicals (S24) and the electrical machinery and apparatus (S31) industries indicate good prospects for sustained growth.

Figure 12.9 shows that small countries lose comparative advantage in the textiles (S17) and the wearing apparel (S18) industries earlier than large and medium-sized countries. As already discussed in the above sections, small countries tend to have better prospects of development in the relatively high-level processing industries such as the chemicals (S24) and the fabricated metals (S28) industries, and small countries can expect to reach levels of development in per capita terms which are comparable to those of large and medium countries. Figure 12.9 shows that even though the electrical machinery and apparatus (S31) industry may also look advantageous for small countries due to the continued and fast increase of value added per capita compared with the growth in productivity, the decline of the industry starts at a much lower level of value added per capita than in large or medium countries (see appendix C). The level of development of the electrical machinery and apparatus industry is much higher in large and medium countries, and its contributions to their economies are much greater.

SPEED AND LEVELS OF INDUSTRIAL DEVELOPMENT

The previous subsections have shown that a country's stage of development, which is associated with endowment structure, and size imply a comparative advantage for specific industries which seem to have a significant effect on manufacturing development at different stages of development. An improvement in productivity is not likely to considerably alter such patterns, although this could potentially extend the survival, in particular, of relatively capital-intensive industries. If countries with similar demographic and geographic conditions generally share patterns of shifts in comparative advantage, do some countries rapidly climb the growth curve of advantageous industries and accelerate the shifts in comparative advantage?

To determine whether productivity growth plays a role in speeding up industrial development, this subsection investigates the relationship between the growth rate of value added per capita and that of productivity. In view of the above discussion, I know that the growth rate of industries changes in accordance with the country's stage of development, and I therefore focus on only a GDP per capita range of US\$ 3,000 to US\$ 6,000, which demonstrates a comparatively linear growth trend for most of the industries, as illustrated in figures 12.1, 12.2, and 12.3. I take the highest and lowest values of the value added per capita of each country, which fall within that range of GDP per capita. Then I take the labor productivity in those two years which correspond to the highest and lowest values of value added per capita and calculate their annual growth rates. I prepare these two data sets for each country that has data in the specified range, and I regress the growth rate of the value added per capita on that of labor productivity for each industry. This analysis uses the data of all available countries together without dividing the countries into three size groups, because only a limited number of countries have data for the given value-added per capita range of each industry.

Table 12.3 presents the results. All coefficients are positive and significant at 95 percent or higher levels. The higher the growth of labor productivity, the faster a country moves in the development trajectories of the eight industries. This correlation is higher for more capital- and technology-intensive industries and lower for labor-intensive ones.[7] The results confirm that productivity growth plays a role in speeding up a country's structural transformation. Productivity growth is especially important for late-emerging, advanced industries while productivity and other factors, such as wage rate, may be associated with the growth of early-emerging labor-intensive industries. Comparative advantage is associated with a specific stage of development, but productivity growth can facilitate the process of moving from one advantage to another by rapidly exploiting the current advantage.

So far the discussion has addressed the trajectories (slope) and speed of manufacturing development. Countries with a similar size have statistically common development patterns, and higher productivity is associated with a faster rate of development. Hence, the slopes of the trajectories and movement on them are linked to development patterns and productivity.

The lines in the figures discussed above are drawn using the intercepts of the fixed-effect model before including country-specific conditions

Table 12.3 Correlations between Growth of Value Added per Capita and Labor Productivity

	Coefficient	t Value	p Value
Food and beverages	0.7614	6.26	0.0000
Textiles	0.4418	3.85	0.0000
Wearing apparel	0.3857	2.57	0.0130
Chemicals	0.8573	7.55	0.0000
Basic metals	1.4851	9.66	0.0000
Fabricated metals	0.8563	4.93	0.0000
Electrical machinery and apparatus	1.0727	5.90	0.0000
Motor vehicles	1.0775	6.37	0.0000

Independent variable: change in labor productivity per year

Dependent variable: change in value added per capita per year

GDP range: US$ 3,000 – US$ 6,000

in order to exemplify the general patterns of industrial development. However, the level of a country intercept, which reflects country-specific conditions, differs from country to country and, in addition to the general pattern and speed of the movement on that pattern, this unique country intercept is the third element which plays a role in a country's manufacturing development.

We identify two types of country-specific conditions. The first type includes country-specific conditions that are ubiquitous and have similar patterns of impact on industries across countries, though the degree or intensity of these conditions differs from country to country. The extent to which such conditions are present in a given country affects the level of an industry's development. The second type of country-specific conditions are not easily discernible and remain a country-specific advantage or disadvantage for manufacturing development even after controlling for all conditions which belong to the first type. For example, natural resource endowments are a country-specific condition that belongs to the first type, because an abundance of resources tends to have a negative effect on the development of certain industries across countries. However, some countries may be capable of effectively managing their natural resources and thus avoid any negative effects on and possibly even promote the development of manufacturing industries. This special capability represents the second type of country-specific conditions and is included in the country fixed effect of our model. We consider the first type of country-specific conditions first to determine how and what types of generally observable country conditions influence manufacturing development. For the second type of country-specific conditions, it is, by nature, only possible for us to imply the underlying factors related to the unique country conditions.

The variables examined for the first type of country-specific conditions are those relating to demographic and geographic conditions over which a government has no or limited control, at least in the short to medium term. The average group-wide patterns are shaped by the country conditions but are nonetheless considered exogenously determined—these patterns are "given" before any individual country policies have an effect. In addition to the size effect accounted for by dividing countries into three size groups whose development patterns statistically differ, variables reflecting the levels of population density and natural resource endowments are included, in addition to the polynomial terms of GDP per capita in the equation (see equation 12.2).

The results are presented in table B.2 of appendix B. The effects of population density and resource endowment on industries are summarized in tables B.4 to B.6 of appendix B, depicting those industries that are most positively and most negatively affected (only statistically significant ones). An abundance of natural resource endowment is considered a negative factor, particularly for large countries, as it reduces the development potential of two thirds of their manufacturing industries. This condition has especially negative effects on capital-intensive industries. It is noteworthy that the electrical machinery and apparatus industry, which is presumed to be a leading industry at a late stage of a country's development, is negatively affected by a high level of resource endowment for large and medium countries. Population density seems to mostly have a positive effect on capital-intensive industries while it usually has the opposite effect on labor and resource intensive industries. Thus, the effects of these demographic and geographic conditions on the industries included in tables 12.4, 12.5, and 12.6 shift the average patterns upwards or downwards, depending on the intensity of the given country's conditions.

After controlling for these given conditions, countries still deviate from the patterns as a result of the second type of country-specific conditions which are captured by country fixed effects. These are, by nature, unique to a country and are barely discernible when using available indicators. Such country-specific conditions are considered to be related to a deeper level of determinants which affect the outcome of manufacturing development. To gain a general overview of what might be linked to country fixed effects, regressions are run to determine the relationship between the extent of country fixed effects and the conditions which seem to remain in place for a fairly long time and affect industrial development. The following results in table 12.7 confirm that the extent of positive deviation relates to a country's unique features, including capabilities, competency, work ethic, or some other special circumstances which impact the level of infrastructure (a useful proxy for this is the share of paved roads in the country), rule-of-law perception, and unit labor costs. These factors relate to the general business climate which changes only through long-term functional government support in education and physical capital improvements.

As is true in the general business climate, there seem to exist some common factors that are important for the success of all manufacturing industries. Table 12.8 classifies large countries, which reported data at least for 12 out of 18 industries, into three groups, depending on whether their

Table 12.4 Large Countries

	Population Density	Resource Endowments
Positive ↑	Food and beverages Coke and refined petroleum Chemicals Rubber and plastic Nonmetallic minerals Basic metals Fabricated metals Machinery and equipment Electrical machinery and apparatus Motor vehicles	
Negative	Tobacco Wearing apparel Wood products Furniture, not elsewhere classified	Food and beverages Tobacco Wood products Paper Coke and refined petroleum Chemicals Nonmetallic minerals Basic metals Fabricated metals Electrical machinery and apparatus Motor vehicles

(Vertical axis label: Marginal effect, ranging from Positive to Negative)

performances across different manufacturing industries are consistent. As seen there, 63 percent of the countries had either above or below performance relative to the average of large countries for more than 80 percent of their manufacturing industries. Only 12 out of 32 countries had mixed performance depending on the industries. This implies the overarching benefits of improving fundamental conditions common across manufacturing industries, such as infrastructure, general levels of education and skills, and political and macroeconomic stabilities.

Table 12.9 depicts, as contributions to R^2, the extent to which income level (GDP per capita), geographic and demographic conditions (population and natural resources), and country fixed effects explain the

Table 12.5 Medium Countries

	Population Density	Resource Endowments
Positive	Coke and refined petroleum Chemicals Rubber and plastic Nonmetallic minerals Basic metals Machinery and equipment	Wearing apparel Paper
Negative	Tobacco Textiles Wearing apparel Paper Furniture, not elsewhere classified	Wood products Electrical machinery and apparatus Motor vehicles Furniture, not else- where classified

Marginal effect (vertical arrow spanning from Negative to Positive)

level of value added per capita of manufacturing industries.[8] GDP per capita makes the largest contributions to R^2 for all country size groups, although its contributions is much lower in small countries than in large and medium-sized countries. Population density and natural resource endowment usually represent only a small fraction of the explanation for manufacturing development. However, our results also indicate that these two factors explain more than 10 percent of the variance in value added per capita of wood products in medium and small countries and of the coke and refined petroleum, machinery and equipment, and electrical machinery and apparatus industries in small countries. While the contributions of GDP per capita to R^2 are lower in small countries relative to the other country groups, the weight of country fixed effects is twice as

Table 12.6 Small Countries

	Population Density	Resource Endowments
	Food and beverages Paper Printing and publishing Chemicals Nonmetallic minerals Machinery and equipment	.
	Textiles Wood products Fabricated metals Motor vehicles Furniture, not elsewhere classified	Nonmetallic minerals

Positive / Negative (Marginal effect)

high in the explanation of manufacturing development in small countries than in medium or large countries. These results confirm that income level is the most important factor associated with manufacturing development for all countries. However, manufacturing development in small countries is relatively more susceptible to country-specific capabilities and circumstances.

Income level has the highest explanatory power for manufacturing development patterns. However, there are certain income levels at which uncertainties of such patterns are relatively high. Figure 12.10 shows the 95 percent confidence intervals of six manufacturing industries in large countries representing the industries of different characteristics. As seen

Table 12.7 Correlations Between the Size of Country Fixed Effects and Business Conditions

	Unit Labor Cost	Rule of Law	Roads
Food and beverages	−0.20 (−6.7)	1.80 (−23.16)	0.07 (−3.97)
Textiles	−0.22 (−3.63)	4.42 (−32.84)	0.94 (−28.08)
Wearing apparel	−0.65 (−18.56)	3.62 (−25.31)	0.72 (−22.96)
Chemicals	−0.66 (−14.1)	1.56 (−10.84)	−0.20(−6.23)
Basic metals	−0.39 (−10.92)	2.19 (−13.19)	−0.07 (−1.52)
Fabricated metals	−0.19 (−4.29)	3.48 (−32.03)	0.78 (−33.36)
Electrical machinery and apparatus	−0.55 (−9.32)	2.87 (−17.3)	0.74 (−21.33)
Motor vehicles	−0.04 (−0.71)	5.60 (−28.98)	1.31 (−33.07)

Note: The dependent variable used for the regressions is country fixed effects. The numbers in parentheses are t values. Unit labor cost was calculated as nominal wage divided by real value added. The variables for the rule of law and road conditions are based on the Worldwide Governance Indicators and the World Development Indicators of the World Bank, respectively.

Table 12.8 Consistency of Manufacturing Performance in Large Countries

1. Consistently high performance across most of the manufacturing industries	Brazil, Canada, France, Germany, Italy, Japan, Republic of Korea, Netherlands, Spain, United Kingdom, United States
2. Consistently low performance across most of the manufacturing industries	Ethiopia, India, Indonesia, Iran, Kenya, Philippines, Turkey, Egypt, Yemen
3. Performance depending on industries	Australia, China, Colombia, Malaysia, Mexico, Morocco, Peru, Poland, Romania, Russian Federation, South Africa, Sri Lanka

Source: Produced by the author based on UNIDO INDSTAT database.

Note: Large countries (with more than 12.5 million of population) are included as they had data to calculate the fixed effects for more than 12 industries. When countries have higher performance than the average of large countries for more than 80 percent of their reported industries, they are put in the first category in the table. When countries have lower performance than the average of large countries for more than 80 percent of their reported industries, they are put in the second category. Countries that fall in neither of the above are placed in the third category.

Table 12.9 Contributions of GDP per Capita, Population Density, Natural Resource Endowment, and Country Fixed Effects to R^2 of Equation (12.2)

	Contributions to R^2 (%)		
	Large	Medium	Small
GDP per capita	82.0	76.2	57.5
Population density and natural resource endowment	1.5%	3.1	2.2
Country fixed effects	16.5	20.7	40.3

in the figures, the confidence intervals tend to be wider at low and high ends of the income range. Similar trends are observed for medium and small countries. This seems to indicate that low-income countries tend to face a high level of uncertainty because of the significant influence of country-specific conditions over manufacturing developments, leading to a wider variance in their performances among countries. However, once the industries take off and start accumulating experience, the differences in the performance among countries at the same income level get smaller. As countries come close to the end of the upper-middle income stage (at around US$ 15,000 GDP per capita in terms of PPP in 2005 constant prices), once again they start having wider differences in performance. The greater uncertainty in manufacturing development from this stage onward often occurs when countries are graduating from manufacturing development through the acquisition of existing technologies from advanced countries and are moving to a stage where they have to take more risks to generate knowledge and technology themselves to directly compete with technology leaders (Lee 2013).

DISCUSSION

The analyses depict the trajectories of manufacturing development, which proceed in accordance with the stage of a country's development and differ in accordance with its demographic and geographic conditions. This chapter has identified the role of comparative advantage, productivity, and country-specific conditions in manufacturing development and how they influence the potential and actual performance of manufacturing industries at different stages of development. This section connects the three factors of manufacturing development by describing the factors' key elements and their interrelationships to elucidate the nature of manufacturing development and to draw some policy implications.

Broadly speaking, countries with comparable demographic and geographic characteristics tend to follow a similar pattern of manufacturing development, even though countries may follow a similar pattern at different output levels. The growth and decline depicted by each development pattern are posited to have overarching influence on manufacturing development and imply the existence of comparative advantage, which in turn relates to a country's endowment structure. Thus, a loss of comparative advantage and the eventual sunset of industries due to a shift in endowment structure are difficult to prevent through productivity

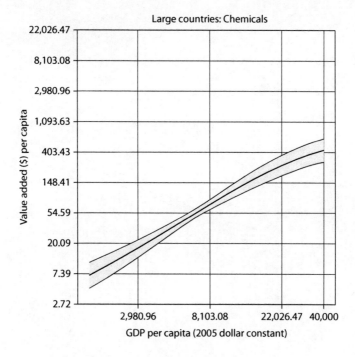

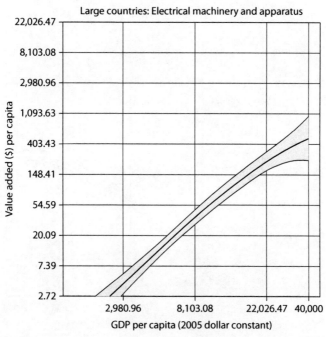

Figure 12.10   Confidence intervals for the estimated patterns, value added (large countries)

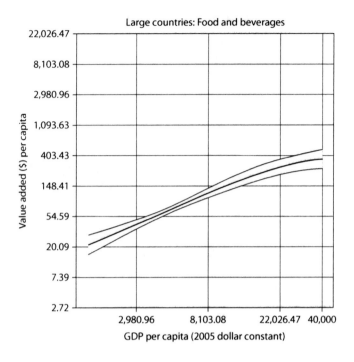

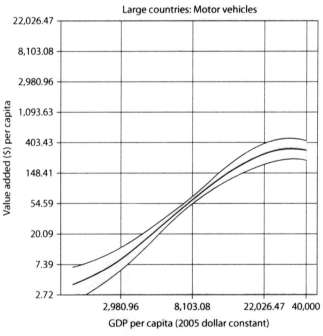

Figure 12.10 (*Continued*)

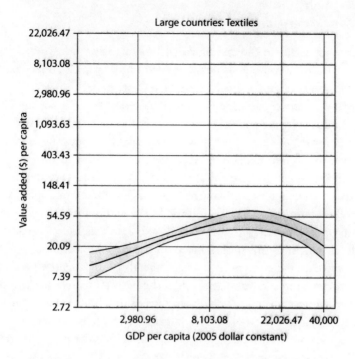

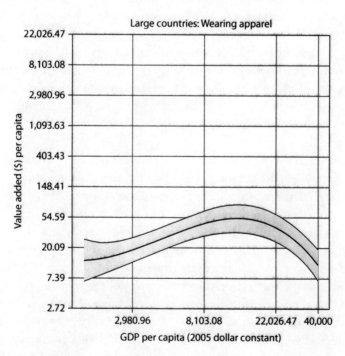

Figure 12.10   (*Continued*)

increase, especially in the case of early labor-intensive industries. Yet a loss of comparative advantage is possibly postponed by such efforts, particularly for late-emerging capital-intensive industries.

In view of the predominant influence exerted by comparative advantage, productivity growth plays an important role in accelerating the pace of development of each industry with a comparative advantage, thus contributing to a faster increase in GDP per capita, which in turn speeds up the shift in comparative advantage and the entire process of manufacturing structural change. Comparative advantage is linked to a specific stage of development; therefore, it is a static factor of development potential at a given time. Productivity growth adds a dynamic aspect of manufacturing development to this static concept of comparative advantage: how fast a country exploits comparative advantage also indicates the pace of the shift in comparative advantage. Besides the two factors relating to a country's endowment structure at a given stage of development and the speed of technological capacity building, a third factor, which relates to country-specific conditions, also plays a role. This includes given geographic and demographic conditions as well as a country's fixed effects—unique circumstances and capabilities which, as shown above, can either increase or decrease the level of manufacturing production by affecting the quality of institutions, infrastructure, and business climate. Such country-specific conditions, which change only slowly, are responsible for the differences in the manufacturing development performance of countries that have different intercept levels, while the slopes of their development trajectories are similar. Our empirical findings are summarized in the following illustration.

Figure 12.11 reveals how comparative advantage, productivity growth, and country-specific conditions together influence manufacturing development. As demonstrated in the average development paths of the industries, countries have a comparative advantage in industry A at a level of US$ 3,000 GDP per capita, but not in industry B, and at the given level of development have little potential of reaching a high level of value added per capita as well as a high growth rate in industry B. Given the dominant influence of development in terms of the level of development and endowment structure, the performance of two countries could differ, even though both focus on industry A in which they have a comparative advantage. Two different countries' performances will continually deviate from the average development pattern of industry A—as indicated by the dotted lines—due to country-specific conditions, such as the levels of

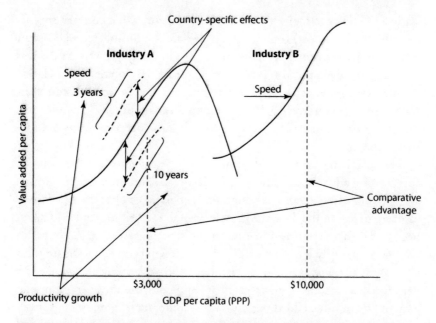

Figure 12.11   Schematic representation of the role of comparative advantage, productivity growth and country-specific conditions in manufacturing development

Source: Created by the author.

resource endowment, population density, capabilities, competency, work ethics, and, through these, levels of costs and infrastructure. Finally, two countries may differ in terms of the time it takes them to move from one level of development (value added per capita) of industry A to another. For example, one country could take three years to increase the same amount of value added per capita of industry A while another may take 10 years. This speed of development is related to the growth of labor productivity. If a country rapidly exploited the comparative advantage of industry A as well as other industries in which its current comparative advantages lie, the country would likely increase its GDP per capita and rapidly shift its endowment structure and hence move its comparative advantage from industry A to, say, industry B, thus speeding up the entire process of manufacturing structural change. Productivity growth in the industries of a country's existing comparative advantage plays a dynamic role in manufacturing development, which influences the pace of structural change. As graphically illustrated, the three factors assume different roles in manufacturing development. Comparative advantage is static and relates to a given stage of development, while country-specific conditions are (almost) time-invariant and are responsible for a persistent difference in performance across time. Productivity growth, in turn, is related to the dynamic aspect of manufacturing development. For clarity, country-specific effects and productivity growth are discussed and illustrated separately; however, they are by no means mutually exclusive. For example, country-specific effects might well influence a country's productivity growth.

The following examples demonstrate how the above elaboration of comparative advantage, country-specific effects, and productivity growth actually manifests in the development experiences of countries. These cases are based on the data of Malaysia, Republic of Korea, and Sri Lanka, because all three countries belong to the same group of large countries and have relatively long time series data, allowing us to investigate their development trajectories. They also have an overlapping range of GDP per capita, which allows us to calculate and compare the average annual growth rate of value added per capita at a comparable development stage.

A set of graphs in figure 12.12 illustrate the actual plots of the real value-added per capita data of the three countries as well as the patterns estimated for the large country group based on the fixed-effect model of the panel data. The observations of the three countries' data indicate that their development patterns follow the estimated pattern (slope) of the group to which they belong remarkably closely. The three countries deviate from the estimated pattern, but their deviations (intercepts) remain more or less constant, at least for a fairly long time, so that they tend to depict the development trajectories in parallel to the estimated patterns.

As indicated by the graphs, Sri Lanka currently has a comparative advantage in relatively labor-intensive industries, such as food and beverages and textiles and wearing apparel, and hence rapid growth in these industries can be anticipated. Malaysia has already lost its advantage in these industries, but can still expect continued growth for some time in the basic metals, fabricated metals, and motor vehicle industries as well as long-term growth in the chemicals and electrical machinery and apparatus industries. In the case of Republic of Korea, the country has already lost or is about to lose its comparative advantage in the basic metals, fabricated metals, and motor vehicle industries, while the electrical machinery and apparatus and chemicals industries are likely to remain advantageous for Republic of Korea in the foreseeable future.

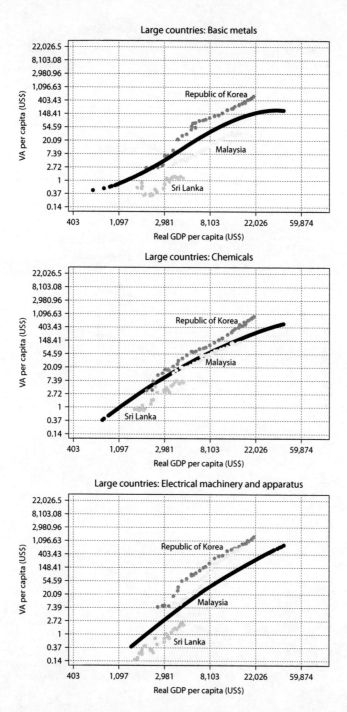

Figure 12.12 Development patterns of value added per capita for large countries and actual country experiences of the Republic of Korea, Malaysia, and Sri Lanka.

Source: Produced by the author based on regression estimations.

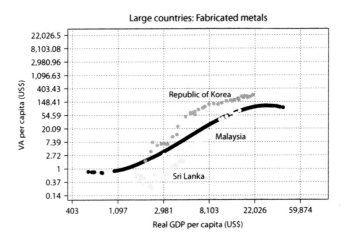

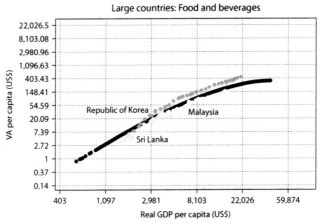

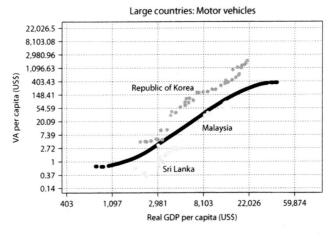

Figure 12.12 (*Continued*)

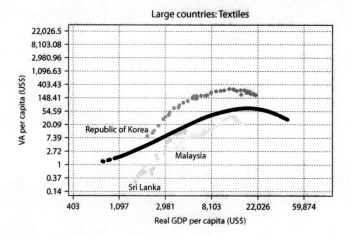

Figure 12.12   *(Continued)*

Although all three countries generally follow the estimated patterns and have comparative advantages that reflect their stage of development, the speeds with which these advantages are exploited—hence, possibly the shift of advantage from one industry to another—differ across the three countries. Table 12.10 shows how fast the manufacturing industries of the three countries moved over the range of GDP per capita from US$ 3,000 to US$ 4,500. This range has been chosen because the data of all three countries overlap over this period of development. For each industry, an average growth rate of value added per capita was calculated by dividing the increase in value added per capita by the corresponding number of years over the selected GDP per capita range. As seen in table 12.10, all eight industries developed much faster in Republic of Korea than in Malaysia. In the textiles and wearing apparel industries, Republic of Korea increased the value added per capita around 20 times faster annually, on average, than Malaysia did, while more capital-intensive industries developed approximately 10 times faster in Republic of Korea than in Malaysia. Over the same stage of development, Sri Lanka's industries, relative to Malaysia's, lagged behind in terms of development speed, with the exception of the textiles and wearing apparel industries.

In addition to development speed, the industries of the three countries differ in terms of the level of value added per capita, even at same stage of development. Although they tend to follow the estimated patterns, the

Table 12.10 Comparison of the Speed of Manufacturing Development Among Malaysia, Republic of Korea, and Sri Lanka

Industry	Malaysia	Republic of Korea	Sri Lanka
Food and beverages	1.46	4.74	0.64
Textiles	0.60	11.49	0.61
Wearing apparel	0.66	13.37	1.43
Chemicals	1.32	3.55	0.19
Basic metals	0.38	3.62	0.03
Fabricated metals	0.24	2.71	0.09
Electrical machinery and apparatus	0.78	7.53	0.10
Motor vehicles	0.40	5.28	0.13

Note: The speed is expressed as an increase in value added per capita divided by the number of years taken over the range of GDP per capita from US$ 3,000 to US$ 4,500.

development trajectories of the countries deviate positively and negatively from the patterns. For all the selected industries, Republic of Korea had higher positive deviations than the others. Indeed, for many industries, Republic of Korea's deviation was one of the highest among the countries included in this research. Malaysia had higher positive deviations than Sri Lanka in more capital-intensive industries. In the case of electrical machinery and apparatus, Malaysia seems to have improved its country-specific advantage from the end of the 1980s and has narrowed the gap with Republic of Korea. Sri Lanka has country-specific advantages or fewer disadvantages in the food and beverages and the textiles and wearing apparel industries. The geographic, demographic, and country-fixed conditions explain such deviations. Considering that the Republic of Korea's and Sri Lanka's conditions are similar in terms of their higher population density and lower natural resource endowment relative to the world median levels, the deviations from the patterns are more likely explained by the second type of country-specific conditions discussed above, which relate to a country's capabilities and other unique circumstances that enhance a country's infrastructure, institutions, and relative cost level.

Based on the above results and analyses, countries are able to derive some general policy guidance for their long-term manufacturing development. First, the manufacturing development patterns in accordance with an increase in GDP per capita indicate in which industries a country has a comparative advantage at a given stage of development. Comparative advantage is associated with the level of a country's development and, therefore, predominantly influences the types of industries in which a country may have the best chance of succeeding at a given stage of development. When a country has a comparative advantage in a certain industry, it can expand this industry while simultaneously increasing labor productivity, occasionally even without increasing productivity by much. Similarly, an industry that is losing comparative advantage can contract while still increasing labor productivity by reducing employment in that industry.

Although the industries with a current comparative advantage may not be expected to have a development path that is as sustainable as that of more advanced industries, it is not advisable for a country to neglect its current advantage and jump into industries that will become advantageous for the country at a much higher income level. A country that targets industries that have no advantage not only would face difficulties developing such industries, but also would be confronted with a slowdown in economic growth due to sluggish developments of both the targeted industries and those in which the country does have a comparative advantage due to resource transfers or policy mismatches. Such slow economic growth would stall GDP per capita growth and consequently slow down the pace of structural change, making the development of more technologically advanced industries unviable for a longer time.

Bearing in mind the timing of change in the comparative advantage from one industry to another, a country's industrialization efforts should be directed toward those industries of current comparative advantage. Such industries should develop faster than other industries and, if the productivity of those industries is improved, can develop even faster, accelerating the pace of structural change. While exploiting the current advantage, countries should also prepare for the industries of the near future by upgrading the levels of education and infrastructure in advance, thus ensuring that these long-term investments provide the appropriate skills and public goods to meet the demands of the industries toward which the country's comparative advantage is shifting.

Even at the same stage of development, countries differ in terms of the level of development of their industries of current advantage. Countries are likely to follow the estimated pattern (changes in slope), but may have different levels of positive or negative deviations at each stage of development. These deviations are related to country-specific effects, including demographic and geographic conditions and other unique features and capabilities. Refer to tables 12.3, 12.4, and 12.5. Countries could consider the likely effects of their demographic and geographic conditions in their manufacturing development strategies. Other country-specific factors included in country fixed effects may also affect the levels of manufacturing development by impacting a country's long-term business climate, such as infrastructure, institutions, and cost competitiveness. Further research is required to identify which unique circumstances and capabilities may create positive deviations in the levels of manufacturing value added per capita across income levels. Country fixed effects are, however, likely to be deeply rooted in culture, history, and regional influence, which implies that econometric studies using readily available indicators may not offer much insight into these effects, because the observed differences reflected in the indicators are probably themselves the result of country fixed effects. In view of this, it may be more meaningful for countries to choose a comparator that belongs to the same size group and has a similar level of GDP per capita, yet enjoys a higher level of manufacturing value added per capita, and to conduct a comprehensive study about the comparator to tease out possible conditions that create systematic differences in manufacturing performance.

The deviation of a given industry's performance from the estimated pattern is usually similar across a country's manufacturing industries because country-specific conditions, which foster or obstruct the long-term performance of a given industry, are often applicable to other industries. In this regard, a country which has a positive deviation in the industry of its current comparative advantage may have a similar degree of positive deviations across manufacturing industries, including more technologically advanced industries, as is the case in Republic of Korea. However, it is not advisable for countries to try to achieve positive deviations in advanced industries with targeted interventions if the industries of current comparative advantage do not demonstrate a positive deviation. For example, according to figure 12.12, if a country has a positive deviation along the top dotted line from figure 12.11, a similar degree of positive deviation in industry B at a GDP per capita level of US\$ 3,000 would probably not distort the country's manufacturing structural change based on comparative advantage. But such a deviation in industry B may not be advisable, if the country is developing industry A along the bottom dotted line. Country-specific information, which stems from this research approach, could thus be used for benchmarking and monitoring a country's manufacturing development.

CONCLUSION

This chapter analyzed the process of manufacturing development in detail by estimating the development patterns of manufacturing industries. The patterns identified in this study indicate the existence of comparative advantage, whose shift is associated with changes in GDP per capita. Even successful countries such as Republic of Korea have generally followed these patterns. What distinguishes countries that have reached the same stage of development and successfully focus on the industries of their comparative advantage from one another in terms of manufacturing performance is the speed at which the advantage of those industries is exploited and the country's unique capabilities and circumstances. The former is associated with a country's labor productivity growth in this study, while the latter affects development based on differences in a country's long-term advantage in infrastructure, institutions, and relative cost levels.

Although still at an embryonic stage, this research suggests how different schools of thought on industrial development, such as comparative advantage, technological development, and functional approaches, all have a place in explaining the performance of industrial development and account for different aspects of development. Future research is needed to further investigate country-specific conditions and how they are translated into long-term country-specific advantages.

APPENDIX A

India has an IIP, but Pakistan does not. Both countries have MVA deflators. To make price adjustments on 1965 data, if Pakistan simply applies its 1965 MVA deflator across industries, the nominal values in 1965 will be increased by 63 percent for all industries. Since 1965, the nominal values in U.S. dollars are higher in terms of U.S. dollars in 1995 (the base year of the IIP), and the values will be higher after adjustments. To reflect subsector-specific inflation trends, e.g., I used India's IIP in 1965 and calculate Pakistan's IIP-based deflators. I used the following equation to arrive at results. Here def = deflator, d.w. = deflator weight, and i.w. = industry weight.

$$\text{Pakistan deflator} = (\text{MVA def} - 1) \times (\text{d.w.} / \text{i.w.}) + 1$$

We then used deflators for each subsector reflecting the industry-specific inflation rate. As seen below, those which have high deflators in India have higher deflators in Pakistan (or in this case, inflators). If I apply these deflators to Pakistan's nominal value, I obtain Pakistan's IIP-based real value added. Again, those industries which had higher deflators had higher real value added, but the total is still the same as it is when an MVA deflator is used. This approach essentially decomposes manufacturing-wide inflation into each industry's inflation rate by using the industry's inflation trend at that time. Using the inflation trend of the neighboring country is reasonable, as manufacturing products are usually tradable and are usually traded more heavily with neighboring countries or with similar trading partners.

1965 data

	India NVA	IIP_RVA	IIP_Def
S1	432,000,000	904,000,000	2.0926
S2	101,000,000	119,000,000	1.1782
S3	231,000,000	544,000,000	2.3550
S4	182,000,000	130,000,000	0.7143
S5	21,000,000	65,200,000	3.1048
S6	383,000,000	1,670,000,000	4.3603
S7	78,100,000	465,000,000	5.9539

	Pakistan NVA	MVA def	MVA def adjusted VA	India def	d.w.	i.w.	Pakistan Def	Pakistan IIP_RVA
S1	103,040,404	1.63	167,955,859	2.0926	0.1059	0.1290	1.5172	156,333,870
S2	89,393,020	1.63	145,710,623	1.1782	0.0596	0.1119	1.3357	119,399,487
S3	99,200,219	1.63	161,696,357	2.3550	0.1192	0.1242	1.6046	159,176,040
S4	119,293,843	1.63	194,448,964	0.7143	0.0361	0.1493	1.1525	137,485,039
S5	120,903,494	1.63	197,072,695	3.1048	0.1571	0.1514	1.6540	199,974,558
S6	125,903,040	1.63	205,221,955	4.3603	0.2207	0.1576	1.8820	236,950,078
S7	141,023,393	1.63	229,868,131	5.9539	0.3013	0.1766	2.0752	292,655,511
Total	798,757,413		1,301,974,583	19.7591	1.0000	1.0000		1,301,974,583

Notes: Def = deflator, VA = value added, RVA = real value added, NVA = nominal value added, IIP_RVA = IIP-based real value added, IIP_def = IIP-based deflator, d.w. = deflator weight, i.w. = industry weight.

If I use the MVA deflator for manufacturing price adjustment for countries without an IIP, I have to also use it for countries with an IIP for the purpose of consistency. For countries with an IIP (e.g., India) I made the following adjustments: I calculated the IIP-based real value added using its own IIP for India. The total IIP-based real value added divided by total nominal value added gives 2.7289. This is different from the MVA deflator of India in 1965, which was 1.573. Thus I had to make adjustments to ensure that all countries would be consistent as far as manufacturing-wide inflation trends are concerned. Hence, I calculated the ratio of the IIP-based manufacturing-wide deflator to India's MVA deflator in 1965. The result is 1.7347. Then I divided the IIP-based real value added by this ratio, 1.7347, to arrive at the IIP-based real value added, which is consistent with the MVA deflator. If I divide the total of this by the total nominal value added, the result is 1.5731. The manufacturing-wide inflation is now consistent with the MVA deflator, albeit each industry's price changes are adjusted in their values.

	India NVA	IIP_RVA	IIP_Def	1963 MVA def	MVA def adjusted IIP_RVA
S1	432,000,000	904,000,000	2.0926	1.5731	521,114,185
S2	101,000,000	119,000,000	1.1782	1.5731	68,597,996
S3	231,000,000	544,000,000	2.355	1.5731	313,590,837
S4	182,000,000	130,000,000	0.7143	1.5731	74,938,987
S5	21,000,000	65,200,000	3.1048	1.5731	37,584,784
S6	383,000,000	1,670,000,000	4.3603	1.5731	962,677,754
S7	78,100,000	465,000,000	5.9539	1.5731	268,050,991
Total	1,428,100,000	3,897,200,000			2,246,555,535

APPENDIX B

Table B.1 Regression Results Based on the FE Estimation Method (GDP Only)

Group	ISIC Code	GDPpc	(GDPpc)^2	(GDPpc)^3	Constant	N	R^2 (Overall)
Small country	15	−22.95***	2.96***	−0.12***	58.72**	354	0.61
Medium country	15	−32.32***	3.97***	−0.16***	88.30***	548	0.79
Large country	15	−3.41	0.81	−0.04*	−0.88	835	0.84
Small country	16	−57.70***	6.65***	−0.25***	166.06***	194	0.29
Medium country	16	−67.66***	8.16***	−0.32***	184.82***	475	0.43
Large country	16	2.34	0.20	−0.02	−18.66	726	0.59
Small country	17	9.15	−0.36	−0.01	−41.15	274	0.00
Medium country	17	−15.57*	2.31**	−0.11***	34.01	592	0.18
Large country	17	−34.00***	4.46***	−0.19***	83.60***	863	0.69
Small country	18	16.39	−0.93	0.00	−71.65	305	0.37
Medium country	18	−27.03**	4.21***	−0.20***	50.36	558	0.38
Large country	18	24.02**	−1.83	0.04	−93.83***	760	0.65
Small country	20	108.30***	−11.46***	0.40***	−335.92***	316	0.02
Medium country	20	−39.10***	4.75***	−0.19***	105.09***	524	0.61
Large country	20	−11.37	1.70**	−0.08**	22.30	787	0.64
Small country	21	−12.06	2.07	−0.10	15.54	246	0.54
Medium country	21	−53.03***	5.93***	−0.22***	157.97***	492	0.74
Large country	21	−5.53	1.02*	−0.05**	3.77	789	0.91

(Continued)

Table B.1 (*Continued*)

Group	ISIC Code	GDPpc	(GDPpc)^2	(GDPpc)^3	Constant	N	R^2 (Overall)
Small country	22	−53.61***	6.26***	−0.24***	150.49***	308	0.78
Medium country	22	−60.39***	7.13***	−0.27***	167.26***	541	0.86
Large country	22	3.56	0.06	−0.01	−23.76	763	0.84
Small country	23	82.55**	−8.03**	0.26*	−279.63**	105	0.39
Medium country	23	26.49	−2.50	0.08	−91.32	260	0.32
Large country	23	−15.32**	2.18**	−0.09***	31.72	574	0.70
Small country	24	−19.79**	1.97*	−0.06	65.16**	305	0.42
Medium country	24	16.71	−1.36	0.04	−64.34	561	0.75
Large country	24	3.61	0.00	−0.01	−22.75	849	0.88
Small country	25	−27.22	3.34*	−0.13**	73.66	261	0.37
Medium country	25	−25.22**	3.61***	−0.16***	51.65	550	0.85
Large country	25	4.83	−0.14	−0.00	−26.94	818	0.86
Small country	26	5.68	−0.34	0.00	−23.36	330	0.54
Medium country	26	−44.29***	5.50***	−0.22***	115.70***	568	0.83
Large country	26	14.79**	−1.18*	0.03	−57.10***	837	0.87
Small country	27	−18.43	2.39	−0.10	45.40	133	0.36
Medium country	27	−20.41*	2.71**	−0.11**	48.68	429	0.67
Large country	27	−31.54***	4.04***	−0.16***	77.91***	682	0.84
Small country	28	−12.47	1.68	−0.07	28.59	338	0.68
Medium country	28	−49.63***	5.98***	−0.23***	134.46***	556	0.84
Large country	28	−41.19***	5.11***	−0.20***	106.88***	804	0.87
Small country	29	−62.28**	6.74**	−0.24**	190.39**	221	0.16
Medium country	29	−6.92	1.60	−0.08	−5.34	471	0.80
Large country	29	−20.40**	2.56**	−0.10**	50.16*	783	0.82
Small country	31	−41.63	4.42	−0.15	130.61	233	0.16
Medium country	31	55.18***	−5.27**	0.17**	−192.18***	529	0.81
Large country	31	8.02	−0.44	0.01	−39.48*	828	0.84
Small country	33	−205.38***	23.75***	−0.90***	581.27***	97	0.59
Medium country	33	87.81***	−9.14***	0.32***	−284.14***	389	0.74
Large country	33	−26.12***	3.45***	−0.14***	59.75**	538	0.79
Small country	34	27.74	−3.65*	0.15**	−63.01	274	0.33
Medium country	34	11.95	−0.55	−0.00	−56.95	525	0.59
Large country	34	−45.21***	5.49***	−0.21***	119.47***	794	0.84
Small country	36	−57.65***	6.53***	−0.24***	170.92***	273	0.03
Medium country	36	−15.43	2.24*	−0.10**	31.86	471	0.69
Large country	36	21.58**	−2.06*	0.07	−74.02**	661	0.80

* $p<0.10$

** $p<0.05$

*** $p<0.01$

Note: ISIC descriptions are as follows: 15–food and beverages, 16–tobacco, 17–textiles, 18–wearing apparel, 20–wood products, 21–paper, 22–printing and publishing, 23–coke and refined petroleum, 24–chemicals, 25–rubber and plastic, 26–non-metallic minerals, 27–basic metals, 28–fabricated metals, 29–machinery and equipment, 31–electrical machinery and apparatus, 33–precision instruments, 34–motor vehicles, 36–furniture, not elsewhere classified.

* $p<0.10$

** $p<0.05$

*** $p<0.01$

Table B.2 Regression Results Based on the FE Estimation Method (All Variables)

Group	ISIC code	GDPpc	(GDPpc)²	(GDPpc)³	RPC	POPD	Constant	N	R² (Overall)
Small country	15	13.28	-1.11	0.03	-0.08	0.62***	-49.78	285	0.13
Medium country	15	-22.13**	2.89***	-0.12***	0.02	-0.02	56.69**	489	0.79
Large country	15	-5.89	1.05*	-0.05*	-1.76***	0.39***	20.84	739	0.66
Small country	16	-14.42	1.92	-0.08	0.31	0.11	31.68	172	0.32
Medium country	16	-40.17***	5.21***	-0.22***	1.00	-0.31***	92.42**	426	0.26
Large country	16	5.88	-0.14	-0.01	-1.89***	-0.34***	-13.55	672	0.45
Small country	17	-13.56	2.12	-0.10	0.05	-0.52***	29.63	249	0.04
Medium country	17	28.13***	-2.18*	0.05	0.11	-0.93***	-104.75***	550	0.00
Large country	17	-28.47***	3.84***	-0.16***	-0.16	-0.12	69.00***	775	0.65
Small country	18	-45.72	5.77	-0.24*	0.07	0.02	118.89	274	0.35
Medium country	18	-2.46	1.93	-0.13**	0.85***	-1.10***	-39.13	514	0.12
Large country	18	18.99*	-1.23	0.02	-0.53	-0.23*	-74.50**	685	0.56
Small country	20	97.45*	-9.75*	0.32*	-0.02	-0.90***	-315.55**	266	0.03
Medium country	20	5.97	-0.22	-0.00	-0.45*	0.29*	-27.36	492	0.35
Large country	20	-5.73	1.13	-0.06*	-1.09**	-0.32***	14.20	723	0.51
Small country	21	-28.13	3.83	-0.16	-0.02	0.73***	61.63	228	0.14
Medium country	21	-90.50***	10.09***	-0.37***	0.39**	-0.41***	267.86***	467	0.63
Large country	21	2.62	0.13	-0.01	-1.04**	-0.10	-11.66	712	0.92
Small country	22	-3.79	1.20	-0.07	-0.04	1.36***	-16.46	273	0.34
Medium country	22	-47.62***	5.72***	-0.22***	-0.29	-0.04	131.14***	510	0.86
Large country	22	13.95**	-1.08	0.03	-1.65***	-0.13	-40.85*	697	0.83
Small country	23	9.54	-0.23	-0.01	-0.02	-0.04	-52.09	93	0.46
Medium country	23	96.71***	-10.23***	0.36***	-0.35	1.29***	-303.15***	235	0.02
Large country	23	-9.93	1.54*	-0.07**	-1.81***	0.45***	30.68	535	0.46
Small country	24	18.85	-2.33*	0.10**	-0.14	1.09***	-51.76	255	0.33
Medium country	24	9.31	-0.84	0.03	-0.03	1.22***	-36.61	529	0.25
Large country	24	-1.65	0.50	-0.02	-2.05***	0.97***	9.30	758	0.51
Small country	25	-37.06	4.39	-0.17	-0.18	0.15	105.58	235	0.18
Medium country	25	-21.89*	3.05**	-0.13**	-0.31	0.65***	47.91	529	0.73

(Continued)

Table B.2 *(Continued)*

Group	ISIC code	GDPpc	(GDPpc)²	(GDPpc)³	RPC	POPD	Constant	N	R² (Overall)
Large country	25	−0.44	0.38	−0.02	−0.72	0.78***	−6.01	755	0.65
Small country	26	−55.27	6.41	−0.24*	−0.44**	0.54***	160.85	280	0.05
Medium country	26	−36.73***	4.57***	−0.18***	−0.08	0.56***	95.28***	522	0.65
Large country	26	12.44**	−0.98	0.03	−1.20***	0.69***	−40.80**	756	0.57
Small country	27	−70.70	7.99	−0.30	0.08	0.33	205.31	116	0.02
Medium country	27	127.84***	−12.89***	0.43***	0.12	0.89***	−422.64***	405	0.08
Large country	27	−38.92***	4.82***	−0.19***	−3.35***	0.71***	126.92***	632	0.49
Small country	28	−36.78	4.49	−0.17	0.03	−0.63***	99.56	283	0.13
Medium country	28	−41.42***	5.14***	−0.20***	0.05	−0.12	107.81**	520	0.82
Large country	28	−41.23***	5.03***	−0.20***	−0.98***	0.78***	114.77***	719	0.61
Small country	29	−214.50***	22.85***	−0.81***	−0.09	0.31*	668.43***	202	0.03
Medium country	29	−10.16	1.83	−0.09	−0.12	0.37**	8.21	453	0.77
Large country	29	−42.33***	4.86***	−0.18***	0.85	1.36***	107.15***	699	0.44
Small country	31	−177.81***	18.66***	−0.65***	−0.35	−0.07	567.17***	210	0.00
Medium country	31	90.67***	−9.38***	0.33***	−1.37***	0.22	−282.81***	503	0.81
Large country	31	5.85	−0.30	0.01	−1.56***	1.12***	−21.06	739	0.62
Small country	33	−201.89*	23.46***	−0.89**	0.44	−0.15	564.93*	85	0.39
Medium country	33	88.85***	−9.32***	0.33***	−0.48	0.21	−281.89***	381	0.69
Large country	33	−22.11**	3.04***	−0.13***	0.54	−0.40*	43.89	527	0.66
Small country	34	41.98	−5.39	0.22	−0.07	−1.00***	−96.37	237	0.19
Medium country	34	87.14***	−8.67***	0.29***	−0.62*	−0.36*	−281.74***	495	0.43
Large country	34	−53.49***	6.35***	−0.24***	−1.94***	0.77***	159.29***	716	0.60
Small country	36	−89.95***	10.26***	−0.38***	−0.01	−0.64***	265.80**	233	0.16
Medium country	36	38.84**	−3.50*	0.10*	−0.58**	−0.79***	−131.76***	434	0.39
Large country	36	28.44***	−2.69**	0.09**	0.29	−0.91***	−97.77***	616	0.46

Note: ISIC descriptions are as follows: 15–food and beverages, 16–tobacco, 17–textiles, 18–wearing apparel, 20–wood products, 21–paper, 22–printing and publishing, 23–coke and refined petroleum, 24–chemicals, 25–rubber and plastic, 26–nonmetallic minerals, 27–basic metals, 28–fabricated metals, 29–machinery and equipment, 31–electrical machinery and apparatus, 33–precision instruments, 34–motor vehicles, 36–furniture, n.e.c.

* p<0.10

** p<0.05

*** p<0.01

APPENDIX C

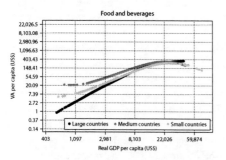

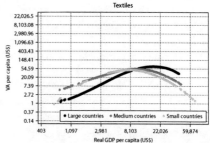

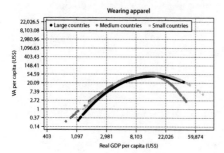

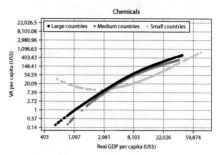

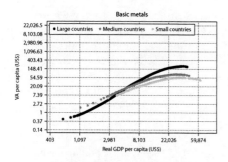

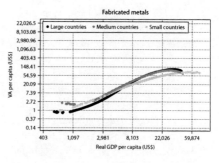

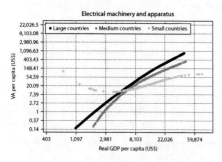

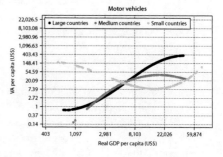

NOTES

The views expressed herein are those of the author(s) and do not necessarily reflect the views of the United Nations Industrial Development Organization. (As provided for in Administrative Circular UNIDO/DA/PS/AC.69 of 17. December 1990). This document has been produced without formal United Nations editing. The designations employed and the presentation of the material in this document do not imply the expression of any opinion whatsoever on the part of the Secretariat of the United Nations Industrial Development Organization (UNIDO) concerning the legal status of any country, territory, city or area or of its authorities, or concerning the delimitation of its frontiers or boundaries, or its economic system or degree of development. Designations such as "developed," "industrialized," and "developing" are intended for statistical convenience and do not necessarily express a judgment about the stage reached by a particular country or area in the development process. Mention of firm names or commercial products does not constitute an endorsement by UNIDO. The opinions, statistical data and estimates contained herein are the responsibility of the author(s) and should not necessarily be considered as reflecting the views of bearing the endorsement of UNIDO.

The author is grateful to: Gorazd Rezonja and Charles Fang Chin Cheng, both consultants at UNIDO, for their assistance in data processing and graphic supports; Ludovico Alcorta, director of Research, Statistics, and Industrial Policy Branch of UNIDO, for his helpful comments; and Niki Rodousakis, UNIDO staff member, for editing and formatting

1. All subsequent references to GDP per capita in this chapter denote GDP per capita in PPP (constant 1995 price).

2. This chapter uses real value added instead of gross output to assess the level of an industry's development. Due to production in global supply chains, an output produced in a country consists of value added originating from various countries. Thus, the use of real value added reflects the level of a country's contribution to an industry's production more accurately regardless of the kind of an output produced in the country, so it is compatible with the analysis of industrial development taking place in global value chains. For this reason, real value-added production data are also preferred to trade data, as the latter shows output rather than value added (only recently has value added been assessed for a limited number of countries and industries in the database, such as "Trade in Value Added" by OECD and WTO). The production data used in this study are more appropriate and comprehensive as they look at value added and cover values added in production for both exports and domestic consumption.

3. Depending on the given country, changes in the weight of quality and products in an industry may not necessarily be regularly updated in IIP. The gradual changes in the valued added share in output may not be appropriately reflected in the IIP despite regular adjustments.

4. First, I determined whether a manufacturing value added deflator (MVA deflator), i.e., a manufacturing sectorwide deflator, could be used for the 70 countries with an IIP. Where this was found to be suitable, a country's MVA deflator could be used to deflate the valued added across manufacturing subsectors within a country for all 120 countries with MVA deflators. To check this, the manufacturing development patterns were estimated for the 70 countries with an IIP and MVA deflators, using both their IIP and MVA deflator. The two estimated patterns based on the IIP and MVA deflator

approaches were compared to determine whether the differences between the two were statistically significant. The two patterns significantly varied for many industries, so I was therefore not able to adjust nominal values by using MVA deflators, which were available for 120 countries.

5. The effects of landlockedness and tropical climate were also tested using the Hausmann-Taylor IV estimator, as these variables are time-invariant. Landlockedness had almost no effect on manufacturing development, and tropical climate tended to negatively affect many capital-intensive industries of medium-sized countries as well as some industries in large countries.

6. The natural resource proxy variable (RPC) was calculated as the difference between exports and imports of crude natural resource commodities and was expressed in per capita terms. The commodities included are those categorized under SITC revision 1 in Codes 2 (crude materials, inedible, except fuels), 32 (coal, coke, and briquettes), 331 (petroleum, crude and partly refined), and 3411 (gas, natural).

7. To determine labor intensity, employment per unit of value added was estimated for 18 manufacturing industries at \$5,000 and \$20,000 per capita GDP, because the labor intensity changes along the income curve. If an industry's labor intensity was higher than the median of 18 manufacturing industries at both income levels, it is considered labor intensive; if lower than the median at both levels, it is considered relatively capital intensive. Labor-intensive industries include wearing apparel, textiles, wood products, fabricated metals, and food and beverages industries. Capital-intensive industries are coke and refined petroleum, tobacco, chemicals, printing and publishing, and electrical machinery and apparatus industries.

8. The contributions of GDP per capita, population density and natural resource endowment, and country fixed effects to R^2 were estimated based on the LSDV method by taking the difference between the R^2 obtained for the regression using all three categories of the variables and that obtained for the regression in which the category was removed. Table 12.9 shows the contributions of each category to R^2 as a mean of 18 manufacturing industries. As this procedure is based on LSDV including country dummies, the R^2 used for this analysis is different from the R^2 in table 2 of appendix B, which is based on the fixed-effect model.

REFERENCES

Chang, Ha-Joon, ed. 2003. *Rethinking Development Economics.* New York: Anthem Press.

Chenery, H. B., and L. Taylor. 1968. "Development Patterns: Among Countries and Over Time." *The Review of Economics and Statistics* 50(4): 391–416.

Clark, C. 1957. *The Conditions of Economic Progress.* New York: Garland.

Felipe, Jesus. 2009. *Inclusive Growth, Full Employment, and Structural Change: Implications and Policies for Developing Asia.* New York: Anthem Press and ADB.

Imbs, Jean, and R. Wacziarg. 2003. "Stages of Diversification." *The American Economic Review* 93(1): 63–86.

Kuznets, S. 1966. *Modern Economic Growth: Rate, Structure, and Spread.* New Haven, Conn.: Yale University Press.

Lee, K. 2013. *Schumpeterian Analysis of Economic Catch-up: Knowledge, Path-Creation, and the Middle-Income Trap?* New York: Cambridge University Press.

Lin, J. 2011. "From Flying Geese to Leading Dragons: New Opportunities and Strategies for Structural Transformation in Developing Countries." Policy Research Working Paper Series, 5702, World Bank.

Lin, J., and H. Chang. 2009. "Should Industrial Policy in Developing Countries Conform to Comparative Advantage or Defy it? A Debate between Justin Lin and Ha-Joon Chang." *Development Policy Review* 27(5): 483–502.

Lin, J., and C. Monga. 2011. "Growth Identification and Facilitation: The Role of the State in the Dynamics of Structural Change." *Development Policy Review* 29(3): 259–310.

Rodrik, D. 2011. "The Future of Economic Convergence." NBER Working Paper Series No. 17400.

Taylor, L. 1969. "Development Patterns: A Simulation Study." *The Quarterly Journal of Economics* 83(2): 220–41.

World Bank. 1993. *The East Asian Miracle.* Washington, D.C.: Oxford University Press.

FURTHER READING

Chenery, H. B., and M. Syrquin. 1989. "Patterns of Development, 1950 to 1983." *World Bank Discussion Paper,* WDP41, Washington, D.C.

Easterly, W., and R. Levine. 2003. "Tropics, Germs and Crops: How Endowments Influence Economic Development." *Journal of Monetary Economics* 50: 3–39.

Fisher, A. G. B. 1939. "Production, Primary, Secondary and Tertiary." *Economic Record* 15: 24–38.

Haraguchi, N., and G. Rezonja. 2011. "Emerging Patterns of Manufacturing Structural Change." Development Policy and Strategic Research Branch Working Paper, 04/2010, UNIDO.

Kader, A. 1985. "Development Patterns among Countries Reexamined." *The Developing Economies* 23(3): 199–220.

Keesing, D. B., and D. R. Sherk. 1971. "Population Density in Patterns of Trade and Development." *American Economic Association* 61(5): 956–61.

Kuznets, S. 1957. "Quantitative Aspects of the Economic Growth of Nations: II. Industrial Distribution of National Product and Labor Force." *Economic Development and Cultural Change* 5(4) Supplement: 1–111.

Maizels, A. 1968. *Exports and Economic Growth of Developing Countries.* London: Cambridge University Press.

McMillan, M., and D. Rodrik. 2011. "Globalization, Structural Change, and Productivity Growth." NBER Working Paper Series No. 17143.

Perkins, D., and M. Syrquin. 1989. "Large Countries: The Influence of Size." In *Handbook of Development Economics,* vol. 2, eds. H. Chenery and T. N. Srinivasan: 1692–753. Amsterdam: North-Holland.

Sachs, J. 2001. "Tropical Underdevelopment." NBER Working Paper Series No. 8119.

Syrquin, M. 1988a. "Patterns of Structural Change." In *Handbook of Development Economics,* eds. Hollis Chenery and T. N. Srinivasan, vol. 1, 203–73. Amsterdam: Elsevier Science Publishers.

Syrquin, M. 1988b. "Structural Change and Economic Development: The Role of the Service Sector." *Journal of Development Economics* 28(1): 151–54.

Syrquin, M. 2007. "Kuznets and Pasinetti on the Study of Structural Transformation: Never the Twain Shall Meet?" International Centre for Economic Research Working Paper, 46.

CHAPTER 13

Does Manufacturing Colocate with Intermediate Services?

ANALYZING THE WORLD INPUT-OUTPUT DATABASE

Ming Leong Kuan

Economic development revolves around the production of goods and services. In extolling the "paramount position of production," John Kenneth Galbraith (1958, 101) described production as measuring "the quality and progress of our civilization." In a world characterized by globalization, growing trade in services has lent support to the notion that both developed and developing countries can prosper by specializing in the development of services. Such a position ignores the manufacturing sector's special historical properties as an engine of economic growth (see Chang, Andreoni, and Kuan 2014) and has led to intense debate.[1]

There are strong theoretical grounds for services to play a larger role than manufacturing as countries attain a more advanced stage of economic development. The standard transformation of economies has involved industrializing from an agrarian society and subsequently deindustrializing to a postindustrial economy. In the early stage of economic development, the output and employment shares of the agriculture sector are large (Fisher 1935; Chenery 1960; Kuznets 1971) as land and labor are channeled toward agrarian activities (Johnston and Mellor 1961).

Consequently, demand-side and supply-side factors drive industrialization. On the demand side, Engel's law states that the share of food expenditure declines as per capita income rises (Clark 1940; Houthakker 1957). On the supply side, resources are freed up for industrial development as the agriculture sector's productivity improves (Rowthorn and Wells 1987; Timmer 1988). Surplus agricultural labor subsequently shifts to the industrial sector (Lewis 1954).

When countries, typically those with more advanced economies, enter the phase of a postindustrial society, services generate greater wealth than manufacturing (Bell 1973) and face stronger demand from a more affluent population (Fisher 1935; Clark 1940). Accordingly, the developed world is viewed as possessing stronger capabilities in services compared to the developing world.

With globalization and the fragmentation of global value chains,[2] a sharper distinction has been drawn between manufacturing and services. In a world that emphasizes trade liberalization and economic specialization, there is the growing belief that countries can afford to specialize narrowly in their comparative advantages and benefit from trade with one another. For instance, high-cost advanced economies are advised to focus on exporting services and leave manufacturing to developing countries (see Brown and Julius 1993; Wood 2009; Bhagwati 2010; Romer 2012). It has also been argued that developing countries can bypass industrialization by concentrating on a services-led path of development (see Baer and Samuelson 1981; Ghani and O'Connell 2014).

By drawing on new data from the European Commission's (2013) World Input-Output Database (WIOD), this chapter analyzes manufacturing-services linkages across industries and over time, and questions whether manufacturing and intermediate services tend to colocate. There are important policy implications for countries. If manufacturing and services need to be geographically proximate, the offshoring of manufacturing activity will lead to the loss of supporting service industries. Ambitions to develop producer services capabilities will in turn depend on the presence of a manufacturing base.

The chapter is organized as follows. The first section, "Literature Review," presents a literature review of manufacturing-services linkages. The second section, "Methodology and Data Source," describes the WIOD and the input-output methodology used. The third section, "Economic Characteristics in the World," provides an overview of manufacturing and services characteristics in the world. The fourth section, "Findings from the WIOD," presents the findings from studying the backward and forward linkages between manufacturing and services in the WIOD. The results reaffirm the strong colocational properties of manufacturing and intermediate services. Finally, the fifth section, "Concluding Remarks," summarizes the main conclusions in the chapter.

LITERATURE REVIEW

Manufacturing and services share a closely interwoven and interdependent relationship (see Britton 1990; Illeris 1996; Daniels and Bryson 2002). Greenfield (1966) described all production as requiring the application of services to transform physical materials. In turn, services can only be performed with physical goods serving as inputs (e.g., medical equipment in a hospital providing healthcare services) or outputs (e.g., published reports by a management consultant) (Walker 1985). At the conceptual level, some definitions of manufacturing include an entire value chain of activities that comprises services such as research and development (R&D), design, logistics, marketing, and aftercare services (Livesey 2006).[3]

Over the past few decades, two forces have increasingly altered the services element in manufacturing. First, the fragmentation of the production process led manufacturers to contract out (or "splinter") service activities that were previously integrated within the firm (Bhagwati 1984). By outsourcing and offshoring these services to specialized service providers, manufacturers benefited from greater cost efficiencies (Houseman 2007). Such a phenomenon resulted in the statistical illusion that manufacturing-services linkages had strengthened even if the economic activity within the country remained unchanged. Importantly, it raised the scope for manufacturing and intermediate services to be produced in different countries.

Second, the "servitization of manufacturing" encouraged manufacturing firms to incorporate new services elements (e.g., aftercare services) to traditional products in order to enhance their competitiveness (Vandermerwe and Rada 1988; Wise and Baumgartner 1999; Baines et al. 2009; Nordås and Kim 2013). Drawing on examples since the nineteenth century, Schmenner (2009) described how manufacturers with poorer capabilities integrated services in order to enact barriers to entry in their industries. In today's context, strong manufacturers such as General Electric, Rolls-Royce, and Xerox undertake vertical integration to differentiate their products from those of their competitors (see Howells 2004; Livesey 2006).

Linkages between manufacturing and services have strengthened, particularly in countries at higher levels of development (Francois and Woerz 2008). Wolfmayr (2008) reported that manufacturing-services linkages, measured by intermediate services as a share of manufacturing output, strengthened in almost all the OECD countries between 1995 and 2000.[4] In the European Union, Wolfmayr (2012) recorded that the share of intermediate services in manufacturing output rose from 14.8 percent to 17.9 percent between 1995 and 2005.[5] Between 1995 and 2007, Falk and Jarocinska (2010) found that the intermediate services demand generated from €1 of manufacturing output in the European Union increased from €0.42 to €0.61.[6]

Nonetheless, the mutual dependence between manufacturing and services appears to be asymmetrical. Early input-output analyses by Park (1989) and Park and Chan (1989) showed that sustained employment and output growth in services was possible only with the concomitant development of manufacturing. Services depended far more significantly on manufacturing inputs (exceeding 35 percent of inputs in most services subsectors) than vice versa. In a study of six advanced economies, Gregory and Russo (2007) illustrated that 24 percent to 31 percent of employment created from an injection of manufacturing demand flowed to the services sector.[7] By contrast, services retained most of the employment gains from increased demand, with only 6 percent to 11 percent of jobs induced in the manufacturing sector. With manufacturing being a major customer of dynamic and high-productivity services, Guerrieri and Meliciani (2005) and Felipe et al. (2013) concluded that the ability of countries to develop such services was tied to the presence and structure of the manufacturing base.

It has been argued that the loss of manufacturing capabilities by countries will eventually lead to the outflow of important manufacturing-related service activities (Cohen and Zysman 1987; Pisano and Shih 2009 and 2012). Given the symbiotic relationship between manufacturing and services, there are grounds for them to colocate. First, the nature of some services (e.g., facility management, rental of factory space, and equipment) requires them to be close to the manufacturing operations that they support. By being nearby, vertically disintegrated producers reduce the costs of interpersonal linkages (Coffey and Bailly 1991).

Second, close proximity between manufacturing and services creates a dynamic industrial environment whereby firms benefit from knowledge spillovers.[8] Drawing on research in the electronics, biotechnology, and pharmaceuticals industries, Pisano and Shih (2009 and 2012) emphasized that growth in manufacturing and services was mutual and reinforcing through the sharing of an "industrial commons." In the industrial commons, there is a collective pool of shared resources (including skilled labor, R&D, and infrastructure) that sustains innovation. By having suppliers and end users (e.g., industries and services such as design and R&D) close by, there is greater potential for better communication and information flows, the exchange of ideas, and innovation (see Porter 2008).

The colocational properties of manufacturing and services were reaffirmed by Andersson (2006) who analyzed employment data for different regions in Sweden. Manufacturing and services were found to colocate in urban regions, with knowledge-intensive manufacturing industries having a stronger influence on knowledge-intensive producer services employment than vice versa.[9]

METHODOLOGY AND DATA SOURCE

This study draws on manufacturing-services linkages among forty countries[10] in the European Commission's (2013) WIOD between 1995 and 2011.[11] The countries span the European Union (twenty-seven countries), Asia and the Pacific (nine countries), North America (two countries), and Latin America (two countries).[12] Annual data were available for thirty-five sectors per country.[13] In 1995, twenty-two developed countries and eighteen major developing countries were represented in the WIOD (table 13.1). By 2011, nine developing countries had become developed.[14]

Together, the forty countries in the WIOD accounted for a significant share of world production (87.8 percent of the world's GDP between 1995 and 2011) (table 13.2). Expectedly, advanced countries with more developed statistical agencies were better represented in the WIOD compared to developing countries.[15] Countries in the WIOD accounted for 90.5 percent of the developed world's GDP between 1995 and 2011, compared to 76.4 percent of the developing world's GDP.

Although broader coverage of developing countries (e.g., African countries) in the WIOD would have been ideal, it is unlikely to affect the results in this chapter significantly. The WIOD includes advanced economies and more-industrialized developing countries which account for a sizable share of global manufacturing and intermediate services output.[16] Between 1995 and 2011, the forty countries produced 89.2 percent

Table 13.1 Forty Countries Represented in the WIOD between 1995 and 2011

Twenty-two Developed Countries in 1995	Eighteen Developing Countries in 1995
Australia, Austria, Belgium, Canada, Cyprus, Denmark, Finland, France, Germany, Greece, Ireland, Italy, Japan, Luxembourg, Netherlands, Portugal, South Korea, Spain, Sweden, Taiwan, United Kingdom, United States	Brazil, Bulgaria, China, **Czech Republic, Estonia, Hungary,** India, Indonesia, **Latvia, Lithuania, Malta,** Mexico, **Poland,** Romania, Russia, **Slovak Republic, Slovenia,** Turkey

Notes: Developed countries correspond to the World Bank's (2015) high-income category while developing countries were in the low and middle income category. Developing countries shown in bold graduated to the category of high-income countries by 2011.

Source: World Bank's analytical income classifications, based on countries in European Commission (2013).

Table 13.2 Summary Statistics in Percent of the WIOD's Forty Countries between 1995 and 2011

	1995–2000	2001–2006	2007–2011	1995–2011
Share of world's GDP	88.7	88.6	85.6	87.8
Share of developed countries' GDP	91.6	91.2	88.4	90.5
Share of developing countries' GDP	74.3	77.2	78.0	76.4
Share of world's manufacturing output	89.4	89.7	88.8	89.2
Share of world's intermediate services output	91.8	92.9	92.5	92.5

Note: In this chapter, intermediate services refer to inputs to the manufacturing sector, unless stated otherwise.

Source: Author's estimates, based on European Commission (2013), DGBAS (2015), World Bank (2015).

of global manufacturing output and 92.5 percent of intermediate services output to manufacturing industries in the world. For brevity in terminology, *intermediate services* in this chapter refer to services inputs provided to the manufacturing sector, unless otherwise stated.

Unlike traditional input-output tables, the WIOD decomposes export flows to the different sectors in other countries. In notational form, the output x_i in country i can be expressed as the following:

$$
x_i = \begin{pmatrix} M_i \\ S_i \\ Z_i \end{pmatrix} = \begin{pmatrix} \alpha_{mm,i} & \alpha_{ms,i} & \alpha_{mz,i} \\ \alpha_{sm,i} & \alpha_{ss,i} & \alpha_{sz,i} \\ \alpha_{zm,i} & \alpha_{zs,i} & \alpha_{zz,i} \end{pmatrix} \begin{pmatrix} M_i \\ S_i \\ Z_i \end{pmatrix}
$$

$$
+ \begin{pmatrix} e_{m,i} \\ e_{s,i} \\ e_{z,i} \end{pmatrix} + \begin{pmatrix} d_{m,i} \\ d_{s,i} \\ d_{z,i} \end{pmatrix} = A_i x_i + e_i + d_i
$$

$$
= \sum_{j=1}^{41} \begin{pmatrix} b_{mm,ij} & b_{ms,ij} & b_{mz,ij} \\ b_{sm,ij} & b_{ss,ij} & b_{sz,ij} \\ b_{zm,ij} & b_{zs,ij} & b_{zz,ij} \end{pmatrix} \begin{pmatrix} M_j \\ S_j \\ Z_j \end{pmatrix}
$$

$$
+ \sum_{j=1}^{41} \begin{pmatrix} d_{m,j} \\ d_{s,j} \\ d_{z,j} \end{pmatrix} = \sum_{j=1}^{41} B_j x_j + \sum_{j=1}^{41} d_j
$$

where manufacturing, services, and others (e.g., agriculture, mining and quarrying, construction, and utilities) are denoted by M, S, and Z respectively; e refers to exports; and d encapsulates the final demand by households and the government, gross fixed capital formation and changes in inventories. Here i spans forty countries, with the forty-first "country" representing the rest of the world (ROW) excluding the forty countries.

Following from the above equation, total services can be decomposed into three categories: (1) intermediate services to manufacturing, (2) intermediate services to nonmanufacturing, and (3) services for final demand, with each category having domestic and exported components. As the emphasis of the chapter is on the colocation of intermediate services with manufacturing, the analysis will focus on the coefficient $b_{sm,ij}$—the service inputs of country i that support the manufacturing industry in country j.[17] When $i = j$, $b_{sm,ij}$ is equal to the technical coefficient $\alpha_{sm,i}$.

The European Commission's (2013) WIOD enhances the scope to analyze global manufacturing-services linkages. Until the release of the WIOD, past input-output analysis had been restricted to studying the technical coefficients in the matrix

$$
\begin{pmatrix}
\alpha_{mm,i} & \alpha_{ms,i} & \alpha_{mz,i} \\
\alpha_{sm,i} & \alpha_{ss,i} & \alpha_{sz,i} \\
\alpha_{zm,i} & \alpha_{zs,i} & \alpha_{zz,i}
\end{pmatrix}
$$

without visibility over the sectoral destinations of exports. Previous studies on manufacturing-services linkages have largely focused on the amm,i, $\alpha_{ss,i}$, $\alpha_{ms,i}$, and $\alpha_{sm,i}$ coefficients (see Park and Chan 1989; Park 1989 and 1994; Guerrieri and Meliciani 2005). By disaggregating

$$
\begin{pmatrix}
e_{m,i} \\
e_{s,i} \\
e_{z,i}
\end{pmatrix}
\text{ to obtain }
\begin{pmatrix}
b_{mm,ij} & b_{ms,ij} & b_{mz,ij} \\
b_{sm,ij} & b_{ss,ij} & b_{sz,ij} \\
b_{zm,ij} & b_{zs,ij} & b_{zz,ij}
\end{pmatrix},
$$

this chapter contributes to the existing input-output literature through the additional analysis of intermediate services flows to other manufacturing industries in the world.

To present general results in this chapter, the thirty-five sectors in the WIOD were categorized into broader groups where necessary (see appendix A). With the focus on manufacturing and services, there was less treatment in analyzing primary industries, utilities, and the construction sector. Manufacturing industries were classified as low-technology (LT), medium-technology (MT), and high-technology (HT) based on their R&D intensity (see OECD 2011).[18] Services were grouped into the following categories: (1) wholesale trade,[19] (2) retail trade,[20] (3) hotels and restaurants, (4) transport,[21] (5) communications,[22] (6) financial services, (7) business services (excluding real estate),[23] (8) real estate activities, and (9) other services.[24]

ECONOMIC CHARACTERISTICS IN THE WORLD

Within a span of 16 years (1995-2010), the distribution of economic activity in the world has shifted considerably (table 13.3). During this period, the contribution of developing countries to global GDP nearly doubled from 15.2 percent to 28.9 percent. Developing countries increased their global shares of both manufacturing value added (VA) and services VA. Led by China, developing countries contributed 37.7 percent of global manufacturing VA in 2010, more than doubling the 15.6 percent share in 1995. Between 1995 and 2010, their share of global services VA also rose from 11.8 percent to 22.8 percent.

Between 1995 and 2010, both developing and developed countries deindustrialized,[25] with the latter group deindustrializing at a faster pace

Table 13.3 Cross-Sectional Distribution in Percent of Economic Activity in the World, 1995–2010

	1995	2000	2005	2010
Share of World GDP (Current US$)				
Developing countries	15.2	17.2	19.2	28.9
Developed countries	84.8	82.8	80.8	71.1
Share of World Manufacturing VA (Current US$)				
Developing countries	15.6	19.8	24.5	37.7
Developed countries	84.4	80.2	75.5	62.3
Share of World Services VA (Current US$)				
Developing countries	11.8	13.3	14.5	22.8
Developed countries	88.2	86.7	85.5	77.2

Notes: Developed countries correspond to the World Bank's (2015) high-income category while developing countries were in the low and middle income category. Services VA included imputed bank service charges, import duties, and statistical discrepancies.

Data source: World Bank (2015).

(figure 13.1). During this period, the share of manufacturing VA fell in developed (19.2 percent to 15.0 percent) and developing (23.0 percent to 21.4 percent) countries.[26] By contrast, the share of services VA rose in both the developed (68.3 percent to 73.6 percent) and developing (47.6 percent to 53.2 percent) economies.

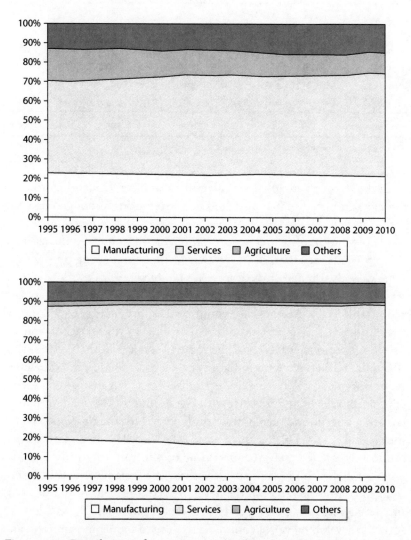

Figure 13.1   Distribution of economic activity (by value-added) in developing and developed countries, 1995–2010

Note: The "Others" category includes mining, construction and utilities.

Data source: World Bank (2015).

Table 13.4 Number and Distribution of Countries Categorized by Share of Manufacturing and Services in GDP, 1995 and 2010

Share in Nominal GDP (%)	Number of Countries				Distribution of Countries (%)			
	Manufacturing		Services		Manufacturing		Services	
	1995	2010	1995	2010	1995	2010	1995	2010
0–15	94	129	1	0	50.0	68.6	0.5	—
15–30	89	53	13	6	47.3	28.2	6.9	3.2
30–45	5	5	39	38	2.7	2.7	20.7	20.2
45–60	0	1	71	57	—	0.5	37.8	30.3
60–75	0	0	55	66	—	—	29.3	35.1
75–90	0	0	9	21	—	—	4.8	11.2
Total countries	188	188	188	188	100.0	100.0	100.0	100.0

Source: Author's estimates, based on World Bank (2015).

Between 1995 and 2010, manufacturing and services also contrasted in their patterns of spatial distribution in the world. Although manufacturing activity became increasingly concentrated in some countries,[27] a similar evolution of spatial concentration was not observed for services. As countries specialized in (or away from) manufacturing production, more were distributed at the upper end (and lower end) of the spectrum representing their share of manufacturing in GDP between 1995 and 2010 (table 13.4). By contrast, countries became increasingly concentrated only at the upper end of the distribution for services, as many developing countries increased the share of services in their economies.

Similar to the VA trends in figure 13.1, both developing and developed economies in the WIOD deindustrialized in terms of manufacturing output between 1995 and 2011, with the decline in the share of manufacturing output once again more pronounced for the developed countries (table 13.5).[28] During this period, both developing and developed countries upgraded their manufacturing basket from LT to MT and HT products. Between 1995 and 2011, the share of LT manufactures in manufacturing output fell in both the developed (39.1 percent to 32.1 percent) and developing (45.6 percent to 37.9 percent) economies. Nonetheless, by 2011, the developing world continued to depend more on manufacturing output and LT manufactures than did the developed world.

Between 1995 and 2011, the share of services output grew in both developed and developing countries (see table 13.5). However, they diverged in their trends for intermediate services. Unlike in advanced

Table 13.5 Cross-Sectional Economic Characteristics of Developed and Developing Economies, in Percent, in the WIOD, 1995, 2003 and 2011

	1995	2003	2011
Developed Economies			
Share of Mfg in total output	30.7	28.2	27.6
Share of HT Mfg in total Mfg output	35.9	40.4	39.4
Share of MT Mfg in total Mfg output	25.0	24.9	28.4
Share of LT Mfg in total Mfg output	39.1	34.7	32.1
Share of Svcs in total output	54.9	58.7	58.5
Share of domestic IS to domestic Mfg in total Svcs output	10.2	9.2	8.7
Share of domestic IS in total IS to domestic Mfg	88.5	86.1	83.5
Developing Economies			
Share of Mfg in total output	35.9	33.7	33.6
Share of HT Mfg in total Mfg output	29.8	31.7	31.2
Share of MT Mfg in total Mfg output	24.7	25.8	31.0
Share of LT Mfg in total Mfg output	45.6	42.5	37.9
Share of Svcs in total output	42.1	46.1	43.8
Share of domestic IS to domestic Mfg in total Svcs output	12.4	11.5	12.7
Share of domestic IS in total IS to domestic Mfg	86.8	88.6	91.9

Notes: Abbreviations for manufacturing (Mfg), services (Svcs), and intermediate services (IS) were used in the table. The shares of low-technology (LT), medium-technology (MT) and high-technology (HT) manufacturing in total manufacturing output may not sum identically to 100.0 percent due to rounding. The economic characteristics for developed and developing countries were based on available data from the forty countries in the WIOD. Unweighted averages of countries are shown in order to represent an average country in the developed or developing economies categories and not skew the numbers toward the economic characteristics of larger countries.

Source: Author's estimates, based on European Commission (2013).

economies, manufacturing industries in developing countries broadly sourced more intermediate services domestically rather than from abroad. Between 1995 and 2011, the share of domestically produced intermediate services fell in developed countries (88.5 percent to 83.5 percent) but increased in the developing world (86.8 percent to 91.9 percent). Increases for developing countries were observed for Bulgaria, India, Indonesia, Romania, and Russia.

Although both developed and developing economies deindustrialized in terms of manufacturing output, domestically consumed manufacturing-related services played a larger role in the production of services in developing countries over time. Between 1995 and 2011, the share of such services in total services output increased for developing countries (12.4 percent to 12.7 percent) but declined steadily for developed countries (10.2 percent to 8.7 percent). Developing countries such as Brazil, Bulgaria, and Russia experienced increases in the contribution of domestically consumed manufacturing-related services to their overall services output.

FINDINGS FROM THE WIOD

Interindustry interdependencies occur through backward and forward linkages between industries (see Hirschman 1958). By using the WIOD, information can be drawn on backward linkages (from manufacturing to the services industries that it draws inputs from) and forward linkages (from the services sector to the domestic and foreign manufacturing industries that it provides inputs to). The use of industry-level analysis allows the strengths of manufacturing-services linkages between different industries to be differentiated.

MANUFACTURING AND SERVICES SHARE STRONG PROPENSITY TO COLOCATE (WITHIN SAME COUNTRY)

The narrative supporting the geographical fragmentation of manufacturing and intermediate services has been premised on globalization and increased production flows across countries. With hyperglobalization (Subramanian and Kessler 2014), global trade has surged in a world characterized by greater integration, increased foreign investment flows, and stronger transnational corporations. The two waves of globalization—the steam revolution until the mid- or late-1980s and the information and communications technology (ICT)[29] revolution from 1980—had reduced, respectively, trade and transmission costs significantly (Baldwin 2014). In addition to the cross-border distribution of economic activities across countries (i.e., internationalization), globalization has enhanced functional integration between geographically dispersed activities (Dicken 2011).

Indeed, the WIOD shows that more services inputs are being sourced from abroad by the manufacturing sector. Between 1995 and 2011, the global manufacturing industry increased its share of imports in total intermediate services from 8.0 percent to 12.4 percent. Almost all manufacturing industries imported a larger share of intermediate services (table 13.6).[30]

Table 13.6 Share of Nonimported Intermediate Services in Percent for Global Manufacturing Industries, 1995–2011

ISIC	Manufacturing Industry	R&D Intensity	Share of Nonimported Intermediate Services in Total Intermediate Svcs			Percentage Point Change (1995–2000 and 2007–2011)
			1995–2000	2001–2006	2007–2011	
20	Wood and wood and cork products	LT	89.5	90.2	89.8	0.3
36, 37	Manufacturing, Nec; recycling	LT	91.9	91.8	91.0	−1.0
19	Leather and footwear	LT	90.0	88.6	88.8	−1.2
15, 16	Food, beverages, and tobacco	LT	91.9	90.9	90.7	−1.2
26	Other nonmetallic mineral	MT	90.2	89.0	89.0	−1.2
27, 28	Basic metals and fabricated metal	MT	90.9	89.3	89.0	−1.9
25	Rubber and plastics	MT	92.9	91.9	90.9	−2.0
34, 35	Transport equipment	HT	92.4	91.5	90.3	−2.1
29	Machinery, Nec	HT	93.0	91.3	90.1	−3.0
21, 22	Pulp, paper, printing, and publishing	LT	92.6	91.3	89.5	−3.1
24	Chemicals and chemical products	HT	90.9	88.6	86.7	−4.2
30, 33	Electrical and optical equipment	HT	93.1	90.0	88.7	−4.4
17, 18	Textiles and textile products	LT	90.2	88.2	85.7	−4.6
23	Coke, refined petroleum, and nuclear fuel	MT	72.2	62.8	60.6	−11.6
15, 37	Total Manufacturing	–	91.2	89.1	87.5	−3.7

Notes: The share of nonimported intermediate services in total intermediate services averages the annual nonimported intermediate services (to each manufacturing sector) as a proportion of total intermediate services output (to the same manufacturing sector) in the world for the time period of analysis. The manufacturing industries were sorted in descending order based on the change (in percentage points) in their shares of nonimported intermediate services in total intermediate services output between the periods 1995–2000 and 2007–2011. The percentage point change in the final column may not correspond identically to manual calculations in the table due to rounding.

Source: Author's estimates, based on European Commission (2013); R&D intensity classifications based on OECD (2011).

Nonetheless, manufacturing continued to source a significant share of its services inputs domestically rather than from abroad. With the exception of the coke, refined petroleum, and nuclear fuel industry,[31] 86 percent to 91 percent of intermediate services were still colocated with manufacturing (within the same country) between 2007 and 2011.[32] Notably, 91 percent of intermediate services to the food, beverage and tobacco, and rubber and plastic industries was still sourced from the same country for the 2007–2011 period. Although globalization and international trade have raised the potential to import intermediate services, manufacturing-services linkages have not fragmented to the extent that different countries can specialize solely in producing only manufacturing or intermediate services.

A similar picture emerges when one analyzes forward linkages from intermediate services to manufacturing industries. Although intermediate services have shown greater export potential since 1995, most intermediate services output continued to be consumed by domestic manufacturing industries (figure 13.2). Individual sectors differed in their "stickiness" to domestic manufacturing activities. At one end, most intermediate services output by the domestically oriented retail and real estate sectors (97 percent to 99 percent) flowed to domestic manufacturing industries. At the other end, trade-related sectors such as transport (particularly water and air transport) and wholesale trade exported a larger share of the intermediate services output to foreign manufacturing industries. Nonetheless, over 80 percent of output in these industries was still consumed within the same country by 2011.

Since the 2008 global financial crisis, intermediate services inputs, particularly from the more tradable sectors, have increasingly been sourced domestically by manufacturing industries in the world (see figure 13.2). The financial services sector illustrates one such example. Between 1995 and 2008, the share of domestically consumed manufacturing-related financial services fell from 94.5 percent to 87.1 percent in tandem with the growth in trade in services. However, the share subsequently rose to 89.3 percent by 2011 as the propensity for intermediate financial services and manufacturing to colocate increased after 2008.

MANUFACTURING-SERVICES LINKAGES
DIFFER ACROSS INDUSTRIES

The WIOD reaffirms the heterogeneous nature of manufacturing industries. Different manufacturing industries have different intermediate

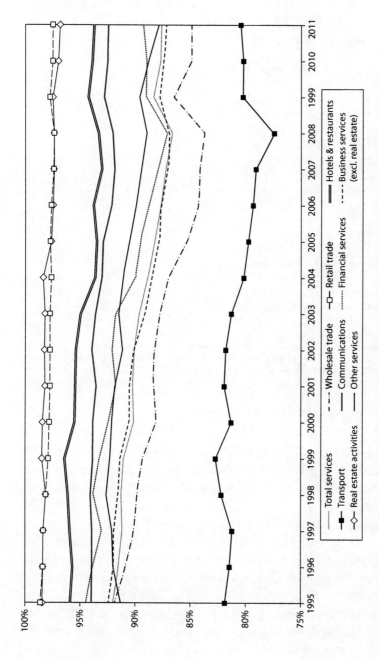

Figure 13.2 Share of Domestically Consumed Intermediate Services in Total Intermediate Services to World Manufacturing, 1995–2011

Source: Author's estimates, based on European Commission (2013).

Table 13.7 Manufacturing Sectors' Dependence on Intermediate Services, 1995–2011

ISIC	Manufacturing Sector	Ratio of Intermediate Services to Mfg Output	Percentage Change (1995–2011)
21, 22	Pulp, paper, printing and publishing	0.238	6.8
24	Chemicals and chemical products	0.215	−11.7
36, 37	Manufacturing, Nec; recycling	0.209	−0.7
15, 16	Food, beverages, and tobacco	0.207	−1.4
26	Other nonmetallic mineral	0.202	−10.5
19	Leather and footwear	0.195	−29.8
30–33	Electrical and optical equipment	0.189	−18.6
20	Wood and wood and cork products	0.186	−14.6
29	Machinery, Nec	0.183	−5.4
25	Rubber and plastics	0.181	−11.7
17, 18	Textiles and textile products	0.179	−15.9
27, 28	Basic metals and fabricated metal	0.165	−16.3
34, 35	Transport equipment	0.165	13.2
23	Coke, refined petroleum, and nuclear fuel	0.146	−11.0
15–37	Total Manufacturing	0.188	−8.5

Notes: The *ratio of intermediate services to manufacturing output* is defined as the average annual intermediate services output (to each manufacturing sector) as a proportion of the manufacturing sector's world output between 1995 and 2011. The manufacturing industries were sorted in descending order based on their ratio of intermediate services to manufacturing output.

Source: Author's estimates, based on European Commission (2013).

services requirements (table 13.7). The publishing (0.24 unit of intermediate services output per unit of manufacturing output) and chemical (0.22 unit) industries relied most on intermediate services. At the other end, the petroleum refining (0.15 unit) and transport equipment (0.16 unit) industries depended least on intermediate services.

The time-series characteristics of several industries stand out (figure 13.3). First, the transport equipment and publishing industries strengthened their backward linkages with the services sector between 1995 and 2011. For the transport equipment industry, backward linkages have steadily increased over time as the sector increased its services demand, particularly for business services and water transport services.[33] Second, the coke, refined petroleum, and nuclear fuel industry was the only industry that did not increase its ratio of intermediate services to

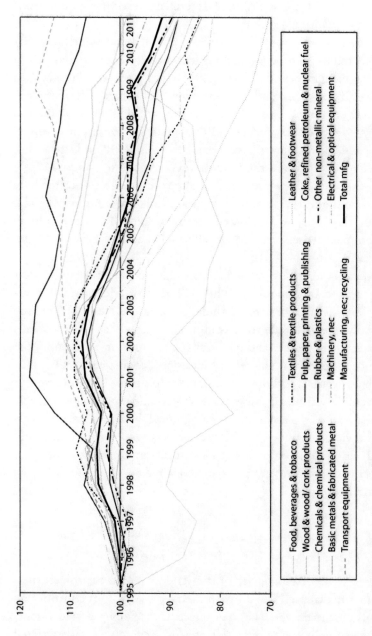

Figure 13.3 Ratio of Intermediate Services Output to Manufacturing Output by Manufacturing Industry, 1995–2011

Note: The ratios were normalised to 100 in 1995.

Source: Author's estimates, based on European Commission (2013).

Legend:

Food, beverages & tobacco
Wood & wood/ cork products
Chemicals & chemical products
Basic metals & fabricated metal
Transport equipment

Textiles & textile products
Pulp, paper, printing & publishing
Rubber & plastics
Machinery, nec
Manufacturing, nec; recycling

Leather & footwear
Coke, refined petroleum & nuclear fuel
Other non-metallic mineral
Electrical & optical equipment
Total mfg

manufacturing output from the 1995 level throughout the entire period of analysis.[34] Third, the leather and footwear industry experienced the most significant decline (30 percent) in its intermediate services requirements to produce each unit of output.

The previous analysis of table 13.6 also revealed that some industries (e.g., coke, refined petroleum, and nuclear fuel) experienced a more significant fragmentation of domestic manufacturing-services linkages than others (wood and wood and cork products). In general, LT industries (e.g., food, beverages, and tobacco; leather and footwear; wood and wood and cork products) decreased their share of nonimported intermediate services at a slower pace than the MT and HT industries did. Among the LT industries, the food, beverage, tobacco, and publishing industries offered better prospects of anchoring related intermediate services than the textiles, leather, and wood industries. Among the HT industries, the transport equipment industry sourced a larger proportion of intermediate services domestically compared to the chemicals and electronics industries.

LT industries tended to require a larger share of intermediate services that were less readily imported, while HT industries demanded intermediate services that were more tradable in nature. For instance, the domestically oriented retail trade comprised a larger share of intermediate services for the leather and footwear (14.7 percent in 2011) and food, beverages, and tobacco (13.9 percent) industries, compared to HT industries such as electrical and optical equipment (9.1 percent) and chemicals (9.4 percent). By contrast, business services—one of the most tradable intermediate services—accounted for a significantly higher share of intermediate services consumed by the chemicals (30.6 percent in 2011) and electrical and optical equipment (28.8 percent) industries, compared to the leather and footwear (12.3 percent) and wood and cork products (13.3 percent) industries.

EXPORTS OF INTERMEDIATE SERVICES OFFER SOME POTENTIAL BUT STILL REMAIN SMALL FOR NOW

Highlighting the heterogeneity of the services sector, manufacturing-related intermediate services differ in their services output contribution and export potential (table 13.8). For instance, the wholesale trade, transport, business services, and retail trade sectors were more greatly affected by deindustrialization because domestically consumed intermediate

Table 13.8 Contribution of Domestically Consumed and Exported Intermediate Services to World Services Output by Services Industries, 1995–2011

Services	Share of Domestically Consumed Intermediate Services (Exported IS) in Total Services Output (%)			Domestically Consumed IS (Exported IS) Growth (% per Annum)
	1995–2000	2001–2006	2007–2011	1995–2011
Wholesale trade	25.9 (2.9)	24.2 (3.7)	23.0 (4.1)	4.5 (9.1)
Transport	15.8 (3.5)	15.6 (3.7)	15.3 (4.0)	5.9 (6.6)
Business services (excl. real estate)	16.8 (1.5)	14.9 (1.8)	14.1 (2.1)	5.5 (9.4)
Retail trade	14.4 (0.3)	14.5 (0.3)	15.5 (0.4)	4.9 (8.5)
Financial services	9.6 (0.7)	7.4 (0.8)	7.9 (1.0)	4.5 (9.3)
Communications	7.7 (0.5)	6.9 (0.5)	6.8 (0.6)	6.1 (7.7)
Hotels and restaurants	5.1 (0.2)	4.3 (0.3)	4.4 (0.3)	4.3 (7.3)
Real estate activities	2.5 (0.0)	2.5 (0.0)	2.5 (0.1)	4.7 (9.7)
Other services	1.8 (0.2)	1.6 (0.2)	1.7 (0.2)	4.9 (7.4)
Total services	9.7 (0.9)	8.8 (1.1)	8.8 (1.3)	5.0 (8.2)

Notes: Numbers in parentheses reflect the exported component of intermediate services (IS). The IS sectors were sorted in descending order by their share of total (domestically consumed and exported) IS in total services output between 2007 and 2011.

Source: Author's estimates, based on European Commission (2013).

services comprised a larger share of their total services output. To compensate for the loss of these intermediate services, deindustrializing countries can aim to increase exports to overseas markets.

Between 1995 and 2011, exported intermediate services grew by 8.2 percent per annum, faster than the 5.0 percent per annum increase in domestically consumed intermediate services. Distributive services played a key role, with wholesale trade and transport services, respectively, accounting for 30.1 percent and 27.0 percent of exported manufacturing-related intermediate services in 2011. This was followed by business services (23.1 percent) and financial services (8.2 percent).[35]

Although intermediate services exports across all industries grew faster than domestically consumed intermediate services output between 1995 and 2011 (see figures in parentheses in the last column of table 13.8 for export growth), the strong growth was driven by low base effects. For instance, the share of exported intermediate services in total financial services output grew by only 0.2 percentage point between the periods 2001–2006 and 2007–2011 despite robust export growth. In comparison, the share of domestically consumed intermediate financial services rose by 0.5 percentage point over the same period. For the period 2007–2011, intermediate financial services serving manufacturing industries contributed 8.9 percent of total global financial services output, of which only 11.5 percent (or 1.0 percent of 8.9 percent) of the intermediate financial services was exported.[36]

By 2011, the contribution of exported manufacturing-related intermediate services to total services output (1.3 percent) was still significantly smaller than that of intermediate services serving domestic manufacturing industries (8.9 percent) (figure 13.4A).[37] Low base effects once again contributed to the strong growth of exported manufacturing-related intermediate services. In absolute terms, intermediate services to domestic manufacturing industries experienced a larger increase than did exported manufacturing-related intermediate services (figure 13.4B).

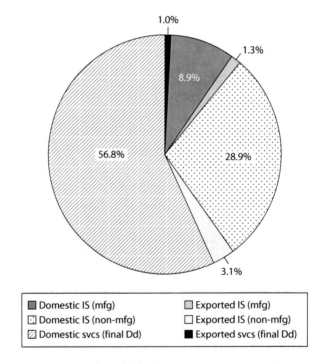

Figure 13.4A   Composition of World Services Output, 2011

Note: World services output comprises services for domestic and foreign final demand, intermediate services to domestic and external manufacturing industries, and intermediate services to domestic and external nonmanufacturing industries.

Source: Author's estimates, based on European Commission (2013).

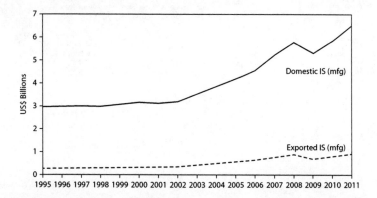

Figure 13.4B   Global Manufacturing-Related Services Output, Domestic and Exported, 1995–2011

Source: Author's estimates, based on European Commission (2013).

SCOPE TO EXPORT INTERMEDIATE SERVICES TO DEVELOPING COUNTRIES CONSTRAINED BY MANUFACTURING INDUSTRIES' LOWER INTERMEDIATE SERVICES REQUIREMENTS

Countries differ in their manufacturing sectors' dependence on intermediate services. Manufacturing in advanced economies (e.g., Ireland, Netherlands, and France) tended to depend more on intermediate services than it did in developing countries, most of which had a below-average ratio of intermediate services to manufacturing output (figure 13.5).[38] For instance, each unit of manufacturing output in Ireland required 0.3 unit of intermediate services between 1995 and 2011, and this dependence on intermediate services grew at one of the fastest rates (2.0 percent per annum) among the WIOD countries. By contrast, China's manufacturing sector required only 0.1 unit of intermediate services to produce each unit of output, with the dependence decreasing over time. As manufacturing production shifted to the developing world, the intermediate services demand by the global manufacturing industry declined from the peak in 2002 (see figure 13.3). By 2011, 0.17 unit of intermediate services was required to produce each unit of manufacturing output in the world, lower than the 0.19 unit of intermediate services needed in 1995.

Differences in the structures of manufacturing industries in developing and developed countries cannot solely explain why their requirements for manufacturing-related intermediate services differ. Between 1995 and 2011, China upgraded the technological content of its manufacturing industry as the HT component of its manufacturing output jumped from 32 percent

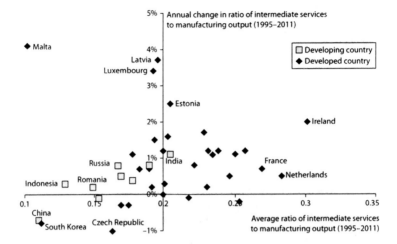

Figure 13.5   Classification of Countries by Ratio of Intermediate Services to Manufacturing Output and Changes in the Ratio, 1995–2011

Source: Author's estimates, based on European Commission (2013).

to 44 percent. By 2006, the HT component of China's manufacturing sector surpassed that of the United States. Nonetheless, although the structure of China's manufacturing sector has become more sophisticated over the years, its intermediate services requirements continued to fall.

One explanation for the difference in the share of intermediate services across countries may be that they differ in the vertical organization of production. Manufacturing firms in developing countries may use more in-house services than those in developed countries. Manufacturing-services linkages are therefore underreported as these integrated in-house services are classified as manufacturing. In these countries, the colocational properties of manufacturing and services will be stronger than official statistics reveal. The scope to export intermediate services to these developing economies will also be more limited.

ECONOMIC CENTER OF GRAVITY OF INTERMEDIATE
SERVICES PRODUCTION FOLLOWS MANUFACTURING
PRODUCTION TO THE EAST

The global economy's center of gravity is shifting toward the East (Grether and Mathys 2010; Quah 2011). A similar picture emerges when one analyzes the spatial movement of manufacturing and intermediate services output using the WIOD (figure 13.6). The mirrored movements of the

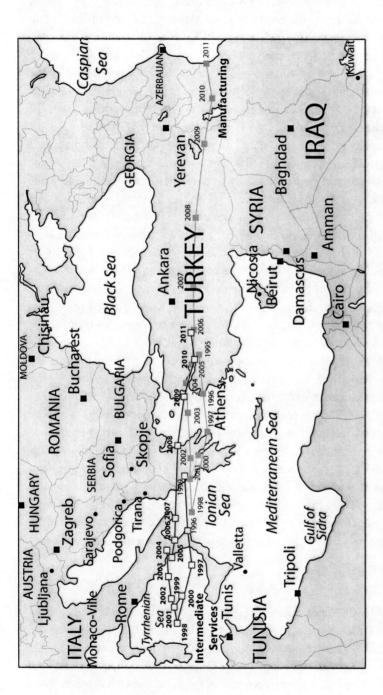

Figure 13.6 Economic Centers of Gravity of Global Manufacturing Output and Intermediate Services Output, 1995–2011

Notes: The economic center of gravity refers to the average location of economic activity for the forty countries (which accounted for 89.2% of global manufacturing output and 92.5% of global intermediate services output between 1995 and 2011) in the WIOD. The geographic coordinates of capital cities were used as the point location of countries.

Source: Author, based on internal estimates using European Commission (2013).

economic centers of gravity of manufacturing output and intermediate services output lend support to the proposition that the offshoring of manufacturing production will eventually lead to the loss of manufacturing-related services (e.g., Cohen and Zysman 1987; Pisano and Shih 2012).

Between 1995 and 1998, the center of gravity shifted westward as the United States and Japan experienced contrasting fortunes in their production of manufacturing and intermediate services. During this period, the United States's share of world manufacturing output rose from 20.3 percent to 23.4 percent while that of Japan fell from 18.9 percent to 13.8 percent.[39] Similarly, the United States gained a larger share of the global intermediate services market (22.1 percent to 25.3 percent between 1995 and 1998) while Japan's global market share declined (17.4 percent to 12.7 percent).

Since its accession to the World Trade Organization (WTO) in 2001, China's rapid development as a global manufacturing powerhouse contributed to the significant shift in the economic center of gravity of manufacturing production toward the East. Between 1995 and 2011, manufacturing output in China expanded by 17.0 percent per annum as its share of global manufacturing output jumped from 5.5 percent to 26.8 percent.[40] From 2007, China overtook the United States to become the world's largest producer of manufacturing output.[41]

The center of gravity of intermediate services output is following the spatial movement of manufacturing production toward the East. Given the propensity for intermediate services to colocate with manufacturing activities, China's strengths in manufacturing contributed to robust growth in its intermediate services output (16.0 percent per annum between 1995 and 2011). Between 1995 and 2011, China gained a significant share of global intermediate services output (from 3.4 percent to 16.1 percent) at the expense of other leading producers in the developed world, such as the United States, Japan, Germany, and France. In 2011, China overtook the United States (15.1 percent of global output) to become the world's largest producer of manufacturing-related intermediate services.[42]

CONCLUSION

Using the WIOD, this chapter reaffirms that manufacturing and services continue to share a strong propensity to colocate. Although international trade and ICT advancements have increased the potential for cross-border flows of services, manufacturing-services linkages have not fragmented to the extent that some countries can specialize as manufacturers while others focus on exporting intermediate services to them. Since the 2008 global financial crisis, manufacturing industries have increasingly sourced tradable intermediate services such as financial services domestically rather than from abroad.

The WIOD provides evidence to suggest that the offshoring of manufacturing production will eventually lead to the loss of manufacturing-related services. Manufacturing industries in developing countries such as China have a different vertical organization of production (e.g., more in-house services) that requires fewer intermediate services from abroad. Given the importance of geographical proximity between manufacturing and services, both manufacturing and intermediate services capabilities are increasingly shifting to the East. Reflecting this trend, China became the largest producer of intermediate services in the world in 2011.

The loss of intermediate services capabilities has important implications for economic development. Francois and Reinert (1996) illustrated the close relationship between income levels of countries and the demand for manufacturing-related producer services. Park (1994) emphasized the critical role indigenous producer services played in sustaining industrial exports and competitiveness. According to Ciccone and Matsuyama (1996), producer services tied to manufacturing were an important source of innovation and an essential part of economic development.

The results from the analysis also show that manufacturing and services are highly heterogeneous and cannot be simplistically classified into two distinct groups for countries to choose from. Within manufacturing and services, different activities are better suited for different countries. Identifying the ideal mix of industries and promoting them through judicious industrial policies remain important priorities for countries seeking to foster positive structural change.

Given their symbiotic relationship, the loss of manufacturing capabilities implies the loss (in developed countries) or foregoing (in developing countries) of important producer services capabilities. Deindustrializing developed countries will need to ensure that the loss of manufacturing and manufacturing-related services can be adequately compensated by the growth of services to nonmanufacturing activities. For developing countries seeking to bypass industrialization by undertaking a services-led path of development, an assessment will need to be made of whether the development of services can be sustainable without the presence of a healthy producer services sector. So far, the historical and empirical evidence continues to reaffirm that countries neglect the manufacturing sector at their own risks because of its healthy interdependencies with other important sectors in the economy.

APPENDIX

SECTORAL CLASSIFICATIONS IN THE WIOD

ISIC	Sector	OECD (2011) Classification	Category
A-B	Agriculture, hunting, forestry, and fishing	—	PI
C	Mining and quarrying	—	PI
15-16	Food, beverages and tobacco	LT: food products, beverages, and tobacco (15-16)	LT
17-18	Textiles and textile products	LT: textiles, textile products, leather, and footwear (17-19)	LT
19	Leather and footwear		
20	Wood and wood and cork products	LT: wood, pulp, paper products, printing, and publishing (20-22)	LT
21-22	Pulp, paper, printing and publishing		
23	Coke, refined petroleum, and nuclear fuel	MLT: coke, refined petroleum products, and nuclear fuel (23)	MT
24	Chemicals and chemical products	HT: pharmaceuticals (2423) MHT: chemicals excluding pharmaceuticals (24 excluding 2423)	HT
25	Rubber and plastics	MLT: rubber and plastic products (25)	MT
26	Other nonmetallic mineral	MLT: other nonmetallic mineral products (26)	MT
27-28	Basic metals and fabricated metal	MLT: basic metals and fabricated metal products (27-28)	MT
29	Machinery, Nec	MHT: machinery and equipment, Nec (29)	HT
30-33	Electrical and optical equipment	HT: office, accounting and computing machinery (30); radio, TV, and communications equipment (32); medical, precision, and optical instruments (33) MHT: electrical machinery and apparatus, Nec (31)	HT
34-35	Transport equipment	HT: aircraft and spacecraft (353) MHT: motor vehicles, trailers and semitrailers (34); railroad equipment and transport equipment, Nec (352+359) MLT: building and repairing of ships and boats (351)	HT
36-37	Manufacturing, Nec; recycling	LT: manufacturing, Nec; recycling (36-37)	LT

ISIC	Sector	OECD (2011) Classification	Category
E	Electricity, gas and water supply	—	Utilities
F	Construction	—	Construction
50	Sale, maintenance and repair of motor vehicles and motor-cycles; retail sale of fuel	—	Retail trade
51	Wholesale trade and commission trade, except of motor vehicles and motorcycles	—	Wholesale trade
52	Retail trade, except of motor vehicles and motorcycles; repair of household goods	—	Retail trade
H	Hotels and restaurants	—	Hotels and restaurants
60	Inland transport	—	Transport
61	Water transport	—	
62	Air transport	—	
63	Other supporting and auxiliary transport activities; activities of travel agencies	—	
64	Post and telecommunications	—	Communications
J	Financial intermediation	—	Financial services
70	Real estate activities	—	Real estate
71-74	Renting of machinery and equipment, and other business activities	—	Business services
L	Public administration and defense; compulsory Social Security	—	Other services
M	Education	—	
N	Health and social work	—	
O	Other community, social and personal services	—	
P	Private households with employed persons	—	

Notes: Primary industries (PI) included agriculture, forestry, fishing, mining and quarrying. OECD (2011) classified manufacturing industries, based on direct R&D intensity, into four categories: high-technology (HT), medium-high-technology (MHT), medium-low-technology (MLT), and low-technology (LT). In the analysis, HT and MHT industries were combined to a single "HT industries" grouping while MLT industries were referred to as medium-technology (MT) industries. This reflected the WIOD's broad sectors (e.g., chemicals and chemical products, and electrical and optical equipment) which had a mix of HT and MHT industries. Classification of the transport equipment sector posed greater difficulty because of its mix of HT, MHT, and MLT industries. A decision was made to reclassify it as a HT industry because (1) it had more ISIC categories falling under HT and MHT industries and (2) the countries in the WIOD were skewed toward those at a more advanced stage of development (with better records of input-output tables), and hence with more advanced industries. "Nec" refers to related industries that were "not elsewhere classified."

Source: OECD (2011), European Commission (2013), and internal classifications.

NOTES

The author expresses gratitude to Ha-Joon Chang for his intellectual guidance and valuable comments. The chapter has also benefited from discussions at both the meeting of the IPD/JICA Task Force on Industrial Policy and Transformation in New York and the 2015 Advanced Graduate Workshop on Poverty, Development and Globalization in Bangalore. In particular, the author would like to thank Joseph Stiglitz, Akbar Noman, Nobuya Haraguchi, and C. P. Chandrasekhar for their useful comments and suggestions. The views expressed in this chapter are those of the author and should not be attributed to the Ministry of Trade and Industry, Singapore.

1. For example, Chang and Bhagwati (2011) had an online debate in *The Economist* on the motion "This house believes that an economy cannot succeed without a big manufacturing base."

2. Globalization has greatly reduced the barriers of distance through lower transportation costs, more seamless communications, and more advanced information and organization technologies. Alongside globalization, the fragmentation of global supply chains across geographical borders lowers costs for firms and increases the potential for countries to specialize in different activities (Helpman 1984; Markusen 1984; Feenstra 1998; Hummels, Ishii, and Yi 2001; Yi 2003). The division of labor across countries now revolves around production activities rather than products, as in the past. Rather than relocating entire manufacturing operations overseas, transnational corporations can now move specific segments of the value chain abroad based on their contribution to the firm's overall objectives (Hanson, Mataloni, and Slaughter 2001). The growing potential for modularization in the manufacturing sector means that, similar to Lego blocks, final products can increasingly be built up from smaller modules which are produced across the world (Berger 2005).

3. Arising from the important role of services such as R&D, engineering, design, sales, and maintenance, manufacturing costs were estimated to account for less than 25 percent of a manufacturer's value-added and production cost in many industries (e.g., electronics) (Hansen 1994, 189; Illeris 1996, 74).

4. Canada, France, and Portugal were the only exceptions.

5. The growth of the share of intermediate services in manufacturing output slowed down in the second period (2000–2005) of Wolfmayr's (2012) analysis.

6. This included the direct intermediate services purchased by manufacturing (€0.15 in 1995; €0.19 in 2007) and the indirect intermediate services used by nonservices inputs in the manufacturing sector (€0.27 in 1995; €0.42 in 2007).

7. Countries in Gregory and Russo's (2007) study included France, Germany, the Netherlands, Spain, the United Kingdom, and the United States. A broader definition of manufacturing (including agriculture, mining and quarrying, public utilities, and construction) was adopted by the authors.

8. The idea of creating positive externalities from localizing related economic activities has its theoretical foundations from Alfred Marshall's (1920) pioneering work on industrial clusters.

9. Andersson (2006) defined knowledge-intensive industries to have a higher proportion of employment with at least three years of university education (above 6 percent for manufacturing; above 10 percent for producer services).

10. Other countries were grouped into a "rest of the world" category.

11. The WIOD (1995–2009) was released to the general public in May 2012. In November 2013, the time series was extended to 2011.

12. Countries were classified into the following geographical regions: *European Union* (Austria, Belgium, Bulgaria, Cyprus, Czech Republic, Denmark, Estonia, Finland, France, Germany, Greece, Hungary, Ireland, Italy, Latvia, Lithuania, Luxembourg, Malta, Netherlands, Poland, Portugal, Romania, Slovak Republic, Slovenia, Spain, Sweden, and United Kingdom), *Asia and the Pacific* (Australia, China, India, Indonesia, Japan, Russia, South Korea, Taiwan, and Turkey), *North America* (Canada and United States), and *Latin America* (Brazil and Mexico).

13. See appendix A for the thirty-five sectors in the WIOD.

14. Poland was classified as a developed country in 2011 on the basis that it surpassed the high-income country threshold in 2010 and 2012, even though it experienced a temporary dip in 2011.

15. For instance, there were no African countries in the WIOD.

16. The agriculture sector tends to play a larger role in developing countries (12.7 percent of GDP between 1995 and 2010) than in developed countries (1.8 percent of GDP) (World Bank 2015).

17. The analysis examines only direct (first-order) economic contributions of manufacturing and services and their second-order effects arising from input-output linkages between the two sectors. Subsequent third-order effects are excluded from the study.

18. LT industries include (1) food, beverages, and tobacco; (2) textiles and textile products; (3) leather and footwear; (4) wood and wood and cork products; (5) pulp, paper, printing, and publishing; and (6) manufacturing, not elsewhere classified (nec); recycling. MT industries include (1) coke, refined petroleum, and nuclear fuel; (2) rubber and plastics; (3) other nonmetallic minerals; and (4) basic metals and fabricated metal. HT industries include (1) chemicals and chemical products, (2) machinery, nec, (3) electrical and optical equipment, and (4) transport equipment.

19. *Wholesale trade* refers to "wholesale trade and commission trade, except of motor vehicles and motorcycles."

20. *Retail trade* includes (1) "sale, maintenance and repair of motor vehicles and motorcycles; retail sale of fuel" and (2) "retail trade, except of motor vehicles and motorcycles; repair of household goods."

21. The "transport" category includes (1) inland transport, (2) water transport, (3) air transport, and (4) other supporting and auxiliary transport activities plus activities of travel agencies.

22. The "communications" category refers to "post and telecommunications."

23. In this definition of business services, real estate activities are classified separately because they are significantly less tradable than the other components of business services. Business services include a diverse range of activities ranging from professional services (e.g., legal, accounting, consultancy, architectural, and engineering activities) to research and development.

24. "Other services" include (1) public administration and defense as well as compulsory social security; (2) education; (3) health and social work; (4) other community, social, and personal services; and (5) private households with employed persons.

25. In this instance, deindustrialization refers to a fall in the share of manufacturing in nominal VA.

26. The agriculture sector's share of GDP also fell in the developed (2.4 percent to 1.4 percent) and developing (16.4 percent to 10.5 percent) countries between 1995 and 2010 (World Bank 2015).

27. Between 1995 and 2003, there was a steady increase in the share of imported intermediate manufacturing inputs by the global manufacturing industry (23.2 percent to 31.2 percent) (European Commission 2013). Thereafter, imported intermediate manufacturing inputs fell as manufacturers started integrating backward into the production of their components, and manufacturing activity became increasingly concentrated in countries. By 2011, the share of imports in total intermediate manufacturing output fell to 27.0 percent.

28. Between 1995 and 2011, the share of manufacturing in total output fell more in developed (30.7 percent to 27.6 percent) than developing (35.9 percent to 33.6 percent) countries (European Commission 2013).

29. Notably, the tradability of services has increased because of rising Internet penetration (Freund and Weinhold 2002) and ICT investments (Guerrieri and Meliciani 2005).

30. Only the wood products industry saw its share of imported intermediate services fall marginally from 10.5 percent in the period 1995–2000 to 10.2 percent in the period 2007–2011.

31. The coke, refined petroleum, and nuclear fuel industry was an outlier compared to the other manufacturing industries, but it still sourced 61 percent of its services inputs domestically between 2007 and 2011.

32. This contrasted with intermediate manufacturing inputs whereby a smaller share (72 percent in 2007–2011) was colocated with manufacturing (European Commission 2013).

33. Between 1995 and 2011, the shares of business services and water transport services in the total intermediate services demanded by the global transport equipment industry, respectively, rose by 3.5 percentage points (from 23.6 percent to 27.1 percent) and 0.8 percentage point (from 1.1 percent to 1.8 percent). During this period, the output of intermediate water transport services and business services, respectively, expanded by 353 percent and 203 percent, greatly surpassing the 134 percent increase in global transport equipment output.

34. The coke, refined petroleum, and nuclear fuel industry is an industry in which advanced economies such as that of the United States have retained their competitiveness. Between 1995 and 2011, it was the only U.S. manufacturing industry that raised its share of global manufacturing output (by 1.0 percentage point) (European Commission 2013). All other U.S. manufacturing industries experienced falls in their shares of global manufacturing output of 4.2 to 12.7 percentage points.

35. Business services appeared to benefit from the offshore outsourcing of previously integrated services in the manufacturing sector until the early 2000s when the phenomenon stabilized. See, e.g., Tregenna (2008), who analyzed the outsourcing of jobs from manufacturing to business services categories including cleaning, security, and professional services. Between 1995 and 2003, the share of business services in

the world's exported manufacturing-related intermediate services output rose from 19.4 percent to reach a high of 25.3 percent. Subsequently, the share stabilized between 22 percent and 25 percent. By comparison, exported intermediate financial services played a smaller role, with its output accounting for only 35.3 percent of exported intermediate business services output by 2011. Between 1995 and 2011, the share of financial services in the output of exported intermediate services rose by only 1.2 percentage points (or 0.07 percentage point per annum).

36. Although the share of intermediate services in total financial services output declined from 11.3 percent to 7.8 percent between 1995 and 2005, it subsequently increased steadily to 9.5 percent by 2011, suggesting that the sector's reliance on the manufacturing sector strengthened (European Commission 2013).

37. Between 1995 and 2011, the share of exported manufacturing-related intermediate services in total services output rose from 0.9 percent to 1.3 percent (European Commission 2013).

38. This result corroborates findings by Francois and Woerz (2008) that countries draw more producer services inputs at higher levels of development. Among the developing countries in 2011, only India's manufacturing sector depended on intermediate services (marginally) above the average level.

39. Between 1995 and 1998, manufacturing output fell by 10.9 percent per annum in Japan but rose by 3.8 percent per annum in the United States.

40. As a comparison, global manufacturing output grew by 5.9 percent per annum between 1995 and 2011.

41. In value-added terms, the United States relinquished its position as the largest manufacturer in the world to China in 2009.

42. As China industrialized, it also developed capabilities in intermediate services exports. Between 1995 and 2011, China's exported manufacturing-related intermediate services grew by 18.5 percent per annum, 3.2 times the rate experienced by the United States (5.7 percent per annum).

REFERENCES

Andersson, M. 2006. "Co-Location of Manufacturing and Producer Services: A Simultaneous Equations Approach." In *Entrepreneurship and Dynamics in the Knowledge Economy*, eds. C. Karlsson, B. Johansson, and R. R. Stough, 94–124. New York: Routledge.

Baer, W., and L. Samuelson. 1981. "Toward a Service-Oriented Growth Strategy." *World Development* 9(6): 499–514.

Baines, T. S., H. W. Lightfoot, O. Benedettini, and J. M. Kay. 2009. "The Servitization of Manufacturing: A Review of Literature and Reflection on Future Challenges." *Journal of Manufacturing Technology Management* 20(5): 547–67.

Baldwin, R. 2014." Trade and Industrialization After Globalization's Second Unbundling: How Building and Joining a Supply Chain Are Different and Why It Matters." In *Globalization in an Age of Crisis: Multilateral Economic Cooperation in the Twenty-First Century*, eds. R. C. Feenstra and A. M. Taylor, 165–212. Chicago: University of Chicago Press.

Bell, D. 1973. *The Coming of Post-Industrial Society: A Venture in Social Forecasting.* New York: Basic Books.

Berger, S. 2005. *How We Compete: What Companies Around the World Are Doing to Make It in Today's Global Economy.* New York: Doubleday.

Bhagwati, J. N. 1984. "Splintering and Disembodiment of Services and Developing Nations." *The World Economy* 7(2): 133–144.

——. 2010. *The Manufacturing Fallacy.* Retrieved January 2, 2015, from Project Syndicate: http://www.project-syndicate.org/commentary/the-manufacturing-fallacy

Britton, S. 1990. "The Role of Services in Production." *Progress in Human Geography* 14(4): 529–46.

Brown, R., and D. Julius. 1993. "Is Manufacturing Still Special in the New World Order?" In *Finance and the International Economy 7: The Amex Bank Review Prize Essays in Memory of Robert Marjolin,* ed. R. O'Brien, 6–20. New York: Oxford University Press.

Chang, H.-J., and J. Bhagwati. 2011. "Economist Debates: Manufacturing: This House Believes that an Economy Cannot Succeed Without a Big Manufacturing Base." *The Economist.* Retrieved October 10, 2015 from: http://www.columbia.edu/~jb38/papers/pdf/The_Economist_com_Debate_Manufacturing.pdf.

Chang, H.-J., A. Andreoni, and M. L. Kuan. 2014. "International Industrial Policy Experiences and the Lessons for the UK." In *The Future of UK Manufacturing: Scenario Analysis, Financial Markets and Industrial Policy,* ed. A. Hughes. London: UK-IRC.

Chenery, H. B. 1960. "Patterns of Industrial Growth." *The American Economic Review* 50(4): 624–54.

Ciccone, A., and K. Matsuyama. 1996. "Start-Up Costs and Pecuniary Externalities as Barriers to Economic Development." *Journal of Development Economics* 49(1): 33–59.

Clark, C. 1940. *The Conditions of Economic Progress.* London: Macmillan.

Coffey, W. J., and A. S. Bailly. 1991. Producer Services and Flexible Production: An Exploratory Analysis. *Growth and Change* 22(4): 95–117.

Cohen, S., and J. Zysman. 1987. *Manufacturing Matters: The Myth of the Post-Industrial Economy.* New York: Basic Books.

Daniels, P. W., and J. R. Bryson. 2002. "Manufacturing Services and Servicing Manufacturing: Knowledge-Based Cities and Changing Forms of Production." *Urban Studies* 39(5–6): 977–91.

DGBAS (Directorate-General of Budget Accounting and Statistics). 2015. *National Statistics Database.* Taipei City: DGBAS.

Dicken, P. 2011. *Global Shift: Mapping the Changing Contours of the World Economy.* New York: Guilford.

European Commission. 2013. *World Input-Output Database.* Brussels: European Commission.

Falk, M., and E. Jarocinska. 2010. *Linkages Between Services and Manufacturing in EU Countries.* SERVICEGAP Review Paper 1. Brussels: European Commission.

Feenstra, R. C. 1998. "Integration of Trade and Disintegration of Production in the Global Economy." *Journal of Economic Perspectives* 12(4): 31–50.

Felipe, J., R. Briones, D. H. Brooks, A. Mehta, and H. Verspagen. 2013. *Asia's Economic Transformation: Where to, How, and How Fast?: Key Indicators for Asia and the Pacific 2013 Special Chapter.* Manila: Asian Development Bank.

Fisher, A. G. 1935. *The Clash of Progress and Security.* London: Macmillan.

Francois, J. F., and K. A. Reinert. 1996. "The Role of Services in the Structure of Production and Trade: Stylized Facts from a Cross-Country Analysis." *Asia-Pacific Economic Review* 2(1) 35–43.

Francois, J. F., and J. Woerz. 2008. "Producer Services, Manufacturing Linkages, and Trade." *Journal of Industry, Competition and Trade* 8(3–4): 199–229.

Freund, C., and D. Weinhold. 2002. The Internet and International Trade in Services. *The American Economic Review* 92(2): 236–40.

Galbraith, J. K. 1958. *The Affluent Society.* Boston: Houghton Mifflin.

Ghani, E., and S. D. O'Connell. 2014. *Can Service Be a Growth Escalator in Low Income Countries?* World Bank Policy Research Working Paper No. 6971. Washington, D.C.: World Bank.

Greenfield, H. I. 1966. *Manpower and the Growth of Producer Services.* New York: Columbia University Press.

Gregory, M., and G. Russo, 2007. "Do Demand Differences Cause the U.S.-European Employment Gap?" In *Services and Employment: Explaining the U.S.-European Gap*, eds. M. Gregory, W. Salverda, and R. Schettkat, 81–108. Princeton, N.J.: Princeton University Press.

Grether, J.-M., and N. A. Mathys. 2010. "Is the World's Economic Centre of Gravity Already in Asia?" *Area* 42(1): 47–50.

Guerrieri, P., and V. Meliciani. 2005. "Technology and International Competitiveness: The Interdependence Between Manufacturing and Producer Services." *Structural Change and Economic Dynamics* 16(4): 489–502.

Hansen, N. 1994. "The Strategic Role of Producer Services in Regional Development." *International Regional Science Review* 16(1–2): 187–95.

Hanson, G. H., R. J. Mataloni, and M. J. Slaughter. 2001. "Expansion Strategies of U.S. Multinational Firms." In *Brookings Trade Forum*, eds. S. M. Collins and D. Rodrik, 245–94. Washington, D.C.: Brookings Institution Press.

Helpman, E. 1984. "A Simple Theory of International Trade with Multinational Corporations." *Journal of Political Economy* 92(3): 451–71.

Hirschman, A. O. 1958. *The Strategy of Economic Development.* New Haven. Conn., and London: Yale University Press.

Houseman, S. 2007. "Outsourcing, Offshoring, and Productivity Measurement in U.S. Manufacturing." *International Labour Review* 146(1–2): 61–80.

Houthakker, H. 1957. "An International Comparison of Household Expenditure Patterns, Commemorating the Centenary of Engel's Law." *Econometrica* 25(4): 532–51.

Howells, J. 2004. "Innovation, Consumption and Services: Encapsulation and the Combinatorial Role of Services." *The Service Industries Journal* 24(1): 19–36.

Hummels, D., J. Ishii, and K.-M. Yi. 2001. "The Nature and Growth of Vertical Specialization in World Trade." *Journal of International Economics* 54(1): 75–96.

Illeris, S. 1996. *The Service Economy: A Geographical Approach.* Chichester: Wiley.

Johnston, B., and J. Mellor. 1961. "The Role of Agriculture in Economic Development." *The American Economic Review* 51(4): 566–93.

Kuznets, S. 1971. *Economic Growth of Nations: Total Output and Production Structure.* Cambridge, Mass.: Harvard University Press.

Lewis, W. A. 1954. "Economic Development with Unlimited Supplies of Labour." *The Manchester School* 22(2): 139–91.

Livesey, F. 2006. *Defining High Value Manufacturing.* London: University of Cambridge Institute for Manufacturing.

Markusen, J. R. 1984. "Multinationals, Multi-Plant Economies, and the Gains from Trade." *Journal of International Economics* 16(3–4): 205–26.

Marshall, A. 1920. *Principles of Economics.* 8th ed. London: Macmillan.

Nordås, H. K., and Y. Kim. 2013. *The Role of Services for Competitiveness in Manufacturing.* OECD Trade Policy Papers No. 148. Paris: OECD.

OECD (Organisation for Economic Co-operation and Development). 2011. "ISIC Rev. 3 Technological Intensity Definition: Classification of Manufacturing Industries into Categories Based on R&D Intensities." OECD, July 7. Retrieved January 2, 2015, from: http://www.oecd.org/sti/ind/48350231.pdf

Park, S.-H. 1989. "Linkages Between Industry and Services and Their Implications for Urban Employment Generation in Developing Countries." *Journal of Development Economics* 30(2): 359–79.

——. 1994. Intersectoral Relationships Between Manufacturing and Services: New Evidence from Selected Pacific Basin Countries. *ASEAN Economic Bulletin* 10(3): 245–63.

Park, S.-H., and K. S. Chan. 1989. "A Cross-Country Input-Output Analysis of Intersectoral Relationships between Manufacturing and Services and their Employment Implications." *World Development* 17(2): 199–212.

Pisano, G. P., and W .C. Shih. 2009. "Restoring American Competitiveness." *Harvard Business Review,* July-August, 114–25.

——. 2012. *Producing Prosperity: Why America Needs a Manufacturing Renaissance.* Boston: Harvard Business Review Press.

Porter, M. E. 2008. *On Competition: Updated and Expanded Edition.* Boston: Harvard Business Press.

Quah, D. 2011. "The Global Economy's Shifting Centre of Gravity." *Global Policy* 2(1) 3–9.

Romer, C. D. 2012. "Do Manufacturers Need Special Treatment?" *New York Times,* Feb 4. Retrieved January 2, 2015: http://www.nytimes.com/2012/02/05/business/do-manufacturers-need-special-treatment-economic-view.html

Rowthorn, R., and J. Wells. 1987. *De-Industrialization and Foreign Trade.* London: Cambridge University Press.

Schmenner, R. W. 2009. "Manufacturing, Service, and Their Integration: Some History and Theory." *International Journal of Operations and Production Management* 29(5): 431–43.

Subramanian, A., and M. Kessler. 2014. "The Hyperglobalization of Trade and Its Future." In *Towards a Better Global Economy: Policy Implications for Citizens Worldwide in the 21st Century,* eds. F. Allen, J. R. Behrman, N. Birdsall, S. Fardoust, D. Rodrik, A. Steer, et al., 216–77. London: Oxford University Press.

Timmer, C. P. 1988. "The Agricultural Transformation." In *Handbook of Development Economics*, vol. 1, eds. H. B. Chenery and T. N. Srinivasan, 275–331. Amsterdam: North Holland.

Tregenna, F. 2008. "Quantifying the Outsourcing of Jobs from Manufacturing to Services." *South African Journal of Economics* 76(S2): S222–S238.

Vandermerwe, S., and J. Rada. 1988. "Servitization of Business: Adding Value by Adding Services." *European Management Journal* 6(4): 314–24.

Walker, R. A. 1985. "Is There a Service Economy? The Changing Capitalist Division of Labour." *Science and Society* 49(1): 42–83.

Wise, R., and P. Baumgartner. 1999. "Go Downstream: The New Profit Imperative in Manufacturing." *Harvard Business Review* 77(5): 133–41.

Wolfmayr, Y. 2008. *Producer Services and Competitiveness of Manufacturing Exports*. FIW Research Report No. 9. Vienna: Federal Ministry of Science, Research and Economy, Austria.

——. 2012. "Export Performance and Increased Services Content in Manufacturing." *National Institute Economic Review* 220(1): R36–R52.

Wood, P. 2009. "Service Competitiveness and Urban Innovation Policies in the UK: The Implications of the 'London Paradox.'" *Regional Studies* 43(8): 1047–59.

World Bank. 2015. *World Development Indicators Database*. Washington, D.C.: World Bank.

Yi, K.-M. 2003. "Can Vertical Specialization Explain the Growth of World Trade?" *Journal of Political Economy* 111(1): 52–102.

ACKNOWLEDGMENTS

This volume is an outcome of the collaboration between the Initiative for Policy Dialogue (IPD) and the Japan International Cooperation Agency (JICA) in the work of IPD's Industrial Policy Task Force directed by Akbar Noman and Joseph Stiglitz. In addition to financial support, JICA staff contributed to the substantive work of the task force including notably Akio Hosono and Go Shimada, who contributed two chapters published in this book. We are most grateful to JICA for funding this work.

In addition to the contributing authors, we gratefully acknowledge the comments of a long list of colleagues (without of course committing them to our analysis or views) and in particular to Yaw Ansu, C.P. Chandrasekhar, Ha-Joon Chang, Wouter Jongbloed, William Johnson, Anush Kapadia, Keun Lee, Kalle Moene, Celestin Monga, Ichiro Tambo, Eric Verhoogen, and Robert Wade. We are very grateful to the two anonymous referees who provided insightful comments on the manuscript. This work would not have been possible without the professional dedication of IPD's Program Manager, Jiaming Ju, who was vital in arranging the task force meetings and coordinating the production process of this volume. A large debt of gratitude is also owed to Kristen Grennan for her excellent contribution to the copyediting of this book and to Florian Schaeffer for his diligent note taking.

Finally, we most gratefully acknowledge the superb help, guidance, and support of Bridget Flannery-McCoy and her team at Columbia University Press.

CONTRIBUTORS

Akbar Noman is an economist with wide-ranging experience of policy analysis and formulation in a variety of developing and transition economies, having worked extensively for the World Bank as well as at the IMF, other international organizations and at senior levels of government. He combines teaching at Columbia University with being a Senior Fellow at the Initiative for Policy Dialogue—a "think tank" headed by Joseph Stiglitz at Columbia University—where his tasks continue to include policy work with governments. His other academic appointments have been at Oxford University (where he was also a student) and the Institute of Development Studies at the University of Sussex.

Joseph E. Stiglitz is a University Professor and cochair of the Committee on Global Thought at Columbia University, the winner of the 2001 Nobel Memorial Prize in Economics, and a lead author of the 1995 IPCC report, which shared the 2007 Nobel Peace Prize. He was chairman of the U.S. Council of Economic Advisors under President Clinton and was chief economist and senior vice president of the World Bank from 1997 to 2000.

Stiglitz received the John Bates Clark Medal, awarded biennially to the American economist under 40 who has made the most significant contribution to the subject. He was a Fulbright Scholar at Cambridge University, held the Drummond Professorship at All Souls College Oxford, and has also taught at M.I.T, Yale, Stanford, and Princeton. He is the author most recently of *The Price of Inequality: How Today's Divided Society Endangers Our Future*.

Antonio Andreoni (PhD, Cambridge) is lecturer in economics at the Department of Economics of the School of Oriental and African

Studies—SOAS, University of London. At SOAS he is also co-research director of the Anti-Corruption Evidence DFID Research Programme Consortium and Leader of the SOAS-IDP Industrial Development and Policy Research Cluster. Also, research fellow at the Institute for Manufacturing, University of Cambridge. His work has appeared in the *Cambridge Journal of Economics*, *Structural Change and Economic Dynamics*, and *Oxford Review of Economic Policy*. He is co-author (with M. Moazam and H.-J. Chang) of *Developing with Jobs* (Palgrave Macmillan) and an advisor to various governments and multilateral organisations including UNIDO, ILO, UNCTAD, UNDP, UN DESA, OECD, BMZ-GIZ, DFID, UK Government Office for Science, and Tanzania MITI.

Mario Cimoli is director of the Division of Production, Productivity and Management and officer in charge of the Division of International Trade and Integration at the United Nations' Economic Commission for Latin America and the Caribbean (ECLAC) and professor of economics at the University of Venice (Ca' Foscari). He obtained his PhD at SPRU (University of Sussex) with a thesis that analyzes the effect of technological gaps and trade on growth in developing economies. In 2004, he was appointed co-director (with Giovanni Dosi and Joseph Stiglitz) of two task forces: Industrial Policy and Intellectual Property Rights Regimes for Development (Initiative for Policy Dialogue, Columbia University, New York). He was also awarded the Philip Morris Chair of International Business (2004) at the Sant'Anna School of Advanced Studies, University of Pisa.

He gives speeches, writes and publishes books and articles on economic issues on industrial policy, science, technology and innovation.

Giovanni Cozzi is senior lecturer in economics at the University of Greenwich (London, UK) and member of the Greenwich Political Economy Research Centre (GPERC). He was Senior Economist at the Foundation for European Progressive Studies (FEPS), Brussels, Belgium and Research Fellow at the Centre for Development Policy and Research (CDPR) at the School of Oriental and African Studies. At CDPR he collaborated on a three-year European Commission FP7 funded project assessing the Challenges for Europe in the World of 2030 (AUGUR). His current research is on fiscal policies, the role of social and physical investment in promoting sustainable growth and employment for women and men, and the role of development banks. Several of his research publications employ the Cambridge Alphametrics Model (CAM), a Structuralist growth model, to project alternative macroeconomic scenarios and their policy implications.

Giovanni Dosi is professor of economics and director of the Institute of Economics at the Scuola Superiore Sant'Anna in Pisa, Italy. He also served as co-director of the 'Industrial Policy' and 'Intellectual Property Rights' task forces at the *Initiative for Policy Dialogue* at Columbia University. Additionally, Professor Dosi is a continental Europe editor of the journal *Industrial and Corporate Change.* He is included in the ISI Highly Cited Research list, denoting those who made fundamental contributions to the advancement of science and technology, and is a corresponding member of the Accademia Nazionale dei Lincei, the first academy of sciences in Italy. His major research areas—where he is author and editor of several works—include Economics of Innovation and Technological Change, Industrial Economics, Evolutionary Theory, Economic Growth and Development, Organizational Studies. A selection of his works has been published in two volumes: *Innovation, Organization and Economic Dynamics. Selected Essays*, Cheltenham, Edward Elgar, 2000; and *Economic Organization, Industrial Dynamics and Development: Selected Essays*, Cheltenham, Edward Elgar, 2012.

João Carlos Ferraz is professor at the Instituto de Economia, Universidade Federal do Rio de Janeiro, Brazil. From May 2007 to May 2016 he was executive director of the Brazilian Development Bank, BNDES, coordinating its research, corporate planning and risk management activities. From June 2003 to May 2007 he headed the Division of Productivity and Management of the United Nations Economic Commission for Latin America and the Caribbean, UN/ECLAC, in Santiago, Chile. He has published extensively in Brazil and abroad, among them, L. Coutinho, J. C. Ferraz, A. Nassif, and R. Oliva (2012) "Industrial Policy and Economic Transformation," in J. Santiso and J. Dayton-Johnson (Eds.), *The Oxford Handbook of Latin American Political Economy* (OUP, Oxford) and J. C. Ferraz, D. Kupfer, and L. Haguenauer (1996), *Made in Brazil: Desafios Competitivos para a Indústria Brasileira* (Editora Campus, Rio de Janeiro), which was named Book of the Year by the Brazilian Publishers Association.

As an economist, **Stephany Griffith-Jones** has researched and provided policy advice on reforming the international and national financial architecture, with an emphasis on public development banks. Griffith-Jones is the current financial markets director of the Initiative Policy Dialogue at Columbia University as well as emeritus fellow at the Institute of Development Studies in the UK. In her work, she has led a number of major international research projects on international finance, development finance, and macro-economic issues. Griffith-Jones has also written or edited over twenty books and numerous journal and newspaper articles, such as *Time for a Visible Hand*, which she co-edited with Joseph Stiglitz and José Antonio Ocampo.

Nobuya Haraguchi is industrial research officer at the Department of Policy, Research, and Statistics of UNIDO in Vienna. He led various research projects for publication including UNIDO Industrial Development Report (2013), Global Green Growth (2015), and Global Value Chains and Development (2015). He has published widely on structural change, patterns of manufacturing and industrial policy and practice. Recently, jointly with Wim Naudé and Adam Szirmai he was editor of the book *Structural Change and Industrial Development in the BRICS*, published by Oxford University Press in 2015. Before joining UNIDO, he taught macroeconomics at St. John's University in the United States. He holds a PhD from the University of London.

Akio Hosono is the current senior research adviser and former director (2011–2013) of Japan International Cooperation Agency Research Institute (JICA-RI). He holds a doctorate in economics from the University of Tokyo. After graduation he served in a variety of posts such as vice-president at Tsukuba University in Tsukuba Science City, Japanese ambassador to El Salvador, and professor at the National Graduate Institute for Policy Studies (GRIPS) in Tokyo, professor at the Research Institute of Economics and Business Administration at Kobe University to name a few. His publications include *Development for Sustainable Agriculture: The Brazilian Cerrado* (with Magno and Hongo, Palgrave MacMillan, 2016); *Chile's Salmon Industry: Policy Challenges in Managing Public Goods* (with Iizuka and Katz, Springer, 2016); *Getting to Scale: How to Bring Development Solutions to Millions of Poor People* (with Chandy, Kharas and Linn, Brookings Press, 2013); *Regional Integration and Economic Development* (with Saveedra and Stallings, Palgrave, 2003); and *Development Strategies in East Asia and Latin America* (with Saavedra, Macmillan, 1998).

Ming Leong Kuan is lead economist at the Ministry of Trade and Industry, Singapore. In the civil service, he has held various portfolios that spanned economic policies related to medium-term economic growth, industrial development, urban planning, demographics, and economic engagement strategies. His research interests include the role of the state in economic development, industrial policy, international trade, and the structural transformation of economies. In recent years, he has worked on projects for various organizations including the United Kingdom's Government Office for Science, the International Labour Organization (ILO), the United Nations Industrial Development Organization (UNIDO), and the Friedrich-Ebert-Stiftung (FES). He holds a PhD from the University of Cambridge, and an MSc from the London School of Economics and Political Science.

Justin Yifu Lin is director, Center for New Structural Economics; dean, Institute of South-South Cooperation and Development; and honorary dean, National School of Development at Peking University. He was the senior vice president and chief economist of the World Bank from 2008 to 2012. Prior to this, Mr. Lin served for fifteen years as Founding Director of the China Centre for Economic Research at Peking University. He is the author of twenty-three books, including *Against the Consensus: Reflections on the Great Recession*; *The Quest for Prosperity: How Developing Economies Can Take Off*; *Demystifying the Chinese Economy,*; and *New Structural Economics: A Framework for Rethinking Development and Policy.* He is a corresponding fellow of the British Academy and a fellow of the Academy of Sciences for Developing World.

Deepak Nayyar is professor emeritus at Jawaharlal Nehru University, New Delhi, where he taught economics for twenty-five years. He is an honorary fellow of Balliol College, Oxford, and was, until recently, Distinguished University Professor of Economics at the New School for Social Research, New York. Earlier, he taught at the University of Oxford, the University of Sussex, and the Indian Institute of Management, Calcutta. He was vice chancellor of the University of Delhi from 2000 to 2005. He also served as chief economic adviser to the Government of India and secretary in the Ministry of Finance from 1989 to 1991. His research interests are primarily in the areas of international economics, macroeconomics and international economics. He has published numerous articles in academic journals and several books, including *Catch Up: Developing Countries in the World Economy*, *Macroeconomics and Human Development*, *Liberalization and Development*, *Trade and Globalization*, *Stability with Growth: Macroeconomics, Liberalization and Development* (co-author), *Governing Globalization: Issues and Institutions*, and *The Intelligent Person's Guide to Liberalization* (co-author).

José Antonio Ocampo is professor in the School of International and Public Affairs, co-president of the Initiative for Policy Dialogue, and member of the Committee on Global Thought at Columbia University. He is also chair of the Committee for Development Policy of the United Nations Economic and Social Council (ECOSOC) and of Colombia's Rural Development Commission. He has occupied numerous positions at the United Nations and his native Colombia, including UN Under-Secretary-General for Economic and Social Affairs, executive secretary of the UN Economic Commission for Latin America and the Caribbean (ECLAC), and minister of finance, minister of agriculture and director of the National Planning Office of Colombia. He has published extensively on macroeconomic theory and policy, international financial issues, economic and social development, international trade, and Colombian and Latin American economic history.

Carlota Perez specializes in the socioeconomic impact of technical change and on the shifting historical context for growth and development. Author of *Technological Revolutions and Financial Capital: the Dynamics of Bubbles and Golden Ages* (Elgar 2002), she has acted as consultant for international organizations such as UNIDO, ECLAC, the World Bank, the IDB and the OECD; for several Latin American governments and for global corporations, including IBM, Cisco, Telefonica and Ericsson. In the early 1980s, with the aim of strengthening companies to survive liberalization, she proposed and was made founding director of Technological Development at the Ministry of Industry in Venezuela. Carlota is Centennial Professor of International Development at the London School of Economics, professor of Technology and Development at TUT, Estonia; and honorary professor at SPRU, University of Sussex.

Go Shimada is associate professor of the University of Shizuoka, visiting scholar of Columbia University, visiting scholar of JICA Research Institute, and adjunct researcher of Waseda University. Prior to this, Dr. Shimada worked for JICA for more than two decades as director, Trade and Investment Division, Department of Industrial Development; special assistant to the President, Office of the President; and first secretary, Permanent Mission of Japan to the United Nations, New York.

He has a PhD from Waseda University and an MA in economics from the University of Manchester. He recently has published chapters in *Industrial Policy and Economic Transformation in Africa* (Noman and Stiglitz, 2015) and *The Last Mile in Ending Extreme Poverty* (Chandy, Kato, and Kharas, 2015), as well as "The Role of Social Capital after Disasters: An Empirical Study of Japan based on Time-Serries-Cross-Section (TSCS) Data from 1981 to 2012" in the *International Journal of Disaster Risk Reduction* (2015).

INDEX

Page numbers in italics indicate figures and/or tables

CPSIA information can be obtained
at www.ICGtesting.com
Printed in the USA
LVOW07*0818070717

540448LV00001B/1/P

9 780231 180504